THE IMAGES OF THE CONSUMER IN EU LAW

This book consists of contributions exploring from different perspectives the 'images' of the consumer in EU law. The images of the consumer form the foundation for various EU policies, more or less directly oriented towards the goal of consumer protection. The purpose of the volume is to establish what visions of the consumer there are in different contexts of EU law, whether they are consistent, and whether EU law's engagement with consumer-related considerations is sincere or merely instrumental to the achievement of other goals. The chapters discuss how consumers should be protected in EU contract, competition, free movement and trade mark law. They reflect on the limits of the consumer empowerment rationale as the basis for EU consumer policy. The chapters look also at the variety of concerns consumers might have, including the cost of goods and services, access to credit, ethical questions of consumption, the challenges of excessive choice and the possibility to influence the content of regulatory measures, and explore the significance of these issues for the EU's legislative and judicial process.

Volume 21 Studies of the Oxford Institute of European and Comparative Law

Studies of the Oxford Institute of European and Comparative Law

Recent titles in this Series

Volume 12: Article 82 EC: Reflections on its Recent Evolution
Edited by Ariel Ezrachi

Volume 13: Prohibition of Abuse of Law: A New General Principle of EU Law?
Edited by Rita de la Feria and Stefan Vogenauer

Volume 14: Constitutional Pluralism in the European Union and Beyond
Edited by Matej Avbelj and Jan Komárek

Volume 15: The Protection of Fundamental Rights in the EU After Lisbon
Edited by Sybe de Vries, Ulf Bernitz and Stephen Weatherill

Volume 16: The Involvement of EU Law in Private Law Relationships
Edited by Dorota Leczykiewicz and Stephen Weatherill

Volume 17: Current Problems in the Protection of Human Rights: Perspectives from Germany and the UK
Edited by Katja S Ziegler and Peter M Huber

Volume 18: Legal Challenges in the Global Financial Crisis: Bail-outs, the Euro and Regulation
Edited by Wolf-Georg Ringe and Peter M Huber

Volume 19: The Unitary EU Patent System
Edited by Justine Pila and Christopher Wadlow

Volume 20: The EU Charter of Fundamental Rights as a Binding Instrument: Five Years Old and Growing
Edited by Sybe de Vries, Ulf Bernitz and Stephen Weatherill

The Images of the Consumer in EU Law

Legislation, Free Movement and Competition Law

Edited by
Dorota Leczykiewicz
and
Stephen Weatherill

·HART·
PUBLISHING
OXFORD AND PORTLAND, OREGON
2018

Hart Publishing
An imprint of Bloomsbury Publishing Plc

Hart Publishing Ltd
Kemp House
Chawley Park
Cumnor Hill
Oxford OX2 9PH
UK

Bloomsbury Publishing Plc
50 Bedford Square
London
WC1B 3DP
UK

www.hartpub.co.uk
www.bloomsbury.com

Published in North America (US and Canada) by
Hart Publishing
c/o International Specialized Book Services
920 NE 58th Avenue, Suite 300
Portland, OR 97213-3786
USA

www.isbs.com

First published in hardback, 2016
Paperback edition, 2018

British Library Cataloguing-in-Publication Data
A catalogue record for this book is available from the British Library.

ISBN: PB: 978-1-50992-117-1
HB: 978-1-84946-544-1

Library of Congress Cataloging-in-Publication Data

Names: Leczykiewicz, Dorota, 1979– editor. | Weatherill, Stephen, editor.

Title: The images of the consumer in EU law : legislation, free movement and competition law / Edited by Dorota Leczykiewicz and Stephen Weatherill.

Description: Portland, Oregon : Hart Publishing, 2016. | Series: Studies of the oxford institute of european and comparative law ; 21 | Includes bibliographical references and index.

Identifiers: LCCN 2015037291 | ISBN 9781849465441 (hardback : alk. paper)

Subjects: LCSH: Consumer protection—Law and legislation—European Union countries. | Consumers—European Union countries.

Classification: LCC KJE6577.I43 2016 | DDC 343.2407/1—dc23 LC record available at http://lccn.loc.gov/2015037291

Typeset by Compuscript Ltd, Shannon

Norbert Reich

Prof D jur and Dr hc mult

September 9th 1937–October 17th 2015

The conference that generated the papers contained in this book was animated and enlivened by Norbert Reich, not only as a presenter and a commentator but also as an energetic and enthusiastic participant in the vivid debates held in the margins of the event. This book is adorned by a chapter written by Norbert Reich, which displays his characteristic intellectual curiosity, astonishing breadth of knowledge and consistent thirst for innovation. Sadly, as we checked the final version of the proofs for the book in October 2015, we learned the news of Norbert's death.

We dedicate this book to Norbert Reich—in admiration, in gratitude, in friendship, and most of all in the secure knowledge that his legacy as a truly great scholar will be long-lasting.

A book is a small tribute. Palaces of marble and gold have been constructed for lesser men than Norbert. But Norbert was a man of letters, for whom academic debate provided treasure. European consumer law will be the poorer for the loss of Norbert Reich from our discussions, but European consumer lawyers will be forever in Norbert's debt for all that he has done to breathe life and intellectual excitement into our subject. His passion and his enthusiasm showed us the way forward. Norbert was known round the world: Norbert was loved round the world. He will never be forgotten.

DL / SW

PREFACE

We are delighted to present this 'book of the conference': the conference was held in Oxford in March 2014 under the auspices of the Oxford Institute of European and Comparative Law (IECL), and this is the book.

Our interest in this project, and our motivation in bringing together the group of experts whose contributions are collected in this volume, was piqued by a strong sense that the image of the consumer in EU law was under-explored. In fact, our feeling was that we should be examining the *images* of the consumer, not the image, and we should be doing so under a suspicion that the 'consumer' is used and quite possibly abused as a means to achieve a wide range of (possibly conflicting) objectives in the EU. We wanted to pin that down. So we proceeded to examine and, courtesy of our team of scholars, have examined the concepts of 'consumer welfare', 'consumer protection' and 'consumer interest' in different contexts of EU law: legislation, free movement law and competition law. That was the rich feast devoured at the conference: that is the material we put before you in this book. We hope and believe we have deepened appreciation of the role played by the consumer in EU law and policy and we eagerly await the further scholarly research which we aspire to provoke.

All our speakers and contributors deserve our warm and sincere thanks, both for the quality of their scholarship and also for their more mundane but, to us as editors, priceless willingness expeditiously to convert their presentations into the final texts contained in this volume. Binesh Hass helped in the conscientious editing of the papers, and we thank him warmly. Jenny Dix, the Administrator of the Oxford Law Faculty's IECL, was, as ever, a pillar of strength in the organisation of the event and provided indispensable support: thank you so much! Stefan Vogenauer, Director of the IECL, was supportive from start to finish both in matters of intellectual ambition and at a more practical level.

The project was generously funded by the John Fell Fund of Oxford University and we are very grateful for that support, which was genuinely indispensable. The Oxford Law Faculty was also supportive: again, sincere thanks are due for this help.

As editors, we are proud and we are privileged that this book appears in a prestigious series that does so much to convey and confirm the high standing of the IECL as a source of intellectual energy. In that vein we thank too Hart Publishing, who are partners in this success.

DL/SW

CONTENTS

LIST OF CONTRIBUTORS

ALBERTINA ALBORS-LLORENS is a University Senior Lecturer at the Faculty of Law, University of Cambridge, and a Fellow and Director of Studies in Law at St John's College. Her research focuses on EU law and competition law. She is co-author of the 5th edition of *Goyder's EC Competition Law* (Oxford University Press, 2009) and has recently published articles, inter alia, in the *Cambridge Law Journal* (2012) and the *Yearbook of European Law* (2014). She was previously a British Academy Post-doctoral Fellow, a Research Fellow and then a Fellow, Tutor, and the Director of Studies in Law at Girton College, Cambridge.

HUGH COLLINS is the Vinerian Professor of English Law at All Souls College, University of Oxford. Formerly he was the Professor of English Law at the London School of Economics. His main research interests lie in the fields of contract law and employment law. His books include *Regulating Contracts* (Oxford University Press, 1999), *Towards a European Civil Code: The Way Forward* (Cambridge University Press, 2008), and *Employment Law* 2nd edn (Oxford University Press, 2010). He is also a member of the editorial committee of the *Modern Law Review* and the *Industrial Law Journal* and of the executive board of the Society of European Contract Law (SECOLA).

GARETH DAVIES is Professor of European Law at VU University Amsterdam. Prior to this he lectured at the University of Groningen and briefly practised as a barrister. His interests are in EU free movement law and constitutional law, and in particular in their interaction. He is one of the authors of Chalmers, Davies and Monti, *EU Law* (Cambridge University Press).

SYBE A DE VRIES is Professor of EU Single Market Law and Fundamental Rights and the Jean Monnet Chair at the Europa Institute of Utrecht University. He is also the coordinator of the FP7 research project 'bEUcitizenship' on European citizenship and a member of the editorial boards of the Journal for European and Economic law (SEW) and the Netherlands Journal for Human Rights (NTM/NJCM-bulletin). In 2010 he was a visiting researcher at the Oxford Institute of European and Comparative Law. Since 2015 he has been an Honorary Judge at the Court of Rotterdam dealing with competition and consumer law cases.

GRAEME B DINWOODIE is the Professor of Intellectual Property and Information Technology Law at the University of Oxford, and Director of the Oxford Intellectual Property Research Centre. He is an elected member of the American Law

Institute, and served as President of the International Association for the Advancement of Teaching and Research in Intellectual Property from 2011 to 2013. In 2008, the International Trademark Association awarded Professor Dinwoodie the Pattishall Medal for Teaching Excellence in Trademark Law.

SIDNEY FREEDMAN, MA (Oxon), Barrister, after practising for a number of years at the Bar in London, worked for Shell and later Rolls-Royce before joining the Competition Department of the European Commission. He was Head of Division in the Consumer Service of the European Commission (1978–1990), where he was responsible for protection of the economic interests of consumers and access to justice. Subsequently, he was Counsellor to a Director-General in External Relations, and covered information and relations with the European Parliament and the Court of Auditors. He was visiting professor at the University of California, Berkeley (1988–1989) and at the University of Washington, Seattle (1998–1999).

DEV S GANGJEE is an Associate Professor in Intellectual Property within the Oxford Law Faculty as well as a Tutorial Fellow at St Hilda's College, and presently Director of the Oxford Diploma in Intellectual Property Law and Practice. His research focusses on branding and trade marks, geographical indications and copyright law, the history and political economy of intellectual property, collective and open innovation and the interface between law and development. He is an Academic Member of the Oxford Intellectual Property Research Centre and a Research Affiliate with IP Osgoode, Canada, and sits on the Editorial Board of the *Modern Law Review*.

STEFAN GRUNDMANN holds the chair of Transnational Private Law at the European University Institute (on leave from Humboldt University where he is a Professor of Private and Business Law). His main areas of expertise and writing include European, German and comparative contract, banking and company law, private law and social theory, transnational law and governance. He is the founding president and also the current president of the Society of European Contract Law (SECOLA), a co-founder and the president of the European Law School (Berlin/London/Paris/Rome/Amsterdam), and a member of the board of the German Society of Comparative Law.

CHRISTOPHER HODGES is Professor of Justice Systems at the University of Oxford, Head of the Swiss Re/CMS Research Programme on Civil Justice Systems at the Centre for Socio-Legal Studies, Oxford, a Supernumerary Fellow of Wolfson College, Oxford, and a (non-practising) solicitor. He has been Erasmus Professor of the Fundamentals of Private Law at Erasmus University in Rotterdam, Honorary Professor at the China University of Political Science and Law in Beijing, Visiting Professor at Leuven University and Visiting Fellow at the Australian National University, Canberra. He has published extensively on EU regulatory, enforcement, redress, dispute resolution and alternative dispute resolution systems.

GERAINT HOWELLS is Chair Professor of Commercial Law and Dean of the Law School at Manchester University; barrister at Gough Square Chambers, London (though not currently practising) and former President of the International Association of Consumer Law. He previously held chairs at Sheffield, Lancaster and Manchester and has been head of law schools at Lancaster and Manchester. His books include *Comparative Product Liability* (Dartmouth Publishing, 1993), *EC Consumer Law* (with Thomas Wilhelmsson, Dartmouth, 1993), *Consumer Product Safety* (Ashgate, 1998), *Consumer Protection Law* (with Stephen Weatherill, Ashgate, 2005), *Handbook of Research on International Consumer Law* (with Iain Ramsay and Thomas Wilhelmsson, Edward Elgar, 2011), *European Fair Trading Law* (with Hans-W Micklitz and Thomas Wilhelmsson, Ashgate, 2013), and *The Tobacco Challenge: Legal Policy and Consumer Protection* (Ashgate 2013).

ANGUS JOHNSTON is Professor of Law and Hoffmann Fellow in Law at University College, Oxford. He has lectured and published widely in the field of EU law and private law, with a particular focus on energy law and various aspects of the internal market. His publications include (with Guy Block) *EU Energy Law* (Oxford University Press, 2012) and (with Simon Deakin) *Markesinis & Deakin's Tort Law* 7th edn (Oxford University Press, 2012).

ALISON JONES is Professor of Law at King's College London and a solicitor at Freshfields Bruckhaus Deringer LLP. Prior to joining King's College, Alison read law at Girton College, Cambridge, worked at Slaughter & May and completed a BCL at Christ Church, Oxford. She is co-author of Jones and Sufrin, *EU Competition Law: Text, Cases, and Materials* 5th edn (Oxford University Press, 2014) and researches principally in the fields of EU competition law and US antitrust law.

DOROTA LECZYKIEWICZ is Associate Professor at the Faculty of Law of the University of Oxford, and a Fellow of St Peter's College. She was previously a Marie Curie Fellow at the European University Institute in Florence and a Leverhulme Trust Early Career Fellow in the Faculty of Law at the University of Oxford. Her research interests include EU and comparative private law, EU fundamental rights, and theory and practice of legal reasoning. She has co-edited *The Involvement of EU law in Private Law Relationships* (with Stephen Weatherill, Hart Publishing, 2013).

VANESSA MAK is a Professor of Private Law at Tilburg University. Her research focusses on the role of private law in the economic regulation of the European (consumer) market. Prior to her appointment in Tilburg, Vanessa held positions as a Lecturer in Law at Oriel College, Oxford and as a postdoctoral researcher at the Max Planck Institute for Comparative and International Private Law in Hamburg. Vanessa has law degrees from Erasmus University Rotterdam and from the University of Oxford, where she obtained her DPhil on *Performance-Oriented Remedies in European Sale of Goods Law* (published with Hart Publishing, 2009).

HANS-W MICKLITZ is Professor of Economic Law at the European University Institute in Florence, on leave from the Jean Monnet Chair of Private Law and European Economic Law at the University of Bamberg. He is Head of the Institute of European and Consumer Law (VIEW) in Bamberg and has provided consultancies for ministries in Austria, Germany, the UK, for the European Commission, OECD, UNEP, GIZ, and Consumers International Den Haag Netherlands/Penang Malaysia. He holds an ERC Grant 2011–2016 on European Regulatory Private Law. He has held visiting positions at the University of Michigan, Ann Arbor and Somerville College, Oxford.

LUCINDA MILLER is Senior Lecturer in Law at University College London. She obtained a doctorate from University College London for a thesis on the Europeanisation of Contract Law which was published as a book entitled *The Emergence of European Contract Law: Exploring Europeanization* (Oxford University Press, 2011). Her research focuses mainly on comparative contract law, EU private law and, more recently, on ethical consumerism as a mode of governance.

IAIN RAMSAY is Professor of Law at the University of Kent, Canterbury, UK. From 1986 to 2007 he was a Professor of Law at Osgoode Hall Law School, York University, Toronto, Canada. His research interests are primarily in credit and insolvency, and regulation of consumer markets at national, regional and international level. He has published widely in these areas. His most recent book is *Bankruptcy in the 21st Century: A Comparison of the US and Europe* (forthcoming with Hart Publishing/Bloomsbury in 2016).

NORBERT REICH is Professor Emeritus at the University of Bremen. He has held visiting professorships at the University of Tartu and the University of Groningen, and a Fernand Braudel Senior Fellowship at the European University Institute in Florence. He is author of *Europäisches Verbraucherrecht* (with Hans Micklitz, Namos, 2003), *Understanding EU Law* 2nd edn (Intersentia, 2005), *European Consumer Law* 2nd edn (with Hans Micklitz, Peter Rott and Klaus Tonner, Intersentia, 2014), *General Principles of EU Civil Law* (Intersentia, 2014) and *Understanding EU Internal Market Law* 3rd edn (with Annette Nordhausen Scholes and Jeremy Scholes, Intersentia, 2015).

CHRISTIAN TWIGG-FLESNER is Professor of Commercial Law at the University of Hull. His research interests lie broadly in the fields of commercial law, consumer law, contract law, and the harmonisation of private law. The focus of his current research is on the concept of 'harmonisation', both in the context of European consumer and contract law and transnational commercial law, the reform (and codification) of consumer law, and on international consumer law. He has published widely on EU consumer and contract law, and is also co-editor for Law of the *Journal of Consumer Policy* (Springer).

STEPHEN WEATHERILL is Jacques Delors Professor of European Law at the University of Oxford, a Fellow of Somerville College, and Deputy Director for European Law at the Oxford Law Faculty's Institute of European and Comparative Law. His research interests embrace the field of European law in its widest sense, although his published work is predominantly concerned with EU trade and consumer law. Among others, he is author of *EU Consumer Law and Policy* 2nd edn (Edward Elgar, 2013), *Cases and Materials in EU Law* 11th edn (Oxford University Press, 2014), and *Consumer Protection Law* 2nd edn (with Geraint Howells, Ashgate, 2005).

1

The Images of the Consumer in EU Law

DOROTA LECZYKIEWICZ AND STEPHEN WEATHERILL

This book is about EU law and areas of law influenced by EU regulation. It is not limited to consumer law. The conceptual focus of the book is on the 'images' of the consumer who is understood, on the one hand, as an actual person whom EU institutions have in mind when they devise regulation and, on the other, as a projected person who will emerge as a result of the regulatory and deregulatory efforts of these same institutions. Exploring the images of the consumer in EU law in their duality enables us to understand both who is actually protected by the regulation and in what situations, and what kind of individual EU law is creating by providing regulatory incentives or disincentives. The transformative effect of EU law on consumers raises questions about the sincerity of the ambitions pursued by the EU in fields which are overtly presented as aimed at a high level of consumer protection. Could it be the case that the goals of EU law, even the goals of EU consumer law, if such can be identified, at the residual level serve goals other than consumer protection?

However, even within the areas where consumer protection is clearly and sincerely the primary objective, it is still valuable to ask about the images of the consumer constituting the basis of the adopted policies. Protecting consumers may mean different things, depending on whose needs, preferences, characteristics and relations are taken as the point of reference. What is at stake is not only the level of protection but also the contexts in which protection is offered, and much depends on choices made by institutions responsible for creating and enforcing regulation.

I. Consumers in EU Law

Consumers are a central component of the European integration project. EU consumers are those who buy goods and services domestically and from other Member States. It is for their financial resources that companies on the EU market are competing and it is their choices which trigger many other transactions.

Of course, we are thinking here primarily of ultimate consumers, a category largely indistinguishable from EU citizens. In the current-day rhetoric the internal market operates for consumers. But if that is the case the law needs to take account also of other values which citizens hold dear. Otherwise EU citizens are reduced to only one aspect of their lives—consumption.

Yet this is where EU law faces a problem, because it is not like national law. It cannot aspire to the systematic coverage achievable by national law. The EU is confined by the principle of conferral, according to which the EU's competences and powers are limited to those granted by its Member States pursuant to the founding Treaties. Article 5(2) TEU declares that 'competences not conferred upon the Union in the Treaties remain with the Member States'. Because there is no general regulatory competence, there can be no general regulation of all matters important for EU citizens. The programme has to be limited and has to respect the limits of Treaty competences. Even the broad authorisation to harmonise laws, Article 114 TFEU, applies only 'for the achievement of the objectives set out in Article 26', that is for the creation of 'an area without internal frontiers in which the free movement of goods, persons, services and capital is ensured in accordance with the provisions of the Treaties'. Article 169(1)(a) TFEU, which is aimed at promoting the interests of consumers and ensuring a high level of consumer protection, refers to Article 114 TFEU as the provision on which EU regulatory action is actually based. Article 169(2)(b) TFEU envisages only EU 'measures which support, supplement and monitor the policy pursued by the Member States'. This is very limited. The negative competence of the EU—free movement and competition law, most conspicuously—is allegedly broader in the sense that it also encompasses acts not covered by the EU's legislative competence (exercised or not yet exercised). But the negative competence is even more directly focussed on internal market objectives than EU legislative initiatives.

One should, however, be careful. Focussing on the internal market does not mean that consumer interests are neglected. There are obvious ways in which the internal market helps consumers—broadens their choice, makes products and services available at more competitive prices, or enables technical innovation, which brings consumers new products. Yet it also exposes consumers to potentially unfamiliar dangers stemming not only from unknown features of products and services but also from the foreign legal environment under which the transactions are often concluded. This is not to say that the internal market is inherently more dangerous than the domestic market. Equally, national law due to its unlimited competence is not by definition more successful in ensuring consumer protection. The law of consumer protection at the national level is also typically fragmented and sometimes idiosyncratic, an amalgamation of material stretching across public and private law that is relevant to the consumer but not created with the consumer specifically in mind. It also tends to be tied to more recent material which has a particular perception of the consumer as a category that requires a degree of protection, with a wider concern to achieve substantive equality or otherwise to compensate for the failings or the inequities of loosened markets. So EU consumer law is relatively less systematic than national consumer law but national consumer law, too, is not typically steered by a single image of the consumer.

The EU's connection to the consumer is arguably stronger precisely because of its limited character and the central importance of the project of completing the internal market. So while EU competences are not limited by reference to consumer interest—that is to say, the EU is not generally empowered to act for consumers—consumer interest, in particular the desire to achieve a high level of consumer protection, is what drives regulation. Article 38 of the Charter of Fundamental Rights now directs that 'Union policies shall ensure a high level of consumer protection' but this lacks precision and in any event the Charter applies only within the scope of EU competence. The same applies to Article 12 TFEU, which states that '[c]onsumer protection requirements shall be taken into account in defining and implementing other Union policies and activities'.

A. Free Movement Law and Competition Law

So why do many believe that the relationship between EU law and consumers is weak, that consumer protection is subsidiary to the internal market project? Part of it is presentational and part of it is substantive. The perception that the EU is not directly engaged with consumers arises because the relevant provisions governing the internal market make no immediate connection to the consumer. This is definitely true of free movement law and competition law.

Free movement law serves to eliminate national measures that partition product and service markets. Removal of barriers to cross-border trade performs the centrally important role of stimulating competition—that is ultimately a matter of consumer policy even if the Treaty avoids spelling it out in those precise terms. Free movement law is supposed to open up space for contractual autonomy, it is supposed to promote consumer choice. It is accordingly broadly interpreted. Moreover, assumptions about the capacity of consumers to absorb information (for example, from labels on packaging) have frequently served to lead to condemnation of more rigid composition rules as unjustified barriers to trade in differently constituted products. There is here an assumption about the capacity of the consumer to process and respond to such disclosed information. *Cassis de Dijon*, decided by the Court of Justice (now the Court of Justice of the European Union—'CJEU') in 1979, is the shining beacon of EU law's image of the consumer even two generations later.[1] It shows how Article 34 TFEU, the Treaty provision governing the free movement of goods, controls local regulatory autonomy in setting technical standards insofar as such rulemaking may cause impediments to the development of an internal market stretching across the territory of the EU. There is a vigorous deregulatory impetus in this case law. It is thematically propelled

[1] Case 120/78 *Rewe-Zentrale AG v Bundesmonopolverwaltung für Branntwein* (*Cassis de Dijon*) [1979] ECR 649.

by a preference for the private autonomy of traders and, only in consequence, of consumers in the market over public regulation.

Competition law, as an element in the Treaty system designed to achieve and maintain undistorted competition in the internal market, is supposed to serve the consumer interest, although here too the Treaty does not spell out a precise image of the consumer and there is certainly room for different understandings of how and why the interest of the consumer should inform the shaping of competition law and policy. 'Consumer welfare' is used frequently as a lodestone but without precisely agreed definitions. In particular—and this is where EU law has a flavour that is conspicuously distinct from US law—the concern for integration may promote a higher level of scepticism of deals that impede cross-border trade even in the absence of demonstrated damage to inter-brand competition—in fact even where inter-brand competition would be enhanced.

In both instances, free movement and competition law, some assessment of the limits of this project are needed. Free movement law does not always disable national competence to act to protect the consumer. It is open to Member States to show an interest of sufficient importance to override the principle of free movement and since one recognised justification for obstructive national rules is the protection of the consumer. There has arisen a heap of cases in which the consumer interest in integration, expressed through condemnation of national laws as unlawful restrictions to inter-State trade, confronts the consumer interest in protection, which in turn finds expression in the readiness to treat national regulations as justified. Courts must decide which interest—which image of the consumer—prevails and why. This is a context-specific inquiry, dependent on the quality of the justifications advanced, but the linking theme is clear: it asks what image of the consumer should drive the internal market. The more one trusts the consumer to enjoy the advantages of choice in an integrated market, the more sceptical one is of national intervention in the market. Conversely an attachment to the virtue of national rules as protective of vulnerable consumers tends to lead to an approach that restrains integration through law, by finding national measures to be justified. And some national measures subjected to scrutiny are nuanced while others are not. In *Buet v Ministère Public*,[2] a ruling that is a candidate as the first and transformative identification of the 'vulnerable' consumer as an image recognised by EU law, the Court approved of French rules designed to protect less educated consumers and wishing to improve it by including explicit reference to the harm shown to have been inflicted on such consumers in the unregulated market.

By contrast, the Court has sometimes been ruthlessly dismissive of detail and context. In *Mars*[3] it famously adopted the irritated manner of a sunbather brushing away a buzzing fly as it rejected the claim that German intervention to

[2] Case 382/87 *R Buet and Educational Business Services (EBS) v Ministère public* [1989] ECR 1235.
[3] Case C–470/93 *Verein gegen Unwesen in Handel und Gewerbe Köln eV v Mars GmbH* [1995] ECR I–1923.

protect consumers could be justified because of the risk of misunderstanding that a '+10%' marking on chocolate bars did not promise a still greater increase in the size of the product because the flash containing the (accurate) '+10%' marking covered more than 10% of the total surface of the wrapping. The Court simply observed that '[r]easonably circumspect consumers may be deemed to know that there is not necessarily a link between the size of publicity markings relating to an increase in a product's quantity and the size of that increase'.[4]

Competition law protects the consumer from restrictive practices and abusive conduct by dominant firms, and here too there is a delicate balance to be struck. Too much intervention may harm business flexibility and innovation to the detriment of the consumer; too little intervention may open up the prospect of a market that operates in an anti-competitive manner to the disadvantage of consumers. Article 101(3) TFEU is one of the very few references to the consumer that was present in the original Treaty of Rome, and it locates the consumer as a threshold in that a condition of exemption holds that the consumer shall take a 'fair share' of the resulting benefit of the collaboration between undertakings. The Commission Guidelines on the application of Article 101(3) offer a fuller explanation,[5] locating an image of the consumer in a broad context apt to accommodate all direct and indirect users of a product. But failure to meet the benchmark is fatal to the enforceability of the agreement. So too Article 102 takes an image of the consumer as a central element in deciding first, whether an undertaking holds a dominant position (where market analysis including the pattern of consumer preference is required), and second, whether it has abused it.

A particular manifestation of the importance of competition law arises where services previously supplied by public authorities are transferred into private hands or where regulation of the sector is loosened. The image of the consumer changes: the consumer is expected to use the market to their advantage. The idea is greater market competition in favour of the consumer: the risk is that the harm to the consumer which had previously prompted the intervention of the state in the first place will re-emerge with gusto and that orthodox competition law will lack the nuance required to address the failures and inequities that taint such markets. The consumer of a service provided under a natural monopoly is not the same as the consumer in a highly competitive and transparent market. The higher the velocity with which this trend moves, the heavier the demands placed on the consumer—from transport, energy, telecommunications, even to health care and education. EU law touches the sensitivities of the matter through recognition of the special case of services of general economic interest, addressed through ad hoc litigation prompting Commission amplification and the arrival of sector-specific and increasingly dense legislative initiatives.

[4] ibid, para 24.

[5] Commission, 'Guidelines on the application of Art 81(3) [now Art 101(3) TFEU] of the Treaty' [2004] OJ C101/97.

B. Legislative Harmonisation

Where the choice falls in favour of protecting the consumer through national initiatives—that is, where national measures are justified—attention shifts from free movement to harmonisation. The shift is institutionally fundamental: away from courts to the legislative process. But the focus is not changed. Once again this is a project driven in the name of the internal market. Legislative harmonisation, on its most simple model, treats the justification of diverse national laws as an impediment to inter-State trade which is apt to cause fragmentation of the EU's internal market. The antidote is to replace national diversity with regulatory homogeneity at the EU level. The EU reduces multiple sources of (national) rules to a single source, which is the EU's chosen harmonised rule. This serves to promote the integration of markets. It is a different route to the internal market. Free movement law operates according to a radically decentralised model, for where national measures cannot be sustained for want of justification it simply causes them to be set aside, opening up trade in goods and services complying with the rules of their state of origin. Competition law, too, evacuates unjustified practices from the market—there is no question of replacing them with EU norms. By contrast legislative harmonisation is a centralising model, locating regulatory responsibility at the EU level. Moreover it does so exclusively under a model of maximum harmonisation. But EU legislative intervention in the name of harmonisation, of which Article 114 is the principal source, is still driven by the imperative of market-making and the assumption holds that the advancement of market integration consequent on the levelling of the playing field that is characteristic of harmonisation will itself serve the consumer interest by widening choice and accelerating market competition. But because harmonisation, in contrast to free movement law, is not apt to create a regulatory vacuum in the terrain in which it operates, it is more than an exercise in driving choice and competition in the market. Where what is being harmonised is national consumer law that obstructs trade, what emerges from the legislative process is EU consumer law. Harmonisation is about *both* integrating the market and about regulating it, in this instance in the name of consumer protection. So, in the development of legislative harmonisation, the EU is forced to develop its own understanding(s)—image(s)—of the consumer and of their need for protection.

Therefore the EU arrives at regulation of the internal market principally through harmonisation pursuant to Article 114 TFEU. At one level this suggests a market bias, and it is plainly true that Article 114 may be released as a basis for (harmonised) consumer law only providing that necessary connection to the market-making project is demonstrated. However, Article 114 is very broad in the sense that only a low threshold needs to be crossed to allow the legislature access to it, and, threshold crossed, it is then easily connected to the legitimate pursuit of wider regulatory values including consumer protection. So EU consumer law, shaped by legislative harmonisation, is in part guided by the choices to which the

EU responds which have already been made (in diverse ways) at the national level, but it is also driven by constitutional commitments found in aforementioned Articles 12 and 169 TFEU and in Article 38 of the Charter.

II. The Consumer as a Distant Beneficiary

The view that the consumer is more likely to be a distant, rather than a direct beneficiary of many EU policies is confirmed by Albertina Albors-Llorens and Alison Jones in a chapter dedicated to competition law (Chapter 3). It discusses in detail how a policy ostensibly motivated by consumer interest incorporates consumer-related considerations only in a very limited way. Albors-Llorens and Jones explain that despite the presence of consumer welfare rhetoric in EU competition law, neither the Commission nor the claimants have to show that the conduct scrutinised under its rules harm the welfare of consumers. Instead the law uses presumptions and indirect assessment of such an effect and in concrete instances generates situations of under- or over-inclusiveness. The authors also point to the difficulty of defining consumer welfare in competition law. Their analysis suggests that the meaning of consumer welfare should be located in contrast to other fundamental policy concepts of competition law, such as market efficiency or 'fair' competition.

Another dangerous phenomenon is that of enlarging the concept of a consumer in such a way that it encompasses not only the ultimate consumer but also intermediaries, effectively covering everyone on the buyer's side. This, on the other hand, enables neglect of certain sub-groups of consumers as long as efficiency gains can be shown for the entire group of consumers. So it is not merely the constant danger of aggregation which rears its ugly head but the fact that among consumers are included smaller and larger retailers. This, combined with the fact that foreclosing competition is presumed to harm consumers and that Article 102 TFEU is virtually extinct as a method of prosecuting exploitative conduct, suggests that competition law desperately needs to refocus on the consumer. This can be partially achieved by enhancing private enforcement of competition law, also discussed by Albors-Llorens and Jones in Chapter 3.

Angus Johnston's chapter on the consumer in energy law shows a more decisive link between the EU energy policy and consumers than the one observed in competition law (Chapter 4). Not only is vulnerability expressly recognised as a relevant consideration in the Gas and Electricity Directives,[6] but consumers are granted specific rights vis-à-vis energy suppliers, who are under a universal service

[6] Directive 2009/72/EC of the European Parliament and of the Council of 13 July 2009 concerning common rules for the internal market in electricity [2009] OJ L211/55, where this obligation is mentioned only in the Directive's preamble; Directive 2009/73/EC of the European Parliament and of the Council of 13 July 2009 concerning common rules for the internal market in natural gas [2009] OJ L211/94.

obligation. What EU energy policy is missing is express retail price regulation, a gap which is particularly telling especially in comparison with the existence of detailed EU rules on network access, including on pricing. Also in the context of EU energy law, a question arises about the correct delineation of relevant groups. Consumers are often clamped together with other 'customers' of energy suppliers. This raises doubts as to whether their particular interest is adequately protected. Johnston may also be seen as echoing Hans Micklitz in Chapter 2 in the way he questions the presumption existing in various parts of EU law against state regulation. Inefficient markets are rarely good for consumers but energy policy based on market principles makes it difficult for states to carry out social welfare policies through energy retail contracts.

III. Vulnerable Consumers

Competition law and energy law are examples of sectors in which the categories used by law are over-inclusive, arguably undermining the entire policy as a vehicle of enhancing consumer interest. One way out of the impasse is by creating the category of vulnerable consumers, which could serve a double function. In policies which use the term 'consumers' to denote all buyers or replace the term 'consumers' with 'customers', the 'vulnerable' consumers could constitute a group whose interest, regardless of the overall direction of the policy in question, could not be neglected. The discussion would then move from defining consumers to defining vulnerability, and in particular to whether its definition should or should not include 'weakness' arising from particular market conditions or from the unequal bargaining power between the consumer and the trader in a given contractual relationship.

Yet vulnerability may also be seen as a concept enabling greater differentiation of consumer *protection* policy where uniform treatment of consumers as a class would create situations of unfairness. It thus touches upon a feature of the image of the consumer in EU law—its frequent singularity and lack of necessary differentiation.

Norbert Reich in Chapter 5 discusses vulnerability in this latter sense. He offers an overview of different forms of vulnerability that the concept should encompass—physical disability, intellectual disability, but also poverty, which, according to the author, in the context of credit and mortgage law, may place the consumer in a particularly weak position, requiring, just like disability, social solidarity. Reich also explains how vulnerability as part of EU contract law poses further challenges to the notion of private autonomy as the foundation of that law. The EU consumer is suspended somewhere between two paradigms of the consumer—one that sees them as autonomous parties to contracts, and the other that accepts their weaknesses in order to ensure that the market which the EU creates and develops is also a social market.

The theme of financial vulnerability is further developed by Iain Ramsay in Chapter 6 with respect to credit law. Ramsay explains that credit, at least in some circumstances, could be conceptualised as a dangerous product. Ramsay investigates at a very deep level the question of the most socially desirable solution to consumer protection in credit law. On the one hand, it could be maintained that access to credit ensures financial inclusion, enhances capabilities and extends the benefits of consumption onto greater numbers of consumers. On the other hand, however, the confidence in the credit market, unsupported by social regulation, arising from excessive reliance on consumer credit as a motor of the economy, questions the correctness of the current permissive policy. Ramsay is of the view that the solution should impose only modest restrictions on access to credit, such as those stemming from the inclusion in EU measures of the obligation of responsible lending. This policy solution is further supported by the finding of behavioural economics with which Ramsay engages in his contribution and which he perceives as a valuable addition to the regulatory process in credit markets. He observes, however, that reliance on behavioural economics poses the danger of the inability to create more generalised rules (the danger of individualism). A very important insight of Ramsay's contribution is the connection between the character of credit markets, on the one hand, and consumer preferences, on the other. The existence of structural factors affecting the position of particular consumers, such as the substitution of credit for social welfare challenges a view whereby financial management should be a matter of individual responsibility for consumers. According to Ramsay, credit is seen in neoliberal terms even though it is clothed as an element of social policy, employing ideologies of equality. This generates difficulties if the ideology of equality is not matched with actual equal wealth among consumers.

The more historical chapter by Sidney Freedman (Chapter 19) reveals that vulnerability was also the image guiding the first consumer-oriented directives in the EU. However, to avoid obvious connotations with vulnerability, consumer protection policy was renamed simply as 'consumer policy'. The hostility with which early proposals for consumer directives were treated by industry, described by Freedman, suggests that the Commission had to tread a difficult path of appeasing those who were afraid of the 'nanny state' and big government and those who saw in consumers victims of dangerous products and unfair market practices. If vulnerability could not openly motivate EU consumer policies, injustice could. This injustice stemmed from various factors which the Commission was trying to address: absence of regulation, lack of remedies, disparities between the laws of the Member States, and protectionist national policies which limited consumer choice and kept unduly high prices.

IV. Confident Consumer

Behavioural economics treads an uneasy terrain between paternalistic regulation and effective regulation. If consumers are to be left with choices, these choices have to be meaningful. How does it fit a system of rules designed for the vulnerable? What convincing argument can be made for protecting the autonomy of consumers if they are all presumed to be vulnerable? This tension is explored in the chapter by Christian Twigg-Flesner (Chapter 7), who presents EU law's resistance to the possibility of waiving consumer rights and its insistence on *ex officio* protection of these rights in the judicial process as examples of paternalism, which are incompliant with the otherwise prevalent image of the confident consumer. Twigg-Flesner lists the different ways in which the image of the confident consumer is assumed. First, EU regulation presupposes that the EU consumer will benefit from information. Second, it is taken for granted that they will benefit from the Single Market. And third, they are presumed to take advantage of better consumer protection laws in other Member States and motivated to shop abroad by the presence of the same floor of rights everywhere. The importance of law in EU consumer policy suggests that disparities between the laws of the Member States and insufficient protection constitute obstacles to the emergence of the confident consumer. So the tension in EU law is within the image of the confident consumer itself, which is regarded to reflect the real consumer (who allegedly does not need protection beyond enhanced information) but partially is also a projected image of someone who will emerge only once disparities between the laws of the Member States are removed.

The image of the confident consumer as a policy goal is also discussed by Stephen Weatherill in Chapter 8. First, Weatherill disagrees with the view which sees cases where national 'consumer protection' laws were struck down as evidence of the definitive direction against consumer protection in EU law. He points out that EU law is obviously interested in consumer safety. EU energy law, passenger law, and the law of audiovisual media services also show that there is more to EU consumer policy than just consumer empowerment by provision of information. Weatherill argues that there are possibilities for further differentiation in the image of the consumer that EU policy uses. The Unfair Commercial Practices Directive[7] does not expect every consumer to become attentive but also protects the vulnerable consumer. The national regulator may advance arguments to show the inappropriateness of the 'average consumer' test as a ground of review for the particular challenged measures against free movement provisions. At the rhetorical level, this differentiated approach could be facilitated by recognising the protection of weaker parties as a general principle of EU law.

A similar theme is taken up by Geraint Howells in Chapter 18, which asks about the 'soul' of EU consumer policy. In the author's view, consumer policy insufficiently engaged with consumer protection is soulless, especially in the changing context of increased maximum harmonisation and the findings about the consumer provided by behavioural economics. Similar to Weatherill, Howells gives

[7] Directive 2005/29/EC of the European Parliament and of the Council of 11 May 2005 concerning unfair business-to-consumer commercial practices in the internal market (Unfair Commercial Practices Directive) [2005] OJ L149/22.

many examples where EU law is more protective of consumers, paying special attention to the vulnerable, or ensuring the fairness and transparency of contractual terms in consumer contracts. However, Howells also sees many dangers, including those posed by the Unfair Commercial Practices Directive, whose side effect is, according to the author, the undermining of protective rules at the national level. Moreover, Howells links the level of substantive regulation of the consumer in the EU with questions about the overall character of the EU. Only regulatory, protective law, according to the author, shows that the EU is concerned with its citizens and is more than a free trade zone.

The theme of the confident consumer appears also in Stefan Grundmann's chapter (Chapter 9). His point of reference is the entire EU contract law, which so far has introduced differentiation only between consumers and traders. Grundmann maintains that this distinction is based on the idea of weakness and as such should not stop at consumers and include also traders where their position in a transaction is that of a 'weaker' party. So as with Weatherill, Grundmann relies on the notion of weakness but draws drastically different conclusions. His view is that paternalistic inroads into contract law should not stem from status (that is as consumers) but rather from substantive reasons concerning the level and the nature of risk involved in a particular transaction. One of the distinctions he offers is between the risk of suffering existential losses and that of suffering purely economic losses. In transactions which create the risk of only economic losses, regulation should only focus on correcting market failures. So the image of the confident consumer, the consumer whose right to self-determination is respected, as the objective of EU policy, should be departed from only where information rules are insufficient because of the consumer's inability to assess risk or due to the supplier's manipulation of cognitive biases or the existing practice of adverse selection.

V. Participants in the Regulatory Process

Hans Micklitz in Chapter 2 starts his analysis with the image of the weak consumer. He argues that EU consumer law was instrumentalised for the enhancement of the internal market. He points to a distinction between producerist and consumerist policies, understood as policies which as their primary focus take account of producers' and consumers' interests respectively. According to Micklitz, it was national consumer law which realised the programme of consumer protection. In the EU 'consumer welfare' is promoted through market efficiency. The other consequence of that is the fragmented character of today's image of the EU consumer. The interests of consumers are no longer linear and the different fora where legislation relevant for consumers is produced make their democratic participation difficult. Just as constitutional patriotism was to replace democracy in the EU, so should constitutionalisation of (consumer) private law create coherence necessary for a meaningful debate about the content of law regulating consumer transactions. Courts will ease that process but should not replace democratically legitimised legislative institutions.

But democratic participation is not the only way in which consumers may influence the regulatory process. Christopher Hodges in Chapter 10 discusses other ways in which consumers may effectively become regulators or influence regulatory choices made by legislative institutions and enforcement bodies, and also change market conditions by directly influencing the behaviour of traders. Hodges points out that the complaints and dispute resolution procedures, such as the Consumer Dispute Resolution mechanism introduced by an EU Directive, enable institutions to collect information on the market.[8] The collected data will allow policymakers to reconstruct actual choices of consumers and envisage more tailored and practically effective policies. Secondly, Hodges observes that one should not underestimate the role of consumers as direct regulators of markets. Through their actions (enforcement actions, consumer feedback) they create pressure on businesses to change their behaviour so that they can maintain a good reputation.

Dorota Leczykiewicz (Chapter 11), on the other hand, focusses mainly on the judicial review process in the EU as a step towards completing the EU's law-making cycle. The review practices of the Court of Justice of the EU are important due to the way in which they affect the legislative process. Leczykiewicz argues in favour of incorporating the principle of preventing regressive redistribution as a standard against which EU law affecting consumer interest should be assessed. In her view the law-making process in the EU is deficient because it does not require the institutions to take account of the question of who bears the regulatory cost and what economic implications consumers will have to face. She maintains that democratic and justice-promoting credentials of the EU require greater discursive engagement with financial burdens which EU policies create for consumers.

VI. Consumers Beyond Consumption

EU consumers have various identities and only a selection of their actual characteristics that can be taken as reference points for legislative policies. This creates a problem. Reducing the consumer to the act of consumption is not only arbitrary but potentially dangerous for all values other than self-gratification. Neoclassical economics presupposes that utility can be measured and that we are all rational utility-maximisers. Welfare economics takes account of other motivations and preferences of consumers but it is notoriously deficient in providing a basis for concrete policy choices. So what can be done and what should be done about values other than self-gratification in the law regulating consumer transactions?

[8] Directive 2013/11/EU of the European Parliament and of the Council of 21 May 2013 on alternative dispute resolution for consumer disputes (Directive on Consumer ADR) [2013] OJ L165/63.

Lucinda Miller in Chapter 12 discusses the question of ethical consumption. At the more descriptive level she asks whether the EU is at all interested in regulating for the ethical consumer. She notes that in reality consumers have a number of identities and only some acts of consumption are related to the image of the consumer which is currently prevalent in EU law. For this reason, Miller sees a negative effect of EU law on the practice of ethical consumption because the emphasis on the 'average' consumer creates policies which discourage consumers from building junctures of solidarity with the community. Collective interest is marginalised, leading to the removal of citizens' discourse from consumption regulation. The evidence of this is the labelling policy of the EU and the decision not to include information about the process of production. This focusses consumer attention on other issues and is not therefore normatively neutral. However, using labelling to provide information about the process of production is still a defective way of protecting the collective interest because it shifts the responsibility for creating a positive change onto the consumer. Consumers become fragmented not only as a group but also individually, within their particular selves, where practical concerns may be pulling them in a different direction from the one in which they are nudged by carefully constructed labels.

Hugh Collins in Chapter 13, on the other hand, considers the ethics of consumption from the perspective of (consumer) contract law. He sees contract regulation supporting ethical consumption as a continuation of an approach in contract law which sees it as an element of social policy, correcting imbalances between parties to the contract and ensuring respect human rights. Similarly to Miller, Collins focusses on negative externalities of contracting, created especially for those outside Europe, where goods retailed and consumed in the EU are produced in large numbers. He makes a strong case for treating human rights or environmental deficiencies in the production process as affecting the 'quality' of products and thereby giving consumers the right to rescind the contract. Contrary to Miller, he ascribes individual consumers a greater role in policing the market and enforcing compliance with human rights and environmental standards. In this way EU contract law could circumvent the obstacles posed by strict separation in international trade law between product and process and the difficulties which Member States have when they wish to impose bans on products relating to labour conditions under which they were produced. Consumers' expectations as to the process of production should, according to Collins, enrich the notion of 'satisfactory quality' in consumer law, although this naturally raises the question of the transformative effect of such an enriched understanding in a situation where empirical evidence shows that consumers do not have any particular process-related expectations.

Gareth Davies in Chapter 14 takes the question of non-consumption-related interests of consumers even further. His main interest is the interaction in EU law between economic and non-economic interests. Davies regrets that economic and social interests are separated as evidenced by an excessively transactional focus of free movement law, endorsed and deepened by the CJEU. As a result, the interests of the consumer as a member of the society and as a citizen in a democracy are undermined. Davies maintains that the Member States have insufficient means in EU law of protecting their rules on product quality, of confining economic activity and of protecting their citizens from burdensome choices which negatively affect their quality of life. While the author notes those instances where the Court and in consequence EU law are not blind to non-economic, non-transactional considerations (gambling, freedom of press, language, moral sensibilities) he maintains that there is a structural imbalance in EU free movement law, which is dangerous to European societies and the feeling of togetherness.

VII. Methods of Constructing the Image of the Consumer

The discussion of the personality of the EU consumer leads our attention to the question of how the image of the consumer which forms the foundation of policies in particular fields is constructed in EU legislative and judicial practice. The law may refer to consumers, their characteristics, preferences and expectations, but in the application of individual tests use assumptions, presumptions and rules of thumb. The choice of the method of constructing the image of the consumer and the level of engagement with empirical evidence tells us two things. First, it enables us to assess the extent to which the image is real or fictional; and second, if it is a fictional image, it reveals whether it is an expression of antecedent policy choices only masquerading as results of a reasoning process based on actual needs and characteristics of EU consumers, or the fictions are there merely as the necessary generalisations ensuring workability of the regulatory framework.

Vanessa Mak in Chapter 16 comes to the conclusion that the image of the consumer in EU law is fictional and is an expression of conscious regulatory choices. She lists various other roles which the EU consumer has to perform in EU law, such as that of relating to mediating competences between the EU and the Member States and that of the rational actor responsible for bringing about the internal market. Mak has a sceptical view of the EU consumer in EU regulatory law concerning contractual transactions. The notion of the 'weak' consumer is in her view used instrumentally to justify regulatory interventions into private law relationships. The 'autonomous' consumer, so dominant in national laws, is absent from EU law which, according to Mak, suggests an insufficient engagement with policy choices made at the national level.

Graeme Dinwoodie and Dev Gangjee in Chapter 15 examine the character of the image of the consumer in EU trade mark law. Their main thesis is that the consumer in that field of law is in parts an empirical and normative construct. They clearly explain areas where actually measured behaviour of consumers is taken into account in the assessment process. They also draw a very useful distinction between the normative and formal concepts of the consumer, and treat formalism as the law's response to applicatory challenges, which do not necessarily make the rules diverge from standards constructed on the basis of statistical evidence, if such was available and reliable. Empirical evidence does play a role in informing judicial decision-making, in particular with respect to such questions as consumer perceptions and market conditions. Empirical evidence may also play a role via national law where EU trade mark law leaves to national procedural rules the regulation of the burden of proof and the way in which the likelihood of confusion, central for the finding of the trade mark's infringement, is to be established. Dinwoodie and Gangjee explain that EU trade mark law has borrowed concepts from free movement law, in particular the concept of the 'average' consumer. This shows that despite the verbal formulations which suggest statistical references, the consumer in EU trade mark law is instrumentalised to maximise its harmonising effects, and for this purpose necessarily requires a normative element. This also explains why in the context of national trade marks the CJEU allows greater reliance on empirical evidence leading to more varied scope of protection, sensitive to particular market conditions and linguistic variations.

Sybe de Vries is, on the other hand, interested in the purely normative aspect of the image of the consumer in EU law (Chapter 17). He explains that the consumer is conceptualised both as responsible for building the internal market and as its beneficiary. The normative image with which EU law operates is constructed by references to various sources, not only the Treaties and the recently introduced concept of 'social market economy' but also the Charter of Fundamental Rights. Free movement law can easily incorporate this normative version of the consumer because it has for a long time used normative standards, such as consumer protection, including the protection of vulnerable consumers, the protection of fundamental rights, including the protection of the child, and the respect for constitutional identities. The framework of free movement law entails that the image of the consumer will be able to adapt to the challenges which the author sets out, such as increased globalisation, informatisation and financial instability of the modern world.

VIII. Who is the EU Consumer?

Being a consumer in the EU market means participating in transactions and using goods retailed and services provided on that market. Simply through these activities consumers are implicated in the EU's market regulation, whether or not we perceive this regulation to be directed towards the interests of consumers. The title of this book implies that the images of the consumer which can be constructed on the basis of careful analysis of EU law are multiple. At the very least we have shown that consumer images are used both as points of reference in policy formation and also as goals of regulation. So who is the consumer which emerges from the review of this broad investigation of EU law?

The EU consumer is certainly someone who still retains contractual autonomy and choice. Consumer transactions are reviewable only to a limited extent. Consumers continue to be entitled to enter into transactions even to their detriment. Moreover, the opened market of the EU gives the EU consumer the opportunity to enhance their autonomy. This image is not restricted to the EU context. The case for deregulation and liberalisation of markets across Europe and beyond has frequently been underpinned by a discourse which assumes that the consumer will benefit from that process. The loosening of State intervention and the increase in the number of suppliers is promoted under an expectation that the consumer will use the market to their advantage, but there is no watertight protection from bad choices.

But the consumer is also someone who, according to policy preferences exhibited by EU law, needs to change and whose habits need to be broken down. The EU consumer is encouraged by law and by permissively treated advertising to buy foreign products and services. This policy goal triggers a whole range of initiatives, strongly related to building consumer confidence not only to participate in the market but also to enter into cross-border transactions. This image of the consumer is visible in both free movement and competition law. In fact, in some respects this image drives the interpretation of those Treaty provisions. The employment of EU law as a means to generate dynamic change in market structures is attached to the role of the consumer. As the Court has (rather loftily) observed, EU law puts to the test national rules which 'crystallize given consumer habits so as to consolidate an advantage acquired by national industries concerned to comply with them'.[9] Also the legislative *acquis* is commonly treated, as a number of chapters in this volume have shown, as a contribution to consumer confidence improving the functioning of the internal market.

The responsibility of EU consumers reaches also the sphere of enforcement. In EU law the consumer is a bearer of enforceable rights. But this image is not without problems. Access to justice is plainly relatively more costly for a consumer than a trader. And most cases in which EU law is pleaded indeed involve litigation by traders, not consumers. It is perfectly plausible to see some such cases as instances of traders litigating as proxies for consumers: *Cassis de Dijon* stands as an enduring example of this model, as public regulation was shaken out by litigation to reveal wider scope for private autonomy.[10] But the fact of the matter is that they were not brought by consumers. There are also occasional examples of consumers (or at least their representatives) reaching the CJEU[11] and examples too of the Court seeking to promote the protection of the consumer by interpreting Treaty

[9] Case 178/84 *Commission v Germany* [1987] ECR 1227; Case 170/78 *Commission v United Kingdom* [1980] ECR 417.

[10] *Cassis de Dijon* (n 1).

[11] Joined cases C–178/94, C–179/94, C–188/94, C–189/94 and C–190/94 *Erich Dillenkofer, Christian Erdmann, Hans-Jürgen Schulte, Anke Heuer, Werner, Ursula and Trosten Knor v Bundesrepublik Deutschland* [1996] ECR I–4845.

provisions as apt for direct enforcement by consumers[12] and by requiring that national procedural rules that obstruct access to justice be set aside in the name of the effectiveness of EU law.[13] In contrast, within legislative *acquis* the role of consumers as enforcers is more visible. National courts act as intermediaries, resolving consumer disputes, but even there enforcement is considered suboptimal and the EU is eager to introduce new solutions such as the Collective Redress mechanism and the Directive on the Consumer Dispute Resolution.[14]

The image of a weak or vulnerable consumer, advocated as the correct paradigm for EU law by many authors in this volume, is obviously in stark contrast with the consumer who is expected to enforce their rights with vigour and determination. The image of the consumer in need of protection sustains aspects of a large number of EU measures of secondary legislation. Protective logic is visible in some measures of general application, such as Directive 93/13, which requires the prohibition of unfair terms in consumer contracts, and Directive 2005/29, which addresses unfair commercial practices.[15] Directive 2005/29 treats the consumer, as it should if adequate protection is to be ensured, as 'economically weaker and less experienced in legal matters' than the trader.[16] A consumer protection rationale operates also in more sector-specific contexts, including supply of credit (especially mortgage credit), alcohol, tobacco, energy and financial services. Patients, too, are treated as 'vulnerable' in the context of the level of safety they are entitled to expect from medical devices.[17] Sometimes the legislative *acquis* might target particular groups of vulnerable consumers (in energy markets, for example, or markets for financial services) or at least, even if in principle of general application, a measure may accommodate the possibility in appropriate circumstances to justify a focus on a particular group of vulnerable consumers.

So the image of the vulnerable consumer is present but its unsystematic treatment in EU law makes its dominance questionable and easily resisted in concrete legislative proposals. The 'average consumer' remains the benchmark. This is problematic if one remembers that harmonisation of laws locates at the EU level the responsibility to secure consumer protection. The average consumer, a largely fictitious and normative construct, should have limits. The real sensitivity surrounds determination of just where those limits should be placed, in particular in the application of free movement and competition law and perhaps less so, but still very significantly, in the shaping of the EU's legislative *acquis*.

12 Joined cases C–295/04 *Vincenzo Manfredi v Lloyd Adriatico Assicurazioni SpA* [2006] ECR I–6619.

13 Case C–168/05 *Elisa María Mostaza Claro v Centro Móvil Milenium SL* [2006] ECR I–10421.

14 Commission, 'Recommendation of 11 June 2013 on common principles for injunctive and compensatory collective redress mechanisms in the Member States concerning violations of rights granted under Union Law' [2013] OJ L201/60; Directive on Consumer ADR (n 8).

15 Council Directive 93/13/EEC of 5 April 1993 on unfair terms in consumer contracts [1993] OJ L95/29; Unfair Commercial Practices Directive (n 7).

16 Case C–388/13 *Nemzeti Fogyasztóvédelmi Hatóság*, judgment of 16 April 2015, para 53.

17 Joined cases C–503/13 and C–504/13 *Boston Scientific Medizintechnik GmbH v AOK Sachsen-Anhalt—Die Gesundheitskasse*, judgment of 5 March 2015, esp paras 39 and 54.

The citizenship status of EU consumers, their capacity to participate in the democratic process, the ability to protect values reaching beyond self-gratification, and the possibility of retaining simultaneous membership in multiple communities—local, national, European—is also the subject of many chapters in this book. The image of the EU consumer as a citizen, largely absent from positive law but much discussed in the literature, insists on a more active understanding of the consumer in the market. It looks more broadly to the consumer as a citizen and to the market as simply an element within society. The starting point for future legal development could be justification in free movement cases where the CJEU has shown sensitivity to broader social and political concerns of the market. The image of the EU consumer as a citizen could also form part of the legislative agenda at EU level. The Court has consistently taken the view that provided an adequate contribution to the functioning of the internal market is demonstrated, there is no objection at all to an EU measure adopted pursuant to Article 114 TFEU taking wider policy objectives such as public health, consumer protection or animal welfare as a 'decisive factor in the choices to be made'.[18] This carries considerable potential in future policy elaboration.

However, even if a whole range of values could effectively be expressed through EU law the problem of the multi-layered nature of regulation of consumer transactions in the EU makes consumers' engagement difficult. EU law competes on this terrain with national law. A particular manifestation of this pattern of regulatory inter-relations addresses the impact of EU legislation on residual national competence. It is, in short, the minimum *versus* maximum debate. An image of the consumer which values the national level as a site of regulatory responsibility is far more likely to favour minimum rulemaking by the EU. Conversely an image of the consumer which is wedded to the smooth functioning of the internal market would drive a strong preference for the EU to adopt rules of a maximum character, shutting out room for divergent choices at the national level.

Consumer law, as with other parts of EU law, is a site of complex and overlapping tiers of governance dominated by the unstable process of jumbled coordination between national and transnational law. And it is not easy to locate one's loyalties. While some are ready to perceive national law as predominantly protective of consumers, and EU law as predominantly Ordoliberal and market oriented, such simplifications can be dangerous, especially in the now more diverse EU of 28 Member States. Equally, the question of the level of democratic participation or democratic deficit between the EU and the Member States has to be approached carefully and does not point to an obvious winner with which loyalty bonds should be formed.

[18] Case C–380/03 *Germany v Parliament and Council* [2006] ECR I–11573, para 43; Case C–58/08 *The Queen, on the application of Vodafone Ltd and Others v Secretary of State for Business, Enterprise and Regulatory Reform* [2010] ECR I–4999, para 36; Case T–526/10 *Inuit Tapiriit Kanatami v Commission*, judgment of 25 April 2013, para 41.

Whichever position one is taking in this debate, it is apparent that the consumer already is and is likely to become an even more important figure in EU law. Part of it stems from the societal consequences of problems associated with consumption and consumerism. Debt as a social problem naturally transcends the consumer sector and, as a consequence of the high levels of borrowing by middle and lower classes from the rich, becomes a factor contributing to the sore of increasing inequality in society. Similarly, EU competitiveness and stability depend on choices made by individuals and the level of their consciousness about these choices' implications for the European economy. If the EU wishes to shape consumer choices and continue to link them with goals unrelated to individual and immediate preferences of consumers, it needs to open its accountability paths to consumers. The consumer has become the new sovereign; political consequences have to follow.

2

The Consumer: Marketised, Fragmentised, Constitutionalised

HANS-W MICKLITZ*

I. Market, State and Society[1]

Using Max Weber's distinction between market, state and society,[2] I will link the consumer to the market (the national and the Internal Market), to the state (the Member States and the EU) and to society (national society and European society). I will try to show how the shift from the national to the European, from the national market to the European market, from the nation state to the EU and from national society to European society has changed the concept of the consumer, roughly from the weak consumer to the circumspect consumer. This means that in order to understand the concept of the consumer one has to compare its former and latter versions; the older and the newer image; the primary concept—the social welfare paradigm where the weaker party enjoys protection through the state—and the degenerated one—where the marketised and fragmentised consumer has

* I would like to thank Marija Bartl (Amsterdam) and Dorota Leczykiewicz (University of Oxford) for their extremely useful comments. The responsibility remains mine alone.

[1] Self-references do not enjoy much reputation. That is why I prefer to point to a number of contributions which serve as background to the current paper and without which my argument might at times appear opaque or undeveloped. On *autonomy*: G Comparato and H-W Micklitz, 'Regulated Autonomy between Market Freedoms and Fundamental Rights in the Case Law of the CJEU' in U Bernitz, X Groussot and F Schulyok (eds), *General Principles of EU Law and European Private Law* (Farnham, Ashgate, 2013) 121–54; on the transformation of the *market state*: together with D Patterson, 'From the Nation State to the Market State: The Evolution of EU Private Law', *EUI Working Paper LAW* 2012/15, also in B van Vooren, S Blockmans and J Wouters (eds), *The EU's Role in Global Governance: The Legal Dimension* (Oxford, Oxford University Press, 2013) 59–78; on *access justice*: 'Social Justice and Access Justice in Private Law' in H-W Micklitz (ed), *The Many Faces of Social Justice in Private Law* (Cheltenham, Elgar, 2011); on the *future of consumer law*: H-W Micklitz, 'Do Consumers and Business need a New Architecture for Consumer Law? A Thought Provoking Impulse' (2013) 32 *Yearbook of European Law* 266.

[2] M Weber, *Wirtschaft und Gesellschaft* 1st edn (1925).

to fight, often in reliance on his or her constitutional rights. This cannot be done without positioning myself in how I see the future of consumer law.

It seems that the European integration project, in particular the impact it has on the market, the state and society, is recently encountering ever stronger resistance—not only in political but also in academic circles. One of the deeper reasons seems to be the fact that the driving force behind the European integration project, what JHH Weiler[3] described as 'European messianism', gradually faded away after the fall of the Berlin Wall. This goes hand in hand with the rise of nationalism in politics and in legal research, often driven by a diffuse sentiment that the world was better in the old times. Politicians and scholars seem to be longing for the time before the European integration project gained pace. At the very least, they long for an arrangement in which Member States had a stronger say and a stronger role in day-to-day politics, which meant that they could defend their particular variation of the values which govern the market, society and state.

There is certainly a need for a kind of taking stock, for a thorough analysis of the reach of the impact of European integration on the market, on the state and on society. My argument is that all three are undergoing transformations and that it is necessary to understand the drivers behind these transformations. This is what I am going to do. The purpose of this chapter is to reconstruct the paths which consumer law has taken in the last 50 years—that is, since the famous declaration of President Kennedy in 1962. I am aware that in doing so I am conveying a message. A choice of explanatory theory is never neutral. So what is the normative message behind this chapter? I would like to put forward the following arguments: (1) the *instrumentalisation* of consumer law to complete the Internal Market to shape a European Market State and to build a European society has reached a stage where it is necessary to start reminding the policy-makers and ourselves that autonomy and the responsibility of the individual formed the foundations of the European Enlightenment; and (2) in the design of the consumer image there is more at stake than economic efficiency, in the meaning of US consumerism, and social justice, in the meaning of EU producerism.[4] We should start caring again about the values of the Enlightenment (autonomy and personal responsibility). It is a mistake to focus only on the values of economic efficiency and social justice.

[3] J Weiler, 'Deciphering the Political and Legal DNA of European Integration: An Exploratory Essay' in J Dickson and P Eleftheriadis (eds), *Philosophical Foundations of European Union Law* (Oxford, Oxford University Press, 2012) 147 arguing that 'political messianism' constitutes the political and legal (cultural) DNA of European integration. This 'messianism' is the direct result of World War Two, condensed in the Schuman Manifesto, resting on the two pillars of European civilisation: 'the enlightenment and the heritage of the French revolution and European Christian tradition'.

[4] JQ Whitman, 'Consumerism Versus Producerism: A Study in Comparative Law' (2007) 117 *Yale Law Journal* 340.

II. The Argument

My central focus is on how the EU consumer is subjected to transformations of the market, the state and society.[5] In a way, these transformations occur consecutively: first the market, then the state and finally society. This results from the shift from the national to the European level, from national markets to the completion of the Internal Market, from nation states being responsible for consumer protection to the EU gradually taking over and turning into the major regulator of consumer law around the world, from the national society in which the consumer has been embedded to the emergence of a European society. Let us recall the major Treaty amendments: the Single European Act, which strengthened the Internal Market in 1986; the Maastricht Treaty, which introduced the Monetary Union in 1991; and the Lisbon Treaty, which made the Charter of Fundamental Rights an integral part of EU law in 2009.

A. Market

The consumer as a societal configuration (*eine soziale Konfiguration*)[6] must be seen as inherently linked to the market for goods and services. From that perspective, what is dominant is their role as a passive or active market participant: buying and selling goods and services and being the subject of extensive regulation to 'protect' their economic interests and their rights against risks to their health and safety. As a result, the consumer cannot exist and be conceptualised without the law which surrounds them. Until the 1970s, markets were first and foremost national markets. The completion of the Internal Market project, promoted through the Single European Act, went hand in hand with a transfer of regulatory power from the nation state to the EU. Today it is primarily EU law which sets the tone. Moreover, since the EU has taken over market regulation, consumer law has taken a different direction. It has to fit what is needed to complete the Internal Market. Consumer law is instrumentalised. The result is what I shall call the 'marketised consumer'.

B. State

The consumer in relation to their 'state'—that is, the nation state—appears as a citizen who participates in the law-making process through exercising their

[5] Though not using this terminology, but telling a similar story of the transformations of consumer law in a different language: S Weatherill, *EU Consumer Law and Policy* (Cheltenham, Edward Elgar, 2005).

[6] What is meant here is that the consumer is a societal actor: they are the product of the society in which they are embedded and they behave and act within the societal boundaries. For the consumer as a societal configuration see T Roethe, *Der Verbraucher—Rechtssoziologische Betrachtungen* (Baden-Baden, Nomos, 2014).

voting rights. They may vote for a political party that is more or less consumer-friendly, which usually comes down to something like paternalism. Linking the market, the state and consumer law explains why there is a broad variety of consumer legislation in the Member States, which reflects the substantial differences in the extent to which consumers may rely on their 'state' to enjoy protection.[7] The Member States have delegated the law-making power to the EU. This affects the consumer as a citizen. Consumer law is made in Brussels and Strasbourg. Voting and participation follows different patterns. Once a directive or regulation is adopted, national parliaments are bound to implement what has been decided in the Council and in the European Parliament. So long as harmonisation aimed to guarantee minimum protection, Member States were free to maintain or introduce standards which went beyond the minimum standards.[8] However, since the Lisbon Council in 2000,[9] the EU is striving for full harmonisation in consumer law.[10] Full harmonisation deprives the Member States from their law-making powers. Any revision is subject to a political majority in the EU decision-making process. Consumer law and consumer policy are centralised in Brussels and at the same time fragmented for each sector. Centralisation and fragmentation are joint processes. This affects the relationship between the EU and Member States. The nation states lose power and importance and the EU is taking over as the enabling state—the market state. The result of all these changes is that the political commitment of consumers is limited to their participation in the election for the EU Parliament and in the consultation processes which are initiated by the European Commission. However, at the same time, consumer participation becomes fragmented. Because it concerns proposals coming from Brussels, it can only be bound to a particular regulatory project—most often the shaping and making of regulated markets.[11]

C. Society

The consumer as a societal actor operates in a societal environment which is largely local and mainly national. Consumers in such a perspective are producers

[7] The Eurobarometer is a wonderful source of information to study the relationship between consumer expectations and state responsibilities <www.ec.europa.eu/public_opinion/index_en.htm> accessed 21 March 2015.

[8] I will not deal with the problem that it is difficult to distinguish between the minimum and the maximum.

[9] European Council, 'The Lisbon Special European Council (March 2000): Towards a Europe of Innovation and Knowledge' <www.europa.eu/legislation_summaries/education_training_youth/general_framework/c10241_en.htm> accessed 21 March 2015 ('The Lisbon Declaration').

[10] Commission, Consumer Policy Strategy 2002–2006 COM(2002) 208 final.

[11] The modes of participation of consumers have attracted more attention from political scientists than lawyers. W Streek, 'The Politics of Public Debt: Neoliberalism, Capitalist Development, and the Restructuring of the State' (2014) 15 *German Economic Review* 143. My analysis from 2009 is somewhat outdated: H-W Micklitz, 'Regulatory Strategies on Services Contracts in EC Law' in F Cafaggi and H Muir Watt (eds), *Regulatory Strategies and New Modes of Governance* (Cheltenham, Edward Elgar, 2009).

in their households[12] and are involved in ground-level societal activities, such as self-organisation and membership in non-governmental organisations. The relationship between the members of society and the state may be modelled on the French or US constitution. For the former, the state constitutes society; for the latter, the society constitutes the constitution.[13] The European integration process affects the relationship between the members of the society and their state. Gradually the relationship becomes looser. For consumers, the changes are most visible in areas where former state monopolies have been replaced by competitive markets. Instead of the state taking care of the basic needs of consumers, they find themselves in a competitive environment where they have to choose the supplier and where regulatory agencies are turning into the major addressees of complaints.[14] Europe has enlarged the societal space—not only through liberalisation, and partly through the privatisation of state monopolies, but also through the strong promotion of the Internet, which at least in theory enables consumers to participate in the internal market more fully. The growing societal space, subject to language barriers, provides ample opportunities for ground-level activities across national borders.[15] The constitutionalisation of the EU was meant to hold European society together and to establish, in its most ambitious variant, the 'United States of Europe', with a constitution and a European civil code. Both projects failed,[16] but what remained is the growing importance of fundamental rights which European citizen consumers may use to fill the empty societal space with legal—that is, constitutional—rules. Although constitutionalisation of private law is not new,[17] it takes a different form at the EU level, because the EU lacks the form of a state, or more precisely because of the market-state character of the EU.[18] In the national context constitutionalisation is embedded into a

[12] For more than 20 years there has been discussion in economics on consumers as producers, a dimension which is usually excluded from a legal analysis.

[13] H Arendt, *On Revolution* 1st edn (New York, Viking Press, 1963).

[14] M Freedland, 'The Marketisation of Public Services' in C Crouch, K Eder and D Tambini (eds), *Citizenship, Markets and the State* (Oxford, Oxford University Press, 2001) 90; H-W Micklitz, 'Universal Services: Nucleus for a Social European Private Law?' in M Cremona (ed), *Market Integration and Public Services* (Oxford, Oxford University Press, 2011).

[15] See R Münch, *Die Konstruktion der europäischen Gesellschaft—Zur Dialektik von transnationaler Integration und nationaler Desintegration* (Frankfurt, Campus, 2008); R Münch, *European Governmentality—The Liberal Drift of Multilevel Governance* (London, Routledge, 2010).

[16] H-W Micklitz, 'Failure or Ideological Preconceptions? Thoughts on Two Grand Projects: the European Con-stitution and the European Civil Code' in K Tuori and S Sankari (eds), *The Many Constitutions of Europe*, (Farnham, Ashgate, 2010).

[17] C Mak, *Fundamental Rights in European Contract Law: A Comparison of the Impact of Fundamental Rights on Contractual Relationships in Germany, the Netherlands, Italy and England* (Alphen aan den Rijn, Kluwer, 2008); S Grundmann (ed), *Constitutional Values and European Contract Law* (Alphen aan den Rijn, Kluwer, 2008); G Brüggemeier, A Colombi Ciacchi and G Comandé (eds), *Fundamental Rights and Private Law in the European Union—A Comparative Overview*, vol 1 (Cambridge, Cambridge University Press, 2010); O Cherednychenko, *Fundamental Rights, Contract Law and the Protection of the Weaker Party* (Munich, Sellier, 2007).

[18] H-W Micklitz (ed), *Constitutionalisation of European Private Law* (Oxford, Oxford University Press, 2014).

national legal, economic and social environment. Courts resolve national conflicts about the reach of consumer protection. Whenever constitutionalisation occurs at the EU level, there is no 'state' at the centre, but a quasi-state at best. There is no homogenous market because the internal market project still remains unfinished. And there is no homogeneous European society. Therefore, a judgment of the Court of Justice of the EU (CJEU) is received in a totally different economic and social environment. These two dimensions should be kept distinct.

III. Marketisation, Fragmentation and Constitutionalisation

The following should be read as an attempt to visualise the various developments and trends which will be analysed in light of the overall distinction between markets, states and societies,[19] characterised and condensed in marketisation, fragmentation and constitutionalisation.

	Marketisation	**Fragmentation**	**Constitutionalisation**
Key actors	Market	Executive and regulatory agencies	Courts
Mode of construction	Market building	Silo building	Society building
Means and function	Regulation and self-regulation	Co-regulation and compliance	Last resort control
Problem solving	Self-executing and private party managed ADR/ODR	Administrative enforcement and supervised ADR/ODR	Serious conflicts—courts as societal agents
Values	Efficiency	Rationalities	Moral values
Images	The rational consumer	Varity of consumer images	The right to be treated as a consumer
Transformations	From a national to a European market	From nation states to supranational executive powers	From institutional protections to individual rights

The reader may have the impression that the transformations described are argued to have taken place in a chronological order. This impression is both correct and incorrect. On the one hand, marketisation constitutes a necessary prerequisite

[19] This last part should be read together with the introduction, more precisely with the explanation of my argument.

for fragmentation. It suffices to recall that liberalisation and privatisation only started in 1986 and were triggered by the adoption of the Single European Act. Yet, the state-controlled part of the market was not completely phased out. The two kinds of market still coexisted. There is an obvious connection between the Internal Market for goods, which has largely been completed, and the Internal Market for services, which is highly fragmented and not yet fully completed. Another trend started with the emergence of a new mode of communication—the Internet. The Internet cuts across all markets. This should be contrasted with more direct forms of communication, which are only possible in the context of a club and which indeed exist only in such a context.[20] Constitutionalisation, understood as the opening up of the common market via the Court of Justice's *Cassis de Dijon* decision, can be first located at the beginning of marketisation. The opening of state markets was a crucial building block for the development of the European Economic Constitution. The series of judgments which started in 1979 would 'only' be evidence of the change from economic to societal rights—from an Economic Constitution to a constitutional order. The result could be described as a constitution with a small 'c'.[21]

Although they are interlinked and interpenetrated, the three contexts in which the consumer appears—the consumer in the Internal Market, the consumer as the focus of the activities of supranational executive agencies, and the consumer as a holder of supranational human and fundamental rights—are in fact three separate 'legal worlds' which exist in parallel and have their own *Eigenleben*, which means that they enjoy an independent existence. What remains to be clarified is whether and how the three legal worlds, with their three different images of the consumer, could be linked. As to whether they should be linked, at this stage I am arguing neither in favour of coherence and against fragmentation, nor in favour of the status quo. My purpose is to establish some kind of rules which would be needed to build some connections between the independent trends and the fragmented field.

A. Marketisation

The marketised consumer is one who is reduced to a market-behavioural function. The consumer society in Europe started in the 1960s. Choice increased tremendously but was restricted to choice between nationally produced products. There were no supermarkets but small shops around the corner with which the consumer formed societal relations. The rise of consumer policy was connected to

[20] L Bernstein, 'Private Commercial Law in the Cotton Industry: Creating Cooperation Through Rules, Norms and Institutions' (2001) 99 *Michigan Law Review* 1724. In the European context standardisation might serve as an example where a close network still dominates, which is very similar to the club mentality described by Bernstein.

[21] N Walker, 'Big "C" or Small "c"?' (2006) 12 *European Law Journal* 12.

the conviction that an increased choice created particular problems for consumer information, for risks to health and safety and for the protection of economic interests because of a lack of appropriate remedies.[22] National consumer law and national consumer policy remained within the boundaries of the nation state. The addressees of the legislation were national consumers and national producers. Responsibility and liability were shaped around the construction of national markets.

In 1979, *Cassis de Dijon* changed this peaceful world dramatically. National legislation which shaped the national economy (cars, foodstuffs, alcohol, cosmetics) had to pass a rationality test.[23] Freedom of choice in an increasing Common Market and *information regulation* instead of *national prohibitions* reduced the opportunities for national voice and for political participation in the shaping of the national economy.[24] First, *Cassis de Dijon* paved the way for the Internal Market project—market integration was achieved through mutual recognition. Mutual recognition was then by and large replaced by harmonisation. The impact on consumer law was immense.[25] Pending harmonisation projects could be adopted on the basis of majority voting. While the effects were first welcomed as an increase in economic freedom, they have recently come under attack due to their cultural and societal consequences, aspects of the European market integration which were previously neglected.[26] Supermarkets instead of retail shops, driving with a car to the supermarket instead of walking to the small shop and chatting with the owner, Internet retail shops heavily promoted by the EU through appropriate regulation so that Internet sales can now replace the dominance of supermarkets. Consumers do not have to leave their home any more: products are brought to their home. The systematic emphasis on Internet sales in the EU not only brings about economic implications between different sales measures—it also has societal implications which touch on the very foundation of society.

I call the process through which the consumer has gone as a result of internal-market integration 'marketisation'. In the 1960s the consumer was very much an object of the societal welfare state. They needed protection and the rhetoric of the weaker party was developed and integrated into national legal systems. This was achieved most obviously through the introduction of mandatory disclosure of information, through making consumer rights in contractual relations binding, and through the control of standard contract terms and of unfair advertising.

[22] See R Nader, who wrote the influential book *Unsafe at Any Speed* (New York, Grossman Publishers, 1965), which triggered the rise of product liability in the US.

[23] C Joerges, 'The Europeanisation of Private Law as a Rationalisation Process and as a Contest of Disciplines—an Analysis of the Directive on Unfair Terms in Consumer Contracts' (1995) 3 *European Review of Private Law* 175.

[24] M Dani, 'Assembling the Fractured European Consumer' (2011) 36 *European Law Review* 362.

[25] H-W Micklitz, P Rott, N Reich and K Tonner, *European Consumer Law* (Cambridge, Intersentia, 2014).

[26] G Davies, 'Democracy and Legitimacy in the Shadow of Purposive Competence' (2015) 21 *European Law Journal* 2.

Marketisation requires a different type of consumer—an active market participant who is ready to 'reap the benefits of the Internal Market'.[27] It has resulted in many trends, and we can now observe many 'from … tos' which mark the path of marketisation. For the purpose of this chapter, a list of the most important changes will suffice. They include: the move from a national societal welfare policy to a consumer policy as a pick-a-pack procedure in Internal-Market building (Article 114 TFEU); the movement from politics (rulemaking through regulation) to markets (as regulators); from regulation to rights (with a strong focus on the individual who is pushed to enforce their individual rights); from consumer protection law (which sees the consumer as the weaker party) to consumer law without protection (which considers the consumer an active market participant); from social justice through mandatory consumer law to market efficiency (whereby each and every rule is submitted to a test whether its stated objectives increase the efficiency of the market); from a consumer policy as protection of economic interests and protection against risks to health and safety (the 1962 declaration of consumer rights by President Kennedy) to a consumer policy which focusses ever more strongly on financial transactions—on borrowing money (consumer credit and mortgages) and granting securities (still very much in the national arena) and consumer investment (MIFID I and MIFID II).[28]

B. The American Challenge

There is more to add. Europe is on the edge of a new paradigm shift: from European producerism—focussing on the protection of consumer—to US consumerism—promoting consumer welfare through market efficiency. The distinction comes from an article by Whitman.[29] Despite all the insistence of citizens in Member States on their cultural and societal particularities, Whitman succeeded in merging the different European approaches in one handsome formula: producerism, which eloquently expresses the common element of all these approaches—concern for consumer protection. The American Law Institute has recently set up a Working Group on the restatement of consumer law. The general reporters are Oren Bar-Gill, Omri Ben-Shahar and Florencia Marotta-Wurgler. All three of them are heavily involved in behavioural economics and conduct research on consumer welfarism.[30] Economic efficiency as a paradigm enshrined

[27] This language stems from the Lisbon Declaration (n 9).

[28] Directive 2004/39/EC of the European Parliament and of the Council of 21 April 2004 on markets in financial instruments [2004] OJ L145/1; Directive 2014/65/EU of the European Parliament and of the Council of 15 May 2014 on markets in financial instruments [2014] OJ L173/349.

[29] Whitman (n 4).

[30] The American Law Institute, 'Restatement of the Law, Consumer Contracts' <www.ali.org/index.cfm?fuseaction=projects.proj_ip&projectid=25> accessed 21 March 2015.

in a liberal market economy (in the meaning defined by Hall and Soskice)[31] drives the re-conceptualisation of consumer law. From the perspective of the economic efficiency paradigm, European consumer law seems dysfunctional due to its unsophisticated reliance on the information paradigm and its strict regulation of standard contract terms. European consumer law also seems counterproductive due to its distorting market effects. It does not account for the fact that consumers are biased, that they over- or underestimate their capacities to take rational decisions, and, last but not least, that this bias-based behaviour may lead to redistributional effects that are detrimental to the most disadvantaged consumers.[32]

US consumer law does not have much to contribute to European consumer law if we look through the rose-tinted glasses of European welfarism. US consumer law is composed of two elements: consumer financial services and class actions. The former failed in the financial crisis[33] and the latter is currently being dismantled, with the support of the US Supreme Court, through the legalisation of arbitration clauses.[34] The US doctrine of unconscionability could be mentioned as a potential antidote. But contrary to the continental equivalent of 'good faith', unconscionability has not yet made its way into the court room—at least not as a substitute for social regulation.[35] So if the EU followed the doctrine of economic efficiency—at least in its radical form[36]—most of the mandatory consumer law that is meant to protect the consumer in all circumstances would be reviewed and would probably not pass the economic efficiency test.

[31] PA Hall and D Soskice, 'An Introduction to Varieties of Capitalism' in PA Hall and D Soskice (eds), *Varieties of Capitalism—The Institutional Foundations of Comparative Advantage* (Oxford, Oxford University Press, 2001). For the update on the developments following the discussion, see D Bohle and B Greskovits, 'Varieties of Capitalism and Capitalism "tout court"' (2009) 50 *European Journal of Sociology* 355, 363, who distinguish four strains of discussion: (1) empirical and methodological questions; (2) social statics; (3) social dynamics; and (4) valid theories about capitalism.

[32] See for an insightful overview on the current strains of discussion, F Esposito, *Consumer Protection in the World of Bounded Rationality: An Attempt to Understand the Contribution of Behavioural Law and Economics* (manuscript, 2014) on file with the author; very helpful review in H Collins, 'O Bar-Gill, Seduction by Contract: Law, Economics, and Psychology in Consumer Markets' (Oxford, Oxford University Press, 2012)' (2014) 77 *Modern Law Review* 1030, who gives an account of the current—mainly US—discussion.

[33] G Trumbull (ed), *Consumer Lending in France and America Credit and Welfare* (New York, Cambridge University Press, 2014); as well as O Bar-Gill, *Seduction by Contract: Law, Economics, and Psychology in Consumer Markets* (Oxford, Oxford University Press, 2012), who is also analysing the mortgage market in the US.

[34] N Reich, 'Negotiation and Adjudication. Class Actions and Arbitration Clauses in Consumer Contracts' in F Cafaggi and H-W Micklitz (eds), *New Frontiers of Consumer Protection—The Interplay Between Private and Public Enforcement* (Cheltenham, Edward Elgar, 2009). See also C Riefa (ed), *Consumer Arbitration* (Middlesex, University of Brunel, 2015), forthcoming.

[35] In respect of Germany, see D Hart, *Allgemeine Geschäftsbedingungen und Justizsystem* (Frankfurt, Kronberg, 1974) who points to the role of courts in using good faith and *bones mores* as a means to submit standard terms to a judicial control, long before the German Act on Unfair Contract Terms (Gesetz zur Regelung des Rechts der Allgemeinen Geschäftsbedingungen, 1976) was adopted.

[36] There are many strands and varieties of approaches in the US debate. While many scholars do not go that far, those representing a more radical approach argue that consumer law, or at least mandatory consumer law, should be abolished.

My point is still slightly different. I would like to change the focus of the EU consumer law debate. Instead of discussing the issues of consumer law from the perspective of the market, we should also look at society. John Rawls, in his letter to Philippe van Parijs, formulated the question, which I think we should ask in Europe today, in the following way:[37]

> One question the Europeans should ask themselves, if I may hazard a suggestion, is how far-reaching they want their union to be. It seems to me that much would be lost if the European Union became a federal union like the United States. Here there is a common language of political discourse and a ready willingness to move from one state to another. Isn't there a conflict between a large free and open market comprising all of Europe and the individual nation-states, each with its separate political and societal institutions, historical memories, and forms and traditions of societal policy. Surely these are great value to the citizens of these countries and give meaning to their life. The large open market including all of Europe is aim of the large banks and the capitalist business class whose main goal is simply larger profit. The idea of economic growth, onwards and upwards, with no specific end in sight, fits this class perfectly. If they speak about distribution, it is [al]most always in terms of trickle down. The long-term result of this—which we already have in the United States—is a civil society awash in a meaningless consumerism of some kind. I can't believe that that is what you want.

The envisaged US–EU trade agreement seems to confirm the preference for the large open market. We see a trend towards more market, more choice and more information, rather than a trend towards the confirmation of a European identity—an identity which can be found in a common language of political discourse through diversity. It is hard to imagine that the so- called *Brussels effect*[38] of EU social standards, which affect the US market, not only but also in consumer law, will be taken off the political agenda.[39] The criticasters of US consumerism have an intellectual hero to whom they can refer. Rawls' statement is moralistic, and the point is whether and to what extent there is room in a globalised economy for divergent social standards, for different images of the consumer. So far, behavioural economics has been too focussed on economic efficiency as its guiding objective, to which all empirical findings are subordinated. However, the irrational, bounded rationale and bias-based behaviour of consumers can be politically mature and might result in resistance against all forms of instrumentalisation. This at least reflects a sociological view of consumer behaviour. Economists tend to ignore the fact that consumers are also societal and political human beings. Socio-legal research is challenging the assumptions—not only those of the law and economics method, but also those of behavioural economics.[40]

[37] J Rawls and P Van Parijs, 'Three letters on The Law of Peoples and the European Union' <https://www.ucl.ac.uk/european-institute/docs/VanParijs_Rawls3Letters.pdf> accessed 21 March 2015.

[38] A Bradford, 'The Brussels Effect' (2012) 107 *Northwestern University Law Review* 1.

[39] See, for a conflict which is paradigmatic of what is about to enter the negotiations, M Djurovic, 'The *Apple Case*: The Commencement of Pan-European Battle Against Unfair Commercial Practices' (2013) 9 *European Review of Contract Law* 253.

[40] Roethe (n 6); S Frerichs, 'False Promises?: A Sociological Critique of the Behavioral Turn in Law and Economics' (2011) 34 *Journal of Consumer Policy* 289.

C. Fragmentation

The fragmented consumer is a phenomenon which is strongly related to marketisation. In the 1960s, the consumer was regarded as a rather homogenous figure. For policymakers and lawyers it was difficult enough to understand and configure this new species, 'the consumer', and to fit this new species into the political and legal context. It will suffice to recall the intellectual battle about the notion of 'the consumer' and its relation to 'the person' or 'the citizen'.[41] The consumer was regarded as a person who was in need of protection against the risks of the consumer society. Nobody thought about attributing a prefix to 'consumer', as in 'vulnerable consumer'. This would have been regarded as a pleonasm.

The more markets the consumer was supposed to conquer, the clearer it became that there was not just one concept of the consumer—the welfarist consumer, the object of societal regulation. It was not only the European market the consumer had to embark on, first by their physical mobility and then also through the Internet. Marketisation has a deeper layer—the economisation of all sorts of activities which had previously remained outside the focus of the market. The rise of the services society and the liberalisation and sometimes privatisation of former public services—which started with telecommunication, energy and transport and which is now about to catch education and healthcare—were not compatible with the rather simple idea of a rational consumer, such as the one behind *Cassis de Dijon*, who needs freedom of choice and information. This development required much more nuanced perceptions and concepts of the consumer.[42] The latest invention is the Single Digital Market—the number two priority of the current President of the European Commission.[43]

This has led to what I will call 'fragmentation'. There is not one single market but various markets, and they are all heavily regulated. Today's consumer shows up in endless variations and it seems as if fragmentation is producing ever more prefixes. Drifting away from the rational consumer—the pareto optimum—to a behaviourally more realistic image opened the floodgates of imagination at the descriptive level.[44] The Wissenschaftliche Beirat beim Bundesministerium für Ernährung, Landwirtschaft und Verbraucherschutz (Scientific Committee at the Federal Ministry of Nutrition, Agriculture and Consumer Protection) distinguishes between the responsible, the confident and the vulnerable (*verantwortlich, vertrauensvoll und verletzlich*) consumer—the threefold distinction still allows

[41] L Azoulai, 'The Making of The European Individual' (seminar paper at EUI, November 2014; his and the other contributions are on file with the author).

[42] L Waddington, 'Vulnerable and Confused: The Protection of "Vulnerable" Consumers Under EU Law' (2013) 38 *European Law Review* 757.

[43] J-C Juncker, 'A New Start for Europe: My Agenda for Jobs, Growth, Fairness and Democratic Change' <http://ec.europa.eu/priorities/docs/pg_en.pdf> accessed 21 March 2015: 'By creating a connected digital single market, we can generate up to €250 billion of additional growth'.

[44] LA Reisch, 'The Place of Consumption in Ecological Economics' in LA Reisch and I Røpke (eds), *The Ecological Economics of Consumption* (Cheltenham, Edward Elgar, 2004).

combining descriptive findings with normative requirements.[45] In that sense behavioural economics is a response to market fragmentation.

Again there are many 'from … tos' that can be observed within the phenomenon of 'fragmentation'. My intention is not to go fully into the details of fragmentation at the level of markets in this chapter. Nor would I like to discuss in detail the consumer images linked to each of the regulated markets. However, the following tendencies can be observed. First, the development from one consumer image to three consumer images—the responsible consumer, the confident consumer and the vulnerable consumer (and any other distinction might equally be defendable). Secondly, the development from the consumer of goods in the old markets to the customer in the markets of regulated services, where the consumer is frequently not even called a consumer. In service market regulation the language is adapted to the particular rationality of the respective markets. That is why in energy and telecoms we find the term 'customer', and in financial services the term 'investor', instead of that of a 'consumer'. Thirdly, the development from the consumer as customer to small- and medium-sized companies, which are from an economic perspective very much like vulnerable consumers when they conclude contracts with multinational companies.[46] Fourthly, the move from horizontal consumer law (the first wave of EU law-making in the 1990s) to ever more sophisticated consumer law rules in vertically regulated markets (the second wave after the year 2000). Fifthly, and even more deeply, we can observe the development from politicisation to de-politicisation. The vertical sectors turn into 'clubs' of service providers, their lawyers, the respective regulatory agencies and the European authorities involved. This looks very much like what Lisa Bernstein has observed in the cotton and diamond industry.[47] Furthermore, we see developments from juridification to de-juridification,[48] from law-making via the legislator to rulemaking via regulatory agencies, from national parliaments to European executive powers (from the legislator to the supranational executive),[49] from binding legislation to co-regulation and self-regulation,[50] from regulation to standardisation, from enforcement via courts to enforcement via regulatory agencies, from collective

[45] With regard to the descriptive level: H-W Micklitz and others, 'Der vertrauende, der verletzliche oder der verantwortungsvolle Verbraucher? Plädoyer für eine differenzierte Strategie in der Verbraucherpolitik' (2010) <www.bmelv.de/SharedDocs/Downloads/Ministerium/Beiraete/Verbraucher politik/2010_12_StrategieVerbraucherpolitik.pdf?__blob=publicationFile> accessed 21 March 2015; on the normative implications, see H-W Micklitz, 'The Future of Consumer Law—Plea for a Movable System' (2013) 2 *Journal of European Consumer and Market Law* 5.

[46] This is not to say that SMEs are always in a weaker position. That is not true. It depends on the market position of the SME. So deep empirical knowledge is needed about what is called today value chains or supply chains.

[47] Bernstein (n 20).

[48] M Bach, *Europa ohne Gesellschaft* (Berlin, Springer, 2008).

[49] M Scholte and M Rijsbergen, 'The Limits of Agentification in the European Union' (2014) *German Law Journal* 1123; A Somek, *Individualism: An Essay on the Authority of the European State* (Oxford, Oxford University Press, 2008).

[50] F Cafaggi (ed), *Reframing Self-Regulation in European Private Law* (Alphen aan den Rijn, Kluwer International, 2006).

action to ADRs/ODRs,[51] from market efficiency to market rationalities. Again, this list is by no means exhaustive.

We might easily agree on the phenomenon of fragmentation, on the shift that it implies from law-making via nation-state parliaments to rulemaking via regulatory agencies, fostering the logic of the market state—the enabling state.[52] The only question is how to deal with it. Is fragmentation a problem? Some ten years ago Thomas Wilhelmsson[53] answered with a clear 'no' to the then emerging tendencies of developing a homogeneous European Civil Code. In his paper on consumer concepts in EU secondary law, Jules Stuyck[54] rejected any claim for more coherence and argued that existing legal doctrine and courts could handle different images of the consumer in their respective contexts. The drafters of the Academic Common Frame of References[55] provided their own answer in that their model of the European Civil Code excluded services from the scope of application unless they were connected to the delivery of a product. The same logic reappears in the so-called Optional Instrument,[56] a project that was officially buried by the European Commission in early 2015. Such an approach reaffirms the difference between, on the one hand, a coherent body of law governed by a single concept of the consumer—at least as it is understood in continental Europe—and on the other hand, whatever is left in the basket: the fragmented markets, the fragmented concepts of consumers and customers—in short, all those activities which account for 70 per cent of gross income in the EU and which mirror fragmentation.

Are we afraid of fragmentation? Do we want to return to the quiet and organised world of the 1950s and 1960s where postal services, energy, transport and

[51] H-W Micklitz, 'The Transformation through Enforcement of European Integration', forthcoming in the *European Review of Private Law*.

[52] See with regard to the international dimension, D Patterson and A Afilalo, *The New Global Trading Order: The Evolving State and the Future of the Trade* (Cambridge, Cambridge University Press, 2008).

[53] T Wilhelmsson, 'Private Law in the EU: Harmonised or Fragmented Europeanisation' (2002) 10 *European Review of Private Law* 77.

[54] J Stuyck, 'Consumer Concepts in EU Secondary Law', paper presented at an interdisciplinary workshop on consumer images organised on 12–13 February 2013 at the Law Faculty of the Ruhr University Bochum (Professors Fabian Klinck and Karl Riesenhuber), to be published in a forthcoming book.

[55] Acquis Group, Principles of the Existing EU Contract Law (Acquis Principles) Contract I (2007) <http://www.acquis-group.jura.uni-osnabrueck.de/ag/dms/ag/dms.php?> accessed 21 March 2015; C Bar and others (eds), *Principles, Definitions and Model Rules of European Private Law, Draft Common Frame of Reference (DCFR)* <http://ec.europa.eu/justice/policies/civil/docs/dcfr_outline_edition_en.pdf> accessed 21 March 2015.

[56] Commission, 'Proposal for a Regulation of the European Parliament and of the Council on a Common European Sales Law' COM(2011) 635 final, see in this context *Common Market Law Review*, which has published a special issue that collects contributions to the conference entitled 'A Law and Economics Approach to European Contract Law', held at the University of Chicago Law School on 27–28 April 2012. All contributions examined various aspects of the Commission's Proposal for a Regulation on a Common European Sales Law (CESL) that was published by the EU Commission, and, with few exceptions, most of them do so from a law-and-economics perspective <www.law.leiden.edu/organisation/publiclaw/europainstitute/news/special-issue-on-common-european-sales-law.html> accessed 21 March 2015.

water were supplied by public services at fixed prices? Where no choice was possible, in which the 'local' incumbent did not only have a monopoly of supply but also invested in societal services like building a swimming pool or maintaining a tennis club, which granted access to all at a low price?

Some of the litigation initiated by consumer organisations seems to indicate that the way back is the way forward. The true story behind a recent judgment of the Court of Justice in *RWE*,[57] concerning the legality of price-increase clauses in standard term contracts, is the struggle of the citizens of Hamburg and Berlin to put pressure on regional governments to buy back privatised energy companies. The reason behind it is that communities in Germany have sold their energy suppliers to one of the big four multinational energy companies in Europe. The subsequent price increases and the dissatisfaction with the marketing practices of RWE pushed consumer advice centres into action. They started collecting claims and in the end won before the CJEU. However, as there is no class action in Germany, only a few customers will benefit from the favourable judgment—namely those who have submitted their claim to the consumer advice centres. The upheaval even went so far that a referendum was initiated in Hamburg and Berlin with the intention to oblige the two cities to buy their energy suppliers back from the big four. These attempts failed not least because the cities did not have the money. What the communities and regions got for the sale of their local or regional incumbents had long been spent. This local protest against EU rules and the EU executive was thus rather disillusioning, but it remains symbolic.[58] It seems as if N Luhmann and G Teubner[59] were right. There is no way back from differentiation. Or is there? Can constitutionalisation bring the different segments of regulated markets closer to each other?

D. Constitutionalisation

The constitutionalised consumer emerges as a means of last resort—not only to overcome marketisation and fragmentation, but also to 'save' consumer protection. Thanks to the references to human and fundamental rights the emphasis could again be placed on 'protection', which would revitalise the societal

[57] Case C–92/11 *RWE Vertrieb AG v Verbraucherzentrale Nordrhein-Westfalen eV*, judgment of 21 March 2013; comment E Terryn, 'Unfair Contract Terms—Statutory Provisions, Price Increase and the Role of the ECJ' in E Terryn and V Colaert (eds), *Landmark Cases of EU Consumer Law—In Honour of Jules Stuyck* (Cambridge, Intersentia, 2013) 677; on the practice of the German courts, see P Rott, 'The Adjustment of Long-Term Supply Contracts: Experience from German Gas Price Case Law' (2013) 21 *European Review of Private Law* 717; the follow-up judgment of the Bundesgerichtshof (BGH) VIII ZR 162/09 of 31 July 2013 has been published in Zeitschrift für Wirtschaftsrecht (ZIP) 2013, 1964. On the overall context, see N Reich, '"I want my money back"—Problems, successes and failures in the price regulation of the gas supply market by civil law remedies in Germany' *EUI Working Paper LAW* 2015/05.

[58] Somek (n 49).

[59] G Teubner constantly reiterates this plea in his writings.

dimension. As mentioned above, social considerations were at the origin of the consumer movement but got somewhat lost in the process of marketisation and fragmentation, where what counts is making the best deal for the best money, etc. Politically speaking, constitutionalisation is intended to introduce and/or to enhance social justice in contract law.[60] Constitutionalisation of consumer law is not really new. It started some 20 years ago in national constitutional courts. The German *Bürgschaftsentscheidung* is paradigmatic of the type of conflicts which are reaching national courts.[61] The case concerned the liability of family members with little or no income for a business loan for which the father had applied, granted by the banks on the condition that the family members served as security. Many of the Member States had their particular version of the *Bürgschaftsentscheidung*, regardless of whether or not they had a constitutional court. As with the cases about German Beer, Italian pasta, British milk and French cheese, this kind of constitutional conflict highlights a change. What has happened? What are the reasons behind consumer litigation in which national constitutional courts have become the means of last resort? Through constitutional litigation on consumer protection issues, courts have established a particular relationship with citizens. Habermas has called this new loyalty, forged in the hearts of consumers in post-war Germany, *Verfassungspatriotismus* (constitutional patriotism).[62] Distrust in parliaments, in national civil courts, and a growing awareness of consumer problems in society via public interest groups and NGOs could be some of the reasons why courts are becoming more important actors in the field of consumer protection.

The constitutionalised consumer upgrades the whole field of consumer law and consumer policy. As a result, it receives *höhere Weihen*—major orders. Consumer law is no longer in the lowlands of market law, the unloved stepchild of private law or public law. It has now reached the holy grail of the constitutional order. Nobody knows the exact figures of constitutional conflicts in the Member States. But we know that the number is increasing: there are a few cases in Germany, many cases in Italy, two in the UK,[63] and now also in France.[64] We also know that the constitutionalisation of consumer law has now reached the European Courts.[65]

[60] H Collins, 'The Constitutionalisation of European Private Law as a Path to Social Justice?' in H-W Micklitz (ed), *The Many Faces of Social Justice in Private Law* (Cheltenham, Edward Elgar, 2011).

[61] German Constitutional Court (BVerfG), judgment of 19 October 1993, 1 BvR 567, 1044/89, BVerfGE 89, 214, 229.

[62] J Habermas, 'Staatsbürgerschaft und nationale Identität' in J Habermas, *Faktizität und Geltung* (Frankfurt, Suhrkamp, 1992).

[63] See *The Office of Fair Trading v Abbey National plc* [2009] UKSC 6, [2010] 1 AC 696, on appeal from (2009) EWCA Civ 116. See also *The Director General of Fair Trading v First National Bank plc* [2001] UKHL 52, [2002] 1 AC 481.

[64] Conseil Constitutionnel, Décision no 2014-690 DC of 13 March 2014, on the constitutionality of the envisaged law on group actions <http://www.conseil-constitutionnel.fr/conseil-constitutionnel/francais/les-decisions/acces-par-date/decisions-depuis-1959/2014/2014-690-dc/decision-n-2014-690-dc-du-13-mars-2014.140273.html> accessed 21 March 2015.

[65] H Micklitz (ed), *The Constitutionalisation of European Private Law* (Oxford, Oxford University Press, 2014).

First, this happened in a somewhat hidden form, without openly addressing the constitutional dimension. Both *Aziz*[66] and *Asbeek*[67] are strongly linked to the problem of housing and the right to have a roof over one's head. The constitutional dimension here is obvious. And so is the societal dimension in *Aziz*, which is paradigmatic for the nearly 5,000 Spanish consumers who have been evicted from their homes because they were no longer able to pay their mortgages. In two recent judgments, *Sánchez Morcillo* and *Kušionová*,[68] the Court of Justice went one step further and openly addressed the constitutional dimension.[69] Constitutionalisation of consumer law should not be equated with problem solving. Courts can do no more than set incentives for the political agenda. This is all the more true for the CJEU, which decides on the interpretation of EU private law rules, but not on the facts.

What does constitutionalisation mean? In the current context it is used in a rather crude form to indicate that the consumer may rely on rights enshrined in the higher strata of the legal order. At the national level, the consumer may refer to fundamental or human rights which are part of the national constitution. At the EU level, the consumer may, since 2000, rely on the European Convention on Human Rights and, since 2009, on the European Charter of Fundamental Rights. The levels—the national and the European—should be kept distinct and certainly deserve to be analysed in more depth.[70] Why is constitutionalisation occurring at the EU level? What is behind the move to constitutionalisation in the EU? Are the reasons the same or is the EU, due to its lack of a functioning civil society, the absence of a European identity and the distance between the peoples and the Union institutions, an even better candidate for the source of constitutional concerns of European citizens? The recent wave of preliminary references in the aftermath of the financial crisis seems to indicate that there is more trust in the CJEU than in national political institutions. Can the preliminary reference procedure help to build a European identity and a European society?

Again within the phenomenon of constitutionalisation we have a number of 'from … tos'. Moving from a lower law to a higher law indicates a degree of

[66] Case C–415/11 *Mohamed Aziz v Caixa d'Estalvis de Catalunya, Tarragona i Manresa (Catalunyacaixa)*, judgment of 14 March 2013. See H-W Micklitz, 'Unfair Contract Terms—Public Interest Litigation Before European Courts Case C–415/11 *Mohamed Aziz*' in Terryn and Colaert (n 57); as a follow-up see the Opinion of AG Wahl in Case C–482/12 *Peter Macinský Eva Macinská v Getfin sro Financreal sro* in which he finds that the Court does not have jurisdiction. However, he discusses *Aziz* in detail as a sort of supplementary argument. Its importance for the EU principle of 'effectiveness' has been emphasised by N Reich, *General Principles of EU Civil Law* (Cambridge, Intersentia, 2013) paras 4.5 and 4.15.

[67] Case C–488/11 *Dirk Frederik Asbeek Brusse and Katarina de Man Garabito v Jahani BV*, judgment of 30 May 2013, para 52.

[68] Case C–169/14 *Juan Carlos Sánchez Morcillo and María del Carmen Abril García v Banco Bilbao Vizcaya Argentaria SA*, judgment of 17 July 2014 and Case C–34/13 *Monika Kušionová v SMART Capital*, judgment of 10 September 2014.

[69] F della Negra, 'The uncertain development of the case-law on consumer protection in mortgage enforcement proceedings: *Sánchez Morcillo* and *Kušionová*', forthcoming in the *Common Market Law Review*.

[70] Extremely helpful: Brüggemeier and others (n 17).

dissatisfaction with the lower law. Fundamental rights are invoked by businesses to strike down consumer protection rules or by consumers to challenge unsatisfactory results in lower courts. The series of references to the CJEU from Romania represent the first variant, while the series of references from Spain represent the second.[71] I will emphasise the second variant, although the two have a lot in common.

Most of the constitutional references to European courts, even if the actions have been brought by individual claimants, in a nutshell highlight a societal problem of high political relevance and of broad societal and economic importance. Quite often this 'problem' is represented before European courts as a national problem, even if it is a widespread phenomenon across the EU, as is the case with all issues arising as a result of the impact of the euro crisis on (over)-indebted consumers. The societal actors in the EU rarely join forces and rarely use the bigger societal space for coordinated legal and/or political action. In that sense the CJEU turns into a forum where the open conflicts about how to deal with the impact of the euro crisis on homeowners finally find some legal attention. This is not a political forum and again the Court is not in a position to 'solve' conflicts, but it can remind national governments and parliaments of their responsibility.[72]

So there is a move away from national and European parliaments as agents of political representation to European courts as the last and true protector of 'justice' in the EU. But can European courts meet the hopes and expectations? Using European courts as agents of societal rights has inherent limits. That is what trade unions, equal opportunities commissions, environmental organisations and consumer organisations have painfully discovered in the last 20 years.[73] However, could it be said that there is a growing preparedness of the CJEU to take the role of a societal agent which compensates for societal deficits in European law-making, just like the Warren Court in the US? This is what Daniel Keleman is convinced of when he speaks of Euro-legalism, of public interest groups involving the CJEU in collective conflict resolution.[74] If Kelemen is right, it would mean that there would be public interest litigation without the most powerful means that the US legal system has provided to consumers—the class action. The story behind over-indebted consumers demonstrates that there is enough backing in the Spanish (maybe even in the European?) society for the CJEU to take a bold step—a finding which confirms that US public interest litigation could only succeed if there were societal support.[75]

[71] For empirical evidence, see I Domurath, G Comparato and H-W Micklitz (eds), 'The Over-indebtedness of European Consumers—a View from Six Countries' *EUI Working Paper LAW* 2014/10.

[72] For a negative example where the coordination is still missing, see H-W Micklitz and I Domurath (eds), *Societal Inclusion of Over-Indebted Consumers in the Aftermath of the Economic Crisis in Europe* (Farnham, Ashgate, forthcoming 2015). For a positive example where the European Consumer Association (BEUC) took the lead in national actions for injunctions against Apple, see Djurovic (n 39).

[73] With regard to anti-discrimination law and consumer law see H-W Micklitz, *The Politics of Judicial Co-operation* (Cambridge, Intersentia, 2005).

[74] D Keleman, *Eurolegalism: The Transformation of Law and Regulation in the European Union* (Cambridge, Harvard University Press, 2011).

[75] J Handler, *Social Movements and the Legal System—A Theory of Law Reform and Social Change* (New York, Academic Press, 1978).

There is more at stake if we agree with Giovanni Comandé, who has argued that the CJEU is building a European society, and even a European identity, via preliminary reference judgments, and in cooperation with national courts and their constituents. How should we understand this transformation? Should we interpret it as the equipping of consumers by the CJEU with a sort of a 'pouvoir constituant'? This would make sense as long as the CJEU used its new role to fill the societal gap created by marketisation and fragmentation.[76] Constitutionalisation via European courts would then result in re-politicisation, since European courts are not in a position to 'solve the problem' pending before them. They have to delegate it back to the national or European political fora. This is exactly what happened in Spain in the aftermath of *Aziz*. However, it has not resulted in a cross-border approach to policymaking. However, the increasing case law of the CJEU on the societal consequences of the euro crisis will certainly establish a new relationship between the court and European consumers.

What about the dangers, limits and risks of constitutionalisation? Can constitutionalisation overcome marketisation and fragmentation; can it provide a link between compartmentalised markets and the resulting different concepts of the consumer? And can it hold together the bits and pieces of consumer law which are drifting apart in all directions, depending on the context and the subject matter? Can it solve the legitimacy crisis caused by the promoted marketisation and by the ever deeper fragmentation which is largely the product of national statutory and EU regulation? Constitutionalisation through courts also raises institutional concerns. In a democracy parliaments are best suited to solve social and economic conflicts and courts, whether national or European, are perhaps not the appropriate actors.[77] What we can expect to emerge, however, are constitutional minimum standards in European private law.[78]

An even more difficult question is whether constitutionalisation can give consumers their autonomy and dignity back.[79] Consumers lost their autonomy and dignity through all the instrumentalisation—first, before *Cassis*, through 'infantilization'[80] and then, after *Cassis*, through overestimation of choice-guided market machines.[81] Consumers were charged with a normative and political burden to always behave as a good and active market participant, as a circumspect and alert customer, to compare prices and to be ready to switch, while looking

[76] Both Bartl and Leczykiewicz are very critical, though for different reasons. Bartl understands constitutionalisation as just the prolongation of marketisation and fragmentation, another variant of a market driven logic of the EU law. However, in light of the recent cases decided along the lines of the financial crisis I would be slightly more optimistic. Leczykiewicz argues that constitutionalisation is just another variant of fragmentation. I disagree for the reasons set out below.

[77] This can be studied in the failed attempts of Advocate General van Gerven to use the proportionality principle in the Sunday trading cases for institution-building purposes.

[78] H-W Micklitz, 'Introduction' in Micklitz (n 65) 23.

[79] I recognise the difficulties of using 'dignity' as a particular German constitutional value in the European context, and even more so in the context of consumer and consumption.

[80] Dani (n 24).

[81] Davies (n 26).

for the next and better offer.[82] Can they be saved from all that through constitutionalisation? I am convinced that the answer to all these questions, even to those related to individual consumer rights, is at the very best a reluctant 'yes', provided constitutionalisation succeeds in securing a form of materialised autonomy in the Weberian sense. However, there remains a strong 'but', as constitutionalisation cannot replace political processes in a society.

Mark Bell has raised the question of whether there is 'a human right and/or a fundamental right to be treated as a worker'.[83] In a similar fashion I would like to ask whether there is a 'fundamental and human right to be treated as a consumer'. In the DCFR circle there was a joke going around which was passed on to me by Fryderyk Zoll: 'get out of the way with all your consumer law rules, which set unbearable thresholds of compliance. I am a mere consumer and all I need is protection!' The question behind the question is whether there is a core to the concept of the worker or the consumer—a core which can be teased out and given constitutional standing. It would entail creating out of the existing concept of the consumer (under primary and secondary EU law) a formula which could pass a constitutionality test. A further question is whether the core is a transnational one which can be condensed into one formula at least for the European context. Only if both steps are successful can the constitutionalisation of consumer law and the concept of the constitutionalised consumer have a future in consumer law.

However, what should be remembered is that the constitutionalised consumer, at the moment, exists only in relation to particular fields of consumer law. Not each and every consumer conflict bears a constitutional dimension. It will be necessary to develop criteria to distinguish between conflicts of lower and higher importance. This means that we have to comb through the woods of consumer law and identify those rules and regulations that have a higher value. Clearly a hierarchy can be established between rights to health and safety and economic rights. However, the euro crisis has demonstrated how conflicts over mortgage contracts can easily obtain a constitutional dimension. The formula which might hold the different fields of consumer law together is the distinction between, on the one hand, *existential* consumer issues such as life-threatening risks to health and safety and threats to our *physical existence*, and, on the other hand, other consumer interests. For the former, consumers should enjoy constitutional standing.[84] For the latter, it should be accepted that they remain below the threshold of constitutional protection. For these issues, national courts, supranational or national executive

[82] See H Unberath and A Johnston, 'The Double-Headed Approach of the ECJ Concerning Consumer Protection' (2007) 44 *Common Market Law Review* 1237, who distinguish between primary community law (average consumer) and secondary consumer law (weaker party); H Micklitz and N Reich, 'The Court and the Sleeping Beauty—The Revival of the Unfair Contract Terms Directive (UCTD)' (2014) 51 *Common Market Law Review* 771.

[83] M Bell, 'Constitutionalisation and EU Employment Law' in Micklitz (n 65) 137.

[84] Admittedly this argument is very much in line with theories on transnational law where basic human rights are said to be respected also by private internationally operating countries.

bodies, or even out-of-court settlements—with or without public monitoring and supervision—would be sufficient. Only such a clear distinction between the constitutional minimum and the societal maximum could protect the integrity of the constitutional right to be treated as a consumer.

IV. Conclusion

Conclusion? Is there a conclusion at all? The state is transforming, and so is private law. The transformation is driven by the EU, but it is supported by the majority of the Member States and the European Court of Justice, which has kept its integrationist model alive for decades. Many consumer activists hope for an activist court that will use constitutionalisation as a remedy for the consequences of the excessive emphasis on market integration and as a way to promote social justice. They have already been disappointed—first, in labour law,[85] and later in environmental protection. However, at that time the constitutional bias was much less clear as there was no Charter of Fundamental Rights yet. It might be the case that the constitutionalisation of consumer law and the consumer will open up a new round of debate about the relationship between the Internal Market and Fundamental Rights.

Those who are more sceptical will argue that constitutionalisation is unlikely to generate all these effects and is more likely going to be just a prolongation of the marketisation ideology. The only difference is that it will now be carried out in the name of fundamental rights and human rights. This would mean that the Charter of Fundamental Rights will be marketised. As half of the preliminary references to the CJEU now rely on the Charter of Fundamental Rights,[86] there is and there will be ample space for the European Court of Justice to shape the constitutionalisation of European private law and hopefully to provide 'general principles' which would start to connect the fragmented bits and pieces of EU law. Academics will have the task of investigating whether the constitutionalised consumer is just another variant in the overall history of consumer protection or whether this concept will turn into a new page in the history of private law—of constitutionalised private law beyond the state through the Charter of Fundamental Rights and not forgetting the European Convention on Human Rights.

[85] Micklitz (n 73).

[86] Personal communication between Judge Marek Safjan (CJEU) and the author.

3

The Images of the 'Consumer' in EU Competition Law

ALBERTINA ALBORS-LLORENS AND ALISON JONES

I. Introduction

This chapter surveys the images of the consumer drawn within the sphere of EU competition law and seeks to provide an underlying explanation for the variety of images drawn. It also elucidates the rationale for the different meanings ascribed to the terms 'consumer' and 'consumer welfare' in the competition law context as compared to that adopted in the consumer law context.

The competition provisions in the Treaty on the Functioning of the European Union (TFEU) make several express references to 'consumers'[1] without defining the term.[2] Further, a number of allusions to the consumer can be found in the jurisprudence, secondary legislation and, most specifically, the Commission's guidance documents. These sources (legislation, case law, decisional practice and

[1] There are three specific references to the consumer in the TFEU competition law provisions: see Art 101(3), Art 102(b) and, in the context of the state aid provisions, Art 107(2)(a), which lists 'aid having a social character, granted to individual consumers' as one of the forms of aid automatically compatible with EU law.

[2] Apart from the reference to 'individual' consumers in Art 107(2)(a) TFEU (as distinguished from the reference to consumers in a generic sense in Arts 101 and 102), the Treaty does not offer a definition of consumer for the purposes of EU competition law. This is not uncommon in EU law. Many key concepts in the Treaty, eg the notions of 'worker' in Art 45 TFEU, and 'undertaking' in the context of the competition provisions themselves, are not defined. In many cases, the case law has filled these gaps. See, for instance, for the definition of *worker*, Case 53/81 *DM Levin v Staatssecretaris van Justitie* [1982] ECR 1035, para 17 and *undertaking*, Case C–41/90 *Klaus Höfner and Fritz Elser v Macrotron GmbH* [1991] ECR I–1979, para 21, where the Court held that an undertaking constitutes 'every entity engaged in economic activities, regardless of the legal status of the entity and the way in which it is financed'. In other cases, the task of giving meaning to undefined concepts has been performed by secondary legislation. For example, consumer protection directives have often defined the consumer as a 'natural person who is acting for purposes which are outside his trade, business, craft or profession' (see Directive 2011/83/EU of the European Parliament and of the Council of 25 October 2011 on Consumer Rights, [2011] OJ L 304/64, Art 2(1)). A common thread that has emerged from this exercise, however, has been that the meaning attributed to these concepts, whilst obviously inspired in the national legal systems, has a distinct and characteristic EU identity. This has not really happened in reference to the concept of consumer in EU competition law.

Commission Guidelines) suggest, at first sight, that, as is the case in other areas of EU law, the image of the consumer painted by the law is not a uniform or monochrome one, but a colourful one, evoking a landscape of diversity. Indeed, these sources variously refer to, or distinguish between, for example: 'consumers' and 'individual consumers',[3] 'direct and indirect users of the products',[4] 'professional end users and final consumers',[5] 'intermediate and ultimate consumers',[6] 'customers and consumers',[7] 'competitors, consumers' and 'final consumers',[8] and 'individual undertakings and consumers'.[9]

This chapter considers this diversity of images and argues that although some loose and inconsistent language is sometimes deployed, when the apparently differing approaches are set within the broader context in which they are used, and against the overarching goals of EU competition law, it can be seen that the interpretations adopted in each scenario are not in fact inconsistent with one another. Rather, the question of how the consumer is characterised and defined in the competition law sphere is dependent upon the context and the part of the competition law process in which it is used. In particular, the meaning of the term 'consumer' adopted fluctuates depending upon whether it is used in the context of: (i) describing the objectives of the competition laws and the consumers that those competition law rules are designed to protect; (ii) identifying persons during the process of determining whether the competition law rules have been infringed and, consequently, their objectives thwarted: for example, when deploying analytical tools or identifying whether particular persons, or groups of persons, have been harmed or benefited by the conduct at issue; or (iii) referring to some of the actors who participate in the enforcement of the substantive competition provisions.

Before focussing on the specific references to consumers that have been adopted in the legislation and jurisprudence, this chapter begins in section II by contextualising the discussion and setting out vital background to it. This section locates the relevance and central importance of the 'consumer' to the competition law enterprise generally, explaining why competition law rules were incorporated within the EU legal order and outlining their objectives. It notes that, although the objectives of the rules have not been made explicit, and have evolved, the emerging view is that their primary goal is, or should be, to prohibit the conduct of undertakings—entities engaged in economic activity[10]—which distorts competition in a way which harms the welfare of consumers and economic

[3] See the references to the wording of Art 107(2) (a) TFEU and that of Arts 101 and 102 TFEU (n 2).

[4] See the Commission Guidelines on the application of Art 81(3) [now Art 101(3) TFEU] of the Treaty (the 'Art 101(3) Guidelines') [2004] OJ C 101/97, para 84.

[5] See the Commission Guidelines on Vertical Restraints [2010] OJ C 130/1, para 56.

[6] See Council Regulation (EC) No 139/2004 of 20 January 2004 on the control of concentrations between undertakings [2004] OJ L 24/1, Art 2(1)(b).

[7] Case 85/76 *Hoffmann-La Roche & Co AG v Commission* [1979] ECR 461, paras 38–39.

[8] Case C–501/06P *GlaxoSmithKline Services Unlimited v Commission* [2009] ECR I–9291.

[9] Case C–52/09 *Konkurrensverket v TeliaSonera Sverige AB* [2011] ECR I–527, para 22. See also discussion of marginal and average consumers, see section III.B.i in this chapter.

[10] See n 2 for the definition of 'undertaking' in EU competition law.

efficiency. Section II then goes on to consider what implications the debate over objectives has for competition law and how it influences the meaning attributed to the term 'consumer' within it. In particular, it considers whether a sole consumer welfare objective is pursued in EU law and, if so, what precisely *consumer welfare* means and *which* consumers' welfare the rules seek to protect.

Section III scrutinises how the interpretation of the competition law rules impacts on the question of how, and to what extent, the interests of the identified consumers are protected in the application of Articles 101 and 102 TFEU and, at the same time, the vision of the consumer drawn, and the role that they play, in this process.[11] It observes that even if a consumer welfare objective is agreed, putting 'consumers' at the core of the competition endeavour, there is considerable disagreement amongst commentators, policy- and law-makers as to how that ambition can be achieved in practice. It will be seen that, in the EU, the Commission or other claimants do not generally have to prove directly that the scrutinised conduct harms the welfare of consumers. Rather, EU law ordinarily tests indirectly for infringements through the application of presumptions and/or indirect assessments of the ability of the undertakings at issue to exercise market power. Consequently a recurrent theme which arises is the tension that exists between pursuing a consumer welfare objective and actually putting in place workable tests which can accurately determine harm or benefit to consumer interests. Because workability may entail a certain crudeness in the tests adopted, an important issue is frequently whether the tests utilised achieve the consumer welfare objective articulated by the Commission or whether, in particular, the rules might at times be either over-inclusive—so sometimes condemning legitimate business practices (creating a risk of false positives or 'Type 1' errors), and so potentially chilling pro-competitive conduct which benefits consumers, or under-inclusive—allowing anti-competitive practices which harm consumers to escape antitrust prohibitions (creating a risk of false negatives or 'Type 2' errors).[12] Furthermore, a second crucial issue that impacts on the application of EU competition law is whether, and if so when, other objectives, in particular the single market objective, can ever trump and therefore override the consumer welfare objective where the goals clash.

Section IV briefly examines the rise of a stronger and more empowered consumer in the context of the public and private enforcement of the EU competition rules, and touches upon the relationship between regulation, consumer and competition law. Section V summarises the findings of this chapter and suggests a taxonomy of the images of the consumer in EU competition law, arguing that this variety of images is apparent rather than real and effectively dependent upon the context in which the term 'consumer' is used. It also concludes that the fluidity

[11] Given the breadth and scope of the Treaty competition rules, this chapter will focus principally on the role of the consumer in the application of Arts 101 and 102 TFEU which, together with the EUMR (n 6), constitute the core competition pillars that apply directly to the conduct of undertakings; see nn 26–27 and accompanying text.

[12] See section III.B in this chapter.

of some of the key concepts that competition law employs and the boundaries within which this discipline operates frequently means that an uncertain correlation exists between the motivation guiding the application of the rules and the promotion of the interests of final consumers.

II. The Objectives of EU Competition Law

A. Why Competition Law? The American Experience

More than 125 jurisdictions around the world now have in place systems of competition law (or antitrust law as they are known in the US).[13] Broadly, such systems are designed to protect the process of competition in which active consumers buy products from suppliers competing vigorously to offer products (and services) which represent the best value for money (in terms of price, quality and choice),[14] and to deal with market imperfections arising, in a free market economy. The question that naturally follows, however, is: why precisely do states wish to protect competition and whose interests do they protect in so doing? The starting point is that without competition law rules, firms may be free to act to distort the process of competition by, for example, colluding or merging with their competitors. Further, firms which win the competitive battle or 'natural' monopolies may be free to act without any competitive restraint being exercised over their behaviour. Many competition law systems now pursue, or purport to pursue, a purely *economic* goal, seeking to prohibit such distortions which preclude the competition process in the free market from delivering products and/or services which offer consumers the best value for money and efficiencies, allocative, productive and/or dynamic. The reality is, however, that most systems have more complex origins, which may suggest a desire to protect a multiplicity of persons and to achieve a multiplicity of objectives, beyond a purely economic one, which do not all necessarily pull in the same direction.

In the US, for example, although it seems clear that the competition laws were initially adopted to meet the public's desire 'to do something' about the trusts which were eliminating competition and competitors and gaining control over a

[13] In contrast, '[u]ntil the mid-20th century less than 10 competition regimes existed worldwide', United Nations Conference on Trade and Development, 'Benchmarking Competition Systems: A Global Survey of Major Institutional Characteristics' <http://unctad.org/en/Pages/DITC/CompetitionLaw/ResearchPartnership/Benchmarking-Competition.aspx> accessed 2 February 2015.

[14] Value for money reflects the fact that consumers' choices between products reflect not only price but also quality, service, functionality, and whether they offer consumers something new and exciting, see A Fletcher, 'Privatisation, Economic Regulation and Competition in the Utilities: Have we got the balance right?' Beesley Lecture Series, <http://competitionpolicy.ac.uk/documents/107435/107584/Amelia+Fletcher+-+Beesley+Lecture+14+Nov+2013.pdf/0dd47fdb-f3b2-41e9-9a24-19b46ef271d4> accessed 2 February 2015.

swathe of core industries (hence they are known in the US as '*anti* trust' law), the exact objective(s) underpinning that desire has been fiercely debated.[15] Indeed, it has been observed that

> the debates and events surrounding the passage of the Sherman Act contain something for everyone. To generations of observers, the Sherman Act's legislative record has supplied a wishing well into which one can peer to glimpse evidence that supports preferred policies.[16]

Scholars have therefore supported competing views as to the legislative intention behind the Sherman Act, arguing that it was introduced to achieve a diverse range of goals, including 'non-economic' ones, for example:[17] to preserve opportunities for firms and individuals to enter a market and compete on the merits and on reasonable open terms (indeed, it was opportunity for small business that had forged the American character); to achieve fairness between big and small businesses and farmers; to prevent unfair wealth transfers from consumers to producers; to block private accumulations of political power and to protect democratic government;[18] to promote consumer welfare; and/or to achieve a combination of these goals.

Although many of these broader objectives undoubtedly influenced the development of US antitrust law, Bork, a leading representative of the Chicago School of Economics, complained that the law cannot achieve such a broad '*pot pourri*' of goals (in particular, protecting smaller competitors may harm competition and consumers), and drew attention to the difficulties that would arise were the different goals to contradict one another and if non-economic goals were to sacrifice the benefits resulting from efficient markets.[19] Bork went on to set out his view

[15] The debates and congressional reports stretch to eleven 'fat' volumes: H Hovenkamp, *The Antitrust Enterprise: Principle and Execution* (Cambridge, Harvard University Press, 2005) 39.

[16] E Gellhorn, WE Kovacic and S Calkins, *Antitrust Law and Economics in a Nutshell*, 5th edn (Eagan, Thomson West, 2004) 23. See also *Northern Pacific Railway v United States* 356 US 1, 4 (1958).

[17] See, eg, RH Bork, *The Antitrust Paradox: A Policy at War with Itself* (New York, The Free Press, 1993) 51; EM Fox and LA Sullivan, 'Antitrust-Retrospective and Perspective: Where Are We Coming From? Where Are We Going?' (1987) 62 *New York University Law Review* 93; R Pitofsky, 'The Political Content of Antitrust' (1979) 127 *University of Pennsylvania Law Review* 1051; RH Lande, 'Wealth Transfers as the Original and Primary Concern of Antitrust: the Efficiency Interpretation Challenged' (1982) 34 *Hastings Law Journal* 65; H Hovenkamp, 'Distributive Justice and the Antitrust Laws' (1982) 51 *George Washington Law Review* 1; L Schwartz, '"Justice" and other Non-Economic Goals of Antitrust' (1979) 127 *University of Pennsylvania Law Review* 1076; Hovenkamp (n 15), 40–41; E Fox, 'The Modernization of Antitrust: A new Equilibrium' (1981) 666 *Cornell Law Review* 1140; G Stigler, 'The Origin of the Sherman Act' (1985) 14 *Journal of Legal Studies* 1.

[18] The American notion of equality ('all men are created equal', Thomas Jefferson, Declaration of Independence 1776) led to a mistrust of power concentrated in the hands of a few, whether private or governmental. The Jeffersonian ideal was diffused power in the hands of citizen farmers and small businessmen, see LA Sullivan and WS Grimes, *The Law of Antitrust: An Integrated Handbook* (MN, West Publishing Group, 2006) 5.

[19] Bork (n 17) 50. 'Antitrust policy cannot be made rational until we are able to give a firm answer to one question: What is the point of the law? ... Only when the issue of goals has been settled is it possible to frame a coherent body of substantive rules.'

that the antitrust laws should pursue only one goal and that goal should be the maximisation of consumer welfare and economic efficiency.[20]

Since then, it has become accepted by the US courts that the antitrust laws do aim to prevent conduct which will reduce competition in such a way that consumer welfare will be harmed; in particular, the Sherman Act is designed as a 'consumer welfare prescription'.[21] Furthermore, and despite initial opposition, there is now widespread agreement between the different schools of thought (Chicago, Harvard and post-Chicago)[22] that the antitrust system is

> technocratic in the sense that antitrust be defined narrowly to examine only those issues that are purely without antitrust's ability to be measured and understood using industrial organization as the basis for economic analysis. This technocratic approach moves non-competition economic considerations to areas such as sector regulation, the legislative process, or executive fiat. Such areas are better equipped than antitrust to deal with political trade-offs between law and policy.[23]

This acceptance still leaves considerable scope, however, for diverging views as to exactly *what* 'consumer welfare' means, and *how* that objective can be achieved.[24]

B. EU Competition Law: The Treaty Context, Early Enforcement and the Emerging Consumer Welfare Objective

Competition policy is one of the foundational areas of competence of the EU institutions. Indeed, the original version of the EEC Treaty provided that its activities should include 'a system ensuring that competition in the [internal market] is not distorted'. It thus embedded the principle of 'undistorted competition' into the fundamental provisions of the Treaty as a mechanism for reinforcing, complementing and implementing other Treaty provisions and tasks, in particular, the functioning of the internal market.[25] The Treaty also incorporated a set of competition provisions which are now found in Articles 101–109 TFEU and secondary legislation. The two key TFEU competition provisions applicable to undertakings,[26] and the focus of this chapter, are Articles 101 and 102, which target,

[20] Bork (n 17) 51. He sets out two related propositions. '(1) The only legitimate goal of American antitrust law is the maximization of consumer welfare; therefore (2) "Competition," for purposes of antitrust analysis, must be understood as a term of art signifying any state of affairs in which consumer welfare cannot be increased by judicial decree.'

[21] *Reiter v Sonotone* Corp 442 US 330, 343 (1979). See also *NCAA v Board of Regents of University of Oklahoma* 468 US 85, 107–08 (1984).

[22] Hovenkamp (n 15) 31–32.

[23] R Blair and D Sokol, 'Welfare Standards in US and EU Antitrust Enforcement' (2013) 81 *Fordham Law Review* 2497, 2505.

[24] Hovenkamp (n 15) 31 and see section II.C of this chapter.

[25] See now Art 3(1)(b) TFEU, which confers exclusive competence to the EU in 'the establishment of the competition rules necessary for the functioning of the internal market'.

[26] For the definition of 'undertaking' in EU competition law see n 2.

respectively, collusive and unilateral anti-competitive behaviour.[27] Article 101(1) prohibits agreements and concerted practices between two or more undertakings which have as their object or effect the restriction of competition and which do not meet the legal exception criteria set out in Article 101(3) (broadly where the restrictions are indispensable to produce sufficient countervailing benefits, a fair share of which are passed on to consumers)[28] whilst Article 102 prohibits abuse of a dominant position.[29] These rules are now supplemented by the EU Merger Regulation ('EUMR'), currently Regulation 139/2004,[30] which prohibits mergers (or 'concentrations') between undertakings which would significantly impede effective competition in the EU.

Although the TFEU sets out specific prohibitions of anti-competitive practices, it neither provides an explanation of what their goals are nor defines the core concepts set out within them, such as what constitutes a 'restriction' of competition, an 'abuse' or a 'dominant position'.[31] It has therefore been for the EU courts to put flesh on these provisions and to elucidate their meaning. Those courts have made it clear that Articles 101 and 102 both have the same goal(s),[32] but have shied away from setting out a plain statement of their objectives. The process of teasing out their aims has therefore been largely an inductive and evolving one which has been surrounded by intense controversy. Some general observations can, however, be made.

First, as a result of the inextricable link between the internal market project and the competition law system set out in the EU Treaties, the Court of Justice and the General Court have interpreted the competition rules so as to prohibit conduct which 'might tend to restore the national divisions in trade between Member States'[33] and so frustrate the most fundamental objectives of the EU, the creation of an internal market.[34] It is clear, therefore, that the EU competition

[27] The TFEU also contains provisions which prevent states from distorting the competitive process. Art 106 TFEU sets out rules to prevent Member States maintaining in force measures contrary to the competition and other Treaty rules and deals with the application of the competition rules (and other rules of the Treaties) to public undertakings and those granted special or exclusive rights by Member States. It contains a limited exemption (Art 106(2)) from the Treaty rules for such undertakings which has been construed narrowly. Art 37 TFEU also requires Member States which have state monopolies of a commercial character to eliminate discrimination between nationals of Member States regarding the conditions under which goods are procured and marketed. Arts 107–109 TFEU contain the rules that apply to the provision of state aid in the EU.

[28] See further section III.B.iv of this chapter. Restrictive provisions in an agreement infringing Art 101 TFEU are void, see Art 101(2) TFEU.

[29] In both cases, a breach of these provisions will only take place if the agreement or practice has an effect, either actual or potential, on intra-Union trade.

[30] Regulation 139/2004 (n 6).

[31] See Arts 101 and 102 TFEU and discussion about the open-ended nature of many provisions in the TFEU in n 2.

[32] Case 6/72 *Europemballage Corporation and Continental Can Company Inc v Commission* [1973] ECR 215, paras 24–25.

[33] Joined Cases 56 and 58/64 *Établissements Consten and Grundig-Verkaufs v Commission* [1966] ECR 299, 340.

[34] For some more recent examples, see Joined Cases C–403/08 and 429/08 *Football Association Premier League Ltd v QC Leisure* and *Karen Murphy v Media Protection Services Ltd* [2011] ECR I–9083,

law rules have been used as an instrument of market integration, meaning that tensions between the single market objective and a purely competition objective can arise.[35] Significantly, and for the purposes of this chapter, it will be seen that the policy of upholding the single market objective has been argued to have had a negative impact on consumer interests in some cases.

Second, it is arguable that the EU's commitment to 'undistorted competition' enshrines multi-faceted goals[36] which permit non-competition, or public policy, factors to play an influential role in the development of EU competition law or aspects of it.[37] For example, it seems clear that early application of the competition rules was influenced, in particular, by Ordoliberal[38] ideas and the desire to protect the competitive process as a mechanism for promoting rivalry, the protection of 'individual economic freedom of action as a value in itself', 'consumer choice' and for restraining abuse of market dominance. Some such views may have encouraged interpretation and application of the competition laws in such a way as to protect competitors themselves, rather than the competitive process (and consumers), to favour small- or medium-sized enterprises, to keep markets open, to protect the process of rivalry between firms and to achieve fairness between firms operating on the market. Although Ordoliberalism does not have significant support as an objective today, some references to it may still be gleaned from the Court's case law.[39]

Further, certain public policy goals, such as environmental protection, administration of justice and public health, appear to have influenced competition law analysis, especially the application of Article 101.[40] Therefore, even though

para 139 (Art 101); Case C–468 *Sot Lélos kai Sia EE v GlaxoSmithKline AEVE Farmakeftikon Proïonton* [2008] ECR I–7139, paras 65–66 (Art 102).

[35] See, eg, section III.B.ii of this chapter.

[36] D Geradin, A Layne-Farrar and N Petit, *EU Competition Law and Economics* (Oxford, Oxford University Press, 2012), 1.70.

[37] Indeed, Art 120 TFEU specifically states that 'the Member States and the Union shall act in accordance with the principle of an open market economy with free competition, favouring an *efficient allocation of resources*', but no specific reference is made to an efficient allocation of resources in the EU competition rules.

[38] See, eg, P Lowe, 'Consumer Welfare and Efficiency—New Guiding Principles of Competition Policy?' (13th International Competition and 14th European Competition Day, Munich, 27 March 2007) <http://ec.europa.eu/competition/speeches/index_2007.html> accessed 2 February 2015; W Möschel, 'The Proper Scope of Government Viewed from an Ordoliberal Perspective: the example of competition policy' (2001) 157 *Journal of Institutional and Theoretical Economics* 4; D Gerber, *Law and Competition in Twentieth Century Europe: Protecting Prometheus* (Oxford, Clarendon Press, 1998) 331–33; and P Behrens, 'The ordoliberal concept of "abuse" of a dominant position and its impact on Article 102 TFEU' in P Nihoul and I Takahashi, *Abuse Regulation in Competition Law*, Proceedings of the 10th ASCOLA Conference, Tokyo 2015.

[39] See, eg, Case C–1/12 *Ordem dos Técnicos Oficiais de Contas v Autoridade da Concorrência*, judgment of 28 Feb 2013, paras 92–93, and see also nn 61–62 of this chapter and accompanying text.

[40] See C Townley, *Article 81 EC and Public Policy* (Oxford, Hart Publishing, 2009) ch 2. For example, in Case C–309/99 *JCJ Wouters, JW Savelbergh and Price Waterhouse Belastingadviseurs BV v Algemene Raad van de Nederlandse Orde van Advocaten* [2002] ECR I–1577, para 97, the Court found that rules adopted in the Netherlands which prohibited members of the Bar practising in full partnership with accountants did not have as their object or effect the restriction of competition. Although the

Articles 101 and 102 do not themselves specifically refer to such public policy goals,[41] the EU Commission and the EU courts have sometimes taken account of these factors, particularly given the context of the rules within the TFEU and the importance that those courts have placed upon teleological and contextual readings of the EU Treaties.[42] Indeed, a complex and controversial issue, which is more alive than ever after the entry into force of the Lisbon Treaty, is whether EU competition law can be legitimately isolated from other EU policies. For example, Article 7 TFEU sets out the principle of consistency between all EU policies and activities and Articles 11 and 12 TFEU provide, respectively, for the integration of environmental and consumer protection requirements in the implementation of other EU policies, which naturally include competition policy.

Third, the emerging view of the European Commission (the Commission), which has sought to modernise its application and interpretation of the competition law rules since the end of the 1990s, and to distance itself from the previous approach based on broader 'public policy' objectives, is that the appropriate goal for Articles 101 and 102, and the EUMR, is 'to protect competition on the market as a means of enhancing consumer welfare and of ensuring an efficient allocation of resources'.[43] The Commission takes the view that pursuit of this goal, which is supported by many commentators, will ensure the efficient functioning of markets to the benefit of consumers and the global competitiveness of EU businesses. Indeed, former Competition Commissioner Joaquín Almunia stressed that consumer welfare is not just a catchy phrase; rather it 'is the cornerstone, the guiding principle of EU competition policy'.[44]

C. Consumer Welfare as an Objective of EU Competition Law: Which Consumers' Welfare Does Competition Law Protect?

The discussion above indicates that it is crucial both to the rationality of any competition law system, and to the question of whose interests it protects, that its goals are well defined. Further, although it is clear that the overall purpose of EU competition law is to ensure a system of undistorted competition within the internal market that can contribute to the achievement of the aims and wellbeing

arrangements restricted services that could be offered and reduced scope for efficiencies, the Court concluded that it was not unreasonable for the Bar Council to take the view that these restraints were necessary for the proper practice of the legal profession.

[41] In fact the Art 101(3) Guidelines (n 4) only refer to economic efficiencies to the exclusion of non-economic considerations. See further R Whish and D Bailey, *Competition Law*, 7th edn (Oxford, Oxford University Press, 2012) 160.

[42] Case C–519/04 P *David Meca-Medina and Igor Majcen v Commission* [2006] ECR I–6991, para 45; *JCJ Wouters* (n 40) para 97 ff; and Case T–193/02 *Laurent Piau v Commission* [2005] ECR II–209, para 102.

[43] Art 101(3) Guidelines (n 4) para 13.

[44] J Almunia, 'Competition—What's in it for Consumers?' <http://europa.eu/rapid/press-release_SPEECH-11-803_en.htm?locale=en> accessed 2 February 2015.

of the EU, the crucial issue of what specific objectives it pursues in order to achieve this overarching goal has not been clarified. Nonetheless, the Commission has, in the course of its process of modernisation, sought to rectify the uncertainty by reiterating its belief that competition rules should be designed to promote consumer welfare and efficiency.

One essential problem with the 'consumer welfare' concept articulated, and which is now championed as the goal of a number of competition law systems around the world, is that it is often used, especially by competition agencies, without clear explanation of what exactly is meant by it and exactly which consumers' welfare it protects. Indeed, when Bork adopted the term it was only rarely used and had no standard meaning in economics.[45] The phrase has thus been described by some as a 'shibboleth'[46] or as 'the most abused term'[47] in modern antitrust analysis.

In the competition law context, the term consumer welfare is ordinarily used as a synonym for one of two things. When Bork used this phrase in his seminal book,[48] he appears to have meant what is now referred to as 'total' or 'social welfare': that is, the objective of maximising efficiency for society as a whole (the sum of producer surplus and consumer surplus—that is total surplus), whoever benefits from those efficiency gains (whether producers or consumers).[49] On this approach, the total welfare of consumers as a class and the 'wealth of the nation' *overall* is used to assess changes in welfare—consequently, everyone in society (whether producers, distributors, retailers or final consumers) is characterised as a 'consumer' and competition law is not concerned with how that wealth is distributed amongst sellers and buyers and the members of society. Rather, so long as winners gain more than losers lose, total welfare is maximised and the conduct should be permitted.[50]

Another view, however, which now appears to have become the standard,[51] is that the objective of the competition law rules should be the maximisation of

[45] G Werden, 'Antitrust's Rule of Reason: Only Competition Matters', 7 <http://papers.ssrn.com/sol3/papers.cfm?abstract_id=2227097> accessed 2 February 2015.

[46] G Werden, 'Essays on Consumer Welfare and Competition Policy', 5 <http://papers.ssrn.com/sol3/papers.cfm?abstract_id=1352032> accessed 2 February 2015.

[47] JF Brodley, 'The Economic Goals of Antitrust Efficiency, Consumer Welfare, and Technological Progress' (1987) 62 *New York University Law Review* 1020, 1032.

[48] Bork (n 17) 90–91.

[49] *Social (total) welfare* is thus the sum of producer surplus (the profits a producer makes by selling goods over the cost of production) and consumer surplus (the difference between what consumers would be prepared to pay for goods and what they do pay). The objection to monopoly, or the exercise of market power, is that it does not just transfer some consumer surplus to producers but that some surplus (the deadweight) is totally lost to the market: Bork (n 17) 90 ('Consumer welfare is greatest when society's economic resources are allocated so that consumers are able to satisfy their wants as fully as technological constraints permit. Consumer welfare, in this sense, is merely another term for the wealth of the nation'). But see, eg, Lande (n 17), esp 88–89.

[50] This is known as a 'Kaldor-Hicks' improvement, see, eg, RJ Van den Bergh and PD Camesasca, *European Competition Law and Economics: A Comparative Perspective*, 2nd edn (London, Sweet & Maxwell, 2006) 29–30.

[51] Werden (n 46) 11.

efficiency but *only* if consumers receive a fair share of the total wealth—so the goal is to maximise *consumer* surplus,[52] and consequently it is this narrower aim which should be identified with consumer welfare. Under this elucidation, consumers are equated with 'buyers' on the market.

In most cases pursuit of either a total or (narrower) consumer welfare objective will achieve the same outcome. In exceptional circumstances, however, pursuit of the consumer welfare objective could result in the prohibition of conduct which results in an increase in efficiency overall, but which creates a transfer of consumer surplus to producers;[53] this concept thus favours buyers over sellers.[54] It is therefore crucial to know which of the outlined approaches the law favours and, consequently, which consumers' interests it protects: whether it is those of *all* of society, some groups within it (all those on the buyer side) and/or some groups more than others (final consumers more than intermediate buyers).[55]

The Commission has not explicitly stated which standard it prefers. Nonetheless, it does appear to have rejected the broader social welfare standard expounded by Bork and to support the narrower consumer welfare standard. In press releases, speeches, policy documents and reports, it continually stresses that it acts for the benefit of European *consumers* and to prevent practices which will result in 'consumer detriment', resulting from higher prices, reduced output or choice or

[52] For the view that the concept of 'consumer sovereignty' or 'consumer choice', 'the possibility and the right, for customers, to choose freely the products/services best corresponding to their needs, and the economic partners they want to deal with', plays an important role in EU competition law, see, eg, P Nihoul, 'Freedom of Choice: The Emergence of a Powerful Concept in European Competition Law' (2012) 3 *Concurrences* 55. See also RH Lande, 'Consumer Choice as the Ultimate Goal of Antitrust' (2001) 62 *University of Pittsburgh Law Review* 503 (but contrast, eg, D Wright and DH Ginsburg, 'The Goals of Antitrust: Welfare Trumps Choice' (2013) 81 *Fordham Law Review* 2405).

[53] eg OE Williamson, 'Economies as an Antitrust Defense: The Welfare Tradeoffs' (1968) 58 *American Economic Review* 18 (Williamson's efficiency trade-off model demonstrates that even a merger which will result in price rises above previous levels may increase total welfare if the cost savings to which it gives rise are greater than the loss suffered by consumers as a result of the reduction in output (the merger produces a net efficiency gain even though it permits the firm to raise its price above its marginal cost)); JB Kirkwood and RH Lande, 'The Fundamental Goals of Antitrust: Protecting Consumers, Not Increasing Efficiency' 84 *Notre Dame Law Review* 191, 224–31.

[54] This approach privileges the buyer (the consumer) above the seller (the producer), assuming the welfare of one is inherently more precious than that of the other and leads therefore to a form of discrimination between the two. A question which consequently is interesting is whether Arts 101 or Art 102 should be concerned not only with the exercise of market power on the sellers' side but also the exercise of market power on the buyers' side (monopsony power). Monopsonists, like monopolists, have power over price as they have the power to reduce the price paid for an input upstream (which also reduces the quantity of input supplied and utilised and, indeed, Art 101 has been applied to buyer cartels and Art 102 specifically prohibits both unfair selling and unfair *buying* prices). Although such conduct inhibits the maximisation of the wealth of society as a whole, it is the input producers upstream that are harmed and the view could be taken that if the competition laws are designed to protect consumers on the buyer side of the market, such conduct should not be condemned unless those holding monopsony power also have market power in the output market: see, eg, T Rosch, 'Monopsony and the Meaning of Consumer Welfare: A Closer Look at Weyerhaeuser' [2007] *Columbia Business Law Review* 353, but contrast G Werden, 'Monopsony and the Sherman Act: Consumer Welfare in a New Light' (2007) <http://ssrn.com/abstract=975912> accessed 2 February 2015.

[55] Werden (n 46) 5–6.

lower quality of goods or services, or diminished innovation. It thus seeks to maintain an undistorted system of competition which will, in turn, deliver consumer benefit. Although the adoption of this narrower standard is not uncontroversial, it does gain some support from the TFEU itself.[56] For example, Article 101(3), which provides the legal exception to Article 101(1) for restrictive agreements that produce countervailing benefits, demands that a 'fair share' of such identified benefits or efficiencies must be passed on to consumers (see further section III.B.iv below). Further, Article 102 specifically states that an abuse of a dominant position may consist of (a) imposing 'unfair' selling prices or unfair trading conditions,[57] (b) 'limiting production, markets or technical development' to the prejudice of consumers, or (c) engaging in discriminatory behaviour ('applying dissimilar conditions to equivalent transactions with other trading parties, thereby placing them at a competitive disadvantage') (see further section III.B.v below). Similarly, Article 2(1)(b) of the EUMR states that there is need to take account of the 'interests of intermediate and ultimate consumers' when assessing the compatibility of a proposed concentration with EU law. In addition, pursuit of a consumer welfare objective—focussing more closely on allocative rather than productive efficiency—may be justifiable on the grounds that it is easier to apply than a social welfare objective and that it is a more palatable objective as it evokes 'ideas of fairness, redistribution, and protection of the many and vulnerable, making this rhetoric attractive to politicians, policy-makers, and competition officials.'[58]

An important issue that presides over the consumer welfare debate in the EU, however, is that, despite support for a consumer welfare approach from the Commission and a number of commentators and practitioners, the case law of the Court does not unambiguously endorse it as the ultimate objective of EU competition law. While, in 2006, two judgments of the General Court, *Österreichische Postsparkasse AG and Bank für Arbeit und Wirtschaft AG v Commission* and *GlaxoSmithKline Services Unlimited v Commission* indicated support for such a goal,[59] subsequent judgments of the Court of Justice have placed greater emphasis on the need to protect not only the interests of consumers, but the interests of competitors and the structure of the market and competition as such.[60] In *TeliaSonera*,[61] for example, the Court held that the function of the Treaty competition rules is precisely 'to prevent competition from being distorted to the detriment of the public interest, individual undertakings and consumers, thereby ensuring the well-being of the European Union'.

[56] See also Art 12 TFEU.

[57] So exploiting customers. However, it also refers to unfair purchase prices; see n 54.

[58] R Nazzini, *The Foundations of European Union Competition Law, The Objectives and Principles of Article 102* (Oxford, Oxford University Press, 2011) 44–45.

[59] Joined cases T-213/01 and T-214/01 *Österreichische Postsparkasse AG and Bank für Arbeit und Wirtschaft AG v Commission* [2006] ECR II-16011, para 115 and Case T-168/01 *GlaxoSmithKline Services Unlimited v Commission* [2006] ECR II-2969 para 118.

[60] *GlaxoSmithKline* (n 8), para 63.

[61] *TeliaSonera* (n 9), para 22.

The Court therefore seems to attach significant importance to competition as a process that should in itself be protected. Although this could be taken to suggest support for broader goals and/or Ordoliberal ideas, it could also support the view that protecting that process, and precluding hindrances to it, benefits consumers—that is, that protecting the market structure from artificial distortions is the best mechanism for protecting the interests of the consumer in the medium to longer term. Further, these statements clearly indicate that the Court considers that the welfare of consumers forms at least part of the EU competition law fabric, even if it is not its sole or core objective. Indeed, in *Post Danmark*,[62] the Grand Chamber of the Court gave a judgment which, although containing no express statement about the objectives of the law, did focus heavily on the effects of the conduct on consumers, and in *Groupement des cartes bancaires v Commission*,[63] the Court placed emphasis on the poor allocation of resources to the detriment, in particular, of consumers that results from certain types of collusive behaviour between firms liable to infringe Article 101. In sum, therefore, important observations, relevant to our examination of the roles of the consumer in EU competition law, are that whilst the Commission has, post-modernisation, enthusiastically adopted consumer welfare as the key objective of EU competition law in its Guidance documents, the Court has been more guarded in ranking it above other equally important objectives: in particular, the single market project and the promotion of competition itself. Further, if it is to be accepted that EU competition pursues, whether solely or primarily, a 'consumer' welfare objective in the narrow sense, a few important conclusions can be drawn about the meaning of 'consumer' and 'consumer welfare' in this competition law context and the way that competition law protects such consumers' interests.

First, a statement that the competition law system pursues a 'consumer welfare' objective denotes that it pursues an economic objective. Although there is a debate in the EU as to whether non-economic or public policy factors can also be taken into account in a competition law assessment (and if so where and how), the consumer welfare objective itself does not seem to incorporate non-economic considerations as it does in the consumer protection realm.[64]

Second, it follows from the structure of the Treaty, which contains a set of prohibitions on anti-competitive behaviour, that the principal focus of the rules is on *eliminating* conduct stemming from anti-competitive agreements, conduct

[62] Case C–209/10 *Post Danmark AS v Konkurrencerådet*, judgment of 27 March 2012.

[63] Case C–67/13P *Groupement des cartes bancaires (CB) v Commission*, judgment of 11 September 2014.

[64] In their seminal work, Averitt and Lande note that competition law seeks to address external market failures that reduce the choices available to consumers and is concerned with the proper functioning of the markets, whilst consumer protection law addresses internal market failures that prevent consumers from making rational choices and thus has the non-economic aim of protecting consumers against deception, asymmetries of information, etc. NW Averitt and RH Lande, 'Consumer Sovereignty: A Unified Theory of Antitrust and Consumer Protection Law' (1996) 65 *Antitrust Law Journal* 713, 713–14. In their view, however, both areas of law complement each other and are bridged by the notion of consumer sovereignty; see also references cited at n 52.

or mergers of undertakings that is liable to harm consumer welfare rather than on actively promoting it through positive action. Consequently, there are some distortions of competition and market imperfections which operate to prevent the process of competition delivering value for money to consumers that competition law cannot reach. In such cases, consumer law and/or regulatory tools might be required, alternatively or additionally, to make markets work more efficiently for the benefit of consumers (see further III.C below).

Third, despite the populist rhetoric that might seem inherent in the slogan 'consumer welfare', such an objective is not designed solely to protect the interests of 'final consumers' (natural persons acting outside their 'trade, business, craft or profession')[65] or individual 'consumers' (persons who purchase goods or services for personal use).[66] Although it will be seen that the EU courts and Commission do sometimes use the term consumer in these narrower senses when making substantive competition law assessments (see further III below) and the Commission has a tendency to emphasise the benefits that the enforcement the competition law rules have for individual citizens, 'consumers' in this technical sense encompasses all those on the buyer side, whether they are indirect or direct users, small or large, natural or legal persons (indeed, many will be businesses), intermediate buyers or final consumers. This broader definition of the consumer concept, although perhaps counterintuitive, is explicable on the basis of the rationale underlying the application of competition law.[67] The rules promote the process of competition for the benefit of all such consumers and do not perform the more protective function performed by consumer law, such as safeguarding the interests of those perceived to be the weaker or more vulnerable party in individual contractual transactions.[68] This broad construction of the term 'consumer' is crucial, as it provides the fulcrum on which secondary assessments and interpretations of the core concepts set out in the competition law rules are based. We return to this point in section III when we consider the role that the consumer plays in competition law assessments.

Fourth, because the consumer welfare objective seeks to protect the interests of the relevant 'consumers' overall, it is frequently necessary, in determining whether

[65] See, eg, the Consumer Rights Directive (n 2), Art 2(1) and the Council Directive 93/13/EEC of 5 April 1993 on unfair terms in consumer contracts [1993] OJ L 95/29, Art 2(b).

[66] See the definition in the Oxford English Dictionary, where a consumer is defined as 'a person who purchases goods or services for personal use'.

[67] See A MacCulloch, 'The Consumer and Competition Law' in G Howells, I Ramsay and T Wilhelmsson (eds), *Handbook of Research on International Consumer Law* (Cheltenham, Edward Elgar, 2011) 79.

[68] ibid, but see the discussion of Ordoliberal ideas in references at n 38 and accompanying text as well as section III.B.v of this chapter and, eg, a report prepared by A Fletcher, A Karatzas and A Kreutzman-Gallasch for the Federation of Small Businesses, 'Small Businesses as Consumers: Are They Sufficiently Well Protected?' (January 2014). Competition agencies might also decide to focus their resources on bringing proceedings in cases which involve harm to a particularly vulnerable group of consumers; see section IV of this chapter. For statements of the protective function of consumer law, see Joined cases C–240/98 *Océano Grupo Editorial SA v Roció Murciano Quintero* [2000] ECR I- 4941, para 25; Case C–168/05 *Elisa María Mostaza Claro v Centro Móvil Milenium SL* [2006] ECR I–10421, paras 25–26.

the rules have been infringed, to weigh the interests of some groups of consumers against those of others. Further, harm to current consumers may have to be weighed against the (more speculative) benefits to future consumers which may be achieved by the conduct in the longer term (and vice versa). Indeed, an approach focussing only on immediate consumer interests might be at risk, in particular, of disregarding the impact of the conduct on competition, productivity and/or innovation and the interests of consumers in the long run (see further III below).[69] The term 'consumer' thus has a general rather than an individual character.

Fifth, the objective pursued may also have an impact upon how the rules are enforced: in particular, how a public enforcement agency determines in what way to devote its resources towards enforcement and whether private enforcement should be permitted and encouraged (see section IV). Finally, it is seen in the section below that even if an overarching consumer welfare objective is agreed and pursued, this is not an easy objective to achieve.

III. Achieving a Consumer Welfare Objective: Consumer Welfare as a 'Guide' in the Application of the Law

A. Introduction: Market Power and Rules and Standards

In the previous section we introduced the idea that the image of the consumer used to define the *objectives* of EU competition law is a wide-ranging one. In this section, we examine more closely how EU competition law seeks to achieve that objective and how the interests of different groups of consumers are taken into account in so doing. This enables us, simultaneously, to analyse other visions of the 'consumer' that emerge in the competition law context, in particular when identified as a tool in the process of making competition law *assessments*.

A particular problem in achieving a consumer welfare objective is that it is not ordinarily realistic or feasible to test directly in an individual case how the conduct at issue has, or will have, an impact upon consumer welfare, because efficiency is difficult to measure. Such an objective does not mean, therefore, that all conduct can, or should, be tested under competition law to see whether it harms or benefits consumer welfare.[70]

Rather, because it is frequently too difficult to measure how conduct affects efficiencies directly, the overarching objective plays a role principally by guiding

[69] See Art 101(3) Guidelines (n 4), para 87, and Case C–238/05 *Asnef-Equifax, Servicios de Información sobre Solvencia y Crédito, SL v Asociación de Usuarios de Servicios Bancarios (Ausbanc)* [2006] ECR I–11125 para 70.

[70] But see, eg, Werden, 'Essays on Consumer Welfare' (n 46), arguing that in the context of merger control consumer welfare can operate as the objective guide and legal test.

or shaping the interpretation of core concepts (such as a 'restriction' of competition or an 'abuse' of a dominant position) and the crafting of tests and/or presumptions to identify such conduct. These tests are guided by economics and, in particular, by an assessment of whether the conduct at issue is liable to interfere with the competitive process and/or to permit the relevant undertakings to exercise market power—'the ability to maintain prices above competitive levels for a significant period of time or to maintain output in terms of product quantities, product quality and variety or innovation below competitive levels for a significant period of time'[71]—and/or achieve offsetting efficiencies. Because they cannot always replicate economists' (frequently conflicting) views,[72] in many cases it is necessary, in considering how to construct legal rules or standards aimed at distinguishing anti-competitive from pro-competitive conduct (to separate the antitrust goats from the beneficial sheep),[73] for a trade-off to be made between the application of more complex standards or clearer bright-line rules. The former require detailed factual and economic analysis, which is more difficult and costly to apply both by undertakings and decision-takers, whilst the latter require less sophisticated analysis and less emphasis on expert economic evidence but which may, consequently, be less accurate in some cases. In making such trade-offs, it will be necessary to consider whether an approach which may sometimes condemn legitimate business practices and allow Type 1 errors is a lesser or greater evil than one which may sometimes allow Type 2 errors.[74]

In the next sections we will consider the references to, and relevance of, the consumer and consumer interests in the framework of five key competition law assessments: (i) the assessment of market power and dominance; (ii) the determination of when presumptions of harm to consumer welfare should be employed in the application of Article 101; (iii) the determination of when presumptions of no harm to consumer welfare should be employed in the application of Article 101; (iv) the balancing of anti and pro-competitive effects in the context of Article 101; and (v) the determination of what constitutes an 'abuse' under Article 102.

B. Substantive Interpretation of the Law: Identifying Anticompetitive Conduct and the Role of the Consumer in Competition Law Assessments

i. The Consumer in the Assessment of Market Power and Dominance

A core concern of competition law is that there should be effective competition in markets and firms should not be able to engage in anticompetitive agreements,

[71] Art 101(3) Guidelines (n 4) para 25.

[72] See, eg, Justice Breyer's dissenting judgment in *Leegin Creative Leather Products Inc v PSKS Inc, DBA Kay's Kloset* 551 US 877 (2007).

[73] ibid.

[74] eg OECD, *Resale Price Maintenance* (2008) <http://www.oecd.org/daf/competition/43835526.pdf> accessed 2 February 2015.

conduct or mergers which will permit them to exercise market power and deprive consumers of the benefits that that competition would otherwise bring, through low prices, choice, quality and/or innovation. Many competition law assessments thus commence with a consideration of the relevant undertaking's (or undertakings') market power.[75]

Article 102, for example, targets only the behaviour of firms that possess a 'dominant position'—a concept which the Court has equated with market rather than commercial power and the ability of the 'dominant firm' to maintain prices above competitive levels[76]—and so might be in a position to exploit that market power and to engage in anticompetitive conduct which excludes competitors from the market. Dominance has been defined by the Court in *Hoffmann-La Roche* as a position of economic strength enjoyed by an undertaking 'which enables it to prevent effective competition being maintained on the relevant market by affording it the power to behave to an appreciable extent independently of its competitors, *its customers and ultimately of the consumers*'.[77]

In this case, it can be seen that the Court refers to 'consumers' more narrowly than in the way identified in the discussion of 'consumer welfare' above, seemingly equating the concept with final consumers and distinguishing them from competitors and other customers (or consumers) operating on the buyer side. Although this might at first appear to suggest a different vision of the term 'consumer', on closer scrutiny, it is seen that it is not in fact symptomatic of an inconsistent approach but is just a reflection of the different context in which the notion is used. Rather, the ostensibly different vision drawn emerges because the final consumer in this case is simply identified as part of the process of ascertaining the features of a dominant firm which distinguishes it from a non-dominant one; in this case, the Court thus equates the ability of the dominant firm to act independently of buyers (direct customers or final consumers) and other suppliers (competitors) with its ability to exercise market power—to maintain higher prices whilst at the same time maintaining a much greater market share than those of its competitors.[78]

The term consumer also appears, and plays an important role, when determining the relevant market in which the competition law assessment takes place; in this case the different categories of consumer again play a distinct role in the process of determining the relevant market, which is simply one step taken on the route to the final determination of whether an infringement of the competition law rules (which harms consumer welfare) has been committed. In competition law, the question of whether one or more firms has/have market power (or a dominant position) is generally determined not directly[79] but indirectly through use of

[75] But see section III.B.ii of this chapter.

[76] Case T–321/05 *AstraZeneca AB and AstraZeneca plc v Commission* [2010] ECR II–2805, para 267 and Case C–457/10 P *AstraZeneca AB and AstraZeneca plc v Commission* [2012] ECR I–000, judgment of 6 December 2012, para 177–81.

[77] *Hoffmann-La Roche* (n 7) paras 38–39, emphasis added.

[78] *AstraZeneca* (n 76).

[79] There is a growing view, however, that, especially in merger analysis, other tools (such as pricing pressure indices) can substitute for traditional analysis based on market definition, market shares and

proxies such as an analysis of market shares and other factors such as barriers to entry into the market. This requires the 'relevant' market on which the undertakings concerned operate to be identified (from both a product and geographic perspective) so that an assessment of the conditions of competition on that market can be made. Where this approach is taken, market definition sets out an important preliminary step which permits the identification of the boundaries of competition between firms, the competitive constraints that the relevant undertaking(s) face from actual competitors, potential new entrants and/or buyers and, consequently, an assessment of whether or not it has sufficient market power, for example, to be found dominant or to restrict competition on that market.[80]

The Court has held that the relevant market consists of products (or services) which are interchangeable with each other but not (or only to a limited extent) interchangeable with those outside it. This interchangeability may be with other products or with the same products from elsewhere; it thus has both a product (the product market) and a geographical dimension (the geographic market). Although the Court has stressed the importance of using qualitative criteria such as characteristics, price and intended use[81] for assessing functional interchangeability, the truth is that these criteria are not always very helpful in shedding light on the core issue that the process is seeking to answer;[82] that is, whether the undertaking or undertakings are operating on markets which may be monopolised. Competition agencies, including the Commission, thus tend now to use less subjective and more scientific mechanisms for determining the relevant markets, in particular, by relying on the hypothetical monopolist, or Small but Significant Non-transitory Increase in Price (SSNIP), test to provide a conceptual framework for their identification. Essentially, the test starts by hypothesising a particular relevant market (for example, a market for bottled sparkling water in France) and then assuming a small (5–10%) rise in the price of that product. It is then asked whether this price increase would cause customers to purchase another product (for example, bottled still water), or to purchase bottled sparkling water from another area, to such an extent that the price rise is unprofitable.

> If substitution were enough to make the price increase unprofitable because of the resulting loss of sales, additional substitutes and areas are included in the relevant market.

concentration measures; see, eg, L Kaplow, 'Why (Ever) Define Markets?' (2012) 57 *Antitrust Bulletin* (special issue); J Farrell and C Shapiro, 'Antitrust Evaluation of Horizontal Mergers: An Economic Alternative to Market Definition' (2010) 1 *BE Journal of Theoretical Economics* 1.

[80] Commission, Notice on the definition of the relevant market for the purposes of Community competition law (Notice on Market Definition) [1997] OJ C372/5, para 10.

[81] Case 27/76 *United Brands Company and United Brands Continentaal BV v Commission* [1978] ECR 207.

[82] They will not shed light when trying to determine, for example, whether or not sparkling mineral water is in the same market as still mineral water, tap water, orange juice, or tonic water. All of these products have similar characteristics and uses. The Commission now recognises the limited usefulness of analysing the characteristics and intended use of a product when defining the market, except as a preliminary step when considering the possible substitutes for a product. See Notice on Market Definition (n 80), para 36.

This would be done until the set of products and geographical areas is such that small, permanent increases in relative prices would be profitable.[83]

The SSNIP test thus requires an assessment of demand substitution (determination of the range of products viewed as substitutes by consumers (or customers) on the buyer side) and supply substitution (whether suppliers are able to switch production to the relevant products and market them in the short term without incurring significant additional costs or risks in response to small and permanent changes in relative prices) to determine whether the hypothetical price rise would be possible.

It is against this background that the use of the term 'consumer' in the Commission's Notice on the definition of the relevant market (the 'Market Definition' Notice)[84] and cases must be understood. The discussion above establishes that in identifying the market, too great an emphasis must not be placed on the subjective viewpoint of any one group, or groups, of consumers. For example, the Commission and Court were criticised in the classic case of *United Brands*[85] for identifying a relevant product market for 'bananas' partly on the basis that there was a distinct group of final consumers (the young, the elderly, the sick) who would not think that bananas could be substituted for other kinds of fruit.[86] The SSNIP test clarifies, however, that the important question in determining whether bananas can be identified as a relevant market which could be monopolised (that is, whether it is an economically meaningful market) is not whether there are some consumers who will not switch to another product following a rise in its price or even whether a majority of consumers will not switch, but whether a *sufficient* number of consumers will switch to make the price rise unprofitable. If therefore it is impossible to discriminate against the 'infra-marginal' customers who cannot, or who will not, switch—in the bananas case, the young, old and sick—by charging them a higher price, then the behaviour of marginal customers (who are able to switch) must be taken into account as it is this (not the behaviour of groups of consumers or even the average consumer) which affects a supplier's pricing decisions and which is, consequently, crucial in the determination of the market.[87]

The Commission stresses the importance of the marginal consumer in its Market Definition Notice. For example, it states that the question to be answered in applying the SSNIP test is whether 'the parties' customers' could switch to substitutes in such volume to make the price increase unprofitable (because of the resulting loss of sales). By way of practical example it states:

In practice, the question to address would be whether consumers of flavour A would switch to other flavours when confronted with a permanent price increase of 5% to 10% for flavour A. If a sufficient number of consumers would switch to, say, flavour B, to

[83] ibid, para 17.
[84] Notice on Market Definition (n 80).
[85] *United Brands Company* (n 81).
[86] ibid, paras 27–34.
[87] See Notice on Market Definition (n 80), para 43.

> such an extent that the price increase for flavour A would not be profitable owing to the resulting loss of sales, then the market would comprise at least flavours A and B. The process would have to be extended in addition to other available flavours until a set of products is identified for which a price rise would not induce a sufficient substitution in demand.[88]

In the Market Definition Notice, the Commission seems to use the terms 'customers' and 'consumers' interchangeably to emphasise the importance of testing consumers' preferences as a whole.[89]

An important practical problem, however, arises in actually applying the SSNIP test. How are customers' (or consumers') reactions to the hypothetical price rise to be gauged? In the EU, the Commission is willing to use both empirical evidence (using preliminary information gathered from, in particular, the investigated firms, their main customers,[90] suppliers and competitors as well as other industry players) and quantitative tests[91] devised by economists.[92] Although such techniques are not panaceas, they can, when used correctly and rigorously, be helpful tools to use within the SSNIP framework. The past and future reactions of consumers (whether intermediate or final) may thus be important to the analysis where relevant evidence is available: for example, evidence of consumers' past behaviour or 'revealed preference' (that is, reaction to past changes in prices)[93] or evidence of how they might behave in the future when making estimations of cross-elasticity.[94]

ii. Presumptions of Harm to Consumer Welfare: Agreements which have as their Object the Restriction of Competition

Defining relevant markets and then assessing whether the conduct at issue facilitates, or will facilitate, the strengthening or exercise of such market power involves complex and time-consuming analysis. Although such analysis is necessary in many cases (see sections (iv) and (v) below), most competition law systems take shortcuts and seek to sidestep a full analysis in cases where anti-competitive effects are very likely (or where they are very unlikely: see (iii) below). For example, competition law systems frequently apply presumptions of illegality to agreements which clearly distort the process of competition and which are always, or virtually

[88] ibid, paras 17–18.

[89] See also Nihoul (n 52).

[90] Consumer questionnaires may have to be treated with some caution, however, as it is recognised that asking hypothetical questions may lead to biased results and that interviewees may, in practice, behave differently from how they answer survey questions.

[91] Notice on Market Definition (n 80), paras 36–43. See also G Monti, *EC Competition Law* (Cambridge, Cambridge University Press, 2007) 135–38.

[92] Including elasticity estimates, tests based on similarity of price movements over time (price correlation analysis), causality calculations, price convergence analysis, evidence of recent substitution in the past available as a result of actual events or shocks in the market ('shock analysis') or critical loss analysis; see, eg, Van den Bergh and Camesasca (n 50) 137.

[93] See Notice on Market Definition (n 80), paras 38–39.

[94] ibid.

always, likely to restrict competition. Clear rules against such obviously pernicious conduct are considered acceptable as they eradicate the need for a claimant to prove, at cost, its adverse consequences. In the EU, Article 101 allows for a (rebuttable) presumption of illegality to be applied,[95] as it prohibits both agreements which have as their object the restriction of competition and those which have such an effect. The Court has made it plain that the words 'object or effect' are alternative,[96] not cumulative, requirements: so if the object of the agreement is found to be 'sufficiently deleterious', it need not be established that it also has a restrictive effect. Complex market analysis and proof of actual or likely effects on competition and consumers are thus avoided[97]—a restriction of competition is assumed. Although an infringement of Article 101 can be avoided by the parties demonstrating that the agreement has off-setting benefits and meets the criteria for legal exception under Article 101(3), in practice discharging this burden is difficult. Indeed, the Commission's view is that such agreements are presumed not to satisfy the conditions of Article 101(3) (so the conduct is generally prohibited by the competition law rules).[98]

A crucially important question therefore is which agreements have as their object the restriction of competition and how is it determined which agreements fall within that object category? Clearly if an overarching consumer welfare objective is to be achieved, best practice suggests that the rule should be drawn on the basis of economic principles so that it yields minimal error costs (especially from over-inclusive presumptions of illegality which may lead to false positives: that is, wrongly presuming that pro-competitive agreements infringe the competition law rules).[99]

The EU courts have held that the objectives, context and content[100] of an agreement are critical to the determination of whether it is 'by its very nature' injurious to competition and restrictive of competition by object. Content, in particular, holds significant weight[101] and jurisprudence establishes that specific agreements, including horizontal cartels[102]—broadly, anti-competitive arrangements between competitors to fix prices, make rigged bids (collusive tenders), establish

[95] In the US, in contrast, a conclusive (and irrebuttable) presumption of illegality is applied in per se cases.

[96] eg Case C–49/92P *Commission v Anic Partecipazioni SpA* [1999] ECR I–4125, para 123.

[97] Even in these cases, however, some assessment of the relevant market is required under EU law to demonstrate that the jurisdictional element of Art 101 TFEU is satisfied—that the agreement appreciably affects trade between Member States; see Case C–439/11 P *Ziegler SA v Commission*, judgment of 11 July 2014.

[98] Art 101(3) Guidelines (n 4), para 46.

[99] See *Groupement* (n 63), Opinion of AG Wahl.

[100] *GlaxoSmithKline* (n 8), para 58.

[101] Although objectives and context may be relied upon both to expand or contract the category; see, eg, A Jones and B Sufrin, *EU Competition Law*, 5th edn (Oxford, Oxford University Press 2014) ch 4.

[102] Case T–374/94 *European Night Services Ltd (ENS), Eurostar (UK) Ltd, formerly European Passenger Services Ltd (EPS), Union internationale des chemins de fer (UIC), NV Nederlandse Spoorwegen (NS) and Société nationale des chemins de fer français (SNCF) v Commission* [1998] ECR II–3141, para 136.

output restrictions or quotas, or share or divide markets[103]—and certain vertical agreements (see further below) are likely to be found restrictive by object. In a recent decision, the Court has reiterated that the category of agreements restrictive of competition by object must be interpreted restrictively and applied to situations where an agreement inherently reveals a 'sufficient degree of harm to competition'.[104]

The assumption of a restriction on competition in relation to cartel activity is uncontroversial. Indeed, as there is growing international acceptance that such activity poses a serious threat to economies and consumers and constitutes 'the supreme evil of antitrust'[105] and 'the most egregious'[106] violation of competition law, many antitrust systems do treat such conduct as an 'automatic' violation of the rules.[107] Parties to cartels deliberately set out to interfere with free competition, to contradict the principles of the free market economy and to act instead to protect the prosperity of the participants as a whole. In addition, such agreements are costly to create and enforce,[108] they harm efficiency (they are estimated to cost society billions)[109] and are 'naked'—'[t]hey seek to restrict competition without producing any objective countervailing benefits'.[110] The direct interference with the free operation of competition justifies the presumption of illegality to all cartels, whatever the parties' market shares, the level of the market at which the cartel operates, the product or service involved and whether or not it can be demonstrated that the cartel has in fact harmed consumer welfare or final consumers. Their likely impact upon welfare (total and consumer) thus operates as a guide for rules because most cartels will reduce 'consumer welfare' and will never increase it.[111] Indeed, in *Groupement des cartes bancaires*, the Court held that since horizontal price fixing by cartels

> may be considered so likely to have negative effects, in particular on the price, quantity or quality of the goods and services, that it may be considered redundant, for the purposes of applying Article [101(1)], to prove that they have actual effects on the market …

[103] Commission, Recommendation of the Council concerning Effective Action against Hard Core Cartels COM(98) 35 final.

[104] *Groupement* (n 63), para 53.

[105] *Verizon Communications v Law Offices of Curtis V Trinko* 540 US 398, 408 (2004); eg OECD, *Fighting Hard Core Cartels: Recent Progress and Challenges Ahead* (2003), and speech of M Monti, 'Fighting Cartels Why and How? Why Should We Be Concerned with Cartels and Collusive Behaviour?' (3rd Nordic Competition Policy Conference, Stockholm, 11–12 September 2000).

[106] COM(98) 35 (n 103).

[107] In the US, for example, cartel arrangements are, because of their pernicious effect on competition and lack of any redeeming virtue, considered to be illegal per se under s 1 of the Sherman Act of 1890, *Northern Pacific Railway Co v United States* 356 US 1, 5 (1958).

[108] Van den Bergh and Camesasca (n 50), s 5.2.1.2.

[109] eg OECD, *Hard Core Cartels—Recent Progress and Challenges Ahead* (2003).

[110] Monti (n 105).

[111] Because cartel agreements are generally 'naked', generating no countervailing benefits of efficiencies, the parties are most unlikely to be able to establish that the criteria of Art 101(3) TFEU (for legal exception) are met.

> Experience shows that such behaviour leads to falls in production and price increases, resulting in poor allocation of resources to the detriment, in particular, of consumers.[112]

The extent to which the object category should be used in relation to agreements other than naked cartel activity is, however, controversial.[113] In the EU it has also been held to encompass vertical agreements[114] containing provisions fixing the minimum prices at which retailers can sell the contract products (resale price maintenance (RPM))[115] and those conferring absolute territorial protection (ATP) on a distributor or otherwise partitioning national markets.[116] Vertical agreements are, however, not ordinarily concluded between competitors but between providers of complementary goods and services. Consequently, they are less 'obviously' anti-competitive than horizontal agreements and provide greater scope for efficiencies. Indeed, a manufacturer of a product will generally want to ensure that its product is distributed in the most efficient manner possible so that it competes more effectively with the products of its competitors. Vertical agreements may, therefore, be used to expand markets through solving free-rider or double marginalisation problems, to lower costs through efficiencies and/or to promote investment and innovation through solving a 'hold up' problem. The assumption that a vertical agreement, which has more ambiguous welfare effects, restricts competition arguably creates a greater risk that false positives will result and the consumer welfare will not be achieved because consumers may be deprived of the benefit of an efficiency-enhancing agreement.

This point is illustrated by the early case of *Consten and Grundig*.[117] In this case the Commission had held that distribution arrangements, which resulted in Consten being granted the exclusive right to sell Grundig products in France (neither Grundig itself nor any other Grundig distributor was entitled to sell the products there) had as its object the restriction of competition. The parties disputed this assessment arguing that the agreement was pro-competitive; it had

[112] *Groupement* (n 63), para 51.

[113] One controversial issue is the question whether an agreement incorporating severe restraints, such as a horizontal price or output restraint, should be characterised as restrictive by object where the restraints are argued to be inherent in, or objectively necessary to, a *pro-competitive* venture, for example, where horizontal price restraints are not 'naked' but are designed, and necessary, to achieve some efficiency-enhancing or other legitimate objective; see, eg, Case C–382/12P *MasterCard Inc and Others v Commission*, judgment of 11 September 2014 and the Commission Staff Working Document, Guidance on restrictions of competition 'by object' for the purposes of defining which agreements may benefit from the *De Minimis* Notice, COM(2014) 249 final 6.

[114] See also, eg, Case C–8/08 *T-Mobile Netherlands BV, KPN Mobile NV, Orange Nederland NV and Vodafone Libertel NV v Raad van bestuur van de Nederlandse Mededingingsautoriteit* [2009] ECR I–4529 and Case C–32/11 *Allianz Hungária Biztosító Zrt v Gazdasági Versenyhivatal*, judgment of 14 March 2013.

[115] eg Case 243/83 *SA Binon and Cie v SA Agence et messageries de la presse* [1985] ECR 2015, para 44.

[116] *Consten and Grundig* (n 33). A dealer has ATP when it is shielded from all competition in the sale of the manufacturer's products (from the manufacturer itself and from other distributors of that manufacturer's products) in that territory.

[117] ibid.

been essential to enable Grundig to penetrate the French market. Indeed, without the promise of ATP, Consten would not have agreed to take the risk of acting as distributor in France as other distributors (outside of France) would have been able to take a 'free ride' upon its promotional and investment efforts there. Although, therefore, the agreement resulted in the existence of only one distributor of Grundig products in France (there was a restriction on competition between distributors of Grundig products—a restriction of *intra-brand competition*), the agreement led to an increase in competition for consumer electronics products in France (that is, there was an increase in *inter-brand competition*) and, consequently, had beneficial effects for consumers. The parties argued, therefore, that the Commission should have conducted a fuller market analysis to determine whether the agreement had as its effect the restriction of competition.[118] The Court, however, upheld the Commission's Decision. The agreement giving Consten the exclusive right of sale of Grundig products in France had as its *object* the restriction of competition so an assessment of its *effect* was deemed unnecessary. It also upheld the Commission's view that the agreement did not meet the Article 101(3) criteria. The Court has reiterated this strict stance towards absolute territorial vertical restraints on several occasions.[119]

This line of cases is important. First, it illustrates how EU competition rules are, in the context of vertical territorial restraints, influenced by the internal market project;[120] concerns about the impact of an agreement on the integration of national markets may therefore outweigh efficiency arguments raised by the parties.

Second, it illustrates more broadly that the more extensive the category of agreements to which a virtually irrefutable presumption of illegality is applied, the greater the risk that some pro-competitive agreements will be condemned, and others deterred, with the effect that competition, and consumers, may be harmed. In the EU the question of whether it is rational or reasonable to apply an assumption of restrictive effects to vertical territorial, and price, restraints and/or whether a change of approach is required, has provoked extensive debate.[121] Some commentators have argued that the presumption is not defensible because of the potential for such agreements to increase inter-brand competition and consumer welfare.

[118] This view was supported by Roemer AG, who considered it to be wrong that Art 101(1) should be applied, on the basis of purely theoretical considerations, to a situation which might, upon closer inspection, reveal no appreciable adverse effects on competition. A restriction could not be established without looking at the market *in concreto* and without taking account of competition between similar products. In a case like this one, where the agreement had already been implemented, the Commission should have made a comparison between two market situations: that after making the agreement and that which would have arisen had there been no agreement. If Grundig had not found an outlet for its products in the absence of supplying a sole concessionaire, the exclusive distribution agreement clearly promoted competition; it would have been necessary for Grundig to gain access to the new market.

[119] See, for a more recent example, *GlaxoSmithKline* (n 8).

[120] See cases cited at n 34 and accompanying text.

[121] eg A Jones, 'Resale Price Maintenance: A Debate About Competition Policy in Europe?' [2009] *European Competition Journal* 425 and J Goyder, 'Is Nothing Sacred? Resale Price Maintenance and the

The application of the EU rebuttable presumption of illegality to these cases is strongly supported by the Commission. The Commission and the Court consistently stress the importance of the competitive process at all levels of the market and have been concerned about arrangements which result in the complete elimination of rivalry and competition (or price competition) between distributors of a manufacturer's product. Further, the Commission has emphasised that the risk of Type 1 errors is minimised as it is always open to the parties to demonstrate that the agreement does in fact produce efficiencies which are passed on to consumers.

Third, and crucially for the purposes of our discussion, this assumption of a restriction of competition demonstrates that where an automatic presumption of harm to consumer welfare is applied, there is no need for any image of the consumer to be drawn, or considered, at the Article 101(1) stage of the assessment. The extent to which consumer interests have *really* been harmed by the anti-competitive behaviour is not examined; it is taken for granted. These consumer interests are only considered at a later analytical stage, in particular if the parties attempt to establish that the Article 101(1) prohibition does not apply because the agreement produces offsetting efficiencies and delivers consumer benefits under Article 101(3) (see section (iv) below).

iii. Presumptions of Legality: Safe Harbours

At the other end of the spectrum, many competition law systems apply a presumption of legality to agreements between parties which are unlikely to have sufficient market power to be able to restrict competition.[122] In the EU, an agreement is presumed to be legal either: (a) where any restriction of competition is liable to be insignificant, or *de minimis*,[123] because of the very weak position of the parties; or (b) because it falls within the scope of one of the EU block exemption regulations (which are directly applicable), so it is presumed to satisfy the conditions of Article 101(3).

Block exemptions have generally been crafted by the Commission,[124] following its experience of examining agreements individually, to grant an 'exemption' under Article 101(3) to categories of agreements which, in its experience, are unlikely to restrict competition and/or are likely to generate efficiencies—in particular, where

EU Policy Review on Vertical Restraints' in Swedish Competition Authority (eds), *The Pros and Cons of Vertical Restraints* <http://www.kkv.se/globalassets/english/research/report-the-pros-and-cons-of-vertical-restraints-18mb.pdf> 173–74 (accessed 6 February 2015).

[122] As Art 102 only applies to the unilateral conduct of undertakings which hold a dominant position (see section III.B.i of this chapter), unilateral conduct (other than mergers) of firms which are not dominant do not fall within the scope of the competition law rules.

[123] In this respect, see Case 5/69 *Franz Völk v SPRL Ets J Vervaecke* [1969] ECR 295 and the Communication from the Commission—Notice on agreements of minor importance which do not appreciably restrict competition under Article 101(1) of the Treaty on the Functioning of the European Union [2014] OJ C291/1 (De Minimis Notice).

[124] They are adopted generally by the Commission, acting in the exercise of delegated powers from the Council.

the parties do not have significant market shares and where the agreements do not contain listed 'hard core restraints'. The list of hard core restraints closely mirrors the object restraints discussed in section (ii) above and reflects the Commission's view that agreements containing such restraints are presumed to violate Article 101 and cannot benefit from a presumption of legality under a block exemption.

Some block exemption regulations pertain to specific sectors (for example, insurance).[125] Others apply more generally, for example, to vertical (Regulation 330/2010),[126] horizontal cooperation (Regulations 1217/2010[127] and 1218/2010)[128] or technology transfer (Regulation 316/2014)[129] agreements.

In the context of block exemptions, therefore, no detailed scrutiny of an agreement that falls squarely within the scope of exemption is required as the Commission has made an *a priori* determination that even if such an agreement restricts competition, it will satisfy the four conditions of Article 101(3), and in particular that *consumers* will receive a 'fair share'[130] of the benefits generated by the agreement (see further section (iv) below).[131] In other words, the benefits that the agreement yields for consumers are taken for granted and presumed; the block exemptions operate as a safe harbour and their protection can only be withdrawn prospectively.[132]

iv. Anti-competitive Effect in the Application of Article 101(1) TFEU and the Balancing of Pro- and Anti-competitive Effects in the Application of Article 101(3) TFEU

Where the two extreme presumptions of legality or illegality do not apply under Article 101, a fuller competition law assessment will be required to determine whether (a) the agreement has as its effect the restriction of competition; and, if so, (b) whether it satisfies the conditions of Article 101(3).

[125] Commission Regulation (EU) No 267/2010 of 24 March 2010 on the application of Article 101(3) of the Treaty on the Functioning of the European Union to certain categories of agreements, decisions and concerted practices in the insurance sector [2010] OJ L83/1.

[126] Commission Regulation (EU) No 330/2010 of 20 April 2010 on the application of Article 101(3) of the Treaty on the Functioning of the European Union to categories of vertical agreements and concerted practices [2010] OJ L102/1.

[127] Commission Regulation (EU) No 1217/2010 of 14 December 2010 on the application of Article 101(3) of the Treaty on the Functioning of the European Union to certain categories of research and development agreements [2010] OJ L335/36.

[128] Commission Regulation (EU) No 1218/2010 of 14 December 2010 on the application of Article 101(3) of the Treaty on the Functioning of the European Union to certain categories of specialisation agreements [2010] OJ L335/43.

[129] Commission Regulation (EU) No 316/2014 of 21 March 2014 on the application of Article 101(3) of the Treaty on the Functioning of the European Union to categories of technology transfer agreements [2014] OJ L93/17.

[130] See section III.B.iv of this chapter.

[131] eg Regulation 330/2010 (n 126), Rec 2.

[132] See esp Council Regulation (EC) No 1/2003 of 16 December 2002 on the implementation of the rules on competition laid down in Articles 81 and 82 of the Treaty [now Arts 101 and 102 TFEU] [2003] OJ L1/1, Art 29(1)(2).

Since in Article 101(1) 'effect' cases a restriction of competition is not assumed, the likely impact of the agreement on inter- (and/or intra-) brand competition must be determined. Indeed, ever since 1966, and its judgment in *Société Technique Minière v Maschinenbau Ulm GmbH*,[133] the Court has recognised that agreements which do not have as their object the restriction of competition, should be assessed in their market context and an economic approach adopted when determining their effect. This position has been reiterated on many occasions. The Commission thus states in its Article 101(3) Guidelines that, in general, to establish that the agreement has as its effect the restriction of competition, a claimant will have to establish that it affects 'actual or potential competition to such an extent that on the relevant market negative effects on prices, output, innovation or the variety or quality of goods and services can be expected with a reasonable degree of probability'.[134]

Consequently, it is not sufficient to look at the contractual restraints in the agreement abstractly but they must be examined in the context in which they operate, encompassing an examination of the market shares and market power of the parties, the market context of the agreement and its effect on actual and potential competition.[135] In 'effect' cases, therefore, an adverse effect on consumer welfare (and consumer interests) is only established where, compared to the situation which would occur in the absence of the agreement, the competitive process is distorted in such a way that negative effects on prices (or other parameters of competition) can be expected. Whether such effects are probable is generally determined indirectly through an examination of the relevant market, the parties' position in that market and the terms of the contract.[136] The examination of the market thus focusses on *likely*, not actual, effects on consumers through negative effects on prices and other parameters of competition. Where such effects can be demonstrated the agreement will be prohibited unless the Article 101(3) legal exception applies: in particular, by establishing that consumers will benefit from other compensating efficiencies such as enhanced quality.[137]

Unless the conditions of one of the block exemptions apply (see (iii) above), it is for those claiming the benefit of Article 101(3)[138] to establish that *all four*[139] of its

[133] In Case 56/65 *Société Technique Minière (LTM) v Maschinenbau Ulm GmbH* (MBU) [1966] ECR 235.

[134] Art 101(3) Guidelines (n 4) para 24. This could be because the agreement restricts actual or potential competition between the parties or between any one of the parties and third parties that could have existed absent the agreement, ibid, paras 25–26. Alternatively, it will have to establish that the agreement restricts a supplier's distributors from competing with each other since potential competition that could have existed between the distributors absent the restraint is restricted.

[135] See Case C–234/89 *Stergios Delimitis v Henninger Bräu AG* [1991] ECR I–935.

[136] Art 101(3) Guidelines (n 4), para 22.

[137] ibid, para 86.

[138] Regulation 1/2003 (n 132), Art 2.

[139] The requirements are cumulative, see Case T–528/93 *Metropole télévision SA and Reti Televisive Italiane SpA and Gestevisión Telecinco SA and Antena 3 de Televisión v Commission* [1996] ECR II–649, para 93 and Case T–65/98 *Van den Bergh Foods Ltd v Commission* [2003] ECR II–4653, para 144, and Case C–68/12 *Protimonopolný úrad Slovenskej republiky v Slovenská sporiteľňa as*, judgment of 7 February 2013, paras 31–34.

criteria are satisfied:[140] (1) that the agreement achieves benefits—improvements in the production or distribution of goods or the promotion of technical or economic progress; (2) that a fair share of those benefits are passed on to 'consumers'; (3) that the agreement does not contain any indispensable restraints; and (4) that it does not eliminate competition in respect of a substantial part of the products in question. There is relatively little current jurisprudence providing clarification as to how these important criteria are interpreted. Consequently, the Commission's Guidelines on Article 101(3)[141] and other Notices also provide helpful guidance to business, shedding light on how the Commission interprets the criteria. When considering how Article 101(3) affects the 'consumer', several important observations can be made.

First, the role of Article 101(3)[142] is to determine whether benefits achieved by the agreement, or restrictive provisions, outweigh negative effects, so that the agreement is on balance pro-competitive:[143] that is, whether it achieves 'appreciable objective advantages of such a character as to compensate for the disadvantages which they cause in the field of competition'.[144] The Commission's current view is that the parties must demonstrate efficiency gains (that is economic benefits, not public policy benefits unless they are used to supplement the economic benefits which the agreement generates), cost efficiencies,[145] and qualitative efficiencies, creating value in the form of new or improved products (dynamic efficiencies),[146] which will result from the economic activity that forms the object of the agreement (that is, there is a causal link between the agreement and the claimed efficiencies)[147] and that there is a pass-on of these efficiencies to consumers.[148]

The Commission, reflecting the overarching consumer welfare goal, interprets the concept of the consumer broadly in this context to encompass:

> all direct or indirect users of the products covered by the agreement, including producers that use the products as an input, wholesalers, retailers and final consumers, ie natural persons who are acting for purposes which can be regarded as outside their trade or profession. In other words, consumers within the meaning of Article [101(3)] are the customers of the parties to the agreement and subsequent purchasers. These customers can be undertakings as in the case of buyers of industrial machinery or an input for further processing or final consumers as for instance in the case of buyers of impulse ice-cream or bicycles.[149]

[140] *Österreichische* (n 59), para 235.

[141] See Art 101(3) Guidelines (n 4).

[142] In early cases much of the Commission's analysis was focussed on Art 101(3), on account of the broad jurisdictional interpretation of Art 101(1). Despite this, published exemption decisions, especially the early ones, did not contain particularly lengthy or sophisticated analysis of the Art 101(3) criteria.

[143] Art 101(3) Guidelines (n 4) para 33.

[144] *Consten and Grundig* (n 33), para 348; *Van den Bergh* (n 139) paras 101 and 139; and *MasterCard* (n 113) para 234.

[145] Art 101(3) Guidelines (n 4) paras 64–68.

[146] ibid, paras 69–72.

[147] ibid, para 45.

[148] ibid, paras 83–104.

[149] ibid, para 84.

The consumer in Article 101(3), as a recipient of off-setting efficiencies, is thus equated with the consumer whose benefit is secured by the consumer welfare objective as a whole. For this reason, this is a different consumer from the one who is the subject of consumer protection law or who is one of the actors in the internal market case law.[150] The final consumer *may* be a recipient of efficiencies but is not necessarily one of them or the only one.

Second, it is clear that not all individual consumers need to derive a benefit from the agreement for Article 101(3) to apply. Rather, 'it is the beneficial nature of the effect on all consumers in the relevant markets that must be taken into consideration, not the effect on each member of that category of consumers.'[151] This approach detaches the analysis of the consumer benefit condition from the effects of an agreement on any individual consumer, or particular group of consumers. The emphasis is placed on the effect of the agreement on consumers *overall*. It is significant that competition law bases this enquiry on factual considerations. By contrast, in other areas of EU law, legal constructs have been used to determine the parameters for the protection for consumers. For instance, the notion of the 'average' consumer has been widely used in free movement[152] and consumer protection[153] law to determine legal standards of protection, and often it has been construed in the light of the objectives that the law has tried to achieve. The average consumer has thus been identified in these areas as a 'reasonably circumspect and well informed consumer';[154] consequently it is understood as embodying a highly competent consumer whose protection should interfere as little as possible with free trade and so trumps the more paternalistic national norms of consumer protection.[155]

Third, '[t]he concept of "fair share" implies that the pass-on of benefits must at least compensate consumers for any actual or likely negative impact caused to them by the restriction of competition found under Article [101(1)].'[156] In other words, the net effect of the agreement must at least be neutral from the perspective of the consumers affected. A thorny issue in this context is whether the pass-on must compensate 'those consumers directly or likely affected by the agreement'.[157]

[150] See section II.C of this chapter.

[151] Case C–238/05 *Asnef-Equifax, Servicios de Información sobre Solvencia y Crédito, SL v Asociación de Usuarios de Servicios Bancarios (Ausbanc)* [2006] ECR I–11125, para 70. See also the recent decision of the Court in *MasterCard* (n 113), para 237.

[152] See, eg, Case C–470/93 *Verein gegen Unwesen in Handel und Gewerbe Köln e.V. v Mars GmbH* [1995] ECR I–1923, para 24 and Case C–210/96 *Gut Springenheide GmbH and Rudolf Tusky v Oberkreisdirektor des Kreises Steinfurt—Amt für Lebensmittelüberwachung* [1998] ECR I–4657, para 31.

[153] See Directive 2005/29/EC of the European Parliament and of the Council of 11 May 2005 concerning unfair business-to-consumer commercial practices in the internal market ('Unfair Commercial Practices Directive') OJ [2005] L149/22, Rec 18.

[154] ibid.

[155] See further C Barnard, *The Substantive Law of the EU*, 4th edn (Oxford, Oxford University Press 2013) 174–76.

[156] Art 101(3) Guidelines (n 4), para 85.

[157] Unless 'the group of consumers affected by the restriction and benefiting from the efficiency gains [on a different market] are substantially the same', Art 101(3) Guidelines (n 4) para 43. Only exceptionally, therefore, where markets are closely related, can efficiencies in separate markets be taken into account.

Although the view that all pro-competitive benefits in all markets should be relevant and weighed against the agreement's anti-competitive effects gains some support from the Court, and, arguably, better accords with the overarching consumer welfare objective pursued,[158] in a recent judgment the Court held, in the context of a two-sided market (in which firms have to compete simultaneously for two groups of customers), that although the consumer benefits requirement relates to:

> the beneficial nature of the effect on all consumers in the relevant markets … in the case of a two-sided system … it is necessary to take into account … all the objective advantages … not only on the market in respect of which the restriction has been established, but also on the market which includes the other group of consumers associated with that system.[159]

However, benefits on one side of the market alone are not sufficient if the restrictive effects occur only on the other side and if the consumers in the two markets are not substantially the same.

A broad reading of the cases also suggests that all consumer benefits, whether current or future, should be taken into account, so both the short- and long-term effects of the agreement may be relevant to the assessment. Indeed, the Commission's Guidelines acknowledge that in assessing this overall impact, the efficiencies created by the agreement may only materialise in the future and that present loss to consumers may be compensated by future gain.[160] Clearly, however, even if future benefits to future consumers are relevant, it may be extremely difficult for the parties to provide convincing evidence that such benefits will result to consumers.[161]

v. *Abuse of a Dominant Position in Article 102 TFEU*

a. Exploitative Conduct: 'Unfair' Pricing and Price Discrimination

An obvious objection to an undertaking holding a dominant position, or with market power, is its ability to 'exploit' its position and its customers and consumers in a way which would be impossible for an undertaking operating on a competitive market. Again, as was seen to be the case in the context of Article 101, the concern here is to prevent exploitation of a broad range of 'consumers', broadly encompassing those on the 'buyer' side of the market and not just final consumers.[162] It is clearly the purpose of Article 102 to prevent such conduct as the provision

158 See Case T–86/95 *Compagnie générale maritime and Others v Commission* [2002] ECR II–1011, para 343. See also, eg, C Townley, 'The Relevant Market: an Acceptable Limit to Competition Analysis?' (2011) 32(10) *European Competition Law Review* 490 (arguing that the Commission's rule against aggregating across markets runs contrary to the EU courts' precedents, creates unacceptable uncertainty, undermines consumer welfare and risks distorting undertakings' investment decisions).

159 *MasterCard* (n 113), para 237.

160 *Compagnie générale maritime* (n 158), paras 87–88. See also paras 44 and 92.

161 See C Townley, 'Inter-generational Impacts in Competition Law: Remembering Those Not Yet Born' (2011) 32 *European Competition Law Review* 580 (arguing that aggregating across generations should be allowed).

162 See *Continental Can* (n 32), para 19, where there is a separation between 'consumers', denoting all customers of a dominant company, and 'trade partners'.

refers specifically to ways in which market power may be exploited: for example, through 'imposing unfair purchase or selling prices or other unfair trading conditions' (Article 102(a)) or engaging in discriminatory behaviour, 'applying dissimilar conditions to equivalent transactions with other trading parties, thereby placing them at a competitive disadvantage' (Article 102(c)). Indeed, early on in the evolution of EU competition law it was questioned whether Article 102 went any further than protecting consumers from exploitation: whether it was *only* intended to forbid exploitative behaviour which harms consumers *directly*.[163]

In 1972 in *Continental Can*, however, the Court, in a seminal judgment, confirmed that Article 102 does not set out an exhaustive list of prohibited conduct[164] and that it *can* be applied to prohibit conduct affecting the structure of the market;[165] it applies to what are now referred to as 'exclusionary' abuses, as well as to exploitative ones, because such practices 'cause consumers harm through their impact on competition';[166] by having the actual or potential effect of foreclosing the market, such practices harm consumer interests *indirectly*. The rationale for prohibiting exclusionary conduct is therefore that by protecting the competitive process,[167] automatic benefits to consumers will be delivered, especially in the long term.

Indeed, something which might perhaps seem surprising to a consumer lawyer is that, following clarification from the Court that Article 102 applies to exclusionary conduct, *most* Article 102 competition law enforcement has focussed on such conduct. The Commission, like many other competition agencies, has rarely intervened in cases which purely involve 'exploitative behaviour'. There is consequently a dearth of decisions and of guidance[168] relating to behaviour that is directly exploitative of, and specifically targets,[169] consumers.[170]

In relation to 'unfair pricing' there may be several reasons for this recalcitrance on the part of competition agencies. First, any such intervention by a competition authority is extremely regulatory in nature and it is well known that there are

[163] eg R Joliet, *Monopolization and Abuse of Dominant Position* (Boston, Nijhoff, 1970) and P Akman, 'Searching for the Long-Lost Soul of Article 82 EC' (2009) 29 *Oxford Journal of Legal Studies* 267.

[164] It has been argued that the width of Art 102(b) means that it should be the test for all exclusionary abuses: JT Lang, 'How Can the Problems of Exclusionary Abuses under Article 102 TFEU Be Resolved?' (2012) 37 *European Law Review* 136. In this case the Court accepted that a dominant undertaking could strengthen its position and eliminate competition by taking over a competitor. On the facts, however, it quashed the Commission's decision because it had failed adequately to define the market and, consequently, to show that the undertaking was dominant.

[165] *Continental Can* (n 32). See also *Le Problème de la Concentration dans le Marché Commun*, Etudes CEE, Série Concurrence No 3 (1966) esp paras 25–27.

[166] *Post Danmark* (n 62), para 20.

[167] ibid and *T-Mobile* (n 114), Opinion of AG Kokott, para 58.

[168] See Commission, Guidance on the Commission's enforcement priorities in applying Article 82 of the EC Treaty [now Art 102 TFEU] to abusive exclusionary conduct by dominant undertakings [2009] OJ C45/7 ('Guidance Paper'), para 5.

[169] ibid, para 7.

[170] Guidance Paper (n 168) is focussed on exclusionary behaviour and only leaves open the possibility of future guidance on exploitative behaviour, see para 7.

acute difficulties involved in ascertaining when a price will be 'excessive'—or as the Court explained, 'one that has no reasonable relation to the economic value of the product supplied'.[171] In addition, it is also questionable whether intervention of this type is desirable because of its potential to have a negative effect on the competitive process—and consumers—in the long run.[172] In the US, for example, the courts have been reluctant to condemn 'monopoly' power thrust upon a firm or achieved through superior skill, foresight and industry.[173] On the contrary they have recognised that such market power provides the signal to attract new competition into the market[174] and a *reward* for innovation and the lawful winning of the competitive battle. In *Verizon Communications v Law Offices of Curtis v Trinko LLP*, Justice Scalia stated:

> The mere possession of monopoly power, and the concomitant charging of monopoly prices, is not only not unlawful; it is an important element of the free-market system. The opportunity to charge monopoly prices—at least for a short period—is what attracts 'business acumen' in the first place; it induces risk taking that produces innovation and economic growth. To safeguard the incentive to innovate, the possession of monopoly power will not be found unlawful unless it is accompanied by an element of anticompetitive conduct.[175]

Although, therefore, it may be accepted that such monopoly pricing harms customers of the dominant firm and consumers of their products in the short run (customers who do not value a product more than the cost of producing that product do not obtain it and static competition is reduced), it is accepted in the US that, in the long run, the conduct may make the market more competitive, by providing incentives both for innovation and new entry into the market.[176]

In the EU, although 'the [EEC] Founding Fathers' faith in competition as a process of rivalry between competitors was not strong enough to tolerate customer/consumer exploitation in the short run',[177] there are nonetheless only relatively rare examples of Commission decisions concerning behaviour that had a direct impact

[171] See *United Brands Company* (n 81).

[172] Three main conceptual challenges suggesting a cautionary approach to excessive pricing cases arguably are that the markets are self-correcting, the prohibition is tantamount to prohibiting the dominant position and that exploitative practices serve an important dynamic role, thereby increasing welfare, see M Gal, 'Abuse of Dominance-Exploitative Abuses' in I Lioanos and D Geradin (eds), *Handbook on European Competition Law: Substantive Aspects* (Cheltenham, Edward Elgar, 2013).

[173] In *United States v Aluminium Co of America (Alcoa)* 148 F 2d 416 (2d Cir 1945).

[174] *Berkey Photo Inc v Eastman Kodak Co* 603 F 2d 263, 294 (2d Cir 1979).

[175] *Verizon Communications v Law Offices of Curtis v Trinko* LLP 540 US 398 (2004).

[176] In the EU it has also been argued that a policy of non-intervention in cases of monopoly pricing should be adopted: both because the competition authority is not qualified to determine what price is appropriate and because the policy would reduce, and possibly forgo, the chance to protect consumers in the future by competition rather than policy intervention; see, eg, J Gual and others, 'Report by the EAGCP—An Economic Approach to Article 82' (July 2005) 11.

[177] L Gyselen, 'Rebates: Competition on the Merits or Exclusionary Practice?' in CD Ehlermann and I Atanasiu (eds), *European Competition Law Annual 2003: What is an Abuse of a Dominant Position?* (Oxford, Hart Publishing, 2006).

on customers or *final consumers*: usually where the case has another dimension—an exclusionary or internal market aspect[178] or where the interests of consumers cannot otherwise be ensured.[179] A good example is the 1999 Commission decision about the 1998 FIFA World Cup,[180] where the Commission investigated the arrangements relating to the sale of entry tickets to the 1998 FIFA World Cup. There, the Commission decided that the French body in charge of the organisation of the 1998 World Cup had abused its position of dominance in limiting markets to the prejudice of consumers by discriminating against consumers outside France because the purchase of entry tickets was conditional on the provision of a postal address in France and telephone reservations could only be made within metropolitan France. In this case, and as well as the harm suffered by consumers, the commitment of the competition rules to the ideal of a single market where there is no direct or indirect discrimination against foreign products or foreign nationals can also be seen in action.

Similarly, although price discrimination is specifically targeted by Article 102, if a consumer welfare objective is pursued there may be good reasons for being cautious about enforcing Article 102(c) in the way that its wording suggests. Price discrimination is a common occurrence in markets as suppliers seek, where possible, to extract from each consumer the maximum that they are willing to pay and to reflect the different demand sensitivities of consumers. Although price discrimination might harm consumers in some circumstances (for example, by allowing a dominant firm to exclude competitors, to diminish consumer choice[181] or to protect their dominant position and so damage the competitive process) where price discrimination is used as a mechanism to enable a firm to increase output by charging each customer its reservation price (and not to decrease output like other monopolistic practices),[182] the practice may benefit consumers that might not otherwise have been able to purchase the product, even though it might harm traders by putting one at a disadvantage vis-à-vis another. A problem inherent in Article 102(c) is that its wording does not seem to require 'welfare losses' but appears designed not only to prevent sellers from impairing the competitive

[178] eg Commission Decision of 29 April 2014 in Case AT.39985—Motorola—Enforcement of GPRS standard essential patents, [2014] OJ C 344/6 and Case 26/75 *General Motors v Commission* [1975] ECR 1367.

[179] eg Guidance Paper (n 168), para 7.

[180] Commission Decision of 20 July 1999 in Case 36888 *1998 Football World Cup* [2000] OJ L5/55. See also eg *Football Association* (n 34) paras 108–109 (the Court made clear that the ownership of an IPR does not necessarily guarantee the right for the owner to demand the highest possible remuneration—only appropriate remuneration which must be reasonable in relation to the economic value of the service provided), Case 238/87 *AB Volvo v Erik Veng* [1988] ECR 6211 and the Commission's investigation into prices in mobile telephone services in the EC (Press Releases IP/98/141, IP 98/707, IP (98) 1036).

[181] See Nihoul (n 52).

[182] Bork (n 17) 394–98. 'If discrimination increases output, it tends to move resource allocation and value of marginal product toward that which would obtain in a competitive industry. A decrease in output has the opposite effect. The impact of discrimination on output, therefore, may be taken as a proxy for its effect on consumer welfare' (395).

position of competitors through price-cutting tactics (primary line injury), but to target the harm occasioned when competition is distorted between buyers and by favouring powerful buyers over smaller buyers without such effective buyer power (secondary line injury), whether or not such conduct is likely to harm consumers downstream. Article 102(c) has undoubtedly been relied upon and applied broadly by the Commission. In recent years, however, it has indicated that it will focus its resources on primary line injury, conduct which unlawfully excludes competitors and allows the dominant firm to acquire or strengthen its dominant position. Indeed, in its 2009 Guidance Paper on enforcement priorities the Commission only sets out its priorities in relation to exclusionary conduct and repeatedly emphasises that it will focus on the types of conduct that are most harmful to consumers.[183]

b. Exclusionary Conduct

A majority of EU jurisprudence therefore focusses on exclusionary conduct which

> through recourse to methods different from that which condition normal competition in products or services on the basis of the transactions of commercial operators, has the effect of hindering the maintenance of the degree of competition still existing in the market or the growth of that competition.[184]

The case law draws a vital distinction between competition on the basis of performance, or competition on the merits, and abusive exclusionary conduct. Where there is prima facie evidence of such exclusionary behaviour, the burden of demonstrating that the practice is objectively justified or that it produces efficiencies that ensure no net harm is likely to arise for consumers—and hence to show that Article 102 should not apply—will fall on the dominant company.[185] Complexity is inherent in these assessments in distinguishing between unlawful exclusionary behaviour and legitimate competition[186] and determining whether such conduct is liable to harm consumer interests and in determining whether any justification for the conduct exists.

The question of how to construct rules to identify and condemn exclusionary behaviour that harms competition and consumers and to differentiate it from competitive conduct in a way which is both sufficiently clear and accurate—so minimising both Type 1 and Type 2 errors—has proved a major challenge.[187]

[183] See Guidance Paper (n 168), para 5.

[184] *Hoffmann-La Roche* (n 7), para 91.

[185] See Guidance Paper (n 168), paras 28–31 and also Case C–95/04 P *British Airways plc v Commission* [2007] ECR I–2331, para 86 and *TeliaSonera* (n 9), para 76.

[186] In this context, the Commission and the Court were consistently criticised for adopting a 'form' based approach, which inferred that certain types of conduct were automatically abusive. In more recent years and particularly following the adoption of the 2009 Guidance Paper (n 168) the Commission has moved to an approach that focusses more on the actual anti-competitive effects of the behaviour of the dominant company.

[187] 'Aggressive, competitive conduct by any firm, even one with market power, is beneficial to consumers. Courts should prize and encourage it. Aggressive, exclusionary conduct is deleterious to

The tendency in the EU has been for the distinction to be drawn through the use of conduct-specific tests. It has often been complained, however, that the EU authorities have been too ready to assume that conduct which may foreclose competitors and/or which may limit individual freedom or equality of opportunity between economic operators and their freedom to compete is abusive (without a need to demonstrate prejudice to consumers) and have consequently imposed too great a responsibility towards the competitive process on the shoulders of dominant firms and set the bar for establishing an abuse of Article 102 too low. In consequence, it has been argued that the tests drawn for identifying abuse may be over-inclusive, deterring dominant firms from engaging in aggressive and legitimate conduct, especially low price competition on the merits which might benefit consumers.[188] Consequently, there is a risk that hard-nosed competition, which may benefit consumers, may be deterred and less-efficient competitors protected.

The Commission has sought to meet this type of criticism by 'modernising' its approach to Article 102[189] publishing first, in 2005, a DG Comp Staff Discussion Paper on the Application of Article 82 [102 TFEU] of the Treaty to Exclusionary Abuses[190] and subsequently, in 2009, Guidance on its Enforcement Priorities in Applying Article 82 [102 TFEU] to Abusive Exclusionary Conduct by Dominant Undertakings (the 'Guidance Paper').[191] The new approach set out in the Guidance Paper does not purport to contain a statement of the law (rather, at times it is in clear tension with it) but conveys the Commission's determination to focus enforcement only on cases where the exclusionary conduct of the dominant firm impairs effective competition by 'foreclosing their competitors in an anticompetitive way, thus having an adverse impact on consumer welfare';[192] that is, to focus 'on safeguarding the competitive process' whilst being mindful of the fact 'that what really matters is protecting an effective competitive process and not simply protecting competitors. This may well mean that competitors who deliver

consumers, and courts should condemn it. The big problem lies in this: competitive and exclusionary conduct look alike': see FH Easterbrook, 'When is it Worthwhile to Use Courts to Search for Exclusionary Conduct?' [2003] *Columbia Business Law Review* 345, 346.

188 Those taking the view that exclusionary conduct is rare, that conduct by single firms frequently has efficiency potential, may believe that too expansive liability will lead to Type 1 errors and chill aggressive behaviour, keep prices high, discourage innovation and encourage less efficient rivals to misuse the competition rules when losing out in the competitive battle; see, eg, Bork (n 17). Others, however, may be more concerned about Type 2 errors and to ensure that rules do not allow dominant firms to place rivals at a disadvantage, to raise their costs, so as to preserve their position of dominance and allow for the exercise of market power; see, eg, TG Krattenmaker and SC Salop, 'Anticompetitive Exclusion: Raising Rivals' Costs to Achieve Power over Price' (1986) 96 *Yale Law Journal* 209.

189 This reform followed its overhaul of the working and application of Art 101 and the EUMR.

190 Commission, Abuse of dominant position (Article 102 TFEU) <http://ec.europa.eu/competition/antitrust/art82/index.html> accessed 2 February 2015.

191 Guidance Paper (n 168).

192 Guidance Paper (n 168), para 19. Anticompetitive foreclosure is defined as 'a situation where effective access of actual or potential competitors to supplies or markets is hampered or eliminated as a result of the conduct of the dominant undertaking whereby the dominant undertaking is likely to be in a position to profitably increase prices to the detriment of consumers'. See also, eg, Lowe (n 38).

less to consumers in terms of price, choice, quality and innovation will leave the market'.[193]

This is not an easy task, however, particularly in the area of pricing, where it is difficult to distinguish between aggressive competition through low pricing (which ordinarily benefits consumers and is promoted by competition law) and low pricing which unlawfully excludes competitors from the market and may damage consumers in the longer run. In determining whether low pricing by a dominant firm should be found abusive, relevant inquiries may be whether an equally efficient competitor[194] can compete (in particular, whether the dominant firm is pricing below its costs) and whether that conduct is liable to produce anticompetitive effects and harm consumers. Another important issue is whether, and if so when, presumptions of illegality should be used. It has been seen that in *Groupement des Cartes Bancaires* the Court of Justice stressed, in the context of Article 101, that the category of agreements restrictive of competition by object must be interpreted restrictively and applied only to situations where an agreement inherently reveals a 'sufficient degree of harm to competition'.[195]

In relation to Article 102, the Commission states in its Guidance Paper that anti-competitive effects do not need to be demonstrated in the case of conduct 'that can only raise obstacles to competition and … creates no efficiencies';[196] such practices are, by their very nature, abusive unless the dominant firm can raise a valid objective justification for its conduct. In the context of pricing, the Court has held (recognising the relevance of the equally efficient competitor) that where a dominant firm engages in predatory pricing, pricing below its average variable costs (AVC), the abusive nature of such conduct is presumed, as the conduct has 'no conceivable economic purpose other than the elimination of a competitor, since each item produced and sold entails a loss for the undertaking'.[197] This presumption is arguably justifiable for if the dominant firm is not covering its variable costs it makes no sense for it to be selling extra units.[198]

In *Post Danmark*, the Court confirmed that, conversely, Article 102 does not prevent an undertaking from acquiring, on its own merits, a dominant position and does not seek to ensure that:

> competitors less efficient than the undertaking with the dominant position should stay on the market … Competition on the merits may, by definition, lead to the departure from the market or the marginalisation of competitors that are less efficient and so less attractive to consumers from the point of view of, among other things, price, choice, quality or innovation.[199]

[193] Guidance Paper (n 168), para 6.
[194] eg Case C–62/86 *AKZO Chemie BV v Commission* [1991] ECR I–03359 and Case C–280/08P *Deutsche Telekom AG v Commission* [2010] ECR I–9555.
[195] *Groupement* (n 63), para 58.
[196] Guidance Paper (n 168), para 22.
[197] Case C–333/94P *Tetra Pak v Commission* ('*Tetra Pak II*') [1996] ECR I–5951 para 41.
[198] eg B Allan 'Article 82: A Commentary on DG Competition's Discussion Paper' (2006) 2 *Competition Policy International* 42, 57.
[199] *Post Danmark* (n 62), paras 21–22.

Nonetheless, there are some circumstances in which the EU condemns pricing practices even where it has not been established that they may exclude equally efficient competitors; for example, where the conduct is designed to ensure exclusivity, so tying customers to the dominant firm, limiting customer choice and restricting competitors' access to the market.[200] A controversial issue in this situation is, however, how a claimant must demonstrate that the conduct of the dominant undertaking is likely to exclude competition or damage the competitive structure in a way that is detrimental to *consumers* (that is to say, how must prejudice to consumers be demonstrated?) and in particular exactly when a presumption of anticompetitive effects can be relied upon.[201]

Even where anticompetitive effects are not assumed proof of actual anticompetitive effect or a high probability that such an effect will arise is generally not required under Article 102 (as is the case in the context of Article 101). Rather, the anticompetitive effects of a dominant firm's conduct tend to be presumed where proof of anticompetitive effects 'which may potentially exclude competitors'[202] and eliminate effective competition is demonstrated. Critics complain that this means that the interests of consumers under Article 102 are too remote. The judgments, however, appear to prefer a construction of Article 102 that will ensure that the process of competition and rivalry between firms is preserved and protected.[203]

Third, like Article 101, Article 102 frequently requires a balance to be achieved between the protection of long- and short-term consumer interests.[204] In many of the leading judgments of the Court on exclusionary behaviour, the long-term

[200] See Case T–286/09 *Intel Corp v Commission*, judgment of 12 June 2014.

[201] In *Intel* (ibid) one important issue raised by the case is whether it is justifiable to apply a presumption of illegality in the context of loyalty rebates even though the dominant firm may be pricing *above* cost and a voluminous literature records possible pro-competitive rationales for them; see eg P Ibáñez Colomo, '*Intel* and Article 102 TFEU Case Law: Making Sense of a Perpetual Controversy' *LSE Law, Society and Economy Working Papers* 29/2014; P Nihoul, 'The Ruling of the General Court in Intel: Towards the End of an Effect-based Approach in European Competition Law?' (2014) 5 *Journal of European Competition Law and Practice* 521; J Venit, 'Case T–286/09 *Intel v Commission*—The Judgment of the General Court: All Steps Backward and No Steps Forward' (2014) 10 *European Competition Journal* 203; R Whish, '*Intel v Commission*: Keep Calm and Carry On!' (2014) *Journal of European Competition Law and Practice*; W Wils, 'The Judgment of the EU General Court in Intel and the So-Called "More Economic Approach" to Abuse of Dominance' (2014) 37 *World Competition: Law and Economics Review* (forthcoming) and articles by A Jones & B Sufrin, D Crane, B Allan, C Ahlborn & D Piccinin, M Dolmans & T Graf and D Neven in 'Symposium: Intel' [2015] 1 *Competition Law & Policy Debate* 28–96.

[202] *TeliaSonera* (n 9), para 64. Rather, to ensure that the evidentiary burden on claimants is not placed too high, the test appears to require it to be demonstrated that 'in a manner tailored to the specificities and facts of each case, that a particular practice "tends" to restrict competition in the sense that it has the potential to hinder competition. It must thus be demonstrated that it is plausible that the practice harms or will harm competition. Abstract, purely hypothetical or remote assertions or theories of harm, which are not linked to the specificities of the case at hand, will thus not suffice', *AstraZeneca* (n 76) Opinion of Mazák AG, paras 62–63.

[203] L Lovdahl Gormsen, 'The Conflict between Economic Freedom and Consumer Welfare in the Modernisation of Article 82 EC' (2007) 3 *European Competition Journal* 329, 337.

[204] See further on this point, S Haukka, 'Consumer Protection and EU Competition Law' in H Kanninen, N Korjus and A Rosas (eds), *EU Competition Law in Context* (Oxford, Hart Publishing, 2009).

effects on consumer interests play an important role.[205] For example, in the context of predatory pricing, it has been seen that it is assumed that a dominant firm which prices its products so low that it is not even covering the marginal cost, or average variable cost, of producing that output commits an abuse of a dominant position. Although it might therefore seem peculiar for competition law to condemn low pricing, one of the very virtues it promotes, the conduct is prohibited as it is presumed that it will exclude equally efficient competitors from the market, deter competitors from entering the market and, after the predatory siege has ended, permit the dominant firm to raise prices and recoup the losses made. Conversely, in some cases competition law will not compel a dominant firm to engage in conduct which would increase competition in the short term (for example, to supply, or to continue to supply, a product which a competitor needs to compete) if, in the longer run, it might discourage innovation by the dominant firm or the competitor.

IV. Enforcement of the Competition Rules as a Tool to Protect Consumer Interests and Gaps and Lacunas

The previous sections have considered the role that the consumer plays in framing the objectives of EU competition law and how those goals have shaped the interpretation of the substantive law. The goals are also crucial, however, to the question of how the laws should be *enforced*. Enforcement actions are, of course, necessary for the substantive law to be clarified and developed, and to ensure that the rules are effective and achieve their overarching objective—in particular, that consumers are protected by ensuring that violations are brought to an end, future violations are deterred and that consumers are compensated for any loss suffered as a consequence of infringements.[206] Where a consumer welfare goal is adopted, therefore, important questions are: how should the interests of 'consumers', or particular groups of consumers, have an impact upon public enforcement (for example, in setting enforcement priorities of public enforcement agencies and in determining the role that consumers should play in public enforcement processes)? And should private enforcement, which involves direct action by consumers to safeguard their own interests, be encouraged? The enforcement arena

[205] eg Case T–201/04 *Microsoft Corp v Commission* [2007] ECR II–3601 in relation to tying practices or the case law on predatory pricing (eg Case T–340/03 *France Télécom SA v Commission* [2007] ECR II–107).

[206] See W Wils, 'The Relationship between Public Antitrust Enforcement and Private Actions for Damages' (2009) 32 *World Competition* 3 and Commission, Green Paper on Damages actions for Breach of the EC Antitrust Rules COM(2005) 672 final, s 1.1 on the common aims and relationship of complementarity between the public and private systems of enforcement.

consequently provides an additional, and more practical, setting for determining how consumer interests should be protected and must, therefore, be referred to in this chapter.

In the EU, although, historically, competition rules were enforced principally by the Commission, a more decentralised system has now emerged, involving a network of competition authorities: the European Competition Network, comprising the Commission and national competition authorities (NCAs),[207] and the courts and tribunals of the individual Member States (the national courts). Consumers benefit both directly and indirectly from the interplay between these two levels of enforcement. Indeed, in the past few years important developments have taken place that are designed to put in place a more effective system of enforcement. These developments have yielded the image of a stronger and more empowered consumer.

On the one hand, most competition law systems depend, to a greater or lesser extent, upon public enforcement. In the EU, the Commission and NCAs focus principally on ensuring that violations are brought to an end and deterred, not on ensuring compensation for victims;[208] the Commission does not have power to award damages to those who have suffered loss, although it is seen below that it has been active in trying to facilitate private actions by victims for compensation. The questions of how competition agencies can best deter infringements, how public enforcement should be divided between the Commission and NCAs and how public enforcement relates to private enforcement are complex ones with their own rich body of literature. However, three important points are drawn out here.

First, enforcement by the Commission follows an integrated administrative model;[209] in proceedings under Articles 101 and/or 102 it acts, pursuant to powers conferred on it by Regulation 1/2003[210] and Regulation 774/2003 (the Implementation Regulation),[211] as an integrated decision-maker, deciding which cases to investigate, whether to initiate proceedings, whether an infringement has occurred and what sanctions should be imposed on undertakings in breach. A noteworthy feature of this process is that interested natural or legal persons that can show a 'legitimate interest' may take part in it in a number of ways: for example, by submitting complaints to the Commission,[212] with the objective of triggering an

[207] Although NCAs have, since 2004, started to perform an ever increasing and important role in EU antitrust enforcement, the Commission has sought to retain its central position 'as the guardian of the Treaty' which 'has the ultimate but not the sole responsibility for developing policy and safeguarding consistency when it comes to the application of [EU] competition law', Commission, Notice on cooperation within the Network of Competition Authorities [2004] OJ C101/43, para 43.

[208] But see, eg, OFT Press Release 88/06 'Independent Schools agree settlement' 19 May 2006 and the provisions on voluntary redress in the UK's Consumer Rights Act 2015, Schedule 8.

[209] See generally Jones and Sufrin (n 101) chs 13 and 15.

[210] The model was first set up by Regulation 17 of 1962 ([1959–1962] OJ Sp Ed 87) and is now set out in Regulation 1/2003 (n 132).

[211] Commission Regulation (EC) No 773/2004 of 7 April 2004 relating to the conduct of proceedings by the Commission pursuant to Articles 81 and 82 of the EC Treaty ('Conduct of Proceedings Regulation') [2004] OJ L123/18.

[212] They may also lodge complaints with NCAs.

investigation (the Commission is not obliged to act on a complaint, however, and may reject it if, following an examination, it decides that the case does not raise sufficient EU (or public) interest),[213] or submitting observations in the course of the Commission proceedings.[214] The modernisation reforms strengthened the role of complainants by encouraging them to inform the Commission about suspected infringements and, importantly, by clarifying the parameters that inform the submission of a complaint, as well as the procedural rights of the complainant. In particular, the 2004 Commission Notice on the Handling of Complaints[215] endorsed the view that not only undertakings, trade and consumer associations[216] but also individual consumers[217]—and here this term seems to be used as a synonym of final consumers—whose economic interests are directly and adversely affected by anti-competitive practices can be held to show a legitimate interest. This view, emphasising the position of final consumers as complainants that may set off the process of public enforcement of the Competition rules, has been upheld by the General Court in its case law. Indeed, in *Österreichische Postsparkasse AG*,[218] the General Court affirmed the broad interpretation of those having a legitimate interest and confirmed that it extends to final consumers who can demonstrate that their economic interests have been harmed. It may be recalled that this judgment was controversial in terms of the discussion on the objectives of EU competition law because it was one of the few cases where the General Court adopted an interpretation favouring a narrow consumer welfare objective and thus adopted an approach that closely resembled the position taken by the Commission in the aftermath of the process of modernisation.[219] Although later case law of the Court of Justice does not so clearly support this goal,[220] the strong endorsement of the final consumer as a complainant that can trigger the Commission investigation remains entrenched in the case law.

Second, not only does the Commission seek, when enforcing Articles 101 and 102, to ensure that infringements are brought to an end, but it is intent on deterring the most serious violations of the competition law rules which cause widespread harm to consumer welfare (such as cartels and serious abuses of a dominant position).[221] To facilitate this, Regulation 1/2003 confers broad powers of investigation and enforcement upon the Commission, which are recognised

[213] See Regulation 1/2003 (n 132), Art 7(2).

[214] See Regulation 773/2004 (n 211), Art 6 and more generally Arts 5–9.

[215] Commission Notice on the handling of complaints by the Commission under Articles 81 and 82 of the EC Treaty [now Arts 101 and 102 TFEU] [2004] OJ C 101/65.

[216] See Case T–37/92 *Bureau Européen des Unions de Consommateurs and National Consumer Council v Commission* [1994] ECR II–285.

[217] See the Commission Notice on the handling of complaints (n 215), para 37.

[218] See Joined cases T-213-214/01 *Österreichische Postsparkasse* (n 59), paras 113–14. The General Court thus emphasised that promoting the rights of consumers as complainants contributed to the attainment of the objectives of competition law, para 115.

[219] See section II.C of this chapter and especially n 63.

[220] Again, see section II.C of this chapter.

[221] See sections III.B.ii and v of this chapter.

by the case law,[222] which it uses to ascertain the existence of potential violations of the EU competition rules. Furthermore, it confers power upon the Commission to: adopt decisions finding an infringement;[223] impose, subject to the principle of proportionality, remedies to ensure that the relevant undertakings bring the infringement to an end (through the issue of a cease and desist order and/or the imposition of other remedies); and fine undertakings that are found to be in breach of Articles 101 and 102, up to 10% of the undertaking's turnover in the preceding year.[224] The levels of fines—especially in relation to cartel activity[225]—have been increasing steadily within this band, especially since the publication of the (current) 2006 Guidelines on the method of setting fines.[226] Although these fines do not provide redress for consumers, the Commission action benefits consumers both by ensuring that that infringement is brought to an end and through precluding future anti-competitive behaviour that might be harmful to them. Indeed, the Commission has stressed that the purpose of these fines is two-fold deterrence: both 'specific' deterrence—by sanctioning the undertakings in question—and 'general' deterrence—through deterring other undertakings from breaching the competition rules.[227] In the cartel context, the Commission, like many other competition enforcement agencies around the world, has sought to deter cartel activity not only through increasing sanctions for those found to have been involved in such activity but by simultaneously utilising a leniency regime as an important anti-cartel enforcement tool which serves to destabilise cartels and to encourage a 'race to confess'.[228] Essentially, if certain conditions are fulfilled, the first undertaking to submit relevant evidence to the Commission is offered immunity and others that cooperate are offered the possibility of reduction in fines.

Third, exactly how a competition authority uses its scarce resources to prioritise cases also has an important impact upon the question of which consumers are benefited. One of the concerns driving the introduction of a decentralised

[222] eg Case 374/89 *Commission v Kingdom of Belgium* [1991] ECR I–3283, para 22.

[223] The Commission also has power to adopt non-infringement and commitment decisions, see Regulation 1/2003 (n 132), Arts 10 and 9.

[224] See Regulation 1/2003 (n 132), Arts 7 and 23(2) and further Commission, Guidelines on the method of setting fines imposed pursuant to Art 23(2)(a) of Regulation No 1/2003 [2006] OJ C210/2, para 32.

[225] eg the fines of €1.47 billion imposed in December 2012 on the producers of TV and computer monitor tubes for two decade-long cartels (Commission Press Release, IP/12/1317).

[226] See Guidelines on the method of setting fines (n 224).

[227] See Communication from the Commission on quantifying harm in actions for damages based on breaches of Article 101 or 102 of the Treaty on the Functioning of the European Union [2013] OJ C167/19, para 1. Despite very high corporate fines there is some concern that even these may not be sufficient to deter the most serious violations—such as cartel activity. Some advocate that individual sanctions—and even criminal sanctions—may be required; see, eg, discussion of this issues in A Jones and R Williams, 'The UK Response to the Global Effort against Cartels: Is Criminalization Really the Solution?' (2014) *Journal of Antitrust Enforcement* 100.

[228] Commission, Notice on immunity from fines and reduction of fines in cartel cases [2006] OJ C298/11. Since 2008, the Commission has also sought where possible to dispose of cartel cases rapidly through reliance on a formal settlement procedure; Commission, Notice on the conduct of settlement procedures [2008] OJ C167/1.

system of enforcement of Articles 101 and 102 was to allow the Commission to focus on the most serious violations of competition law.[229] Many competition authorities, including the Commission, devote significant resources to the detection and punishment of cartels. Often these relate to products, for example lysine or vitamins, which are not purchased by final consumers. Nonetheless, they cause harm to customers (such as farmers) who in turn may pass price increases down to consumers—so it is generally assumed that the harmful effects of such illegal price fixing cascade down to consumers. In some other cases, however, the Commission, NCAs (particularly those integrating consumer protection functions) and/or appeal courts, have shown in their decisional practice and judgments a direct focus on conduct which has an impact upon final consumers[230] or particular groups of consumers, such as vulnerable consumers.[231]

On the other hand, private civil actions may provide direct remedies to, and compensation for, victims of competition law infringements. They are therefore a mechanism for directly protecting consumers by allowing them to bring proceedings which will result in infringements being brought to an end and/or reparation being provided for the harm that they have suffered as a result of anti-competitive practice. Furthermore, private litigation has an additional beneficial indirect effect on consumer interests by deterring future infringements and ensuring compliance with the competition rules.[232] A number of important reforms have taken place over the past few years in the context of private enforcement with the objective of strengthening the position of the consumer as an enforcer of the EU competition rules before the national courts.

Early on in its jurisprudence, the Court recognised that Articles 101(1), 101(2) and 102 were directly effective, and hence could be enforced by private parties before the national courts.[233] Despite this recognition, however, a very limited culture of private enforcement was prevalent, partly due to the centralised system of enforcement that applied before the enactment of Regulation 1/2003.[234] Alongside

[229] See Regulation 1/2003 (n 132), Rec 3.

[230] See, eg, *Price-fixing of Replica Football Kit*, decision of the OFT of 1 August 2003 [2004] UKLR 6 and *Hasbro UK Ltd/Argos Ltd/Littlewoods Ltd*, decision of the OFT of 2 December 2003 [2004] UKLR 717, and the decisions of the Competition Appeal Tribunal in Cases 1021/1/03 and 1022/1/03 *JJB Sports v OFT* [2004] CAT 17 and Cases 1014 and 1015/1/03 *Argos Ltd v OFT* [2004] CAT 24.

[231] See the decision of the Competition Appeal Tribunal in Case No 1044/2/1/04 *JJ Burgess and Sons v Office of Fair Trading and W Austin and Sons and Hardwood Park Crematorium Ltd and Consumers' Association* [2005] CAT 25, paras 320 ff and esp para 335 on the vulnerability of the consumers involved.

[232] See the Communication of the Commission on quantifying harm in actions for damages (n 227) para 2. See A Komninos, 'Public and Private Antitrust Enforcement in Europe: Complement? Overlap?' (2006) 3 *The Competition Law Review* 1, 9; R Nazzini and A Nikpay, 'Private Actions in EC Competition Law' (2008) 4 *Competition Policy International* 107, 109.

[233] Case 127/73 *Belgische Radio en Televisie and Société belge des auteurs, compositeurs et éditeurs v SV SABAM and NV Fonior* [1974] ECR 51, para 15.

[234] The fact that national courts and NCAs could not apply TFEU, Art 101(3) prior to the Competition Rules Regulation coming into force meant that it was hard for them to participate in a comprehensive way in the enforcement process; see, eg, Jones and Sufrin (n 101) ch 14.

the process of modernisation, the main impulse for the development of private enforcement of the EU rules followed from the decisions of the Court in *Courage v Crehan*[235] and *Manfredi*,[236] where the Court recognised that a private party that suffers harm as a result of anti-competitive behaviour has a right to compensation, *as a matter of EU law*. Although the volume of private litigation has begun to grow dramatically in some Member States, such as the UK, Germany and the Netherlands, the EU as a whole continues to present a stark contrast to the US where there is a culture of antitrust litigation and where a large proportion of competition cases are litigated privately.[237] Indeed, because the procedural and substantive rules governing these claims are regulated by national law, private litigation is being hampered by a multiplicity of differing obstacles which vary from jurisdiction to jurisdiction and by a lack of clarity over the question of what demands and constraints the EU law principles of effectiveness and equivalence impose on those national rules. For example, it is unclear whether the principles of effective judicial protection and of effectiveness of EU law, stressed in the Court's *Crehan* and *Manfredi* judgments, requires that indirect purchasers (as well as direct purchasers) should have standing to bring antitrust proceedings and/or whether defendants should be able to raise a defence that a claimant should be denied recovery on the grounds that it has passed on an overcharge to its customers.

The answer to this question would appear to depend on how the principle of effectiveness is to be interpreted and, specifically, whether it suggests that the principal purpose of private enforcement is the attainment of corrective justice, with deterrence operating merely as a socially beneficial by-product of such actions, or whether private enforcement is simply a tool to increase enforcement, deter violations and punish violators.[238] If the Court were to elevate the deterrent function of private enforcement higher than its 'compensation function' it might accept the compatibility with EU law of national rules which concentrate antitrust claims in the hands of those most likely to sue, for example, direct purchasers, and simplify antitrust actions for damages, for example, by precluding a passing on defence.[239] Such an approach might ensure that strong incentives to sue[240] are provided and

[235] Case C–453/99 *Courage Ltd v Bernard Crehan and Bernard Crehan v Courage Ltd* [2001] ECR I–6297.

[236] Cases C–295–297/04 *Vincenzo Manfredi v Lloyd Adriatico Assicurazioni* [2006] ECR I–6619.

[237] eg W Kolasky, 'Antitrust Litigation: What's Changed in Twenty-Five Years' (2012) 27 *Antitrust* 9 and B Rodger (ed), *Comparative Private Enforcement and Collective Redress Across the EU* (Alphen, Kluwer Law International, 2014).

[238] eg P Nebbia, 'Damages Actions for the Infringement of EC Competition Law: Compensation or Deterrence?' (2008) 33 *European Law Review* 23, 28; K Roach and MJ Trebilcock, 'Private Enforcement of Competition Laws' (1996) 34 *Osgoode Hall Law Journal* 461, 496; F Hoseinian, 'Passing-on Damages and Community Antitrust Policy—An Economic Background' (2005) 28 *World Competition* 3, 7; R Nazzini, 'The Objective of Private Remedies in EU Competition Law' (2011) 4 *Global Competition Litigation Review* 131, 139–40.

[239] See the approach of the US Supreme Court in *Hanover Shoe Inc v United Shoe Machine Corp* 392 US 481 (1968) and *Illinois Brick Co v Illinois* 431 US 720 (1977).

[240] In contrast, provision for apportionment of recovery through the distribution chain, increases the overall costs of recovery through injecting extremely complex issues into the case; at the same time

that difficult issues of remoteness and tracing of injury are avoided. In contrast, if it were to elevate the compensation function over the deterrent one, it may require national law to ensure compensation to *any* claimant (whether a direct or indirect purchaser) who has suffered loss in consequence of anti-competitive activity and permit rules which deny recovery to claimants that have passed loss down the chain.

In 2013, the Commission published a package of measures designed to remove this type of uncertainty and the principal obstacles to full compensation for anti-trust victims and to ensure that private and public enforcement operate harmoniously together.[241] This comprised the proposal of an EU Directive on Antitrust Damages actions,[242] a Recommendation on common principles for injunctive and compensatory collective redress,[243] and a Communication on the quantification of harm for damages.[244] All of these initiatives indicate a new layer of protection of consumer interests at the level of enforcement. For instance, the Directive, which was adopted in November 2014 and has to be transposed by Member States into their national laws by 27 December 2016, emphasises the principle of *full* compensation for any natural or legal person who has suffered harm—even if they had not purchased directly from the undertaking or undertakings infringing competition law.[245] It also creates a rebuttable presumption that cartels cause harm.[246] Although the Directive does not attempt to adopt a complete harmonised framework, it incorporates provisions relating to discovery (so claimants will have easier access to evidence); protection of leniency and settlement documents; joint and several liability (for any participant in an infringement subject to certain exceptions for recipients of immunity and small and medium sized enterprises); the effect of NCA decisions; establishment of clear limitation periods; the

such an apportionment would reduce the benefits to each plaintiff by dividing the potential recovery among a much larger group.

[241] See N Dunne, 'The Role of Private Enforcement within EU Competition Law' (2013–14) 16 *Cambridge Yearbook for European Legal Studies* 143, for a thorough examination of these recent reforms.

[242] Commission, Proposal for a Directive of the European Parliament and the Council on certain rules governing actions for damages under national law for infringements of the Competition law provisions of the Member States and the European Union COM(2013) 404 final. On 17 April 2014, the Parliament adopted a text of the directive that was agreed between the Parliament and the Council and which included some amendments to the original Commission proposal. The Directive was formally adopted in November 2014, see Directive 2014/104/EU on certain rules governing actions for damages under national law for infringements of the competition law provisions of the Member States and of the European Union [2014] OJ L349/1.

[243] Commission, Recommendation of 11 June 2013 on Common principles for injunctive and compensatory redress mechanisms in the Member States concerning violations of rights granted under Union Law [2013] OJ L201/60.

[244] Communication on quantifying harm in actions for damages (n 227).

[245] See Antitrust Damages Actions Directive (n 242), Art 3. See also further, the recent decision of the Court in Case C–557/12 *Kone AG v ÖBB-Infrastruktur AG*, judgment of 6 June 2014, which has held that a national ban on damages for customers of a undertaking that is not party to a cartel but which has benefited from the conditions of umbrella pricing created by the cartel and has set prices higher than expected under competitive conditions is contrary to Art 101.

[246] See Antitrust Damages Actions Directive (n 242), Rec 47 and Art 17(2).

legal consequences of passing on (the Directive establishes a rebuttable presumption that indirect purchasers suffer some level of overcharge harm); and consensual dispute resolution.

Likewise, the Commission hopes that the introduction of a set of common principles in the field of collective redress will help to ensure that effective compensation is obtained in mass harm situations; consequently, it might result in a more empowered consumer who is able, by joining claims with others, to get access to justice and pursue infringements of competition law, particularly where the cost of individual action may otherwise have acted as a deterrent.[247] As, however, the recommendation is that collective redress systems should, as a general rule, be based on the 'opt-in' principle (under which claimant parties are formed through directly expressed consent of their members), there is some concern that such classes will encompass only a small percentage of the antitrust victims.[248]

Finally, the Commission's guidance on quantifying harm is principally intended to bolster the effectiveness of the right to compensation.[249] As former Commissioner Almunia explained, this new legislation seeks to 'democratise' enforcement by making damages actions more readily available to victims of anti-competitive practices.[250] The final consumer is clearly a prominent beneficiary of these initiatives alongside other victims of anti-competitive practices in the production and distribution chain.

Private and public enforcement are thus closely connected. In particular, both systems work towards the protection of consumer interests and the empowerment of consumers. Public enforcement actions have a facilitating effect on private enforcement; a Commission decision finding a competition law infringement may be relied upon to establish the existence of a breach[251] and may provide evidence helpful in establishing causation and harm.[252] Private actions can reinforce public enforcement by increasing deterrence by increasing the resources available for the prosecution of competition law infringements[253] and filling any 'enforcement

[247] See the Recommendation on collective redress (n 243) Rec 9. This rationale also applies to other areas of EU law and hence why the principles of the Commission Recommendation are not solely applicable in the field of competition law but also horizontally to consumer protection, environmental protection, data protection, financial services and other areas where claims for injunctions or damages in respect of breaches of EU law are relevant, Rec 7.

[248] See R Lande, 'The Proposed Damages Directive: The Real Lessons from the United States' March 2014 *CPI Antitrust Chronicle* 2, 6 (recovery in the EU will also be severely limited if lawyers are not allowed to receive contingency fees; 'the vast majority of consumer-victims and small business-victims' may therefore 'continue to be uncompensated').

[249] See Communication on quantifying harm in actions for damages (n 227), para 11.

[250] J Almunia, 'Looking Back at Five Years of Competition Enforcement in the EU' (Global Antitrust Enforcement Symposium, Georgetown Law, Washington DC, 10 September 2014).

[251] The Directive provides that NCA infringement decisions are binding on national courts within that same Member State. Final decisions of an NCA may, however, be presented before the national courts of another Member State as at least prima facie evidence of a competition law infringement (Art 9 of the Directive).

[252] Wils (n 206), 15–16.

[253] Nazzini and Nikpay (n 232) 111.

gap', and by increasing the likelihood of detection and increasing the cost of non-compliance.

Difficult decisions may have to be taken, however, where the interaction between the two enforcement systems becomes strained or where a conflict arises. For example, in *Pfleiderer* a tension arose between the need to ensure, on the one hand, the effectiveness of the right to compensation available to victims of anti-competitive practices and, on the other, the effectiveness of the leniency programmes, which are a crucial aspect of the public enforcement of the Commission in its fight against cartels.[254] The key question in that case was whether a victim of a cartel pursuing an action for damages before the national court should be provided access to the file of the German competition authority that included documents provided by applicants for leniency. The Advocate General neatly explained the dichotomy arising in the case. On the one hand, he pointed to the need to ensure the efficiency of the EU leniency programmes. This would be undermined if self-incriminating documents that participants in a cartel submitted in their application for leniency were then communicated to victims of the cartel which would use them as a basis of actions for damages at national level.[255] On the other, he referred to the right to compensation for harm suffered as a result of anti-competitive behaviour.[256] In the context of ensuring the effectiveness of this right, the information provided by a leniency applicant could evidently help a third party in preparing an action for damages under Article 101.[257] The Advocate General then made a choice, according primacy to the EU interest in securing an effective public enforcement of competition policy and, indirectly, the common market objectives, over the interests of private claimants. Following this rationale, it would seem that the direct interests of specific consumers that are victims of anti-competitive practices could rank second to the effectiveness of the general system of public enforcement and the wider public interest. However, a more long-term view of this approach is that the system of public enforcement indirectly benefits consumer interests *as a whole* by promoting general deterrence. The Court was more cautious than the Advocate General and left the balancing exercise between those two objectives to be performed by national courts on a case-by-case basis. Although the Court has since held that a total ban on disclosure is contrary to the principle of effectiveness in EU law,[258] it again confirmed that it is for the national court to decide whether access should be granted or refused and the conditions that apply. In other words, the Court has not made a clear choice between the objectives of the leniency programmes and the direct interests of individual consumers seeking compensation for the harm that they have suffered as a result of anti-competitive practices and thus has sent the implicit message that these two objectives are, in principle, equally important. The Directive, however, overrides

[254] Case C–360/09 *Pfleiderer AG v Bundeskartellamt* [2011] ECR I–5161.
[255] ibid, para 38 of the Opinion of the AG.
[256] See *Courage* (n 235) and *Vincenzo Manfredi* (n 236).
[257] *Pfleiderer* (n 254), paras 36–37 of the Opinion of the AG.
[258] Case C–536/11 *Bundeswettbewerbsbehörde v Donau Chemie AG*, judgment of 6 June 2013.

this solution, providing that national courts must not order disclosure of leniency and settlement documents in national proceedings.

Criticism may be levelled against some aspects of these recent reforms concerning private enforcement. For example, it could be argued that a bolder, more holistic approach should have been adopted in the Directive tackling a greater number of the areas of legal ambiguity that exist. Further, that because the Recommendation on collective redress takes the form of 'soft law' and recommends only systems based on the opt-in principle, the extent to which it will be able to bolster the position of the consumer is uncertain. However, overall, the consumer seems to have secured an increasingly prominent place in the context of the enforcement of the EU competition rules. Enforcement legislation and guidance documents refer more explicitly to the final consumer as an independent actor in EU competition law than in the context of the substantive law, and the initiatives briefly considered above suggest a strong trend towards the empowerment of the consumer in this field.

One final important point to note, however, is that the EU competition rules cannot reach all conduct or features of a market, which result in the process of competition working sub-optimally so that it does not deliver to consumers products or services which represent the best value for money. Articles 101 and 102 and the EUMR target certain types of conduct of undertakings which distort the process of competition:[259] anti-competitive agreements, mergers and unilateral conduct of dominant firms. It has been seen, however, that Article 102 does not provide an ideal mechanism for dealing with exploitative conduct of an undertaking which holds a dominant position in the market. In addition, standard ex post competition law may not be able to reach 'tacit collusion'[260] between undertakings operating on an oligopolistic market or easily deal with other structural problems that may arise on a market (for example access to key infrastructure) or markets that fail because of blockages that occur on the demand side of the market. In such cases it may be features of the market other than the conduct targeted by these competition provisions which result in the market not operating efficiently.

In such situations consumer law and regulation may play a role in filling the gaps that competition law cannot reach. Consumer law, for example, seeks to deal with some obstructions to the demand side of the market by striving to ensure that consumers have access to accurate information which they can act on and by protecting them against unfairness, deception or undue pressure. Regulation may plug any holes still left by competition and consumer law. Thus in some sectors,

[259] But see also the provisions that apply to the activities of the state, citations at n 27.

[260] Broadly, tacit collusion occurs where undertakings operating on some oligopolistic markets set their prices 'as if' there had been some explicit collusion between them. Oligopolists may recognise their interdependence and, without explicitly agreeing to do so, align their conduct and charge supra-competitive prices as a rational response to market circumstances. Market conditions may therefore dictate that, without any communication between the undertakings, they align their behaviour in a manner which maximises the profits of the players involved but reduces efficiency and the welfare of consumers.

such as energy and telecommunications, for example, sophisticated regulatory regimes may be required, in particular, to ensure access to essential infrastructure and facilities and to regulate the terms upon which access is given. Further, many jurisdictions confer broad powers upon competition agencies to conduct sector inquiries or market studies or investigations, in order to allow them to scrutinise closely markets that they believe may be malfunctioning and to discover the root cause.

V. Conclusions

The competitive process in a free market economy drives efficiency and delivers benefits to consumers by ensuring that the goods and services they receive represent the best value for money. One, if not the principal, goal of the competition rules is to ensure that markets operate efficiently so that the welfare of consumers is maximised. As a result, frequent references to 'consumers' and to 'consumer welfare' are found in the competition law context. Despite this, the exact meaning of these concepts has not been clearly elucidated in the legislation and the case law, suggesting that a more comprehensive attempt to clarify the position of the consumer in the framework of EU competition law is required. This article has, therefore, aimed to provide a taxonomy of those references and a more systematic analysis of the role of the 'consumer' and 'consumer interests' in EU competition law. In doing so, it has considered the position of the consumer in three main contexts: in defining the objectives of EU competition law; in the application of the substantive rules; and in the enforcement of these rules. This section summarises the main findings of this chapter.

There is, first of all, the primary question: *who* is the consumer referred to and protected by the competition rules? Unlike other areas of EU law, where the consumer is defined by the case law or legislation as a final user of goods and/or services (and different images of it are drawn such as the 'average' consumer or the 'vulnerable' consumer), the only comprehensive definition provided of the term 'consumer' in the competition law context is that set out in the Commission Guidelines on the application of Article 101(3). There, the consumer is construed in very wide terms to encompass all direct and indirect users of a product, with the result that the interests of a broad contingent of economic actors (intermediate buyers, retailers, final consumers, etc) are included. This definition accords with the Commission's view that the overarching objective of the rules is to protect competition on the market as a means of enhancing consumer welfare and of ensuring an efficient allocation of resources. This understanding of the objectives of competition law has proved to be a key issue in ascertaining the role of the consumer in EU competition law. Although the Commission's view that consumer welfare is the cornerstone of EU competition law has not been endorsed by the Court, it is generally accepted that 'consumer welfare' is at least one important objective of competition law. In addition, it seems clear that, although this term has been assigned a variety of meanings—ranging from narrow notions of consumer surplus, to broad ones equated with 'total' or 'societal' welfare—both the Commission and the wording of the TFEU seem to support the narrower definition of consumer welfare.

It has also been seen that pursuit of a consumer welfare objective may require trade-offs between different groups of consumers to be made as it concentrates on the maximisation of the welfare of consumers as a whole. Thus, despite Commission rhetoric which emphasises the position of the final consumer as the key beneficiary of the competition rules, the protection of the interests of *final* consumers, who are the essential consideration in other areas of EU law such as consumer law or internal market law (when consumer protection is invoked as a derogation to the provisions on free movement), is just *one* element that is taken into account. Rather, competition law seeks to protect their interests by ensuring that competition is not distorted, in particular by cartels, anti-competitive mergers and the unlawful exclusionary conduct of dominant firms, and assumes that the benefits of competitive markets will cascade down to them.

This chapter has established that it is this broad perception of the 'consumer' that is used implicitly in many cases involving the application of the substantive competition rules and that this conclusion is not undermined by some examples of narrower images of the consumer being drawn. Rather, in most cases where a narrower definition of the consumer is adopted, the consumer identified is simply one playing a part in the more detailed analytical process of considering whether the competition laws apply or have been infringed: for instance, in the determination of the relevant product market or as a reference point in determining how particular groups of consumers have been or may be affected by particular conduct and consequently whether a restriction of competition or an abuse of dominant position has been committed. Thus, in spite of an apparent diversity of images of the consumer, it has been argued that the term 'consumer' is a chameleonic concept which simply adapts to the (competition law) context in which it is used.

To the inherently nebulous view of the objectives of competition law, more uncertainty is added by the use of assumptions and presumptions and indirect assessment to test the legality of market behaviour rather than an actual determination of harm. The focus of the analysis tends to be in the identification of behaviour that is detrimental to competition itself. Further, a competition law system may sometimes decline to condemn behaviour which harms consumers in the short term (for example, exploitative behaviour) in order to protect competition which, in turn, will deliver long-term benefits to consumers. Conversely, there may be behaviour (for example, predatory pricing) that may be prohibited even if it promotes consumer interests in the short term if it will damage the competitive process in the longer-run. The result is that the long-term and short-term interests of consumers must be weighed, and that the latter might be preferred where they coincide more easily with the benefits that the competitive process is supposed to deliver. It seems, therefore, that both in terms of the objectives and of the application of the Competition rules, these rules are applied not to protect directly or come to the aid of final consumers but on the premise that these consumers will draw indirect benefits from the protection of the process of competition. This analytical process, based upon legal presumptions and the assumption of long-term benefits, suggests a degree of remoteness from final consumer interests.

In contrast with the uncertainties that surround the application of the substantive rules, the consumer has seen a strengthening of its position in the context of the enforcement of the competition rules. The recent reforms, both in the field of the public and private enforcement of Articles 101 and 102, have developed and fortified avenues and mechanisms for the consumer to be able to defend their interests in the face of anti-competitive behaviour. Here, the final consumer has begun to emerge as an actor in its own right and as part of the drive to ensure the effectiveness of the substantive rules.

Ultimately, competition law is enforced to promote the process of competition, with the understanding that this will, in turn, deliver benefits to consumers. Consumers are therefore shown a 'promised land' that will take some time to be reached. As far as final consumers—and what they can expect from competition law—are concerned, the way in which the competition rules are applied conjures up the image of a house of cards, intricately built but without a thoroughly solid foundation. The fact that strong mechanisms of enforcement have been developed to ensure that consumers can take action in cases where there has been a breach of the competition rules is a welcome move, but it does not make up for the fact that the actual role of consumer interests in substantive assessments is far from clear. Whether this lack of clarity can be sustained today is questionable, particularly given the obligations imposed by Article 12 TFEU and Article 38 of the EU Charter on Fundamental Human Rights. However, the full implications of these provisions for EU competition law remain to be seen.

4

Seeking the EU 'Consumer' in Services of General Economic Interest

ANGUS JOHNSTON

I. Introduction

From an EU consumer law perspective, we would typically understand the 'consumer' as a private, human (that is, natural, non-body corporate) person who purchases goods or services for purposes outside their business, trade or profession.[1] Yet, as will become clear in what follows, case law and legislation in the field presently under consideration shows an often bewildering range of usages which may overlap and interact in a difficult, or at least unclear, fashion. Traditionally, many of the sectors covered by the idea of providing a service of general economic interest ('SGEI') have fallen within the ownership, control or strong oversight of the state and public bodies: telecommunications, railways, postal services, electricity and gas all spring to mind as key, and often complex, illustrations. Yet movements to privatise and/or liberalise many such sectors have introduced more familiar EU law ideas of free trade and competition, and have brought with them ideas of consumer welfare familiar to competition lawyers, with the concomitant advent of service recipients as customers and/or consumers. Alongside all of this remains the issue of how to ensure access to such goods and services once state control over their provision has been loosened and (largely) left to oversight by independent regulators. The combination of these goals and challenges has created an often difficult web of legislative provisions, lines of case law and guidance documents from national and European executive bodies, all of which form the substance of much of what will be discussed below.

[1] See, among numerous possible examples: Council Directive 93/13/EEC of 5 April 1993 on unfair terms in consumer contracts [1993] OJ L95/29 ('Unfair Terms in Consumer Contracts Directive'), Art 2; Directive 1999/44/EC of the European Parliament and of the Council of 25 May 1999 on certain aspects of the sale of consumer goods and associated guarantees [1999] OJ L171/12 ('Consumer Sales and Guarantees Directive'), Art 1(2)(a); and Directive 2011/83/EU of the European Parliament and of the Council of 25 October 2011 on consumer rights [2011] OJ L304/64 ('Consumer Rights Directive'), Art 2(1).

It is noteworthy, however, that the focus of much of this activity has been upon the restructuring and reorganisation of such sectors, while paying rather less attention—at least originally—to the position and role of these 'new' consumers, their potential problems and contributions. Perhaps the overriding theme of the present paper is the general, structural presumption of much of what one might call 'traditional' EU law that the interests of consumers will best be advanced via the processes of liberalisation and competition,[2] *unless* it can clearly be shown otherwise and that the pursuit of 'other' goals beyond competition, free trade and the like is in itself justifiable. Over time, various legislative developments have made inroads into this presumption. The purpose here is not to provide an exhaustive coverage of all of those situations where SGEI issues have concerned consumers or of the case law of the EU courts and decisional practice of the Commission on these topics; rather, first, terminological difficulties will be highlighted, followed by an attempt to trace developments in the energy sector in particular, with reference to where the EU law analysis has traditionally located consumer-related arguments and issues. This leads into consideration of how these topics have made their way to the EU level in Treaty amendments, case law and particularly a raft of legislation concerning the Internal Energy Market and related developments; finally, the specific example of energy retail price regulation is summarised, before some concluding thoughts are offered about the image(s) of the consumer which have emerged from the discussion. Those images are multi-faceted, sometimes conflicting in how they are portrayed, and may be valued for their own intrinsic worth but also relied upon to paint pictures with a rather broader brush on the national canvas, at least from time to time.

II. Terminology, Overlaps, (Lack of) Clarity

One of the great difficulties presented by the combination of these two broad areas of EU law is the array of terminology used by courts, legislators and commentators, often in a mutually inconsistent or overlapping fashion. A myriad of Venn diagrams might be required to illustrate how these various terms might fit together or sit alongside one another, but this is not the place to offer such a swathe of diagrams. Rather, there follows a small sample of these terminological problems, drawn from various areas/sectors which have sought to address the position of consumers in the context of SGEIs. These are places where the 'consumer' appears and: provokes intervention for them and them alone; acts as a basis for other policies, expanding out to 'protect' others; and/or is then hidden, subsumed or assumed within other terms, rules and goals.

[2] eg G Howells and S Weatherill, *Consumer Protection Law*, 2nd edn (Aldershot, Ashgate, 2005) 1–8.

Competition law has typically distinguished between consumers and their welfare,[3] on the one hand, and those undertakings which compete with each other to supply consumer demand on the other. On occasion, competition law analysis uses the term 'consumer' broadly to encompass all those who buy products or services, which is more akin to the more generic term 'customer'. At times, the relatively weak position of small and medium sized enterprises ('SMEs') vis-à-vis larger undertakings has led to more lenient treatment under competition law for such entities, in the expectation that an enhancement in competition between producers might be enhanced on grounds of quality (of product or service), innovation, etc, or because it would maintain competition between supply chains. Certain national consumer laws have taken this insight concerning the weaker position of SMEs as grounds for extending the protection of consumer law to cover SMEs as well as traditional 'consumers'.[4] Where issues concerning SGEIs arise in the context of competition law—for example, attempts to reserve capacity on natural monopoly transmission lines or interconnection cables[5] or to conclude long-term power or gas purchase agreements[6]—then these notions of consumer welfare in the competition law sense (of maximising economic efficiency so as to generate a consumer surplus (that is, gains which are shared fairly with consumers)) may need to be weighed against the pursuit of other goals of potential importance to consumer interests (such as ensuring constant and reliable energy supplies[7] to all, or at least vulnerable, customers).

In the energy sector (which will be discussed in more detail in section III, below), the early focus was upon customer choice as one of the key drivers of developing a well-functioning Internal Energy Market ('IEM').[8] More recently, the

[3] While acknowledging that there is wide scope for disagreement and nuance about what exactly 'consumer welfare' means and how best it might be pursued. For discussion, see the contribution of Albertina Albors-Llorens and Alison Jones in this volume, and the references cited therein.

[4] See, eg, in the present context the extension in UK telecoms law of various consumer protection provisions to 'small business customers' (ie with 10 workers or fewer): General Conditions of Entitlement (GC) ss 9.3(a) and 14.

[5] eg Commission, 'UK-French electricity interconnector opens up, increasing scope for competition' (IP/01/341, 12 March 2001); Case C–17/03 *Vereniging voor Energie, Milieu en Water v Directeur van de Dienst uitvoering en toezicht energie* [2005] ECR I–4983 and the discussion in K Talus and T Wälde, 'Electricity interconnectors in EU law: energy security, long term infrastructure contracts and competition law' (2007) 32 *European Law Review* 125.

[6] eg Commission Decisions: *Electricidade de Portugal/Pego* (Case IV/34.598) Commission Decision [1993] OJ C265/3; and *Synergen* (Case COMP/E-4/37.732) Commission Decision [2002] IP 02/792; and discussion in K Talus, 'Long-term Natural Gas Contracts and Antitrust Law in the European Union and the United States' (2011) 4 *Journal of World Energy Law and Business* 260 and A Johnston and G Block, *EU Energy Law* (Oxford, Oxford University Press, 2012) paras 8.121–8.171.

[7] See Talus and Wälde (n 5) and K Talus, 'Long-term Gas Agreements and Security of Supply—Between Law and Politics' (2007) 32 *European Law Review* 535.

[8] eg the lengthy debates over the definition of 'eligible customers' in the 1st Package IEM Directives in 1996 and 1998: see A Johnston, 'Maintaining the Balance of Power: Liberalisation, Reciprocity and Electricity in the European Community' (1999) *Journal of Energy and Natural Resources Law* 121, 125–27 and the references cited therein.

potential vulnerability[9] of some customers[10] has been acknowledged on various grounds (isolated locations, connection only to the electricity grid and not the gas network, etc) and the idea of 'energy' and/or 'fuel poverty'[11] has gained significance, as has the question of 'critical services' needing to continue to function in the event of a supply crisis. Some of these categories almost exclusively contain persons we would comfortably identify as 'consumers' (particularly the first two listed in the preceding sentence), while the providers of critical services will not themselves be consumers and yet will have claims to priority supply because of their need to provide goods and services for various key purposes (healthcare, heating, transportation), many of which are crucial because of the consumer's vital requirements, even though others will also benefit from such preference being given to critical services.

In the telecommunications sector, terms such as 'consumer' have regularly overlapped with other notions such as:

— 'subscribers'[12] (which could obviously encompass consumers who pay for their services via subscription);

[9] On the notion of the 'vulnerable consumer' in EU law, see Directive 2005/29/EC of the European Parliament and of the Council of 11 May 2005 concerning unfair business-to-consumer commercial practices in the internal market [2005] OJ L149/22 ('Unfair Commercial Practices Directive'), Art 5(3) and Rec 34 to the Consumer Rights where certain indicia (eg age, physical or mental infirmity) of vulnerability are identified; and see further the contribution of Norbert Reich in this volume.

[10] See the Second Package of EU IEM Directive 2003/54/EC of the European Parliament and of the Council of 26 June 2003 concerning common rules for the internal market in electricity [2003] OJ L176/37 ('Electricity Directive') and Directive 2003/55/EC of the European Parliament and of the Council of 26 June 2003 concerning common rules for the internal market in natural gas [2003] OJ L176/57 ('Gas Directive'), under Art 3(5) of the former and Art 3(3) of the latter, which both refer to 'vulnerable customers' and indicate certain measures to protect such customers that might be 'appropriate'; in the 3rd Package, this protection is enhanced to an obligation on Member States to take such appropriate measures (see Arts 3(7) and 36(h) of the Third Electricity IEM Directive 2009/73/EC of the European Parliament and of the Council of 13 July 2009 concerning common rules for the internal market in natural gas and repealing Directive 2003/55/EC [2009] OJ L211/94 and Arts 3(3)–(4), and 40(h) of the Third Gas IEM Directive 2009/72/EC of the European Parliament and of the Council of 13 July 2009 concerning common rules for the internal market in electricity and repealing Directive 2003/54/EC [2009] OJ L211/55), while leaving it up to Member States to define the concept of 'vulnerable customers' for itself.

[11] See Rec 50 to the Third Electricity IEM Directive (n 10) and Rec 53 to the Third Gas IEM Directive (n 10). For discussion of the issue in the UK context, see B Boardman, *Fixing Fuel Poverty: Challenges and Solutions* (London, Earthscan, 2010); and for a broader economic overview, see L Chester, 'Energy Impoverishment: Addressing Capitalism's New Driver of Inequality' (2014) 48 *Journal of Economic Issues* 395. Note that while much (press) coverage on rising electricity prices is dedicated to blaming these on various environmental measures like the EU Emissions Trading System or subsidies to support the deployment of renewable energy generation, in other parts of the world the advent of renewables is viewed as a potentially vital contribution to ameliorating and even removing energy poverty: eg K Steiner-Dicks, 'The Socio-economic Power of Wind Energy in Remote Areas' (19 January 2015) <http://social.windenergyupdate.com/emerging-markets/socio-economic-power-wind-energy-remote-areas> accessed 6 April 2015, focussing upon South Africa and Latin America; and Out-Law, 'Renewable energy 'generating net financial benefit for South Africa', says study' (30 January 2015) <www.out-law.com/en/articles/2015/january/renewable-energy-generating-net-financial-benefit-for-south-africa-says-study> accessed 6 April 2015.

[12] Art 2 of the Electronic Communications (Universal Service) Order 2003/1904: 'any person who is a party to a contract with the provider of a public electronic communications service for the supply of such service'.

- 'customers'[13] (including those providing telecoms services to those downstream, who pay for access to spectrum, wires/cables and the like: these intermediaries (for want of a better term) are clearly customers of the network owner); and
- 'end users'[14] of telecoms services (which, again, is a category obviously covering both businesses and households, and thus consumers).

More broadly, across what is often called the 'utilities sector', various terms remain in use which hark back to earlier approaches to the provision of such services by the state or through state-owned or controlled entities, or to the transition from that situation to one of gradual liberalisation and privatisation. Thus, the very notion of a 'utility company' is closely connected to the idea of the supply of essentials to customers, such as water, light and heat; while the idea of 'Public Service Obligations' ('PSOs') connotes the public importance of the provision of such goods and services, the fact is that the public authorities (that is, government or similar) have specified these obligations, and that duties are imposed upon suppliers of such essentials to ensure that they are provided. These terms—'utility' and 'PSO'—are themselves regularly a cover or proxy for consumer interests, while also containing the potential to be used for the achievement of other goals less obviously directed towards the welfare and benefit of all or even any consumers.

Finally, some regulatory regimes make a point of using broader categories than just 'consumers' when laying out the duties to be performed by a national regulatory authority ('NRA'). Thus, under its mandate the UK's Office of Communications ('Ofcom')—created[15] to be a converged regulator of the electronic communications industries—is required to further both the interests of 'citizens in relation to communications matters' and of 'consumers in relevant markets, where appropriate by promoting competition'.[16] While this formulation clearly differentiates between consumers and citizens, Ofcom's mission statement sought to combine the two: 'Ofcom exists to further the interests of citizen-consumers through a regulatory regime which, where appropriate, encourages competition',[17] an approach based upon the idea 'that every individual affected by the communications sector and thus its regulation is both a citizen … and a consumer'.[18] The problems that might arise from this pair of duties and their potential inconsistency *inter se* (including the risk that too strong a focus on investment and competition

[13] See GC Part I, which covers those to whom a network or service is provided.

[14] Communications Act 2003, s 151 clearly covering customers of the provider *and* those who are authorised by a customer to make use of the service (eg family members in a household).

[15] By the Office of Communications Act 2002.

[16] Communications Act 2003, s 3(1). See the discussion by Gareth Davies elsewhere in this volume, which touches upon the notion of the (EU) consumer treated purely as an individual actor and party to transactions, rather than addressing the broader, collective, societal interests that might be embodied in thinking of the individual as a citizen.

[17] Ofcom Annual Plan 2005/6, 9.

[18] Ofcom, *A Case Study on Public Sector Mergers and Regulatory Structures* (2006) <www.ofcom.org.uk/files/2010/07/public_sector_merger_case_study.pdf> 66, accessed 6 April 2015.

might lead to neglect of the broader interest of citizens) were much debated when the Communications Bill faced Parliamentary scrutiny during 2002 and 2003,[19] and have also eventuated in practice in some cases.[20] The details listed in the Communications Act 2003 concerning Ofcom's duties are extensive. There are:

- the 'things which ... Ofcom are required to secure' (section 3(2));[21]
- the things to which it must have regard in all cases (namely transparency, accountability, proportionality, consistency and correspondence between targets and needs: section 3(3));
- those to which it must have regard where they appear relevant (section 3(4)(a)–(m)); and
- those specifically relevant to fulfilling the interests of consumers (choice, price, quality of service and value for money: section 3(5)).

Where such duties may conflict *inter se* in any given case, the 2003 Act instructs Ofcom 'to secure that the conflict is resolved in the manner they think best in the circumstances' (section 3(6)), subject to a requirement to give priority to some specific duties over others (in particular, those duties arising under EU law (sections 4 and 25)). The wide range of matters to be taken into account in fulfilling its functions and meeting its various duties create difficult challenges—both for Ofcom in performing these functions and for those affected by Ofcom's approach—not least since this myriad of overlaps and interactions, even in the definitional question of whose interests should be upheld, protected and/or advanced (consumers or citizens), makes the formulation of concrete arguments difficult. This brief excursion into some detail concerning the UK's telecoms rules hopefully provides an idea of the way in which arguments about the goals to be pursued by regulatory regimes intended to secure the provision of SGEIs become embodied in the legislative instruments which then guide and govern such NRAs when carrying out their functions. This point about the content and consistency of legislative instruments (both internally and *inter se*) is one to which we will return below in the energy law context (section III.D below).

Others contributions to this volume have looked in detail at various elements which address some of these questions: I highlight these questions of terminology here because their challenges and uncertainties have been witnessed in some aspects of utilities liberalisation, PSOs and SGEIs. Uncovering the very notion of the 'consumer' and how (if at all) it is used in this area is thus already something of a tricky challenge on many issues; and that is before one starts to examine both the

[19] ibid 4, 8, 17 and 44–45.

[20] In particular in the conduct of Ofcom's periodic reviews of Public Service Broadcasting across the UK: access to the relevant documentation is available at: <http://stakeholders.ofcom.org.uk/broadcasting/reviews-investigations/public-service-broadcasting/psb-review-3/> accessed 14 April 2015. At the time of writing, Ofcom's consultation has closed its Third Review on this subject and a Report is awaited.

[21] A long list, including: optimal use of the spectrum (s 3(2)(a)); availability of a wide range of various services across the UK (s 3(2)(b) and (c); and maintaining a plurality of providers (s 3(2)(d)).

similarities and differences between the various sectors which might fall under the heading of SGEIs, with each of their different and difficult balancing acts between various competing goals and interests. Of necessity here, I will focus mainly on one of these sectors—energy—but will endeavour in places to make cross-references to other sectors where these may prove illuminating.

III. Serving the 'Best Interests' of Consumers

A. SGEIs

First, however, a prior question needs to be addressed: what counts as an SGEI under EU law?[22] The term appears in Article 106(2) TFEU, which provides that:

> Undertakings entrusted with the operation of services of general economic interest … shall be subject to the rules contained in the Treaties, in particular to the rules on competition, in so far as the application of such rules does not obstruct the performance, in law or in fact, of the particular tasks assigned to them. The development of trade must not be affected to such an extent as would be contrary to the interests of the Union.

In its earliest paper on the subject in 1996,[23] the Commission defined SGEIs as 'market services which the Member State subject to specific public service obligations by virtue of a general interest criterion' (as distinct from the broader notion of services of general interest (SGIs), which encompass both market and non-market services). In 2000, it added the point that SGEIs are 'different from ordinary services in that public authorities consider that they need to be provided even where the market may not have sufficient incentives to do so.[24] This is not to deny that in many cases the market will be the best mechanism for doing so.'[25]

Such services have been said to involve characteristics of continuity, universality and equality, and for some they also concern issues of transparency and even affordability.[26] The last of these elements has often been viewed as controversial

[22] For general terminological discussion, see U Neergaard, 'Services of General Economic Interest: The Nature of the Beast' in M Krajewski and others (eds), *The Changing Legal Framework for Services of General Interest in Europe: Between Competition and Solidarity* (The Hague, TMC Asser Press, 2009) ch 1.

[23] Commission Communication, 'Services of general interest in Europe' [1996] OJ C281/03.

[24] On which see: D Helm, J Kay and D Thompson, 'Energy Policy and the Role of the State in the Market for Energy' in P Stevens (ed), *The Economics of Energy*, vol 2 (Cheltenham, Edward Elgar, 2000) 415; and L Hancher and S Janssen, 'Shared Competences and Multi-Faceted Concepts—European Legal Framework for Security of Supply' in B Barton and others (eds), *Energy Security—Managing Risk in a Dynamic Legal and Regulatory Environment* (Oxford, Oxford University Press, 2004) 87–88.

[25] Commission, Services of General Interest in Europe (Communication) COM(2000) 580 final, s 14.

[26] Case C–265/08 *Federutility v Autorità per l'energia elettrica e il gas* [2010] ECR I–3377, Opinion of AG Ruiz Jarabo Colomer, paras 54–55: this led him to conclude (para 56) that 'the objective of preventing undesirable and disproportionate price rises which would be detrimental to consumers constitutes

in some contexts, although affordability consistently appears in definitions of universal service obligations ('USOs'),[27] which are typically viewed as a 'classical case' of defining an SGEI mission.[28] These attempts at generalising the criteria are clearly ripe to cover what one might term 'conventional utilities' such as the supply of electricity (*Almelo*),[29] gas (*Federutility*),[30] water[31] and telecommunications,[32] and the basic postal service (for example, *Corbeau*),[33] but recent cases have expanded the potential scope for SGEIs to areas such as pension schemes (*Albany*),[34] ambulance services (*Ambulanz Glöckner*)[35] and private medical insurance (*BUPA*).[36]

Now we are in a position to address the analytical location of EU law arguments concerning SGEIs, PSOs and the like, to set up the position for assessing how the protection of the 'consumer' (in whichever of her many guises) might be viewed under EU law.

B. The Classical Route

i. Introduction

Typically, national measures which have sought to secure the provision of SGEIs have raised the matter of justifying Member State rules which prima facie raise competition or free movement problems. Nihoul has provided a very helpful thematic analysis of the positive and negative aspects for (various types of) consumers of the introduction of competition in the utilities sectors at the heart of

grounds for 'general economic interest' which, provided [that Directive 2003/55/EC's] other conditions are met, would justify public intervention in respect of prices for the supply of natural gas'. We will return to this question of affordability and 'reasonable prices' below (section III.D.i.b).

[27] eg H Cremer and others, 'Universal Service: An Economic Perspective' (2001) 72 *Annals of Public and Cooperative Economics* 5, 7, and generally paying close attention to the restrictions which USOs impose upon an undertaking's pricing policy: without such restrictions, high-cost service recipients would simply not be served as it would be uneconomic to do so. This also clearly shows the presumption of cross-subsidisation involved in meeting USOs in the face of heterogeneity of service recipient profiles.

[28] COM(2000) 580 (n 25), s14.

[29] Case C–393/92 *Municipality of Almelo and others v NV Energiebedrijf Ijsselmij* [1994] ECR I–1477.

[30] See citations at n 26.

[31] Commission Decision of 4 November 1982 amending Decision 82/371/EEC relating to a proceeding under Art 85 of the EEC Treaty [1982] OJ L167/65.

[32] See Directive 2002/22/EC of the European Parliament and of the Council of 7 March 2002 on universal service and users' rights relating to electronic communications networks and services [2002] OJ L107/51 (Universal Service Directive), esp ch 4.

[33] Case C–320/91 *Criminal proceedings against Paul Corbeau* [1993] ECR I–2533.

[34] Case C–67/96 *Albany International BV v Stichting Bedrijfspensioenfonds Textielindustrie* [1999] ECR I–5751.

[35] Case C–475/99 *Firma Ambulanz Glöckner v Landkreis Südwestpfalz* [2001] ECR I–8089.

[36] Case T–289/03 *British United Provident Association Ltd (BUPA), BUPA Insurance Ltd and BUPA Ireland Ltd v Commission* [2008] ECR II–81.

our discussion of SGEIs.[37] Thus, the introduction of competition has enabled consumers to change their supplier in search of better prices and/or service, with a concomitant improvement in a consumer's bargaining position vis-à-vis businesses due to the possibility of shifting to another provider. As a result, companies are pushed to perform better on price, customer relations, quality of service and the like: in short, innovation and productivity are incentivised and rewarded. Further, consumers are encouraged to become more active in enquiring into, and looking after, their own interests with regard to the supply of such goods and/or services. All of these consequences of the liberalisation process can be said to be benefits provided (or at least encouraged) by the introduction of competition into the provision of such services, along with the various rights (for example, to choose supplier, to move to a new supplier) and protections (for example, availability of information concerning prices, terms and conditions, and access to networks to enable various different service providers to have access to consumers) needed to facilitate such competition.

At the same time, the simple availability of the option for a consumer to shift supplier does not resolve any pre-existing problems or disputes. Looking forward, problems may still subsist for consumers even after the introduction of competition. Companies faced with new competitive pressures may succumb to seeking revenues, even at the expense of treating consumers better (in the hope of attracting new, or retaining existing, business); this may even extend to illegal behaviour where competitive pressure is strong and the ease and credibility of enforcement measures against such action are weak. A different version of this behaviour involves what one might term 'over-promising' all kinds of bells and whistles to the consumer (such as über-rapid broadband speeds) to tempt them to switch, but then failing to deliver such performance in providing the service (whether at all or at best only inconsistently). Finally, it is clear that in this competitive environment the service provider is engaging with consumers in order to earn revenue (whether to turn a profit as a privatised, commercial entity, or at least to cover the overall costs of providing the service on an ongoing basis): some consumers are better placed than others to pay the prices demanded and in a timely fashion, and thus are the more attractive targets of such competition for business. Other consumers may thus not see the expected benefits of competition at all, or at least only to a much lesser degree. Where service providers would not otherwise choose to supply such consumers where it would be unprofitable/uneconomic to do so, intervention is required to ensure that access to essential services is maintained.[38]

[37] P Nihoul, 'The Status of Consumers in European Liberalisation Directives' in D Parry and others (eds), *The Yearbook of Consumer Law 2009* (Farnham, Ashgate, 2009), esp section 2, 'Principles', which this and the subsequent paragraph summarise. See further, P Nihoul and P Rodford, *EU Electronic Communications Law*, 2nd edn (Oxford, Oxford University Press, 2011) chs 4 (on USOs, etc) and 5 (User Protection and Dispute Resolution) and E Newman, 'Consumer Protection and Telecommunications' in I Walden (ed), *Telecommunications Law and Regulation* 4th edn (Oxford, Oxford University Press, 2012) ch 9.

[38] For a relatively early, and admirably clear, identification of the issue in the energy sector, see W Patterson, 'Can Public Service Survive the Market? Issues for Liberalised Electricity' (1999) 4 *Royal Institute of International Affairs Briefing Paper, New Series*; see also the references in n 24 above.

ii. Locating the Analysis

Returning to the location of such arguments within the Treaty framework, such measures have thus regularly been ranged against other 'fundamental' or 'primary' EU law rules, which have as their own basic raison d'être the promotion of trade and competition to enhance consumer (and thus, it is argued,[39] overall societal) welfare. One example among many is provided by the case of *RTT v GB-Inno-BM*: there, laying down the telephone equipment specifications which had to be met for connection of equipment to the national network had been delegated to the incumbent and monopoly public telephone operator.[40] It was found that this had assisted the incumbent in facilitating the restriction or elimination of competition in an ancillary activity, and thus amounted to a breach of competition law, to the detriment of consumer choice, price and quality competition.

Therefore, since such an analysis locates such national measures as derogations from fundamental Treaty rules, justifying such measures has sometimes proved difficult due to the Court's tendency to construe the scope of such derogations narrowly, limiting them to what is strictly necessary to safeguard the justifiably protectable interest in question.[41] So, in the *Commission v Netherlands (Energy import/export)* case, the Court baldly stated: '[b]eing a provision permitting derogation from the Treaty rules, Article [106](2) TFEU must be interpreted strictly'.[42] To provide a flavour of the kinds of national measures involved, in that same case Article 34 of the Dutch Electricity Act 1989 prohibited the importation of electricity into the Netherlands except where this was carried out by the SEP, which was the association of cooperating electricity producers. This prohibition was clearly at odds with Article 37 TFEU, which forbids all discrimination concerning the conditions of sale and supply. The Dutch government relied upon Article 106(2) TFEU to justify this statutory prohibition on imports, arguing that without such a prohibition the planning of electricity supply within the Netherlands would be rendered excessively difficult. The other *Energy Import/Export cases* decided in 1997 involved very similar measures concerning electricity and also gas in some countries.[43] Various cases have shown an unwillingness on the part of the Court to accept Member State derogations in such sectors: a clear set of examples is provided by the slew of 'Golden Shares' judgments handed down by the Court over the past 15 years: typically, these have concerned the restrictions that such shares held by Member States place upon the free movement of capital (but sometimes

[39] As discussed at length by the contribution of Albors-Llorens and Jones in this volume.

[40] Case C–18/88 *RTT v GB-Inno-BM* [1991] ECR I–5941.

[41] See its judgments on Treaty derogations in general, such as Case C–451/03 *Servizi Ausiliari Dottori Commercialisti* [2006] ECR I–2941, para 45.

[42] Case C–157/94 *Commission v Kingdom of the Netherlands* [1997] ECR I–5699, para 37.

[43] *Commission v Kingdom of the Netherlands* (n 42); Case C–158/94 *Commission v Italian Republic* [1997] ECR I–5789; Case C–159/94 *Commission v French Republic* [1997] ECR I–5819, and Case C–160/94 *Commission v Kingdom of Spain* [1997] ECR I–5851 (collectively, '*Energy Import/Export cases*').

also the impact upon freedom of establishment);[44] and, in almost all cases,[45] the Commission's complaint against the Member State has been upheld by the Court.[46] The Member State assertion in such cases is generally that there is a need for a special share held by the public authorities (or some similar regime of control or authorisation) to ensure that changes in shareholdings and overall ownership do not operate so as to endanger the essential supply of key public goods or services (such as energy supplies). On some occasions, the Member State has failed to show that the actual goal was really pursued by its golden share or equivalent rules,[47] while in other cases the Court has rejected the restrictions created by such regimes as disproportionate in nature (for example because their trigger threshold was too low, or prior authorisation was required rather than ex post facto opposition to any particular action by the company).[48] Thus, despite acceptance that such goals *may* be justifiable in general terms, the practical application of such derogations would seem to have left relatively little leeway to Member States.

However, in light of the evolving case law across a wide range of areas, one could argue that the last 25 years have seen at least to some extent a gradual shift of the balance back in favour of Member State choice and discretion in this area. Thus, in those same *Energy Import/Export cases*,[49] the Court required more of the Commission in discharging its burden of proof that the Member State's rules were

[44] See Case C–326/07 *Commission v Italian Republic* [2009] ECR I–2291 (discussed by J van Bekkum, 'Golden Shares: A New Approach' (2010) 7 *European Company Law* 13).

[45] The exception is Case C–503/99 *Commission v Kingdom of Belgium* [2002] ECR I–4809.

[46] Case C–376/98 *Federal Republic of Germany v European Parliament and Council* [2002] ECR I–4731 and Case C–483/99 *Commission v French Republic* [2002] ECR I–4781 (decided, along with *Commission v Kingdom of Belgium* (n 45) separately but handed down on the same day, by a Full Court of 11 judges) (noted by H Fleischer in (2003) 40 *Common Market Law Review* 493); then Case C–463/00 *Commission v Kingdom of Spain* [2003] ECR I–4581, and Case C–98/01 *Commission v United Kingdom* [2003] ECR I–4641, Case C–174/04 *Commission v Italian Republic* [2005] ECR I–4933; Joined cases C–282 and 283/04 *Commission v Netherlands* [2006] ECR I–914; Case C–112/05 *Commission v Federal Republic of Germany* ('*Volkswagen*') [2007] ECR I–8995 (Gr Ch); Case C–274/06 *Commission v Kingdom of Spain* [2008] ECR I–26 (Summ), Case C–207/07 *Commission v Kingdom of Spain* [2008] ECR I–111 (Summ), and *Commission v Italian Republic* (n 44); see, inter alia, the discussions by A Emch, 'News from Luxembourg—Is the New EU Investment Law Taking Shape?' (2008) 9 *Journal of World Investment & Trade* 497; M O'Brien, 'Annotation of Case C–326/07' (2010) 47 *Common Market Law Review* 245; and more broadly, S Gerner-Beuerle, 'Shareholders Between the Market and the State—The VW Law and Other Interventions in the Market Economy' (2012) 49 *Common Market Law Review* 97, and J van Bekkum, 'Cross-border Investments in Undertakings and the Future of EU Company Law' (2014) 25 *European Business Law Review* 811.

[47] eg *Commission v Italian Republic* (n 44) para 46 ff.

[48] See the differences in the results in *Commission v French Republic* (n 46) above and *Commission v Kingdom of Belgium* (n 45): the French rules in the former case required prior authorisation of company decisions and granted very wide discretion to the Minister without publication of possible grounds for approval or refusal; the Belgian rules in the latter case, meanwhile, laid out objective criteria and were subject to effective judicial review (see, further, Fleischer (n 46) for discussion).

[49] See K Talus, *EU Energy Law and Policy: A Critical Account* (Oxford, Oxford University Press, 2013) 33–38 for an account of the various facets of these cases, their implications and place in the evolution of such issues in EU energy law.

incompatible with the common market:[50] the touchstone was whether the enterprise would not be able to fulfil its public duties, not the much higher threshold that the Member State must show that the enterprise's financial viability would be threatened as the Commission had argued in its submissions.[51] The Court also emphasised—in the context of those cases, which involved Article 258 TFEU enforcement actions brought by the Commission—that it was for the Commission to prove the allegation that EU law obligations had not been met by the Member State(s) concerned:

> Whilst it is true that it is incumbent upon a Member State which invokes Article [106](2) to demonstrate that the conditions laid down by that provision are met, that burden of proof cannot be so extensive as to require the Member State, when setting out in detail the reasons for which, in the event of elimination of the contested measures, the performance, under economically acceptable conditions, of the tasks of general economic interest which it has entrusted to an undertaking would, in its view, be jeopardized, to go even further and prove, positively, that no other conceivable measure, which by definition would be hypothetical, could enable those tasks to be performed under the same conditions.[52]

Further, and in a similar vein, the Court in *Altmark* provided a series of criteria that must be satisfied by Member States if State aid scrutiny for compensation for providing public services is to be avoided,[53] which bear a strong resemblance to a combination of procurement rules and the substance of what is now Article 106(2) TFEU. Thus, where an undertaking receives compensation from the state for the performance of public services, and is obliged under PSOs to provide such services,[54] then that remuneration does not amount to State aid, provided that:

> 89. [f]irst, … the recipient undertaking … actually [has] public service obligations to discharge, and the obligations [are] clearly defined]. …
> 90. Second, the parameters on the basis of which the compensation is calculated must be established in advance in an objective and transparent manner …
> 92. Third, the compensation cannot exceed what is necessary to cover all or part of the costs incurred in the discharge of public service obligations, taking into account the relevant receipts and a reasonable profit for discharging those obligations. …

[50] ibid; and see, further, the annotation by PJ Slot, 'Annotation' (1998) 35 *Common Market Law Review* 1183. This approach is now reflected in the text of Art 14 TFEU, which obliges the EU and the Member States to 'take care that such services operate on the basis of principles and conditions which enable them to fulfil their missions'.

[51] *Commission v Kingdom of the Netherlands* (n 42), para 43.

[52] ibid.

[53] Case C–280/00 *Altmark Trans GmbH and Regierungspräsidium Magdeburg v Nahverkehrsgesellschaft Altmark GmbH, and Oberbundesanwalt beim Bundesverwaltungsgericht* [2003] ECR I–7747.

[54] Which might include security of energy supply: Spain's imposition of an obligation to purchase domestic coal to reduce import dependence (alleging the risk of import disruptions was a supply security problem) was recently accepted in *Public Service Compensation Linked to a Preferential Dispatch Mechanism for Indigenous Coal Power Plants* (State Aid Case 178/2010) Commission Decision <http://ec.europa.eu/competition/state_aid/cases/236267/236267_1150043_151_1.pdf> accessed 9 April 2015 and, when challenged, the General Court as a PSO which could be adopted under Art 106(2) TFEU: Case T–57/11 *Castelnou Energía, SL v Commission*, judgment of 3 December 2014.

93. Fourth, where the undertaking … is not chosen pursuant to a public procurement procedure which would allow for the selection of the tenderer capable of providing those services at the least cost to the community, the level of compensation needed must be determined on the basis of an analysis of the costs which a typical undertaking, well run and adequately provided with means … so as to be able to meet the necessary public service requirements, would have incurred in discharging those obligations, taking into account the relevant receipts and a reasonable profit for discharging those obligations.

The significance of importing these ideas into the definition of what counts as 'State aid' for the purposes of what is now Article 107(1) TFEU was that this relieved the Member State of the obligation to notify to the Commission for approval such measures offering compensation in return for public service provision. While the criteria are relatively specific, their general thrust has been to provide Member States with more room to manoeuvre when entrusting the task of public service provision to various actors at national level. In the specific issues considered in what follows, it will emerge that this relative freedom has proved easier to exercise in some ways than others.

iii. Some More Specifics

a. Freedom to Define

To break some of these case law points down further, it must first be noted that it is for Member States to define what qualifies as an SGEI (*France v Commission* (*Telecoms terminal equipment*)[55] and *Commission v Netherlands* (*Energy Import/ Export*).[56] A wide discretion is available to Member States in doing so, as was held by the CFI in *Fred Olsen v Commission*,[57] and this point was cited and emphasised in the *BUPA* case,[58] where the CFI made a clear link to shared and even very limited EU competence, in a subsidiarity-like approach:

167. That prerogative of the Member State concerning the definition of SGEIs is confirmed by the absence of any competence specially attributed to the Commission and by the absence of a precise and complete definition of the concept of SGEI in Community law. The determination of the nature and scope of an SGEI mission in specific spheres of action which either do not fall within the powers of the Community … or are based on only limited or shared Community competence … remains, in principle, within the competence of the Member States.

This freedom has also been emphasised by the Commission:[59]

In areas that are not specifically covered by [EU] regulation Member States enjoy a wide margin for shaping their policies, which can only be subject to control for manifest error.

[55] Case C–202/88 *French Republic v Commission* [1991] ECR I–1223, para 12.
[56] Case C–157/94 *Commission v Kingdom of the Netherlands* (n 42), paras 39–40.
[57] Case T–17/02 *Fred Olsen, SA v Commission* [2005] ECR II–2031, para 216.
[58] *British United Provident Association* (n 36), para 166.
[59] eg Communication from the Commission on services of general interest in Europe [2001] OJ C17/4, para 22.

> Whether a service is to be regarded as a service of general interest and how it should be operated are issues that are first and foremost decided locally.

Where, however, EU legislation *does* regulate a given area, then that Member State margin of discretion can be narrowed, often significantly if the EU rules are far-reaching and detailed in their coverage.

b. Justifiable Goals

Nevertheless, the *goals* or *objectives* pursued by the Member State must be assessed for compatibility with EU law: thus, in the *Dusseldorp* case[60] the protection of the environment had to be accepted at the EU level as an appropriate objective for national measures, both in general and abstract terms, *and* in the specific goal(s)[61] pursued by such measures. Similarly, in the *Energy Import/Export cases* and the various *Golden Shares* judgments, the Court was careful to draw upon earlier cases where goals like security of energy supply had been pleaded and accepted.[62] Further, later Commission documents concerning SGEIs have drawn upon the *Altmark* case[63] to assert that

> the entrustment of a 'particular public service task' implies the supply of services which, if it were considering its own commercial interest, an undertaking would not assume or would not assume to the same extent or under the same conditions. … [I]t would not be appropriate to attach specific public service obligations to an activity which is already provided or can be provided satisfactorily and under conditions, such as price, objective quality characteristics, continuity and access to the service, consistent with the public interest, as defined by the State, by undertakings operating under normal market conditions. As for the question of whether a service can be provided by the market, the Commission's assessment is limited to checking whether the Member State has made a manifest error.[64]

This is consistent with the assessment of Vedder and Holwerda[65]—examining the application of the *Altmark* case in subsequent judgments of the Court of Justice of the European Union (CJEU)—that greater deference is shown to Member State

[60] Case C–203/96 *Chemische Afvalstoffen Dusseldorp v Minister van Volkshuisvesting, Ruimtelijke Ordening en Milieubeheer* [1998] ECR I–4075, concerning protection of the environment as such an objective.

[61] ibid, which there concerned the Netherlands' goal of ensuring the incineration of dangerous waste, a task entrusted to a particular undertaking and which was to be supported by national measures (including an export ban, resulting in an obligation to use that undertaking's disposal services) to ensure the economic viability of that undertaking (paras 12–22 and 62–68).

[62] Like Case 72/83 *Campus Oil Limited v Minister for Industry and Energy* [1984] ECR 2727 and *Almelo* (n 29).

[63] Itself not strictly about Art 106(2) but rather about the definition of whether compensation promised to an undertaking providing a public service (*in casu* bus transport in a German city) qualifies as State aid within Art 107(1) TFEU.

[64] Commission, On the application of the European Union State aid rules to compensation granted for the provision of services of general economic interest COM(2011) 9404 final, paras 47–48; for essentially identical wording, see also Commission, European Union framework for State aid in the form of public service compensation COM(2011) 9406 final.

[65] H Vedder and M Holwerda, 'The European Courts' Jurisprudence after *Altmark*; Evolution or Devolution?' in E Szyszczak and JW van de Gronden (eds), *Financing Services of General Economic Interest: Reform and Modernization* (The Hague, TMC Asser Press, 2011) ch 3.

autonomy so far as the *creation* of SGEIs is concerned[66] than where the Court is faced with questions about the *operation* of such SGEIs, in particular where public service activities are undertaken in combination with, or within the sphere of, commercial and competitive activities.[67]

c. Types of Proceedings and Procedures

Also, it should be emphasised that such questions may arise under various types of different EU law proceedings; this will have a concomitant impact upon the burdens of proof to be satisfied in any litigation, as well as affecting the approach likely to be taken to satisfying the requirement that such national measures are proportionate in their impact upon the *prima facie* EU law rule or goal. First, where a Member State has notified a national SGEI measure for clearance under the State aid rules, it is clear that that Member State must satisfy the Commission that the relevant criteria are met if the sums to be paid are to be justified: for example under the *Altmark* criteria, either an effective and transparent competitive tendering process must be used[68] or the compensation payable for the performance of the service must be determined on the basis of a well-run and adequately equipped undertaking (that is, a benchmarking or comparison exercise with an efficient undertaking). The latter criterion has caused many and notorious difficulties[69] for Member States, the Commission and the EU courts,[70] chiefly because there will rarely be any real-life appropriate comparator to utilise, so that other proxies must be found, based—in the Commission's view,[71] at least—upon not

[66] Citing the *BUPA* judgment (n 36). See also M Klasse, 'The Impact of *Altmark*: The European Commission Case Law Responses' in Szyszczak and van de Gronden (n 65), who doubts that the Commission's decisional practice concerning the *Altmark* criteria either provides clear guidance for Member States and public service providers as to the stability of their arrangements, or allows for the possible flexibility evinced by the *BUPA* judgment concerning the question of the efficiency required of the (hypothetical) comparator undertaking.

[67] Using the example of Case C–209/10 *Post Danmark A/S v Konkurrencerådet*, judgment of 27 March 2012, which involved an allegation of abuse of dominant position under what is now Art 102 TFEU, in the context of a postal undertaking which was also subject to a USO with regard to some categories of mail.

[68] eg *Security of Supply Ireland (CADA)* (Case N 475/2003) Commission Decision [2003] OJ C34/3, esp para 57.

[69] eg JD Braun and J Kühling, 'Article 87 EC and the Community courts: from revolution to evolution' (2008) 45 *Common Market Law Review* 465.

[70] eg Joined cases C–341/06 P and C–342/06 P *Chronopost SA and La Poste v Union française de l'express (UFEX)* [2008] ECR I–4777, where the CJEU rejected the CFI's approach because there was no possibility of comparing the incumbent La Poste's position with a private sector undertaking: this necessitated an assessment of the level of compensation provided by reference to those cost elements which were objective and verifiable, covering appropriate variable and fixed costs, as well as an adequate return on capital invested. See also the judgment of the CFI in *BUPA* (n 36). Both of these cases showed a departure from strict efficiency assessments and comparisons due to the context involved. Contrast *DSB* (Case C 41/08) Commission Decision [2011] OJ L7/1, para 284 ff, where the difficulty of drawing comparisons was used to justify a finding that the Member State had not proved that its approach met the efficiency requirement.

[71] See Commission Decisions: *Postbus Lienz* (Case 16/2007) Commission Decision [2009] OJ L/306/26, para 86; and *Southern Moravia Bus Companies* (Case 3/2008) Commission Decision [2009] OJ L97/14, paras 82–83.

simply actual costs in a given sector but some attempt objectively to establish the costs of an (hypothetical) efficient undertaking. The case law and decisional practice have tended to show a stricter attitude adopted by the Commission, leaving Member States less room for manoeuvre, and a somewhat more lenient approach taken by the EU courts, perhaps particularly the CJEU.

Then, one should compare Article 258 TFEU enforcement actions with references for a preliminary ruling. Under the former, the Commission must positively establish its case that national rules concerning, here, SGEIs amount to a breach of EU law; under the latter, as a result of the jurisdictional division under Article 267 TFEU,[72] it will typically[73] be for national courts to assess justifiability on the facts. A useful illustration of the operation of Article 267 is provided by the judgment of the Dutch court in the *Gemeente Almelo* case,[74] which rejected reliance upon the SGEI justification on the facts when the case returned to the national level from the Court of Justice.[75] This has knock-on consequences for the need to engage with 'less restrictive alternatives' to the measures/rules actually adopted by a Member State in the case in question, under the proportionality rubric: there is some evidence that national courts have generally proved more lenient than the Court in finding that national measures are justifiable and proportionate,[76] which might lead one to think that greater leeway from the Court concerning SGEIs (as highlighted previously in this section) would be used even more broadly at national level.[77]

[72] Case 104/79 *Pasquale Foglia v Mariella Novello (No 1)* [1980] ECR 745; Case 244/80 *Pasquale Foglia v Mariella Novello (No 2)* [1981] ECR 3045; and see Case C–206/01 *Arsenal Football Club plc v Matthew Reed* [2002] ECR I–10273 and, overturned on appeal, *Arsenal Football Club plc v Matthew Reed* [2003] EWCA Civ 696.

[73] Although sometimes the Court will assert that it has all of the information required to reach a conclusion on a particular point, thus effectively taking the decision on the facts for the national court: eg Case C–169/91 *Council of the City of Stoke-on-Trent v B & Q* [1992] ECR I–6654, paras 12–17. For a very recent example of some ambivalence on this issue, see Case C–518/13 *The Queen, on the application of Eventech Ltd v Parking Adjudicator*, judgment of 14 January 2015 (compare paras 57 and 61).

[74] *Municipality of Almelo* (n 29), and see L Hancher's annotation (1997) 34 *Common Market Law Review* 1509 also covering the national court's decision on the return of the case from the ECJ.

[75] The Arnhem court held (judgment of 22 October 1996, rolnr. 87/280) that the parties had not adduced any evidence on which it could be concluded that the statutory task (electricity distribution) would have been impossible to carry out in the absence of the conclusion of the exclusive contracts.

[76] See the discussion in M Jarvis, *The Application of EC Law by National Courts: The Free Movement of Goods* (Oxford, Oxford University Press, 1998), esp chs 6 (on the 'rule of reason') and 7 (on Art 36 EC, now Art 36 TFEU): both offer evidence and criticism of national courts' ready acceptance of the justifiability of national measures on the basis of skimpy evidence and scant reasoning. See also H Micklitz, *The Politics of Judicial Co-operation in the EU: Sunday Trading, Equal Treatment and Good Faith* (Cambridge, Cambridge University Press, 2005) ch 2 (esp 126 ff, on the attitudes of the national judges which sent the references for a preliminary ruling to the Court and then dealt with the Court's answers).

[77] Although it should be acknowledged that there are examples of national courts refusing on the facts to uphold the State's reliance upon such derogations—see *Almelo* (n 29)—and sometimes the CJEU's own reasoning offers a route which allows national courts to protect individuals affected by (eg) trade-restrictive national rules while still leaving room for the State to implement correctives or palliatives to satisfy the proportionality requirement. On this latter point, see Case C–142/05

Further, it must not be forgotten that—assuming that EU competence exists and other hurdles such as subsidiarity, proportionality and fundamental rights under EU law can be surmounted—EU harmonisation legislation can effectively cover this field in certain sectors, by stating the policy objectives in that sector, and even providing detailed rules on which PSOs may or even must be adopted, as well as requiring consumer protection measures to be implemented at national level (see further below, section III.D).

Cases which explicitly refer to the position of consumers and requirements of consumer protection under the heading of SGEIs and/or PSOs, however, are really very small in number, and such references are often at best oblique or implicit. So, in the *Corbeau* case[78] reliance was placed upon the universal postal service obligations of the Belgian Post Office as concerning serving less accessible areas or providing essential services not otherwise economically viable under normal market conditions. The implication is that some vulnerable consumers (including those in remote areas) would see adverse effects. A similar point about universal service and the need for uninterrupted electricity supplies to consumers was assumed in *Gemeente Almelo*;[79] and in *Albany* one might view the obligation for employers to affiliate to a sectoral pension scheme—and the associated exclusive right granted to sectoral pension funds to manage such supplementary schemes—as having been seen as necessary to protect the collective (consumer) interest in affordable pension provision to supplement the limited State pension available.[80] Otherwise, the general assumption underlying the case law generated by the provisions on free movement, competition and State aid seems to be that free trade, competition and liberalisation are what is needed to defend and advance (inter alia) consumer welfare, which is seen as synonymous with the interests of consumers. Where positive, particular instances have arisen where such forces fail to protect or empower the consumer sufficiently, this has led to a range of reactions at EU level, to which we now turn.

C. Leading to Various EU-level Reactions

As experience grew case-by-case with the assessment of national measures concerning SGEIs—whether through State aid notifications under Article 108 TFEU

Åklagaren v Percy Mickelsson and Joakim Roos [2009] ECR I–4273, paras 36–43, discussed by M Derlén and J Lindholm, 'Article 28 EC and Rules on Use: a Step Towards a Workable Doctrine on Measures Having Equivalent Effect to Quantitative Restrictions' (2010) 16 *Columbia Journal of European Law* 191, esp 228.

[78] *Corbeau* (n 33).

[79] *Almelo* (n 29); here, the term 'consumers' is used explicitly by the Court (para 48). However, the Court seems to understand this term to include 'local distributors or end-users', suggesting that the assumption that the USO involved was only partly in service of 'consumers' understood in the narrower sense prevalent in modern consumer (protection) law (as discussed in section II, above): while distribution networks are of course the crucial conduit for serving the genuine consumer, they also serve commercial customers and public bodies.

[80] *Albany International* (n 34), paras 103–22.

or case law coming before the EU courts via Articles 258, 263 and 267 TFEU—this generated a range of reactions on the EU legal and policy level, with a view to clarifying the EU law requirements faced by Member States in this field. The Commission contributed to this process by the adoption of various decisions, sometimes of general application but mainly on specific cases. It developed a range of Guidelines for Member States, and adopted Communications, both on the basis of the experience gained.

The Member States, meanwhile, pursued various additions to the founding Treaties in the field of SG(E)Is at different stages and via different routes. Since 1997 there has been a specific provision on SGEIs, now to be found in Article 14 TFEU:

> Without prejudice to *Article 4 [TEU]* or to Articles 93, 106 and 107 [TFEU], and given the place occupied by services of general economic interest in the shared values of the Union as well as their role in promoting social and territorial cohesion, the Union and the Member States, each within their respective powers and within the scope of application of the Treaties, shall take care that such services operate on the basis of principles and conditions, *particularly economic and financial conditions*, which enable them to fulfil their missions. *The European Parliament and the Council, acting by means of regulations in accordance with the ordinary legislative procedure, shall establish these principles and set these conditions without prejudice to the competence of Member States, in compliance with the Treaties, to provide, to commission and to fund such services.*

The *italicised* text was added by the Treaty of Lisbon.[81] After the introduction of Article 16 EC (as it was first numbered) by the Treaty of Amsterdam in 1997 but prior to the Lisbon Treaty, there had been debate about whether this provision was mere window dressing, adding little to the substantive provisions (like Article 106 TFEU) already contained within the Treaties or whether it amounted (or would amount, in time) to a genuine 'constitutionalisation' of public services within the Treaty framework, enhancing MS autonomy and even serving to guide future EU legislation.[82] The entry into force of the Treaty of Lisbon in December 2009 amended the provision in various ways. First, the text of Article 14 TFEU now specifies that the relevant conditions crucial to fulfilling the functions of SGEIs concern economic and financial matters; second, it now includes legislative powers for the EU. It has been suggested[83] that this leaves the EU with two—potentially competing—legal bases upon which to adopt measures concerning SGEIs: Articles 14 and 106(3) TFEU, the former for the Council and European Parliament, and the latter for the Commission. To this, the present author would add a further category, which concerns the pursuit of internal market goals

[81] And the final italicised sentence concerning legislative competence is much softer in tone and content than the original wording in the now defunct Treaty Establishing a Constitution for Europe [2004] OJ C310/1, which simply read: 'European laws shall define these principles and conditions' (Art III-6).

[82] For discussion see, eg, M Ross, 'Article 16 EC and Services of General Economic Interest: From Derogation to Obligation' (2000) 25 *European Law Review* 22 and W Sauter, 'Services of General Economic Interest and Universal Service in EU Law' (2008) 33 *European Law Review* 172.

[83] Sauter (n 82).

where these overlap with sectors appropriate to SGEIs. In some areas, this category will be covered by Article 114 TFEU (as evinced by the 2009 IEM Directives' reliance, in part, upon the old Article 95 EC,[84] and by the continuing reliance upon Article 95 EC for universal service measures in the telecoms sector);[85] in future, EU measures in the energy sector will surely be based upon Article 194 TFEU. As will be discussed further below (section III.D), the IEM Directives contain a range of PSOs which should be understood as safeguarding the provision of certain key aspects of SGEIs in the energy sector and it seems highly unlikely that the advent of the new last sentence of Article 14 TFEU will cause the EU legislature to shift away from its reliance upon sector-specific competences.[86]

The Lisbon Treaty also served to attach Protocol No. 26 on SGIs to the TEU and TFEU, which clarifies in its Article 1 that the 'shared values' referred to in Article 14 TFEU:

> include in particular:
>
> — the essential role and wide discretion of national, regional and local authorities in providing, commissioning and organising [SGEIs] as closely as possible to the needs of the users;
> — the diversity between various [SGEIs] and the differences in the needs and preferences of users that may result from different geographical, social or cultural situations;
> — a high level of quality, safety and affordability, equal treatment and the promotion of universal access and of user rights.

At the same time the EU Charter of Fundamental Rights acquired legally binding force by virtue of Article 6(1) TEU.[87] Article 36 of that Charter—originally included by the Convention which drafted the Charter back in 1999–2000[88]—addresses the question of *access* to SGEIs:

> The Union recognises and respects access to services of general economic interest as provided for in national laws and practices, in accordance with the [TFEU], in order to promote the social and territorial cohesion of the Union.

[84] eg Directive 2009/72/EC (n 10), which employs Arts 47(2), 55 and 95 EC.

[85] ibid, as most recently amended by Directive 2009/136/EC of the European Parliament and of the Council of 25 November 2009 amending Directive 2002/22/EC on universal service and users' rights relating to electronic communications networks and services, Directive 2002/58/EC concerning the processing of personal data and the protection of privacy in the electronic communications sector and Regulation (EC) No 2006/2004 on cooperation between national authorities responsible for the enforcement of consumer protection laws [2009] OJ L337/11: both are based solely upon Art 95 EC (now Art 114 TFEU).

[86] See Case C–490/10 *European Parliament v Council of the European Union*, judgment of 6 September 2012, and the discussion of the potential difficulties which may be encountered under the new Art 194 TFEU in A Johnston and E van der Marel, '*Ad Lucem*? Interpreting the New EU Energy Provision, and in particular the Meaning of Article 194(2) TFEU' (2013) 22 *European Energy and Environmental Law Review* 181, and the references cited therein.

[87] Charter of Fundamental Rights of the European Union [2010] OJ C83/389.

[88] Charter of the Fundamental Rights of the European Union of the European Parliament, the Council and the Commission [2000] OJ C364/8; on which process, see C McCrudden, 'The Future of the EU Charter of Fundamental Rights' *Jean Monnet Working Papers* 2001/10; and J Schönlau, *Drafting the EU Charter: Rights, Legitimacy and Process* (Basingstoke, Palgrave Macmillan, 2005).

As one commentator has noted, '[i]t is difficult to see what the contribution of Article 36 of the Charter is in view of the general Treaty exemptions to the free movement rules, the mandatory requirements and Article 106(2) TFEU'.[89] In any event, its emphasis chimes harmoniously with the approach of Article 14 TFEU, both in its wording and its reference to Article 4 TEU: the role of SGEIs in general has been emphasised and strengthened in the Treaties and some EU role in this field is acknowledged, with a more explicit recognition of the social dimension;[90] *but* the framers of the Treaties have also been anxious to emphasise that the primary role is played by the Member States, even if the substance of their additions and self-reassurances is viewed as relatively unclear and imprecise,[91] and the implications thereof were—and remain—difficult to predict with great confidence.[92]

D. Beginning to Incorporate Elements within EU (Sectoral) Legislation

Whatever the frustrations of this Treaty framework and its application by the Commission and the EU judicature, the foregoing discussion has served to sharpen the need to focus upon the evolution and detail of sector-specific EU legislation which concerns SGEIs in general, and the position of consumers in particular. Here, this will be examined primarily through the lens of the evolution of this issue in the EU's Internal Energy Market *acquis*, although reference will be made to other areas to offer comparisons or developments on some topics.

In general the EU-level starting point in the energy sector very much focussed upon the consumer welfare gains to be achieved through the liberalisation process and the introduction of customer choice of supplier and competition where possible throughout the energy value chain.[93] Further, where Member State energy

[89] PJ Slot, 'Public Distortions of Competition: The Importance of Article 106 TFEU and the State Action Doctrine' in U Neergaard and others (eds), *Social Services of General Interest in the EU* (The Hague, TMC Asser Press, 2013) ch 10, esp 249.

[90] U Neergaard, 'Services of General (Economic) Interest: What Aims and Values Count?' in U Neergaard and others (eds), *Integrating Welfare Functions into EU Law—From Rome to Lisbon* (Copenhagen, DJØF Publishing, 2009) 206. This insight, allied with cases arising concerning social services (such as healthcare and pension provision) has generated a growing literature focussing upon SG(E)Is and PSOs as part of a broader shift in focus in the EU Treaties towards recognition of values of solidarity and social market economy. See, eg, M Ross, 'The Value of Solidarity in European Public Services Law' in Krajewski and others (n 22) ch 4 and M Ross, 'SSGIs and Solidarity: Constitutive Elements of the EU's Social Market Economy?' in Neergaard and others (eds), *Social Services of General Interest* (n 89) ch 5; and U Neergaard, 'In Search of the Role of "Solidarity" in Primary Law and the Case Law of the European Court of Justice' in U Neergaard and others (eds), *The Role of Courts in Developing a European Social Model—Theoretical and Methodological Perspectives* (Copenhagen, DJØF Publishing, 2010).

[91] A point enhanced or exacerbated (depending upon one's inclinations) in the energy sector by the wording and structure of Art 194 TFEU: see Johnston and van der Marel (n 86).

[92] Sauter (n 82) 173.

[93] eg Commission, Staff Working Paper: First benchmarking report on the implementation of the internal electricity and gas market SEC (2001) 1957, generally and esp 3 and 5 (concerning price levels as indicators of competitive activity).

systems were organised under state ownership and/or control, electricity or gas suppliers provided a public service ensuring supply to consumers, so that references to consumer protection and PSOs were very much expected to remain at national level. Thus, references to such concepts in EU-level measures were limited, and slow to develop. Yet as experience with the implementation and application of each package of IEM measures has been gathered, the subsequent measures have contained more extensive and detailed references to consumers or issues of importance for consumer protection in liberalising energy markets.

i. *Tracking the Evolution of More Far-reaching Liberalisation in the Energy Field, in Parallel with Growing Reference to Position of Consumers/Customers*[94]

a. The Customer as (Simply) a Market Participant

In the early years, there was an acknowledgment in EC legislation that the free play of market forces might not guarantee the achievement of other important goals such as, inter alia, consumer protection. This led to the inclusion of a provision which acknowledged that Member States could impose PSOs upon energy companies.[95] Article 3(2) of Directive 96/92/EC provided that:

> Having full regard to the relevant provisions of the Treaty, in particular Article 90 [EEC, now Article 106 TFEU], Member States may impose on undertakings operating in the electricity sector, in the general economic interest, public service obligations which may relate to security, including security of supply, regularity, quality and price of supplies and to environmental protection. Such obligations must be clearly defined, transparent, non-discriminatory and verifiable; they, and any revision thereof, shall be published and notified to the Commission by Member States without delay. As a means of carrying out the abovementioned public service obligations, Member States which so wish may introduce the implementation of long-term planning.[96]

In practice, this essentially sought to replicate the main conditions established by the Court in its case law, although the various possible interests which could

[94] Note here that the analysis has been developed on the basis of the English language versions of the relevant legislation: I am well aware that a full coverage of the definitional questions will require a more wide-ranging treatment of the terminology used across the EU's official languages. Yet confining oneself to looking purely at the English usage in the relevant materials already provides ample evidence to substantiate the general point concerning consistency, coherence and interactions, as I hope will be shown in what follows hereafter.

[95] eg Recs 9, 13, 17 and 19 to Directive 96/92/EC of the European Parliament and of the Council of 19 December 1996 concerning common rules for the internal market in electricity [1997] OJ L27/20, and Recs 12–16 to Directive 98/30/EC of the European Parliament and of the Council of 22 June 1998 concerning common rules for the internal market in natural gas [1998] OJ L204/1.

[96] In the subsequent First Gas IEM Directive 98/30/EC (n 95), there was added to the end of its Art 3(2): 'taking into account the possibility of third parties seeking access to the system', showing already an evolution in concerns to ensure access for competitors to the networks to contribute to the development of competition in the sector. This is now reflected in the current version of the text of Art 3(2) in both the Third Electricity IEM Directive 2009/72/EC (n 10) and Third Gas IEM Directive 2009/73/EC (n 10).

be protected by such PSOs were specified, presumptively limiting the scope for Member State PSOs to pursue other goals in this sector.[97] Indeed, allied with the requirement that information on such national measures concerning PSOs and USOs be provided to the Commission, this facilitates the gathering of information on the operation of the energy sector in general, and provides the basis for assessing whether further measures need to be taken at the EU level (whether to ensure high standards of public service or to address market foreclosure which might be caused or exacerbated by PSO measures).[98] Otherwise, in line with the competition and liberalisation paradigm, references to categories which might include consumers were typically to 'customers', with a focus upon their eligibility to choose between suppliers.[99] This functioned as a measure of the degree of market opening under the First and Second Package Directives, and was part of the design to bring the benefits of choice and competition to energy customers.

Then, from the Second IEM package onwards, the focus shifted to addressing how to facilitate customers in switching their supplier, to ensure such choice could be exercised and competition could be effective. The Second Electricity[100] and Gas[101] IEM Directives specifically instructed the Commission to report on the extent of actual customer switching and tariff renegotiation,[102] and various Commission[103] and other[104] documents emphasised the importance of this topic now that the category of customers eligible to do so would continue to grow and ultimately encompass all customers, including those at household level. In the Third Package, this issue: has been added to the objectives[105] and duties[106] of the National Regulatory Authority; has found a place in Articles 3(3) (Electricity) and 3(7) (Gas), which impose an obligation upon Member States to 'ensure that the

[97] On the nature of this list as indicative, rather than exhaustive, see AG Ruiz-Jarabo Colomer in *Federutility* (n 26), para 45, and the discussion of C Suykens and B Delvaux, 'Price Regulation in the Energy Sector in the EU—Here to Stay?' in B Delvaux, M Hunt and K Talus (eds), *EU Energy Law and Policy Issues*, vol 4 (Antwerp, Intersentia, 2013) ch 9, esp 224–26.

[98] See Talus (n 49) 89–91 and the references cited therein.

[99] See Art 19 of Directive 96/92/EC (n 95) and Art 18 of Directive 98/30/EC (n 95), and note that Art 3(3) in both Directives specifically identifies a 'Community interest' (in the context of what is now Art 106(2) TFEU) as 'competition with regard to eligible customers'.

[100] Electricity Directive (n 10).

[101] Gas Directive (n 10).

[102] Arts 29(3) of the Electricity Directive and 31(3) of the Gas Directive, respectively.

[103] eg: Commission, Completing the internal energy market (Communication) COM(2001) 125, 8; and the extensive references to this competition indicator throughout the Commission's First benchmarking report (n 93) and in its Second benchmarking report on the implementation of the internal electricity and gas market SEC(2002) 1038 (updated in SEC(2003) 448).

[104] ERGEG, 'Obstacles to Supplier Switching in the Electricity Retail Market—Guidelines of Good Practice and Status Review' (10 April 2008), which emphasised that a mere declaration that all customers are eligible to switch will not in fact ensure that this is possible if network operators (especially at the distribution level) do not enable this to happen and instead act obstructively so as to protect their interests as market actors, rather than market facilitators (at 4).

[105] viz, 'contributing to the compatibility of necessary data exchange processes for customer switching' (Directive 2009/73/EC (n 10), Art 40(h)).

[106] viz, 'monitoring the level and effectiveness of market opening and competition at wholesale and retail levels, including … switching rates' (Directive 2009/73/EC (n 10), Art 41(1)(j)).

eligible customer is in fact able easily to switch to a new supplier'; and features in Articles 3(5)(a) (Electricity) and 3(6)(a) (Gas), where Member States are obliged to ensure that contractually compliant switching by a customer must be effected by the operators concerned within three weeks. All of this underlines switching's key role[107] in empowering the customer so that the anticipated benefits of competition can be realised. These elements suggest that EU-level energy legislation had begun strongly to acknowledge the role played by the customer, but tended to view that role as market participant and agent of liberalisation.

b. More Protective Provisions

Yet it must also be emphasised that other important (protective) issues and values began to be recognised and addressed more specifically and in greater detail, particularly from the Second IEM Package onwards. One key contribution in this regard was the establishment of a universal service requirement[108] in electricity (but not gas) supply for all household customers, as well as (where the Member States 'deem it appropriate') small enterprises. Where both categories are protected by such a universal service obligation (USO), recital 45 to the Third Electricity IEM Directive allows Member States to distinguish between measures aimed at households and small enterprises. Article 3(3) of the Second Electricity IEM Directive explained that such universal service involves 'the right to be supplied with electricity of a specified quality within their territory at reasonable, easily and clearly comparable and transparent prices'. To that end, 'Member States shall impose on distribution companies an obligation to connect customers to their grid', and a supplier of last resort may be appointed to ensure such universal service.[109] These provisions have been maintained largely unchanged in the current legislation, although it is now emphasised in Article 3(3) of the Third Electricity IEM Directive that prices must also be 'non-discriminatory'.

[107] For discussion of the details of the switching process, see Johnston and Block (n 6), paras 7.46–7.57.

[108] The postal sector, too, typically involves the imposition of a USO on the former incumbent monopoly (in the UK, Royal Mail) but not new market entrants, which typically cherry-pick profitable market segments: the cost of maintaining USOs in postal services has come under increasing scrutiny as competition in other market segments has increased, undercutting the scope for cross-subsidy of the USO from other activities. For discussion in the UK context (where the reduction in physical mail and its replacement with e-letters, combined with growing competition in the direct delivery market, has since 2008 raised questions about the ongoing viability of the 6-days-a-week direct delivery USO), see Harker and others, 'CCP Consultation Response on Competition in the UK Postal Sector' <http://competitionpolicy.ac.uk/documents/8158338/8261737/CCP+Response+-+BIS+-+Competition+for+UK+Postal+Sector.pdf> accessed 10 April 2015.

[109] For discussion of the pros and cons of such suppliers of last resort, see ERGEG, 'Status review of the definitions of vulnerable customer, default supplier and supplier of last resort' (E09-CEM-26-04, 16 July 2009), esp 7–8 and 31. In essence, the danger is that the incumbent supplier is usually the one designated and time limits upon how long they can serve in that capacity for any given customer are not usually imposed. This may serve to limit and even discourage competition among suppliers in a national system.

It is worth highlighting here that these USO provisions offer a broad conception of supply security, encompassing regular supply of specified quality and at a reasonable price, which is a matter of some contention in wider discussions of the concept of security of energy supply;[110] further, recital 47 to the third Directive links the content and further strengthening of PSOs (including the USO) to ensuring that 'all consumers, especially vulnerable ones, are able to benefit from competition and fair prices'. This last statement potentially conflates a number of different issues and terms: we will come to the definition of the 'vulnerable' category in a moment, but the notion of 'fair prices' here is linked directly to the benefits of 'competition', which might be thought at least potentially to conflict with the idea that prices must be 'reasonable'. By all accounts, the prevalence in many Member States of state intervention in regulating energy prices suggests that some national governments and regulators share the perception that some final customers need protection from competitive prices if the amounts they are to pay are to remain 'reasonable'. This issue of price regulation will be discussed briefly below (section III.D.iv). Finally, with regard to the USO, it should be noted that the advent of this category is beneficial for *some* categories of customer, insofar as it might otherwise not be economic to supply them with electricity, but for the remainder the impact is to pass on to them the costs of supplying those protected by that USO, effectively socialising the cost of such supplies. This is consistent with the broad terms of Articles 3(10) (Electricity) and 3(7) (Gas), which instruct Member States to 'implement appropriate measures to achieve the objectives of social and economic cohesion and environmental protection': specific reference is made here to 'adequate economic incentives ... for the maintenance and construction of necessary network infrastructure', which are clearly crucial for meeting the USO in electricity and various other PSOs in both electricity and gas, but which leave it to the Member States to define which categories of customers might need such extra attention or protection.

With regard to various sub-categories of customers, the later iterations of the EU's IEM Directives have begun to acknowledge that it may be justifiable for Member States to maintain or introduce special rules for the protection of what are almost always referred to as 'vulnerable customers'.[111] The word 'vulnerable'

[110] On which see Johnston and Block (n 6), paras 9.01–9.20, and the references cited therein. Contrast the position under 2005/89/EC of the European Parliament and of the Council of 18 January 2006 concerning measures to safeguard security of electricity supply and infrastructure investment [2006] OJ L33/22 (Electricity Security of Supply Directive) (and indeed the Regulation (EU) No 994/2010 of the European Parliament and of the Council of 20 October 2010 concerning measures to safeguard security of gas supply [2010] OJ L295/1 ('Gas Supply Security Regulation')), which do not seem to encompass a notion of supply at reasonable prices within their conceptions of 'security of supply': see the definition of 'security of electricity supply' in Art 2(b) of Directive 2005/89/EC. NB, further, that the specific measures in Art 3(2) and Annex I of the Third IEM Directives do not address broader 'security of supply' notions, but focus upon continuity, quality and reliability of supplies. For analysis of these measures, see Johnston and Block (n 6), para 10.12 ff.

[111] For treatment of the notion of the 'vulnerable consumer' in EU law more broadly, see Norbert Reich's contribution in this volume, and the references cited therein.

is nowhere to be found in the First Package legislation, but began to be of significance from the Second Package onwards,[112] and the vulnerable customer appears at many points in the Third Package Directives, in the contexts of PSOs and the objectives of the NRA.[113] Yet still no definition has been offered of the category of 'vulnerable customers':[114] this was due to the difficulties of allowing for those who use energy sources other than gas and electricity as a heat source, and the volatility of energy prices relative to income levels, meaning that measures like the proportion of income spent on energy would not provide a consistent and coherent standard.[115] Thus, the definition of the vulnerable customer is left to the Member States, although they are *obliged* to define that concept—'which may refer to energy poverty and, inter alia, to the prohibition of disconnection … to such customers in critical times'—and 'appropriate measures' must be taken and 'adequate safeguards' implemented. Again, no definition is offered of 'energy poverty' or 'critical times'[116] in the Third Package Directives, so while the categories of issues which are to be addressed by Member States are relatively clearly defined, significant discretion remains at the national level both in choosing the methods to be used to address such issues[117] and in defining those customers whose positions are covered by such measures and safeguards.[118] Another such category concerns customers in 'remote areas', which have moved from an optional category in the Second Package Directives which Member States 'may' protect[119] to a positive *obligation* under Articles 3(7) (Electricity) and 3(3) (Gas) under the current rules; again, there is no EU-level definition of such 'remoteness', leaving Member States to specify where exactly will be covered.

[112] See Recs 2 and 24, and Art 3(5) of the Second Electricity IEM Directive (n 10), and Rec 2 and Art 3(3) of the Second Gas IEM Directive (n 10).

[113] Recs 37, 45, 50 and 53, Arts 3(7) and (8), and 36(h) of the Electricity Directive; and Recs 33, 47 and 50, and Arts 3(3) and (4), and 40(h) of the Gas Directive.

[114] For a definitional attempt in the biomedical ethics sphere, but drawing upon a much more general (and often legal) philosophical approach to the issue, see N Tavaglione and others, 'Fleshing Out Vulnerability' (2015) 29 *Bioethics* 98: '[o]ne can define vulnerable persons as those having a greater likelihood of being wronged—that is, of being denied adequate satisfaction of certain legitimate claims' (98), before going on to develop what might count as 'legitimate claims' (particularly interestingly in the contexts of 'social provision' (102–03) and 'communal belonging' (104–05)), while acknowledging the need for further thought concerning what amounts to 'special protection' and how to address problems of allocating resources and choosing between requirements when they cannot all be satisfied (106).

[115] C Jones (ed), *EU Energy Law—Volume I: The Internal Energy Market—The Third Liberalisation Package*, 3rd edn (Leuven, Claeys and Casteels, 2010) 417.

[116] In the UK, eg Ofgem has set up 'Guaranteed Standards of Performance', under which payments will be made to customers who face long power cuts during severe weather incidents: these led to significant payments to customers after the Christmas 2013 storms and inadequate response thereto from two southern distribution network operators—Ofgem, 'SSE and UKPN pay out £8 million following Christmas storms' (24 July 2014).

[117] eg it has emerged that Ofgem may use the proceeds from fines to benefit charities and funds for vulnerable customers: 'Ofgem penalises three energy firms a total of £4.6m' *Financial Times* (London, 12 December 2014) (concerning fines imposed for breach of environmental (not consumer) obligations).

[118] For some discussion, see Johnston and Block (n 6), paras 7.84–7.96.

[119] Second IEM Directives: Arts 3(5) of the Electricity Directive and 3(3) of the Gas Directive.

More generally, growing levels of detail have been provided in EU energy legislation concerning the position of consumers. Some of these are found in the main body of the Directives, while a wide range of others appear under the label 'measures on consumer protection' in Annex I of the Third Electricity and Gas IEM Directives, although in the same vein as section II (above) we must highlight that the wording of the remainder of that Annex refers mostly to 'customers' when expounding the various protections envisaged.[120] This is, perhaps, an unhelpful terminological elision, not least since Article 3 of each Directive refers to 'customer protection' in its title, and Articles 3(7) (Electricity) and 3(3) (Gas) specifically refer to the measures in Annex I as the minimum which must be implemented with regard to 'household customers'. These infelicities make the scope of some of these provisions in themselves more difficult to apply, and that is before one moves to ask how they might interact with other EU legislative measures specifically directed towards protecting the 'consumer', where that individual is identified as a term of art rather than what in the Third Package Directives sometimes seems little more than a stylistic choice.

Then, we must note that some of these ostensibly protective provisions also interact with others, in the interests of providing the customer with the requisite information to ensure the proper functioning of the competitive process, and avoiding that its operation might in fact operate in a manner exploitative of the consumer.[121] So, Member States must ensure that there is access to information concerning a consumer's consumption data (see Articles 3(5) (Electricity) and 3(6) (Gas)), allied with various provisions in Annex I concerning services, prices, tariffs and conditions (1(a)), the means of accessing information on various topics (including the switching procedure itself), and the fact that there may be no charge for changing supplier. As the Commission has noted, '[t]aken together, these new provisions … are designed to make it easier for consumers to understand their own consumption, to use this information either to compare it with offers from other energy suppliers, or to allow other suppliers to have access to their consumption data so as to provide them with a new offer of supply'.[122]

[120] The exceptions are to be found in paras 1(f) and (h), and 2 of Annex I to each of the Third IEM Directives (n 10): see Table 1 in the text for details of their substance.

[121] Note the link here to Directive 2006/32/EC of the European Parliament and of the Council of 5 April 2006 on energy end-use efficiency and energy services [2006] OJ L114/64, which requires that 'final customers' have made available to them a 'reasonable amount of information … in clear and understandable terms … in or with their bills [etc]', encompassing a wide range of issues (Art 13 *juncto* Recs 12 and 29). This may also be conceptualised more broadly as empowering consumer choice 'in which their active participation as an agent of change within the energy market is to be encouraged on the basis of efficiency and ecology' rather than simply as a coldly lowest-cost, economically rational actor (J Davies, *The European Consumer Citizen in Law and Policy* (Basingstoke, Palgrave Macmillan, 2011) 160, where Crouch is also cited on the citizenship concept of choice: 'if one is part of a universe defined by a certain citizenship, then one is entitled to participate in the choices which it makes available': C Crouch, 'Citizenship and Markets in Recent British Education Policy', in C Crouch and others (eds), *Citizenship, Markets and the State* (Oxford, Oxford University Press, 2001) 125)).

[122] Commission, Interpretative Note on Directive 2009/72/EC concerning Common Rules for the Internal Market in Electricity and Directive 2009/73/EC concerning Common Rules for the Internal Market in Natural Gas: Retail Markets, Staff Working Paper (22 January 2010) 5.

As for the other, important, elements of Annex I in the two current Directives, Table 1 summarises the relevant rights and obligations concerning consumer protection, to provide an overview of their substance and evolution from the Second to the Third Package legislation. Many of these relate to transparency and information provision requirements,[123] typically in response to consumer complaints about poor and sometimes obstructive practices by suppliers in the years following the Second IEM Package,[124] and overall 'high levels of consumer protection' are to be ensured (Articles 3(7) (Electricity) and 3(3) (Gas)).

These developments have taken place hand-in-hand with a growing enhancement of the role of the NRA in each Energy Package, in particular with regard to national retail markets and consumer protection measures. This is not the place to offer a detailed account of this evolution; suffice it here[125] to note that the key focus has been upon specifying more fully the objectives, duties and powers of the NRA to ensure that they can fulfil their enhanced role[126] with regard to the retail market under the Third Package IEM Directives of 'ensuring that customers benefit from the efficient functioning of their national market, of promoting effective competition, and of helping to ensure consumer protection'.[127]

c. Links to Specific EU Rules on Consumer Protection?

Annex I in each of the Third Package IEM Directives makes clear that its provisions are to operate 'without prejudice to the EU rules on consumer protection', so that the various rules on unfair terms, distance selling, doorstep selling, unfair commercial practices (etc) all continue to apply to energy consumers.

Yet there is some experience in the telecommunications sector in the UK that these did not adequately protect consumers against misselling. Ofcom took action by introducing various General Conditions on sales and marketing of fixed-line and mobile services, eventually leading to a general Code of Practice concerning domestic and SME customers on sales and marketing (May 2005). This, in turn, led in 2007 to mobile network operators adopting their own voluntary code on misselling, and eventually to the inclusion of provisions in the general conditions for both mobile (2009) and fixed-line (2010) services, providing a tougher regime.[128]

[123] Including a single point of contact through which customers can access such information: Arts 3(12) of the Electricity Directive and 3(9) of the Gas Directive.

[124] See Johnston and Block (n 6) 177.

[125] See, further, ibid, ch 5 and paras 7.112–7.117.

[126] See Arts 37(1)(j) of the Electricity Directive and 41(1)(j) of the Gas Directive concerning market opening, and competition at wholesale and retail levels, covering (inter alia): prices, prepayment systems, switching and disconnection rates, complaints, and distortions of competition, including bringing relevant cases to the competition authorities. Again, much of this provision relates directly to the customer/consumer as market participant and the NRA's function in developing that role.

[127] Arts 36(1)(g) of the Electricity and 40(1)(g) of the Gas Directive.

[128] Operators must not engage in dishonest, misleading, deceptive or aggressive conduct, or contact the customer in an inappropriate manner; staff must be trained and it must be ensured that agents also comply. See, generally, the discussion by Newman (n 37).

Table 1: 'Consumer Protection' measures in Annex I

Annex I provision	Details	Electricity 2003	Gas 2003	Electricity 2009	Gas 2009
Right to a contract specifying	— identity and address of supplier — services, quality, time for initial connection — types of maintenance service — means for getting information on tariffs and maintenance charges — duration, renewal and termination of services/contract, right of withdrawal — compensation and refund for poor service quality — method for initiating dispute settlement procedures	(a), 1st para	(a), 1st para	1(a), 1st para	1(a), 1st para
	— information reconsumer rights, including complaint handling, clearly communicated through billing or on website	—	—	1(a), 1st para, 8th indent	1(a), 1st para, 8th indent
Conditions	— fair — known well in advance — role of intermediaries	(a), 2nd para	(a), 2nd para	1(a), 2nd para	1(a), 2nd para
Adequate notice of	— intention to modify conditions — right of withdrawal — increase in charges	(b)	(b)	1(b)	1(b)
Ensure customers free to withdraw	— … if do not accept new conditions notified	(b)	(b)	1(b)	1(b)

(continued)

Table 1: *(Continued)*

Annex I provision	Details	Electricity 2003	Gas 2003	Electricity 2009	Gas 2009
Receive transparent information on	— applicable prices and tariffs — standard terms and conditions reaccess to and use of services	(c)	(c)	1(c)	1(c)
Offered a wide range of payment methods		(d)	(d)	1(d)	1(d)
	— which do not unduly discriminate between customers	—	—	1(d)	1(d)
	— prepayment systems fair and adequately reflective of likely consumption	—	—	1(d)	1(d)
Cost-reflective terms and conditions		(d)	(d)	1(d)	1(d)
General terms and conditions	— fair and transparent — clear and comprehensible language — protection against unfair or misleading selling methods	(d)	(d)	1(d)	1(d)
	— not including non-contractual barriers such as excessive contract documentation	—	—	1(d)	1(d)
No charge for changing supplier		(e)	(e)	1(e)	1(e)

(continued)

Table 1: *(Continued)*

Annex I provision	Details	Electricity 2003	Gas 2003	Electricity 2009	Gas 2009
Complaint handling procedures	— simple and inexpensive	(f)	(f)	1(f): **and** transparent out-of-court, preferably within 3 months	1(f): **and** transparent out-of-court, preferably within 3 months
	— enabling fair and prompt dispute settlement	—	—		
	— system for reimbursement or compensation	(f)	(f)	1(f)	1(f)
	— right to a good standard of service and complaint handling from service provider	—	—	1(f)	1(f)
Access to Universal Service in electricity	— must inform customers about their rights thereunder	(g)	—	1(g)	—
Rights to be supplied with gas	— of specified quality — at reasonable prices	—	(g)	—	1(g)
Consumption data at customer's disposal (see Articles 3(5)(b) (Electricity) and 3(6) (Gas)	— able to give access to metering data to any registered supply undertaking — Member States to define format for data, and procedure for access for customers and suppliers — no additional charges for this service	—	—	1(h)	1(h)
Properly and frequently informed of consumption and costs	— to enable to regulate own consumption — time-frame taking account of customer's metering equipment — due account of cost-efficiency of such measures — no additional charges for this service	—	—	1(i)	1(i)

(continued)

Table 1: *(Continued)*

Annex I provision	Details	Electricity 2003	Gas 2003	Electricity 2009	Gas 2009
Receive final closure account	— within 6 weeks of change of supplier	—	—	1(j)	1(j)
Implementation of intelligent metering systems	— enabling active participation of consumers in supply market			2	2
	— may be subject to economic assessment of costs and benefits, form of technology and time-frame				
	— Member States to prepare timetable for implementation			2, 3rd para: target of up to 10 years	2, 3rd para: no target mentioned
	— if assessment of smart meters positive, then target of at least 80% of consumers covered by 2020			2, 4th para	—
	— Member States or designated competent authority to ensure interoperability of metering systems within its territories (taking account of best practice and development of IEM)			2, 5th para	2, 4th para

In the UK energy sector, Ofgem has more recently been active in this area of misselling as well, imposing fines on various energy supply companies (for example Npower in December 2008[129] and SSE in April 2013).[130] As of mid-2013, 14 full-scale investigations had been conducted by Ofgem under various consumer law powers (doorstep selling, distance selling, and the licence condition requiring operators to have procedures in place to prevent misselling), leading to over £35m in fines and £6m in redress payments to consumers.

In this area, we now have two recent CJEU judgments on the interaction between the consumer protection provisions of the IEM Directives (there, the Second Package provisions) and the Unfair Terms in Consumer Contracts Directive 93/13/EEC: *RWE Vertrieb*[131] and *Schulz and Egbringhoff*.[132] These judgments have started to clarify the relationship between these provisions and the impact upon that relationship of national mandatory rules (evident in the analysis in both cases and applied on the facts in *Schulz*). In *RWE Vertrieb*, the Court first pointed out that, as found by the national courts, the relevant national mandatory rules laid down in the relevant national regulation (the AVBGasV,[133] which empowered a gas supplier unilaterally to vary gas prices without giving reasons for doing so) actually did not apply to the contracts in question. Rather, the terms and conditions incorporated into those contracts referred to the AVBGasV, but the regulation's material scope did not cover those special contracts but only applied to standard tariff contracts. As a result, Article 1(2) of the Unfair Terms in Consumer Contracts Directive 93/13/EEC[134] could not operate so as to allow the existence of national mandatory statutory or regulatory rules to exclude the application of that Directive to the present special contracts: the rationale for such exclusion is that, in passing such rules, 'it may legitimately be supposed that the national legislature struck a balance between all the rights and obligations of the parties to certain contracts'.[135] On the facts in *RWE Vertrieb*, that legislative balance did not extend to the intention of the parties to apply those rules to a contract beyond the scope of—here—the AVBGasV, especially when the legislature had specifically chosen not to include such special contracts thereunder.[136] Otherwise, it would

[129] Ofgem Press Release, 'Ofgem Fines Npower for Misselling of Energy' (22 December 2008) <https://www.ofgem.gov.uk/ofgem-publications/76436/221208ofgem38.pdf> accessed 10 April 2015 (with a fine of £1.8m imposed).

[130] Ofgem Press Release, 'Ofgem Fines SSE £10.5 Million for Misselling' (3 April 2013) <https://www.ofgem.gov.uk/ofgem-publications/76232/sse-press-release.pdf> accessed 10 April 2015. The £10.5m fine was the largest yet imposed by Ofgem for misselling.

[131] Case C–92/11 *RWE Vertrieb v Verbraucherzentrale Nordrhein-Westfalen*, judgment of 21 March 2013.

[132] Joined cases C–359/11 and C–400/11 *Schulz v Technische Werke Schussental* and *Egbringhoff v Stadtwerke Ahaus*, judgment of 23 October 2014.

[133] *Verordnung über Allgemeine Bedingungen für die Gasversorgung von Tarifkunden*, 21 June 1979, BGBl 1979 I, p 676.

[134] Unfair Terms in Consumer Contracts Directive (n 1).

[135] *RWE-Vertrieb* (n 131), para 28.

[136] ibid, paras 29 and 33.

be too straightforward for suppliers to circumvent the review of the unfairness of non-individually negotiated terms safeguarded by the Directive.[137] The Court then went on to offer guidance on how to assess whether such a term allowing price variation complied with the requirements of good faith, balance and transparency laid down in Articles 3 and 5 of the Unfair Terms Directive and Article 3(3) of the Second Gas IEM Directive 2003/55/EC, concluding that:

> it is of fundamental importance:
>
> — whether the contract sets out in transparent fashion the reason for and method of the variation of those charges, so that the consumer can foresee, on the basis of clear, intelligible criteria, the alterations that may be made to those charges. The lack of information on the point before the contract is concluded cannot, in principle, be compensated for by the mere fact that consumers will, during the performance of the contract, be informed in good time of a variation of the charges and of their right to terminate the contact if they do not wish to accept the variation; and
>
> — whether the right of termination conferred on the consumer can actually be exercised in the specific circumstances.[138]

From the facts set out in the judgment, it seemed tolerably clear that the terms in the special contracts involved would not meet these requirements, although of course the Court left it to the national court to apply these principles to the facts of the case. It was also notable that the Court used Article 3(3) and the relevant provisions of Annex A to the Second Gas IEM Directive to provide the energy supply context and further details with which the assessment under the Unfair Terms Directive should be conducted.[139] The Court expressly acknowledged the recognition by the EU legislature that there may be a legitimate interest in the supplier being able to alter the prices in charges for providing gas to consumers in such ongoing and indeterminate contractual relationships,[140] but confirmed that such a standard term was still subject to the consumer protection requirements laid down by both of those Directives.

Meanwhile, the relevant contracts in the *Schulz* case *were* subject to the AVBGasV: thus, consistently with the ruling in *RWE Vertrieb*, the Unfair Terms Directive could not assist Ms Schulz in her defence against her gas supplier's claim for payment of sums owing, which included the four times that the supplier had increased gas prices during the period from 1 January 2005 to 1 January 2007. Instead, she relied upon Article 3(3) of the Second Gas IEM Directive, in conjunction with its Annex A. In the parallel *Egbringhoff* case, the claimant sought reimbursement of the extra sums charged and which he had paid (without prejudice),

[137] ibid, para 30–31.
[138] ibid, para 55.
[139] ibid, paras 50–54.
[140] ibid, para 46, referring to the second sentence of point 2(b) and point (d) of the Annex to Unfair Terms in Consumer Contracts Directive (n 1) and from point (b) of Annex A to the Gas Directive.

with interest, after his supplier had increased electricity[141] and gas prices on several occasions. He relied upon that same provision, as well as Article 3(5) of the Second Electricity IEM Directive 2003/54/EC *juncto* its Annex A. In its judgment concerning the 'rights of customers',[142] the Court emphasised the need to ensure a high level of consumer protection with regard to the transparency of contract terms and conditions, and even emphasised that '[c]consumer protection concerns underpin the provisions of Directives 2003/54 and 2003/55 .... Those concerns are closely linked both to the liberalisation of the markets in question and to the objective, also pursued by those directives, of ensuring a stable electricity and gas supply'.[143] It then went on to hold that:

> 47. ... in order to be able to benefit fully and effectively from those rights and to take an informed decision as to whether to terminate the contract or to challenge the adjustment of the supply price, customers must be given adequate notice, before that adjustment takes effect, of the reasons and preconditions for the adjustment, and its scope.
>
> 48. Consequently, national legislation such as that at issue in the main proceedings, which does not ensure that, in those circumstances, the information referred in the preceding paragraph is communicated to a household customer with adequate notice does not meet the requirements set out in Directives 2003/54 and 2003/55.

This approach, and the inapplicability on these facts of the unfair terms Directive, underscore the important contribution of the development of consumer protection provisions *within* the framework of the second IEM Directives, which have been enhanced by the third IEM package Directives in 2009: even national mandatory rules may be subjected to a measure of scrutiny with regard to various customer rights. At the same time, it should be remembered that the full panoply of such consumer protection offered by the rest of the EU consumer law *acquis* will apply only insofar as it does not contain exceptions like those found in Article 1(2) of the Unfair Terms Directive. In this regard, the Consumer Rights Directive 2011/83/EU[144] expressly applies to contracts for the supply of gas and electricity (Article 3(1))—although where more specific requirements exist in the Third IEM Directives (concerning in particular information provision) then these take priority (Article 3(2)). And it seems clear that the Commission will continue to emphasise its potential significance for the energy sector, as well as aiming to develop further information provision initiatives and guidelines.[145]

[141] In which sector there existed the AVBEltV (*Verordnung über Allgemeine Bedingungen für die Elektrizitätsversorgung von Tarifkunden* (21 June 1979, BGBl 1979 I, 684)), which was replaced by the StromGVV (*Verordnung über Allgemeine Bedingungen für die Grundversorgung von Haushaltskunden und die Ersatzversorgung mit Elektrizität aus dem Niederspannungsnetz, Stromgrundversorgungsverordnung* (26 October 2006, BGBl 2006 I, 2391)), which together applied to Mr Egbringhoff's situation across the time period in question and fulfilled the same mandatory rules function as that performed by the AVBGasV in *Schulz*.

[142] NB, not 'consumers', in accordance with the wording of most of the provisions of each Annex A.

[143] *Schulz* and *Egbringhoff* (n 132) para 40.

[144] Consumer Rights Directive (n 1).

[145] See Commission, A European Consumer Agenda—Boosting Confidence and Growth COM(2012) 225 final, paras 4.3 and 4.4, where energy is emphasised as a key focus.

Also here, we should emphasise the acknowledgment by the CJEU in *Schulz* and *Egbringhoff* that, where mandatory national rules apply due to the need to provide for a supplier of last resort so as to ensure that a USO is respected (as was indeed the case on the facts of both of those cases):

> [a]s those suppliers of electricity and gas are required, in the framework of the obligations imposed by the national legislation, to enter into contracts with customers who request this and who are entitled to the conditions laid down in that legislation, *the economic interests of those suppliers must be taken into account in so far as they are unable to choose the other contracting party and cannot freely terminate the contract.*[146]

While this point does not receive any attention in the remainder of the judgment, it may yet prove of no little significance for suppliers faced in the future with arguments based upon the reasoning in *Schulz*: the willingness of the Court to accept the need to consider the supplier's economic interests here shows potential interactions with the approach taken to PSOs in the cases under Article 106(2) TFEU (and, indeed, *Altmark*) discussed above (sections III.B.i and III.B.ii). One could speculate whether the Court's reasoning in the *Alemo-Herron* judgment[147] concerning the inclusion of freedom to conduct a business—and its incorporation of the principle of freedom of contract—in Article 16 of the Charter of Fundamental Rights of the EU[148] might be used to bolster claims that such supplier interests be respected in a proportionate fashion. This might seem no less paradoxical an argument here in the consumer protection scenario than in the employee protection context of *Alemo-Herron* itself,[149] and typically the Court has shown a willingness to interpret EU consumer legislation to provide far-reaching protection for the consumer,[150] as well as a refusal to give much weight to the argument in consumer cases to date.[151] Still, the link to the need to ensure 'the performance, under economically acceptable conditions, of the tasks of general economic interest which [the Member State] has entrusted to an undertaking'[152] would be relevant in a

[146] *Schulz* and *Egbringhoff* (n 132), para 44 (emphasis added).

[147] Case C–426/11 *Alemo-Herron v Parkwood Leisure*, judgment of 18 July 2013, discussed (critically) by J Prassl, 'Freedom of Contract as a General Principle of EU Law? Transfer of Undertakings and the Protection of Employer Rights in EU Labour Law' (2013) 42 *Industrial Law Journal* 434.

[148] [2010] OJ C83/389.

[149] Eg in other recent cases, the Court has emphasised that 'the freedom to conduct a business is not absolute, but must be viewed in relation to its social function [and may] be subject to a broad range of interventions on the part of public authorities which may limit the exercise of economic activity in the public interest' (Case C–281/11 *Sky Österreich v Österreichischer Rundfunk*, judgment of 22 January 2013, paras 45–46. In *Alemo-Herron* (n 147), the distinction relied upon by the Court was that the UK measure adversely affected the 'core content' (*Sky Österreich*, para 49) or 'very essence' (*Alemo-Herron* (n 147), para 35) of that freedom, in a way that it had not found in the *Sky Österreich* case.

[150] eg H Unberath and A Johnston, 'The Double-headed Approach of the ECJ Concerning Consumer Protection' (2007) 44 *Common Market Law Review* 1237, esp 1252 ff and, generally, S Weatherill, *EU Consumer Law and Policy*, 2nd edn (Cheltenham, Edward Elgar, 2014); and N Reich and others, *European Consumer Law*, 2nd edn (Antwerp, Intersentia, 2014).

[151] See Case C–12/11 *Denise McDonagh v Ryanair Ltd*, judgment of 31 January 2013, paras 60–64, where the EU objective of ensuring a high level of protection for consumers was emphasised.

[152] Case C–157/94 *Commission v Kingdom of the Netherlands* (n 42), para 43: see the discussion in section III.B.ii, above.

situation such as that in *Schulz*, where the energy supplier concerned has been appointed as a supplier of last resort (as discussed above, both in this section and in section III.D.i.b).

ii. Yet there are still Shortcomings

In spite of this clear development over time towards greater concern for and attention to the position of what we might style 'genuine' consumers (see the discussion in section II, above) within the EU's energy legislation, various difficulties remain with the *acquis* as it stands. First, many such 'protections' are in reality concerned with creating and facilitating the competitive process (on the assumption that consumers will benefit therefrom), *rather* than real *protection* for consumers. (This also links to questions of energy *prices*, set by market forces or regulated in some way and for some categories of customer: see, below, section III.D.iv.)

Second, the adoption of secondary legislation can (and does, to an extent) add greater specification of what types of interest should/must be protected via PSOs, *but*, due to the overall goals of liberalisation, trade and competition in the EU energy sector being pursued by that legislation, it also *limits* the range of issues on which Member States are *allowed* to adopt PSOs: see Article 3(2) in both of the Third IEM Directives.[153] This operates to restrict some of the points made in the foregoing analysis (see section III.B.iii.a, above) concerning Member State freedom to define and adopt PSOs. Of course, for some this is less of a problem and more a welcome degree of guidance from EU level about which sorts of measures are allowed to be introduced by Member States, thus reducing the scope for unilateral national action to hinder trade and competition. For others, these developing EU law incursions into national regulatory autonomy on sensitive topics such as public service provision and the protection of weaker, vulnerable and/or remote consumers are: politically (democratically) less legitimate and responsive than national regulation; and rendered potentially less effective due to their framing by market liberalisation goals in the EU's energy legislative *acquis* (as discussed in section III.B above).

Third, the substantive detail of such matters in EU legislation can leave much to be desired, often as a result of the compromises necessary among Member States, and between Council and European Parliament, to secure passage of a given measure. In some cases, this serves to preserve a significant measure of Member State autonomy, while at the same time leaving a risk that national measures may not adequately address the consumer protection issues in a given area. This is exemplified by the failure to define at EU level what certain categories might include: for example the notion of 'vulnerable customer' in the Third IEM Directives is

[153] There is some debate about this: compare Suykens and Delvaux (n 97) with T Deruytter, W Geldhof and F Vandendriessche, 'Public Service Obligations in the Electricity and Gas Markets' in B Delvaux, M Hunt and K Talus (eds), *EU Energy Law and Policy Issues*, vol 3 (Antwerp, Intersentia, 2012) ch 3.

highlighted, but exactly who qualifies under this category is left to Member States to define. Once such customers have been identified by national law, the Third IEM Directives do at least provide a range of 'appropriate measures' that Member States might take, but the language of these provisions is more hortatory than prescriptive. In other cases, references in different EU legislative instruments across the energy field can be to similar categories, yet the usage may be inconsistent and potentially confusing when considered alongside each other. So, 'household customers' appear in Article 3(7) of the Third IEM Directives in reference to possible Member State 'consumer protection' measures as listed in Annex I (for a summary, see Table 1, above). They also appear as 'protected customers' in Article 1(1) of Regulation 994/2010/EU on Gas Supply Security, where Member States are allowed to add others[154] to that category: protected customers are then used by the Regulation in defining the 'supply standard' required of gas supply undertakings (Article 8 of the Regulation), which obliges gas supply undertakings to ensure gas supply in the face of particular serious events concerning extreme weather or the disruption of the single largest piece of gas infrastructure. Here, such customers are used as a yardstick for obligations imposed upon undertakings, with a view to protecting the continuity of gas supplies to households: while this may not confer rights upon household customers to such supplies (the point has never been tested before a court), it would seem to establish protection for that group of customers. Yet Article 8(4) of that Regulation provides that these supply standards may not impose an undue burden upon undertakings, and Article 8(6) requires that supplies to protected customers must not prejudice the functioning of the internal market and should be at a price which respects the market value of the supplies. Here, then, the notion of security of supply being safeguarded for household customers would not necessarily seem to include a notion of fair or reasonable prices (compare the discussion of the USO in electricity above).[155]

iii. Broader Questions Concerning the Interaction Between Various Different Pieces of EU Legislation and Policy, and their Implications for the Position of Customers/Consumers

Of course, these questions arise in sectors other than energy, as evinced (for example) by the work of Nihoul looking at the status and protection of consumers (mainly) within the telecoms/e-communications sector,[156] alongside the more UK-focussed work of Newman on telecommunications.[157] But coverage of these issues in the energy sector has been relatively limited to date, hence the reason to focus upon that sector here. As discussed above (in section III.D.i.c), one area

[154] Specifically, SMEs, essential social services and district heating installations: Art 2(1) of Regulation (EU) No 994/2010 (n 110).

[155] See the text at n 110 and ff.

[156] Nihoul (n 37); and see, further, Nihoul and Rodford (n 37), esp chs 4 and 5.

[157] Newman (n 37).

of uncertainty in EU energy law concerned the interaction between general EU consumer law and the sector-specific rules developed in each of the (to date) three IEM legislative packages. The *RWE Vertrieb* and *Schulz* cases have brought a measure of clarity on these questions, as outlined in the preceding section.

To put matters of interaction into the broader sectoral context, the final impact of various environmental and supply security policies has raised wide-ranging questions concerning energy supply. Various actors in the debate have questioned:

— the functioning of the energy market, and infrastructure investment and development (alleging collusion or at least structural problems leading to price co-ordination);
— energy regulatory (un)certainty and its impacts upon the raising of finance and making investment decisions; and/or
— subsidy levels offered to support various energy activities, and their implications for State finances, the competitiveness of domestic businesses and the concomitant increase in the cost of living for households (both specifically concerning energy prices and more broadly, given the contribution of energy costs as an input into most other goods and services in one way or another).

These phenomena can be observed in different ways and to different degrees of intensity across the EU,[158] and are open to various interpretations depending upon the particular national legal, political and economic contexts in which they have arisen.

In the present, consumer-related context, however, recent years have seen a sharpening focus upon subsidy levels and their *impact upon prices*, both for consumers/household customers *and* for business customers. These effects can be enhanced or exacerbated (depending upon your point of view) by *national-level choices* as to how to pursue EU and/or national environmental policy goals: for example, in general the price for an emissions allowance under the EU's Emissions Trading System sets the carbon price applicable to those installations which have obligations under the system,[159] but in the UK the view was taken that this led to

[158] To take but one example, both the UK and Spain sought retrospectively to change the rules applicable to certain subsidies for renewable energy generation: the former failed in the courts (*Secretary of State for Energy and Climate Change v Friends of the Earth* [2012] EWCA Civ 28) due to the interpretation of the relevant primary legislation as not having conferred such a power to make retrospective changes (ibid paras 41–52, *per* Moses LJ), but the latter succeeded in the face of judicial challenges (various judgments of the Supreme Court, most recently JUR2014/14099 (13 January 2014), and the Constitutional Court: SSTC 109/2014 (26 June 2014) and Case 96/2014 (12 June 2014)). The difference seems to lie in the fact that the UK scheme in question was relatively small-scale, and had a limit on the amount of funding made available by the Treasury, whereas the Spanish scheme was much broader and involved subsidies paid from the State budget, which raised very serious financial questions at a time of austerity in Spain in the wake of the financial crisis, spiralling government debt and costs of bond issues, etc. Thus, for the Spanish courts, the connection made to a situation of economic urgency justified the retrospective changes made to subsidy levels. I am grateful to Ms Irene Maria Ruiz Olmo for our discussions on these Spanish cases.

[159] Directive 2003/87/EC of the European Parliament and of the Council of 13 October 2003 establishing a scheme for greenhouse gas emission allowance trading within the Community [2003] OJ L275/32, as amended by Directive 2009/29/EC of the European Parliament and of the Council of

a carbon price which was both too low and too volatile to encourage low-carbon investments. As a result, the UK introduced a tax designed to create a carbon price floor, working in conjunction with the EU ETS:[160] yet fears that the price pressure that this added to customers' energy (particularly electricity) bills led to the freezing of that tax regime at 2014 levels (instead of escalating as planned) less than a year after it had entered into operation.[161] Similarly, subsidies offered to encourage more rapid deployment of renewable electricity generation installations may add to the prices ultimately paid by customers where they are set up so that costs are passed through from generators, via network companies at transmission and distribution level, to final customers (both business and consumer). The Court's judgment in the famous *PreussenElektra* case[162] facilitated this route for Member States—thanks to its conclusion that carefully designed national systems in which the state played no role in collecting, channelling or allocating the funds collected in order to subsidise renewables, and where the customer ultimately paid for that cost (so that the funds were provided neither by the state nor through state resources)—meaning that such subsidies did not amount to notifiable State aid under Article 107 TFEU.[163]

In response to criticisms about the price implications of such energy policy measures, debates have developed about whether price increases are solely or even mainly due to such policy decisions and support instruments, or whether other causes might be (more) important. Thus, there may be:

— technical difficulties in incorporating new technologies into an older grid system; or

23 April 2009 amending Directive 2003/87/EC so as to improve and extend the greenhouse gas emission allowance trading scheme of the Community [2009] OJ L140/63.

[160] For discussion, see A Johnston, 'United Kingdom Report' in J Laffranque (ed), *The Interface between the Energy, Environment and Competition Rules of the European Union*, 541–45.

[161] HM Revenue and Customs, 'Carbon price floor: reform and other technical amendments' (19 March 2014) <https://www.gov.uk/government/publications/carbon-price-floor-reform> accessed 10 April 2015: '[t]his measure caps the UK-only element of the CPF at £18 per tCO2 from 2016–17 until 2019–20 to support UK business competitiveness and helps to restrain increases in household energy bills, while still maintaining the incentive to invest in low-carbon generation'. For comment see, eg, M Hope, 'Budget 2014: Why freezing the carbon price floor is a symbolic blow to the UK's climate commitment' *The Carbon Brief* (18 March 2014) <http://www.carbonbrief.org/blog/2014/03/budget-2014,-why-shed-a-tear-the-unloved-carbon-price-floor> accessed 10 April 2015.

[162] Case C–379/98 *PreussenElektra AG v Schleswag AG* [2001] ECR I–2099; the Court also refused to hold that the national purchasing obligation plus feed-in tariff amounted to an unjustifiable restriction upon the free movement of goods under Art 34 TFEU, and recent judgments (while engaging in more detailed assessment of the reasons why, and conditions under which, this would be justifiable) have not changed its approach on the free movement aspect of the question either: Case C–573/12 *Ålands vindkraft AB v Energimyndigheten*, judgment of 1 July 2014 and Joined cases C–204 to 208/12 *Essent Belgium NV v Vlaamse Reguleringsinstantie voor de Elektriciteits- en Gasmarkt*, judgment of 11 September 2014.

[163] For analysis, see Johnston and Block (n 6) 12.173–12.178, augmented by coverage of more recent cases in A Johnston, 'The Impact of the New EU Commission Guidelines on State Aid for Environmental Protection and Energy on the Promotion of Renewable Energies' in T Sveen (ed), *EU Renewable Energy Law: Legal Challenges and New Perspectives* (Oslo, Marlus 446, 2014) 23–31.

— rising wholesale prices of inputs (natural gas) or when wholesale prices on the spot markets appear to be falling then those companies which have entered into longer-term contracts to ensure gas supplies may see delays before sufficient proportions of their supplies benefit from such price drops, so as allow energy prices to customers to be reduced; or
— issues created by national market design (for example in the UK, gas-fired electricity generation tends to set the market price, which can both overcompensate some generators where gas prices and electricity demand are high, but also under-compensate where gas prices are low); or
— anti-competitive or market-manipulative behaviour on the part of energy supply companies. There have been various allegations of this in the UK, which have led to investigations,[164] and in 2014 a reference for investigation of the supply and acquisition of energy in Great Britain to the new Competition and Markets Authority,[165] in the wake of criticisms that have gone as far as to call for structural remedies to break up the big energy supply companies.

It should be noted that pressure to investigate the energy supply system more broadly in the UK is coming from consumers/households and representative groups, regulators[166] and political parties[167] (particularly as electioneering has ground into high(er) gear from late 2013 onwards),[168] but also from businesses complaining about energy input costs harming their competitiveness within Europe and indeed the wider world economy. It is clear that business pressure to improve competitiveness of domestic goods and services was a key driver behind the freezing of the UK's carbon tax in March 2014, for example. Thus, even here, while elements influencing political and regulatory responses to the functioning

[164] eg Ofgem, 'Addressing Market Power Concerns in the Electricity Wholesale Sector—Initial Policy Proposals' (Ref 30/09, 30 March 2009), after Ofgem had abandoned a Competition Act investigation into SSE and Scottish Power practices (on 19 January 2009); and Office of Fair Trading, 'Off-Grid Energy—Decision not to make a market investigation reference to the Competition Commission' (1401, 21 December 2011), concerning domestic heating oil.

[165] CMA, 'Energy market investigation' (Opened, 26 June 2014; case page: <https://www.gov.uk/cma-cases/energy-market-investigation> accessed 10 April 2015); a final report is currently expected in November or December 2015.

[166] eg Austria's E-Control criticising high energy retail margins in the household sector: see NERA, 'Global Energy Regulation' Issue 187 (December 2014) 3.

[167] Perhaps as a reflection of public criticisms of government for failings which government would ascribe to undertakings in the privatised, liberalised energy sector, reflecting a perception of being held accountable for behaviour which has been shifted from the State's control to that of market forces and associated (but independent) regulators (in competition law and various sectors, such as energy). For use of this disconnect to oppose privatisation in general, see A Dorfman and A Harel, 'Against Privatization as Such' (29 January 2015) <http://papers.ssrn.com/sol3/papers.cfm?bstract_id=2557409> accessed 10 April 2015.

[168] eg: 'Labour would freeze energy prices until 2017, says Ed Miliband' *The Guardian* (London, 24 September 2013); 'Politicians lost in energy wilderness' *The Times* (London, 17 October 2013); the debate on energy price freezes held at the Labour Party conference in September 2014 (see <https://www.youtube.com/watch?v=qGayT970Zz8> accessed 10 April 2015); and the comments of D Helm, 'Electricity and Energy Prices' Energy Futures Network (13 February 2014) <http://www.dieterhelm.co.uk/node/1374> accessed 10 April 2015.

and development of the energy supply system are often clearly focussed upon the need to protect the position of consumers, many of the key decisions seem only to be taken once pressure has been brought to bear by businesses: benefits may then flow through to the consumer in the form of lower prices (or at least more modest price increases) of both energy and other goods and services.

This focus on energy prices sets up a short case study of energy retail price regulation as an example of the tensions in using PSOs to justify national 'protective' measures, complicated by the presence of now quite extensive secondary legislation.

iv. Energy Retail Price Regulation and EU Law

This is not the place for a detailed analysis of the legal requirements for, and restrictions upon, energy retail price regulation by the state under EU law.[169] In brief summary, such price regulation may take various forms: most commonly, it consists of state approval of prices and/or the imposition of price caps upon energy supplies at the retail stage. The most common feature of retail price regulation is that prices are set at levels equal to or *below* competitive market prices, with the goal of ensuring that eligible customers are provided with energy at a 'reasonable' price. Within retail price regulation, one can distinguish between:

— 'general' or 'blanket' price regulation, where all customers within a defined group (households, SMEs) receive regulated prices (usually with a possibility to opt out and seek a better deal on the market, although given the price levels set, this is rarely an attractive option); and
— 'targeted' price regulation, which is focussed on specific, narrowly defined categories of customers: for example the vulnerable, the elderly, and/or those in receipt of social assistance.

Such energy retail price regulation can have various distortive effects. It has various impacts upon market functioning and competition in general (for example where price components are set too low and the proportion of customers covered is too large that competition is restrained), as well as resulting effects upon investment and new market entry: such entry or investment may be discouraged, delayed and/or misdirected. These effects can be felt at the level of network infrastructure (for example delaying or mis-planning grid reinforcement, new interconnections, and the development of smart grids) and at other levels (for example discouraging or delaying the construction of new generation capacity,[170] or the development and

[169] Ongoing joint work involving the present author is nearing completion, upon which the summary here is based. For a useful and succinct summary of price regulation in public utilities more generally, see A Heimler, 'Antitrust Enforcement and Regulation: Different Standards but Incentive Coherent?' in TK Cheng and others (eds), *Competition and the State* (Stanford, Stanford University Press, 2014) ch 6, esp 110–12 (and the references cited therein).

[170] Which may also endanger supply security if (eg) adequate electricity generation capacity is not maintained.

deployment of smart metering). Also, retail price regulation may damage consumer interests in the longer term,[171] when contrasted with the often painfully short-term focus of political accountability and processes.

As far as EU law is concerned, it is clear that the underlying assumption of the EU's internal energy market regime is that market forces and competition will deliver 'reasonable prices', even though there are no explicit provisions on retail price regulation in the *acquis* (by contrast with, for example, detailed rules concerning network access (pricing, terms and conditions, the role of NRAs, etc)). In the judgments in the *Federutility*[172] and *ENEL produzione*[173] cases, the Court relied upon the structure and logic, purpose and scheme of the EU's IEM Directives (there, from the Second Package)[174] to conclude that they required that retail energy supply prices must be set by supply and demand, through the mechanisms of eligible customers having a choice of supplier, and suppliers with the right to deliver across networks to their customers.[175]

One might pause for a moment here, and consider how one might conceive of the 'reasonableness' of prices in this context. Price-setting by the operation of market forces could be seen as 'fair' (in an 'input legitimacy' or procedural sense), although this depends upon confidence in the well functioning of the market in any system: as noted above, in the UK doubts have been expressed about this recently, with wide-ranging potential consequences. Yet even with a functional market, such prices may still be viewed as 'unreasonable' (in an 'output legitimacy' / substantive sense), if one were to focus upon absolute cost levels (especially as a proportion of household disposable income): this assessment is likely to be exacerbated by the ongoing difficult economic situation in many EU Member States.

In any event, the approach in *Federutility* thus leaves state retail price regulation as an exception to the basic rule, and thus in need of proper justification by any Member State intending to impose such regulation. This is because of the damage that price regulation can cause in otherwise competitive markets: in particular, artificially low regulated prices will discourage supplier switching by customers,[176] affecting new market entry incentives and ossifying market conditions to the detriment of new entrants. Thus, while it is acknowledged that high market

[171] Raising problems about the difficulty of comparison with the unprovable, counterfactual 'what might have been' scenario, had there been no competition and market opening.

[172] *Federutility* (n 26).

[173] Case C–242/10 *ENEL produzione v Autorità per l'energia elettrica e il gas* [2011] ECR I–13665.

[174] But it is clear that, with the various enhancements concerning unbundling, third party access and NRAs, the Court's analysis seems all the more apposite under the Third Package IEM Directives (n 10).

[175] This is bolstered by Art 3(1) of the Third Package IEM Directives (n 10), requiring Member States to implement the Directives' provisions with a view to achieving 'a competitive, secure and environmentally sustainable market'.

[176] As state-set prices will be lower than those available on the open market; this shows the likely conflict between retail price regulation and the strong focus—especially in the Third Package (n 10)—of the EU energy *acquis* on facilitating and encouraging customers in switching supplier, as discussed in section III.D.i.a of this chapter.

concentration may translate into excessive end-user prices, justifying a measure of price regulation, there is also a danger that price regulation can create or cement such market concentration. The legislative framework does recognise that there is a need for adequate protection for energy customers: as discussed above (section III.D.i.b), Article 3 of the Third IEM Electricity and Gas Directives clearly covers the imposition of PSOs upon energy undertakings, which may include the 'price of supplies'. Member States must respect the Treaty (especially Article 106 TFEU) when doing so. The exceptional status of such price regulation is confirmed by wording of the provisions in the Third Electricity IEM Directive making such regulation possible: Article 3(3) emphasises that Member State PSOs must not impede market opening; and Article 3(2) makes clear that PSOs must guarantee equal access for EU-based electricity undertakings to national customers.

With regard to such justifications under EU law, the case law (the *Federutility* and *ENEL produzione* cases) to date has focussed upon the issues of necessity and proportionality. It is, first, for the Member State to show the *need* to impose PSOs (under Article 106(2) TFEU) to ensure retail prices remained at a reasonable level.[177] Then, to establish the proportionality of such national rules and their effect upon the competitive market:

— the *duration* of PSOs must be limited to that necessary to achieve the objective. The Court emphasised that one way of showing this would be for the national law to require periodic reassessment by the NRA or government of the ongoing need for such intervention via price regulation. The inclusion of a 'sunset clause' which would end the operation of such price regulation might be a suitable device in this regard, particularly in conjunction with periodic reviews and the possibility of ending such price regulation earlier than originally provided for by the national rules;[178]
— the *scope* of coverage of such PSOs must also be justified clearly, both *ratione personae* and *ratione materiae*. For example, can the Member State justify price regulation which would set the same prices for households as large industrial customers?[179] Presumptively, this may be a real challenge to justify.[180] *Ratione materiae*, the key issue will be whether the method of intervention chosen actually addresses the cause(s) of the problem(s) identified. In particular, the Member State regulatory measure should be limited to the price component 'directly influenced upwards by those specific circumstances' falling within the measure's objectives.[181]

[177] *Federutility* (n 26), para 32.

[178] See Suykens and Delvaux (n 97) 236–38.

[179] *Regulated electricity tariffs in France—extension of the procedure* (State Aid Case 17/07) Commission Decision 2009/C 96/08 [2009] OJ C96/18.

[180] See Commission, 'Energy infringements, Country Fact Sheets—Portugal' cited in Suykens and Delvaux (n 97) 231.

[181] *ENEL Produzione* (n 173), para 48.

What are the implications of this brief analysis for the justifiability of energy retail price regulation? First, the conditions laid down by the Court point towards the need to restrict national measures in this area to targeted, and not across-the-board, price regulation. Second, these judgments suggest that there are concerns about using price regulation for the 'protection' of large and medium-sized companies: it would surely be better to reform markets. Such businesses find it much easier to participate strongly in markets and there is an express reference to 'households' and SMEs in Article 3(3) of the Third IEM Electricity Directive, which provides the foundation for such PSOs. Third, even some household and/or consumer-focussed regulation might prove problematic, if it could be shown that less onerous and more precisely targeted measures were available: for example, such interests might be better protected through the taxation and/or social welfare systems.[182] This is all dependent upon the flexibility or intrusiveness of the approach adopted under the proportionality test at EU level and in possible national court cases. As was highlighted in section III.B above, one can compare the more permissive standards applied in the *Energy Import/Export cases* with the stricter line taken in (inter alia) the *Dusseldorp* case. After legislative developments in the energy sector, the strength of the focus on market opening, competition and customer choice creates a strong presumption against such state regulation, as evinced in the reasoning in *Federutility* and *ENEL Produzione*.[183] All of this shows that certain consumer protection concerns *may* be accommodated by the EU's energy *acquis* in the form of state interventions to regulate retail prices, but also that the design of such national measures must be carefully focussed and limited if they are to be proportionate in their effects; it also indicates that Member States have often tended to seek to maintain broader price regulation schemes covering a wider range of customers than might be justifiable, and that the Commission is alive to these practices and views them with no little suspicion.

IV. Conclusions: Uncovering the 'Image of the Consumer' in Liberalising Sectors

After these often difficult points of detail from legislation and case law alike, what is the 'image of the consumer' which we are beginning to uncover in areas involving services of general economic interest, in particular in the energy sector? Where

[182] It should be noted that this reliance upon alternative protective mechanisms may be criticised where such systems are not well developed or organised at national level: where, eg, there is very widespread electrification in a country, while tax systems face fraud and corruption and social welfare rules are at best nascent, then the broad coverage of the electricity supply system may be a better way of reaching those who are vulnerable to high electricity retail prices: I am grateful to participants in the conference where this paper was first presented for raising this point.

[183] Although it should be noted that, on the facts, the Court held in *ENEL Produzione* (n 173) that the relevant legislation did not preclude the relevant Italian measures (para 89).

the consumer is referred to directly (on which see sections II and III above), they regularly appear in legislation, competition and free movement case law as the 'trickle-down' beneficiary of the proper working of markets, competition and trade, and at times little more than that. A number of so-called 'consumer protection' measures discussed above are really more about market building, monitoring and facilitation (via NRA duties and powers, etc), rather than involving any real attempt to address the disadvantageous position of the consumer in the ways to which we have become accustomed in the EU's broader consumer law *acquis*.

Or is this evaluation too harsh? A careful examination of the material discussed above would—it is submitted—suggest that EU law in this area (in conjunction with national practice under that framework) is slowly evolving to provide a more nuanced picture of the consumer as an (economic) actor who needs information, clarity and mechanisms to facilitate market participation, while still needing protection of their more vulnerable characteristics and sub-groups.[184] Thus, EU legislation has: obliged Member States to ensure that universal service is provided in the electricity sector; required Member States to offer protection for vulnerable customers; maintained the application of 'ordinary' EU consumer law in such sectors; and provided the framework within which such protection can be expanded at national level in codes of practice and formal licence conditions. At the same time, EU law has highlighted the need for careful and ongoing regulatory scrutiny and enforcement, both of the market-actor-facilitating measures and of those aimed at protecting the consumer against misselling and other unsavoury practices which may be employed by energy suppliers in an attempt to sign up more customers. The national- and EU-level measures and actions discussed in sections III.D.i.b and III.D.i.c, above, illustrate growing and often significant contributions in these areas.

At the same time, there is also evidence that (some) Member States (sometimes) may seek to use the (perceived and genuine) woes of the consumer to justify broader state interventions, pursuing policy goals extending to SMEs and even large businesses as energy customers. This emerges most clearly from the energy retail price regulation example discussed above (section III.D.iv), from which it becomes clear that there may be difficult, broader questions to answer about the energy market liberalisation process in general. The Court's case law and the Commission's practice would suggest that there is a pressing need for Member States to refocus carefully upon categories of consumers to be protected and the goals which their national measures seek to achieve. Yet broader reactions by commentators, regulators and politicians might indicate that such Member State price regulation is symptomatic of a wider loss of trust in competition and markets to

[184] Davies (n 121) esp ch 5, would, one feels, go further, and suggest that the myriad of information provision, dispute settlement and consultative or representative fora being developed in the sector show a relatively developed (if clearly still developing—eg environmental awareness and contributions are, for him, still nascent) picture of the 'European Consumer Citizen', focussed on access and choice rights, as well as duties and obligations as market actors (ibid, chs 1–4).

deliver such sensitive 'essential services'. And the cynic might suspect that such arguments involve thinly disguising a desire to regain political control over subjects capable of generating significant criticism of the national government and/or parliament. This last point links back to the implications of price regulation for NRA independence, which is required under the Third IEM Directives: the theory is that such independence puts the NRA in a position to avoid political fads, whims and short-termism, aiming to exercise its functions in the interests of liberalisation, trade and competition, while also protecting the consumer. Yet a political desire to be seen to champion the interests of the consumer—particularly in times of economic recession or stagnation, budget cuts and austerity—may run the risk of undermining the functioning of these crucial systems in the future, whether such politics reflect genuine consumer concerns or unfulfillable promises made in the search for votes as elections loom.

5

Vulnerable Consumers in EU Law

NORBERT REICH

I. The Concept of Vulnerability

A. Who is a 'Vulnerable Consumer'?

The concept of 'vulnerable consumer' has entered EU law. But who is a 'vulnerable consumer'? Vulnerability is a notion which raises sympathy but lacks precision. No one wants to hurt the vulnerable. But how should this sentiment be translated into rules which determine the position of the vulnerable on the market? Should the vulnerable be protected from standard market practices or should they rely exclusively on social support?

In order to get closer to defining this rather new and still imprecise concept, we should look at instances of legal regulation where some aspect of vulnerability plays a role. This very first overview must necessarily be a superficial and limited one. It will only relate to persons in their position as consumers, and not as 'workers' or self-employed persons. The overview will be limited to so-called 'horizontal' relations, namely contract relations. It will not be concerned with 'vertical' relations between an individual and the state, the Union, or some other public law body, such as social security agencies. The overview will refer to a few examples from Member State contract laws that have developed detailed concepts and instruments aimed at protecting minors, adult persons with physical or intellectual deficiencies and, more recently, older people with Alzheimer's, all of whom are considered to need help against unfair contracting and other unfair trading practices. Much more controversial has been the position of poor citizens, particularly in the context of financial services and services of general economic interest, who may be excluded from certain services altogether because the market seems to follow the logic 'The Poor Pay More', as the famous study of the American sociologist David Caplovitz of 1967 has shown.[1]

[1] D Caplovitz, *The Poor Pay More* (New York, Free Press, 1967); even though most of the data are outdated, the social and intellectual insight of the study is still valuable today. For a more recent study on Australia, see T Wilson and others, 'Protecting the Most Vulnerable in Consumer Credit Transactions' (2009) 32 *Journal of Consumer Policy* 117.

The manner of dealing with the issue of vulnerability obviously differs among jurisdictions. It is recognised to pose particular problems in the area of the internet, where the contracting parties do not know (or do not want to know) each other. The constitutional value of protecting citizens against exploitation due to the situation of infirmity may easily conflict with liberal ideas on freedom of contract and party autonomy. Articles 21 and 23 of the Charter on non-discrimination may entail requirements incompatible with Articles 16 and 17 guaranteeing market freedoms. When rules on the limits of contractual freedom resulting from the person's (usually the consumer's) personal circumstances are developed, it is also necessary to keep in mind the situation of third parties.

Community law first became concerned with the issue of 'vulnerable consumers' (the term was not used at the time) in the *Buet* judgment of 1989.[2] The case concerned the proportionality of a French prohibition on canvassing of educational material vis-à-vis the Treaty provisions on free movement of goods. Normally, the right of withdrawal would be considered sufficient protection of consumers. The French legislator saw the issue somewhat differently and the Court of Justice (CJEU) agreed with that perspective:

> It is necessary … to point out that there is greater risk of an ill-considered purchase when the canvassing is for enrolment for a course of instruction or the sale of educational material. The potential purchaser often belongs to a category of people who, for one reason or another, are behind with their education and are seeking to catch up. That makes them particularly vulnerable when faced with salesmen of educational material who attempt to persuade them that if they use that material they will have better employment prospects. Moreover, as is apparent from the documents, it is as a result of numerous complaints caused by such abuses, such as the sale of out-of-date courses, that the legislature enacted the ban on canvassing at issue.[3]

French law contains a special provision on *abus de faiblesse* in Articles L-122-8–L-122-10 Code de la consummation, the predecessor of which was before the Court in *Buet*. It goes back to legislation from 1972, which was amended several times. The definition of *faiblesse* is linked to certain types of transaction, in particular:

— visites à domicile;
— démarchage par téléphone ou télécopie;
— sollicitations personalisées;
— réunions ou excursions organisées;
— transaction faite dans des lieux non destinés à la commercialisation;
— transaction conclues dans une situation d'urgence.

An *abus de faiblesse* by a professional is punishable; the contract is *nul et de nul effet* (Article L-122-8, paragraph 5). *Faiblesse* is defined as '*circonstances … que cette personne n'était pas en mesure d'apprécier la portée des engagements qu'elle prenait*

[2] Case 382/87 *R Buet and Educational Business Services (EBS) v Ministère public* [1989] ECR 1235.
[3] ibid, para 13.

ou de déceler les ruses et artifices déployés pour la convaincre à y souscrire, ou font apparaître qu'elle a été soumise à une contrainte'. The professional is presumed to have been aware of the *faiblesse* or the *ignorance* of the consumer. Yet the provisions have been criticised as incorrectly worded and seem not to play an important role in practice.[4] The question of their relation to the provisions on commercial practices and direct consumer sale, fully harmonised by Directive 2005/29 and Directive 2011/83 respectively, has not been addressed by the French legislator in the preparation of the new edition of the Code de la consommation of 2014. Calais-Auloy and Temple do not see any problem with the full harmonising effect of Directive 2005/29.[5] Whether the Directive does indeed have such an effect is doubtful. It is also not certain whether the outcome in *Buet* would still be the same today given the current state of EU law after the adoption of Directive 2011/83 with its full harmonisation approach to 'off-premises' contracting.

As far as EU law is concerned, it has entered the complex field of regulation for consumer vulnerability only recently. As a general principle, definitions of vulnerability are left to Member States. EU legislation respects national definitions even if divergences among them lead to market segregation. In this respect the logic of *Buet* is followed. The Draft Regulation of a Common European Sales Law ('CESL'), in the abbreviated version adopted by the EP, that is, limited to e-commerce, contained a host of mandatory consumer provisions. Despite that, the Draft Regulation deliberately left out the question of consumer vulnerability. The Draft Common Frame of Reference ('DCFR'), on the other hand, had some specific rules on liability of children and supervised persons in Articles VI.-3:103–104.

It may come as a surprise that despite the complex and value-laden nature of the issue, EU civil law in recent times, perhaps somewhat haphazardly, has engaged with the issue of consumer vulnerability. The debate is still nascent and clear concepts, rules, remedies or procedures have not yet emerged. What in my view can be observed is that consumers, as private persons, may suffer from three different kinds of 'vulnerability'. Each of these types raises the question of an adequate legal response in the event of its exploitation by the market. The three types of vulnerability are:

— physical disability;
— intellectual disability; and
— economic disability.

Furthermore, in my opinion, 'consumer vulnerability' needs to be distinguished from 'consumer weakness' in a contractual situation, which is fairly typical in the context of transactions between professional and consumers.[6]

[4] J Calais-Auloy and H Temple, *Droit de la Consommation* 8th edn (Paris, Dalloz, 2010) paras 132–38.
[5] ibid, paras 132–37.
[6] N Reich, *General Principles of EU Civil Law* (Cambridge, Intersentia, 2014) paras 2.5 and 2.11.

B. The 'Physically Disabled' Consumer

The physically disabled person has entered EU law mostly via anti-discrimination provisions regulating labour relations. Article 21 of the Charter lays down a broad prohibition on discrimination on the grounds of, among others, disability. The Framework Directive 2000/78 provides what remedies have to be available to victims of disability discrimination in employment relations. Disability was the subject-matter of the Court's judgment in *Navas*[7] where the Court held, rather controversially, that 'a person who has been dismissed by his employer solely on account of sickness does not fall within the general framework laid down for combating discrimination on grounds of disability by Directive 2000/78'. On 2 July 2008 the Commission proposed to extend the principle of equal treatment between persons irrespective inter alia of disability to civil law relations outside the labour market, in particular to consumer markets concerning 'goods and services available to the public, including housing'. The proposal has been met with strong resistance from Member States and was not adopted by the outgoing European Parliament.[8] It is doubtful that the Directive will be adopted by the new Parliament because it requires unanimity in the Council, as laid down in Article 19(1) TFEU.

Because Directive 2000/78 is a minimum harmonisation measure Member States remain competent to introduce legislation protecting the disabled also outside employment relationships. Many countries have exercised this possibility. Sections 19 and 20 of the German 'Allgemeine Gleichbehandlungsgesetz' ('AGG') extend the principle of non-discrimination to civil law relations of a 'mass' character (*Massengeschäfte*) and to insurance contracts. An example of behaviour violating German law would be a refusal to offer disabled persons hotel accommodation or access to a restaurant. Such conduct is regarded as unjustified discrimination and is prohibited because hotel and restaurant services are usually offered to the broad public and not on the basis of individual characteristics.[9]

C. The 'Intellectually Disabled' Consumer

A recent paper by Lynden Griggs, an Australian scholar, discusses the concept of 'intellectual disability' and the responses of her common law jurisdiction to the

[7] Case C–13/05 *Sonia Chacón Navas v Eurest Colectividades SA* [2006] ECR I–6467; for criticism, see E Howard, 'EU Equality Law: Three Recent Developments' (2011) 17 *European Law Journal* 785, referring to the UN Convention on the Rights of Persons with Disabilities which includes persons with chronic diseases.

[8] Commission, Implementing the Principle of Equal Treatment Between Persons Irrespective of Religion or Belief, Disability, Age or Sexual Orientation COM(2008) 426 final; for discussion, see AS Vandenberghe, 'Proposal for a new Directive on Non-discrimination' [2011] *Zeitschrift für Europäisches Privatrecht* 235.

[9] For details, see S Bittner in U Rust and J Falke (eds), *AGG Allgemeines Gleichbehandlungsgesetz: Allgemeines Gleichbehandlungsgesetz. Mit weiterführenden Vorschriften. Kommentar* (Berlin, Erich Schmidt-Verlag, 2007) s 19, para 12.

question of protecting those who are at risk of this kind of vulnerability.[10] Aware of the difficulties of defining the concept of 'intellectual disability', she reviews the extensive discussion of appropriate legal responses unfolding in her jurisdiction. On the basis of studies in social psychology, Griggs regards as intellectually disabled those persons who have limited rights and resources to exercise the range of choices possible in a given consumer market.[11] She observes that Australian courts vacillate between protecting intellectually disabled consumers and taking account of the limited awareness of the professional contract partner. Against this background, Griggs develops a principle of 'transactional responsibility', which does not require the proof of knowledge of disability on the part of the professional contract partner. Instead, what makes the professional party liable is 'transactional neglect'. According to Griggs,

> [w]hat we need is a subtle move towards transactional responsibility, or to establish liability, transactional neglect. The hard law of the common law should also be complemented by something akin to representation agreements as has occurred in Canada, with this acknowledging the need for a person-centred approach to assist the individual with an intellectual disability.[12]

This is certainly an interesting concept, the discussion of which will be taken up later.

I am not aware of any similar studies originating in EU countries. The comprehensive study of Schiek and others goes into great detail of the different aspects of non-discrimination law in the EU,[13] but the discussion does not include consumer transactions. Member States have very different approaches to regulating for intellectual disability of consumers.

D. The 'Economically Marginalised Consumer'—'The Poor Pay More'

'Vulnerability' may also stem from the difficult economic situation of the consumer. This may be the result of unemployment, illness, separation from one's

[10] L Griggs, 'The Consumer with an Intellectual Disability—Do We Respond, if so, How?' (2013) 21 *Competition and Consumer Law Journal* 146.

[11] ibid 149, 163 with reference to a study by A McClimens and M Hyde, 'Intellectual Disability, Consumerism, and Identity: To Have and to Have Not' (2012) 16 *International Journal of Intellectual Disabilities* 135, 137 and 141.

[12] Griggs (n 10) 163. This should be compared with the concept of *culpa in contrahendo* present in some continental jurisdictions. However, while *culpa in contrahendo* is focused on contracting, Griggs seems to be more concerned with advertising, which makes her observations more relevant in the European context for Art 5(3) of Directive 2005/29/EC of the European Parliament and of the Council of 11 May 2005 concerning unfair business-to-consumer commercial practices in the internal market [2005] OJ L149/22. In German law, in particular after the BGB reform of 2002, *culpa in contrahendo* is specially regulated in s 241(2) BGB (*Pflicht zur Rücksichtnahme*) and it can give rise to a claim on damages according to s 280(1) BGB.

[13] D Schiek and others (eds), *Non-discrimination Law* (Oxford, Hart Publishing, 2007).

partners, unforeseen life circumstances or even an extended lifestyle leading to over-indebtedness. The unresolved question is whether economic vulnerability is exclusively a problem of social law or also of civil law. Caplovitz, in an empirical study conducted 45 years ago, concluded that people who are already 'poor' will have only the following two options before them: to forgo major purchases or to allow themselves to be exploited.[14] Has anything changed since 1967? Economics tells us that the poor's predicament is the result of market efficiencies by which a risk premium is charged to those who are more likely to not be able to pay their debts. Some of these debts arise from receiving services of general economic interest, such as energy, communication or housing. Because access to financial services market is often dependent on paying a risk premium, calculated specifically for a particular consumer, reliance on financial products to gain access to services of general economic interest makes those services even more expensive to poorer consumers, whose creditworthiness is likely to be lesser than those of richer consumers.

An example of such a pattern is the situation on the UK payment services market, which gave rise to the bank charges case, decided in 2009 by the UK Supreme Court.[15] The case concerned the concept of 'core terms' in Article 4(2) of Directive 93/13.[16] UK banks debited to consumers 'not in credit' a range of charges, such as 'overdraft excess charges', 'guaranteed paid item charges', 'unpaid item charges', and 'paid item charges'. These charges made up about 30 per cent of the banks' revenue from payment services. In some respects clients 'not in credit', more likely those who were less affluent, heavily subsidised those 'in credit', that is those who were better off and did not have to pay these charges. In contrast to the High Court and the Court of Appeal, the UK Supreme Court did not object to this practice. Lord Walker said in his speech that '[t]he services that banks offer to their current account customers are a comparable package of services'.[17] As a result, the excessive charges for debit accounts, which typically hit poor consumers who often had

[14] Caplovitz (n 1) 180. Of course the economy has changed since the time when Caplovitz conducted his empirical studies—but have the options available to the poor changed as well?

[15] *Office of Fair Trading v Abbey National plc & Others* [2009] UKSC 6, [2010] 1 AC 696 (on appeal from [2009] EWCA Civ 116), critical comments by S Whittaker, 'Unfair Contract Terms, Unfair Prices and Bank Charges' (2011) *Modern Law Review* 106; M Kenny, 'Orchestrating Consumer Protection in Retail Banking: Abbey National in the Context of Europeanized Private Law' [2011] *European Review of Private Law* 43; M Kenny and J Devenny, 'A Comparative Analysis of Bank Charges in Europe: *OFT v Abbey National plc* Through the Looking Glass' in M Kenny and J Devenny (eds), *Consumer Credit, Debt and Investment in Europe* (Cambridge, Cambridge University Press, 2012) 212. The Supreme Court was referring to its earlier decision in *Director General of Fair Trading v First National Bank* [2001] UKHL 52, [2002] 1 AC 481; for a critical analysis see H-W Micklitz, 'Case Note: House of Lords—*Fair Trading v National Bank*' (2006) 2 *European Review of Contract Law* 471; H-W Micklitz, 'Zum englischen Verständnis von Treu und Glauben in der Richtlinie 93/13/EWG' [2003] *Zeitschrift für Europäisches Privatrecht* 865; H-W Micklitz, *The Politics of Judicial Co-operation* (Cambridge, Cambridge University Press, 2005) 418.

[16] Council Directive 93/13/EEC of 5 April 1993 on unfair terms in consumer contracts [1993] OJ L95/29.

[17] Whittaker (n 15) para 40.

to pay an additional penalty, did not come under the ambit of legal control envisaged by the Unfair Terms in Consumer Contracts Directive.

In a recent paper, Domurath suggested that the concept of vulnerability should be taken as the general normative standard for all consumer credit and mortgage law.[18] She lists four reasons for that conclusion: absence of the actual freedom of contract in consumer transactions, a small number of reasonably circumspect consumers, inefficiency and unsuitability of the information paradigm in consumer credit and mortgage law, and the need to build a European model of social justice, which so far, because of the limited EU competences in private law, focused mainly on consumers' access to the market.

Domurath argues for the concept of 'universal financial services', in the context of which the consumer would receive special protection due to her economic vulnerability.[19] The model for such regulation is to be found in the Commission Proposal for a Payment Account Fees Directive.[20] The Commission proposal refers to 'vulnerable' consumers as those with few economic resources. However, the author makes no distinction in her analysis between the 'weak' and the vulnerable consumer. Her critique of the normative model of consumer in credit and mortgage law and of the reliance on information duties as a solution to perceived problems is certainly correct. Moreover, an average consumer is unlikely to understand the information provided and is unable to take an informed decision. But this does not make every consumer confronted with an offer of financial services 'vulnerable'. In my view, the concept of vulnerability should be restricted to consumers who are in need of the basic financial services and who, because of their economic situation, do not have access to them at all or who only have such access at unreasonable prices. It follows that economic vulnerability should be approached as a problem of exclusion. The objective of the Commission Proposal for a Payment Account Fees Directive is aimed exactly at combating the problem of exclusion from the financial market arising from 'economic disability'.

The Mortgage Credit Directive 2014/17/EU of 4 February 2014 contains in Article 7 detailed provisions laying down 'conduct of business obligations' of credit providers, including those concerning 'creditworthiness assessment' (Article 16).[21] These provisions are intended to prevent over-indebtedness of consumers who

[18] I Domurath, 'The Case of Vulnerability as the Normative Standard in European Consumer Credit and Mortgage Law—An Inquiry into the Paradigms of Consumer Law' (2013) 2 *Journal of European Consumer and Market Law* 124, 133–35.

[19] ibid 135.

[20] Commission, Proposal for Directive of the European Parliament and of the Council on the comparability of fees related to payment accounts, payment account switching and access to payment accounts with basic features COM(2013) 266 final, now Directive 2014/92/EU of the European Parliament and of the Council of 23 July 2014 on the comparability of fees related to payment accounts, payment account switching and access to payment accounts with basic features [2014] OJ L257/214.

[21] Directive 2014/17/EU of the European Parliament and of the Council of 4 February 2014 on credit agreements for consumers relating to residential immovable property [2014] OJ L60/34

cannot serve their debts and therefore may become 'economically vulnerable'.[22] At the same time the Directive wants to make access to credit possible without discrimination, as provided in Recital 6, which refers to 'financial inclusion':

> This Directive should therefore develop a more transparent, efficient and competitive internal market, through consistent, flexible and fair credit agreements relating to immovable property, while promoting sustainable lending and borrowing and financial inclusion, and hence providing a high level of consumer protection.

II. Consumer Concepts in EU Law

A. The Possible Impact of the 'Vulnerability' Concept on Existing EU Consumer Law

Before I establish whether EU law engages with all three aspects of 'consumer vulnerability', I think it is necessary to recall the very different normative paradigms which EU consumer law has been using so far. These are the paradigms of the 'informed consumer' and the consumer as the 'weaker party'. Both standards have received intensive treatment in the literature and will not be discussed exhaustively here. Recent research has focussed on the behavioural aspects of consumer rules, which inspires a reality-based interpretation of the adopted normative models.[23] For present purposes, a few remarks will suffice. The question which I will address is whether there is another normative standard appearing in EU law which could lead to a different approach to consumer protection in the EU.

B. The 'Informed Consumer' Standard

Community and now Union law proceed from the premise that the EU consumer should be an 'informed consumer'. Consumer protection understood as a form of social protection is generally the responsibility of Member States within the framework of minimum harmonisation measures, as recognised by the CJEU in *Buet*.[24] Under the new framework of total but targeted harmonisation,

[22] For a first assessment concerning German law see F Schäfer, 'Wohnimmobilienkreditrichtlinie—Geschichte und Umsetzung im Verbraucherdarlehensrecht' (2014) 6 *Verbraucher und Recht* 207.

[23] See for a broader discussion N Reich, 'The Social, Political and Cultural Dimension of EU Private Law' in R Schulze and H Schulte-Nölke (eds), *European Private Law—Current Status and Perspectives* (Munich, Sellier, 2011) 57 and 66; more recently, M Engel and J Stark, 'Verbraucherrecht ohne Verbraucher (Consumer Law without Consumers)?' [2015] *Zeitschrift für Europäisches Privatrecht* 32, 38–46 with further references to behavioural research (*Verhaltensforschung*).

[24] *Buet* (n 2). See also J Stuyck in L Krämer and others (eds), *Law and Diffuse Interests* (Baden-Baden, Nomos, 1997) 287, G Howells and T Wilhelmsson, *EC Consumer Law* (Aldershot, Ashgate, 1997) 315–20, S Weatherill 'Justifying Limits to Party Autonomy in the Internal Market—EC Legislation in

Member States' discretion in the field of social protection depends on the scope of application of EU measures. In the area of consumer credit, under Directive 2008/48/EC, questions of social protection of the consumer-debtor against usury, default and insolvency are left to Member State law. EU consumer protection law generally belongs to economic, not social, law. A somewhat more 'social approach' has been attempted in Article 28 of the Mortgage Credit Directive, which concerns 'arrears and foreclosure'. Even there, however, the provision leaves much discretion to Member States as to how to implement these consumer protective measures. Article 11(1)(g) on the standard information to be included in advertising requires Member States to ensure that any advertising of credit agreements includes 'a general warning concerning possible consequences of non-compliance with the commitments linked to the credit agreement'. It is of no surprise that the information requirements are mandatory for Member States and, in consequence, for credit providers while the social protective provisions on foreclosure and arrears remain more or less optional.

The Union legislator—and to an even larger extent the Commission—rely on the effects of the internal market and competition in delivering consumer welfare. For liberal authors, the right to free choice constitutes the core ingredient of the European economic constitution[25] because it is necessary for the exercise of the individual rights of the citizens to participate in cross-border transactions in accordance with Community law. Consumer protection extends these liberties to 'passive citizens'.[26] According to this view consumer protection excessively limiting the freedom of contract may hamper rather than enhance market integration.[27]

Consumer protection measures adopted by the EU focussing on the right to information reflect the policy choices taken by the Treaty, as visible in the wording of Article 169 TFEU.[28] They are regarded as compatible with a market economy. Socio-political, distributive demands are less important.[29] These issues are left to Member States in accordance, one could argue, with the principle of subsidiarity. It is because of the principle of subsidiarity that Wilhelmsson objects to excessive

the Field of Consumer Protection', H-W Micklitz, 'A Comment on Party Autonomy and Consumer Regulation in the European Community—A Plea for Consistency' in S Grundmann, W Kerber, and S Weatherill (eds), *Party Autonomy and the Role of Information in the Internal Market* (Berlin, de Gruyter, 2001) 185–87 and 200 and E Hondius 'The Protection of the Weak Party in a Harmonised European Contract Law' (2004) 27 *Journal of Consumer Policy* 245.

[25] The critical discussion thereof can be found in M Kenny, *The Transformation of Public and Private EC Competition Law*, (Berne, Stämpfli, 2002) 86–93 and in B Lurger, *Grundfragen der Vereinheitlichung des Vertragsrechts in der EU*, (Wien, Springer, 2002) 396–400.

[26] Reich (n 6) paras 1.5–1.9.

[27] C Kirchner, 'Justifying Limits to Party Autonomy in the Internal Market—Mainly Consumer Protection' in Grundmann, Kerber, and Weatherill (n 24).

[28] For an overview, see the contributions in Grundmann, Kerber and Weatherill (n 24).

[29] cf T Wilhelmsson, *Social Contract Law and European Integration* (Aldershot, Dartmouth, 1995); differing opinion C Willet, 'Can Disallowance of Unfair Contract Terms Be Regarded as a Redistribution of Power in Favour of Consumers?' (1994) 17 *Journal of Consumer Policy* 471.

unification of European contract law where 'social values' are unlikely to be adequately considered.[30]

C. The 'Weaker' Consumer in the Case Law of the CJEU

As far as the application and the interpretation of EU consumer directives are concerned, the practice of the CJEU shows a tendency to emphasise the *protection of the consumer as a weaker party* in a contractual relationship.[31] In *Schulte*, the CJEU required Member States

> to ensure that their legislation protects consumers who have been unable to avoid exposure to such risks [incurred because of not knowing of their right of cancellation under the Doorstep Directive 85/577, NR], by adopting suitable measures to allow them to avoid bearing the consequences of the materialisation of those risks.[32]

Lurger rightly describes this approach of the Court as exhibiting preference for the 'principle of solidarity and fairness'.[33]

The CJEU has quite often been criticised by consumer protection activists for its inability to engage with the reality of the problems consumers face. Too often was the Court prepared to merge consumer interest with the Internal Market rationale. One outstanding example is the so-called *Heininger* saga, where even a series of repeated references to the CJEU did not lead to a real improvement of the legal position of consumers, and this despite the Court's pronouncements in *Schulte*.[34]

More recently, however, the CJEU seems to be taking a more active stand in protecting consumer interests. The new battlefield is the interpretation of Directive 93/13/EC. Here a steady influx of references, in particular from the new Member States, but also from the Member States suffering more severely in the euro crisis (for example, Spain), is matched by the Court's readiness to take consumer protection 'much more seriously'.[35] In order to understand the protective ambit of the Unfair Terms Directive, as interpreted by the CJEU, it is helpful to recall a

[30] T Wilhelmsson, 'Private Law in the EU: Harmonised or Fragmented Europeanisation?' [2002] *European Review of Private Law* 77, 84. For a similar view, see N Reich, 'A European Contract Law or an EU Contract Law Regulation for Consumers?' (2005) 28 *Journal of Consumer Policy* 383.

[31] Case C–481/99 *Georg Heininger and Helga Heininger v Bayerische Hypo- und Vereinsbank AG* [2001] ECR I–9945, para 38.

[32] Case C–350/03 *Elisabeth Schulte and Wolfgang Schulte v Deutsche Bausparkasse Badenia AG* [2005] ECR I–9215, para 101.

[33] Lurger (n 25) 380.

[34] H-W Micklitz, 'The Relationship between National and European Consumer Policy—Challenges and Perspectives' in C Twigg-Flesner and others (eds), *The Yearbook of Consumer Law 2008* (Aldershot, Ashgate, 2007) 35–66.

[35] H-W Micklitz and N Reich, 'Von der Klausel- zur Marktkontrolle' [2013] *Zeitschrift für Europäisches Wirtschaftsrecht* 457; H-W Micklitz and N Reich, 'The Court and Sleeping Beauty—The revival of the Unfair Contract Terms Directive' (2014) 51 *Common Market Law Review* 771. The leading case is Case C–415/11 *Mohamed Aziz v Caixa d'Estalvis de Catalunya, Tarragona i Manresa (Catalunyacaixa)*, judgment of 14 March 2013.

statement from the *Penzügij Lizing* judgment,[36] which the Court makes repeatedly to justify its more consumer protective interpretation of the Directive:

> according to settled case-law, the system of protection introduced by the Directive is based on the idea that the consumer is in a weak position vis-à-vis the seller or supplier, as regards both his bargaining power and his level of knowledge. This leads to the consumer agreeing to terms drawn up in advance by the seller or supplier without being able to influence the content of those terms.
>
> The Court of Justice has also held that, on account of that weaker position, Article 6(1) of the Directive provides that unfair terms are not binding on the consumer. As is apparent from case-law, that is a mandatory provision which aims to replace the formal balance which the contract establishes between the rights and obligations of the parties with an effective balance which re-establishes equality between them.
>
> In order to guarantee the protection intended by the Directive, the Court has also stated that the imbalance which exists between the consumer and the seller or supplier may be corrected only by positive action unconnected with the actual parties to the contract.

This case law overtly concerns only Directive 93/13 but the Court's approach should be regarded as indicating more generally the Court's understanding of the objectives of EU consumer law. In B2C transactions party autonomy is tipped in favour of the consumer as a typically weaker party. The business or professional party is regularly seen to be in a stronger bargaining position.

It is hard to predict where this development will lead. The CJEU is narrowing down the leeway of the Member States to set their own protective standards within the framework of EU measures. In this way, the CJEU seems to be counterbalancing the much harsher market-orientated philosophy motivating the European Commission, and to some extent also the European legislator.

D. The 'Vulnerable' Consumer Standard[37]

If we look at the concept of 'vulnerable consumers' as it emerges from existing EU legislation, it seems to encompass still rather superficially those who cannot, or can no longer, cope with the requirements of modern consumer society. Some consumers run the risk of being isolated from social and economic life, be it by over-indebtedness, illness, or lack of possibilities to communicate. There is also a growing problem of 'social deprivation'. This group of consumers was the focus of the national consumer policies of the 1960s and 70s. The political movement of those decades concentrated on protecting the weaker, in particular vulnerable, persons without differentiation. In the Lisbon Strategy, the EU mentioned, for the

[36] Case C–137/08 *VB Pénzügyi Lízing Zrt v Ferenc Schneider* [2010] ECR I–10847, paras 46–48.

[37] This section follows N Reich and others, *European Consumer Law* 2nd edn (Cambridge, Intersentia, 2014) para 1.36a.

first time explicitly, the existence of different types of consumers. It speaks of, as a separate group, people 'living below the poverty line and in social exclusion'.[38]

Improved information and market transparency are of little help to vulnerable consumers when the goal is to enable them to lead self-determined lives. It is rather the targeted improvement of infrastructure, and intelligent, realistic schemes of providing advice, that enable consumers, including vulnerable consumers, to participate independently in economic and social life. If one declares inclusion and social participation as the objective, as the EU does, then one also has to take care of 'vulnerable consumers'.[39] Amazingly enough, the vulnerable consumer has entered the European consumer policy agenda. Recital 34 of the Consumer Rights Directive ('CRD') 2011/83/EU insists that:

> In providing that information, the trader should take into account the specific needs of consumers who are vulnerable because of their mental, physical or psychological infirmity, age or credulity in a way which the trader could reasonably be expected to foresee. However, taking into account such specific needs should not lead to different levels of consumer protection.

However, the obligation mentioned in the recital did not make it into the provisions of the CRD in the form of specific information requirements!

Legal recognition of this new type of consumer is closely linked to the liberalisation of the energy and telecommunication markets, which was forcefully promoted by the European Commission after the adoption of the Single European Act. The guarantee of supply for everybody was added to the concept of universal services. The universal service obligation not only refers to vulnerable consumers but actually includes them in its protective realm by giving them certain basic rights. For the first time the concept appears in Directive 2002/22/EC on universal services and users' rights relating to electronic communications networks and services (Universal Service Directive).[40]

Article 1(1) of the Universal Service Directive aims to ensure the availability throughout the Community of good-quality publicly available services through effective competition and choice. It also aims to deal with circumstances 'in which the needs of end-users are not satisfactorily met by the market'. According to recital 7, the Directive's objective is to ensure 'the same conditions [of] access, in particular for the elderly, the disabled and for people with special social needs'. Directive 2009/140/EC has not changed the terms defined in Article 2 of Directive

[38] Commission, Communication from the Commission: Europe 2020: A strategy for smart, sustainable and inclusive growth COM(2010) 2020 final.

[39] Scientific Advisory Board on Consumer and Food Policies at the Federal Ministry of Consumer Protection, Food and Agriculture (BMVEL), 'The Consumer—Trusting, Vulnerable or Responsible? Plea for a Differentiated Strategy in Consumer Policy' <www.bmelv.de/SharedDocs/Downloads/EN/Ministry/Trusting-Vulnerable-Responsible-Consumer.pdf> accessed 28 May 2015.

[40] Directive 2002/22/EC of the European Parliament and of the Council of 7 March 2002 on universal service and users' rights relating to electronic communications networks and services (Universal Service Directive) [2002] OJ L108/51.

2002/21/EC. For the first time disabled persons are granted special rights.[41] In the Internal Market in Electricity Directive 2003/54/EC and the Internal Market in Natural Gas Directive 2003/55/EC,[42] the so-called second generation of the liberalisation of the energy markets, the European Commission coined the notion of the 'vulnerable customer'.[43] In light of the increasing problems of social exclusion as a consequence of the liberalisation of the Single European Market, the EU further tightened its approach in Directive 2009/72/EC of 13 July 2009.[44] However, the EU has left it to Member States to define the term of the vulnerable consumer, as Article 3(7) of the Directive indicates.

The differentiation between categories of consumers in Directive 2005/29/EC on Unfair Commercial Practices can also be considered to have an impact on the approach traditionally adopted in contract law, which usually starts from a rather abstract and uniform concept of 'persons'. Interestingly the Directive does not speak of the 'vulnerable consumer', but of 'consumers whose characteristics make them particularly vulnerable' to unfair commercial practices. This concept includes consumers whose 'age, physical or mental infirmity or credulity … render them susceptible'. Poverty does not account for the concept of vulnerability.[45] The law does not define the characteristics of the 'normal addressee of an advertisement', to whom the Directive refers as the 'average consumer'.

Finally, the more recent Regulation on consumer online dispute resolution ('ODR')[46] refers to 'vulnerable users' in its Article 5 concerning the most inclusive possible access and use of the ODR-platform by all, including 'vulnerable users ("design for all")'. The Regulation, does not, however, contain a definition of 'vulnerable users'.

Persons with physical disabilities, on the other hand, have entered EU law in different regulations relating to passenger transportation, even though the concept of 'vulnerability' is not used in their respect. Article 2(1) of Regulation 261/2004 talks of persons with 'reduced mobility' who require special services and attention

[41] Arts 7 and 23a of Directive 2009/136/EC of the European Parliament and of the Council of 25 November 2009 amending Directive 2002/22/EC on universal service and users' rights relating to electronic communications networks and services, Directive 2002/58/EC concerning the processing of personal data and the protection of privacy in the electronic communications sector and Regulation (EC) No 2006/2004 on cooperation between national authorities responsible for the enforcement of consumer protection laws [2009] OJ L337/11; for an evaluation see A Nijenhuis in F Benyon, *Services and the EU Citizen* (Oxford, Hart Publishing, 2013) 56.

[42] Directive 2003/54/EC of the European Parliament and of the Council of 26 June 2003 concerning common rules for the internal market in electricity [2003] OJ L176/37; Directive 2003/55/EC of the European Parliament and of the Council of 26 June 2003 concerning common rules for the internal market in natural gas [2003] OJ L176/57.

[43] Compare Art 3(5) Directive 2003/54/EC and Art 3(3) Directive 2003/55/EC (both n 42).

[44] Directive 2009/72/EC of the European Parliament and of the Council of 13 July 2009 concerning common rules for the internal market in electricity and repealing Directive 2003/54/EC [2009] OJ L211/55.

[45] See Directive 2005/29/EC, Art 5(3), which moreover requires them to be an 'identifiable group'.

[46] Regulation (EU) No 524/2013 of the European Parliament and of the Council of 21 May 2013 on online dispute resolution for consumer disputes (Regulation on consumer ODR) [2013] OJ L165/1.

by airlines.[47] If my information is correct, there is as yet no case law of the CJEU concerning the extent of assistance that airlines are obliged to provide for vulnerable passengers because of their reduced mobility. One reason may be the remarkable extension of the obligations of airlines by the CJEU, for instance in cases of interruption of the traffic due to an eruption of the Icelandic volcano Eyjafjallajökull, leading to the closure of airspace. There the Court used Article 9 of the Regulation to grant entitlements to stranded passengers, which were unlimited in time and value and did not distinguish between the different types of passengers.[48] One could argue that in these circumstances every passenger was in some way an ad hoc 'vulnerable consumer' with reduced mobility, not due to their personal situation but due to the closure of air traffic.

III. The Need to Define the Place and Scope of the 'Vulnerable Consumer' Concept

A. 'Vulnerability' in the Concept of 'Vulnerable Consumer' and a Challenge to the Seemingly Incompatible Concept of 'Party Autonomy'

The practical impact of the introduction of the concept of 'vulnerable consumer' into EU law is still hard to evaluate. However, it is clear that EU consumer law is changing its outlook. Today it is fair to assume that the vulnerable consumer concept stands side-by-side with the informed consumer concept. The overview of the different situations leading to 'vulnerability' of the consumer in section 1, and the still very scant and rather contradictory treatment of vulnerability in EU law, outlined in section 2, raise doubts as to whether a new paradigm of EU consumer law is indeed emerging. In my view the EU consumer law *acquis* vacillates between two seemingly conflicting poles that require coordination: consumer protection based on the concept of party autonomy and consumer protection based on the image of the consumer as a weaker party.[49]

[47] Regulation (EC) No 261/2004 of the European Parliament and of the Council of 11 February 2004 establishing common rules on compensation and assistance to passengers in the event of denied boarding and of cancellation or long delay of flights [2004] OJ L046/1. The Commission's proposal for amending the regulation, Regulation of the European Parliament and of the Council amending Regulation (EC) No 261/2004 establishing common rules on compensation and assistance to passengers in the event of denied boarding and of cancellation or long delay of flights and Regulation (EC) No 2027/97 on air carrier liability in respect of the carriage of passengers and their baggage by air COM(2013) 130 final of 13 March 2013 has been critically discussed by M Rostin, (2013) 2 *Journal of European Consumer and Market Law* 138; I will not go into this discussion.

[48] Case C–12/11 *Denise McDonagh v Ryanair Ltd*, judgment of 31 January 2013.

[49] I have tried to develop this in greater detail in chs 1, 2, and 5 of my *General Principles of EU Civil Law* (n 6).

The vulnerable consumer standard may be seen as a sort of 'flexibilisation'[50] of a rather formal approach toward consumer protection, in particular in areas where the classical instruments of information duties, mandatory standards and judicial remedies do not offer sufficient protection to persons who due to certain disabilities are unable to fully enjoy the possibilities of a free and competitive market, including the adequate judicial protection, required by Article 47 of the Charter and Article 19(1), paragraph 2 TEU. Depending on the area of law—in our case it is contract law—different answers will be given to the question of whether the traditional instruments of dealing with consumer issues correspond to the requirements of a 'social market economy', referred to in Article 3(3) TEU. I will give some examples, without any attempt to offer a complete survey, of situations where there might be incompatibility between the traditional instruments of consumer protection and the concept of a social market.

B. Deficits in Consumer Information: The Problem of Adequate Remedies

Let us first focus on the issue of information provided to 'vulnerable consumers'. We should look at it in terms of its negative impact, where we would like to impose prohibitions, and in terms of positive obligations which we would like to impose on producers and suppliers. The former concerns the definition of 'misleading information' which should focus on the subject-matter to which particular advertising and marketing messages are referring. The latter concerns positive obligations to make information on product and service quality, contract terms and so on understandable for consumers with intellectual deficiencies. Both of these aspects are regulated in Article 5(3) of the Unfair Commercial Practices Directive ('UCPD') (below III.C) and in recital 34 of the Consumer Rights Directive. They relate to the intellectual disabilities of consumers. While, to the best of my knowledge, there is still no case law on this point, the 'transactional neglect' principle advocated by Griggs, which I have explained above, is the one which EU law has already adopted. The 'transactional neglect' principle can be found in the wording of recital 34 of the CRD relating to the 'reasonable expectation' of the trader, where the vulnerability of certain groups of consumers has to be taken into account. Unfortunately, this concept has not been expressly included in the information requirements of Articles 5 and 6 CRD. However, it could certainly be imposed on the trader by way of a 'consumer-friendly interpretation' of the Directive and by reference to Article 169 TFEU and Article 38 of the Charter. Information which is not understandable for the targeted group of intellectually disabled consumers

[50] H-W Micklitz, 'Do Consumers and Businesses need a New Architecture of Consumer Law?' German version originally presented to the 69th Deutsche Juristentag (German Lawyers' Association) in Munich (2012); English translation in (2013) 32 *Yearbook of European Law* 266 (at 293 the discussion of the vulnerable consumer, at 349 a plea for a flexible system).

implies absence of information as such, the consequence of which will have to be drawn in accordance with national law, in case it is found that the CRD does not give a conclusive answer.[51]

C. Advertising and Sales Promotion: How does One Define the Targeted Group?[52]

To the extent that commercial practices are addressed to a distinct group of consumers, the yardstick should be the level of understanding of the average member of that group. Article 5(3) UCPD mentioned above refers to consumers who because of their mental or physical infirmity, age, or credulity are particularly vulnerable to commercial practices or the underlying product (including services). The Directive has a normative component as it entails an evaluation of the content of the advertising message. Recitals 18 and 19 shed light on the objectives of this provision. The EU is obviously thinking of children and seniors, who should not be protected to a greater extent per se but only where commercial practices or products are particularly appealing to them. The judgement as to whether an advertisement is aimed at groups of particularly vulnerable consumers is difficult to make. Evaluation of the advertisements' spillover effects is remarkably problematic. Advertisements which are addressed to adults can also reach children. This is particularly true in the age of the internet. Depending on the interpretation, the yardstick of control varies. According to Article 5(3) it is necessary to distinguish between a situation where the trader could reasonably be expected to foresee that the commercial practices can materially distort the economic behaviour of a clearly identifiable group of consumers who are particularly vulnerable, and a situation where such an expectation would not be reasonable. The indication in Article 5(3) and the recitals, that the practices cause or are likely to cause distortion with regard to a group of vulnerable consumers, suggests that there is a subjective element in the assessment concerning the knowledge of the advertiser in the design and choice of the advertising content.

D. The Special Case of Long-Term Contracts for Services of General Economic Interest

The needs of 'economically disabled' and therefore 'vulnerable consumers' have been addressed, as explained above, in recent EU Directives concerning services of general economic interest, that is, telecommunications and energy services.

[51] Reich and others (n 37) para 9.7.
[52] The following part is taken from ibid, para 2.27.

As Micklitz has observed, these directives embody the paradigm of 'access justice',[53] a particular conception of EU law.

The most important elements of EU regulation of services of general economic interest have been, on the one hand, the internal market approach, and on the other, the so-called 'universal service obligation' of providers.[54] The imposition of the universal service obligation is to some extent required by the principle of 'access to services of general economic interest' enshrined in Article 36 of the Charter. It stipulates that the right of access to such services has to be 'provided for in national laws and practices, in accordance with [Union law], in order to promote the social and territorial cohesion of the Union.' Legislation will have to clarify how the framework developed by the EU will incorporate the issue of free choice in access to services and non-discrimination between 'consumers' more traditionally understood and other users. It is not yet clear whether Member States must include protective rules for low-income consumers in their private laws, which would guarantee them access to energy supply and protection against cut-offs, as laid down by Article 3(7) of Directive 2009/72. The relevant provisions on universal services are not unconditional and precise enough to have direct effect. They may, however, be used in the interpretation of Member State contract laws, for instance with the effect of making disconnections from supply conditional on certain procedural requirements. However, to my knowledge no case law of the CJEU has yet developed in this area.

E. Contract Law and Basic Financial Services

As mentioned above, on 8 May 2013 the Commission published a Proposal for a Directive on the comparability of fees related to payment accounts, payment account switching, and access to payment accounts with basic features.[55] This has become Directive 2014/92/EU, to be implemented by 18 September 2016.[56] According to the Directive, economically disabled consumers are to be guaranteed access to some basic financial services, such as a non-debit bank account. It does not mention 'vulnerable consumers' but is intended to combat social exclusion and over-indebtedness, a frequent problem of economically vulnerable

[53] H-W Micklitz, *The Many Concepts of Social Justice in the European Private Law* (Cheltenham, Elgar, 2011) 34; see my review in (2013) 50 *Common Market Law Review* 1523.

[54] P Rott, 'Consumers and Services of General Interest: Is EC Consumer Law the Future?' (2007) 30 *Journal of Consumer Policy* 53; N Reich, 'Crisis of Future of European Consumer Law?' in D Parry and others (eds), *The Yearbook of Consumer Law 2009* (Farnham, Ashgate, 2009); H-W Micklitz, 'The Visible Hand of European Regulatory Civil Law' (2009) 28 *Yearbook of European Law* 3; Micklitz (n 50) 310; M Bartl, 'The Affordability of Energy: How Much Protection for the Vulnerable Consumer?' (2010) 33 *Journal of Consumer Policy* 225; P Rott, 'The Low-Income Consumer in European Private Law' in K Purnhagen and P Rott (eds), *Varieties of European Economic Regulation—Liber amicorum Hans Micklitz* (Berlin, Springer, 2014).

[55] COM(2013) 266 final (n 20).

[56] Directive 2014/92/EU (n 20) art 29(2).

consumers. Article 14 of Directive 2014/92, entitled 'Non-discrimination', requires Member States to ensure that consumers are 'not discriminated against on the basis of their nationality or residence or by reason of any other ground as referred to in Article 21 of the Charter, when those consumers apply for or access a payment account within the Union'. Article 15 establishes a right of access to a basic payment account for consumers in any Member State. It also imposes an obligation on Member States to designate at least one payment service provider responsible for offering a basic payment account. Article 16 specifies the list of payment services that a payment account with basic features should include.

At the time of writing, political, economic and legislative implications of the Directive are not yet clear. Article 15 concerning non-discrimination has a particularly broad scope of application in the field of basic financial services, including—unlike Directive 2000/78[57]—'disability', as well economic grounds such as 'property'. Much will depend on the willingness of Member States to designate one or several 'universal' payment service providers. The proposed right of 'access' to payment services without discrimination may have the effect of transforming payment systems in the EU, despite their heterogeneity, into a 'service of general economic interest' (without, however, a 'universal service obligation' and 'direct effect'). They would in principle still be based on civil law but subjected to special rules that go beyond the traditional concepts of private autonomy and freedom of contract.[58] Such developments in the law on payment services were criticised by Herresthal[59] as incompatible with the fundamental right of the freedom of contract under Article 16 of the Charter. If the state is forced (under EU law) to offer consumers with problems (who usually classify as 'economically vulnerable consumers' in our terminology) access to a bank account, it will have to compensate the chosen bank if such an account cannot be offered without a loss to the bank. The solution seems not only quite far-fetched but also one-sided in the way it places all its emphasis on the autonomy of the consumer (facilitated by access to a bank account) and forgets about the resulting obligations of designated providers of financial services, who are asked to offer their (usually profitable) facilities to a broad range of persons without any discrimination.

IV. Does the Concept of 'Vulnerable Consumer' Challenge the Principle of Party Autonomy?

This chapter was intended as a first overview of the still-elusive concept of 'vulnerable consumer' in EU law and the controversial legal consequences which

[57] *Chacón Navas* (n 7); also Rott, 'The Low-Income Consumer' (n 54) 682.

[58] Reich (n 6) para 3.19a.

[59] C Herresthal, 'Grundrechtscharta und Privatrecht—Die Bedeutung der Charta der Grundrechte für das europäische und das nationale Privatrecht' [2014] *Zeitschrift für Europäisches Privatrecht* 238.

may flow from its incorporation. EU law is at an experimental stage, as references to different legal acts have shown. A few observations can nevertheless be made. First, vulnerability resulting from physical disability could be regulated by reference to the principle of solidarity. Civil law, despite the central place of freedom of contract, includes provisions motivated by the principle of solidarity. Such a view of contract law is, moreover, supported by fundamental rights considerations. Under Article 26 of the Charter disabled persons are entitled to benefit from measures ensuring their 'participation in the life of the community'.[60] Civil law provisions motivated by the principle of solidarity must be regarded as introducing a justified limitation on the freedom to conduct a business, which includes freedom of contract, and is protected not in an absolute manner but 'in accordance with Union and national law and practices'.[61] Therefore, the extension of the principle of non-discrimination on the grounds of disability in Article 21 of the Charter beyond employment relations[62] to issues of 'access to goods and services available to the public' seems mandated by primary EU law. This is particularly the case if the Charter is interpreted in the light of the UN Convention on the Rights of Persons with Disabilities, which requires state parties to the Convention to enhance the possibility of their 'independent living and social inclusion'.[63] This has now been realised by Directive 2014/92 with regard to basic financial services.

As to intellectually disabled consumers, they usually receive protection under the laws of Member States in the form of special rules concerning liability for misrepresentation and fraud. *Abus de faiblesse* may even be an independent ground of liability. EU law's intervention takes the form of reshaping information requirements in order to adapt them to the needs of this special group of consumers. This is already visible in EU law on commercial practices, but not yet—except for a general policy statement in recital 34 of the Consumer Rights Directive—in EU contract law. Member States should be obliged to introduce, under the requirements of EU law concerning national remedies, sanctions for violations of the duty to provide adequate information to intellectually disabled persons, if the supplier knew or should have known of the disability. It is in this area that the principle of 'transactional responsibility', as developed by Griggs,[64] may be helpful.

Most controversial is the question of how one ought to address the needs of consumers suffering from 'economic disabilities'. These difficulties are inherent in a legal system designed for a market economy, based on the freedom of contract. Such an orientation of the legal system usually excludes the use of contract law as an instrument of redistribution. 'The Poor Pay More' seems to be the 'iron law' of such an

[60] The importance of Art 26 as an 'interpretative aid' is discussed by O'Brien in S Peers and others (eds), *The EU Charter of Fundamental Rights—A Commentary* (Oxford, Hart Publishing, 2014) para 26.83–91.

[61] Reich (n 6) para 1.13.

[62] Council Directive 2000/78/EC of 27 November 2000 establishing a general framework for equal treatment in employment and occupation [2000] OJ L303/16.

[63] O'Brien (n 60) paras 26.31–45.

[64] Griggs (n 10).

economy. But as with every law, there are arguably important exceptions to that approach. Some of these exceptions have been introduced by the EU regime of SGEI. It has been recognised in such important areas as the provision of energy, telecommunication, transportation, and in the future also of some elementary financial and internet services, that the market has to be regulated extensively. Access to services of general economic interest is guaranteed, as can be seen in Article 36 of the Charter, 'in order to promote the social and territorial cohesion of the Union'.[65] With regard to access to basic payment services, Article 15 of Directive 2014/92, with its reference to Article 21 of the Charter, excludes 'property' as a justified ground for discrimination. However, national laws and practices are called upon to implement this fundamental principle, and it is at this juncture that the EU directives discussed above play a decisive role.

[65] Its interpretative importance despite the vagueness and the 'tenuousness of an individual right' has been stressed by E Szyszczak in her comment on Art 36 of the Charter, para 36.52, in Peers and others (n 60).

6

Changing Policy Paradigms of EU Consumer Credit and Debt Regulation

IAIN RAMSAY*

I. Introduction

The Great Recession of 2008 posed fundamental questions about the optimal role of household credit and debt in an economy[1] and challenged existing policy paradigms about regulation of credit markets: 'The standard orthodoxy was that people made rational decisions when given sufficient information, that markets are self-correcting and that … if you oversee distribution channels—the right products get to the right people. All three orthodoxies failed.'[2] A 'series of waves of major customer detriment' in financial services in the decades leading up to the crisis substantiated this diagnosis.[3] Household credit, traditionally the Cinderella

* This chapter relates to a research project, 'Personal Insolvency in an Age of Austerity', funded by a Leverhulme Trust research fellowship. Thanks to Maria Gomes for research assistance and Toni Williams and participants at the Oxford conference for comments on an earlier draft.

[1] eg A Turner, 'Escaping The Addiction to Private Debt Is Essential for Long-Term Economic Stability' (Frankfurt Speech, Frankfurt, 10 February 2014) <www.ineteconomics.org/blog/institute/adair-turner-escaping-addiction-private-debt-essential-long-term-economic-stability> accessed 1 January 2015.

[2] Martin Wheatley (former head of the UK Financial Conduct Authority), 2012, quoted in I Ramsay and T Williams, 'The Crash that Launched a Thousand Fixes: Regulation of Consumer Credit after the Lending Revolution and the Credit Crunch' in K Alexander and N Moloney (eds), *Law Reform and Financial Markets* (Cheltenham, Edward Elgar, 2011) 221. See also E Engelen and others, *After the Great Complacence: Financial Crisis and the Politics of Reform* (Oxford, Oxford University Press 2011) 160: 'crisis … often raises questions about the limits of technical knowledge and practice'.

[3] See Financial Services Authority, *Product Intervention* (2011) Discussion Paper DP11/1: 'Looking back over the past twenty years what we see is a series of waves of major customer detriment—products missold, huge and rising numbers of complaints … and then intervention to require compensation … And as the waves followed one after another it became increasingly obvious that there are problems in retail financial services which were not going to be solved simply by demanding fair disclosures in the sales processes—that there are deep reasons why retail financial services markets do not work smoothly'. The payment protection insurance misselling scandal in the UK resulted in over £20 billion in compensation; in France issues of insurance sales have also given rise to concerns.

of financial services,[4] was in the spotlight as the trigger of the crisis. The Great Recession morphed into the Eurozone crisis, and mortgage foreclosures, over-indebtedness and household deleveraging became policy problems for EU technocrats and the International Monetary Fund ('IMF')[5] during the bailout of several EU states.[6] EU and international reforms[7] since the crisis aim to improve the quality of *ex ante* regulation, recognising that credit may be a potentially dangerous product, requiring a product safety approach to regulation.[8] The crisis also brought about a rearrangement of the regulatory architecture in several Member States as a response to perceived regulatory failures. At the EU level, the new European Banking Authority took up a consumer protection mandate.[9] The Mortgage Credit Directive represents a more consumer protective approach than the earlier

See, eg, 'Assurance-emprunteur: l'ACP saisie de l'affaire' *Les Echos* (Paris, 24 December 2012). See in Germany the *Heininger* saga, in Netherlands the Dexia scandal.

[4] Colin Crouch notes in a comparative study of household debt in varieties of European capitalism that 'interest in household debt' had 'developed only in very recent years'. C Crouch, 'Employment, Consumption, Debt and European Industrial Relations Systems' (2012) 51 *Industrial Relations* 389, 406. For greater interest in the macro- and micro-political economy of household credit see, eg, M Prasad, *The Land of Too Much: American Abundance and the Paradox of Poverty* (Cambridge MA, Harvard University Press, 2012); J Logemann, *The Development of Consumer Credit in Global Perspective* (Basingstoke, Palgrave, 2012); G Trumbull, *Consumer Lending in France and America: Credit and Welfare* (New York, Cambridge University Press, 2014).

[5] See, eg, IMF, *World Economic Outlook* (2012) ch 2; World Bank, *Report on the Treatment of Insolvency of Natural Persons* (2013). In EU see C Cuerpo and others, 'Indebtedness, Deleveraging Dynamics and Macro Economic Adjustment' (2013) European Economy Economic Papers 477.

[6] Ireland, Portugal, Greece and Latvia. Spain was also requested to introduce a personal insolvency law by the European Semester and the IMF. It introduced a limited form of discharge for individuals in late 2013. See further discussion in I Ramsay, 'Two Cheers for Europe: Austerity, Mortgage Foreclosures and Personal Insolvency Policy in the EU' in H-W Micklitz and I Domurath (eds), *Consumer Debt and Social Exclusion in Europe* (Farnham, Ashgate, 2015).

[7] See discussion in I Ramsay, 'Consumer Credit Regulation After the Fall: International Dimensions' (2012) 1 *Journal of European Consumer and Market Law* 24.

[8] This idea was promoted by Elizabeth Warren in E Warren, 'Unsafe at any Rate' (*Democracy*, Summer 2007): 'Consumers can enter the market to buy physical products confident that they won't be tricked into buying exploding toasters and other unreasonably dangerous products. They can concentrate their shopping efforts in other directions … Consumers entering the market to buy financial products should enjoy the same protection'. See, eg, Financial Stability Board, *Consumer Finance Protection with Particular Focus on Credit* (26 October 2011): 'The global financial crisis brought into focus how the effects of irresponsible lending practices can quickly spread beyond national borders'; OECD, *G20 High Level Principles on Financial Consumer Protection* (Paris, October 2011): 'All G20 members and other interested parties should assess their national frameworks for financial consumer protection in the light of these principles and promote international cooperation to support the strengthening of financial consumer protection in line with, and building on these principles'. See also European Supervisory Authorities, *Joint Position of the European Supervisory Authorities on Manufacturers' Product Oversight and Governance Processes* (2013) JC–2013–77.

[9] See Regulation (EU) 1093/2010 of the European Parliament and of the Council of 24 November 2010 establishing a European Supervisory Authority (European Banking Authority ['EBA']) [2010] OJ L331/12. Art 1(5) includes enhancing consumer protection within the objectives of the EBA. Art 9 (tasks related to consumer protection and financial services) indicates that the 'Authority shall take a leading role in promoting transparency, simplicity and fairness in the market for consumer financial products and services'. This includes monitoring and the adoption of guidelines and recommendations for promoting 'convergence of regulatory practice' 9(2), issuing warnings 9(2), achieving a coordinated approach to regulation and supervision of product innovation 9(4), and temporarily prohibiting or restricting activities that threaten the orderly functioning and integrity of financial markets 9(5).

2008 Consumer Credit Directive.[10] It strengthens regulation on the supply side of the market and requires the Commission to submit by 2019 a comprehensive report assessing the wider challenges of private over-indebtedness linked to credit activity.[11]

These international developments in consumer finance regulation, often organised around the G20 principles of financial consumer protection and involving the creation of a new network of national, regional and international actors, may result in a transnational paradigm of consumer finance regulation.[12] I use the term 'paradigm' in Peter Hall's sense of 'a framework of ideas and standards that specifies not only the goals of policy and kind of instruments that can be used to attain them, but also the very nature of the problems they are meant to address'.[13] Paradigms link scholarly and political ideas and interests—the Washington consensus is a classic example.[14] Understanding stability and change in paradigms requires an attention to history and the role of interest groups, institutions and ideas. Academic ideas may become embedded in the thinking of technical bureaucracies (for example, the EC Commission and the IMF). If the expert knowledge underpinning a paradigm is questioned or loses credibility, this sets the scene for a paradigm conflict.

This chapter discusses EU policy paradigms about credit and debt, focussing primarily on the development of EU credit directives. Section II outlines the political economy of EU credit policymaking associated with the 2008 Consumer Credit and 2014 Mortgage Credit Directive, charting the effects of the Great Recession and Eurozone crisis on policy. Section III situates the emerging EU paradigm in the context of economic and contemporary theoretical writing on the role of consumer credit in society. It outlines critical approaches to the role of consumer credit and its regulation to throw into sharp relief the potential and limits of the EU paradigm as well as ideas about the vulnerability of the consumer in credit markets. Section IV concludes.

The EBA Consumer Trends report for 2014 includes 'indebtedness and responsible credit; misselling, household borrowing, and financial literacy' under 'trends and issues'. The EBA monitored the passage of the EU mortgage directive and issued two opinions in 2013 on good practices for responsible mortgage lending and treatment of borrowers in mortgage payment difficulties. It indicates in its 2014 report that they may be converted into guidelines.

[10] See Directive 2014/17/EU of the European Parliament and of the Council of 4 February 2014 on credit agreements for consumers relating to residential immovable property [2014] OJ L60/34 ('Mortgage Directive' or 'Mortgage Credit Directive'); Directive 2008/48/EC of the European Parliament and of the Council of 23 April 2008 on credit agreements for consumers [2008] OJ L133/66.

[11] ibid, Art 45: 'Further initiatives on responsible lending and borrowing'.

[12] See further T Williams, 'Continuity, Not Rupture: The Persistence of Neoliberalism in the Internationalization of Consumer Finance Regulation' in T Wilson (ed), *International Responses to Issues of Credit and Over-Indebtedness in the Wake of the Crisis* (Farnham, Ashgate, 2013). See World Bank, *Good Practices for Financial Consumer Protection* (2012).

[13] P Hall, 'Policy Paradigms, Social Learning and the State: The Case of Economic Policymaking in Britain' (1993) 25 *Comparative Politics* 275, 279.

[14] S Babb, 'The Washington Consensus as Transnational Policy Paradigm: Its Origins, Trajectory and Likely Successor' (2012) 20 *Review of International Political Economy* 1.

EU credit regulation is part of the ground rules of a 'competitive social market economy'.[15] We might construct initially the contrasting ideas of 'consumer credit as lubricant' and 'consumer credit as potentially dangerous product'. The former favours increased access whereas the latter may restrict access to protect against the risks of over-indebtedness and its associated social costs. The latter has a long legal and regulatory history; the former is a more modern construct. Both ideas influence EU credit policy and the crisis provided the possibility for a shift towards a policy paradigm, which promises to embrace *both* competition and product safety.

This paradigm envisages competition driven by responsibilised (confident) consumers in a market where toxic products[16] and systematic misselling are minimised by effective public regulation and *ex ante* obligations of responsible lending. The recent Mortgage Directive diagnoses a need for reform in 'irresponsible lending and borrowing caused by market and regulatory failure, the general economic climate and low levels of financial literacy'.[17] Suitably upskilled and financially responsible borrowers will drive competition. Insolvency law will provide a re-entry to the market for the responsible consumer—who must usually wait three to five years for this re-entry.[18] This approach paints an image of a contractual relationship located somewhere between the classical conception of self-interested actors and that of a fiduciary relationship. Ideas drawn from behavioural economics increasingly provide an expert knowledge base for this paradigm both in identifying problems and fashioning remedies. Attempting to combine a 'lubricant' and 'potentially dangerous' image of credit may entail continuing political conflict over the ground rules of a credit market.

Non-discriminatory market access and the avoidance of financial exclusion link the economic and 'social market' EU narrative on credit and debt.[19] Financial inclusion implies access to appropriate credit products which address income smoothing and consumption needs. Responsible lending can ensure that a product is suitable for an individual's needs. Responsible lending may have the potential for some modest exclusion of consumers from the market (for example for first time buyers, the credit impaired and self-employed)[20] but may be justified

[15] See discussion in D Schiek (ed), *The EU Economic and Social Model after the Global Crisis: Interdisciplinary Perspectives* (Farnham, Ashgate, 2013).

[16] Note the difficulties of defining 'toxic product'.

[17] Mortgage Directive, Rec 4.

[18] Almost all Member States of the EU now have insolvency or debt adjustment laws which permit a discharge for individuals. Hungary and Romania are the exceptions.

[19] See, eg, Commission, Proposal for a Directive of the European Parliament and of the Council on the comparability of fees related to payment accounts, payment account switching and access to payment accounts with basic features COM(2013) 266 final. Hans Micklitz argues that the dominant social model of EU policy has focussed on access to production and consumption markets rather than protection from the markets (H-W Micklitz, 'Social Justice and Access Justice in Private Law' *EUI Working Paper LAW* 2011/02). See the discussion of the *Test-Achats* decision, Case C–236/09 *Association belge des Consommateurs Test-Achats ASBL v Conseil des ministres* [2011] ECR I–773, by D Mabbett, 'Polanyi in Brussels or Luxembourg? Social Rights and Market Regulation in European Insurance' (2013) 8 *Regulation and Governance* 1.

[20] See Financial Services Authority, Mortgage Market Review (2011) Consultation Paper CP11/31.

by superior creditor information on credit risk, consumer behavioural biases and also as a method of collective 'hands-tying' for lenders, preventing irrational exuberance. The financial inclusion agenda in the EU has had a modest impact in driving alternative models of financial provision which may be important in the current lending environment;[21] and alternative models of financial service which involve state subsidies might contravene EU competition law. Financial inclusion as a social objective fits with a conception of social rights contributing to market objectives, such as greater productivity, rather than permitting an individual to stand outside the market.[22] The development of personal insolvency as a response to the growth of over-indebtedness in EU states[23] becomes a means of addressing financial and social exclusion from the market, providing 'not a hand out but a hand up', without necessarily solving the longer-term problems of insolvents.[24] Social exclusion began as a concept in France during the 1970s as an alternative to class based discourse on inequality and exploitation. Daniel Béland argues that it 'legitimizes modest policy reforms entirely compatible with moderate understandings of economic liberalism and [is] ultimately unable to fight the social evils this idea refers to'.[25]

Some preliminary points. First, consumer credit assumes a distinction between production and consumption credit. However, consumer credit is often used to finance small business. Many European businesses are unincorporated and family-run. Significant percentages of personal insolvencies are related to business failures.[26] This creates not only practical difficulties for policy definitions, but also for framing coherent policy images.[27] The EU promotes both entrepreneurialism and the responsible consumer. The risk-taking entrepreneur is often deluded as to her chance of success[28] but this may have social value in promoting innovation

[21] The Commission conducted studies on Financial Services Provision and Prevention of Financial Inclusion under the auspices of DG Employment, Social Affairs and Equal Opportunities. See Centre for European Policy Studies (CEPS), 'Financial Services Provision and Prevention of Financial Exclusion' (2008, funded by the Commission). Microfinance is promoted primarily for facilitating entrepreneurialism.

[22] See, eg, V Schmidt, 'Ideas and Discourse in Transformational Political Economic Change in Europe' in G Skogstad (ed), *Policy Paradigms, Transnationalism and Domestic Politics* (Toronto, University of Toronto Press, 2011) 46–47. See discussion in M Dawson, *New Governance and the Transformation of EU Law* (New York, Cambridge University Press, 2011).

[23] For a survey see I Ramsay, 'Between Neo-Liberalism and the Social Market: Approaches to Debt Adjustment and Insolvency in the EU' (2012) 35 *Journal of Consumer Policy* 421.

[24] See CA Lopes and C Frade, 'The Way into Bankruptcy: Market Anomie and Sacrifice among Portuguese Consumers' (2012) 35 *Journal of Consumer Policy* 477, 477: 'The improvement of the insolvency procedures will not resolve the situation of financial distress if the structural causes persist, such as unemployment and deterioration of salaries and cuts in social benefits.'

[25] D Béland, 'The Social Exclusion Discourse: Ideas and Policy Change' (2007) 35 *Policy and Politics* 123.

[26] See Ramsay (n 23).

[27] See the discussion of differing approaches to definition of consumer in credit in H-W Micklitz, J Stuyck and E Terryn (eds), *Cases, Materials and Text on Consumer Law* (Oxford, Hart Publishing, 2010) 380.

[28] See the discussion of optimism and entrepreneurialism in D Kahneman, *Thinking Fast and Slow* (London, Penguin, 2013). He notes that although most surveys indicate that entrepreneurs vastly overrate their chances of success, 'optimism even of a mildly delusional nature, may be a good thing'.

and the EU Commission promotes a liberal individual bankruptcy discharge to support entrepreneurialism. This also benefits consumers but is an unintended consequence of the policy and may not fit snugly with images of the responsible consumer.[29]

Second, the EU wishes to achieve an 'efficient competitive single market for credit' as part of a single market for financial services.[30] Although convergence is growing in levels of household debt between the new and old EU states, consumer credit markets remain persistently national.[31] Consensus does not exist at the EU level on issues such as the creation of a European credit database,[32] often viewed as a central ground rule for the establishment of a single market, or interest rate ceilings, and distinct policy images of the economic and social value of credit may exist within different Member States,[33] along with a plurality of norms.[34]

Finally, the EU initially drew a rough distinction between issues which it deemed appropriate for full harmonisation, generally those which facilitate credit market growth, and social issues such as the treatment of over-indebtedness more appropriate to national regulation or the 'soft' approaches associated with the Open Method of Co-ordination. The coherence of this asymmetric approach to governance of credit policy is challenged by the crisis. Debt overhang became a problem for economic growth and the EU was increasingly enmeshed in national

[29] See Commission, Recommendation of 3 December 2014 on a new approach to business failure and insolvency COM(2014) 1500 final. It notes that 'although consumer over-indebtedness and consumer bankruptcy are also not covered by the scope of this recommendation, Member states are invited to explore the possibility of applying these recommendations also to consumers since some of the principles followed in this Recommendation may also be relevant for them'.

[30] eg Commission, Green Paper on Retail Financial Services COM(2007) 226 final.

[31] eg Commission, White Paper on Integration of Mortgage Credit Markets COM(2007) 807 final: 'The Commission recognizes that consumers predominantly shop locally for mortgage credit'. See also Ipsos and London Economics, *Study on the Functioning of the Consumer Credit Market in the EU* (London, London Economics, 2014) x–xi.

[32] The expert group on credit histories could not agree on the creation of a European credit database. See DG Internal Market and Services, *Report of the Expert Group on Credit Databases* (2009). However, it did agree that 'credit data sharing between creditors is considered an essential element of the financial infrastructure that facilitates access to finance for consumers'. For a more sceptical view of credit reference agencies see A Rona-Tas, 'The Role of Credit Bureaus in Globalized Economies—Why They Matter Less Than We Think and How They Can Matter More' in Micklitz and Domurath (n 6). The Conseil constitutionnel in France recently struck down a proposed *fichier positif* for consumer credit as a disproportionate intrusion on privacy rights. See Decision no 2014–690 DC of 12 March 2014.

[33] Gunnar Trumbull describes the distinct policy images of credit in France and the UK, the former being more distrustful of credit and the need to protect consumers from the market, the latter focussing on the importance of access. See G Trumbull, *Strength in Numbers: The Power of Weak Interests* (New York, Cambridge University Press, 2012) ch 5 and see discussion in I Ramsay, 'Culture or Politics? Models of Consumer Credit Regulation in France and the UK' in T Wilson (ed), *International Responses to Issues of Credit and Over-Indebtedness in the Wake of the Crisis* (Farnham, Ashgate, 2013). See also Logemann (n 4) on the legacy of Ordoliberalism on German approaches to credit.

[34] eg in the UK, the distinct approach and assumptions of the Financial Ombudsman Service and the courts to issues of fairness. Compare *Harrison v Black Horse* [2011] EWCA Civ 1128, [2012] Lloyd's Rep IR 521, with Ombudsman decisions cited in I Ramsay, *Consumer Law and Policy* (Oxford, Hart Publishing, 2007) 454–56.

insolvency policies and developing common insolvency rules as part of the entrepreneurialism agenda.[35]

II. The Political Economy of Consumer Credit Regulation

Lucia Quaglia argues that EU policy outcomes in financial services are likely to represent either (a) the battle of the systems, (b) the Commission as the core actor, or (c) the influence of transnational capital.[36] We might expect EU consumer credit law and its implementation to be skewed towards the interests of finance capital which represents a relatively well-organised and concentrated industry in comparison with the diffuse and fragmented consumer interest where consumers may have cross-cutting interests as debtors and potential borrowers.[37] Households are now a major profit centre for financial institutions and competition to increase shareholder returns stimulates a continuing search for extracting these profits.[38] The technical complexity of credit law—where the devil is often in the detail—would also seem to favour financial interests' ability to influence policy. Financial services law may also be skewed since the financial industry (at least in the UK) is a notorious repeat player in litigation, able to pursue the long run, choosing appropriate test case litigation and settling cases which might result in unfortunate precedents.[39] Since credit law is layered onto existing civil or common law principles, these principles may represent this accumulation over time of advantages by RP creditors. This was one reason for the creation of the Financial Ombudsman Service in the UK which might apply general norms of fairness in disputes between individuals and financial institutions.[40]

35 This is primarily through the European Semester, the Troika and see Commission, Recommendation (n 29).

36 L Quaglia, 'The "Old" and "New" Politics of Financial Services Regulation in the European Union' (2012) 17 *New Political Economy* 515.

37 To a certain extent I am simplifying here since there may be divisions within finance capital. See generally S Hix and B Høyland, *The Political System of the European Union* 3rd edn (Basingstoke, Palgrave, 2011) ch 7.

38 PD Santos, 'On the Content of Banking in Contemporary Capitalism (2009) 17 *Historical Materialism* 180, 180–81. 'Banking has become heavily dependent on lending to individuals and the direct extraction of revenues from ordinary wage earners … Banks mediate access to housing, consumer goods, health care and education'.

39 Hugh Collins describes the 'extensive strategic litigation' by the UK banks to water down the requirements in relation to the protection of guarantors in *Barclays Bank v O'Brien* [1992] EWCA Civ 11, [1993] QB 109. See H Collins, 'Regulating Contract' in C Parker and others (eds), *Regulating Law* (Oxford, Oxford University Press, 2004) 21. A recent example is the settlement by Black Horse finance (a subsidiary of Lloyds Bank) when an appeal to the Supreme Court was granted in *Harrison & Anor v Black Horse Ltd* [2011] EWCA Civ 1128, [2012] Lloyd's Rep IR 521. See also the discussion of the *Heininger* saga in Germany in Micklitz (n 19).

40 See Financial Services and Markets Act 2000, ss 128–30 for the scope of the fair and reasonable test and also the discussion in S Gilad, 'Why the Haves Do Not Necessarily Come Out Ahead in

However, concentrated interests may be vulnerable (because they are concentrated and visible) and therefore regarded as less legitimate than those representing diffuse groups.[41] A political entrepreneur may galvanise public opinion by capitalising on a crisis, associating her campaign with widely shared values, and undermining conventional expert analysis. Elizabeth Warren achieved this in the US through her promotion of a product safety conceptualisation of credit regulation and the associated concept of a Consumer Finance Protection Bureau. Timing may be all important here: her 2007 article appeared just as the crisis unfolded. David Vogel explains the differences in EU and US food and safety policies in terms of the higher political salience of risks after scandals such as BSE in the EU and changes in the policy preferences of key decision makers.[42] Crises provide higher political salience but the long-term impact will depend on the extent to which ideas become embedded in the work of implementing agencies.

The contrasting stories of the 2008 Consumer Credit Directive and 2014 Mortgage Credit Directive are illuminating. A genealogy of the 2008 Consumer Credit Directive seems to confirm the influence of finance capital over the EU law-making process from the outset of policy making in the 1970s.[43] Work on consumer credit harmonisation began in the 1960s and 70s with a series of draft proposals which were systematically critiqued by the relatively well-organised banking lobby. The original 1987 Directive, enacted under the constraints of an unanimity requirement, provided primarily information remedies and a minimal set of protections against potentially unfair terms and enforcement processes. The 1995 review[44] of this Directive proposed amendments to place it 'at the level of average of the Member States'.[45] It identified the new 'widespread' European problem of over-indebtedness and proposed that professionals be held responsible to debtors for 'providing advice, as in the case of Belgian law' and suggested that

Informal Dispute Resolution' (2010) 32 *Law and Policy* 283, suggesting that the FOS approach may reduce the repeat player advantage.

[41] Trumbull (n 33).

[42] D Vogel, *The Politics of Precaution: Regulating Health, Safety, and Environmental Risks in Europe and the United States* (Princeton, Princeton University Press, 2012).

[43] For the politics of the Consumer Credit Directive see S Franken, 'The Political Economy of the EC Consumer Credit Directive' in J Niemi, I Ramsay and W Whitford (eds), *Consumer Credit, Debt and Bankruptcy* (Oxford, Hart Publishing, 2009) ch 7; M Hartlapp and C Rauth, 'The Commission's Internal Conditions for Social Re-regulation: Market Efficiency and Wider Social Goals in Setting the Rules for Financial Services in Europe' (2013) 2 *European Journal of Government and Economics* 25, 34–35. For an account of the development of EU policy since the 1960s to the late 1970s see P Latham, 'Consumer Credit and the EEC—A European View' in R Goode (ed), *Consumer Credit Legislation* (London, Butterworth, 1977). For the banking view see RF Brennan, 'Consumer Credit and the EEC—A Banking View' in the same volume. For a general overview of credit developments, see P Rott, 'Consumer Credit' in H-W Micklitz, N Reich and P Rott, *Understanding EU Consumer Law* (Cambridge, Intersentia, 2009).

[44] See Commission, Report on the operation of Directive 87/102/EEC for the approximation of the laws, regulations and administrative provisions of the Member States concerning consumer credit COM(95) 117 final.

[45] ibid, para 15.

usury laws might be harmonised at the European level.[46] Countries with major financial industries such as the UK, Germany and the Netherlands were sceptical of these initiatives. Over-indebtedness was generally viewed as a social issue best addressed at the national level. The Commission continued to develop reforms as part of the single market initiative. DG Sanco, the relatively new consumer DG, was given responsibility for the 2002 draft.[47] Little consultation occurred with the financial industry before the initial proposal, which drew on research by consumer lawyers. The original Directive proposed total harmonisation of community rules with the country of origin principle—noting presciently that this was a 'politically charged test case' in the context of qualified majority voting.

The Commission's 2002 draft directive, which included rules on all phases of consumer credit transactions, was intended to achieve a balance of market growth, increased access and consumer protection. It was intended to balance access and protection. Gunnar Trumbull suggests that these are the contrasting 'legitimating narratives' in consumer credit regulation. Either of these narratives may dominate in a country and provide a common frame of reference for political coalitions. Thus in the UK both mainstream consumer and business groups have generally favoured increased access and opposed measures such as price controls on credit because of their potential limitation of access. In 2005 a coalition of these mainstream groups lobbied the House of Lords not to adopt an amendment to consumer credit legislation which would have introduced interest rate ceilings.

The Commission had difficulties in selling its overall package of reforms to both financial and consumer interests, perhaps because of the comprehensiveness of the proposals with a variety of objectives. The dominant policy image in the media of the 2002 draft became that of protection, identified with a patronising image of the consumer, and unworkable consumer protection which would limit consumer choice.[48] The legislative history of the 2008 Directive reads like a case study in public choice analysis of consumer policy. Financial interests operating through the European Parliament, their national governments (particularly in the UK and Germany), and the Commission (particularly DG Market, which did not agree with Sanco) succeeded in gutting many of the provisions of the original Directive.[49] The responsible lending provisions were associated with market

[46] ibid, para 177.

[47] Not DG Market, which usually addressed financial services, had greater expertise, and was closer to the financial industry. The EU official with responsibility for the initial draft was Belgian and Belgian law already contained a responsible lending provision. This may have influenced the insertion of responsible lending provisions in the initial draft.

[48] The German Banking Association claimed that the inclusion of overdrafts in the Directive would make them unavailable in Germany ('Consumer Credit Directive—New Law Raises Hackles—Susana Fernandez Caro Reports on Negative Responses to the European Commission's Draft Legislation Promoting "Responsible Lending"', *The Banker* (London, 1 June 2003) quoting Stephan Steuer, chief counsel of the Association of German Banks, that 'ultimately the overregulation proposed in the EU consumer credit directive would effectively put an end to overdrafts').

[49] See Franken (n 43). The European Parliament heard from 20 national and European financial lobbyists and one consumer group. By 2005 the modified Directive contained no duty to consult

exclusion and increased costs.[50] The Directive's image of a paternalistic consumer protection jarred with the increased dominance of a 'democratisation of credit' image associated with the Anglo-Saxon (neoliberal) model of credit. The main EU consumer group BEUC was also not unreservedly in favour of the draft Directive and the Commission could not establish a coalition of support. Ironically a few months after the enactment of the Directive in 2008, Lehman Brothers crashed along with confidence in the idea of increased credit access as welfare enhancing. A limited concept of responsible lending[51] survives which has had international influence[52] as a 'policy image' of a 'European' model of lending.

In contrast, the introduction of the draft Mortgage Directive in 2011 took place against the background of international post-crisis measures of consumer protection in financial services. Consumer financial protection had a high public salience, if measured by media coverage. The crisis provided the opportunity for civil society groups to influence the agenda of reform. The OECD, tasked in 2010 by the G20 with developing principles of financial consumer protection, conceptualised the exercise initially as purely technocratic not requiring consultation with consumer groups. However, after pressure from international consumer groups and an intervention by Christine Lagarde, consumer groups were consulted and the final document indicates the various consultations conducted by the drafting group.[53] The high-level G20 principles are 'voluntary' but the document requests that all G20 members 'and other interested economies should assess their national frameworks for financial consumer protection in the light of these principles'. The Mortgage Directive, after modification by the European Parliament, refers to the congruence of its provisions with those of the G20 principles.

The genealogy of the Mortgage Directive contrasts with the earlier Consumer Credit Directive. The Commission, through DG Market, had worked for several years on preparatory work on mortgage regulation. DG Market was viewed by consumer groups as closer to financial interests and the NGO, ALTER-EU exposed in 2009 the domination of expert EU financial committees by industry groups, arguing that the Commission had been captured by financial interests. Early work on harmonising mortgage regulation embraced the market goals of improving

databases: responsible lending was limited to assessing the creditworthiness of the debtor and providing advice to the debtor to put her in a position to make an informed choice; voluntary insurance premiums were not included in APR. Unfair terms, guarantors and rules on repossession were not included; a light touch for overdrafts, small loans and mortgages excluded.

[50] In the UK mortgage lenders and the British Bankers Association critiqued the initial draft, commissioned a report by a consultancy firm which indicated the detrimental effects of the Directive on the credit industry and credit availability, and lobbied the European Parliament.

[51] Taking together Art 5, particularly 5(6), and Art 8 on creditworthiness. See also Recs 26 and 27, 'promotion of responsible lending practices throughout the transaction'.

[52] eg in Australia. See also World Bank, *Consumer Protection in Financial Services* (2012) and G20 High Level Principles on Financial Consumer Protection (2011) principle 6.

[53] For a useful discussion of the role of international civil society groups in this process of reform see L Kastner, '"Much Ado About Nothing?": Transnational Civil Society. Consumer Protection and Financial Regulatory Reform' (2014) 21 *Review of International Political Economy* 1313. See also Williams (n 12).

competitiveness, product diversity and choice and more efficient enforcement of mortgages, reflecting a 'lubricant' model of credit. These goals were modified in the White Paper of 2007, just after the first reverberations of the sub-prime mortgage crisis.[54] While continuing to emphasise the integration of the EU mortgage market to the efficient functioning of the EU financial system the paper recognised the potential dangers of product innovation and the need to regain consumer confidence by sanctioning irresponsible lending. The Commission also established an expert group on credit histories, initiated a consultation on responsible lending and borrowing, published a communication on financial education, and sponsored studies on interest rate ceilings noting that their potential limitation on cross-border lending should be balanced against the fact that 'they may fulfil an important social and consumer protection role'.

The 2011 proposal for a directive outlined its objectives as twofold: creating an efficient and competitive single market with a high level of protection and promoting financial stability by ensuring that mortgage credit markets operate responsibly.[55] The policy diagnosis now was that reform was necessary because of 'irresponsible lending and borrowing caused by market and regulatory failure, the general economic climate and low levels of financial literacy'.[56] The proposal included a Staff Working Paper on national measures to avoid foreclosure procedures noting that 'losing the family home after having lost one's job has intolerable social and human implications for both borrowers and their families'.[57] This report was intended to 'provide inspiration' for Member States rather than a benchmark but the Commission would continue to monitor default rates closely. No specific provisions on foreclosure and default were contained in the original proposal for a directive.

The European Parliament, in contrast to its approach to the Consumer Credit Directive, widened the scope of the Mortgage Directive to include issues of financial education and post-contractual relations, and strengthened existing provisions in the Directive. Consistency with the FSB international principles was added as an objective with references in specific recitals.[58] The final version,

[54] See Commission, White Paper on Integration of Mortgage Credit Markets (n 31) para 45. See also DG Internal Market and Services, *Towards More Responsibility and Competitiveness in the European Financial Services Sector* (2010).

[55] 'The mortgage credit directive "has to be seen in the context of efforts to create an internal market for mortgage credit and against the background of the financial crisis" … addressing irresponsible lending and borrowing is therefore an important element in financial reform efforts' (Commission, Proposal for a Directive of the European Parliament and of the Council on credit Agreements relating to Residential Property COM(2011) 142 final, 2).

[56] Mortgage Directive, Rec 4.

[57] See Commission, Staff Working Paper: National Measures and practices to avoid foreclosure procedures for residential mortgage loans—Accompanying document to the Proposal for a Directive of the European Parliament and of the Council on credit agreements relating to residential property SEC(2011) 357 final, 11.

[58] eg Mortgage Directive, Rec 3: 'Union's regulatory framework … robust, consistent with international principles', Rec 55: 'member states … should be encouraged to implement the Financial Stability Board's Principles for Sound Residential Mortgage Underwriting Practices'.

developed through the 'trilogue' procedure,[59] contains: (1) increased specificity on competent authorities, including a requirement that they should have adequate resources;[60] (2) an obligation on Member States to support the education of consumers in relation to responsible borrowing and debt management;[61] (3) more detailed provisions to ensure that the internal structure of creditor remuneration and commissions do not encourage excessive risk taking; (4) more specific responsible lending obligations, including prohibition of significant reliance on asset value lending;[62] (5) greater regulation of credit intermediaries; (6) regulation of loans denominated in foreign currencies;[63] and (7) provisions to encourage creditors to exercise reasonable forbearance before foreclosure proceedings are initiated, capping default charges and ensuring best effort prices are achieved from foreclosure sales.[64] Several of these measures responded to the experiences of Member States with debt problems as a consequence of the imposition of austerity in the wake of the Eurozone crisis.[65] The general approach appears to be influenced by the UK Financial Services Authority (FSA) handbook, including its high-level principles to 'treat customers fairly'. Full harmonisation only applies to the standardised information disclosure, calculation of the APRC and responsible lending obligations.

A high level of consumer protection, preventing another mortgage crisis and addressing the problems of indebted homeowners justified these amendments to the Commission's original Directive. The EU Commission hailed it as a measure which demonstrated that the EU was a 'citizen's Europe' close to the problems of everyday life and that the Directive, 'required to meet the commitments made in the G20 "places" the EU at the forefront of global mortgage legislation'.[66] Although many of the proposals are vague and hortatory (for example, on foreclosure), the European Banking Authority may promote greater convergence in supervisory

[59] This is a small group of the Commission, Parliament and Council which attempts to achieve agreement on differences. See Joint Declaration on Practical Arrangements for the [Ordinary Legislative] Procedure [2007] OJ C145/2. Chalmers and others raise concerns about the transparency of this process suggesting that 'only very well connected actors have the opportunity to lobby these informal processes because they can know where they are taking place or who is important within them'. D Chalmers, G Davies and G Monti, *European Union Law: Cases and Materials* 2nd edn (Cambridge, Cambridge University Press, 2010) 109.

[60] Mortgage Directive, Art 5.

[61] ibid, Art 6. Art 6(2) commits the Commission to publishing an assessment of financial education and identify examples of best practices.

[62] ibid, Art 18(3), and see Art 20 requiring verification of consumer's income.

[63] ibid, Art 23.

[64] Art 28.

[65] I discuss these issues further in I Ramsay, 'Two Cheers for Austerity: Mortgage Foreclosure and Personal Insolvency Policy in the EU' in Micklitz and Domurath (n 6).

[66] 'Nous avons donc avec ce texte un des exemples—auxquels je tiens comme vous, Mesdames et Messieurs les députés—de cette Europe concrète, de cette Europe citoyenne proche des gens, de leurs problèmes, de leurs difficultés ou de leurs éléments de leur vie quotidienne … ce sera une preuve de cette Europe citoyenne et concrète à laquelle nous travaillons.' Michel Barnier, Commissioner DG Market, plenary session of the European Parliament held in Strasbourg on 10 September 2013 (13507/13).

practices. It has signalled that it may introduce guidelines on responsible lending and foreclosure practices. The Directive was adopted by a qualified majority with some Member States unhappy with the extension of the scope and provisions of the original draft of the Directive.[67]

The different political backgrounds to the Consumer Credit and Mortgage Directive have resulted in unjustified distinctions in the levels of regulation of mortgage and non-mortgage credit in the EU with, for example, higher responsible lending obligations in mortgage credit. Lower income consumers probably use unsecured and high-cost credit more, sometimes as a method of supplementing limited budgets. Problems of irresponsible lending exist in unsecured credit markets, particularly those associated with high-cost credit such as payday and SMS loans, but consensus does not exist on common approaches to protection in these markets, in particular on the use of interest rate ceilings.[68]

The politics of consumer credit law must also account for the role of the Court of Justice of the EU ('CJEU'). The ability to use the preliminary reference procedure to obtain low-cost access to the CJEU may confer some power on diffuse interests such as consumers to pursue reform and political campaigns[69] with several cases relating to consumer credit.[70] The CJEU in *Aziz* underlined the importance of due process in relation to repossession of the family home, drawing indirect inspiration from Article 7 of the Charter of Fundamental Rights of the EU.[71] This development might be analogised to the US Supreme Court jurisprudence of the late 1960s and early 1970s which applied the Fourteenth Amendment due

[67] Luxembourg, Latvia and Estonia abstained. Austria, the Czech Republic, the UK and Bulgaria expressed some reservations. See Council of the European Union, 'Council Adopts Directive on Mortgage Credits' (Press Release, 28 January 2014) 5564/14 presse 23.

[68] See DG Internal Market and Services, 'Summary of Public Responses to Consultation on Interest Rate Restrictions in the EU' (15 June 2011) <http://ec.europa.eu/internal_market/finservices-retail/docs/policy/irr_summary_en.pdf> accessed 3 January 2015.

[69] See discussion in H-W Micklitz, 'Judicial Activism of the ECJ and the Development of the European Social Mode in Anti-discrimination and Consumer Law', *EUI Working Paper LAW* 2009/19.

[70] eg Case C–76/10 *Pohotovosť sro v Iveta Korckovska*, order of 3 April 2014 (sub-prime lender charging an undisclosed 95% APR and 0.25% daily default interest to disabled person on invalidity pension). See R Minarechová, 'Pohotovosť Claims Flood the Courts' *The Slovak Spectator* (18 March 2013). See also cases such as Case C–264/02 *Cofinoga Mérignac SA v Sylvain Sachithanathan* [2004] ECR I–2157, which was a reference by a 'radical' French judge, and Case C–565/12 *LCL Le Credit Lyonnais v Fesih Kalhan* [2014] OJ C151/4.

[71] Case C–415/11 *Mohamed Aziz v Caixa d'Estalvis de Catalunya, Tarragona i Manresa (Catalunyacaixa)*, judgment of 14 March 2013, para 61 (though without express reference to Art 7). See the later direct reference by Advocate General Wahl in Case C–482/12 *Peter Macinský, Eva Macinská v Getfin sro, Financreal sro*, [2014] OJ C184/22, para 82: 'where the property concerned by the procedure at issue is the consumer's home, there must be specific guarantees. Failure to provide such guarantees may prove problematic from a fundamental rights perspective. Indeed, the loss of a family home is one of the most extreme forms of interference with the rights of the consumer. As respect for the home is a right guaranteed under Article 7 of the Charter of Fundamental Rights of the European Union, in the light of which Directive 93/13 must be interpreted, any person at risk of an interference of this magnitude should be able to have the proportionality of such a measure reviewed by an independent judicial body.' See also *Rousk v Sweden* App no 27183/04 (ECtHR, 25 October 2013 final) (lack of effective procedural safeguards against repossession and sale by Swedish tax authorities violation of Art 8).

process rights to creditors' remedies.[72] This 'embedding' of credit markets through minimum standards at the European level complements the provisions of the Mortgage Directive. The CJEU has not, however, articulated a coherent theory of unfairness in consumer credit contracts,[73] although authors document cases where the Court has been sensitive to the complexities of financial services and the need for higher levels of consumer protection.[74]

III. EU Consumer Credit Policy and Theories of Consumer Credit

A. Conventional Analyses and the Behavioural Challenge

Dominant economic theory before the crash assumed the importance of financial deepening, facilitating greater access to finance including debt as a method of promoting growth and development.[75] Credit could play an important role in lifecycle budgeting, balancing saving and spending and income smoothing. Households who are liquidity-constrained may commit future income to meet present consumption needs. Since lifetime earnings are 'hump shaped', younger consumers may be expected and encouraged to borrow more against their future income expectations in order to accumulate capital assets. A market comprising consumers uncertain about using credit and lenders uncertain about recovering money lent might result in suboptimal lending patterns, and regulation could encourage greater confidence by both parties to commit to long-term credit and drive demand. Even poor consumers could benefit from credit for income smoothing.

[72] eg *Sniadach v Family Finance Corp* 395 US 337 (1969). This trend was halted, however, by the later *Flagg Bros v Brooks* 436 US 149 (1978), which declined to strike down private repossession under the 'due process' clause of the Constitution on the basis that such seizure did not constitute 'state action'.

[73] Occasional references to the inchoate 'weaker' party or the greater complexity of financial service contracts. See Case C–265/12 *Citroën Belux NV v Federatie voor Verzekerings- en Financiële Tussenpersonen (FvF)*, judgment of 18 July 2013, [2014] 1 CMLR 26.

[74] 'Financial services are, by nature, complex and entail specific risks with regard to which the consumer is not always sufficiently well informed.' ibid, para 39, upholding the general Belgian prohibition on combined offers as applied to a combined offer of free insurance coverage with purchase of a new Citroen. Recognised also in Directive 2005/29/EC of the European Parliament and of the Council of 11 May 2005 concerning unfair business-to-consumer commercial practices in the internal market [2005] OJ L149/22 (Unfair Commercial Practices Directive or UCPD). Niamh Moloney refers to cases such as Case C–384/93 *Alpine Investments BV v Minister van Financiën* [1995] ECR I–1141 and Case C–222/95 *Société civile immobilière Parodi v Banque H Albert de Bary et Cie* [1997] ECR I–3899. N Moloney, *How to Protect Investors: Lessons from the EC and the UK* (New York, Cambridge University Press, 2010). Eurobarometer in 2005 noted that Europeans perceive finances and their financial priorities as complicated.

[75] For a statement of economic orthodoxy see G Bertola, R Disney and C Grant (eds), *The Economics of Consumer Credit* (Cambridge MA, MIT Press, 2006) ch 1.

This lifecycle model of credit[76] continues to be influential both in financial literacy strategies and explaining higher levels of debt in certain age categories. It suggests that policy should maximise non-discriminatory access to credit and facilitate financial innovations which expand liquidity in the market—such as securitisation. 'Democratising credit' could expand an individual's opportunities to manage their finances. This conception was one leg of the original draft of the Consumer Credit Directive which recognised the 'lubricant' role of credit.

The rise of behavioural economics provides a corrective to this approach. It has proved attractive to policy makers[77] in consumer financial services markets where individuals often make long-term decisions with uncertain outcomes[78] and where changes in personal circumstances might have substantial effects on ability to repay. Behavioural economics has moved rapidly since the early 2000s from the fringes of consumer policy to the corridors of power. Behavioural analysis provides an alternative to the hyperrationality of traditional economics and might provide a systematic framework for understanding the concept of the 'vulnerable consumer'[79] in financial services. This concept, which may relate to situational

[76] See F Modigliani and R Brumberg, 'Utility Analysis and the Consumption Function: An Interpretation of Cross-Section Data' in K Kurihara (ed), *Post Keynesian Economics* (London, George Allen and Unwin, 1955).

[77] Examples include the various DG Sanco initiatives (eg guidelines on the UCPD which recommend that judges take into account the latest insights of behavioural economics in interpreting the provisions of the UCPD), EU conferences on behavioural economics, the appointment of Sendil Mullainathan to the CFPB, its use by the OFT and the Behavioural Insight team. See Financial Services Authority, *The Turner Review: A Regulatory Response to the Global Banking Crisis* (2009). The first research paper of the new Financial Conduct Authority in the UK concerns the role of behavioural economics. See Financial Conduct Authority, *Applying Behavioural Economics at the Financial Conduct Authority* (2013). For a useful discussion of its influence, see P Lunn, 'Behavioural Economics and Policymaking: Learning from the Early Adopters' (2012) 43 *The Economic and Social Review* 423. For recent overviews see J Mehta (ed), *Behavioral Economics in Competition and Consumer Policy* (Norwich, ESRC Centre for Competition Policy, 2013) and see the articles in (2011) 10 *American Economic Review Papers and Proceedings*, eg E Kamenicka, S Mullainathan and R Thaler, 'Helping Consumers Know Themselves' (2011) 101 *American Economic Review Papers and Proceedings* 417. See Commission, *Consumer Decision Making in Retail Investment Services—A Behavioural Perspective* (November 2010) <http://ec.europa.eu/consumers/archive/strategy/docs/final_report_en.pdf> accessed 28 May 2015.

[78] eg discussion in Moloney (n 74) 67–81.

[79] For discussion in the UK, see *Wilson v First County Trust* [2003] UKHL 40, [2004] 1 AC 816, where the House of Lords refers to 'the vulnerability of those members of the public who resort to pawnbrokers'. See also Office of Fair Trading, *Vulnerable Consumers and Financial Services—The Report of the Director General's Inquiry* (1999). For a discussion of the vulnerable consumer in credit regulation see S Brown, 'European Regulation of Consumer Credit: Enhancing Consumer Confidence and Protection from a UK Perspective?' in J Devenney and M Kenny (eds), *Consumer Credit, Debt and Investment in Europe* (New York, Cambridge University Press, 2011). Consumer Focus identifies in *Tackling Consumer Vulnerability* (2012) the following factors as creating the risk of vulnerability: 'lack of self-confidence, low literacy/numeracy, low/insecure income, being unemployed, being responsible for high level of care for another person, having a physical impairment, having mental health problems, living in social rented housing, living in a lone parent household'. At the EU level the UCPD has a relatively limited category of vulnerable consumers. The Mortgage Credit Directive implicitly accepts a concept of vulnerability in the responsible lending provisions intended to prevent debt overcommitment in housing loans. These measures, although a response to the subprime mortgage crisis, apply to all home buyers—primarily middle income consumers.

or structural factors, personal characteristics or exogenous events, is more often described than analysed.

Behavioural economics has both a scientific and normative aspect. Its scientific findings demonstrate a large number of heuristics and biases associated with consumer preferences, beliefs and decision-making processes.[80] Central findings are that individuals do not measure utility by wealth but by reference to gains and losses from a reference point—usually the status quo, that the consequent framing of a choice is crucial, and that individuals are generally loss averse—except in situations where individuals face very bad choices when they may be risk-seeking. Tastes are not fixed but depend on a 'reference point'[81] which might include 'what other people think'. Thus the unsustainable nature of a housing boom may be supported by individuals observing on a continuing basis the behaviour of their neighbours and friends so that although they might at some level know that the boom is unsustainable, the contrary seems to be validated by peer behaviour.[82] This form of behaviour suggests that policy focussed on individual behaviour, such as financial literacy, may be relatively ineffective and that collective hands-tying may be necessary either through macro-economic controls on lending, or effective forms of responsible lending which can have a counter-cyclical effect.

Given the findings of behavioural economics, the more difficult question is framing a policy response. The normative aspect of behavioural economics has been associated with *Nudge* and libertarian paternalism[83] with measures which are 'easy and cheap to avoid' for the sophisticated consumer. The most common techniques advocated are: more simple and standardised disclosures informed by behavioural analysis, cooling-off periods, and the use of a variety of default rules which may be more or less 'sticky'. Measures which might limit choice such as product or term prohibitions should generally be avoided.[84] This approach respects consumer choice and the avoidance of paternalism. These policies are also attractive because they promise significant change from inexpensive initiatives. EU policymaking has embraced altering defaults,[85] making disclosures less

[80] The tripartite distinction is taken from S DellaVigna, 'Psychology and Economics: Evidence from the Field' (2009) 47 *Journal of Economic Literature* 315. The Financial Conduct Authority outlines 10 key biases, namely, preferences—present bias, reference dependence and loss aversion, regret and other emotional driven preferences; beliefs—overconfidence, extrapolation, projection bias; decision making—mental accounting and narrow bracketing, framing salience and limited attention, decision-making rules of thumb, persuasion and social influence. Financial Conduct Authority, *Applying Behavioural Economics* (n 77).

[81] See generally Kahneman (n 28). For reviews of Kahneman, see, eg, A Shleifer, 'Psychologists at the Gate: A Review of Daniel Kahneman's *Thinking Fast and Slow*' (2012) 50 *Journal of Economic Literature* 1080.

[82] See S Farrazi and B Cynamon, 'Inequality and Household Finance During the Consumer Age' [2013] *Levy Economics Institute Working Paper Archive* no 752.

[83] R Thaler and C Sunstein, *Nudge* (New Haven, Yale University Press, 2008). The identification of *Nudge* with behavioural economic policymaking is of course not inevitable.

[84] eg Thaler and Sunstein reject Lauren Willis's call for prohibition on certain types of mortgage because 'it prohibits contracts that may be mutually beneficial'; ibid 137.

[85] eg Directive 2011/83/EU of the European Parliament and of the Council of 25 October 2011 on consumer rights [2011] OJ L304/64, Art 22.

complex,[86] and warnings about the consequences of default. Shaping consumer choice might include helping consumers to 'know themselves'[87] and their distinct preferences through, for example, annual statements on fees and charges on credit cards.[88]

No logical connection exists, however, between the scientific analyses and libertarian paternalism. A response to a recognition that credit problems with high-cost credit are caused by impulsiveness—myopia caused by presentism—could be a policy which limits access, price controls or product regulation. Tom Baker and Peter Siegelman justify bans on point of sale payment protection insurance (PPI), a measure adopted in the UK, through the application of a behavioural model to this market.[89]

Daniel Kahneman argues that individual decision making often represents system 1 thinking, which operates intuitively, 'automatically and quickly', rather than system 2 cognitive analysis, which involves effortful conscious analysis. Increased reliance on system 1 seems to be associated with a cluster of emotions such as 'good mood, creativity, gullibility'.[90] A 'happy mood' loosens the controls of system 2. Much advertising of course attempts to exploit system 1 and Marianne Bertrand and others illustrate how credit advertising may exploit system 1 in selling credit.[91] EU consumer credit regulation, however, is often premised on triggering system 2 thinking, but Kahneman suggests that in many cases this will not happen. Within the traditional legal frame the 'reasonably circumspect consumer' should discount emotional suggestions and appeals as 'mere puffs'.[92] However, the behavioural findings support Avner Offer's comment that 'puffs like anchoring are effective even when known to be untrue … the legal attitude is

[86] eg ESIS and Mortgage Directive, Rec 41: 'Consumer research has underlined the importance of using simple and understandable language in disclosures provided to consumers.'

[87] Kamenicka, Mullainathan and Thaler (n 77).

[88] Thaler and Sunstein (n 83) propose RECAP (Record, Evaluate and Compare Alternative Prices), which would have two aspects: a requirement on firms to make public (online) their fee schedules (eg for credit cards, mobile phones etc) and a usage disclosure requirement on the provider to send a consumer an annual listing of all the fees which had been incurred. They assume that private firms would emerge to permit easy comparison of the costs which other service providers would have levied. The UK government as part of its midata initiative agreed with the UK cards association to introduce an annual usage disclosure requirement in relation to credit cards along with the creation of a site which permits individuals to assess different scenarios for paying off bills might work.

[89] See T Baker and P Siegelman, 'Protecting Consumers from Add-On Insurance Products: New Lessons for Insurance Regulation from Behavioural Economics' (2013) 20 *Connecticut Insurance Law Journal* 1. In the UK, see Competition Commission, *Payment Protection Insurance Investigation Order* (2011).

[90] Kahneman (n 28).

[91] See M Bertrand and others, 'What's Advertising Content Worth? Evidence from a Consumer Credit Marketing Field Experiment' (2010) 125 *Quarterly Journal of Economics* 263. '[I]ncluding a photo of an attractive woman increases loan demand by about as much as a 25% reduction in the interest rate. The evidence also suggests that advertising content persuades by appealing "peripherally" to intuition rather than reason.'

[92] See Unfair Commercial Practices Directive, Rec 19. In the UK see The Consumer Protection from Unfair Trading Regulations 2008, para 2(6).

misconceived; it applies the test of reason to claims that are designed to bypass the filter of reason'.[93] Regulation might focus on psychological appeals which exploit system 1.[94]

Behavioural analysis may be a useful addition to policymaking in credit markets. But I would make the following caveats. First, it may be quite complex to apply,[95] involving substantial empirical evidence, and continuing monitoring to assess effectiveness and unintended consequences. For example, the idea of introducing minimum payments warnings on credit cards was attractive as a response to behavioural failures in consumer credit markets, but proved complex to apply and seemed to have the unintended consequence of reducing the amounts repaid.[96] Second, many policies based on behavioural economics focus on changing consumer behaviour when the evidence from large systemic scandals such as payment protection insurance in the UK suggest that it is pathologies in organisational behaviour within firms which is a prime source of problems.[97] It is difficult to 'upgrade' consumers to adequately fight against the consequences of these pathologies.[98] Third, the insights of behavioural economics are primarily for the legislator or regulator rather than a judge who might find difficulties in incorporating the insights into individual cases.[99] The effects of over-optimism and underestimation of risks on consumer behaviour may have influenced the decision in *Ashbourne Investments* on unfair terms, but the judge could find empirical support for his position in the OFT submission on the behaviour of consumers in signing up for gym contracts.[100]

Finally, behavioural analysis indicates that preferences are unstable and depend on institutional context. This undermines the distinction between policies designed

[93] A Offer, *The Challenge of Affluence* (New York, Oxford University Press, 2006) 109.

[94] See the various cases before the English Advertising Standards Authority concerning social irresponsibility of payday lenders in their ads. See Advertising Standards Authority, <http://www.asa.org.uk/Rulings/Adjudications/2013/10/WDFC-UK-Ltd/SHP_ADJ_232698.aspx> accessed 3 January 2015.

[95] eg the model outlined in O Bar Gill, 'The Behavioral Economics of Consumer Contracts' (2008) 92 *Minnesota Law Review* 749.

[96] See D Navarro-Martinez and others, 'Minimum Required Payment and Supplemental Information Disclosure Effects on Consumer Debt Repayment' (unpublished) <http://www.ucl.ac.uk/lagnado-lab/publications/harris/NavarroMartinez_JMR.pdf> accessed 3 January 2015.

[97] eg discussion of PPI cases in Williams (n 12) and see cases such as *HFC Bank* in Ramsay (n 34) 397–407.

[98] eg Financial Services Authority, *Financial Capability: A Behavioural Economics Perspective* (2008) 69.

[99] The Commission in its guidance on misleading actions under the UCPD does suggest that national courts and administrative authorities might assess misleading practices by reference to the 'current state of scientific knowledge, including the most recent findings of behavioural economics.' See Commission, Staff Working Document: Guidance on the Implementation/Application of Directive 2005 29/EC Unfair Commercial Practices SEC(2009) 1666.

[100] 'The average consumer tends to overestimate how often he will use the gym once he has become a member and further unforeseen circumstances may make continued use of its facilities impractical. Indeed it is … a notorious fact that many people join such gym clubs having resolved to exercise regularly but fail to attend at all after two or three months. Yet having entered into the agreement, they are locked into paying monthly subscriptions for the full minimum period'. *OFT v Ashbourne Management Services* [2011] EWCA 1237 (Kitchin J) para 164.

to give individuals what they want and those based on paternalism. It problematises policymaking based on revealed preferences.[101] We cannot assume that such preferences necessarily express what people want. This poses challenges for normative economics and foregrounds the role of market ground rules in constituting and shaping markets. These rules may be private or public and include the 'rules of the game', such as social norms. The creation of credit markets in Eastern Europe after the fall of Communism foregrounded the importance of legal rules and institutions in constituting a consumer credit market.[102] It highlighted the role of 'taken for granted' background rules in mature consumer credit economies. We should therefore avoid thinking about government 'intervention' in credit markets—with its assumption of a natural state free from regulation.[103] Governments create affordable housing credit markets through guarantees, mortgage subsidies, homeownership biases in the tax system, planning regulations, etc. They may provide social loans or facilitate the growth of *Sparkassen*-style non-profit institutions. Credit markets are instruments of both economic and social policy which may shape consumer preferences.[104]

A useful example of the contrast between neoclassical approaches and behavioural approaches concerns conceptualisations of vulnerability and the lower-income credit consumer. John Gathergood, in an econometric study of consumer over-indebtedness,[105] concludes that lack of self-control is associated with over-indebtedness. Lack of self-control also correlates with lower-income households, those who are 'unmarried with children, with less education, lower rates of employment and higher rates of unemployment, lower rates of outright homeownership'. His suggested policy responses are to either limit immediate access to credit for this group through a required cooling-off period or more effective financial literacy. This analysis links class (lower income) with individual characteristics. In contrast Sendhil Mullainathan and Eldar Shafir in *Scarcity* (2013) suggest that lower-income consumers have similar behavioural biases to other consumers but that the pressures of poverty make it difficult to focus, resulting in a 'tunnelling' of

[101] eg S Heap, 'What is the Meaning of Behavioural Economics?' (2013) 37 *Cambridge Journal of Economics* 985; A Santos, 'Behavioural and Experimental Economics: Are They Really Transforming Economics?' (2013) 35 *Cambridge Journal of Economics* 705.

[102] eg A Rona-Tas and A Guseva, *Plastic Money—Constructing Markets for Credit Cards in Eight Postcommunist Countries* (Stanford, Stanford University Press, 2014).

[103] Joseph Stiglitz and Andrew Weiss pointed out that because of adverse selection, markets for credit do not clear like other markets and credit would be rationed. J Stiglitz and A Weiss, 'Credit Rationing in Markets with Imperfect Information' (1981) 71 *American Economic Review* 76.

[104] See W Schelkle, 'A Crisis of What? Mortgage Credit Markets and the Social Policy of Promoting Homeownership in the United States and Europe' (2012) 40 *Politics and Society* 59, 60: 'Comparative welfare state research has barely started analyzing social policies in their relationship with financial markets generally'. G Trumbull, 'Credit Access and Social Welfare: The Rise of Consumer Lending in the United States and France' (2012) 40 *Politics and Society* 9. For the role of ground rules in shaping credit markets see I Ramsay, 'Consumer Law, Distributive Justice and the Welfare State' (1995) 15 *Oxford Journal of Legal Studies* 177.

[105] See J Gathergood, 'Self Control Financial Literacy and Consumer Over-indebtedness' (2012) 33 *Journal of Economic Psychology* 590.

vision. The poor are often as well informed as affluent individuals but they have much smaller room for errors in decision making and therefore must make better-quality decisions. The many pressures on their time mean that they are more likely to be myopic in decision making and not attentive to long-term costs. They refer to the problem as an absence of 'bandwidth', represented by scarcity of money, unpredictability of income, and lack of buffers. Policy solutions might change the institutional context of lending along with measures which radically reduce the costs of decision making. Mullainathan and Shafir's focus on the context of decision making provides a contrasting explanation of vulnerability to individualistic explanations which 'assume that the problem lies with the person' and imply policies to change the consumer rather than the institutional framework.

A further example concerns payday loan regulation in the UK, where a debate has existed over price and terms regulation. The Financial Conduct Authority (FCA) commissioned Europe Economics to assess the consequences on consumers of FCA proposals to regulate this market including limits on 'rollovers'—which can result in spiralling debt.[106] Empirical evidence suggested that borrowers could be divided into 'payday copers', 'moderate risk borrowers' and 'high risk borrowers'. The analysis expressed concern because some moderate risk and payday copers might have more restricted access to loans. 'Payday copers' were individuals who 'prefer payday loans as they are wary of revolving credit and overdraft models'. However, the existing preferences of this group are a consequence of the institutional context of the present structure of revolving credit and overdrafts. We cannot assume that using a payday loan is a choice which they would prefer in a different lending environment.

B. Critical Approaches to Consumer Credit

Behavioural economics draws attention to how market ground rules and context shape choices. Since the crisis more critical approaches have drawn attention to wider structural factors affecting credit markets. Aldo Barba and Massimo Pivetti outline a 'loans for wages' model.[107] Since the late 1970s household incomes for middle- and lower-income consumers have stagnated in many countries and inequality has increased.[108] This creates problems for maintaining demand since wealthier individuals tend to save more than lower income consumers who have a 'higher marginal propensity to consume'. One response is to make credit more easily available. Increased credit use was 'an effort by low and middle income

[106] See Europe Economics, *A New Consumer Credit Regime* (London, 3 October 2013).

[107] See A Barba and M Pivetti, 'Rising Household Debt: Its Causes and Macro-economic Implications—A Long Period Analysis' (2009) 33 *Cambridge Journal of Economics* 113. For references to recent literature on this model see Farrazi and Cynamon (n 82). See also G Dumenil and D Levy, *The Crisis of NeoLiberalism* (Cambridge MA, Harvard University Press, 2012).

[108] See J Ostry, A Berg and C Tsangarides, *Redistribution, Inequality and Growth* (IMF Staff Discussion Note, 2014).

households to maintain as long as possible their relative standards of consumption in the face of persistent changes in income distribution in favour of households with higher incomes'.[109] Rajan describes this strategy of credit for income pithily as 'let them eat credit'.[110] In some EU countries housing credit acted as a form of 'privatized Keynesianism'[111] where individuals could borrow against rising house prices and use homes as a source for further credit.

The rise in inequality in many countries is also relevant. Thomas Piketty argues[112] that returns on capital are outstripping income from increased growth, causing a potentially increasing level of inequality and concentration of wealth in society. He notes that financial capital is primarily held by the richest decile, who search for high returns for their savings. Lending to lower-income groups has provided an increasingly profitable investment with the growth of sophisticated technologies of risk-based pricing. Doug Henwood noted presciently in 1995 that 'the middle and lower classes have borrowed more to stay in place: they've borrowed from the very rich who have gotten richer. The rich need a place to earn interest on their surplus funds, and the rest of the population makes a juicy lending target.'[113] The payday or SMS loan is the symbol of a contemporary credit market where the very wealthy (represented by capital funds—the ultimate owners of some UK payday loan companies) lend to lower-income consumers at very high prices so that the latter can make ends meet.[114] The Competition and Markets Authority concluded that the major payday loan companies make supra-normal profits.

Some writers conceptualise creditor–debtor relations as a defining characteristic of contemporary neoliberalism which embraces individualisation of responsibility for managing biographical risks as the state downloads this responsibility to the individual. The individual becomes an 'entrepreneur of the self'[115] investing in her human capital and managing debt often against an unstable economic background. Maurizio Lazzarrato develops these themes in his recent text *The Making*

[109] Barba and Pivetti (n 107) 121–22.

[110] R Rajan, *Fault Lines: How Hidden Fractures Still Threaten the World Economy* (Princeton, Princeton University Press, 2010) 21 and 8–9: 'Cynical as it may seem, easy credit has been used as a palliative throughout history by governments that are unable to address the deeper anxieties of the middle class directly'.

[111] The idea of 'privatised Keynesianism' is developed in C Crouch, *The Strange Non-Death of Neoliberalism* (Cambridge MA, Polity Press, 2011).

[112] T Piketty, *Capital in the Twenty-First Century* (Cambridge MA, Harvard University Press, 2014).

[113] D Henwood, *Wall Street* (New York, Verso, 1995) 64–65.

[114] See Competition and Markets Authority, *Payday Lending Market Investigation Provisional Findings Report* (2014); L Hyman, 'The Politics of Consumer Debt: US State Policy and the Rise of Investment in Consumer Credit 1920–2008' (2012) 644 *The Annals of the American Academy of Political and Social Science* 40, 48. 'Whereas in the post war period the 1 percent paid the 99 percent in wages after 1970 the 1 percent increasingly just lent the 99 percent money'.

[115] See M Foucault, *The Birth of Bio-Politics Lectures at the Collège de France* 1978–79(Basingstoke, Palgrave Macmillan, 2008); M Lazzarrato, *The Making of Indebted Man: An Essay on the Neo-Liberal Condition* (Cambridge MA, MIT Press, 2012) Lazzarrato argues that 'contemporary neo-liberal policies produce a human capital or 'entrepreneur of the self' more or less indebted and more or less poor but always precarious.'

of the Indebted Man. He argues that the growth of a debt-dominated economy limits the power of sovereign states, disciplines firms through shareholder capitalism and shapes the subjectivity of the indebted man as 'an entrepreneur of the self [who] is restricted to managing, according to the terms of business and competition, its employability, its debts, the drop in wages and income and the reduction of public services.'[116]

A debt economy requires a specific form of subjectivity—where individuals develop a way of life, discipline, attitudes and conduct appropriate to the 'indebted man [sic], who should learn to exploit credit markets appropriately'.[117] Although fewer traditional sites of discipline exist, the growth of technologies of credit scoring and credit bureaux perform a significant sorting, channelling and disciplining role. Individuals are encouraged to check and learn how to improve their credit rating just as one might with cholesterol levels. The enormous growth in 'care of the self' techniques—such as the worldwide financial literacy movement to make consumers perform more like the rational actor model of neo-classical economics—shape this subjectivity.[118] Financial literacy fits with new forms of governance associated with neoliberalism which attempt to manage the subject of consumption through education, and expert advice.[119] Neoliberalism does not mean, therefore, the absence of the state. Facilitating market growth and ensuring market confidence requires substantial state action. The consumer is enlisted as a regulatory subject[120] in making credit markets competitive (for example, through enhanced switching) and policing 'internalities'[121]—such as impulsiveness or myopia—which may result in over-indebtedness or obesity.[122] This is the world of the responsible borrower.

Lazzarrato develops earlier critiques of the disciplining effects of credit.[123] Other Marxist-inspired analyses focus on the extent to which neoliberalism and

[116] Lazzarrato (n 115) 94.

[117] ibid 104.

[118] ibid 38: 'Learning how to "live with debt" has now been made part of certain American school curricula'.

[119] eg N Rose, *Powers of Freedom: Reframing Political Thought* (Cambridge, Cambridge University Press, 1999).

[120] See T Williams, 'Empowerment of Whom and for What? Financial Literacy Education and the New Regulation of Consumer Financial Services' (2007) 29 *Law and Policy* 226. See D Marron, '"Informed, educated and more confident": Financial Capability and the Problematization of Personal Finance Consumption' (2013) 17 *Consumption Markets and Culture* 491. See discussion of this theme in Moloney (n 74) 47–67. See discussion in relation to EU in V Mak and J Braspenning, '*Errare humanum est:* Financial Literacy in European Consumer Credit Law' (2012) 35 *Journal of Consumer Policy* 307.

[121] In contrast to traditional economic rationale of externalities. For references, see G Loewenstein and others, 'Can Behavioral Economics Make Us Healthier?' [2012] *British Medical Journal* 1.

[122] Margaret Atwood highlights the increasing discussion of 'Debt as the New Fat'. See M Atwood, *Payback: Debt and the Shadow Side of Wealth* (Toronto, Anansi, 2008) 41.

[123] See J Baudrillard, 'The Consumer Society' in J Baudrillard, *Selected Writings* (Stanford, Stanford University Press, 2000) 81. Lendol Calder drew on Baudrillard to argue that the instalment plan in the US imposed a discipline similar to Taylorist factory discipline. Lazzarrato argues that in contemporary society with fewer traditional 'sites of discipline' such as the factory, we have moved to a society of control (see G Deleuze, 'Postscript on the Societies of Control' (1992) 59 *October* 3). See also I Ramsay, 'Consumer Credit Society and Consumer Bankruptcy: Reflections on Credit Cards and Bankruptcy

privatisation of many public responsibilities have provided an opportunity for increased exploitation by financial institutions of individuals through creating future claims on wages. Susanne Soederberg coins the term 'debtfare state' to describe how high-cost credit is a form of 'secondary exploitation' of workers through the credit market, in addition to the exploitation associated with the capital–labour relationship.[124] Like Lazzarato, she views this form of secondary exploitation as a dominant aspect of contemporary neoliberalism. Secondary exploitation is legitimated through the ideology of the 'democratization of credit' and individualised forms of 'consumer protection' which mask the structural inequalities between lender and borrower. The debtfare state substitutes individualised credit for social welfare. Within this perspective, regulation of high-cost credit is legitimating an industry which should not exist.

What are the implications of these critiques of the role of household credit? First, they should make us wary of individualistic explanations of the rational/vulnerable distinction and the need to be aware of the background context of credit transactions. The concept of the 'vulnerable consumer' in EU law includes both structural and personal characteristics of the consumer. But the conception of 'vulnerability' has a tendency towards the individualisation of problems as reflecting individual weaknesses. Second, individualisation may also privilege remedies intended to address perceived individual weakness such as financial literacy. Financial capability and literacy have become central topics in regulation.[125] There is, however, much that is untested in relation to financial literacy studies and its recommendations.[126] Third, recognition of the social role of credit underlines the extent to which the role of household credit markets in society dovetails with other public policies on issues such as unemployment protection, housing, the financing of education and health. Generous unemployment provision may reduce the need for credit and prevent individuals from needing to declare insolvency. The EU policy paradigm of credit provides limited protection from the market, attempting to ensure better access and the ability of individuals to manage credit. Other EU policies may limit the ability of states to provide social safety nets. As these are reduced, the more limited safety nets associated with the credit market, such as insolvency, become more important. In the case of housing debt, the importance of homeownership in the EU makes effective safety

in an Informational Economy' in J Niemi, I Ramsay and W Whitford (eds), *Consumer Bankruptcy in Global Perspective* (Oxford, Hart Publishing, 2003) 38–39.

[124] S Soederberg, *Debtfare States and the Poverty Industry: Money, Discipline and the Surplus Population* (Abingdon, Routledge, 2014) 37.

[125] eg Art 9 of EBA Regulation (n 9); Financial Services and Markets Act 2000, s 3; Mortgage Credit Directive. The EBA 2014 Consumer Trends notes financial literacy as a common area of concern among National Supervisory Agencies.

[126] See Williams (n 123) and L Willis, 'Against Financial Literacy-Education' (2008) 94 *Iowa Law Review* 197. For a review see *Financial Capability—A Behavioural Economics Perspective* (n 98); J Michael Collins and C O'Rourke, 'Financial Education and Counselling—Still Holding Promise' (2010) 44 *Journal of Consumer Affairs* 483. C Arthur, *Financial Literacy Education: Neoliberalism, the Consumer and the Citizen* (Rotterdam, Sense Publishers, 2012).

nets for homeowners a priority. Minimum standards on foreclosures are only one modest step to achieve that objective. Fourth, an economy dependent on consumer debt may not be sustainable in the long run, leading to bubbles and crashes which threaten financial stability, coupled with a continuing need to reintegrate individuals into the credit system—achieved in the US by a generous bankruptcy system. Crashes may create externalities for other countries—witness the effects of the sub-prime mortgage debacle in the US. The model may also be associated with increased leverage—over-indebtedness among lower middle and lower income populations living with high levels of household debt—the new precariat.[127]

IV. Conclusion

The credit as lubricant and product safety model suggest conflicting policies and images of credit, although both can be linked to market expansion through the objective of increased market confidence for credit. In that sense they are both neoliberal. The relative balance between these images and their associated policies depends on the continuing politics of credit and debt policy implementation in the EU, which takes place now in many sites and against the background of international standards. The EU asymmetry of economic and 'social' regulation—with the latter consigned to national regulation—does not seem sustainable where increasingly the regulation of the treatment of over-indebtedness is discussed in the context of the single market and how its regulation contributes to economic objectives.

Less discussion now occurs of the larger questions which were raised in the immediate wake of the crisis about the role of consumer credit in the economy and the forms of delivery—such as through public institutions subject to more democratic control. Behavioural economics recognises the importance of ground rules for credit markets but then retreats to a policy mode of libertarian paternalism or ensuring better choices within existing markets. A further line of inquiry could rather be to focus on the broader conditions of choice in a society where individual capabilities depend on 'economic, social and political arrangements'.

[127] See G Standing, *The Precariat: The New Dangerous Class* (London, Bloomsbury, 2011).

7

The Importance of Law and Harmonisation for the EU's Confident Consumer

CHRISTIAN TWIGG-FLESNER

I. Introduction

The objective of this chapter is to explore one particular feature of the consumer image in EU consumer legislation—the notion of the 'confident consumer'. Consumer confidence is an objective which is frequently cited in policy documents,[1] with a lack of confidence in buying goods and services in another EU Member State being cited as a reason for EU action, but the notion of the 'confident consumer' is under-explored.[2] Although it is possible to identify the key features of the confident consumer, there are contradictions between the notion of the confident consumer and the relevant legal rules, which is bordering on the paradoxical. One possible explanation for this is the way the EU has gone about in creating its *acquis* on consumer law, based as it is on a harmonisation approach driven by the internal market imperative. The dominant theme is that law is essential to increase consumer confidence in the internal market, and that attaining this goal requires that there is a common level of consumer protection law in force across all of the EU Member States. The EU's approach is to equip consumers with a set of common legal rights, some focussing on directly or indirectly providing information about all aspects of a particular transaction to a consumer, whereas others are concerned with the performance of the contract itself. However, this enabling approach (or 'empowerment') is combined with a heavily paternalistic straightjacket which seems to be inconsistent with the idea of

[1] eg, Commission, A European Consumer Agenda—Boosting Confidence and Growth COM(2012) 225 final.

[2] eg, in H-W Micklitz and others, *European Consumer Law* (Antwerp, Intersentia, 2014), the discussion of the consumer concept concentrates on the informed, vulnerable and weaker notions of the consumer, but not the confident one; see 45–52.

a confident consumer—for example, the absolute mandatory nature of the rules emanating from the various directives.

This chapter argues that the EU's notion of the 'confident consumer' overemphasises the significance of law, and harmonised law in particular, as an end in itself, without considering properly (i) all the various issues which affect consumer confidence, and (ii) whether the legal rules adopted by the EU really help to boost consumer confidence. It will first consider the 'consumer confidence' notion as reflected in the various directives, and link this to the general notion of the 'average consumer' before examining how the substantive provisions in these directives reflect the objective of enhancing consumer confidence. This will also take into account relevant judgments of the Court of Justice of the European Union ('CJEU') on the interpretation of particular provisions. It will then argue that too much emphasis has been put on law for law's sake at the expense of establishing what legal rules would promote consumer confidence, particularly in the internal market.

II. 'Consumer Confidence'

Increasing consumer confidence has become a dominant justification for many EU directives in the field of consumer law,[3] although this notion did not make an explicit appearance in the recitals to a consumer law directive until the Injunctions Directive. In Recital 5 to that Directive, the difficulties caused by ensuring compliance with consumer law where infringements have cross-border effects are said to be 'likely to diminish consumer confidence in the internal market'. In Recital 5 to the Consumer Sales Directive,[4] it is stated that the 'creation of a common set of minimum rules of consumer law, valid no matter where goods are purchased' within the EU, would 'strengthen consumer confidence' and encourage participation in the internal market. The next mention of 'consumer confidence' is in the Directive on the Distance Marketing of Financial Services.[5] This Directive was adopted to facilitate the marketing of financial services to consumers throughout the EU to increase consumer choice and to enable them to choose financial services 'that are best suited to their needs. In order to safeguard freedom of choice, which is an essential consumer right, a high degree of consumer protection is

[3] The rise of the 'consumer confidence' justification was critiqued convincingly in T Wilhelmsson, 'The Abuse of the "Confident Consumer" as a Justification for EC Consumer Law' (2004) 27 *Journal of Consumer Policy* 317.

[4] Directive 1999/44/EC of the European Parliament and of the Council of 25 May 1999 on certain aspects of the sale of consumer goods and associated guarantees [1999] OJ L171/12 (Consumer Sales Directive), Rec 5.

[5] Directive 2002/65/EC of the European Parliament and of the Council of 23 September 2002 concerning the distance marketing of consumer financial services [2002] OJ L271/16.

required in order to enhance consumer confidence in distance selling'.[6] Moreover, 'the establishment of a legal framework governing the distance marketing of financial services should increase consumer confidence'.[7]

The concept then reappears in the recitals to the Unfair Commercial Practices Directive.[8] Recital 4 alludes to the existence of diverse national rules on unfair commercial practices which results in the creation of barriers for both traders and consumers to taking advantage of the single market. In addition, these barriers 'make consumers uncertain of their rights and undermine their confidence in the internal market'. A further reference to consumer confidence is then found in Recital 13, which states that 'in order to support consumer confidence the general prohibition [in Art 5] should apply equally to unfair commercial practices which occur outside any contractual relationship between a trader and a consumer or following the conclusion of a contract and during its execution'.

Finally, in the Consumer Rights Directive, the importance of increasing consumer confidence through harmonising directives is among the main reasons given in the Directive's recitals. Having noted that the volume of cross-border traffic in distance sales via the internet appears low, particularly when compared with the growth of online sales in domestic markets,[9] 'disproportionate fragmentation'[10] of consumer protection laws is identified as undermining consumer confidence in the internal market.[11] The full harmonisation of consumer information and the right of withdrawal in distance and off-premises sales would 'considerably increase legal certainty',[12] which in turn would boost cross-border sales.

If these various instances of the 'consumer confidence' notion are taken together, interesting clues emerge about what, in the views of the EU legislature, makes for a 'confident consumer'. First, a confident consumer is one who wishes to take advantage of the single market and is therefore, at least in principle, a consumer interested in cross-border shopping. Moreover, a confident consumer is aware of consumer protection law, in particular of the law in their jurisdiction, and also aware of the fact that there are differences in the laws of the various Member States. Further still, the confident consumer seemingly puts a great deal of weight on the law—for, according to the various recitals mentioned earlier, ensuring that there are no (significant) variations in the consumer laws between the various Member States will boost consumer confidence. Finally, it seems that a confident consumer is also a consumer who will benefit from information to help

[6] Directive 97/7/EC of the European Parliament and of the Council of 20 May 1997 on the protection of consumers in respect of distance contracts [1997] OJ L144/19, Rec 3.

[7] ibid, Rec 5.

[8] Directive 2005/29/EC of the European Parliament and of the Council of 11 May 2005 concerning unfair business-to-consumer commercial practices in the internal market (Unfair Commercial Practices Directive) [2005] OJ L149/22.

[9] Directive 2011/83/EU of the European Parliament and of the Council of 25 October 2011 on consumer rights [2011] OJ L304/64 ('Consumer Rights Directive'), Rec 5.

[10] ibid, Rec 6.

[11] ibid.

[12] ibid, Rec 7.

him make the right decision about which goods and services to purchase, where, and on what terms.

III. Boosting Consumer Confidence: Law Matters

Going by the recitals to directives noted above, a confident consumer in the eyes of the EU is a consumer who regards law as fundamental to that confidence, who knows about the law that applies in their home Member State, and who is consequently deterred from looking beyond their national borders because of the diversity of legal rules which exist. So in order to increase consumer confidence, there has to be greater uniformity of legal rules. This very basic model of a confident consumer leads to the assumption that the focus of EU activities will be on greater uniformity of rules as an objective in its own right, without necessarily considering the suitability of those rules specifically for encouraging consumers to make greater use of the internal market. To substantiate this critical stance towards the notion of the confident consumer, it is necessary to consider the substantive legal rules adopted by the EU.

There is a sizeable body of EU directives on matters relating to consumer protection in place now, although these deal with particular aspects of consumer law, and the EU has thus far not introduced more detailed and broader legislation in this area.[13] Nevertheless, it is possible to find numerous instances which reflect the view of the confident consumer as one primarily concerned with law, in particular provisions which assume that a consumer is knowledgeable about the law and that their confidence will be increased if there is a harmonised set of consumer law in force across the EU. The following section will therefore survey several areas of EU consumer law in order to illustrate how they reflect this particular notion of the confident consumer. Some provisions concentrate on improving the flow of information about all aspects of a transaction to consumers, whereas others, for want of an immediate rationale for the content of these rules, seek to create a harmonised set of rules on certain matters.[14] The focus will be on: (i) the importance of information about the law, both concerning goods/services and about the terms of a contract; (ii) the right of withdrawal; (iii) the CJEU's interpretation of the unfairness test in the Unfair Contract Terms Directive,[15] and (iv) the regulation of consumer sales contracts.

[13] In the run-up to the proposal for the Consumer Rights Directive presented in 2008, there were indications that the Commission would put forward a very ambitious directive, and whilst the proposal was for a directive with more detailed rules and for full harmonisation, it was much less extensive than the Green Paper preceding it suggested. The Directive as adopted is, of course, more modest still.

[14] For the purposes of this chapter, it is not necessary to provide a full account of the various features of EU consumer law. A more detailed overview can be found in ch 3 of C Twigg-Flesner, *The Europeanisation of Contract Law* 2nd edn (London, Routledge, 2013).

[15] Council Directive 93/13/EEC of 5 April 1993 on unfair terms in consumer contracts [1993] OJ L95/29.

A. Law, Information and Confident Consumers

Based on what has been said so far, in the EU's vision, law is the key means of boosting consumer confidence, and this is pursued by creating a set of common legal rules which are applicable throughout the EU.[16] However, there is very little by way of indication as to how the substance of these rules might be designed. The only indication as to one area which is regarded as important is the provision of information about the goods/services as well as the terms of a contract. Although there is no explicit link between the notion of the 'confident consumer' with that of the 'average consumer' developed through the case law of the CJEU in the context of the free movement provisions,[17] the combination of the 'confident consumer' justification in the Recitals to the Unfair Commercial Practices Directive ('UCPD') with the utilisation of the 'average consumer' concept in the substantive rules of the UCPD suggests that the confident consumer also has the attributes of the average consumer as one who 'is reasonably well-informed and reasonably observant and circumspect, taking into account social, cultural and linguistic factors'.[18] So the confident consumer is one who is also a reasonably well-informed consumer, which means that in order to boost consumer confidence, it is necessary to introduce legal rules to ensure that consumers are provided with information. This is reflected in EU provisions and CJEU case law in a variety of ways. It is well known that a key tool in the EU consumer law arsenal is the requirement to provide consumers with all sorts of information, both during the pre-contractual stage and once a contract has been concluded.[19] As EU consumer law evolved from 1985 through to 2011, the requirement to provide information has become more and more detailed, culminating in Articles 5 and 6 of the Consumer Rights Directive.[20] Article 5 stipulates eight different categories of information which need to be provided to a consumer before a contract which is not an off-premises or distance contract is concluded. For off-premises and distance contracts, Article 6 lays down 20 categories of information (although not

[16] The perspective taken in this chapter is on the consumer. The harmonisation programme of the EU is seen to be as much for the benefit of traders as consumers, as it is also intended to make it easier for traders to sell to consumers from other Member States by providing a common set of consumer protection requirements.

[17] cf H Unberath and A Johnston, 'The Double-Headed Approach of the ECJ Concerning Consumer Protection' (2007) 44 *Common Market Law Review* 1237.

[18] Unfair Commercial Practices Directive, Rec 18.

[19] Examined in detail, eg in H Schulte-Nölke, C Twigg-Flesner and M Ebers (eds), *EC Consumer Law Compendium* (Munich, Sellier, 2008) 482–96.

[20] The now-repealed directives on contracts negotiated away from business premises (Council Directive 85/577/EEC of 20 December 1985 to protect the consumer in respect of contracts negotiated away from business premises [1985] OJ L 372/31) and distance selling (Directive 97/7/EC of the European Parliament and of the Council of 20 May 1997 on the protection of consumers in respect of distance contracts [1997] OJ L144/19) also contained requirements to provide information, although in the former directive, this was limited to information about the right of withdrawal, and whilst the catalogue of information was more detailed in the Distance Selling Directive, it was nowhere near as comprehensive as the requirements in the Consumer Rights Directive.

all of these will be applicable in any given context). However, what is not clear is why the various items of information are regarded as important for increasing consumer confidence—the provisions in the Consumer Rights Directive seem to be a product of an ever-increasing list of items to be provided as the body of EU consumer law measures has grown. All that this Directive achieves is a standardisation of the information requirement across the EU, but just how this helps with consumer confidence remains unclear. Rather, it seems to fit with the general theme that harmonised law is enough for increasing consumer confidence.

Alongside the positive obligation of providing information to consumers through the Consumer Rights Directive, there are indirect information obligations in the Unfair Commercial Practices Directive, through its prohibitions of misleading actions and misleading omissions.[21] These similarly seek to ensure that consumers are provided with a large amount of information before making a transactional decision. In addition to these general information duties, there are also specific information duties for the contracts covered by the directives on the Distance Marketing of Financial Services,[22] Timeshare[23] and Consumer Credit.[24]

As well as requiring the various items and categories of information to be given to consumers, the various directives also contain rules on the form and method of provision. The requirements include that the information is given in 'plain and intelligible language',[25] is legible,[26] is provided in writing or on another durable medium,[27] and in some instances even in a specific language.[28]

So whilst the central focus of EU consumer law on ensuring that consumers are supplied with a lot of information is obvious, what is less clear is whether this drive towards providing more and more detailed information really has the effect of increasing consumer confidence, or whether it simply creates a higher risk of consumer confusion as the volume of information becomes overwhelming.[29] Little attention has been paid to this issue; instead, the main concern appears to have been to create a fully harmonised set of information duties, and this seems to have been motivated largely by a desire to have a common set of rules for the sake of it rather than because a coherent justification for introducing these particular requirements has been given.

[21] Unfair Commercial Practices Directive, Arts 6(1) and 7(4).

[22] Directive 2002/65/EC, Art 4.

[23] Directive 2008/122/EC of the European Parliament and of the Council of 14 January 2009 on the protection of consumers in respect of certain aspects of timeshare, long-term holiday product, resale and exchange contracts [2009] OJ L33/10, Arts 3–5.

[24] Directive 2008/48/EC of the European Parliament and of the Council of 23 April 2008 on credit agreements for consumers and repealing Council Directive 87/102/EEC [2008] OJ L133/66, Art 4 and Annex II, 'Standard European Consumer Credit Information'.

[25] eg, Consumer Rights Directive, Art 8.

[26] eg, ibid, Art 6.

[27] eg, Consumer Credit Directive, Arts 5(1) and 6(1).

[28] eg, Timeshare Directive, Art 5(1).

[29] O Ben-Shahar and CE Schneider, *More Than You Wanted to Know—The Failure of Mandated Disclosure* (Princeton, Princeton University Press, 2014).

i. Information about Contract Terms

The information theme can also be identified in the Unfair Contract Terms Directive. According to this Directive, a term which has not been individually negotiated is regarded as unfair 'if, contrary to the requirement of good faith, it causes a significant imbalance in the parties' rights and obligations arising under the contract, to the detriment of the consumer'.[30] The interpretation of this notion by the CJEU will be considered in the next section, but here, it needs to be noted how much emphasis is placed on information even in this directive. The CJEU has said that the Unfair Terms Directive is based on the assumption that a consumer is in a weaker position than a seller/supplier both with regard to their bargaining strength and knowledge about a particular transaction, and that the Directive effectively compensates for this (at least with regard to terms which a consumer was unable to negotiate).[31] Thus, Recital 20 makes it clear that a consumer 'should actually be given an opportunity to examine all the terms', which implies that before a consumer concludes a contract, he or she should be able to familiarise himself with all the terms of that contract. As the CJEU said in *RWE Vertrieb AG v Verbraucherzentrale NRW*,[32]

> [i]nformation, before concluding a contract, on the terms of the contract and the consequences of concluding it is of fundamental importance for a consumer. It is on the basis of that information in particular that he decides whether he wishes to be bound by the terms previously drawn up by the seller or supplier.[33]

This assumes that a consumer would want to read the terms of a contract in advance and consider these carefully before deciding whether to conclude that contract—but how often will a consumer really want to do this?

This is further emphasised by the requirement in Article 5 that written terms must always be drafted in plain and intelligible language—a provision at least in part designed to make it easier for a consumer to decide whether to conclude a contract (assuming, of course, that consumers really do read all the terms of a contract before proceeding). Interestingly, the CJEU has recently amplified the scope of this requirement, holding that the requirement that a term is in plain and intelligible language had to be understood in a broad sense and not merely limited to the question of whether a term is 'formally and grammatically intelligible',[34] and that consequently, a consumer must be able to evaluate on the basis of clear, intelligible criteria, the economic consequences resulting from the term.[35] As well

[30] Unfair Contract Terms Directive, Art 3(1).

[31] eg Case C–484/08 *Caja de Ahorros y Monte de Piedad de Madrid v Asociación de Usuarios de Servicios Bancarios (Ausbanc)* [2010] ECR I–04785, 27.

[32] Case C–92/11 *RWE Vertrieb AG v Verbraucherzentrale Nordrhein-Westfalen eV*, judgment of 21 March 2013.

[33] ibid, para 44.

[34] Case C–26/13 *Árpád Kásler and Hajnalka Káslerné Rábai v OTP Jelzálogbank Zrt*, judgment of 30 April 2014, para 71.

[35] ibid, para 73.

as emphasising the breadth of the information requirement in this Directive, it also underlines the link between the confident consumer and the average consumer's characteristics of observance and circumspection. Moreover, it suggests that a confident consumer will also read the terms of a contract carefully and consider the implications of these—but one may doubt whether this really is the case, at least in the context of frequent transactions.

B. Right of Withdrawal

The objective of ensuring that consumers are able to make a well-informed purchasing decision is further supported by the widespread use of the right of withdrawal. First introduced in the Doorstep Selling Directive, it has since been utilised for both off-premises and distance contracts generally, as well as the specific contracts such as those for consumer credit or timeshare contracts. In some instances, the rationale for providing consumers with a right of withdrawal is the fact that the context in which a contract was formed could be said to be one where the consumer might have been under some pressure (for example, in the consumer's home), but in most instances it is provided because the consumer was not able fully to assess all the features of the goods or services to be acquired. Thus, where goods are bought online, the consumer is not able to examine or test the goods, which is why they are given an opportunity to do so on receiving those goods.[36] If, following this examination, they are unsuitable or he or she does not like them, they can exercise their right of withdrawal and return the goods for a refund. The existence of a (now fully) harmonised right of withdrawal could be seen to be promoting consumer confidence, because it might give consumers the confidence to buy goods/services online, safe in the knowledge that they can change their mind. However, the practicalities of exercising this right could undermine this confidence—indeed, consumers might be put off by the need to arrange for the return of goods and consequently ignore the existence of the right of withdrawal.

C. Regulating the Substance of Consumer Transactions

Although much of EU consumer law focusses on the process of contract formation and the difficulties consumers might encounter in the run-up to making the decision to enter into a contract, there are some provisions which deal with the content of particular contracts and aspects of performance. In particular, the Unfair Contract Terms Directive can be used to police the fairness of contract terms which were not individually negotiated, that is standard form contracts,

[36] Note the provision made in the Consumer Rights Directive which limits the consumer to doing only what is necessary to test/try out the goods before deciding whether to exercise the right of withdrawal (Art 14(2)).

and the Consumer Sales Directive focusses on the obligations of a seller to supply goods which meet certain expectations as to quality and fitness, and provides remedies for circumstances where these expectations have not been met. These provisions also reflect the assumption that law is central to consumer confidence, and that a confident consumer is knowledgeable about the law and that boosting that confidence requires harmonised laws.

i. The Unfairness Test in the Unfair Contract Terms Directive

The importance for the confident consumer of knowing about the law is reflected in the guidance given by the CJEU on the interpretation of the unfairness test in Article 3 of the Unfair Contract Terms Directive. A term will be unfair if it (i) is contrary to the requirement of good faith and (ii) causes a significant imbalance in the rights and obligations of the parties, to the detriment of the consumer. In *Freiburger Kommunalbauten*,[37] the CJEU noted that Article 4 of the Directive requires that all the circumstances surrounding the conclusion of the contract need to be taken into account when applying the fairness test, which includes the consequences of the term under the applicable national law.[38] This was developed further in *Banco Español*,[39] where the CJEU observed that the assessment of whether a term causes a significant imbalance to the consumer's detriment requires consideration of the rules of national law that would apply in the absence of the term under challenge.[40] In assessing whether this would then be against good faith, a court has to consider whether a seller/supplier dealing fairly and equitably with a consumer could reasonably assume that the consumer would have agreed to the term if there had been individual negotiation.[41] This surely presupposes that a consumer would be aware of the rules of national law as they would apply and would also be capable of establishing how their legal position would change if they were to agree to the term. In other words, this assumes that consumers will know a lot about their national law—an assumption consistent with the 'confident consumer' notion.

ii. Consumer Sales Contracts

The other main directive dealing with the substance and performance of a contract is the Consumer Sales Directive. This Directive requires that goods delivered to a consumer must be in conformity with the contract (Article 2). Where goods are not in conformity, the consumer is entitled to a number of remedies, starting

[37] Case C–237/02 *Freiburger Kommunalbauten GmbH Baugesellschaft and Co KG v Ludger Hofstetter and Ulrike Hofstetter* [2004] ECR I–3403.

[38] ibid, para 21.

[39] Joined Cases C–537/12 and C–116/13 *Banco Popular Español SA v Maria Teodolinda Rivas Quichimbo, Wilmar Edgar Cun Pérez* and *Banco de Valencia SA v Joaquín Valldeperas Tortosa, María Ángeles Miret Jaume*, order of 14 November 2013.

[40] ibid, para 65.

[41] ibid, para 66.

with either repair or replacement, and moving on to price reduction or rescission of the contract (Article 3). Article 2 lists a number of factors which are taken into account in determining whether goods meet the requirement of conformity with the contract (Article 2(2)(a)–(d)). But even these substantive rights are not absolute and are dependent on what information about the goods is available to a consumer. Thus, Article 2(3) states that there will not be a lack of conformity if the consumer 'was aware, or could not reasonably be unaware' of a fault or other matter which would otherwise mean that the goods are non-conforming. So if the specific faults are disclosed to the consumer before a contract is made, the seller will not be liable. This effectively puts the burden on the seller to provide all the information he or she has about the goods in advance so as to reduce the likelihood that he or she may be held liable for any faults.[42] It is therefore possible to analyse Article 2 from the perspective of improving information to consumers, whether as a clear obligation to disclose information,[43] an 'indirect information requirement',[44] or merely an 'encouragement to provide information'.[45] However, this is not unique to the Consumer Sales Directive, and corresponding provisions of domestic law could be analysed in a similar way.[46] So this approach is not particularly novel and is certainly not distinct, which leads to a more general question about why these rules were regarded as being important for consumer confidence and how this is reflected in the substantive provisions. The reasons for this Directive can be gleaned from its recitals. Thus, the internal market is the key driving force (not least because of the Directive's legal base, which, like all other directives in this sphere, is a predecessor to what is now Article 114 TFEU), which means that 'consumers resident in one Member State should be free to purchase goods in the territory of another Member State *on the basis of a uniform minimum set of fair rules* governing the sale of consumer goods'.[47] As the italicised words reveal, a uniform (albeit minimum) set of rules is key to getting consumers to shop abroad. This is reinforced in Recital 3, which notes the disparity of national laws on the sale of consumer goods. Recital 4 then emphasises the importance of those con-

[42] Art 2 cannot be purely considered in terms of information, because there is also an element of risk allocation for hidden faults inherent in this provision. This means that a seller can be liable for hidden defects even though he had no knowledge of them, nor the obvious means of discovering them.

[43] See, eg, K Riesenhuber, 'Party Autonomy and Information in the Sales Directive' in S Grundmann, W Kerber and S Weatherill (eds), *Party Autonomy and the Role of Information in the Internal Market* (Berlin, De Gruyter, 2001).

[44] See T Wilhelmsson, 'Private Law Remedies against Breach of Information Requirements of EC Law' in R Schulze, M Ebers and HC Grigoleit (eds), *Informationspflichten und Vertragsschluss in Acquis communautaire* (Tübingen, Mohr Siebeck, 2003).

[45] C Twigg-Flesner, 'Information Disclosure about the Quality of Goods—Duty or Encouragement?' in G Howells, A Janssen and R Schulze (eds), *Information Rights and Obligations* (Farnham, Ashgate, 2005).

[46] cf S Hedley, 'Quality of Goods, Information, and the Death of Contract' [2001] *Journal of Business Law* 114, examining the corresponding provisions of the Sale of Goods Act 1979.

[47] Consumer Sales Directive, Rec 2 (emphasis added).

sumers who want to shop abroad for the internal market and how the absence of common rules on the sale of consumer goods poses a risk to this. Finally, Recital 5 then argues that common rules will strengthen consumer confidence in the internal market. The remaining recitals then explain what the substantive provisions of the Directive are intended to achieve, but there is nothing further about how these rules will encourage consumers to shop abroad, other than the mere fact that there will be a standard set of rules. In short, consumers will become more confident merely because there are uniform rules in place—no matter how good the quality of these rules might be (and this Directive is far from easy to understand), and how suitable they might be for the specific challenges posed by buying goods in another Member State. The means of improving consumer confidence is simply to harmonise the law—irrespective of the content of the harmonised rules.

iii. Confident Consumers and the Law

This section has demonstrated how the argument that law is crucial for the confident consumer is borne out in the various substantive rules of EU consumer law. It was seen that the EU's conception of the confident consumer regards law as central and harmonised law as an important tool for raising consumer confidence without necessarily being concerned with the content of the law. Indeed, the focus on law for law's sake and the lack of proper coordination between the various directives (as well as the failure to articulate a coherent vision for consumer policy) is evident.

D. The Mandatory Nature of Consumer Law

The previous two sections argued that the EU's confident consumer notion entails that such consumers are very familiar with their national laws, and need harmonised laws to be able to participate in the internal market. The importance of law to the confident consumer is further illustrated by the fact that consumers cannot shake off or modify those legal rights which are given to them by EU consumer law. Article 25 of the Consumer Rights Directive is but one example of this:

> If the law applicable to the contract is the law of a Member State, consumers may not waive the rights conferred on them by the national measures transposing this Directive. Any contractual terms which directly or indirectly waive or restrict the rights resulting from this Directive shall not be binding on the consumer.

This is a double-lock on consumer rights: first, contractual terms which might limit consumer rights are not binding on a consumer—irrespective of whether such a term was individually negotiated or not. Secondly, this Article makes it clear that *consumers* are not permitted to waive their rights. It is clearly essential to prevent unilateral attempts by a trader to use standard contract terms or other means to restrict or exclude consumer rights. However, the EU's 'confident consumer' vision, with its emphasis on the active use of law by consumers, does lead one to ask why a consumer is prevented from deciding actively and without any pressure from a trader not to take the benefit of specific consumer rights. One might even suggest that this is a paradox within the confident consumer image. On the one hand, it is assumed that a confident consumer knows his or her legal rights and therefore is able to act taking full account of the law, but on the other, the consumer is also seen as incapable of deciding whether he or she wishes to modify their legal rights, perhaps in exchange for better contracting terms in a given context. The vision of the confident consumer suggests that he or she would have the legal wherewithal to choose whether to take the full benefit of their legal rights or not—but they are effectively precluded from having that choice.

It needs to be stressed that the point made here should not be understood as endorsing an approach which would permit consumers to waive their rights easily and on a regular basis—the danger of abuse of such an option is obvious.[48] However, with law having been given such a central position in the EU's confident consumer image, it is important to highlight inconsistencies such as this.

E. The Obligation on Courts to Act on their own Motion

A further example of how important the law is for the EU's conception of the confident consumer is the obligation developed in the CJEU's case law which requires national courts dealing with a dispute between a consumer and a trader to raise the unfairness of a contract term even if the consumer has not pleaded this.[49] At first, this was recognised simply as a power for national courts in *Oceano Grupo Editorial SA v Quintero*,[50] but it soon developed into an obligation. Thus, in *Mostaza Claro*,[51] the CJEU held that a national court hearing an action for the annulment of an arbitration award must determine of its own motion whether the arbitration clause in a contract is void for being an unfair term, even though the consumer did not plead the unfairness of the term. In *Pannon v Győrfi*,[52] the CJEU confirmed that if a national court has all the factual and legal information available to it to assess the unfairness of a term, it is required to do so of its own motion. If the court concludes that a term is unfair, then it must not uphold it. The upshot of all of these cases is that consumers might see the unfairness of a

[48] And in practical terms, a consumer can choose not to attempt to enforce their legal rights if they have encountered a problem, but to take other action such as complaining generally, or switching suppliers. See, eg, KPN Morel, TBC Poiesz and HAM Wilke, 'Motivation, Capacity and Opportunity to Complain: Towards a Comprehensive Model of Consumer Complaint Behaviour' (1997) 24 *Advances in Consumer Research* 464.

[49] Case C–488/11 *Dirk Frederik Asbeek Brusse and Katarina de Man Garabito v Jahani BV*, judgment of 30 May 2013.

[50] Joined Cases C–240 to 244/98 *Océano Grupo Editorial SA v Roció Murciano Quintero* [2000] ECR I–4941.

[51] Case C–168/05 *Elisa María Mostaza Claro v Centro Móvil Milenium SL* [2006] ECR I–10421.

[52] Case C–243/08 *Pannon GSM Zrt v Erzsébet Sustikné Győrfi* [2009] ECR I–4713.

term raised in national court proceedings, with potentially serious consequences if the term is found to be unfair and the contract cannot continue without that term. Yet, the CJEU has limited the potential severity of this by holding that if the consumer, aware of the court's assessment on unfairness, does not seek the non-application of the term, then it can remain binding.[53] This is another paradox because a consumer is given the right to waive the rights they have under the Unfair Contract Terms Directive—indeed, Articles 3(1) and 6(1) make it clear that once the unfairness of a term has been established, it is not binding on a consumer automatically without this having to be pleaded and so there is no choice given to a consumer under the Directive. It also seems to run against the strict mandatory nature of consumer law. That said, whilst this is an apparent inconsistency, it reflects a more sensible approach which does respect the autonomy of a consumer to act independently.

F. Domestic Law Follows a Consumer

As well as preventing a consumer from contracting out of his legal rights, EU law also ensures that the consumer's domestic law follows him in certain circumstances when participating in cross-border shopping. Thus, under Article 6(1) of the Rome–I Regulation,[54] the law applicable to a consumer contract is the law of the country where the consumer has his habitual residence, provided that

(i) either the trader pursues his commercial or professional activities in the country where the consumer has his habitual residence; or
(ii) the trader by any means directs such activities to that country or to several countries including that country.

In *Pammer v Schlüter*,[55] the CJEU confirmed that websites could be regarded as a 'directed activity' if the trader has 'manifested its intention to establish commercial relations with consumers from one or more other Member States, including that of the consumer's domicile'.[56] A clear statement by the trader on the website that goods or services are offered in one or more Member States, and these states are mentioned by name, or the paid inclusion in search engines accessed from particular Member States, would be pointers in that direction.[57] Additionally,

> the international nature of the activity at issue; … telephone numbers with the international dialling code; use of a top-level domain name other than that of the Member State

[53] ibid, para 33.
[54] Regulation (EC) 593/2008 of the European Parliament and of the Council of 17 June 2008 on the law applicable to contractual obligations (Rome I) [2008] OJ L177/6.
[55] Joined Cases C–585/08 and 144/09 *Peter Pammer v Reederei Karl Schlüter GmbH & Co KG* and *Hotel Alpenhof GesmbH v Oliver Heller* [2010] ECR I–12527.
[56] ibid, para 75.
[57] ibid, para 81.

> in which the trade is established … or the use of neutral top-level domain names such as '.com' or '.eu'; … mention of an international clientele composed of customers domiciled in various Member States[58]

could all be relevant; as would the website offering a language or currency different from that of the Member State where the trader is established.[59] This is potentially quite a broad conception of the 'directed activity' criterion, and this view is reinforced by *Mühlleitner v Ysufi*.[60] An Austrian consumer looking for a new car accessed a German search platform, and her search results included the website of a German car dealership. She contacted the defendants by telephone, and whilst the car she wanted had already been sold, the dealership suggested another car and emailed details to the consumer. The claimant then travelled to Hamburg to conclude the contract and took delivery of the car. The Austrian Supreme Court took the view that this amounted to a directed activity,[61] because the dealership had included the international dialling code on its website and it knew that the consumer lived in Austria. In *Emrek v Sabranovic*,[62] a consumer from Saarbrücken in Germany travelled to a car dealer in France (in a town close to the border) to buy a second-hand car. The dealer's website included both French and German telephone numbers with their international dialling codes, but the consumer had not even seen the website. A dispute arose and one question before the courts was whether the dealer had been involved in a directed activity. The German court concluded that the dealer had directed his activities to Germany, but then sought guidance from the CJEU as to whether a causal link between the directed activity and the decision to conclude the contract was required. The CJEU held that this was not the case, as adding a causal link requirement would undermine consumer protection.[63]

The objective pursued by Article 6(1) (and the corresponding provision on jurisdiction in Article 15(1)(c) of the Brussels–I Regulation,[64] which gave rise to the cases mentioned above) is clearly important: consumers should not unexpectedly be faced with a situation where a trader operating from a jurisdiction with lower consumer protection standards can rely on the law of that jurisdiction to undermine consumer protection standards in the consumer's home jurisdiction. However, the rather generous interpretation given by the CJEU could be seen as unduly favouring consumers who are actively seeking to shop abroad. This is entirely consistent with the EU's take on the confident consumer needing to be assured of having a standard set of legal rights (and consequently to be able to take

[58] ibid, para 83.

[59] ibid, para 84.

[60] Case C–190/11 *Daniela Mühlleitner v Ahmad Yusufi and Wadat Yusufi*, judgment of 6 September 2012.

[61] OGH, 18 October 2012, 4 Ob 172/12s.

[62] Case C–218/12 *Lokman Emrek v Vlado Sabranovic*, judgment of 17 October 2013.

[63] ibid, para 24.

[64] Council Regulation (EC) No 44/2001 of 22 December 2000 on jurisdiction and the recognition and enforcement of judgments in civil and commercial matters [2001] OJ L 12/1.

their rights—of which they are of course fully aware) with them when responding to a trader's directed activity. However, it does mean that traders might unexpectedly be faced with a situation where they have to comply with consumer protection rules from another Member State (which, despite harmonisation, are still quite diverse), or where action is taken against them in the courts of another Member State. So whilst this approach might boost consumer confidence, it would have the opposite effect on some traders.

IV. The Paradox of the Confident Consumer as a Legalistic Consumer

The discussion thus far has demonstrated that the EU notion of the confident consumer assumes that for a consumer to be confident to utilise the opportunities offered by the internal market, there needs to be extensive harmonised law. There are two general points of attack for any criticism of this position: first, the broad assumption that harmonised law is going to boost consumer confidence in itself is open to question; second, even if harmonised law can have the effect of increasing consumer confidence, it may be questioned whether the substantive rules adopted by the EU actually have this effect.

The first criticism essentially urges some caution about the significance that should be attached to harmonised law for boosting consumer confidence. The EU frequently cites consumer concerns over variations in their rights and in enforcement as an obstacle to greater participation in the internal market,[65] but there is insufficient evidence to suggest that greater harmonisation will reduce these concerns to a sufficient extent. This leads to the second criticism, which reflects a concern raised by Thomas Wilhelmsson some time ago in his critique of the use of the 'confident consumer' notion to justify the adoption of EU consumer law measures.[66] Wilhelmsson concluded that there was limited evidence in support of the assertion that harmonised legislation would boost consumer confidence, but even to the extent that the law might have that effect, the approach adopted by the EU had not actually had this effect. He focusses on the lack of an 'easily accessible and reliable counterparty'[67] which would make it easier for consumers to resolve disputes which may arise in the performance of a contract—in other words, his criticism is that EU law could increase consumer confidence by making it much easier for consumers to deal with problems but that current substantive rules fail to do so. This conclusion is undoubtedly correct and, in fact, reflects a much more fundamental problem of EU consumer law: the fact that it

[65] eg Commission, The Consumer Conditions Scoreboard—Consumers at Home in the Single Market (Luxembourg, Office for Official Publications of the European Union, 2012) 3–4.

[66] Wilhelmsson (n 3).

[67] ibid, 333.

has focussed too much on establishing common rules (whether of a minimum or maximum level of harmonisation) and not enough on assessing whether these rules would really support consumers in taking advantage of the opportunities offered by the single market.[68]

As noted, the EU's approach to boosting consumer confidence in the internal market is premised on the assumption that standardised rules across the internal market will go a long way towards achieving this objective. There can be little doubt that law has some role to play in facilitating consumer utilisation of the internal market, although it remains debatable just how significant this role is. One factor in this regard is the substantive content of the legal rules put into place. The starting point surely must be identifying what specific legal obstacles there are to consumer confidence in the internal market, and then to design legal rules which are specifically aimed at reducing or eliminating such obstacles. However, the general approach of the EU has been to assume that the mere existence of legal differences is a major obstacle and that eliminating legal differences by adopting whichever harmonised rules would suffice—but little attention, if any, has been given to whether the particular rules adopted would really boost consumer confidence specifically in the internal market. This is, in fact, an inconsistency between the EU's conception and implementation of the consumer confidence concept.

To pursue the confident consumer as envisaged by the EU through the adoption of legislation requires not only that harmonised legal rights are provided *but also* that these rights will have as their focus the objective of increasing confidence in the internal market. Providing consumers with strong legal protection has the potential of improving their confidence (although this will depend on how clearly expressed their rights are and how easy they are to apply and enforce), but if the objective is not only to boost consumer confidence generally but to do so with the specific focus on the internal market, then it follows that legal rules must be designed in such a way as to improve consumer confidence in cross-border shopping. In other words, laying down a common standard should not be the sole objective, but additionally, this common standard must satisfy the requirement that it would specifically enhance confidence in the internal market, that is cross-border shopping. The implication of this is that EU rules should be designed specifically with a focus on the cross-border context. This would entail one of two things: (i) the harmonisation of consumer laws would produce national rules which are designed for a cross-border context, which would mean that purely domestic situations would be governed by rules which might not be suitable; or (ii) that a distinction is drawn between cross-border transactions, which are governed by EU law, and domestic transactions, which remain subject to domestic law. The EU has hitherto adopted the approach of harmonising domestic laws without making a distinction between cross-border and domestic transactions,

[68] This is a point made elsewhere, arguing for a clearer focus on cross-border transactions: see C Twigg-Flesner, *A Cross-Border-Only Regulation for Consumer Transactions in the EU—A Fresh Approach to EU Consumer Law* (New York, Springer, 2012).

which means that, if the consumer confidence objective is to be attained, the substantive rules stemming from harmonising directives need to ensure that they are geared towards dealing with the obstacles to consumer confidence when engaging in cross-border shopping.

This then leads to one potential objection which needs to be addressed: the distinction between a domestic and an internal market/cross-border focus implies that there are two distinct spheres which require potentially different responses. This could be regarded as being incompatible with the whole notion of an internal market. Thus, Stephen Weatherill observed that:

> An internal market requires regulation of some matters that might appear of purely local interest: it verges on the paradoxical to treat matters as internal to a single Member State within an EU market that is itself 'internal'.[69]

This suggests that the internal market should be treated as one entity, and that no single jurisdiction should, in a given set of circumstances, be treated as distinct from the remainder of the internal market. Objectively, this point of view makes perfect sense, but it does sit somewhat uneasily with reality. The make-up of the EU as a conglomerate of 28 or so national entities with diverse political, economic and cultural identities makes it rather difficult to treat the EU as a single homogenous market, decades of legislative and other initiatives to create just that notwithstanding. And, perhaps more importantly, individual consumers are much more likely to take a 'national' focus when it comes to buying goods and services (perhaps with the exception of those in border regions), so from the perspective of the individual, the distinction between 'domestic' and 'cross-border' might be quite crucial. On that basis, consumer confidence might well be increased if it focusses on specific rules for the cross-border context[70]—but this is not what has happened at EU level thus far.

V. Room for Some Harmonisation

This discussion has concentrated on the provision of individual rights to consumers, which has concluded that the EU's confident consumer image means that EU legislation should focus on the specific issues raised by cross-border contracts rather than harmonisation generally, because the EU's concern is with consumer confidence in the internal market.

However, there are aspects of consumer law where EU action has perhaps a much greater potential of boosting consumer confidence: measures which

[69] S Weatherill, 'The Consumer Rights Directive: How and why a quest for coherence has (largely) failed' (2012) 49 *Common Market Law Review* 1279, 1308–09.

[70] eg, direct producer or even network liability: see R Bradgate and C Twigg-Flesner, 'Expanding the Boundaries of Liability For Quality Defects' (2002) 25 *Journal of Consumer Policy* 345.

directly regulate the safety and quality of products (rather than giving consumers individual rights of action where products are unsafe[71] or of poor quality).[72] If consumers can be assured that enough is being done to ensure that goods sold throughout the EU must (and do) comply with strong safety and quality standards, then that might do more to boost confidence in the internal market than trying to create a single set of individual consumer rights. For example, the proposed new regulation on consumer product safety[73] could, if adopted, be a much more significant contribution in this regard. So when it comes to legislation which regulates products and services directly, rather than measures seeking to provide consumers with individual rights for when things go wrong, the EU could achieve more in helping consumers feel more confident in the internal market.

Moreover, the EU's focus on strong enforcement mechanisms for consumer law also needs to be acknowledged as a positive development. These include what might be called 'non-individual enforcement mechanisms', that is the powers given to enforcement bodies and consumer associations to take action against traders. They are an important element of EU consumer law, particularly useful for dealing with cross-border issues.[74] This should be giving consumer some confidence that the actions of traders are policed and that individual action is not the sole route by which infringements can be tackled.

VI. Confident Consumers Without Law?

The preceding discussion discussed the assumption of EU consumer law that, in order to be confident, consumers need law and harmonised law in particular in order to be confident about utilising the opportunities offered by the internal market. It was argued that this is overstating the relevance of law from the perspective of consumers. However, even if consumers are concerned with variations in the level of legal protection between the various Member States, this still does not inevitably lead to the conclusion that the only way of increasing consumer confidence is to agree a harmonised set of detailed, and at times fairly technical, legal rules. Often, the practical differences between the various jurisdictions will be less pronounced than might be feared, and many differences are more likely to be of

[71] eg, under Council Directive 85/374/EEC of 25 July 1985 on the approximation of the laws, regulations and administrative provisions of the Member States concerning liability for defective products [1985] OJ L210/29.

[72] As is the case under the Consumer Sales Directive.

[73] Commission, Proposal for a Regulation of the European Parliament and of the Council on Consumer Product Safety and Repealing Council Directive 87/357/EEC and Directive 2001/95/EC COM(2013) 78 final.

[74] Regulation (EC) No 2006/2004 of the European Parliament and of the Council of 27 October 2004 on cooperation between national authorities responsible for the enforcement of consumer protection laws (the Regulation on consumer protection cooperation) [2004] OJ L364/1.

concern to lawyers than consumers (or business). If there are significant variations which could create a real surprise for consumers, then it might be enough to focus on appropriate consumer education to highlight the main differences, without having to try to eliminate them through harmonisation for the sake of it. On the other hand, if there are legal rules that could be introduced to make it genuinely easier to shop abroad, then these will be worth pursuing, whether through harmonising national laws outright, or through the adoption of measures with a specific cross-border focus. However, the link between confident consumers and extensive harmonisation is unconvincing.

That leaves the question of what else could be done to improve consumer confidence. Rather than focussing on law, it seems that consumer confidence is more likely to be enhanced by educating consumers about being a consumer—that is to make them much more aware of how different sectors operate, what to expect, and what to look out for. Consumer education is one of the Treaty-based objectives of EU consumer policy (Article 169 TFEU) and there are important initiatives in place,[75] but it seems that the EU focusses too much on rights and not sufficiently on practical action.

VII. Conclusions

This chapter has explored the notion of the 'confident consumer' and highlighted two key features: the importance of information and the importance of law. The notion of a 'confident consumer' as one who places a great deal of significance on consumer law has been a central theme in the development of EU consumer law throughout much of the EU's harmonisation programme. The shaky foundations of this as a justification for taking action at the EU level are obvious,[76] and it seems that the desire to harmonise aspects of consumer law was perhaps less influenced by a desire to address the real concerns consumers might have than to give the impression that the EU takes the interests of its citizens as consumers seriously—even if the substantive rules which have been put into place are a fairly mixed bag in terms of genuinely improving consumer protection.

The objective of increasing consumer confidence is undoubtedly a good one, and one that does need to be taken seriously. However, as this chapter has sought to demonstrate, the EU's notion of a 'confident consumer' overemphasises the role of detailed legal rules in boosting consumer confidence. This might be because there is some confusion as to how the 'consumer confidence' notion is conceived at the EU level: on the one hand, there is an assumption (supported by some empirical evidence) that consumer confidence benefits from strong legal rights, and on

[75] eg, the 'Consumer Classroom' website <http://www.consumerclassroom.eu> accessed 10 February 2015.

[76] cf Wilhelmsson (n 3).

the other, the use of the 'confident consumer' to justify the adoption of harmonising legislation in the belief that this alone will make consumers become more confident about cross-border shopping.

The role of EU law in this regard requires a re-evaluation in order to consider where it is best deployed. If the focus of EU consumer law is to be on increasing consumer confidence in the internal market, then whatever substantive legal rules are adopted should be designed to address the particular legal problems consumers will encounter in this context, and not simply maintain the position that *any* harmonised or uniform set of legal rules will do the job. This would mean focussing on those legal obstacles which might prevent consumers from going beyond their home market—and effectively mean adopting a distinction between domestic and cross-border transactions, with the EU's focus on the latter.

If, on the other hand, the objective is to boost consumer confidence across the EU generally, without trying to encourage more consumers to shop outside their home Member State, then detailed legal rules might not be the best way of achieving this. It seems likely that most consumers will only have a very general awareness of consumer law, so perhaps the best way forward would be to use directives in their literal meaning of the EU Treaty and set out broad objectives to be achieved, rather than detailed legal rules, which could then be reflected in the laws of the Member States. That way, all consumers could be reassured that, in general terms, there is sufficient commonality across the EU.

However, in addition to consumer *law*, the *practicalities* of everyday consumer transactions and the obstacles for accessing the internal market might be much more significant. These range from basics such as language issues and transport costs (in the case of goods) to concerns about finding a solution when something has gone wrong. Lawyers might think strong consumer law with a detailed set of rules on cross-border enforcement and litigation are the answer, but it seems unlikely that consumers would share this—and, after all, EU consumer law purports to promote consumer confidence—not consumer lawyers' confidence. So, if there is ever going to be, at some future point, another review of EU consumer law, it is suggested that the starting point would be to think seriously about what the purpose of EU consumer law should really be—and what is really required to boost consumer confidence.

8

Empowerment is not the only Fruit

STEPHEN WEATHERILL

I. An Agenda of Empowerment

In May 2012 the European Commission published its document *A European Consumer Agenda—Boosting confidence and growth*'.[1] It presented a rather startling image of the consumer:

> *Empowered* and confident consumers can drive forward the European economy. Well designed and implemented consumer policies with a European dimension can enable consumers to make informed choices that reward competition, and support the goal of sustainable and resource-efficient growth, whilst taking account of the needs of all consumers. This European Consumer Agenda identifies the key measures needed now to *empower* consumers and boost their trust. It sets out measures to put consumers at the heart of all EU policies as means to achieve the Europe 2020 goals … *Empowering* consumers means providing a robust framework of principles and tools that enable them to drive a smart, sustainable and inclusive economy. *Empowered* consumers who can rely on a robust framework ensuring their safety, information, education, rights, means of redress and enforcement, can actively participate in the market and make it work for them by exercising their power of choice and by having their rights properly enforced.[2]

The italicised emphasis on *empowerment* in this quotation is my own addition, but the thematic reliance on empowerment in the Commission's agenda set out in this extract and, in fact, throughout the document is strikingly bold and firmly to the forefront of the vision presented.

I do not disagree with the value of empowerment in consumer law. But consumer law needs to be about *more* than empowerment. It may seem a small shift to prefer to address 'consumer law' over 'consumer protection law', but it is a shift that carries with it an enormous risk that the protective instinct that underpins the development of the law, driven by the appreciation that in some circumstances

[1] Commission, A European Consumer Agenda—Boosting Confidence and Growth COM(2012) 225 final.

[2] ibid 2.

the market will harm the consumer, or at least some consumers, will be diluted or even lost. A vision based exclusively on empowerment is too narrow.

And this is historically clear. EU consumer policy—which is now 40 years in the making—is in part about empowerment, but only in part. There is much more to it. There is protection. There is concern for vulnerability. There is readiness to look beyond formal equality. These features are visible in free movement law and they are visible too in the EU's legislative *acquis*. Both the judicial and the political institutions of the EU have long embraced a range and a pattern of consumer images, varying according to the context. So although empowerment of the consumer is in some contexts a worthy paradigm, in other contexts it verges on a dangerous complacency. In other contexts again it is simply not what the EU seeks to achieve at all.

This chapter is therefore concerned to urge that empowerment of the consumer is a virtuous quest in some contexts, but that it should be accompanied by a richer and broader understanding of the nature and purpose of the EU's law of consumer protection. The message, then, is that the Commission's emphasis on empowerment must not become an *exclusive* emphasis on empowerment.

II. Empowerment and Free Movement

The Court's landmark ruling in *Cassis de Dijon* is concerned with empowerment.[3] By finding the German rules that obstructed the marketing of French-produced blackcurrant liqueur to be both a trade barrier and unjustified in the general interest, the Court was interpreting EU law to open up the (German) market, so that purchasing decisions would be taken by (German) consumers, unconfined by public regulation of the composition of the relevant product. The ruling equipped (what is now) Article 34 TFEU with a sharpened deregulatory bite. Technical standards could be attacked as impediments to free movement rather than left in place, fragmenting the EU market along national lines, pending the completion of the laborious process of adopting common rules through EU legislative intervention. This is readily understood as empowerment through choice—the consumer in the market is freed of the oppressive (and protectionist) restrictions anachronistically applied by German law.

Many of the early cases decided by the Court dealing with national rules alleged to serve the protection of the economic interests of the consumer are of exactly this type. In *Walter Rau v de Smedt* the Court ruled that a Member State may not prohibit sale of imported margarine in cone-shaped packaging where local rules insisted on cube-shaped packaging.[4] As the Court illuminatingly explained, such

[3] Case 120/78 *Rewe-Zentral AG v Bundesmonopolverwaltung für Branntwein* (*Cassis de Dijon*) [1979] ECR 649.

[4] Case 261/81 *Walter Rau Lebensmittelwerke v De Smedt PvbA* [1982] ECR 3961.

a rule imposes additional costs on imported products by requiring their repackaging in order to comply with the requirements in force on the target market.[5] The protective effect enjoyed by local producers was demonstrated by the fact 'that despite prices appreciably higher than those in some other Member States there is practically no margarine of foreign origin to be found on the Belgian market'.[6] There could be no sensible justification for such a measure. The risk of consumer confusion was plainly too slight to justify such a heavy-handed intervention. The assumption underlying the application of EU free movement law in such circumstances is that it is far better that the measure be set aside to promote an integrated market for margarine, within which consumers can exercise choice and, as a matter of orthodox economic theory, enjoy lower prices in consequence on the release of competition in the (Belgian) market.

In *Deserbais* the Court adopted the same approach in finding French rules governing the fat content of cheese to be unjustified.[7] The message is: let the consumer choose between differently made cheese! In *Verein gegen Unwesen in Handel und Gewerbe Köln eV v Mars GmbH* German rules allegedly designed to prevent unfair competition which banned a particular form of product packaging were found by the Court to be unjustified.[8] The packaging would, the Court considered, not mislead a 'reasonably circumspect' consumer. The same model may be found in the law dealing with the free movement of services too. *Commission v France* was a challenge to French rules laying down qualification requirements for persons wishing to offer services as tourist guides.[9] Anyone could acquire such a qualification. There was no direct discrimination based on nationality. In practice, just as in *Cassis de Dijon* imported products made according to different standards would tend not to meet local rules, so too in the case of tourist guides those who were not based in France would typically find their qualifications wanting when they wished to act in France. There was an obstacle to the cross-border provision of services. And the Court, opting for a market solution in preference to public regulation, decided that the qualification rules could not be justified. The Court observed that competition between tour operators would ensure the hiring of competent guides and that accordingly a state licensing regime governing access to the profession could not be justified.[10] Consumers could take care of themselves adequately without the need for such public intervention and, in fact, setting aside the licence requirement would permit tourists to choose a guide 'who is familiar with their language, their interests and their specific expectations'.[11]

[5] ibid, para 13.

[6] ibid, para 14.

[7] Case 286/86 *Ministère public v Gérard Deserbais* [1988] ECR 4907.

[8] Case C–470/93 *Verein gegen Unwesen in Handel und Gewerbe Köln eV v Mars GmbH* [1995] ECR I–1923.

[9] Case C–154/89 *Commission of the European Communities v French Republic* [1991] ECR I–659.

[10] ibid, para 20.

[11] ibid, para 19.

It is possible to understand these cases as involving a collision between different conceptions of the consumer interest: on the one hand, that expressed through the national rules on product composition or qualification requirements and on the other that expressed through the application of EU free movement law. The 'reasonably circumspect' consumer identified in *Mars* is the lever. He or she is taken to prefer consumer choice expressed through the application of free movement law. This is an instrumental consumer—a consumer who is empowered enough not to need regulation of the market in such circumstances and who is empowered further by the wider choice that is made available by opening up the local market to cross-border competition. And clearly EU law serves to promote deregulation. However, the context is highly relevant. In truth the national rules at stake in these cases do not deserve to stand. They do not deserve to be treated as measures of consumer protection at all. These cases all involve absurd attempts to present protectionist rules that favour producer interests as measures of consumer protection. The Court will not have it. The aggressive application of EU free movement law is conditioned by the lack of sincerity in the arguments advanced by the regulator. Consumers are better off without such rules—they are better off in a market opened up to competition and choice.

But this vision of empowerment through enhanced market competition does not always prevail. It is crucial that the deregulatory cutting edge of EU free movement law is not absolute. As the Court puts it, 'the fact that one Member State imposes less strict rules than another Member State does not necessarily mean that the latter's rules are disproportionate and hence incompatible with Community [now Union] law'.[12] So rules may be shown to be justified and standards may therefore vary from state to state according to local preference. A regulating state may set tougher standards than its competitors—if it can justify them. And if a regulating Member State is sincere, the Court is receptive to its arguments. This limits the deregulatory potential of EU free movement law.

So, for example, *Buet* concerned a French rule which went beyond giving consumers the right of cancellation required by the so-called 'Doorstep Selling' Directive, which mandated only minimum rules.[13] France had chosen to apply a ban on canvassing at private dwellings for the sale of educational material. This protected consumers against ill-considered purchases to a degree that the EU legislature had not thought necessary—and moreover to a degree that went beyond what other Member States thought necessary. It was challenged as an obstacle to inter-state trade by a firm that sold English-language teaching material which earned 90% of its turnover by such canvassing at private dwellings.[14] The Court, however,

[12] eg in connection with the free movement of goods, Case C–294/00 *Deutsche Paracelsus Schulen für Naturheilverfahren GmbH v Kurt Gräbner* [2002] ECR I–6515, and in connection with the free movement of services Case C–3/95 *Reisebüro Broede v Gerd Sandker* [1996] ECR I–6511.

[13] Case 382/87 *R Buet and Educational Business Services (EBS) v Ministère public* [1989] ECR 1235.

[14] ibid, para 2. Today there would arise a question whether this is enough to bring the matter within the scope of Article 34 TFEU. For discussion in this context of the impact of Joined cases C–267/91 and

found the rules capable of justification. The centrally important point was that the French rules were, unlike those in *Cassis* and the other peculiar cases considered above, targeted at particular sensitivities and particular products. The Court placed careful emphasis on the greater risk of an ill-considered purchase

> when the canvassing is for enrolment for a course of instruction or the sale of educational material … [because] the potential purchaser often belongs to a category of people who, for one reason or another, are behind with their education and are seeking to catch up.[15]

That, the Court observed, 'makes them particularly vulnerable'.[16] It noted too that the French ban had been enacted 'as a result of numerous complaints caused by such abuses, such as the sale of out-of-date courses'.[17] And it added that 'since teaching is not a consumer product in daily use, an ill-considered purchase could cause the purchaser harm other than mere financial loss that could be longer lasting'.[18] Accordingly EU free movement law did not serve to deregulate the (French) market. Instead it was interpreted to grant respect to the local regulatory choice designed to protect particularly vulnerable consumers. This is a vision that stretches the sensitivity of EU consumer law beyond a narrow focus on empowerment.

In similar vein *A-Punkt Schmuckhandels GmbH v Claudia Schmidt* concerned the prohibition of home jewellery parties in Austria.[19] If this was found to be a barrier to inter-state trade, a matter for the national court to determine,[20] then the Court of Justice was open to the possibility of finding it to be justified despite its restrictive effect on commercial freedom. The Court noted that the rule was apt to:

> take account of the specific features associated with the sale of silver jewellery in private homes, in particular the potentially higher risk of the consumer being cheated due to a lack of information, the impossibility of comparing prices or the provision of insufficient safeguards as regards the authenticity of that jewellery and the greater psychological pressure to buy where the sale is organised in a private setting.[21]

This is focused—targeted—consumer protection. *Buet* involved a class of consumers vulnerable for want of education, *A-Punkt* concerned consumers who may be vulnerable in a particular setting (at home). In neither case is what is at stake untargeted overregulation of the type which the Court was asked to examine in *Cassis de Dijon*. Where the national regulator has identified a particular need for protection and crafted a law that is appropriately nuanced and specific, the Court responds by judging its justifiability with respect for that nuance. *Buet* and

C–268/91 *Keck and Mithouard* [1993] ECR I–6097 see S Weatherill, *EU Consumer Law and Policy* 2nd edn (Cheltenham, Edward Elgar, 2013) 37–39.

15 ibid, para 13.
16 ibid.
17 ibid.
18 ibid, para 14.
19 Case C–441/04 *A-Punkt Schmuckhandels GmbH v Claudia Schmidt* [2006] ECR I–2093.
20 A delicate 'post-*Keck*' question: cf n 14.
21 *A-Punkt* (n 19), para 29.

A-Punkt stand for the limits of empowerment promoted by EU free movement law. And the same theme is found in recent cases in the services sector.

In *DKV Belgium* the Court addressed Belgian rules restraining an increase in premium rates for 'individual room' coverage in hospitalisation insurance.[22] The Court found this was a restriction on the right of establishment and the freedom to provide services. But it was receptive to the justification of the particular Belgian rules. It referred to the permissible objective of protecting consumers against sharp, unexpected increases in insurance premiums, though it left it to the national court to ascertain whether or not the chosen system of national regulation went beyond what is necessary in order to achieve that objective.

Citroën Belux concerned a commercial practice engaged in by Citroën consisting of a free offer of comprehensive insurance for six months on the purchase of a Citroën vehicle.[23] This was challenged in Belgium as a prohibited 'combined offer'. This falls within the material scope of Directive 2005/29 on unfair commercial practices,[24] which applies a regime of maximum harmonisation, and so would normally provide a complete answer to the question of whether the practice is fair or not, to the exclusion of Belgian preference. But Article 3(9) of Directive 2005/29 excludes financial services from the maximum harmonisation regime and states instead that Member States may apply more restrictive rules. This is explained by the Directive's Preamble on the basis that:

> Financial services and immovable property, by reason of their complexity and inherent serious risks, necessitate detailed requirements, including positive obligations on traders. For this reason, in the field of financial services and immovable property, this Directive is without prejudice to the right of Member States to go beyond its provisions to protect the economic interests of consumers.

The measure therefore already openly steers thinking towards the particularly pressing need for supplementary protection in this sector, should a Member State choose to provide it. This mirrors *Buet*, which concerned the 'Doorstep Selling' Directive,[25] although in *Citroën Belux* the EU measure does not generally set only minimum standards, but rather it is minimum in character only in its targeting of a particular sector, that of financial services. And the Court found stricter Belgian rules to be justified. It displayed a sector-specific sensitivity, and accepted that 'financial services are, by nature, complex and entail specific risks with regard to which the consumer is not always sufficiently well informed'.[26] It added that a combined offer of which one component is a financial service

[22] Case C–577/11 *DKV Belgium v Association belge des consommateurs Test-Achats ASBL*, judgment of 7 March 2013.

[23] Case C–265/12 *Citroën Belux NV v Federatie voor Verzekerings- en Financiële Tussenpersonen (FvF)*, judgment of 18 July 2013.

[24] Directive 2005/29/EC of the European Parliament and of the Council of 11 May 2005 concerning unfair business-to-consumer commercial practices in the internal market ('Unfair Commercial Practices Directive') [2005] OJ L149/22.

[25] Council Directive 85/577/EEC of 20 December 1985 to protect the consumer in respect of contracts negotiated away from business premises [1985] OJ L372/31.

[26] *Citroën Belux* (n 23), para 39.

tends to lack transparency as regards the conditions, the price and the exact content of that service. So

> such an offer may well mislead consumers as to the true content and actual characteristics of the combination offered and, at the same time, deprive them of the opportunity of comparing the price and quality of that offer with other corresponding services from other economic operators.[27]

It is perfectly possible to disagree. Some may feel this is yet more overregulation of the market, as petty as that swept aside with disdain in *Cassis de Dijon*. That is a legitimate point of discussion. However, the fact that the Court upheld the rule as a contribution to consumer protection shows that the Court is not aggressively deregulatory in its application of free movement law where it faces sincere and targeted arguments for justification—even if one might be a little sceptical on the facts as to how strong this justification really is.

One can look more broadly too, beyond these classic consumer cases, to identify the Court's willingness to approve scepticism about the virtues of market solutions. So, for example, *Essent NV* concerns Dutch rules prohibiting privatisation in the gas sector.[28] The Court is receptive to justifications rooted in consumer protection and energy security, and offers ringing endorsement of the virtues of public ownership as a means to address matters such as cross-subsidisation, promote transparency and ensure investment.[29] In *Ministero dello Sviluppo economico* the Court agreed that fixing minimum tariffs might be justified despite its restrictive effect on the provision of certification services where it could be shown that unrestricted price competition might induce damage to the independence of the certifying bodies.[30]

The consumer is not necessarily empowered by market integration. The consumer may be exposed to harm. This is part of the Court's assessment of the justification of national Measures. And today Article 12 TFEU and Article 38 of the Charter of Fundamental Rights, which both assert a constitutional commitment to the protection of the consumer, support this openness to justification of national measures even where they impede trade integration. So EU free movement law is not only about empowerment. It recognises too the limits of empowerment.

III. Empowerment and the Legislative *Acquis*

Where the EU legislature decides to replace diverse state measures that hinder integration by an initiative of harmonisation of laws, the aim is to put in place

[27] ibid.

[28] Joined cases C–105/12 to C–107/12 *Staat der Nederlanden v Essent NV and Essent Nederland BV and Eneco Holding NV and Delta NV*, judgment of 22 October 2013.

[29] See esp ibid, paras 56, 58, 59 and 65.

[30] Case C–327/12 *Ministero dello Sviluppo economico v SOA Nazionale Costruttori*, judgment of 12 December 2013.

a single set of rules apt to underpin the creation and maintenance of an internal market. In this sense harmonisation is an instrument of market-making. Indeed, the key provision in the Treaty which authorises the adoption of measures of harmonisation, Article 114 TFEU, is explicitly connected to Article 26 TFEU, which sets out the definition of the internal market as 'an area without internal frontiers in which the free movement of goods, persons, services and capital is ensured in accordance with the provisions of the Treaties'.

This is an exercise in deregulation. On the simplest model, 28 different (national) regimes are reduced to one common (EU) regime. But the market is not simply deregulated, it is simultaneously also regulated because the EU rule becomes the (common) basis for the regulation of the sector in question. In fact, it is more helpful to describe this not as regulation, but as reregulation in order to capture the notion that the EU is reacting to and replacing diverse patterns of national regulation.

Accordingly harmonisation of laws is conventionally and correctly understood as a vertical transfer of regulatory responsibility from Member States to the EU. Diverse national measures are replaced by a common EU standard. This may wholly exclude the scope for divergent national rules—maximum harmonisation, whereby the EU rule becomes ceiling and floor. Or it may conserve the possibility for stricter national rules—minimum harmonisation, whereby the EU rule becomes the floor only. This process serves to integrate and to deregulate the EU market, but also to reregulate it, according to the standard and technique chosen by the EU.

This re-regulatory consequence has been fully acknowledged by the Court. Provided that the conditions for recourse to Article 114 TFEU as a legal basis are fulfilled, the EU legislature 'cannot be prevented from relying on that legal basis on the ground that public health protection is a decisive factor in the choices to be made'; and in the light of the commitment of key provisions such as Articles 114(3) and 168 TFEU to public health concerns, the harmonised rule 'may consist in requiring all the Member States to authorise the marketing of the product or products concerned, subjecting such an obligation of authorisation to certain conditions, or even provisionally or definitively prohibiting the marketing of a product or products'.[31] Similarly provided that the conditions for recourse to Article 114 TFEU as a legal basis are fulfilled—that is, provided there is in short a market-making contribution found in the measure of harmonisation—there can be no constitutional objection that the protection of animal welfare is a decisive factor in the choices to be made.[32] And in similar vein

[31] eg Cases C–154/04 and C–155/04 *The Queen, on the application of Alliance for Natural Health and Others v Secretary of State for Health and National Assembly for Wales* [2005] ECR I–6451; Case C–380/03 *Federal Republic of Germany v European Parliament and Council of the European Union* [2006] ECR I–11573.

[32] Case T–526/10 *Inuit Tapiriit Kanatami and Others v Commission*, judgment of 25 April 2013.

where diverse and market-fragmenting national measures of consumer protection are subjected to the discipline of harmonisation, the result is that the EU must and does make choices about what shall be the shape, content and intensity of its own (harmonised) consumer protection rules.

This fits into an agenda of empowerment. The consumer is invited to treat the EU market as integrated because he or she is protected in the same (harmonised) way wherever he or she chooses to shop. The vision is of an active consumer, confident about shopping across borders. But it is also concerns (re-)regulation of the market.

The heavy emphasis in the legislative *acquis* on the mandatory disclosure of information to consumers as a regulatory technique fits into an agenda of empowerment. The assumption is that the consumer is able to use the disclosed information in order to bargain more effectively and thereby to secure the benefits of a more transparent and competitive market. It is, of course, a questionable assumption on several levels.[33] One might question whether consumers use information in the way envisaged by theory. Even if they (or at least some) do, one might question whether that is really enough to correct the operation of the market. The model of information disclosure will serve consumers ill if it legitimates the use of pernicious commercial tactics under a false assumption that consumers are sufficiently alerted to the risks by legal rules. Empowerment-through-information is an important part of EU consumer law, but as a general observation, by no means confined to the EU, it remains a contested concept.

However, in reviewing the EU's legislative *acquis* involving the harmonisation of laws pertaining to consumer protection, there is more than empowerment on show. The EU legislative *acquis* includes important rules that protect the consumer from harm, and it is inadequate to regard them merely from the standpoint of achieving empowerment. Mandatory information disclosure is not the limit of the EU's regulatory preoccupation. The EU's Directive 2001/95 on General Product Safety does not mandate that consumers be provided with information about unsafe products.[34] It requires that unsafe products be excluded from the market. But it is not only in the matter of consumer health and safety that the EU's legislative *acquis* adopts a model more ambitious than mere information disclosure. In protecting the economic interests of consumers too, the EU has chosen to require that some practices be excluded from the market.

[33] eg H-W Micklitz, 'The Expulsion of the Concept of Protection from the Consumer Law and the Return of Social Elements in the Civil Law: a Bittersweet Polemic' (2012) 35 *Journal of Consumer Policy* 283; G Howells, 'The Potential and Limits of Consumer Empowerment by Information' (2005) 32 *Journal of Law and Society* 349; C Willett and M Morgan-Taylor, 'Recognising the Limits of Transparency in EU Consumer Law' in J Devenney and M Kenny (eds), *European Consumer Protection: Theory and Practice* (Cambridge, Cambridge University Press, 2012).

[34] Directive 2001/95/EC of the European Parliament and of the Council of 3 December 2001 on general product safety [2002] OJ L11/4.

A. Unfair Terms

Directive 93/13 harmonises rules governing unfair terms in consumer contracts.[35] And, in short, it forbids such terms. The system of protection implemented by the Directive has been vividly captured by the Court as 'based on the idea that the consumer is in a weak position vis-à-vis the seller or supplier, as regards both his bargaining power and his level of knowledge'; and that this 'leads to the consumer agreeing to terms drawn up in advance by the seller or supplier without being able to influence the content of those terms'.[36] The Directive requires the Member States to provide that unfair terms shall not bind the consumer. This is made explicit in Article 6(1), which the Court has described as a mandatory provision which aims to replace the formal balance which the contract establishes between the rights and obligations of the parties with an effective balance which re-establishes equality between them.[37] This, then, is a direct check on the enforceability of contractual terms which is motivated by concern to tackle the imbalance that flows from permitting contractual freedom free rein in the relationship between the trader and the consumer. So intervening in freedom of contract is rationalised on the basis that preserving freedom of contract in imbalanced relationships is not freedom at all but rather licence for the powerful to impose on the weak.

This mantra has concrete consequences for effective consumer protection. So, for example, *Árpád Kásler* concerned the interpretation of Directive 93/13 in the context of a challenge to a term dealing with the exchange rate applicable to repayment of a loan denominated in a foreign currency.[38] The ruling raises several points of interest but of central present relevance was the consideration given by the Court to the proviso in Article 4(2) of the Directive that assessment of the unfair nature of terms shall relate neither to the definition of the main subject matter of the contract nor to the adequacy of the price 'in so far as these terms are in plain intelligible language'. This, the Court concluded, imposes a 'requirement of transparency' which, given the consumer's 'position of weakness', must be interpreted broadly.[39] Accordingly the requirement that a contractual term must be drafted in plain intelligible language stretches beyond formal grammatical

[35] Council Directive 93/13/EEC of 5 April 1993 on unfair terms in consumer contracts [1993] OJ L95/29.

[36] eg Case C–472/11 *Banif Plus Bank Zrt v Csaba Csipai and Viktória Csipai*, judgment of 21 February 2013, para 19.

[37] eg Case C–168/05 *Elisa María Mostaza Claro v Centro Móvil Milenium SL* [2006] ECR I–10421, para 36; Case C–137/08 *VB Pénzügyi Lízing Zrt v Ferenc Schneider* [2010] ECR I–10847, para 47; Case C–618/10 *Banco Español de Crédito SA v Joaquín Calderón Camino*, judgment of 14 June 2012, paras 40 and 63; Case C–472/11 *Banif Plus Bank Zrt v Csaba Csipai and Viktória Csipai*, judgment of 21 February 2013, para 20; Case C–415/11 *Mohamed Aziz v Caixa d'Estalvis de Catalunya, Tarragona i Manresa (Catalunyacaixa)*, judgment of 14 March 2013, para 45; Case C–470/12 *Pohotovosť sro v Miroslav Vašuta*, judgment of 27 February 2014, paras 39–41. See Weatherill (n 14) ch 5.

[38] Case C–26/13 *Kásler Árpád, Káslerné Rábai Hajnalka v OTP Jelzálogbank Zrt*, judgment of 30 April 2014.

[39] ibid, paras 71–72.

intelligibility to encompass also a transparent explanation of how the term shall operate in order to ensure that the consumer is in a position to evaluate on the basis of clear criteria the economic consequences.[40] So, in the particular circumstances, the contract should set out transparently exactly how the mechanism of conversion for the foreign currency shall operate. If it does not, the relevant term does not escape review pursuant to Article 4(2) of the Directive.

It should be conceded that the Court's case law cannot be adjudged remorselessly consistent. So, for example, *Asociación de Consumidores Independientes de Castilla y León v Anuntis Segundamano España SL* concerned Spanish rules on territorial jurisdiction which worked to the advantage of the trader rather than the consumer representative association seeking to act against unfair terms.[41] The Court's perception that an *individual* consumer is in an inferior position has provoked it to interpret EU law, specifically Directive 93/13, in order to rescue consumer litigants from the damaging consequences of such procedural rules,[42] but it refused to extend this logic to the case of a consumer representative association. The judgment seems to be based on an assumption that consumer representative associations are powerful enough to counteract the economic power of suppliers even where suppliers are privileged by domestic procedural rules, but this, though probably sometimes true, is likely frequently to be false. The Court could and arguably should have left open the possibility for a national court to explore whether a particular association is adequately resourced or not, but instead it subordinated the concern for effective consumer protection to the preservation of national choices about procedural economy. However, the majority of its case law concerning Directive 93/13 makes the opposite choice. *Árpád Kásler* is more typical than *Asociación de Consumidores Independientes*. Article 12 TFEU and Article 38 of the Charter may be expected to act as an increasingly prominent frame for this pro-consumer interpretative approach, but they exert no transformative effect, for the Court's anxiety to treat the legislative *acquis* as infused with sensitivity to the needs of consumer protection is long-standing.[43] So, as a detailed and inspiring examination has concluded the Court is going 'far beyond laying down minimum standards' and is 'developing hand in hand with the consumers and citizens what has been called a "European civil society"'.[44]

This is not inconsistent with the agenda of empowerment. Perhaps, in a sense, it *is* empowerment. It might be understood as empowerment through regulation: private autonomy is promoted by laws that address substantive inequality.

[40] ibid, para 75.

[41] Case C–413/12 *Asociación de Consumidores Independientes de Castilla y León v Anuntis Segundamano España SL*, judgment of 5 December 2013; and see similarly Case C–470/12 *Pohotovosť sro v Miroslav Vašuta*, judgment of 27 February 2014.

[42] eg *Claro* (n 37).

[43] S Weatherill, 'Article 38—Consumer Protection' in S Peers, T Hervey, J Kenner and A Ward (eds), *The EU Charter of Fundamental Rights: A Commentary* (Oxford, Hart Publishing, 2014).

[44] H-W Micklitz and N Reich, 'The Court and Sleeping Beauty: The Revival of the Unfair Contract Terms Directive' (2014) 51 *Common Market Law Review* 771, 806.

However, I think it is more complex and sophisticated than 'empowerment'. It is driven by a concern to protect consumers from unacceptably exploitative practices in the EU's internal market, whether the harm is caused by deliberate commercial chicanery or by simple lack of full understanding of what is on offer in a complex market. It is a (re-regulatory) choice which reveals the EU's concern to achieve adequate levels of protection for all consumers, whether empowered or not. And the Court commonly supplements the legislative regime when offered the opportunity to rule on the compatibility with EU law of national procedures which cramp the Directive's intended effective protection of the consumer.

B. Unfair Commercial Practices

Directive 2005/29 protects the consumer from unfair commercial practices.[45] Like Directive 93/13, its legal base is (what is now) Article 114 TFEU, so it is in formal terms a measure dedicated to the creation of the EU's internal market. But at the same time it involves a choice about the re-regulatory standard to be applied (in common) by the Member States, and that standard is clearly infused by the need to protect consumers. And so Article 1 identifies the 'purpose' of the Directive as twofold: to contribute to the proper functioning of the internal market and achieve a high level of consumer protection. Indeed, the very first Recital in the Directive's Preamble highlights that the Treaty—then Articles 153(1) and (3)(a) EC, now Articles 12 and 169 TFEU—provides that the EU 'is to contribute to the attainment of a high level of consumer protection' by the measures it adopts pursuant to the competence to introduce market-making legislative harmonisation. Today Article 38 of the Charter would add further support to the constitutional linkage between market-making and the protection of the consumer.

The core of the regime is contained in Article 5(1). It could not be more textually simple: 'Unfair commercial practices shall be prohibited.' In pursuit of definitional clarity Article 5(2) amplifies the notion of unfairness. A commercial practice shall be treated as unfair if (a) it is contrary to the requirements of professional diligence[46] and (b) it materially distorts or is likely to materially distort the economic behaviour[47] with regard to the product of the average consumer whom it reaches or to whom it is addressed or of the average member of the group when

[45] Directive 2005/29/EC, Unfair Commercial Practices Directive (n 24). See B Keirsbilck, *The New European Law of Unfair Commercial Practices and Competition Law* (Oxford, Hart Publishing, 2011); S Weatherill and U Bernitz (eds), *The Regulation of Unfair Commercial Practices under EC Directive 2005/29: New Rules and New Techniques* (Oxford, Hart Publishing, 2007); C Willett, 'Fairness and Consumer Decision Making under the Unfair Commercial Practices Directive' (2010) 33 *Journal of Consumer Policy* 247.

[46] Defined in Art 2(h) to mean 'the standard of special skill and care which a trader may reasonably be expected to exercise towards consumers, commensurate with honest market practice and/or the general principle of good faith in the trader's field of activity'.

[47] Defined in Art 2(e): 'to materially distort the economic behaviour of consumers' means using a commercial practice to appreciably impair the consumer's ability to make an informed decision, thereby causing the consumer to take a transactional decision that he would not have taken otherwise.

a commercial practice is directed to a particular group of consumers. The Directive proceeds to amplify control that shall in particular be directed at commercial practices that are misleading and those that are aggressive. And the Directive is maximum in character, with small exceptions only,[48] which means not only that Member States shall suppress practices that count as unfair within the meaning of the Directive but also that, in so far as a matter falls within the material scope of the Directive, they shall allow practices that do not count as unfair.

One could understand this as 'empowering' in the sense that ensuring protection induces confident consumers to treat the internal market as viable. But, as already argued above, it seems to me to be an unhelpfully narrow understanding of the purpose of the EU's chosen form of market regulation to focus (only) on empowerment. Directive 2005/29 is about *protection* from, or at least within, the market.

Moreover, although in many respects Directive 2005/29 adopts the Court's model of an attentive consumer in establishing a benchmark for judging 'unfairness', it (like the Court's case law) also accommodates an understanding of the need to consider vulnerable consumers. Article 5(3) of the Directive provides that:

> Commercial practices which are likely to materially distort the economic behaviour only of a clearly identifiable group of consumers who are particularly vulnerable to the practice or the underlying product because of their mental or physical infirmity, age or credulity in a way which the trader could reasonably be expected to foresee, shall be assessed from the perspective of the average member of that group. This is without prejudice to the common and legitimate advertising practice of making exaggerated statements or statements which are not meant to be taken literally.

So here the average consumer is to be considered not in the abstract but rather in its appropriate regulatory context. The purpose of Article 5(3) is to allow scope for the suppression of practices that would not harm the average consumer in the general population but would have a particular impact within a clearly identifiable group of consumers. Accordingly, at least where the preconditions of Article 5(3) are met, the Directive does not prohibit targeted protection of particular groups of vulnerable consumers.

I have argued that Article 5(3) should be read with reference to the Court's case law under Article 34 TFEU, which accepts that a system of consumer protection which can be shown to target protection of a particular group of consumers should be assessed on its own terms, and should not be swept aside on an unthinking application of the broad 'average consumer' test.[49] That is to say, if the law is not designed to deal with a problem which would concern the average consumer, it must not be assessed as if it were so designed. This, of course, does not mean that the Court will not look hard at the claims made in support of the law. Frequently, as the case law examined above reveals, the claimed advantages of national measures

[48] *Citroën Belux* (n 23).
[49] S Weatherill, 'Who is the "Average Consumer"?' in Weatherill and Bernitz (n 45).

do not stand up to close scrutiny. But in principle a regulator can advance arguments designed to show the inappropriateness of the 'average consumer' test as a basis for reviewing a particular challenged measure, and the Court will in principle be receptive to such contextual arguments. This is how Article 5(3) should be read. It serves as an invitation to the regulator to demonstrate just how and why a particular practice should be suppressed as incompatible with the Directive's control even though it is a practice that would not distort the behaviour of the 'average consumer' in the general population. So the Directive—as EU consumer law generally, in both legislative and judicial practice—is not blind to the needs of particular disadvantaged or vulnerable groups. Quite the contrary: it accepts the place of such targeted measures of consumer protection. It requires only that choices made by regulators be properly explained and justified, under an assumption which holds that national measures which restrict cross-border trade require such justification because, by impeding market integration, they damage the consumer interest in a more efficiently functioning market which delivers wider choice and competition on price and quality.

Admittedly, the features of vulnerability to which Article 5(3) chooses to draw attention are limited: 'mental or physical infirmity, age or credulity'. What of educational attainment? Income? Ethnicity? There is a considerable amount of empirical research into patterns of consumer deception and the list in Article 5(3) has convincingly been described as 'quite arbitrary' in its restrictive approach by Stuyck, Terryn and Van Dyck, who call for an empirical inquiry into the correlation between the characteristics of certain groups of consumers and the likelihood of vulnerability to particular practices.[50] I agree with this. It is important that the Directive be interpreted in a way that is receptive to the whole range of possible vulnerabilities and disadvantages with which particular groups of consumers are burdened. As a matter of detailed interpretation, the way to achieve this under Article 5(3) of the Directive is to take a broad view of what may be regarded as 'credulity'. More generally, one should appreciate that the vision of the consumer in EU judicial and legislative practice is sophisticated enough to take account of a broad sweep of possible vulnerabilities and disadvantages. This is mandated today by Article 12 TFEU and Article 38 of the Charter.

C. Vulnerable Consumers—And Beyond

Protection of 'vulnerable' consumers also appears in the EU's legislative *acquis* governing energy supply. So, for example, Directive 2009/72 establishes common rules for the internal market in electricity, and includes provision for universal service and the protection of vulnerable consumers. Here is another area in

[50] J Stuyck, E Terryn and T Van Dyck, 'Confidence through Fairness? The New Directive on Unfair Business-to-Consumer Commercial Practices in the Internal Market' (2006) 43 *Common Market Law Review* 107, 121–22.

which the EU's understanding of the needs of consumer protection reaches some distance beyond empowerment.[51] Admittedly, the actual content of the protective rules themselves may be less strong than one might wish, and certainly the EU regime cannot be considered comprehensive. It is moreover lacking the definitional clarity that would be required to deliver a consistent and even protective regime across all the Member States. But the evolving pattern of legislative activity at EU level reveals an increasingly dense network of rules. The bare fact that the EU *acquis* touches on universal service and consumer vulnerability *at all* is already revealing of a move towards guaranteed social protection, not choice alone, in the market. This nudges the debate towards consumers as citizens, and even broader still (and beyond the scope of this chapter) towards consumer rights as human rights.[52]

Something more assertive than empowerment through information disclosure is found in the protection of passengers on air transport. This is secured by Regulation 261/2004, which establishes common rules on compensation and assistance to passengers in the event of denied boarding and of cancellation or long delay of flights.[53] This takes as its legal base Article 80 EC, which is now, in an amended form, Article 100 TFEU. It authorises EU legislation in the sea and air transport sectors and asserts in its Preamble a concern to aim at ensuring a high level of protection for passengers. This regime appears to have real practical significance judged by the growing amount of case law generated before the Court of Justice on its scope and intent. It is case law which has been criticised for its perceived overgenerous interpretation of the scope of protection. So, for example, in *Sturgeon* the Court interpreted the Regulation to cover not only passengers on cancelled flights but also those on delayed flights.[54] This is not expressly foreseen by the Regulation. It was achieved by an interpretative stretch, based on reference to the context and objectives of the legislative scheme, and open to sceptical review.[55] Subsequently in *Germanwings* the Court was politely asked by the Landgericht Köln to reconsider its approach, and especially whether its ruling in *Sturgeon* amounted to a violation of the principle of separation of powers.[56] Unsurprisingly the Court disagreed and blandly restated that *Sturgeon* was a matter of legitimate interpretation of a legislative text. That is an intriguing

[51] For detail see A Johnston and G Block, *Energy Law in Europe* (Oxford, Oxford University Press, 2012) ch 7.

[52] I Benöhr, *EU Consumer Law and Human Rights* (Oxford, Oxford University Press, 2014).

[53] Regulation (EC) No 261/2004 of the European Parliament and of the Council of 11 February 2004 establishing common rules on compensation and assistance to passengers in the event of denied boarding and of cancellation or long delay of flights [2004] OJ L46/1.

[54] Joined cases C–402 and C–432/07 *Christopher Sturgeon, Gabriel Sturgeon and Alana Sturgeon v Condor Flugdienst GmbH and Stefan Böck and Cornelia Lepuschitz v Air France SA* [2009] ECR I–10923.

[55] For discussion, see S Garben, 'Sky-high controversy and high-flying claims? The Sturgeon case law in light of judicial activism, euroscepticism and eurolegalism' (2013) 50 *Common Market Law Review* 15; F Le Bot, 'La protection des passagers aériens dans l'Union européenne' (2013) 49 *Revue Trimestrielle de Droit Européen* 753.

[56] Case C–413/11 *Germanwings GmbH v Thomas Amend*, judgment of 18 April 2013.

debate. For present purposes it suffices to locate this regime as a contribution by the EU legislative process to a protective pattern which transcends empowerment and an instance of the Court as a 'socially activist' institution.[57]

Denise McDonough v Ryanair Ltd allowed the Court to assess the scope of the obligation to provide care for passengers in the event of cancellation of a flight imposed by Regulation 261/2004 in the light of the Charter of Fundamental Rights.[58] The background to the dispute was the notoriously disruptive eruption of the Eyjafjallajökull volcano in Iceland in the spring of 2010. The reference directed attention only to Articles 16 and 17 of the Charter, dealing with freedom to conduct a business and the right to property respectively, but the Court in its ruling drew on Article 38 governing consumer protection. The Court concluded that the obligation imposed on airlines by Regulation 261/2004 struck 'a fair balance' between the several Charter rights at stake.[59] Therefore, it did not breach Articles 16 and 17 of the Charter. The EU is a legitimate *regulator* of markets.[60]

This is admittedly a niche area of legal regulation and it tends to reinforce the impression of EU intervention as a patchwork. However, passengers using railways,[61] ships,[62] buses and coaches[63] also enjoy a degree of protection in the event of delays and cancellations under measures adopted pursuant to the Title on Transport in the TFEU or its predecessor, and there is an additional significant layer of protection established under international agreements. Accordingly, provided one appreciates that coverage is far from comprehensive, the label EU 'travel law' or 'passenger law' is not far-fetched.[64] And it is about more than empowerment.

Directive 2010/13 on Audiovisual Media Services supplies another good example of how harmonisation is concerned not only with integrating the EU market through the adoption of common rules but also with the choice of the type of (re-)regulatory standards that the EU should prefer.[65] The Directive provides in Article 9 that Member States shall ensure that audiovisual commercial communications for alcoholic beverages shall not be aimed specifically at *minors*; and

[57] Garben (n 55), 36; cf Micklitz and Reich, 'The Court and Sleeping Beauty: The Revival of the Unfair Contract Terms Directive' (n 44).

[58] Case C–12/11 *Denise McDonagh v Ryanair Ltd*, judgment of 31 January 2013.

[59] ibid, para 64.

[60] cf Case C–544/10 *Deutsches Weintor eG v Land Rheinland-Pfalz*, judgment of 6 September 2012; Case C–283/11 *Sky Österreich GmbH v Österreichischer Rundfunk*, judgment of 22 January 2013; Case C–101/12 *Herbert Schaible v Land Baden-Württemberg*, judgment of 17 October 2013.

[61] Regulation (EC) No 1371/2007 of the European Parliament and of the Council of 23 October 2007 on rail passengers' rights and obligations [2007] OJ L315/14.

[62] Regulation (EU) No 1177/2010 of the European Parliament and of the Council of 24 November 2010 concerning the rights of passengers when travelling by sea and inland waterway [2010] OJ L334/1.

[63] Regulation (EU) No 181/2011 of the European Parliament and of the Council of 16 February 2011 concerning the rights of passengers in bus and coach transport [2011] OJ L55/1.

[64] cf J Karsten, 'Travel Law' in C Twigg-Flesner (ed), *The Cambridge Companion to European Union Private Law* (Cambridge, Cambridge University Press, 2010).

[65] Directive 2010/13/EU of the European Parliament and of the Council of 10 March 2010 on the coordination of certain provisions laid down by law, regulation or administrative action in Member States concerning the provision of audiovisual media services (Audiovisual Media Services Directive) [2010] OJ L95/1.

Article 12 adds that Member States shall take appropriate measures to restrict on-demand audiovisual media services which might seriously impair the physical, mental or moral development of *minors*. Directive 2010/13's Preamble declares that '[m]easures taken to protect the physical, mental and moral development of minors and human dignity should be carefully balanced with the fundamental right to freedom of expression as laid down in the Charter on Fundamental Rights of the European Union'. And the measure itself shows that restraint on that freedom is capable of being justified. Here is more—sector-specific, targeted—protection mandated by EU law.

This is not designed to offer an exhaustive survey. The point is simply that it is possible to piece together a number of areas of the EU's legislative *acquis* which reveal concern for the vulnerable consumer, embracing topics as diverse as unfair commercial practices, transport, energy, food, credit, and SGEIs.[66] The EU's Treaty mandate grants it no general distributive aspiration, but nor is it confined to a narrow, exclusively functional preoccupation with market efficiency. There is public law, there is private law—there is elision of the divide between the two. The provision of information to the consumer has strong claims to have been the first 'principle' of EU consumer law to emerge in concrete fashion. It did so in the context of both the application of the proportionality control over justifications advanced in the context of free movement and also in the EU's legislative *acquis*. But there is plainly far more to it than mere transparency, even if it remains contested how much more there is to EU contract law and, wider still, EU private law—and how much more there *should* be.[67]

The Parliament's recent resolution on a strategy for strengthening the rights of vulnerable consumers has it right:

> the ambition for EU consumer policy should be a high level of empowerment and protection for every consumer … the single market must also ensure a high level of protection for all consumers, with a special focus on vulnerable consumers in order to take into account their specific needs and strengthen their capabilities.[68]

[66] The material is helpfully assembled by M Friant-Perrot, 'Le consommateur vulnerable à la lumière du droit de la consummation de 'Union européenne' (2013) 49 *Revue Trimestrielle de Droit Europeen* 483; also L Waddington, 'Vulnerable and Confused: The Protection of "Vulnerable" Consumers under EU Law' (2013) 38 *European Law Review* 757.

[67] See, eg, for diverse assessment T Wilhelmsson, 'Varieties of Welfarism in European Contract Law' (2004) 10 *European Law Journal* 712; J Basedow, 'Freedom of Contract in the European Union' (2008) 16 *European Review of Private Law* 901; J Davies, 'Entrenchment of New Governance in Consumer Policy Formulation: a platform for European Consumer Citizenship Practice?' (2009) 32 *Journal of Consumer Policy* 245; H-W Micklitz, 'The Expulsion of the Concept of Protection from the Consumer Law and the Return of Social Elements in the Civil Law: a Bittersweet Polemic' (2012) 35 *Journal of Consumer Policy* 283; C Herresthal, 'Constitutionalisation of the Freedom of Contract in European Union Law' in K Ziegler and P Huber (eds), *Current Problems in the Protection of Human Rights—Perspectives from Germany and the UK* (Oxford, Hart Publishing, 2013).

[68] European Parliament resolution of 22 May 2012 on a strategy for strengthening the rights of vulnerable consumers [2013] OJ C264 E/11.

Moreover, there is a convincing case to be made that protection of the weaker party constitutes a general principle of EU law.[69] The material on consumer protection forms an important part of that case. This is something richer than 'empowerment'.

D. Vulnerability and Choice of Model of Harmonisation

Vulnerability—and weakness—is certainly a complex and multi-dimensional issue, and EU law reflects that in only a fragmented way. Accordingly there is a good argument that EU rules should leave space for national choices about how to protect particular groups of vulnerable consumers whose particular needs cannot be satisfactorily addressed by rules adopted at EU level. Some of the free movement case law fits this model. *Buet* was a ruling which authorised French rules as compatible with free movement law in circumstances where there was already an EU Directive mandating protection at a lower level than that chosen by France.[70] It was the fact that the Directive explicitly required that its rules be treated as only a minimum standard that ensured it was possible to assess the justifiability of the stricter French intervention. This is a perspective that counsels strongly against maximum harmonisation, which would in principle close off the possibility even to consider the desirability of stricter measures than the agreed EU norm.

This is a contested issue. In *EU Consumer Policy Strategy 2007–2013: Empowering consumers, enhancing their welfare, effectively protecting them*, the Commission, in pursuit of an internal market driven by 'empowerment', was dismissive of the virtue of minimum harmonisation.[71] Its Green Paper on the Review of the Consumer Acquis went so far as to exclude the model of 'minimum harmonisation' as an option for the future.[72] And the proposal for a Regulation of the Parliament and the Council on a Common European Sales Law took the opportunity to lament the damage done to regulatory uniformity in the internal market by past preference for minimum harmonisation.[73] The Commission is clearly right to assert that the minimum model of harmonisation damages the unity of the internal market. Member States may and do set stricter national rules within the scope of the EU measure, and this denies a 'level playing field' for trade. But the maximum model of harmonisation has disadvantages too, which are not always acknowledged, still less accepted, by the Commission. Stricter national rules are disallowed, which prevents national choice and flexibility. Consumer protection

[69] See especially N Reich, *General Principles of EU Civil Law* (Cambridge, Intersentia, 2014) ch 2.

[70] *Buet* (n 13).

[71] Commission, EU Consumer Policy Strategy 2007–2013: Empowering consumers, enhancing their welfare, effectively protecting them COM(2007) 99, esp 7.

[72] Commission, Green Paper on the Review of the Consumer *Acquis* COM(2006) 744 final.

[73] European Commission, Proposal for a Regulation of the European Parliament and of the Council on a Common European Sales Law COM(2011) 635, 5.

is set at the level chosen by the EU—it cannot be raised by national law, and, moreover, if the EU maximum is *lower* than existing national standards, then in those states the EU causes a reduction in protection.

The issue is whether the costs of this vertical transfer of regulatory responsibility from the Member States to the EU outweigh the benefits, or vice versa. That is a debate that has been pursued with vigour.[74] The assumption on which this chapter is based is that maximum harmonisation should be regarded as the exception and minimum harmonisation as the norm in order to preserve space for national initiatives that reflect the sheer diversity of consumer experience and preference across the regulatory terrain of the EU's internal market. In the matter of consumer protection, a complex and multi-faceted ambition, the EU cannot do it all.

IV. Conclusion

This chapter commenced with the Commission's 2012 document *A European Consumer Agenda—Boosting confidence and growth.*[75] Nothing in that document contradicts what I argue here. The Commission does not deny the richer, wider, deeper heritage of EU consumer law. But it does not embrace it either. Provided that empowerment is treated as just one element of EU consumer protection law, I have no objection. But if empowerment confines or excludes other concerns—if EU consumer protection law is to be converted into EU consumer law or dissolved into some generalised EU law of market freedom—then not only will the proud history of the EU's work in the field have been betrayed but so too will the constitutional commitments found in particular in Article 12 TFEU and Article 38 of the Charter have been violated. EU consumer law is understandable as a means to promote and achieve empowerment—but not only that. It is about, in short, protection too. EU consumer (protection) law is built on EU rules—but not only EU rules. It is built on national rules too. And, in looking at EU consumer (protection) law, this chapter advances these claims at both the descriptive and the normative level.

[74] eg S Weatherill, 'The Consumer Rights Directive: How and Why a Quest for "Coherence" Has (Largely) Failed' (2012) 49 *Common Market Law Review* 1279; S Weatherill, 'Maximum versus Minimum Harmonization: Choosing between Unity and Diversity in the Search for the Soul of the Internal Market' in N NicShuibhne and L Gormley (eds), *From Single Market to Economic Union: Essays in Memory of John A Usher* (Oxford, Oxford University Press, 2012); N Boeger, 'Minimum Harmonisation, Free Movement and Proportionality' in P Syrpis (ed), *The Judiciary, the Legislature and the EU Internal Market* (Cambridge, Cambridge University Press, 2012); F Gomez and R Ganuza, 'An Economic Analysis of Harmonization Régimes: Full Harmonization, Minimum Harmonization or Optional Instrument?' (2011) 7 *European Review of Contract Law* 275.

[75] COM(2012) 225 (n 1).

9

Targeted Consumer Protection

STEFAN GRUNDMANN

I. Introduction

Consumer contract law has been important for the development of European contract law. It has in fact been so important that—at least in the beginning—the term European consumer law was even more prominent than European contract law.[1] If, then, a new concept of the consumer in European contract law is to be discussed, a broader question is raised for the whole of European contract law about how far differentiation should go with respect to the protection of 'weaker' parties more generally. This chapter puts that question even more broadly, because it considers whether consumer law (in Europe) is to be conceived and understood primarily as an instrument of individual protection or rather as a tool of market functioning at large—that is, establishing a level playing field. It asks too what consequences would flow from the one conception or the other. Indeed, a new interest in images of the consumer—their

[1] See, in particular, G Howells and T Wilhelmsson, *EC Consumer Law* (Aldershot, Ashgate, 1997); N Reich, *Europäisches Verbraucherrecht—eine problemorientierte Einführung in das europäische Wirtschaftsrecht* 3rd edn (Baden-Baden, Nomos, 1996); then N Reich and H-W Micklitz, *Europäisches Verbraucherrecht—eine problemorientierte Einführung in das europäische Wirtschaftsrecht* 4th edn (Baden-Baden, Nomos, 2003); N Reich and others, *European Consumer Law* 2nd edn (Antwerp, Intersentia, 2013); S Weatherill, *EU Consumer Law and Policy* 2nd edn (Cheltenham, Edward Elgar, 2013); also G Howells and S Weatherill, *Consumer Protection Law* 2nd edn (Aldershot, Ashgate, 2005). See, on the other hand, for the completely changed concept of a European contract law (and indeed a law of business transactions mainly) C Kirchner, 'Europäisches Vertragsrecht' in H-L Weyers (ed), *Europäisches Vertragsrecht* (Baden-Baden, Nomos, 1997); and much more broadly S Grundmann, *Europäisches Schuldvertragsrecht—das Europäische Recht der Unternehmensgeschäfte (nebst Texten und Materialien zur Rechtsangleichung)* (Berlin, de Gruyter, 1999); S Grundmann, 'The Structure of European Contract Law' (2001) 4 *European Review of Private Law* 505; C Quigley, *European Community Contract Law* (London, Kluwer, 1997); for a more recent contribution, see K Riesenhuber, *EU-Vertragsrecht* (Tübingen, Mohr-Siebeck, 2013). This has become the official term since 2001–03, see, for instance: Commission, Communication to the Council and the European Parliament on European Contract Law COM(2001) 398 final; Commission, Communication to the European Parliament and the Council of 15 March 2003—A more coherent European Contract Law—An Action Plan COM(2003) 68 final; Commission, Green Paper on policy options for progress towards a European Contract Law of 1 July 2010 for consumers and businesses COM(2010) 348 final.

differentiation and the foundations—would seem to have arisen.[2] In this chapter, it is argued that consumer protection is to be conceived against the background of a continuum of weaker parties, not only consumers (see section II) and that for this reason a general and formal mode of protection can be justified only insofar as it is grounded in the function of contracting. In other words, just because of their *personal status* as consumers, consumers should enjoy only such protection as is aimed at an informed autonomous taking of decisions. On the other hand, paternalistic inroads into such (informed) autonomy need to be justified not only by such a personal status, but by additional *substantive reasons* (see section III). On the other hand, players other than consumers, namely professionals (in small or medium sized enterprises (SMEs) for instance), also enjoy protection when it can be justified positively with a view to enhancing an informed autonomous decision-taking capacity. This chapter therefore argues that within the area of consumer protection, the regime should no longer be differentiated (mainly) according to different types of consumers, but with respect to substantive reasons concerning the amount of risk. This is the core of this contribution. The cross-border or multi-level dimension should, however, not be completely neglected (see section IV) because choices about the territorial scope of application play a significant role in deciding how far protection actually reaches.

II. The Person of the Consumer or Weaker Party—A Simple Model

A. Images of the Consumer—Introductory Remarks on a Functional Model

The traditional (and first) image of the consumer was established by the Court of Justice of the European Union (CJEU) for the fundamental freedoms. The Court recognised consumer protection as a category relevant within the interpretation and application of the fundamental freedoms.[3] Later, the CJEU transposed the same concept to EC secondary law, including contract law.[4] In both cases, the consumer was to be reasonably well-informed and reasonably observant and circumspect.

With regard to the fundamental freedoms, the CJEU first characterised national rules as impediments to the free movement (of goods) even if they applied both to

[2] See also F Klinck and K Riesenhuber (eds), *Verbraucherleitbilder: Interdisziplinäre und europäische Perspektiven* (Berlin, De Gruyter, 2015).

[3] Case 120/78 *Rewe-Zentral AG v Bundesmonopolverwaltung für Branntwein* (*Cassis de Dijon*) [1979] ECR 649.

[4] Case 210/96 *Gut Springenheide GmbH and Rudolf Tusky v Oberkreisdirektor des Kreises Steinfurt—Amt für Lebensmittelüberwachung* [1998] ECR I–4657. The criterion is described (in the holding) as this: 'an average consumer who is reasonably well-informed and reasonably observant and circumspect'.

domestic and foreign supply, at least if, at the same time, they *de facto* put a heavier burden on foreign supply, for instance by imposing higher costs of compliance. In a second step, even more relevant for present purposes, the Court characterised consumer protection as a mandatory reason of public good, which might justify an impediment to trade. The latter should, however, only be the case if the rule protecting consumers imposed a proportionate burden: that is to say, if a reasonably well-informed and reasonably observant and circumspect consumer could not have adequately been protected in a less intrusive (less stringent) way. It was in this way that the first image of the consumer was created. In the leading case of *Cassis de Dijon*, the national norm attacked had forbidden the use of the term liqueur (Likör)—for instance on the label—below a certain percentage of alcohol, supposedly justified to prevent German consumers from drawing false conclusions. The CJEU, however, saw a less stringent means to reach this goal in the form of the mere declaration of the percentage of alcohol on the label (an indication which the labels of *Cassis de Dijon* already contained). This indication would be sufficient to inform adequately any reasonably well-informed and reasonably observant and circumspect consumer and leave them the choice of whether to buy the product. The Court then treated secondary EC law in the same way, specifically in relation to misleading advertising. Advertising was seen as misleading only if a reasonably well-informed and reasonably observant and circumspect consumer gathered incorrect information from it.

It is this case law (among other factors) which led to a critique in European private, specifically contract, law that this body of law has been shaped in a way that is too one-sided and purely instrumentalist. It was said that only one goal was important for this body of law, that of (internal) market integration.[5] In consumer law, the call for more 'differentiation' with respect to images of the consumer and needs for protection can be seen as an answer to this critique, a critique which sees the model currently in place as being too market-liberal, too 'instrumentalist'. The claim is indeed that more consumer groups should be differentiated according to their distinct needs of protection and should be treated differently: the (particularly) vulnerable consumer,[6] the hasty consumer,[7] the consumer with inferior

[5] Namely C Joerges, 'Verbraucherrecht und Marktökonomik—eine Kritik ordnungstheoretischer Eingrenzungen der Verbraucherpolitik' in C Joerges and others (eds), *Wirtschaftsrecht als Kritik des Privatrechts—Beiträge zur Privat- und Wirtschaftstheorie* (Königstein, Athenäum, 1980). To some extent, see also N Reich and others (n 1) 70–86, esp 78 ff and Howells and Weatherill (n 1) 85–91, esp 89.

[6] For a partly critical comment, see H-W Micklitz, 'The Expulsion of the Concept of Protection from the Consumer Law and the Return of Social Elements in Civil Law: A Bittersweet Polemic' (2012) 35 *Journal of Consumer Policy* 283, 294–96; J Stuyck, 'The Notion of the Empowered and Informed Consumer in Consumer Policy and How to Protect the Vulnerable Under Such a Regime' (2006) 1 *The Yearbook of Consumer Law* 167, 180–85; L Waddington, 'Vulnerable and Confused: The Protection of 'Vulnerable' Consumer under EU Law' (2013) 38 *European Law Review* 757; T Wilhelmsson, 'The Informed Consumer v the Vulnerable Consumer in European Unfair Commercial Practices Law—A Comment' in G Howells and others (eds), *The Yearbook of Consumer Law* 2007 (Aldershot Ashgate 2007).

[7] See citations at n 6.

bargaining power,[8] and the uninformed consumer. More generally, the broad range of cognitive errors and biases ('bounded rationality') was seen as relevant both from the perspective of legal policy and of doctrinal interpretation.[9] In this respect, Article 5(2)(3) of the Unfair Commercial Practices Directive is of particular interest as it states,[10] for the whole area of advertising and commercial practices, that particularly vulnerable groups of consumers might be protected more intensely.

This confirms, on the one hand, that such a differentiation can be considered in European contract law, but at the same time belies the critique that secondary EU law is exclusively shaped according to a goal of market integration. This—most prominent—example of differentiation according to consumer groups also raises the question whether the differentiation may be better explained by recourse to the *function of contracting*, that is, considering the very case at hand which has been regulated by this rule. In its simplest form, the argument in the strand of literature focussing on the function of contracting is that contract law, just like other regulatory law, stems from a democratic legislature, whose primary goal is, as it should be, overall welfare. It is the democratic legislature that to this end leaves individuals a large scope of autonomy, the overall welfare consideration being the fact that party autonomy fosters creativity, spontaneity, and better use of dispersed knowledge. It follows that, according to this literature, the (overall) function of contract in a society justifies both a high level of party autonomy and its limits, where the overall welfare consideration does not apply.[11]

B. Consumers—A Heterogeneous Group

When differentiation and heterogeneity among consumers are discussed, the focus is mainly on their different capabilities, such as the reasonably well-informed, hasty, particularly vulnerable consumer and so on. This should not distract attention

[8] J Stuyck, 'Consumer Concepts in EC Secondary Law' in Klinck and Riesenhuber (n 2) and H Unberath and A Johnston, 'The Double-Headed Approach of the CJEU Concerning Consumer Protection' (2007) 44 *Common Market Law Review* 1237. First hints towards this direction (all on the EC Standard Contract Terms Directive) are indicated in Joined cases C–240/98 to C–244/98 *Océano Grupo Editorial SA v Rocić Murciano Quintero* [2000] ECR I–4941, para 25; Case C–168/05 *Elisa María Mostaza Claro v Centro Móvil Milenium SL* [2006] ECR I–10421, para 25; Case C–243/08 *Pannon GSM Zrt v Erzsébet Sustikné Győrfi* [2009] ECR I–4713, para 22; Case C–40/08 *Asturcom Telecomunicaciones SL v Cristina Rodríguez Nogueira* [2009] ECR I–9579, para 29; Case C–137/08 *VB Pénzügyi Lizing v Ferenc Schneider* [2010] ECR I–10847, para 46.

[9] See, for instance, R Incardona and G Poncibó, 'The Average Consumer—The Unfair Commercial Practices Directive and the Cognitive Revolution' (2007) 30 *Journal of Consumer Policy* 21, which focussed, however, on the Unfair Commercial Practices Directive (Directive 2005/29/EC of the European Parliament and of the Council of 11 May 2005 concerning unfair business-to-consumer commercial practices in the internal market (Unfair Commercial Practices Directive) [2005] OJ L149/22).

[10] Directive 2005/29/EC (n 9).

[11] See more extensively L Raiser, 'Vertragsfunktion und Vertragsfreiheit' *Festschrift Deutscher Juristentag* (1960) 101–31, and explanation in S Grundmann, 'Negotiation, Contract Function and Justice of Consensus' in S Grundmann, H-W Micklitz and M Renner (eds), *Private Law Theory* (forthcoming 2015).

from another type of heterogeneity, which might be even more important. Over the entire population (after all, we are all consumers in one situation or another) there stretches a continuum of variations. For the sake of clarity, I will refer only to its two extremes. On the one hand, we have the well-educated and informed, typically also the well-to-do consumer, who has decent access to legal advice (for instance, a high government official or professor). On the other hand, we have the poorly informed and much less well-to-do consumer (for instance, the worker who does not possess any of the relevant qualifications). The important aspect of this differentiation—which, at first glance, looks very similar to that between the reasonably well-informed and the hasty or the vulnerable consumer—is not so much that consumers in both groups are not equally 'strong' or 'vulnerable'. The important aspect is rather that they typically have diverging interests. While in company law, heterogeneity of different groups of shareholders—shareholders with dispersed ownership, minority shareholders or large block-owners having control—is seen as the real basis for the discussion and accordingly protective measures are mainly shaped with a view to their diverging interests, this aspect is mostly neglected in consumer law.

This aspect is, however, also paramount in the context of regulating consumer transactions. In particular, it is important for a proper design of consumer law because strong consumer protection is typically not capable of protecting primarily weak consumers or protecting them in the same way as stronger consumers. This is so because in most areas of private law, such as those of contract, corporate, and commercial law,[12] a redistribution towards consumers as a whole can be undone by the supply side of the market. In B2C transactions the supply side of the market incorporates the costs of higher consumer protection into prices. In competitive markets, this is even the rule.[13] As such, this would not be very problematic, even though all would have to carry the price of increased protection of those harmed. The protection granted can be (valued) higher than the price increase (loss of money). However, this insight has to be combined with the observations about the heterogeneous nature of consumers as a group mentioned above. There is a very tangible risk that within this heterogeneous group strong consumer rights (or strong rights for the 'weaker' party, more generally) favour the strongest and most well-to-do. This is the group which in the case of damages claims is most likely to succeed. This is further exacerbated where liability of the

[12] L Kaplow and S Shavell, 'Should Legal Rules Favor the Poor? Clarifying the Role of Legal Rules and the Income Tax in Redistributing Income' (2000) 29 *Journal of Legal Studies* 821, 823.

[13] The path-breaking analysis is R Craswell, 'Passing on the Costs of Legal Rules—Efficiency and Distribution in Buyer-Seller Relationships' (1991) 43 *Stanford Law Review* 361. On the Common European Sales Law (Commission, Proposal for a Regulation of the European Parliament and of the Council on a Common European Sales Law COM(2011) 635 final), see G Wagner, 'Zwingendes Vertragsrecht' in H Eidenmüller and others, *Revision des Verbraucher-Acquis* (Tübingen, Mohr-Siebeck, 2011) 44–46. Kaplow and Shavell (n 12) (and some other articles before that) develop their famous 'double distortion' argument according to which redistribution not only distorts the incentive to be productive (also in tax law) but also cannot be undertaken successfully at all in contract law (second distortion) and certainly less successfully than in tax law.

trader is strict because the well-to-do group is likely to have the highest claims—the material losses they suffer are likely to be relatively high and their labour incapacity in case of personal injury will cost much more (and the medical costs will not in most cases be borne by public health care). Moreover, this group will typically have easier access to legal advice, and therefore it is very likely that they will make use of the rights more extensively and in order to claim much higher sums. The risk, then, is that strongly redistributive consumer rights fall to be paid for by all consumers (the losses are socialised), while the gains are mostly 'privatised' by the most well-to-do and best informed. This leads to redistribution towards the rich![14]

C. Consumers—Too Narrow a Group

It is, of course, not a new observation that in the general contract law some groups, including also businesses, may be in need of 'systemic protection'.[15] Highly prominent as a (potential) legislative manifestation of this perspective is the proposed Common European Sales Law.[16] It is primarily conceived as an instrument for protection in unequal bargaining power situations. For this reason, its personal scope of application is restricted (at the EU level) to contracts with the participation of at least one consumer or SME.[17]

For this chapter, however, this observation is important only as a contrasting scenario. It serves to elucidate the functional design of consumer protection and to show how this logic would continue to apply outside consumer protection, that is, outside B2C transactions. For reasons of legal certainty, it may well be advisable to use a simple criterion of demarcation, such as the distinction between consumers and professionals (businesses), a distinction which is fundamental for European contract law. If, however, the need to justify regulation is also taken into consideration, it seems that the simple and rough criterion of status could only 'sufficiently' justify a particular type of regulation, namely regulation aimed at facilitating market functioning. Such regulation would help consumers make more informed use of their choices and for this reason it would create less profound inroads into party autonomy.[18] If, on the other hand, regulation is more paternalistic and

[14] O Ben Shahar and O Bar-Gill, 'Regulatory Techniques in the Consumer Protection: A Critique of European Consumer Contract Law' (2013) 50 *Common Market Law Review* 109; H-B Schäfer and C Ott, *Lehrbuch der ökonomischen Analyse des Rechts* 4th edn (Heidelberg, Springer, 2005) 138 ff and Wagner (n 13) 45 ff.

[15] See, for instance, V Roppo, 'From Consumer Contracts to Asymmetric Contracts—A Trend in European Contract Law?' (2009) 5 *European Review of Contract Law* 304.

[16] COM(2011) 635 final (n 13).

[17] ibid, Art 7.

[18] Note, on this characteristic of disclosure rules, that on the one hand, they are mandatory, on the other, however, they leave party autonomy intact and are even aimed at facilitating its use. On this point, see S Grundmann, 'Information, Party Autonomy and Economic Agents in European Contract Law' (2002) 39 *Common Market Law Review* 269; W Schön, 'Zwingendes Recht oder informierte

has the effect of substituting consumer choice in favour of mandatory substantive rules, and thus also of restricting potential offers by businesses, a formal and general criterion of status (of the consumer) seems too weak a justification. In the following analysis I will argue that the more paternalistic regulation can only be justified if a *substantive criterion*, and not the consumer status, is used.

Before entering into the details of this type of justification, at least a short comment should be made on the other dimension mentioned. For businesses too—and not only SMEs—regulatory measures of protection are much easier to justify when they are primarily facilitating and enhancing market functioning, thereby affecting party autonomy less profoundly. For this reason, disclosure rules are quite important also for B2B transactions, albeit considerably less than in B2C transactions. Regulation in large parts of capital market law and in investment services law in particular (MiFID)[19] are good evidence of this. In this area, many professionals are 'lay persons' when compared to capital markets intermediaries and professional market participants. The information model protects businesses here as well, with a view to enhancing autonomous decision taking. While it would go beyond the scope of this chapter to explain the details of the information model, at least one point needs to be stressed here. Investment services are an area which, according to the categories used below, should be seen as 'existential' (see below section III.B). Investment of disposable capital is not only paramount for businesses, but is also extensively used for retirement savings and other forms of management of personal assets. Indeed, rules such as the 'know-your-customer' rule are consistent with this characterisation. Where they have not investigated the matter themselves, providers of investment services are not permitted to start from the presumption that their clients are sufficiently informed or experienced.

III. The Content of the Protection of Consumers—A Simple Model

A. Consumer Protection as a Goal in Itself?—The Link to Market Structure

Any discussion would seem to be superfluous on the point that consumer protection should not be seen as an aim in itself, but should instead be justified

Entscheidung—zu einer (neuen) Grundlage unserer Zivilrechtsordnung' in A Heldrich and others (eds), *Festschrift für Claus-Wilhelm Canaris* (München, CH Beck, 2007) 1191. For the whole of company law, see U Grohmann, *Das Informationsmodell im Europäischen Gesellschaftsrecht* (Berlin, De Gruyter, 2006). A general survey can be found in S Grundmann, W Kerber and S Weatherill (eds), *Party Autonomy and the Role of Information in the Internal Market* (Berlin, De Gruyter, 2001).

[19] Directive 2004/39/EC of the European Parliament and of the Council of 21 April 2004 on markets in financial instruments [2004] OJ L145/1.

by convincing reasons, the so-called 'mandatory reasons of public good'. From the overall welfare perspective, consumer protection can go both so far that it becomes detrimental and not far enough. Two examples from the sub-prime loan crisis of 2008 and, ensuing from this, the world financial crisis of 2008 are good illustrations of both dimensions. The subprime borrowers who (foreseeably) were unable to pay back their loans from income or existing assets were in some states 'protected' by mandatory 'walk-away clauses', which allowed them to give up the homes bought and to free themselves from any other obligation incurred. These clauses may well have encouraged them to care even less whether they had the capacity to pay back the loans. On the other hand, too little consumer protection was granted against the strategic (ab)use of consumer over-optimism or other cognitive errors. Banks designed loans in such a way that no interest was due in the first one or two years. Consumers who moved into the homes purchased with those loans were then 'stuck', even though the lending banks typically had known that the interest due in subsequent years could not be paid from the consumers' assets or salaries. This strategy violated the so-called duty of 'responsible lending'—which, of course, in virtually none of the US state jurisdictions had been adopted as a rule and even in European private law was disputed at that time.[20] In any case, because remedies (both voidability of the loan contract and a claim for damages) were introduced only later—if at all—they did not apply to the subprime loans which triggered the crisis.

The two most recent large-scale projects of European consumer law nourish the impression that many see consumer protection as an aim in itself. There seems to be a trend no longer to question but only to increase the level of consumer protection once achieved: always to aim for 'more stringent' or 'most stringent' levels of protection. For the optional Common European Sales Law the strategy was very explicitly chosen to install a level of protection which would be no lower than that of *any* national consumer law or at least as high as (and typically also higher than) existing EU consumer harmonisation. This entails the highest level of protection (the first possibility) or at least one well above the EU level of the so-called minimum-standard harmonisation (which, of course, all national laws have had to introduce already—the second possibility).[21] For the EU Consumer

[20] On this concept and on the dispute about whether a duty of responsible lending is enshrined in EU law, see Y Atamer, 'Duty of Responsible Lending' in S Grundmann and Y Atamer (eds), *Financial Services, Financial Crisis, and General European Contract Law—Failure and Challenges of Contracting* (Alphen, Kluwer, 2011), 179; C Hofmann, 'Die Pflicht zur Bewertung der Kreditwürdigkeit' (2010) 25 *Neue Juristische Wochenschrift* 1782, 1785 ff. For mortgage loans, this duty has been introduced very clearly recently in Art 19(5) of Directive 2014/17/EU of the European Parliament and of the Council of 4 February 2014 on credit agreements for consumers relating to residential immovable property [2014] OJ L60/34 (Mortgage Credit Directive). See also this Directive's Art 7.

[21] For the first possibility, see D Staudenmayer, 'The Common European Sales Law—Why do We Need It and How Should It Be Designed?' in G Alpa and others (eds), *The Proposed Common European Sales Law—the Lawyers' View*, (Munich, Sellier, 2013) 17. For the second possibility, see COM(2011) 635 (n 16), Rec 11: 'The rules should maintain or improve the level of protection that consumers enjoy under Union consumer law' (conceived as the average of the transposing measures already existing in all Member States).

Rights Directive,[22] on the other hand, the argument was made that the level of protection had to be higher than that of the two directives it replaced (both of which had introduced a harmonised minimum standard) for the very reason that some Member States had introduced more stringent national rules and therefore retaining the level adopted in the earlier directives as a full or maximum harmonisation standard would have decreased the average protection in the EU already in existence. In other words an increased level of consumer protection was established at the EU level without any attempt to justify this by substantive reasons.[23]

Therefore, the very model of harmonisation or unification is of itself seen as sufficient justification for increasing a level of protection at the EU level previously adopted, just because some Member States have unilaterally introduced more stringent national law. These national peaks are now used to determine the European level or, at least, to influence the overall trend for the future, and this occurs without discussion about substance at the EU level. What is important here is that this trend is purely mechanical and points in only one direction—'more stringent consumer protection'. The upwards trend suppresses unprejudiced discussion about whether consumers really want to pay extra for such increases in protection.

Even if such a mechanical approach is rejected, one question would still have to be raised; whether a 'mandatory reason of public good' for the adoption of rules aimed at consumer protection is to be accepted only in the context of structural market failures, or also in the case of individual shortcomings of consumers, such as cognitive errors which can be found in certain (albeit also larger) groups of consumers. This seems to be the fundamental question of consumer protection policy today. When answering this question, considerations about the heterogeneity of groups of consumers and their interests need to be kept in mind. The answer should, however, not be given in the abstract, but with reference to concrete groups of cases. The following differentiations would seem to be crucial.

B. Existential versus Economic Loss

Not all damages or losses affecting consumers are of the same importance. Even though it may not always be easy to draw the line, it would seem to be highly

[22] Directive 2011/83/EU of the European Parliament and of the Council of 25 October 2011 on consumer rights [2011] OJ L304/64 (Consumer Rights Directive).

[23] G Howells and R Schulze, 'Overview of the Proposed Consumer Rights Directive' in G Howells and R Schulze (eds), *Modernising and Harmonising and Consumer Contract Law* (Munich, Sellier, 2009) 25; M Tamm, *Verbraucherschutzrecht—Europäisierung und Materialisierung des deutschen Zivilrechts und die Herausbildung eines Verbraucherschutzprinzips* (Tübingen, Mohr-Siebeck, 2011) 301 ff and 312; K Tonner and K Fangerow, 'Directive 2011/83/EU on Consumer Rights: A New Approach to European Consumer Law?' (2012) 2 *Journal of European Consumer and Market Law (euvr)* 67, 76. For a discussion of the proposal, see H-W Micklitz and N Reich, 'Crónica de una Muerte Annunciada: The Commission Proposal for a "Directive on Consumer Rights"' (2009) 46 *Common Market Law Review* 471, 516; K Tonner and M Tamm, 'Der Vorschlag einer Richtlinie über Rechte der Verbraucher und seine Auswirkungen auf das nationale Verbraucherrecht' (2009) 64 *Juristenzeitung* 277, 282.

plausible as a starting point to distinguish day-to-day economic loss from losses which put at risk the very existence of a consumer. It is therefore not surprising that the CJEU does not apply the standard of the reasonably well-informed and reasonably observant and circumspect consumer when personal integrity (health and life) is at stake. In these cases the Court requires measures such as warnings which adequately protect the hasty and incautious consumer as well as the intellectually less capable consumer.[24] Against such risks all consumers are to be protected, not only those who are reasonably observant and circumspect. Reference to the ranking of different constitutional values and rights in several charters of fundamental rights can easily justify the prominent role of health and human life as values which are 'existential' and rank higher than day-to-day economic loss. The same is true for other inviolable rights of the person.

It is, however, not only these rights of the person which qualify as 'existential'. In some cases economic loss may also be 'existential' in this sense. This, however, is only the case when the loss affects the existence of the consumer as such, that is, when there is a substantial and not merely illusory risk of financial distress. One important legal development in this respect is, of course, the introduction of a particular form of consumer insolvency (with discharge after a probationary period of some years) in combination with mutual recognition under the EU Insolvency Regulation.[25]

In contract law, the area which stands out as most intimately related to (the risk of) financial distress is consumer credit. The legal rules cover 'dangerous' activities broadly because the term 'consumer credit' encompasses all transactions giving rise to long-term liabilities (those not discharged with the transaction itself). These liabilities carry the risk that circumstances may change later on (such as divorce or unemployment), creating unexpected problems of payment and thus triggering financial distress (insolvency). In this context two precautions should be taken by credit institutions. First, they should assess correctly the capacity for payment of interest and of the sum owed at the moment when the liability is incurred, and second, they should illustrate and explain properly the risk stemming from subsequent unexpected developments. For the latter, however, it is difficult to ask for more than a 'sufficiently clear' warning. As there are always risks of future adverse developments, asking for more than a clear warning would necessarily imply that consumer credits are forbidden whenever future risks of unexpected developments cannot be excluded. And this, on the other hand, would lead to significant restrictions on the accessibility of credit to consumers.

[24] Case C–220/98 *Estée Lauder Cosmetics GmbH & Co OHG v Lancaster Group GmbH* [2000] ECR I–117, esp 128 (reference to the general standard only where 'a mistake as to the product's characteristics cannot pose any risk to public health'); Case C–99/01 *Criminal proceedings against Gottfried Linhart and Hans Biffl* [2002] ECR I–9375, esp para 31 (same quotation).

[25] Council Regulation (EC) No 1346/2000 of 29 May 2000 on insolvency proceedings [2000] OJ L160/1.

The legal measures which address these risks were first the EC Consumer Credit Directive of 1986 (not by chance was this the first EC legal measure in the field of contract law, if we exclude, of course, some specific measures triggered by and aimed at addressing some particular scandalous situations, such as the peculiar practices of doorstep selling in Mallorca), and then the second EC Consumer Credit Directive of 2008, and most recently the Mortgage Credit Directive of 2014.[26] Their content can be summarised. The risk that creditworthiness is assessed incorrectly at the *moment of contract formation* was addressed by the 1986 Directive by information rules alone, specifically by requiring indication of the aggregated costs of the credit on a yearly basis and indication of the annual percentage rate in order to make competing offers more easily comparable. The 2008 Directive introduced additional information duties, with a particular reference to the risk of subsequent adverse developments. It required the lender to warn the consumer about the typical risks (such as unemployment and divorce) and about other more general risks. These rules do not, however, contain a duty to present sample calculations, which would make the information more concrete. Neither do they introduce a duty to explain the risks verbally. The 2008 Directive did not dare to take the more demanding substantive step to introduce a duty of responsible lending according to which the lender would be obliged to conduct an assessment of the consumer's situation in their interest. Such a duty, proposed but not introduced by the Directive, would have protected the customer, including those not sufficiently circumspect, by providing that a violation of the duty would trigger a claim for damages or eliminate the consumer's duty to pay interest or to pay back the loan at all (limiting liability to restitution of the existing enrichment). Such a duty of responsible lending has, however, been introduced in the 2014 Directive, but only for mortgage loans to consumers (secured by residential premises). This step can be seen to some extent as a reaction to the 2008 subprime loan and financial crisis.[27]

More intensive protection in the area of 'existential' risk, which creates a 'safety net', strengthens the case for different treatment of day-to-day economic loss. In this latter situation, it should be taken into account that in a heterogeneous group of consumers there are (different) winners and losers according to the level of consumer protection which is applied. Comparative advertising can, for instance, facilitate the best choice for the reasonably circumspect consumer, while it may induce hasty consumers into error. At the same time, since advertising is often one

[26] Council Directive 87/102/EEC of 22 December 1986 for the approximation of the laws, regulations and administrative provisions of the Member States concerning consumer credit [1987] OJ L42/48; Directive 2008/48/EC of the European Parliament and of the Council of 23 April 2008 on credit agreements for consumers [2008] OJ L133/66; Mortgage Credit Directive (n 20).

[27] See references at n 20 and, more extensively, see I Domurat, 'The Case of Vulnerability as the Normative Standard in European Credit and Mortgage Law' (2013) 3 *Journal of European Consumer and Market Law (euvr)* 124; M Renner in *Staub'scher Großkommentar Handelsgesetzbuch* vol 10, 4th part (Berlin, De Gruyter, 2015), paras 650–55.

of the most accessible channels of information, forbidding comparative advertising may lead to losses for the reasonably circumspect consumer. In this context it may be pointed out that other chances in life, not related to law, are also distributed according to how much effort and intelligence are invested in decision-making. Circumspect behaviour tends to help. In my view, there is no strong argument in favour of 'correcting' this result to the potential detriment of those who are reasonably circumspect. Thus, it would seem sensible to regulate the problem of day-to-day economic loss only where the market as such needs facilitation or corrective measures, while the (individual) protection of those who are or cannot be circumspect should be focused on situations of 'existential' loss. I will explain the details of this proposition in the following section.

C. Protection via Information versus Protection via Mandatory Substance

European consumer law has been shaped from the outset predominantly under the paradigm of the information model. It is still so today. The prime strategy is to level out the (most important) informational asymmetries which consumers face with respect to their professional counterparts. This should empower consumers to take more informed and circumspect—yet autonomous—decisions. This is true for disclosure rules, for withdrawal rights (which allow consumers a short period of time to gather the information which was unavailable to them because the marketing technique employed hindered them from doing so), and this is also true for rules on liability for incorrect information. This trend has often been described and does not need to be discussed here in detail.[28]

For the current discussion, it is important to point out that most of information rules are designed for consumers who are reasonably observant and circumspect. As explained by reference to comparative advertising, a consumer protection model based on information rules can operate to the detriment of hasty, non-diligent consumers, who neglect the information. Two more examples from among the core contract types may illustrate this in still more detail.

The Directive on Payment Systems rules that banks may credit the amount transferred to the international bank account number (IBAN, formed in an internationally standardised way) without checking the name of the recipient.[29] This helps the large number of observant and circumspect customers because it reduces transaction times by half, increases legal certainty, allows a more rapid use

[28] See references above at n 18. For a systematic assessment of all legal measures in European contract law (then extant) with a view to see how far they contain (mostly mandatory) *information/disclosure* duties or mandatory *substantive* rules/duties, see S Grundmann, 'The Structure of European Contract Law' (2001) 9 *European Review of Private Law* 505.

[29] Directive 2007/64/EC of the European Parliament and of the Council of 13 November 2007 on payment services in the internal market [2007] OJ L319/1, Art 74.

of money, the payment of smaller interest, an easier use of rebates, and so on. On the other hand, hasty customers lose the safety net that would apply were banks to correct their errors made when filling out the transfer forms.[30] More generally, the Directive on Payment Systems introduced a model based on incentives and favouring rational and observant behaviour. It did so also with respect to loss of payment cards by introducing a wholesale liability of €150 (irrespective of fault, which is difficult to prove in such a mass transaction market). This liability serves as an incentive to behave cautiously. At the same time, full liability for losses is limited to cases in which the customer behaved in a grossly negligent way.

A similar approach can be seen with respect to sales contracts in the Consumer Sales Directive.[31] Initially, the proposal was that that 'average quality' (without defects) should be required as the mandatory objective standard. In the version adopted, however, the standard of reasonable expectations of the average observant consumer was introduced. It applies only when the course of negotiations and the contract formed could not be interpreted differently, revealing, for example, also only implicitly, that a lower quality was accepted.[32] This new approach (in the adopted version) does nothing about the errors which hasty consumers can make. On the other hand, the objective standard that was first proposed could have wiped out certain lines of products or added considerable uncertainty to the conditions of their marketing, with a high risk of noticeable price increases. This is particularly relevant for low-budget products, functioning products but with certain defects, and potentially also for used products.

A consistent trend always to demand more consumer protection is nevertheless noticeable. In some areas, such as financial services,[33] the trend is followed for good reasons. It has over the last decade led to a more severe critique of the information model. The critique points mainly to two issues.[34] On the one hand, it is observed that consumers often cannot 'digest' the information given. This is mainly because the amount of information prescribed has dramatically increased, the information cannot be given in an understandable way, and it may be misleading, reach beyond the (intellectual) capacity of consumers, or not include the truly important information. All this entails a *lack of utility in the information*. On the other hand, it is also pointed out that the information is, or may be, not only useless but even harmful to the consumer because giving information is often seen

[30] On this issue (and also on the fact that because of the so-called MOD97-10 procedure the money transferred is typically not credited to an incorrect account, but returned and time is lost): S Grundmann in *Staub'scher Großkommentar Handelsgesetzbuch*, vol 10, 3rd part (Berlin/New York, de Gruyter, 2015) paras 329–31.

[31] Directive 1999/44/EC of the European Parliament and of the Council of 25 May 1999 on certain aspects of the sale of consumer goods and associated guarantees [1999] OJ L171/12.

[32] See, for example, S Grundmann, in M Bianca and S Grundmann (eds), *EU Sales Directive—Commentary*, (Leuven, Intersentia, 2002) Art 2, paras 1–8.

[33] See citations at n 18.

[34] For the critique in the most radical form, see O Ben-Shahar, 'The Myth of "Opportunity to Read" in Contract Law' (2009) 5 *European Review of Contract Law* 1.

as an excuse for rejecting claims by disappointed consumers (*harmfulness of the information*).

The critique of the information model is convincing in some respects. In my view, however, it throws the baby out with the bath water. It asks for a fundamental reform of the information model and, as long as these are not taken, the critique will probably continue to increase. To assess the critique in a more analytical way it is helpful and indeed indispensable to start out from a distinction which is today universally accepted in behavioural economics, even though the founding fathers of research on bounded rationality did not make it clear.[35] It is a distinction between two situations in which the consumer may find themselves. On the one hand, the consumer can be in a situation in which they are unable to access the relevant information or in which they can do so only at prohibitively high cost, excessively higher than for the consumer's counterpart—a professional supplier. This is true of hidden characteristics of a product or a service and applies also to standard contract terms. The initiator of such terms will typically use them many times, thereby greatly reducing the costs of their drafting, sometimes even to a few cents per use, while the terms are used by the consumer often just once, only in the particular transaction. This imposes disproportionate information costs on the consumer, for instance in terms of time, which are much higher for them than for the supplier. Such situations lead to 'structural' information asymmetries, that is to market failures. Initially they were mistakenly seen as situations in which consumers act in a boundedly rational way.

The second situation concerns cases where rationality is really limited; cases of bounded rationality in the narrow sense (so-called 'cognitive errors'). This affects consumers differently depending on their level of education,[36] business

[35] H Simon,'A Behavioural Model of Rational Choice' (1955) 69 *The Quarterly Journal of Economics* 99 (1955); H Simon, 'Theories of Decision-Making in Economics and Behavioral Science' (1959) 49 *The American Economic Review* 253; then on bounded rationality more specifically (from the abundant literature), see D Kahneman and A Tversky,'Judgment under Uncertainty—Heuristics and Biases' (1974) 185 *Science* 1124; D Kahneman and A Tversky,'Prospect Theory: An Analysis of Decision under Risk' (1979) 47 *Econometrica* 263–291; A Tversky and D Kahneman, 'Extensional versus Intuitive Reasoning—The Conjunction Fallacy in Probability Judgment' (1983) 90 *Psychological Review* 293; A Tversky and D Kahneman,'Rational Choice and the Framing of Decisions' (1986) 59 *The Journal of Business* 251; and C Jolls, *Behavioral Economics and the Law* (Boston, Now Publishers, 2011).

[36] Already, the seminal article by Kahneman and Tversky, 'Judgment under Uncertainty' (n 35) summarised the ample empirical studies made by the authors in the sense that experienced and highly educated actors (including professionals) are also subject to biases and do not necessarily learn from losses made due to the influence of biases. On the other hand, however, firms and educated persons show tendency for strategic planning and take systemic precautions in order not to be influenced by certain biases. In fact, several studies report significant and negative correlations between levels of bounded rationality and intelligence: see, eg, D Kahneman and S Frederick, 'A Model of Heuristic Judgment' in K Holyoak and R Morrison (eds), *The Cambridge Handbook of Thinking and Reasoning* (Cambridge, Cambridge University Press, 2005) 278–79; S Frederick, 'Cognitive Reflection and Decision Making' (2005) 19 *Journal of Economic Perspectives* 25; G Mitchell,'Why Law and Economics' Perfect Rationality Should not be Traded for Behavioral Law and Economics' Equal Incompetence' (2002) 91 *Georgetown Law Journal* 67, 83–119 and esp 94–98; K Stanovich and R West, 'Individual Differences in Reasoning: Implications for the Rationality Debate?' in T Gilovich, D Griffin and D Kahneman (eds), *Heuristics And Biases* (Cambridge, Cambridge University Press, 2002) 434–37; KE Stanovich, 'On the

understanding, attentiveness, statistical training,[37] and so on. They can be overoptimistic, they can more easily be seduced by certain ways of presentation and, because of the effects of 'framing', they can disregard other aspects of the transaction, which would have been more important for them, given their preferences.

The structure of general market failures have been investigated for decades and regulatory approaches in their respect have been much discussed. The matter is, however, different for cognitive errors. One important aspect is that they can also be helpful and not only detrimental. They can speed up decision taking, for instance by leading to disregarding certain inessential aspects.[38] More importantly, however, cognitive errors do not affect all consumers as a group. Some consumers are affected more than others, and some not at all. The question of which strategy of protection is preferable in the face of cognitive errors will be answered below (see below section III.D).

In the case of genuine market failures arising from (structural) informational asymmetries, a two-step strategy continues to be highly convincing. In a first step, one should attempt to even out the information asymmetry as far as possible, with a view to empowering consumers to take their own sufficiently informed autonomous decisions. If the informational load is too heavy, the best starting approach is not to abandon the information model, but to look for ways of reducing the load, while maintaining in the information the really important content and making it transparent. This solution could involve determining the order in which the information is to be given, from the most important to the less important, perhaps highlighting those three or four items which are most important for most consumers. Today, the European legislature might well have to work more intensely on the techniques which would render information more focussed, rather than extend and 'complete' the list of all possible pieces of information to

Distinction between Rationality and Intelligence: Implications for Understanding Individual Differences in Reasoning' in Holyoak Morrison (above). While one must be careful not to generalise, they show that a higher degree of *bounded* rationality often correlates with *lower* intelligence, an important exception being overconfidence (KE Stanovich and RF West, 'Individual differences in reasoning: Implications for the rationality debate?' (2000) 23 *Behavioral and Brain Sciences* 645). Simultaneously, persons with lower IQs have lower levels of education and socio-economic wealth. See, more generally, also P Hacker, 'Overcoming the Knowledge Problem in Behavioral Law and Economics: Bounded Rationality, Decision Theory, and Autonomy' (forthcoming 2015) (on file with author).

[37] In 1983, Nisbett, Krantz, Jepson and Kunda published a seminal piece on the use of statistical heuristics in everyday reasoning: R Nisbett and others, 'The Use of Statistical Reasoning in Everyday Inductive Reasoning' (1983) 90 *Psychological Review* 339. They concluded that due to the widespread use of such implicit statistical approaches, people with training in statistics would fare better even in routine reasoning tasks of everyday life. In a host of studies, they were able to show that statistical training leads to (a) a more 'statistical' approach to reasoning tasks in general and (b) to more statistically correct reasoning in particular (357–59). Subsequent studies confirmed and expanded their findings, see, eg, F Agnoli and D Krantz, 'Suppressing the Natural Heuristics by Formal Instruction: The Case of the Conjunction Fallacy' (1989) 21 *Cognitive Psychology* 515–50; F Agnoli, 'Development of Judgmental Heuristics and Logical Reasoning: Training Counteracts the Representativeness Heuristic' (1991) 6 *Cognitive Development* 195.

[38] See, most prominently, D Kahneman, *Thinking, Fast and Slow* (New York, Farrar, Straus and Giroux, 2011).

be given to consumers. Only when the information content cannot be shaped in such a way that a reasonably observant, circumspect consumer could 'digest' it at a reasonable price or with reasonable effort should a second type of regulation, mandatory substantive law and control, be considered.

The core example is the control of standard contract terms. The reason for mandatory substantive law in this context is, as already explained above, that no information rule could give the consumer the opportunity to know properly the content of those standard contract terms at a price/effort which is roughly similar to the one which the professional (a very regular user) of those terms has to invest. Given that this is the core example of mandatory substantive regulation, it is not at all astonishing that much more than half of the recent case law of the CJEU on European contract law has been concerned with the Unfair Contract Terms Directive.[39] The information model, on the other hand, is more straightforward, of course, if we exclude from it regulation for existential losses and the issues associated with the formal requirements of withdrawal rights. Conversely, fixing the right level of substantive mandatory protection is problematic.

D. Protection Because of Bounded Rationality?

The main problem of substantive mandatory rules led by the concern for the 'bounded rationality' of consumers has already been identified. Problems which affect the market as a whole—because all customers cannot gather a particular type of information and therefore there is a general market failure—have to be distinguished from cases in which individual heuristics may lead to decisions which do not reflect the consumer's particular preferences ('cognitive errors'). The latter may well affect large groups of consumers. Yet, they are structurally less problematic for the whole market and entail a different type of treatment.

The literature providing guidelines on how one should regulate for cognitive errors is extensive.[40] Therefore, and within the space available in this chapter, I will name only one guideline: the view that the distinction between day-to-day economic losses and 'existential' losses should serve as the starting point for cases of bounded rationality. In the case of general market failures, regulation can be justified both on the grounds of (prevention of) adverse selection (economic theory) and of the need to promote self-determination (a constitutional argument).[41] In the case of boundedly rational individual heuristics, however, this

[39] See survey on the case law by B Kas and H-W Micklitz, 'Overview of Cases before the CJEU on European Consumer Contract Law (2008–2013)—Part I and II' (2014) 10 *European Review of Contract Law* 1 and 189.

[40] See citations at n 29.

[41] On the interdisciplinary foundations of the principle of auto-determination (*Selbstbestimmung*) and ensuing responsibility (*Selbstverantwortung*), see, for the most complete account, K Riesenhuber (ed), *Das Prinzip der Selbstverantwortung* (Tübingen, Mohr-Siebeck, 2011).

is not the case. The market does not tend structurally towards adverse selection. Moreover, the choice of heuristics is also part of the consumer's self-determination ('is my time too precious for me to care?').

There may be exceptions to the general principle that individual heuristics, even if boundedly rational, should not warrant regulatory intervention. One such exception can be found in situations in which cognitive biases not only have an effect on individual decisions but have been used systematically by enterprises to push ('manipulate') the other side of the market towards decisions which are not only hasty, but which are contrary to the (typically assumed) consumer interest. In other words two factors need to be present to justify regulatory intervention: cognitive bias and suppliers' manipulation. On the other hand, the risks of adverse selection and of significant inroads into consumers' self-determination are on their own sufficient to justify regulatory intervention. This also explains the difference between Articles 5(2) and 5(3) of the Unfair Commercial Practices Directive.[42]

E. Caveat: Enforcement

There is one 'caveat' to the explanations given. Enforcement, specifically procedural tools of enforcement, has not been discussed here. It constitutes a subject in and of itself. Enforcement may well be an area where consumer law is 'special', that is, profoundly different from substantive law because the need for protection is the highest. This relates mainly to 'access to justice' (class actions, alternative dispute resolution and legal aid). The need arises generally from three facts. First, claims for damages and damages awards are often rather small, per se and in relation to the costs of enforcement, which leads to consumer apathy with respect to enforcement. Second, some groups of consumers just cannot afford litigation. Third, some groups of consumers may not have sufficient information and education to assess chances of success and to understand the steps that have to be taken. Enhancing enforcement not only aims at protecting individual consumers but also, and just as important, at general deterrence. Enhancing enforcement also means reducing the risk of future disregard of consumers' rights.

Besides 'access to justice', there are other reasons for which enforcement is a highly important issue for consumer law. The probability that consumers will sue seems so low under the current regime of civil procedure (at least in some areas) that there are enterprises which apparently prefer (quite systematically) not to honour even the most obvious claims against them because non-compliance costs them less. Even legally knowledgeable persons (such as the author) have been subject to such strategies in mobile phone and air transportation markets. This

[42] See references above at n 9. The differentiation can be traced back to Case C–159/09 *Lidl SNC v Vierzon Distribution SA* [2010] ECR I–11761, para 56, and before that in Case C–39/97 *Canon Kabushiki Kaisha v Metro-Goldwyn-Mayer Inc Case* [1998] ECR I–5507, para 29, and Case C–342/97 *Lloyd Schuhfabrik Meyer & Co GmbH v Klijsen Handel BV* [1999] ECR I–3819, para 17.

seems to indicate that the incentives to abandon such strategies, which would at the same time benefit the consumer, are not strong enough. This, on the other hand, entails that we should discuss again the introduction of punitive damages ('treble damages') for certain situations. Such situations could for example include cases in which after due notice and explanation by the consumer (the 'second chance') enterprises do not honour claims and which the court then holds to be 'obviously well founded',[43] cases in which it is highly likely that the particular enterprise tries to make strategic use of consumer apathy. The instrument introducing punitive damages should, however, be clearly delimited so as to create the appropriate mix of incentives and minimise the risk that whole industries will lobby against such an instrument. To this end, punitive damages should be limited to clear cases of abuse and moreover the rules should ideally contain an indicative list. Moreover, considerations of general deterrence should act as guidelines for courts.

Accordingly, the 'caveat' for enforcement is to be understood as encompassing both the procedural questions and questions of substantive law relating to issues of enforcement.

IV. The Territorial Scope of Consumer Protection

The reach of protection depends to a considerable extent on the territorial scope of its application. Therefore, the question of how to target consumer protection should not be asked only from a substantive law perspective (above sections II and III) but also from a 'conflict of laws' perspective. This dimension has to be assessed primarily not in a dogmatic way by assessing the case law of the Court of Justice on this issue, but rather from a legal policy perspective. Let us look at the example of how the concept of minimum harmonisation should be understood in EU law.

The concept of minimum harmonisation can be understood in two ways. The first holds that compliance with the minimum standard in one country does not yet imply that offers made under this (national) law are marketable in this shape in the whole of the internal market: that means that no full home country principle applies to offers made on the basis of a national law even though they are in full compliance with the (minimum) European harmonised standard. Under this understanding of the concept of minimum harmonisation, an additional and more stringent national consumer law can be imposed on offers from another Member State in the targeted market provided that the additional and more stringent national law is justified by mandatory reasons of public good in the normal way.[44] The second way to understand the concept of minimum harmonisation

[43] A legal basis might be Art 13, second phrase, of the Unfair Commercial Practices Directive, which states that '[t]hese penalties [imposed on unfair commercial practices] must be … dissuasive.'

[44] In this sense, see namely B Smulders and P Glazener, 'Harmonization in the Field of Insurance Law through the Introduction of Community Rules of Conflict' (1992) 19 *Common Market*

holds that harmonisation specifies (for internal market transactions) the amount of consumer protection which is strictly necessary, that is, the amount which is supported by *mandatory reasons of public good*. This standard therefore exhausts any scope for national measures that are stricter. More stringent national rules can be imposed but only in purely domestic transactions (as the fundamental freedoms and their liberalising effect do not apply), but not to cross-border internal market transactions. The second understanding of the concept of minimum harmonisation is supported by the fact that it stems from primary EU law and is therefore superior to the Rome–I Regulation or (formerly) the Rome Convention (see also their Articles 23 and 20 respectively)[45] on which the first understanding is based.

This second understanding is preferable, in my view, mainly from a legal policy perspective. Two strands of justification stand out. First, it 'respects' more faithfully the intentions of the EU legislature. The relevant Regulation is here given the effect whose creation, after all, is the necessary condition of using Article 114 TFEU as the Regulation's legal basis. There is a legal basis in the Treaty for minimum harmonisation measures (only) if they contribute to the building of the internal market. The view preferred here achieves this goal because, up to the harmonised level, it genuinely creates a situation similar to a market governed by one law only (an 'internal market'). Suppliers from Member States can make their offers for the whole of Europe under *one* law (their home country law), as long as the EU's minimum standard is respected.

Moreover, this understanding of the concept of minimum harmonisation would make EU measures a source of not only minimum standards but also as the source of the *one relevant standard* for (cross-border) internal market transactions (a maximum standard).[46] At the same time, this would honour the (implicit)

Law Review 775, 797; W-H Roth, 'Die Freiheiten des EG-Vertrages und das nationale Privatrecht—Zur Entwicklung internationaler Sachnormen für europäische Sachverhalte' (1994) 1 *Zeitschrift für Europäisches Privatrecht* 5, 31 ff; W-H Roth, 'Transposing "Pointillist" EC Guidelines into Systematic National Codes—Problems and Consequences' (2002) 10 *European Review of Private Law* 761, 771–74; and, undecided, M Dougan, 'Minimum Harmonization and the Internal Market' (2000) 37 *Common Market Law Review* 853, 863–85.

[45] In this sense, see N Bernard, 'The Future of European Economic Law in the Light of the Principle of Subsidiarity' (1996) 33 *Common Market Law Review* 633, 646 ff; S Grundmann, 'Internal Market Conflict of Laws—From Traditional Conflict of Laws to an Integrated Two Level Order' in A Fuchs, H Muir Watt and É Pattaut (eds), *Les conflits de lois et le système juridique communautaire* (Paris, Dalloz, 2004) 12–16 and 22–27; I Klauer, 'General Clauses in European Private Law and "Stricter" National Standards: The Unfair Terms Directive' (2000) 8 *European Review of Private Law* 187, 201–10; and also P Martin, 'Le droit social communautaire: droit commun des États membres de la Communauté européenne en matière sociale?' (1994) 30 *Revue trimestrielle de droit européen* 609; E Steindorff, *Grenzen der EG-Kompetenzen* (Heidelberg, Recht and Wirtschaft, 1990) 84; P Mengozzi, 'La seconda direttiva bancaria, il mutuo riconoscimento e la tutela del'interesse generale degli Stati Membri' [1994] *Rivista di diritto europeo* 447, 459 ff; and more extensively K Riesenhuber, *System und Prinzipien des Europäischen Vertragsrechts* (Berlin, De Gruyter, 2003) 146–70.

[46] This is such an important aim for the European legislature that it even introduces radically new legislative techniques such as full harmonisation or optional instruments for its achievement (Recs 2–5 of the Consumer Rights Directive (Rec 5 quotes as the impediment 'the different national consumer protection rules imposed upon the industry') and Recs 13–15 of the Common European Sales

statement made by the EU legislature that the standard in a given minimum harmonisation Directive exhibits the level of protection which is absolutely necessary from the European perspective, a standard which is supported by EU-widely accepted mandatory reasons of public good. Reasons of subsidiarity allow national legislatures to have the option to introduce or maintain additional (more stringent) 'regional' consumer protection law for their own domestic markets, even though EU mandatory reasons of public good would support or require them.

The second strand of justification might be still more important. It concerns competition in Europe in the broad sense. The understanding of consumer protection advocated here allows for more regulatory competition (between national legislatures). In the case of full harmonisation, such competition is completely abolished. In the case of the sole optional instrument drafted so far, the (proposal for a) Common European Sales Law (CESL), such competition might well be much more restricted than is commonly believed, at least if its shape is the one proposed so far. Regulatory competition could, on the other hand, develop in the case of an alternative design.[47]

In choosing between the two concepts of minimum harmonisation—one imposing a full home country principle and the other allowing Member States to impose additional rules if they can be justified by mandatory reasons of public good—it is necessary to keep in mind that only the former ensures regulatory competition. Under the full home country principle, the level of consumer protection of the target Member State market meets that applicable on the market of the foreign supplier and the consumer in the target market can choose. A foreign supplier, by autonomous choice, could offer their products and services accompanied by the target market consumer law, thus offering two competing standards, potentially at different prices. Certainly this solution would have to be made operational by easily understandable disclosures of the level(s) of consumer protection. The aim of such disclosure could not, of course, be a fully informed consumer. Consumers do not generally know their domestic law and it is unlikely that they would get to know a foreign law to make comparisons. What such disclosure could, however, achieve—if it were clear enough—is a situation where the consumer knows under which law they will fall. So even though the consumer would not know the applicable law they could nevertheless feel more at ease because they would have an overall perception of what the applicable law should guarantee.

Law). Compare the different modes of maximum harmonisation in the Consumer Rights Directive, on the one hand, and in the (optional) Common European Sales Law. For much broader comments on this, see S Grundmann, 'Costs and Benefits of an Optional European Sales Law (CESL)' (2013) 50 *Common Market Law Review* 225, 229–34. For a comparison of the advantages and disadvantages of the three approaches (minimal harmonisation, full harmonisation, and the Optional Instrument), see S Grundmann, 'The EU Consumer Rights Directive—Optimizing, Creating Alternatives, or Dead End?' (2013) 18 *Uniform Law Review* 98, 120–26.

[47] For more detail and the overview of literature supporting and criticising that view, see Grundmann, 'Costs and Benefits …' (n 46).

Independent of these considerations about regulatory competition (whose existence and significance in consumer law is disputed by many authors), one more aspect relating to competition is of importance. The EU Commission rightly points out, when advocating the adoption of its proposal for the CESL, that markets in small Member States raise particular problems. There the market is often characterised by monopolies or oligopolies. Moreover, enterprises from other (larger) Member States often prefer not to make offers in those smaller states because the volume of trade expected is too small to pay for the costs of obtaining knowledge about the unknown consumer law standards. If the minimum harmonisation concept is understood in the way advocated here, this would change the situation dramatically for those smaller Member States and for the consumers residing in them. Competition, real competition, not 'only' regulatory competition, and indeed powerful competition, would be free to flow into these markets to challenge the monopolies and oligopolies.

The chance to break up monopolistically or oligopolistically structured markets in a good number of smaller Member States in a situation where optional and fully harmonised instruments seem increasingly unrealistic for most parts of contract law would seem to be the strongest policy argument in favour of the proposal made here. This proposal envisages a market order based on trust in the EU legislature's ability to create a sufficiently adequate level of consumer protection, which justifies full free circulation of offers in the internal market. In the larger Member States, which have fewer problems with monopolistically or oligopolistically structured markets, and which may at the same time have more stringent consumer laws, there are in most cases enough domestic offers even in the face of a more stringent level of consumer protection. If consumers are more satisfied with these offers, they will remain available. With respect to the problem of multi-level governance and interplay of legal orders this model is also part of what I mean by 'targeted consumer protection'.

V. Conclusion

Three basic proposals can be derived from the observations made above. First, the risk of day-to-day economic loss is regulated in EU consumer law only (or mostly) by disclosure rules, which are designed for reasonably well-informed and circumspect consumers. This policy choice is convincing. More stringent consumer rules would bring losses also for those who are circumspect and, perhaps, or even most of all, for those least well-to-do. Second, the risks of existential loss should be addressed by rules which also favour the less circumspect consumer. With respect to both strands of regulation, substantial reform may well be needed, for instance, to address the problems of 'information overkill' or in order to select the appropriate amount of warning in consumer credit law about risks relating to future unexpected developments. But even though the current law needs amendments in core places, the overall disposition of existing regulation in EU consumer law is correct. Thirdly, the bounded rationality of consumers should not be seen as a general reason for introducing regulation. It should serve as a legislative rationale but only in exceptional cases where regulatory measures are specifically justified, for instance in cases of strategic use of cognitive errors by business, which can be characterised as an unfair commercial practice.

10

The Consumer as Regulator

CHRISTOPHER HODGES*

I. Traditional Images: Regulators, Traders, and Consumers

The traditional view of a market assigns separate and distinct roles to different categories of actors. The fundamental ultimate bilateral relationship is that between traders and consumers. In modern markets, however, independent third parties play a crucial role as regulators. A 'regulator' can be broadly defined as a body charged with surveillance, investigation, and enforcement of market trading and consumer trading law. The role of the regulator can have the important enforcement function of removing and preventing illegal or fraudulent traders from operating in the market, through use of strong public powers of prohibition and prosecution, but most regulators' activities are directed at ensuring that traders undertake their lawful activities in compliance with the law and associated codes. In the latter function, traders' activities are recognised as being of value to society, but the *manner* in which they are performed is the focus. The objective is to ensure that the manner of performance is consistent with the rules of society and of the market, rather than, in the first situation noted above, to prevent trading entirely.

Thus, the traditional image of a regulator is a public authority that is charged by the legislature with a mission to ensure that an area of law is observed, and endowed with powers such as oversight, inspection and enforcement. However, the behaviour of traders can be affected by a number of external impulses and not just the activities of public authorities. Private sector bodies can play significant roles in oversight, inspection and enforcement. Self-regulation by trade associations is widely seen. For example, the Wettbeverbzentrale, a business association, plays a central role in the enforcement of unfair competition law in Germany. In the United Kingdom, enforcement of advertising is undertaken by private bodies such as the Advertising Standards Authority and the Prescription Medicines

* Research funding has been received from the Swiss Reinsurance Company Limited, the European Justice Forum, and the international law firm CMS.

Code of Practice Authority. Sectoral codes of conduct are widely used in various Member States.

Further enforcement activity can be undertaken by consumer associations. Consumer associations have for some time possessed power to take action in protecting the general consumer interest through seeking injunctions to stop illegal action by traders in breach of specified consumer protection Directives.[1] However, this mechanism has hardly been used on a cross-border basis by consumer associations, and only to a limited extent by public authorities.[2] Some Member States have national arrangements in which consumer associations play an active role in enforcement of consumer trading law, albeit alongside other private or public organisations. A leading example is the work in Germany of the various Verbraucherzentralen, acting alongside the Wettbeverbzentrale in the enforcement of unfair competition law. In many other states, however, consumer associations are largely inactive in exercising enforcement functions.

In contrast to the image of strong traders and powerful enforcers, the corresponding traditional image of consumers would be a diverse mass of individual purchasers, who are not coordinated and so possess little or no power, vulnerable to exploitation by traders in exchange transactions. There may be asymmetries of information, of voice, and of ability to take effective enforcement action. It is precisely because of such asymmetries that an important rationale for the function of regulators arises, so as to assist and redress the vulnerability of consumers.

But this chapter argues that these images, while undoubtedly retaining validity, are changing and can be viewed in new ways that transform the roles of consumers and regulators. There are three aspects of change to which I would like to draw attention.

II. Outline of the Argument

This chapter argues that the critical new development is the prospect of highly effective mechanisms for the resolution of consumer-to-trader ('C2B') complaints and disputes, through the creation of a pan-European framework of consumer dispute resolution ('CDR') entities covering all business sectors. This structure provides not just a means for raising and resolving more C2B disputes than is possible under the existing civil procedure systems in most Member States, but also a mechanism for capturing extensive data from consumer inquiries and complaints. A CDR system has to be designed so as to enable such information to be

[1] Directive 2009/22/EC of 23 April 2009 on injunctions for the protection of consumers' interests [2009] OJ L110/30, Arts 1–3; formerly Directive 98/27/EC of 19 May 1998 on injunctions for the protection of consumers' interests [1998] OJ L166/51.

[2] U Docekal and others, *The Implementation of Directive 98/27/EC in the Member States* (Bamberg, Institute for European Business and Consumer Law, 2005).

captured and recycled: not every CDR system currently has this facility but the more advanced ombudsmen systems do operate this way.

The ability of a legal system to feed back extensive data on the market activities of traders through CDR entities to consumers, markets and regulators provides a very powerful means of identifying non-compliance and new trends that can be addressed. In this way, the dispute resolution system adopts a significant extra function as a regulatory system. In this way, the consumer—acting individually and through aggregation of the data provided—can and will play a critical role by providing information that has a direct regulatory effect. Hence, it is not far-fetched to view the consumer as functioning at least in part as a co-regulator of market behaviour: indeed, without effective consumer involvement, the regulatory effects that transparency and feedback mechanisms are designed to produce just would not occur.

Viewing consumers as regulators is entirely consistent with recent scholarship and theory on modern regulatory systems, in which effects on behaviour can be produced by a wide range of actors other than a public enforcement agency. Regulatory systems are viewed as comprising multiple actors, and effects are achieved through open and meta systems.

III. Distinguishing Public and Private Enforcement

This analysis of how consumers can affect the behaviour of traders by acting as regulators involves an important shift away from traditional notions of viewing consumers as having the means to enforce their rights, and from viewing private enforcement—and even enforcement of law itself—as the principal means of affecting traders' behaviour.

For some time, there has been a strand of consumer rhetoric that has talked of 'empowering' consumers by giving them rights that they can then enforce themselves by 'taking the law into their own hands'. It may be questioned whether such rhetoric has in practice any real substance, or chance of realising concrete effects, and whether it has been seen as either a myopic view of reality or a conscious political fraud on consumers. It is very rare for individual consumers to attempt to enforce legal rights through the courts. The vast majority of consumer disputes involve very small sums of money, in relation to which no rational person would waste money or time in pursuing.[3] The cost–benefit balance in relation to bringing a legal action in respect of the overwhelming number of consumer–trader disputes is wholly disproportionate. At this point, a snapshot image of

[3] C Hodges, 'Consumer Redress: Ideology and Empiricism' in K Purnhagen and P Rott (eds), *Varieties of European Economic Law and Regulation—Liber Amicorum for Hans Micklitz* (Heidelberg, Springer, 2014).

many consumers would reveal disappointment, frustration, anger, impotence, vulnerability, despair and exploitation.

For too long, reliance has been placed on access to courts and lawyers in 'enforcing rights' through private litigation. But the transactional costs are disproportionate and claims will not tend to be brought (as a result of what economists term rational apathy) unless an external funder steps in, such as public funds (legal aid) or private legal expenses insurance ('LEI'). However, legal aid is a dead duck in post-financial crisis economies and many consumer claims are too small for LEI. Consumer advice centres can be effective if they are funded, resourced and available. But both small claims mechanisms and aggregation of individual claims in collective actions can now be seen as disappointingly empty mechanisms that consumers do not find attractive because they do not satisfy the criteria of user-friendliness, speed, low cost, and effective outcomes.[4] For example, the EU cross-border small claims mechanism is hardly used by consumers,[5] and the Commission's proposed revisions[6] are directed at SMEs and not at consumers—the Commission's documentation hardly mentions consumers.[7]

An analysis of the extent to which private enforcement of law is ineffective as a mechanism of enforcement of rights is outside the scope of this chapter—and would need to be extensive in terms of empirical data. But if there is at least some truth in the idea that there are significant limitations to the current effectiveness of private enforcement, then questions arise over how effective individual or collective private enforcement might be in relation to controlling traders' *behaviour*, and whether other means of affecting behaviour are available and might be more effective.

Furthermore, some thought needs to be devoted to exactly *how* the future behaviour of individuals and trading organisations is affected by techniques of public or private enforcement, or by other means. Although that issue is too extensive to be addressed in this chapter, it is suggested that the idea that the changes in behaviour by a trader result from individual acts of enforcement, whether after that trader or another trader has been 'enforced against', deserves close scrutiny and justification, since serious doubts can be raised about its validity. The idea that

[4] C Hodges, 'Collective Redress: A Breakthrough or a Damp Sqibb?' (2014) 34 *Journal of Consumer Policy* 67.

[5] Commission, Report on the application of Regulation (EC) No 861/2007 of the European Parliament and of the Council establishing a European Small Claims Procedure COM(2014) 225 final.

[6] Commission, Proposal for the regulation of the European Parliament and the Council COM(2013) 794 final.

[7] C Crifò, 'Europeanisation, Harmonisation and Unspoken Premises: The Case of Service Rules in the Regulation on a European Small Claims Procedure (Reg. No. 861/2007)' (2011) 30 *Civil Justice Quarterly* 283 ('an ungainly juggernaut'; 'the legal landscape appears, far from simplified, further complicated'); XE Kramer, 'Small Claim, Simple Recovery?' (2011) 1 *ERA Forum* 119. See also XE Kramer and EA Ontanu, 'The Functioning of the European Small Claims Procedure in the Netherlands: Normative and Empirical Reflections' (2013) 3 *Nederlands Internationaal Privaatrecht* 319 ('the number of cases handled in the ESCP is limited. … Apparently consumers still find it difficult to find their way to this procedure … the duration of the procedure is on average three to five months').

private enforcement through individual litigation actions—and even collective actions—has an inevitable, lasting, and widespread effect on traders' behaviour can be seriously challenged. *Does* the result of a single court action taken by private parties under civil law affect the ongoing behaviour of the particular defendant, or of other similar defendants? *How* does this occur? An injunction in relation to a specific breach of law, such as an aspect of advertising or unfair contract term, might affect the individual defendant, and might even apply as a matter of law to other traders, but does it *in fact* affect their ongoing behaviour, and of how many of them? So-called rogue traders and internet scammers break the law repeatedly and only strong public enforcement appears effective against them. The business practices of even major reputable traders can adversely affect many consumers,[8] and continue despite private enforcement actions. The assertion, for example, that tort law or civil litigation have sufficient regulatory effect to justify being relied on as a principal means of affecting traders' behaviour has been known for some time to be strikingly unsupported by empirical evidence.[9] Considerably more behavioural and empirical research is needed to establish satisfactory answers to these questions.

It may only be where enforcement is accompanied by ongoing *scrutiny* of behaviour across a marketplace, backed by relevant public enforcement powers, that change may effectively be produced, such as where public systems (now supplemented by ombudsmen) are in place, or maybe a private body acting in a quasi-public function as in Germany.

IV. Business Systems and Feedback

This examination of the regulatory role of consumers begins not by looking at consumers but by analysing how businesses operate. The operation of businesses of any size is based on management *systems* that control all the firm's activities. Systems control product and service design, marketing, operation, and financial functions. Public regulatory systems are designed to operate so as to integrate with firms' internal business systems. For example, international, European and national standards prescribe quality systems, which not only form the basis of firms' internal operating systems but also form the basis of many regulatory systems.

[8] See the cases against Apple and various airlines and communications companies noted in Consumer Justice Enforcement Forum, *Guidelines for Enforcement of Consumer Rights* (May 2013) <http://www.cojef-project.eu/IMG/pdf/Conclusions_document_cases__FINAL_8_May.pdf> accessed 26 December 2014.

[9] A leading critique of the assumptions of deterrence and the economic analysis of law is D Dewees, D Duff and M Trebilcock, *Exploring the Domain of Accident Law* (New York, Oxford University Press, 1996).

A quality system has two broad functions. First, it specifies a system of controls on all relevant activities. Second, it mandates the constant cycling of information on how the firm's activities are performing. The simple objective is to ensure that activities are undertaken consistently in accordance with a specified protocol and are kept constantly under review, so that deviations and improvements can be identified and addressed. The system is portrayed as a continuous circling of information, which is evaluated and acted upon.

The continuous circling of information of course requires all of the relevant information first to be captured. Regulatory systems have developed during the past 40 years from focussing on design and production aspects to encompass also post-marketing information, so that firms can learn how their products and services are performing in use, and what users think of them. Indeed, the capture of as much relevant information as possible from consumers has long been regarded as vital by many retailers who operate in highly competitive markets. Such retailers have built well-resourced and highly effective customer care departments, which demonstrate extraordinarily crusading zeal in attempts to capture as much information from their customers as possible, whether good or bad, since the information has considerable commercial value.[10] In sectors where competition is less effective, it may be important for government or regulators to impose pressure on traders to improve complaint handling systems and practice, as has recently occurred in relation to financial services in the UK.[11]

Further examples illustrate a general shift in both business practice and regulatory systems in the past 40 years from just pre-marketing to both pre- and post-marketing controls. One example is the continuous evolution of the regulatory system for medicinal products, where initial controls focussed exclusively on pre-marketing requirements (especially extensive requirements for animal toxicology tests, and clinical trials in volunteer and patient humans, before detailed expert evaluation of safety before the grant of a marketing authorisation).[12] Such pre-marketing requirements have been extended very significantly since 1965, but the real focus of safety has been the addition of requirements to evaluate post-marketing safety data (adverse reaction reports) and the construction of the pharmacovigilance system, roughly from the mid-1990s.[13] Similar expansions in

[10] See the customer care departments of a leading pharmacy retailer and manufacturer of a wide range of consumer goods noted in C Hodges, 'Best Practice in Customer Care in the UK', in C Hodges, I Benöhr and N Creutzfeldt-Banda (eds), *Consumer ADR in Europe* (Oxford, Hart Publishing, 2012) ch 12.

[11] Financial Conduct Authority, *Complaint Handling* (November 2014) <http://www.fca.org.uk/static/documents/thematic-reviews/tr14-18.pdf> accessed 28 May 2015.

[12] The first measure was Directive 65/65/EEC of 26 January 1965 on the approximation of provisions laid down by Law, Regulation or Administrative Action relating to proprietary medicinal products [1965] OJ L22/369.

[13] Directive 93/39/EEC of 14 June 1993 amending Directives 65/65/EEC, 75/318/EEC and 75/319/EEC in respect of medicinal products [1993] OJ L214/22 and Council Regulation (EEC) No 2309/93 of 22 July 1993 laying down Community procedures for the authorization and supervision of medicinal products for human and veterinary use and establishing a European Agency for the Evaluation of Medicinal Products [1993] OJ L214/1. See further Regulation (EC) No 726/2004 of the European

post-marketing controls can be identified in relation to the regulatory system for general product safety,[14] and the many product types regulated under the New Legislative Framework.[15]

One manifestation of these changes in focus can be seen in the extensive concentration by consumer businesses from around 1990 onwards on ensuring that product production, distribution, and marketing systems were capable of being operated in *reverse*, in order to enable safety recalls to be effected. Systems had previously been designed to operate in one forward direction only, placing products on the market, whereas the increased availability of safety data and emphasis on safety *in use* required systems to enable products to be removed from the market as well.

Similarly, product liability law, enshrined in the EU in the 1985 Directive, has traditionally focussed on whether a product is defective *at the time it is placed into circulation*.[16] That Directive has never been significantly amended, and contrasts with the evolution of product liability law in the US, where the 1998 Third Restatement of Torts adopted four classifications of types of product liability that, crucially, added in liability for *post*-marketing activities of a manufacturer, notably in failure to warn claims. Such post-marketing liability is, of course, catered for under national fault liability rules. In practice, the first concern of both manufacturers and regulators following identification of a serious safety issue is not with

Parliament and of the Council of 31 March 2004 laying down Community procedures for the authorisation and supervision of medicinal products for human and veterinary use and establishing a European Medicines Agency [2004] OJ L136/1; Directive 2001/83/EC of the European Parliament and of the Council of 6 November 2001 on the Community code relating to medicinal products for human use [2001] OJ L311/67. And now Directive 2010/84/EU of the European Parliament and of the Council of 15 December 2010 amending, as regards pharmacovigilance, Directive 2001/83/EC on the Community code relating to medicinal products for human use [2010] OJ L348/74; Regulation (EU) No 1235/2010 of the European Parliament and of the Council of 15 December 2010 amending, as regards pharmacovigilance of medicinal products for human use, Regulation (EC) No 726/2004 laying down Community procedures for the authorisation and supervision of medicinal products for human and veterinary use and establishing a European Medicines Agency, and Regulation (EC) No 1394/2007 on advanced therapy medicinal products [2010] OJ L348/1, Commission Implementing Regulation (EU) No 520/2012 of 19 June 2012 on the performance of pharmacovigilance activities provided for in Regulation (EC) No 726/2004 of the European Parliament and of the Council and Directive 2001/83/EC of the European Parliament and of the Council [2012] OJ L159/2, and 'Good Pharmacovigilance Practice Guidelines' (*European Medicines Agency*) <http://www.ema.europa.eu/ema/index.jsp?curl=pages/regulation/document_listing/document_listing_000345.jsp> accessed 28 May 2015.

[14] Compare Directive 92/59/EEC of 29 June 1992 on general product safety [1992] OJ L228/24 and Directive 2001/95/EC of the European Parliament and of the Council of 3 December 2001 on general product safety [2001] OJ L11/4.

[15] Compare the requirements of the New Legislative Framework in Regulation (EC) No 765/2008 of the European Parliament and of the Council of 9 July 2008 setting out the requirements for accreditation and market surveillance relating to the marketing of products [2008] OJ L218/30 and Decision No 768/2008/EC of the European Parliament and of the Council of 9 July 2008 on a common framework for the marketing of products [2008] OJ L218/82. See also extensions proposed in the 2013 'Product Safety and Surveillance Package' described in Commission, Communication on more product safety and better market surveillance in the Single Market for products COM(2013) 74 final.

[16] Directive 85/374/EEC of 25 July 1985 on the approximation of the laws, regulations and administrative provisions of the Member States concerning liability for defective products [1985] OJ L210/29.

liability for compensation but with the need to recall a product, so as to reduce the risk to consumers and the liability exposure of the relevant traders.

So, there has been an evolution in both business and regulatory systems from exclusively focussing on pre-marketing activities to also encompassing post-marketing activities and on how consumers experience products and services. But how do traders and regulators get their information? Virtually every regulatory system requires *traders* to keep and report relevant safety information *to regulators*. But these requirements do not cover every type of activity, especially outside issues relating to physical safety, although reporting requirements exist in relation to, for example, financial institutions.[17] Regulators can receive information direct from consumers, such as on serious illegal activity, but this source of information is undeveloped in almost every country. So, where do traders obtain their information? How do they get information from multiple customers? Some traders, especially those in competitive retail markets, have developed highly active customer care functions, but the equivalence of a wide-ranging business focus on customers' experiences, akin to the generic 'recall revolution' of the 1990s, has yet to occur across all areas of consumer trading. However, this chapter suggests that it is in the process of emerging. Before considering how such a development is occurring, it is helpful to consider more closely the means for the enforcement of law.

V. Regulatory Theory: Multiple Regulators

It is also useful to reflect on recent understandings of regulatory law and its enforcement as involving multiple actors and various techniques of influencing behaviour. These theories open the door for the exclusively bilateral model of trader–regulator to be broadened so as to encompass shareholders, employees, and *consumers* as being able to affect business behaviour and, therefore, to be regarded as functioning as at least quasi-regulators.

Regulatory theory has developed significantly in the past 40 years, largely as a result of empirical analysis by socio-legal scholars of what regulators actually do 'on the ground, out there', rather than on the basis of theoretical assumptions about 'how law works'. Traditional ideas of 'command and control' regulation (a regulatee does what a regulator requires) have largely given way to the idea that the behaviour of 'a business', and of the people in it, can be affected by many internal and external influences.

Ayres and Braithwaite's idea of regulatory tripartism (involving regulator, regulated, and third parties)[18] was developed by Gunningham and Grabosky with

[17] In the UK, see Financial Conduct Authority, *Systems Reporting* (2014) <http://www.fca.org.uk/firms/systems-reporting> accessed 28 May 2015.

[18] I Ayres and J Braithwaite, *Responsive Regulation: Transcending the Deregulation Debate* (Oxford, Oxford University Press, 1992).

the concept of 'Smart Regulation', referring to a form of regulatory pluralism that seeks to harness not just governmental bodies but also business structures and third parties in controlling business activities.[19] In this viewpoint, behaviour is 'in the hands not of governmental officials but of the myriad individuals employed in the private sector' and that, often, more can be achieved by harnessing the enlightened self-interest of the private sector than through command and control regulation.[20] Parker proposed the concept of 'decentered regulation'.[21] Grabosky and others also described 'regulation of regulation', in which regulators oversee sector or firm level regulatory schemes, also known as meta-regulation.[22]

The key point to note for present purposes is the idea that 'enforcement' by a public authority may not be necessary in order to achieve changes in traders' behaviour. In other words, the views of customers or the general public can affect traders' activity, directly or indirectly, for example through the expression of visible opinion (complaints) or commercial power (switching to another supplier). SMEs often think that they comply until it is pointed out by a person that they respect that they are in fact not complying, and then they respond to information and suggestions about how to improve.[23] Both large and small companies that rely on maintaining their reputations in order to trade successfully can be responsive to external influences that have the potential to adversely affect a reputation.

For these reasons, regulatory and market systems often aim to enable extensive accurate information on traders, products, services, and markets not only to be accessible to potential customers but also that actual customers can feed back their opinions on service levels. In analytical terms, the system should operate as a very large quality system, which constantly churns information so as to drive improvements in outputs.

[19] N Gunningham and P Grabosky, *Smart Regulation. Designing Environmental Policy* (Oxford, Oxford University Press, 1998); see also N Gunningham, 'Enforcement and Compliance Strategies' in M Cave, R Baldwin and M Lodge (eds), *The Oxford Handbook of Regulation* (New York, Oxford University Press, 2010).

[20] N Gunningham and P Grabosky, *Smart Regulation—Designing Environmental Policy* (Oxford, Oxford University Press, 1998).

[21] J Black, 'Critical Reflections on Regulation' (2002) 27 *Australian Journal of Legal Philosophy* 1.

[22] P Grabosky, 'Using Non-Governmental Resources to Foster Regulatory Compliance' (1995) 8 *Governance: An International Journal of Policy and Administration* 527; C Parker and J Braithwaite, 'Conclusion' in C Parker and others (eds), *Regulating Law* (New York, Oxford University Press, 2004); C Parker, 'Meta-regulation: Legal Accountability for Corporate Social Responsibility' in D McBarnet, A Voiculescu and T Campbell (eds), *The New Corporate Accountability: Corporate Social Responsibility and the Law* (Cambridge, Cambridge University Press, 2007); C Coglianese and E Mendelson, 'Meta-Regulation and Self-Regulation' in M Cave, R Baldwin and M Lodge (eds), *The Oxford Handbook of Regulation* (New York, Oxford University Press, 2010); J Bomhoff and A Meuwese, 'The Meta-Regulation of Transnational Private Regulation' (2011) 38 *Journal of Law and Society* 138.

[23] See Department for Business, Innovation and Skills, *Large Businesses and SMEs: Exploring How SMEs Interact with Large Businesses* (19 October 2012) <http://www.bis.gov.uk/assets/biscore/enterprise/docs/e/12-1196-exploring-how-smes-interact-with-large-businesses> accessed 28 May 2015; Department for Business, Innovation and Skills, *SMEs: The Key Enablers of Business Success and the Economic Rationale for Government Intervention* (7 December 2013) <https://www.gov.uk/government/uploads/system/uploads/attachment_data/file/266304/bis-13-1320-smes-key-enablers-of-business-success.pdf> accessed 28 May 2015.

A familiar example of inbuilt feedback is the function of rating transactions of online traders, whose aggregated scores are available to potential purchasers, and who are removed from the online platform by the platform operator if a certain number of adverse comments are received from customers.

On the other hand, literature on 'responsibilisation' has queried the extent to which consumers should be drawn into the regulatory net as 'risk regulators' and the appropriateness of regulatory and policy initiatives to build capable, independent, and informed financial actors who can take on responsibility for welfare provision.[24] Instead, there has been a call for finance to be 'humanised', and more attention given to the 'patience gene'.[25]

VI. Consumer ADR

The 'game changer' that transforms resolution of consumer–trader disputes and opens the door to empowering consumers as regulators is the EU Consumer ADR Directive.[26] Explanations on how CDR mechanisms currently work, and the power that they can enlist if the opportunity is now seized to develop them sensibly, exist elsewhere.[27] CDR systems are developing into swift, cheap and effective dispute resolution systems, which are often easy to use and free to consumers.

The position is about to undergo revolutionary change and development. A pan-EU network of CDR entities is being created, and every trader who is covered by a CDR scheme will have to provide specified information on that scheme, and notify a consumer who has an unresolved complaint of the CDR entity to which the complaint may be submitted.[28] An online dispute resolution (ODR) platform will enable complaints against traders in another Member State to be directed at the relevant CDR body in the other State.[29] The existing CDR system in almost every Member State will be reformed in some way. As a result, the ability of consumers to complain, and have their valid complaints effectively and swiftly resolved, should be significantly enhanced. This is not to say that the CDR system in 2015 will function perfectly, since further development will be necessary.

[24] T Williams, 'Empowerment of Whom and for What? Financial Literacy Education and the New Regulation of Consumer Financial Services' (2007) 29 *Law & Policy* 226; I Ramsay, 'Consumer Law, Regulatory Capitalism and New Learning in Regulation' (2006) 28 *Sydney Law Review* 9.

[25] RJ Sciller, 'Democratising and Humanizing Finance' in RS Kroszner and RJ Shiller (eds), *Reforming U.S. Financial Markets* (Cambridge MA, MIT Press, 2011).

[26] Directive 2013/11/EU of the European Parliament and of the Council of 21 May 2013 on alternative dispute resolution for consumer disputes ('Directive on consumer ADR') [2013] OJ L165.63.

[27] Hodges, Benöhr and Creutzfeldt-Banda (n 10); C Hodges, I Benöhr and N Creutzfeldt-Banda, 'Consumer-to-Business Dispute Resolution: The Power of CADR' (2012) 13 *ERA Forum* 199.

[28] Directive 2013/11/EU (n 26), Arts 5 and 13–15.

[29] Regulation (EU) No 524/2013 of the European Parliament and of the Council of 21 May 2013 on online dispute resolution for consumer disputes and amending Regulation (EC) No 2006/2004 and Directive 2009/22/EC (Regulation on consumer ODR) [2013] OJ L165/1.

But the impending change is revolutionary in scope and in the ability to deliver outcomes.

The significant point for present purposes arises from the fact that a major attraction of CDR systems is that, if they have particular design features, they function not just in resolving disputes (and, indeed, more disputes than hitherto). They also enable the data about the subject-matter of individual complaints and inquiries, and of the traders that are involved, to be collated, aggregated and fed back. As noted above, this ability to feed back extensive data, both aggregated and individualised, is an essential part of most enhanced regulatory systems. But it is certain CDR systems that are capable of generating the required data. In contrast, this is *not* a function of which courts are capable. The publication of the CDR market data allows regulators, consumers and others to see what is actually happening in the marketplace, and to take appropriate action—supporting good traders, and shunning bad ones or taking enforcement action against them.

Thus, the CDR mechanism has enormous potential to assist in affecting trading and market behaviour, improving standards and identifying poor practice. Again, this regulatory function needs to be developed further, but existing experience is very encouraging from CDR entities such as the UK's Financial Ombudsman Service, Communications Ombudsman, Energy Ombudsman, Legal Ombudsman, ABTA complaint system and Motor Codes complaints systems.[30]

For example, the Financial Ombudsman Service currently receives 1.2 million inquiries annually from consumers, which turn into around 500,000 formal disputes. The sheer volume of such information provides banks, the Financial Conduct Agency and consumers with extensive information on what is happening in the marketplace, which banks are misbehaving and what trends are emerging that need attention. Regulatory or enforcement action is now commonplace and consumers can exercise choices to switch or exit if they wish (although competition needs improvement in this sector).

VII. Conclusion

The CDR mechanism at last affords a practical, effective means of raising small complaints and obtaining effective outcomes. CDR can process both individual and mass claims. Further, a CDR system in which complaint data is recycled affords not only proper access to justice but also real enfranchisement of consumer rights. These are the mechanisms that should be taken forward. More remains to be done in redesigning these new systems and making sure that the full advantages can be realised in practice, so it is on such aspects that effort should now be directed. But

[30] For details on how these organisations operate, see Hodges, Benöhr and Creutzfeldt-Banda (n 10).

consumers are now given significant *voice* and the mechanisms to use that voice in a significant regulatory capacity. The regulatory effect arises from the aggregation of data from multiple claims, but so its power is dependent on the input of multiple individual items of information. This system therefore has a strong alignment with democratic principles: individual votes count. There is an inherent and inescapable link between individual contributions and the collectivised voice. Hans Micklitz has referred earlier in this volume to 'fragmentisation', but the CDR system can provide an effective mechanism for linking and reconstructing multiple discrete, individual voices.

The regulatory benefits of a CDR scheme cannot become functional reality without the involvement of multiple consumers as active, collaborative participants, feeding back comments, suggestions and complaints. The CDR Directive merely establishes the framework of CDR entities, ensures a regulatory system for them that should support trust in their quality, and imposes information requirements on traders who use them. It is premature for CDR membership to be obligatory for all traders and for decisions to be binding. Both legal and practical obstacles need to be overcome if such changes were to be made—and it is possible that such mandatory provisions might not be necessary. But the CDR Directive is a watershed and a catalyst. CDR systems and membership are clearly expanding and in several Member States are already sufficiently established so as to operate with the regulatory effects described above. The key is to design CDR and regulatory systems so that they can operate as described, and in the process work not only effectively but also efficiently. Well-functioning systems should be capable of reducing regulatory burdens on business through operating on the basis of transparency and reputational principles, thereby delivering better regulation benefits.

In short, the snapshot of unhappy consumers noted earlier in this chapter is capable of being transformed into confident, empowered and economically active consumers—operating not just as agents of consumption but also as regulators of market behaviour and a collective force supporting good trading behaviour.

11

Regulatory Cost, the Consumer, and the EU Constitutional Framework

DOROTA LECZYKIEWICZ*

I. Affordability of Products and Services and Other Goals of the EU

This chapter investigates the question of whether EU law takes account of consumers' economic interests when it uses their finances to pursue policies focussed on goals other than *affordability* of products and services for consumers. For this purpose the chapter first establishes what types of interests consumers are able to defend against encroachment by EU legislative agendas. Given the fact that protection against excessive regulatory cost for consumers is not one of the 'juridified' interests in EU law (it has not been translated into a right) the chapter investigates two additional questions. First, it explores whether product affordability is a concept which consumers can use to challenge excessive EU regulatory cost. Second, the chapter reflects on the question of how consumers' non-juridified interests are recognised in EU constitutional discourse. The starting assumption of the chapter is that to the extent that certain interests cannot be expressed in the formal parlance of EU law, controlled to a large extent by the Court of Justice of the EU (CJEU) in the process of constitutional review, they remain neglected in the legislative process. The chapter uses the term 'EU constitutional framework' to encapsulate two types of constraints which affect the legislative process in the EU. First, the legislator is constrained by the wording of Treaty provisions and Protocols, and now the Charter of Fundamental Rights. Second, the Court's review practices play a major role in moulding the way in which policy choices are justified and the language used to express them in individual measures.[1] In this light, the chapter

* The research leading to these results has received funding from the Seventh Framework Programme FP7-MC-IEF under grant agreement n° 623734.

[1] S Weatherill, 'The Limits of Legislative Harmonisation Ten Years after Tobacco Advertising: How the Court's Case Law has become a "Drafting Guide"' (2011) 12 *German Law Journal* 827; D Leczykiewicz, '"Constitutional Justice" and Judicial Review of EU Legislative Acts' in D Kochenov, G de Búrca and A Williams (eds), *Europe's Justice Deficit?* (Oxford, Hart Publishing, 2015).

investigates whether the cost of policies for consumers is one of the considerations which the EU legislator has been obliged to take into account as a result of the pattern of the Court's assessment of validity. It therefore focusses on the way in which the Court of Justice deals with arguments about excessive regulatory cost for consumers when it assesses an EU measure's compliance with competence conferring provisions and the principle of proportionality. It will be shown that the only way in which consumers can successfully present the argument of the measure creating excessive economic burdens for them is by way of aligning their position with that of business and arguing that the business interest has been subjected to disproportionate interference. Moreover, as will be shown below, the investigation of economic implications for consumers is not one of the compulsory elements of the pre-legislative assessment. EU law possesses no general safeguards against regressive redistribution and relies almost entirely on the instrument of market competition to keep prices low for consumers. It follows that one of the images of the consumer which is still missing from EU law is that of the party financing the regulatory programmes adopted by the EU.

My purpose in this chapter is *not* to question EU regulatory programmes on the mere ground that they may generate costs for consumers. Instead, I would like to question the conceptual framework of a legal system which indirectly encourages regressive redistribution because of a curious asymmetry with which the interests of business, on the one hand, and of consumers, on the other, are treated. While the constitutional process, both legislative and judicial, is mindful of the effects of regulatory initiatives on business, creation of financial burdens for consumers is not only absent from the list of constitutional considerations but it is occasionally used as a positive justification for proposed measures.

II. Consumer Interest Beyond Rights

The 2012 Commission Communication 'A European Consumer Agenda—Boosting confidence and growth' stated that '[i]f the Single Market is to continue to be a success, there need to be improvements in market participants' trust in the effective and efficient enforcement of [consumers'] rights and the availability of adequate redress mechanisms'.[2] This translated into two objectives: the effective enforcement of consumer law and the development of efficient ways of solving consumer disputes. These policy statements reveal what role consumers are ascribed in the EU. The EU consumer is foremost 'a market participant'. Their trust is to be improved inter alia by making enforcement of their 'rights' more effective and efficient. This is then reflected in the objective of effective enforcement of 'consumer law' as the source of rights that consumers need to be able to enforce in order, presumably, to

[2] Commission, A European Consumer Agenda—Boosting Confidence and Growth (Communication) COM(2012) 225 final, 10.

have more trust in the single market. It follows that, in the Commission's view, the image of the EU consumer is strongly related to that of a right-holder.

Yet enforcement of consumer rights is not, in EU law, the exclusive prerogative of consumers. The Commission 'enforces' rights on behalf of consumers by monitoring the implementation of consumer directives by and the subsequent enforcement efforts of the Member States. Many consumer Directives ascribe a prominent role for public regulators and consumer organisations.[3] The remedies available to consumers are, however, centred on two issues—dispute resolution and remedying loss resulting from violations of consumers' rights. Without a dispute or without a violation of a right, the EU consumer remains marginalised in the legal enforcement machinery. One could ask, what is the consumer meant to enforce if none of their legal rights have been violated? I will argue in this chapter that consumers have a stake, and therefore should participate, in the legal enforcement machinery envisaged in EU law beyond the terrain delineated to them by the scope of rights they formally possess under that law. The enforcement machinery and its functions are understood here broadly, and in particular to include the procedure of judicial review of EU legislative acts. For this reason, I will be interested in any form of argumentative participation in proceedings before the CJEU that enables consumers to protect their interests regardless of whether these interests have been translated into legal rights. Such participation should be distinguished from 'public interest litigation' where court proceedings are initiated by a litigant who is not in possession of legal rights and whose objective is to bring about broader public interest benefits. While a public interest litigant may be motivated by a private interest, the presence of that interest is not the defining feature of public interest litigation. Indeed, those who support public interest litigation usually claim that it should *not* be dependent on showing a private interest by the claimant. However, 'public interest litigation' is rejected in many jurisdictions. The CJEU denies standing for non-governmental organisations in the context of direct actions intended to challenge the validity of an EU act.[4] The situation is different if the interest of an individual bringing the action is affected. Such an applicant is in principle able to show 'individual concern', one of the necessary

[3] Council Directive 93/13/EEC of 5 April 1993 on unfair terms in consumer contracts (Unfair Terms Directive) [1993] OJ L95/29; Directive 2006/114/EC of the European Parliament and of the Council of 12 December 2006 concerning misleading and comparative advertising [2006] OJ L376/21; Directive 2002/65/EC of the European Parliament and of the Council of 23 September 2002 concerning the distance marketing of consumer financial services and amending Council Directive 90/619/EEC and Directives 97/7/EC and 98/27/EC [2002] OJ L271/16; Directive 2005/29/EC of the European Parliament and of the Council of 11 May 2005 concerning unfair business-to-consumer commercial practices in the internal market (Unfair Commercial Practices Directive) [2005] OJ L149/22; Directive 2008/122/EC of the European Parliament and of the Council of 14 January 2009 on the protection of consumers in respect of certain aspects of timeshare, long-term holiday product, resale and exchange contracts [2009] OJ L33/10; Directive 2011/83/EU of the European Parliament and of the Council of 25 October 2011 on consumer rights [2011] OJ L304/64.

[4] Case C–321/95 P *Stichting Greenpeace Council (Greenpeace International) v Commission* [1998] ECR I–01651.

conditions of admissibility of a challenge to a legislative act.[5] Still, it is virtually impossible for an individual who is an applicant in a direct action against a legislative act to succeed on the issue of standing before the CJEU unless their position is distinguishable from that of other individuals whose interests were also affected by the same measure.[6]

This chapter does not, however, deal with the obstacles consumers—as individuals, that is non-privileged applicants in direct actions—face when they bring such actions against an EU measure. Access to the CJEU is frequently ensured at the national level because national courts are bound by the principle of effective judicial protection. Yet the obligations of national courts stemming from the principle of effective judicial protection are activated only when the applicant has an 'EU right', or at least a clearly recognised legal interest under EU law.[7] National courts are required to enable access to judicial proceedings, apply EU consumer law granting rights *ex officio*, ensure that the consumer is fully compensated if they have suffered harm and disapply any conflicting national provisions making the exercise of EU consumer rights less attractive.[8] Obligations relating to access to judicial proceedings imposed on national courts by EU law benefit also those consumers or consumer organisations which would like to challenge validity of EU acts, and not only those who would like to rely on incompatibility of national rules with EU law. For this reason I do not think that the main obstacle to bringing challenges based on the ground of an excessive cost for consumers is that of the limited *procedural* access to a court. In my view, what restricts the ability of the consumer to appear before the Court of Justice or the national court is the absence of a juridified interest. Thus, it is first necessary to establish what consumer interests have so far been juridified by EU law and investigate whether any of them could be used as a gateway to a constitutional challenge based on the excessive regulatory burden for consumers of an EU policy.

[5] See Art 263 TFEU and Case C–583/11 P *Inuit Tapiriit Kanatami v Parliament and Council*, judgment of 3 October 2013.

[6] Case 25/62 *Plaumann & Co v Commission* [1963] ECR 199; *Inuit Tapiriit Kanatami* (n 5).

[7] Case C–432/05 *Unibet (London) Ltd and Unibet (International) Ltd v Justitiekanslern* [2007] ECR I–2271, paras 42–44: 'while it is, in principle, for national law to determine an individual's standing and legal interest in bringing proceedings, Community law nevertheless requires that the national legislation does not undermine the right to effective judicial protection … it is for the national courts to interpret the procedural rules governing actions brought before them, such as the requirement for there to be a specific legal relationship between the applicant and the State, in such a way as to enable those rules, wherever possible, to be implemented in such a manner as to contribute to the attainment of the objective … of ensuring effective judicial protection of an *individual's rights under Community law*' (emphasis added).

[8] Joined cases C–240/98 to C–244/98 *Océano Grupo Editorial SA v Rocío Murciano Quintero* [2000] ECR I–4941; Case C–168/05 *Elisa María Mostaza Claro v Centro Móvil Milenium SL* [2006] ECR I–10421; Case C–404/06 *Quelle AG v Bundesverband der Verbraucherzentralen und Verbraucherverbände* [2008] ECR I–2685; Case C–243/08 *Pannon GSM Zrt v Erzsébet Sustikné Győrfi* [2009] ECR I–4713.

III. The Consumer and EU Law

The role in which the consumer appears in EU law is primarily that of a market participant. On the one hand, the consumer is seen as entitled to be able to pursue valuable activities other than consumption. In order to be able to focus on these other activities, while still maintaining some level of participation in the market, the consumer has to delegate or abdicate some of their protective responsibility to the state or another political organisation, such as the EU. Only then will they not be 'consumed' by the need to protect themselves against exploitation by other market participants. On the other hand, the EU consumer is expected to perform an active role in market monitoring and in effectuating competition and cross-border trade. It follows that for the EU legislator the consumer is primarily a contracting party of a trader. The trader owes the consumer a series of duties, such as the duty of information and the duty not to include in a standard contract unfair terms under the sanction of their invalidity. The consumer is someone who needs a cooling-off period so that they become more willing to shop at a distance, including online, and remedies in the event the product which they bought differs from the contractual description. The consumer is also someone whose behaviour may be affected by misleading advertising and other unfair market practices. However, the EU consumer is not seen as someone who is interested in the level of prices for goods and services. As a result, EU policies are not routinely motivated by the desire to keep prices low for consumers. Obviously, there are important exceptions. According to Article 39 TFEU the objectives of the common agricultural policy include ensuring 'that supplies reach consumers at reasonable prices'. EU competition law focusses on the level of prices for consumers.[9] When competition law fails as an effective tool in achieving the lowering of prices for consumers the EU may decide to step in and regulate directly the prices of the services in question. An example of such a situation was the adoption by the EU of the Roaming Regulation.[10]

EU policy in the field of telecommunication is implemented by means of a number of Directives, whose primary function is to enhance competition within this field. The Roaming Regulation is aimed at ensuring that 'users of terrestrial public mobile telephone networks when travelling within the Community do not pay excessive prices for Community-wide roaming services when making or receiving voice calls'[11] and for this purpose it sets the maximum charges at retail level through the introduction of a 'Eurotariff'. The Regulation applies horizontally, which means that it is a direct source of rights for consumers. The Preamble to the Regulation explains that

[9] See Albertina Albors-Llorens and Alison Jones in this volume.

[10] Regulation (EC) No 717/2007 of the European Parliament and of the Council of 27 June 2007 on roaming on public mobile telephone networks within the Community [2007] OJ L171/32.

[11] ibid, Rec 16.

> [t]he high level of the prices payable by users of public mobile telephone networks ... is a matter of concern for national regulatory authorities, as well as for consumers and the Community institutions. ... Reductions in wholesale charges are often not passed on to the retail customer. Although some operators have recently introduced tariff schemes that offer customers more favourable conditions and lower prices, there is still evidence that the relationship between costs and prices is not such *as would prevail in fully competitive markets.*[12]

In *Vodafone* the Court of Justice was asked to review the Roaming Regulation.[13] The proportionality challenge concerned precisely the capping by the Regulation not only of the wholesale but also of the retail prices of roaming services. The mobile phone companies argued that the negative economic consequences which they faced as a result were excessive. The Court rejected this argument. Consumer protection entailed protecting consumers against high levels of charges.[14] In the absence of competitive pressure which would otherwise bring the prices of roaming services down in the world of capped wholesale prices, capping retail prices was proportionate.[15] It follows from the Court's judgment that price regulation by the EU is justified when it is motivated by the goal of consumer protection (understood to include the lowering of prices for consumers), especially if past practice shows that competition law had failed as a mechanism of bringing the prices down. This confirms that low prices are, or can be, part of the EU's market-making policy. As Weatherill explains, the level of consumer protection forms part of 'the quality of the environment (re-)regulated by the EU'.[16] In *Vodafone* that 'quality' was attained by capping the prices of roaming services for consumers.

The Roaming Regulation is, however, an exception. The standard approach of the EU, if it engages with the question of the level of prices at all, is to impose an obligation to ensure availability of the service at an undefined 'reasonable' or 'affordable' price on the Member States (such as in the Electricity and Gas Directives, the Universal Service Directive).[17] The Electricity and Gas Directives have

[12] ibid, Rec 1 (emphasis added).

[13] Case C–58/08 *The Queen, on the application of Vodafone Ltd and Others v Secretary of State for Business, Enterprise and Regulatory Reform* [2010] ECR I–4999.

[14] ibid, para 60.

[15] ibid, para 69.

[16] S Weatherill, 'Article 38—Consumer Protection' in S Peers, T Hervey, J Kenner and A Ward (eds), *The EU Charter of Fundamental Rights: A Commentary* (Oxford, Hart Publishing, 2014) 1005.

[17] Directive 2009/72/EC of the European Parliament and of the Council of 13 July 2009 concerning common rules for the internal market in electricity [2009] OJ L211/55 (Electricity Directive), where this obligation is mentioned only in the Directive's preamble; Directive 2009/73/EC of the European Parliament and of the Council of 13 July 2009 concerning common rules for the internal market in natural gas [2009] OJ L211/94 (Gas Directive), where the obligation appears in the Annex on Consumer Protection Measures, Art 1(g): 'Without prejudice to Community rules on consumer protection, in particular Directive 97/7/EC of the European Parliament and of the Council of 20 May 1997 on the protection of consumers in respect of distance contracts and Council Directive 93/13/EEC of 5 April 1993 on unfair terms in consumer contracts, the measures referred to in Article 3 are to ensure that customers [are] connected to the gas system are informed about their rights to be supplied, under the national legislation applicable, with natural gas of a specified quality *at reasonable prices*' (emphasis added); Directive 2002/22/EC of the European Parliament and of the Council of 7 March 2002 on universal service and users' rights relating to electronic communications networks and services (Universal Service Directive) [2002] OJ L108/51.

as their objective, inter alia, the supply of energy to consumers at a 'reasonable price'.[18] However, the Directives themselves guarantee the consumer only that their contract with the supplier specifies the means by which up-to-date information on all applicable tariffs and maintenance charges may be obtained, that they are given adequate notice of any intention to modify contractual conditions and are informed about their right of withdrawal when the notice is given, and receive transparent information on applicable prices and tariffs.[19] The CJEU has given some teeth to these modest price-related entitlements in the Electricity and Gas Directives. In *Invitel*[20] it held, applying the Unfair Terms Directive,[21] that the contractual term on variation of the price was unfair unless it set out the reasons and methods of variation and the consumer's right to terminate the contract.[22] In *Schulz*[23] the Court held that a high level of consumer protection entailed the consumer's right to challenge adjustments to the prices of gas and electricity, even though this right was not explicitly granted by the Directives.[24] According to the Court, the existence of the right to challenge adjustments to the price explained why adequate notice of modifications to tariffs had to be given. Without such notice price adjustments were contrary to EU law.[25] Any additional price-related entitlements of consumers had to come from national law.

The Universal Service Directive[26] is another measure intended to protect the interest of consumers in low prices. It uses the concept of 'affordable price', which is connected to the requirement of the service's 'universality'. According to Recital 4 in the Preamble to the Directive, '[e]nsuring universal service (that is to say, the provision of a defined minimum set of services to all end-users at an affordable price) may involve the provision of some services to some end-users at prices that depart from those resulting from normal market conditions'.[27] The Directive obliges national regulatory authorities not only to monitor the market for communication services and enhance competition on that market but also to cap prices for those undertakings which impose 'excessive prices' on consumers.[28] Contracts with 'end-users' should specify the 'particulars of prices

[18] Recs 45 and 50 of the Electricity Directive and Rec 43 of the Gas Directive.

[19] Annex I Measures on Consumer Protection, Art 1(a), (b) and (c) to both Directives.

[20] Case C–472/10 *Nemzeti Fogyasztóvédelmi Hatóság v Invitel Távközlési Zrt*, judgment of 26 April 2012.

[21] Directive 93/13/EEC (n 3).

[22] *Invitel* (n 20), para 24.

[23] Joined cases C–359/11 and C–400/11 *Alexandra Schulz v Technische Werke Schussental GmbH und Co KG and Josef Egbringhoff v Stadtwerke Ahaus GmbH*, judgment of 23 October 2014.

[24] ibid, paras 45–46.

[25] ibid, para 55.

[26] Directive 2002/22/EC (n 17).

[27] See also Recs 7 and 8 and Arts 1(2) and 3(1) of the Directive. 'Affordable price means a price defined by Member States at national level in the light of specific national conditions, and may involve setting common tariffs irrespective of location or special tariff options to deal with the needs of low-income users. Affordability for individual consumers is related to their ability to monitor and control their expenditure' (Rec 10).

[28] Art 17(2).

and tariffs and the means by which up-to-date information on all applicable tariffs and maintenance charges may be obtained' (Article 20(1)(d)). Consumers are also guaranteed a right to transparent and up-to-date information on applicable prices and tariffs. However, these duties materialise only when the Member States enact implementing legislation because the obligations are not imposed directly on service providers and the Directive is not horizontally directly effective.

The three isolated contexts described above, energy, communication and roaming services, the EU consumer is seen as someone who pays and whose financial interests should be protected. As a result, the EU is empowered to regulate the given market, even to impose price caps, and the Member States retain extensive market interventionist competences in order to ensure reasonableness or affordability of prices. But in all the examples described above, the high level of prices for consumers, which the EU legislation was addressing, did not per se result from excessive and compliance-costly regulation. Instead, it stemmed from absence of effective competition. In the context of energy and communication services it was the fundamental importance of ensuring universal access to the services which justified the EU's indirect regulation of prices.[29] It follows that these measures and their constitutional validity under EU law do not provide adequate examples of how that law responds to regulatory cost created *by* EU legislation. Therefore, we need to look at examples of EU regulation where the measure neither capped the prices nor addressed market failures causing excessive prices for consumers. We need to look at measures that regulate the manufacturing, distribution and sale of goods and services. It is accepted that in a very competitive market consumers are only moderately affected by such regulatory measures in terms of prices they pay. But in a less competitive market, or a market with small price elasticity of demand, consumers do effectively bear the economic burden of these measures.

Because in many markets perfect competition is not accomplished, and the price elasticity of demand is limited, it would be logical for EU law to approach consumers as burden-bearers of regulatory activities. I will explain below that surprisingly this image of the consumer is not part of the EU's constitutional landscape. Neither Treaty provisions on EU competences nor the grounds of judicial review of EU legislative acts necessitate a discussion about the cost of a reviewed act for the consumer. In particular, the principle of proportionality, as applied by the Court of Justice in cases of validity review, has proved incapable of fostering a discourse on the regulatory cost borne by consumers. This could be contrasted with EU policy statements. The Commission's 'European Consumer Agenda' of 2012 shows the concern, in the section on 'Social exclusion, vulnerable consumers and accessibility', for 'a very significant fall in income or purchasing power [of consumers]', which increases 'the risk of social exclusion and the risk that citizens are

[29] The fundamental importance of access to the energy and communication services explains why they are covered by the universal service obligation.

unable to afford essential goods and services'.[30] The EU Consumer Policy Strategy for 2007–2013 listed as one of its objectives the aim '[t]o enhance EU consumers' welfare in terms of price, choice, quality, diversity, affordability and safety'.[31]

The more general question which emerges from the discussion included in this chapter concerns the notion of 'consumer protection' in EU law. The particular importance of this notion stems from its Treaty-embedding. Article 4(1) TEU mentions 'consumer protection' as one of the competences which the EU shares with the Member States. Article 12 TEU states that 'consumer protection requirements' are to be taken into account in defining and implementing other Union policies and activities, and Title XV of the TFEU is entitled 'consumer protection', which is indirectly defined as 'protecting the health, safety and economic interests of consumers, as well as … promoting their right to information, education and to organise themselves in order to safeguard their interests'.[32] 'Consumer protection' has also been elevated in the EU to the status of a fundamental right,[33] although it is unclear what significance in practice this change will have for EU law.[34] Given its explicit presence in the Treaties the notion of 'consumer protection' participates in legitimising Union action. Yet, its capacity to vest Union action with legitimacy depends on the concept's democratic and justice-promoting credentials. In the following section I will look briefly at the role of 'consumer protection' in establishing the existence of the EU's competence and then discuss the implications of the principle of proportionality for the position of excessive burdens for consumers in the EU constitutional framework. The question of whether consumer protection entails ever higher levels of regulation, regardless of the financial implications for consumers, is a topical one in a situation where a real possibility exists that some consumers can be priced out of the market and the ability of traders to conform to demanding regulatory obligations is not uniform in different regions of the EU.[35]

IV. Validity of EU Acts

Validity of acts adopted by the EU depends on their compliance with a number of criteria. Article 263 TFEU lists 'lack of competence, infringement of an essential

[30] COM(2012) 225 final (n 2).

[31] Commission, EU Consumer Policy Strategy 2007–2013—Empowering consumers, enhancing their welfare, effectively protecting them (Communication) COM(2007) 99 final.

[32] Art 169(1) TFEU.

[33] Art 38 of the Charter of Fundamental Rights: 'Union policies shall ensure a high level of consumer protection.'

[34] Weatherill (n 16).

[35] D Caruso, 'The "Justice Deficit" Debate in EU Private Law: New Directions' *Boston University School of Law Working Paper* No 12–42 and '*Qu'ils mangent des contrats*: Rethinking Justice in EU Contract Law' in D Kochenov, G de Búrca and A Williams (eds), *Europe's Justice Deficit?* (Oxford, Hart Publishing, 2015) 373–75.

procedural requirement, infringement of the Treaties or any rule of law relating to their application, or misuse of powers' as possible grounds of an EU measure's invalidity. Competence review, understood narrowly, refers to the existence of a Treaty competence for Union action. The Court assesses whether a measure of a given content is covered by the transfer of powers effectuated by the Treaty provision cited in the measure as its basis. Competence-conferring provisions of the Treaty often stipulate the goal to be achieved, rather than the subject-matter. Thus, famously, Article 114 TFEU 'appl[ies] for the achievement of the objectives set out in Article 26', that is for the creation of 'an area without internal frontiers in which the free movement of goods, persons, services and capital is ensured in accordance with the provisions of the Treaties'. The peculiar feature of the EU's competence arrangement is that none of the positive competence provisions has as its main objective consumer protection.[36] Even Article 169(1) TFEU, which is aimed at promoting the interests of consumers and ensuring a high level of consumer protection, refers to Article 114 TFEU as the provision on which EU regulatory action is actually based (subsection (a)). Where the link between consumer protection and the internal market is abandoned in Article 169(1), namely its subsection (b), the Treaty empowers the EU to introduce measures which only support, supplement and monitor the policy pursued by the Member States.[37] It follows that for most EU measures linked to consumer protection the competence to adopt them has to be established independently from the objective of consumer protection, as required by Article 114 TFEU, even if its 'high level' is to be taken as the base.[38] The Treaty is silent on what the concept of 'consumer protection' and its 'high level' entail. It has traditionally been understood to mean extensive rather than limited regulation, although not the highest standard found among the Member States.[39] Not only is there no presumption in favour of liberalisation, which in the case of very competitive markets would translate into lower prices for consumers, there is also no clear direction from the competence provisions that competences exist only where it is legitimate to ask the consumer to make the additional expense.

Moreover, it is often the case that consumer protection measures are adopted on the basis of other competence conferring provisions. To ensure equal access to goods and services regardless of gender or race the EU has adopted legislation under Article 19 TFEU, which defines the EU's competence as that involving

[36] For more on the EU's consumer protection competence, see S Weatherill, *EU Consumer Law and Policy* (Cheltenham, Edward Elgar Publishing, 2013).

[37] ibid, 17–18.

[38] Case C–380/03 *Federal Republic of Germany v European Parliament and Council* (*Tobacco Advertising*) [2006] ECR I–1573. Para 3 of Art 114 states: '[t]he Commission, in its proposals envisaged in paragraph 1 concerning health, safety, environmental protection and consumer protection, will take as a base a high level of protection, taking account in particular of any new development based on scientific facts. Within their respective powers, the European Parliament and the Council will also seek to achieve this objective'.

[39] Weatherill, *EU Consumer Law and Policy* (n 36) 72.

combating discrimination rather than consumer protection.[40] Consumers using transport services are granted new rights by EU law by measures adopted on the basis of the Treaty Title concerning Transport.[41] Interestingly, EU competences regarding Transport do not possess any specific objective or objectives. According to Article 90 TFEU the common transport policy realises simply 'the objectives of the Treaty'.[42]

It follows that the only part of the broader competence review that shows some openness to arguments relating to financial burdens for consumers is that of *proportionality*. In the remaining part of the paper I will discuss its potential to restrict regulatory choices of the EU law-makers vis-à-vis the consumer burden.

V. The Double Importance of Proportionality

There are two reasons why proportionality carries a heavy normative load in the EU. Both of them relate to the question of legitimacy of the EU's action. Legitimacy may be approached from a purely procedural perspective. There, what seems to matter is whether those who are affected by legislation could participate in the legislative process (legitimacy as self-government) and whether they would have accepted the legislation in a rational discourse (legitimacy stemming from the respect for private autonomy of citizens).[43] A procedural approach to legitimacy offers fewer insights into the content of reasons which are permitted and accepted in the rational discourse than a substantive approach. One could argue that it draws an insufficient connection between substantive and participatory rights in the sense that the possibility to participate in the law-forming discourse for dispersed individuals, such as consumers, is often contingent on the existence of substantive rights giving them voice if not in the legislative process, then at least in the constitutional review process. Moreover, the procedural version of deliberative democracy presupposes an active engagement of the lawmaking institutions in a communicative action. Even if such responsiveness is actually achieved in a concrete case it still remains open which 'reasons' or 'arguments' qualify as 'rational' and therefore universally acceptable. Validity of conclusions depends on the existence, and not only on the acceptance, of such reasons.

[40] Council Directive 2004/113/EC of 13 December 2004 implementing the principle of equal treatment between men and women in the access to and supply of goods and services [2004] OJ L373/37; Council Directive 2000/43/EC of 29 June 2000 implementing the principle of equal treatment between persons irrespective of racial or ethnic origin [2000] OJ L180/22.

[41] Title VI of the TFEU.

[42] Art 90 TFEU: 'The objectives of the Treaties shall, in matters governed by this title, be pursued within the framework of a common transport policy' (emphasis added). Action aimed at improving consumer protection is not mentioned as one of the explicit modes of 'implementing Article 90' TFEU but is laconically described as laying down 'any other appropriate provisions' (Art 91(1)(d) TFEU).

[43] J Habermas, *Between Facts and Norms* (Cambridge MA, MIT Press, 1996) 107.

In practice, acceptability of arguments in a particular legal system is a conventional matter. Laws develop their argumentative structures through institutional acts of justification. Particularly important in this context is the role of review courts whose judgments affect the substance of acceptable arguments in two ways. First, they influence the choice of arguments made by legislative institutions when they decide which arguments are necessary and/or sufficient to justify a particular conclusion (existence of a competence to act, proportionality, compliance with higher-ranking norms of a legal system, such as fundamental rights etc). Second, review courts themselves use arguments to justify their conclusions as to the correct interpretation of legal provisions or the necessity to lay down a rule of particular content. This reasoning process is particularly important in the formation of the argumentative canon. Also in EU law, certain arguments are 'good' arguments because they have the potential to influence the reasoning of the Court of Justice.[44] But 'good' arguments of EU law, those that form the canon, do not necessarily include all claims which from the perspective of some normative theory we would regard as relevant. This creates a logical space for reflecting on whether the argumentative structure of EU law succeeds in substantively legitimising the EU's action. The role of the Court of Justice is extensive because it cannot be convincingly maintained that the set of claims on which it can draw is materially restricted by the wording of the Treaties. As I have argued elsewhere, Treaty provisions shape the Court's reasoning in constitutional review cases only in a very limited way.[45] This on the other hand means that the Court exercises substantial control over the range of arguments which 'work' in EU law. Inability to express certain interests in EU law is usually due to absence of the necessary language among concepts and principles endorsed, controlled and developed by the Court of Justice.

If we apply these observations to the principle of proportionality we notice that the principle on its own (its verbal inclusion into EU law) is insufficient to generate positive effects for EU action's legitimacy. Instead, what is needed is a set of conventions, that is, judicial practices, surrounding the principle of proportionality. If we believe that the Union's legitimacy depends on generating substantive positive effects (for example, promoting justice) we might expect one of the fundamental legitimising principles, the principle of proportionality, to be based on the substantive approach.[46] The substantive claim on which I focus here is that of *distributive justice*. While we may dispute whether distributive justice is necessary for a legal system's legitimacy, it is usually accepted that at least in some cases taking steps to achieve distributive justice contributes to legitimacy. While it is contested whether distributive policies imposing equalisation of wealth among

[44] Here, 'good' means acceptable and persuasive to the extent of being binding on relevant courts.

[45] Leczykiewicz (n 1).

[46] This should be distinguished from the 'output legitimacy' which focusses more directly on effectiveness in government, rather than any substantive set of values. See FW Scharpf, *Governing in Europe* (New York, Oxford University Press, 1999).

the members are just and should be introduced, it is usually accepted that justice requires that regressive redistribution should not be encouraged or facilitated by law. In turn, a legal system which fails at giving citizens argumentative tools to challenge regressive redistribution could be seen as insufficiently legitimised.

The question is then whether prevention of regressive redistribution is one of the factors in the proportionality assessment carried out in EU law. Article 5(4) TEU defines the principle of proportionality as requiring that 'the content and form of Union action shall not exceed what is necessary to achieve the objectives of the Treaties'. According to Article 5 of the Protocol on the Application of the Principles of Subsidiarity and Proportionality, '[a]ny draft legislative act should contain a detailed statement making it possible to appraise compliance with the principles of subsidiarity and proportionality. This statement should contain some assessment of the proposal's financial impact'.[47] Moreover, according to the same Article, '[d]raft legislative acts shall *take account of the need for any burden*, whether financial or administrative, falling upon the Union, national governments, regional or local authorities, economic operators *and citizens*, to be minimised and commensurate with the objective to be achieved'. A burden falling on citizens is, according to the Protocol, a relevant consideration. From this it would normally follow that the argument that consumers carry an excessive burden should be accepted as 'good', that is, relevant and binding on the Court, even if the Court nevertheless decides that the objective justified the burden.

Yet the Court does not actually apply the formulation we find in the Protocol to test the proportionality of EU measures. Instead, it uses a test which avoids an inquiry into the cost–benefit analysis carried out by the EU legislative institutions. The test is:

> [w]ith regard to judicial review of [proportionality], it should be noted that the Community legislature must be allowed a broad discretion in an area such as that in issue in the present case, which involves political, economic and social choices on its part, and in which it is called on to undertake complex assessments. Consequently, the legality of a measure adopted in that area can be affected only if the measure is manifestly inappropriate having regard to the objective which the competent institutions are seeking to pursue ...[48]

The practical effect of the broad discretion test is that the only circumstance which the Court takes into account when assessing proportionality is that of whether the EU action was or was not 'manifestly inappropriate' to attain the stated objective. Secondly, as is that of also visible from the afore-cited paragraph, the Court, through the formula it uses, is not willing to empower itself to control the choice of the objective pursued by the EU legislature. The legislative objective must, at least in some remote sense, refer to one of the Treaty objectives of the EU so that existence of the competence is established. However, within these impre-

[47] Emphasis added.

[48] Joined cases C–453/03, C–11/04, C–12/04 and C–194/04 *The Queen, on the application of ABNA Ltd v Secretary of State for Health and Food Standards Agency* [2005] ECR I–10423, para 69.

cise boundaries the legislator remains free to define the concrete objective to be pursued. When 'consumer protection' is used as the secondary objective it may mean the objective of disincentivising the consumer from smoking, of protecting consumers from a contractual term's unfairness, of remedying the effects of flight cancellations, or of strengthening the position of consumers in the event of unilateral changes to energy tariffs, just to name a few.

How does this affect the proportionality review in cases where the regulatory cost is borne by consumers? Let us first look at the *IATA* case,[49] in which the Court was asked to assess the validity of Regulation No 261/2004.[50] The Regulation guarantees passengers the right to assistance, care and compensation in the event of the flight's cancellation, denied boarding and long delay. One of the challenges concerned the validity of a provision restricting the possibility of air carriers to use the defence of extraordinary circumstances.[51] The applicants argued that the restriction was insufficiently justified by the EU legislator and therefore breached the duty to give reasons under Article 253 EC (now Article 296 TFEU). Following its standard approach, the Court did not challenge the legislator's overarching assumption that consumer protection entailed compensating passengers in the event of flight cancellation or its long delay. 'Serious inconvenience' which such occurrences cause was regarded to justify the Community's regulation of air carriers' liabilities. And the burden of proof was placed on the applicants to show that damage resulting from the cancellation and delay for the passengers was an 'insignificant phenomenon'. The EU legislator, on the other hand, did not have to show that the volume of incidents was sufficiently high to justify an intervention.[52] The Court also accepted the legislator's assumption that realisation of the objective of protecting passengers entailed the introduction of 'standard and effective compensatory measures'. Such measures might require restricting the air carriers' access to the defence of extraordinary circumstances, and the legislature was not asked to submit any further reasons why and in which circumstances availability of the defence should be restricted.[53]

[49] Case C–344/04 *The Queen, on the application of International Air Transport Association and European Low Fares Airline Association v Department for Transport* [2006] ECR I–403.

[50] Regulation (EC) No 261/2004 of the European Parliament and of the Council of 11 February 2004 establishing common rules on compensation and assistance to passengers in the event of denied boarding and of cancellation or long delay of flights [2004] OJ L46/1.

[51] According to Art 5(3) of the Regulation No 261/2004 '[a]n operating air carrier shall not be obliged to pay compensation in accordance with Article 7, if it can prove that the cancellation is caused by extraordinary circumstances which could not have been avoided even if all reasonable measures had been taken'.

[52] *IATA* (n 49), para 71: 'It is also not in dispute that the various kinds of damage suffered by passengers in the event of cancellation of, or a long delay to, a flight exist. It has not been established, nor indeed has it been asserted, that incidents of this nature amount to no more than an insignificant phenomenon. Neither Article 253 EC nor any other provision indicates that, in order for the Community measure at issue to be valid, it would have to contain precise figures justifying the need for action on the part of the Community legislature.'

[53] ibid, para 72.

Finally, the Court addressed the question of the measure's proportionality. The applicants argued that the duties to assist, care for and compensate passengers prescribed by Regulation No 261/2004 were disproportionate by reason of the considerable financial charges which they imposed on air carriers. The Court identified its task as involving answering the question of whether 'the measures adopted [were] manifestly inappropriate in the light of the regulation's explicit objective, that relating to strengthening protection for passengers'.[54] The criteria adopted for determining the varying passengers' entitlement (the length of the delay, the time taken to inform of the flight's cancellation) 'did not appear' to the Court to be 'unrelated to the requirement of proportionality'.[55] Two paragraphs of the judgment expressly address the issue of regulatory cost. The applicants were trying to draw a connection between the price of the ticket and the obligations imposed on them in the event of cancellation and long delay. Intending to keep the prices of tickets low they suggested that the proportionate solution would be to vary the duties of air carriers against the price paid for the ticket.[56] It was the applicants' mistake not to articulate the underlying concern more directly. The cost of compliance with the Regulation inevitably raises the prices of tickets. It is true that this makes low-cost airlines less competitive and affects their profits. But behind that also lurks a much deeper question about the prices of tickets paid by consumers. The Court was completely blind to this issue and simply held that 'the harmful consequences to which a delay gives rise and which Regulation No 261/2004 seeks to remedy are in no way related to the price paid for a ticket'.[57] The CJEU was equally unreceptive to arguments about the excessive financial burdens for air carriers. While the Court did not demand concrete figures from the EU legislator, it demanded them from the applicants. Because they failed to give figures on the frequency of delays and cancellations the costs for air carriers were described as merely 'theoretical'. The Court then added that 'in any event [the costs did not] enable it to be regarded as established that those effects would be out of proportion to the interest in the measures'.[58] Proportionality review was in fact reduced to one line in the judgment where the Court declared that financial burdens could not, in principle it seems, challenge the validity of measures pursuing a legitimate objective.

[54] ibid, para 83.

[55] ibid, para 85.

[56] Low-cost airlines also argued that it breached the principle of equal treatment to impose on them the same obligations as those borne by all other carriers, without drawing any distinction on the basis of their pricing policies and the services that they offer (para 94). The Court nevertheless held that: 'the damage suffered by passengers of air carriers in the event of cancellation of, or a long delay to, a flight is similar *whatever the airline with which they have a contract and is unrelated to the pricing policies operated by the airline*. Accordingly, if the Community legislature was not to infringe the principle of equality, having regard to the aim pursued by Regulation No 261/2004 of increasing protection for all passengers of air carriers, it was incumbent upon it to treat all airlines identically' (para 98).

[57] ibid, para 88.

[58] ibid, para 89.

The Court's judgment in *Nelson* consolidates the approach whereby the regulatory cost is incapable of constituting a relevant consideration in assessing the measure's validity as an aspect of the Court's assessment of proportionality.[59] The case concerned the validity of Articles 5 to 7 of Regulation No 261/2004. In an earlier judgment,[60] the Court held that passengers whose flights had been delayed should be treated, for the purposes of the application of the right to compensation, as passengers whose flights had been cancelled. The applicants in *Nelson* argued that under this interpretation the relevant provisions of the Regulation were invalid, inter alia, because imposing the obligation to pay compensation to passengers whose flights were merely delayed, but not cancelled, was disproportionate. This time, the applicants explicitly linked the issue of proportionality of the expansively interpreted provisions to the financial impact of such rules on passengers. Yet also in this case the Court remained unmoved. Only one sentence of the judgment is devoted to the possible increase of consumer fares:

> no specific evidence has been submitted to the Court which could lead to the conclusion that the payment of compensation in the event of long delays to flights would give rise to an increase in fares or a reduction in the number of flights from local airports and services to outlying destinations.[61]

Once again, the burden of proof is placed on the applicants, not the EU legislator, to show that the payment of compensation would give rise to an increase in fares. Moreover, the Court relies on *Vodafone*, a case which concerned, as we have seen, a measure *capping prices* of a consumer service, to argue that 'the importance of the objective of consumer protection … may justify even substantial negative economic consequences for certain economic operators'.[62] This further strengthens the impression that the Court is not treating the type of implications for consumers as a distinctive feature of a particular measure.

VI. Encouraging Regressive Redistribution

The legitimacy credentials of the principle of proportionality are also undermined by the fact that the way the Court reasons with respect to this principle not only removes the cost for consumers from the range of relevant considerations but, paradoxically, treats it as a circumstance pointing to the measure's *compliance* with the principle of proportionality. The case of *McDonagh* concerned the interpretation, not the validity, of the same Regulation No 261/2004.[63] The claimant was a

[59] Joined cases C–581/10 and C–629/10 *Emeka Nelson and Others v Deutsche Lufthansa AG*, judgment of 23 October 2012.

[60] Joined cases C–402/07 and C–432/07 *Christopher Sturgeon, Gabriel Sturgeon and Alana Sturgeon v Condor Flugdienst GmbH* [2009] ECR I–10923.

[61] ibid, para 83.

[62] ibid, para 81.

[63] Case C–12/11 *Denise McDonagh v Ryanair Ltd*, judgment of 31 January 2013.

passenger who claimed compensation before the Irish court for the cost of accommodation and subsistence which she incurred during the time she was stranded as a result of the Icelandic volcano's eruption. She argued that these costs were caused by Ryanair's failure to provide her with 'care' when her flight was cancelled. Under Article 5 of the Regulation air carriers are obliged to provide care to passengers even if the flight was cancelled due to extraordinary circumstances.[64] Ryanair argued that the principle of proportionality required that these obligations be restricted in time or by amount. The Court of Justice rejected this argument. It held that 'air carriers should, as experienced operators, foresee costs linked to the fulfilment, where relevant, of their obligation to provide care and, furthermore, *may pass on the costs incurred as a result of that obligation to airline ticket prices*'.[65] The fact that air carriers were able to and did pass on the cost of their increased responsibilities to passengers constituted the Court's explanation for why the interpretation of the Regulation which the Court selected complied with the principle of proportionality.

Another example is provided by the *Test-Achats* case.[66] In this case the Court held that the use of sex as a factor in the calculation of premiums and benefits for the purposes of insurance and related financial services would not result in differences in individuals' premiums and benefits from 21 December 2012. It reached this conclusion by invalidating Article 5 of the Directive on equal treatment between men and women in the supply of goods and services.[67] The Court was not at all concerned about the financial consequences of its ruling for the respective groups of consumers. Arguably, this was in line with the intention of the EU legislator. The Proposal for the Directive[68] stated that the insurance companies estimated that it was likely that prices for the different types of insurance would need to settle at a figure somewhere above the average of the current prices for women and men so as to provide a sufficient safety margin against the risk of an imbalance of risks in the scheme.[69] The Commission noted this consequence

[64] Regulation 261/2004 introduced rules on compensation and assistance in the event of denied boarding, short-notice cancellation, long delay and involuntary downgrading. Depending on the circumstances of travel disruption, the Regulation requires air carriers to provide passengers with assistance (meals, refreshments, telephone calls and hotel accommodation), offer rerouting and refunds, pay flat-rate compensation, and proactively inform passengers about their rights. The air carrier is not obliged to pay financial compensation if it can prove that the cancellation or delay was caused by 'extraordinary circumstances', although obligations of care and assistance are still upheld in these circumstances.

[65] *McDonagh* (n 63), para 49 (emphasis added).

[66] Case C–236/09 *Association Belge des Consommateurs Test-Achats ASBL v Conseil des ministres* [2011] ECR I–773.

[67] Council Directive 2004/113/EC (n 40).

[68] Commission, Proposal for a Council Directive implementing the principle of equal treatment between women and men in the access to and supply of goods and services COM(2003) 657 final. This claim seems in principle to be substantiated by the adverse selection mechanism.

[69] Commission, 'Commission Staff Working Paper "Proposal for a Council Directive implementing the principle of equal treatment between women and men in the access to and supply of goods and services" Extended Impact Assessment' SEC(2003) 1213, 17.

and used it to show that the impact of the proposed Directive on business would be acceptable.[70]

I am not arguing here that the increased cost for the consumer is not an appropriate price which society should pay for equal treatment between men and women. Nor do I disagree with AG Kokott in her opinion in the *Test-Achats* case that '[p]urely financial considerations, such as the danger of an increase in premiums for a proportion of the insured persons or even for all of the insured persons, do not in any event constitute a material reason which would make discrimination on grounds of sex permissible'.[71] However, I would not go so far as to argue that consumers should be discouraged from putting forward arguments of excessive financial burden even in the case of equal treatment legislation. So I remain surprised by how easy it is for the EU legislator to use an argument that the cost of regulation has been passed on to the consumer and how receptive the Court of Justice is to this argument. This means that the Court is concerned only about consumers for whom the increase in the price is offset by the benefit arising from more extensive obligations of the traders. The interests of remaining consumers are overlooked, and consumer organisations, even if they were interested in bringing a challenge against consumer rights which make goods and services more costly, have no legal principle on which they could base their argument of illegality.

VII. The Promise of Impact Assessments

The European Commission introduced an impact assessment system in 2002 to structure and support the development of EU policies.[72] It was only in 2005 that the Commission started to include in its report the assessment of economic, social and environmental dimensions. The most recent Commission's guidelines on impact assessment state the following:

> You should always identify who is affected by the impacts and when. Options that would be beneficial for society as a whole may have positive and negative impacts that *are spread unevenly across society* and over time. You should consider two distinct types of distributional impacts: impacts on different social and economic groups: identifying 'winners' and 'losers' can help you to anticipate obstacles to the proposed action and may point to the need to change its design, or to introduce measures to mitigate the negative impacts. For example, a proposal may be beneficial for consumers, but have costs which fall mainly on enterprises. There may be distributional effects even within a given group

[70] ibid. See the Commission's impact assessment accompanying Commission, Proposal for a Council Directive on implementing the principle of equal treatment between persons irrespective of religion or belief, disability, age or sexual orientation COM(2008) 426 final, for similar observations.

[71] *Test-Achats* (above n 66), Opinion of AG Kokott, para 68.

[72] For more on EU impact assessment, see ACM Meuwese, 'Inter-institutionalising EU Impact Assessment' in S Weatherill (ed), *Better Regulation* (Oxford, Hart Publishing, 2007) 287.

(eg between SMEs and larger companies, between market entrants and incumbents, *between low-income and higher-income households*, etc). Finally, the impacts may differ between Member States or regions … impacts on existing inequalities: you should for instance compare regional, gender impacts and impacts on vulnerable groups of the proposed action to see if it is likely to leave existing inequalities unchanged, aggravate them, or help to reduce them. This is not a simple matter: for example, differences between male and female lifestyles may mean that a proposal which appears to be neutral as regards gender equality will in practice have different impacts on men and women.[73]

For example, the impact assessment report prepared in relation to the Proposal for the Consumer Rights Directive reviews various policy options against the following criteria:[74]

Point 5.2:

(a) Economic effects, including: compliance/administrative costs of public authorities; increased /reduced costs for businesses such as administrative and compliance costs or costs for handling complaints and returns, legal advice, etc; consumers and other indirect effects for example on prices; consumer and business awareness and confidence; effects on SME and, effects on the internal market and competition.
(b) Social effects, including the level of consumer protection, consumer empowerment, employment, etc.

It follows that, in principle, impact assessments should enable a more thorough discussion about economic implications of particular regulatory choices for consumers. This could then feed into the Court's review of proportionality. As the *Vodafone* judgment shows, impact assessments may be crucial in the Court's proportionality review in two respects.[75] First, they provide evidence that the EU is addressing a real problem whose causes are known and which could not be addressed by alternative, less intrusive, means. Second, they direct the Court's attention to relevant considerations. Thus, an assessment of policy options also in the light of their financial burdens for consumers could steer the Court's proportionality review in the direction of contemplating the significance of the regulatory cost not only for business but also for consumers.

However, so far impact assessment reports have not been seriously engaging with this issue of consumer financial burden. For example, in the impact assessment report prepared in relation to Air Passenger Rights Regulations, consumer cost appears in two contexts.[76] First, it is mentioned in the context of a financial

[73] Commission, Impact Assessment Guidelines SEC(2009) 92, 33 (emphasis added).

[74] Commission, Impact Assessment Report Accompanying the Proposal for a Directive of the European Parliament and of the Council on consumer rights SEC(2008) 2544, 26.

[75] *Vodafone* (n 13), para 65.

[76] Commission, Impact Assessment accompanying the document Proposal for a regulation of the European Parliament and of the Council amending Regulation (EC) No 261/2004 establishing common rules on compensation and assistance to passengers in the event of denied boarding and of cancellation or long delays of flights and Regulation (EC) No 2027/97 on air carrier liability in respect of the carriage of passengers and their baggage by air SWD(2013) 62 final.

impairment suffered by airline companies due to the fact that their obligations under the Regulations were initially unclear and, as a result, the increases in prices that the airline companies imposed on passengers proved insufficient to cover the cost of these new obligations. Second, consumer cost is discussed as a factor which demotivates air carriers from seeking compensation from third parties responsible for delays, cancellation and lost luggage. Consumer cost does not appear, however, in the report as a consideration relevant for the level of ticket prices as such, and therefore as a constraint on the extent to which the EU consumer should be 'protected' in particular circumstances and on the EU's capacity to insist on full compliance with the Regulations. As we have seen, this incomplete reasoning is later replicated by the Court of Justice.

Moreover, the constitutional status of impact assessment reports is still unclear. In the light of the existing case law of the Court, it would be an exaggeration to accord impact assessment reports the status of even 'soft law'. In *Afton Chemical* the applicant challenged the validity of a provision from the Fuel Quality Directive,[77] a Directive concerning a reduction of greenhouse gas emissions by introducing specifications of petrol, diesel and gas-oil and thereby changing previous EU rules on the quality of petrol and diesel fuels,[78] on the ground that the EU legislator failed to comply with the principle of proportionality and the precautionary principle. The Directive limited the use of certain metallic additives (MMT) in fuel. Afton Chemical manufactured and sold MMT worldwide. The Commission's proposal for the Directive did not include any provision limiting the use of MMT in fuel and it was the Parliament's Committee on Environment, Public Health and Food Safety that wanted the use of MMT to be banned completely. The impact assessment carried out for the Commission's proposal did not indicate that metallic additives should be prohibited or that their use in fuel should be limited. The Court observed first that the impact assessment was binding on neither the Council nor the Parliament, which under the co-decision legislative procedure laid down by Article 251 EC were entitled to make amendments to that proposal.[79] Compliance with proportionality depended on whether

> in exercising its discretion, the European Union legislature attempted to achieve a degree of balance between, on the one hand, the protection of health, environmental protection and consumer protection and, on the other hand, the economic interests of traders, while pursuing the objective assigned to it by the Treaty to ensure a high level of protection of health and environmental protection.[80]

[77] Case C–343/09 *Afton Chemical Limited v Secretary of State for Transport* [2010] ECR I–7027.

[78] Art 1(8) of Directive 2009/30/EC of the European Parliament and of the Council of 23 April 2009 amending Directive 98/70/EC as regards the specification of petrol, diesel and gas-oil and introducing a mechanism to monitor and reduce greenhouse gas emissions and amending Council Directive 1999/32/EC as regards the specification of fuel used by inland waterway vessels and repealing Directive 93/12/EEC [2009] OJ L140/88, to the extent that it inserted a new Art 8a(2) and 8a(4) to (6) in Directive 98/70/EC of the European Parliament and of the Council of 13 October 1998 relating to the quality of petrol and diesel fuels and amending Council Directive 93/12/EEC [1998] OJ L350/58.

[79] *Afton Chemical* (n 77), para 30 and then repeated in para 57.

[80] ibid, para 56.

An attempt to achieve a degree of balance between the conflicting interests is, in the Court's view, sufficient to satisfy the requirement of proportionality even against the background of a more in-depth impact assessment report.

All this leaves impact assessment reports in an uncertain place. It is likely that the Court will invoke them only when their conclusions match those intended for the judgment. Even if the report predicts extensive costs for consumers, the Court may always invoke the importance of the legislative objective or the broad margin of legislative discretion to hold that the measure was proportionate. Therefore, it is unlikely that the impact assessment will aid the translation of excessive financial burdens for consumers from a mere consideration into a strong argument against the measure's proportionality.

VIII. Ideologies of EU Regulatory Law

It follows from the above that both EU constitutional law and the institutional practice remain weak on addressing the issue of the regulatory cost borne by the consumer. This may seem surprising given the liberal outlook of the main consumer protection competence, Article 114 TFEU. However, as it is often underlined, Article 114 TEU does not empower the EU simply to adopt market regulatory measures. As explained in the *Tobacco Advertising* judgment, the focus of Article 114 TFEU is on trade *between the Member States*. It follows that consumer protection does not constitute an independent aim. Rather, it is employed in the project of Internal Market building. A high level of consumer protection is needed in order to boost consumer confidence.[81] As a result, Article 114 TFEU can follow only two mutually reinforcing rationales: free movement and paternalism. The concept of 'consumer confidence' enables the EU legislator to avoid tension between them.[82] The image of the EU consumer is thus still based on that presented in the Consumer Policy Action Plan 1999–2001. There the consumer is

[81] See, eg, Commission, Proposal for the Directive on unfair commercial practices COM(2003) 365 final, para 15, where consumer confidence is described as necessary in order to encourage consumers to shop abroad and a high level of protection as a means of enhancing consumer confidence, then reflected in Rec 2 of the Unfair Commercial Practices Directive. See also Directive 1999/44/EC of the European Parliament and of the Council of 25 May 1999 on certain aspects of the sale of consumer goods and associated guarantees [1999] OJ L171/12, Rec 5; Directive 2002/65/EC of the European Parliament and of the Council of 23 September 2002 concerning the distance marketing of consumer financial services [2002] OJ L271/16, Rec 3; Directive 2008/48/EC of the European Parliament and of the Council of 23 April 2008 on credit agreements for consumers [2008] OJ L133/66, Rec 8.

[82] The European Economic and Social Committee did notice the tension and criticised the Commission for prioritising the Internal Market (3.1.1) and for a bias towards transparent and efficient markets (3.1.2), both exemplified by a shift to maximum harmonisation. See European Economic and Social Committee, Opinion of the European Economic and Social Committee on the Communication from the Commission to the Council, the European Parliament and the European Economic and Social Committee: EU Consumer Policy Strategy 2007–2013—empowering consumers, enhancing their welfare, effectively protecting them COM(2007) 99 final [2008] OJ C162/20.

presented as someone who depends on protection. This entails protection of all consumers, not just the vulnerable, and that is why so many EU measures have a paternalistic outlook. In Consumer Policy Strategy 2002–2006 consumers once again are to be protected 'at the highest level' and the issue of economic implications for consumes of such far-reaching protection is not discussed.[83] The special needs of low-income consumers are to be taken into account only in the context of services of general interest.

The systemic blindness of EU law to considerations of distributive justice, also in its more modest form of preventing regressive redistribution, raises questions about the ideology which is being engrained by the EU through its regulatory initiatives.[84] Disregard for the issue of whether the cost of regulation is passed to the consumer, and a review of proportionality which encourages such consequences, means that EU regulatory law fails as a system of distributive justice.[85] What has to be appreciated is that focussing on economic implications of regulatory proposals does not serve exclusively neoliberal goals.[86] At the moment, the principle of proportionality works against progressive redistribution because it focusses exclusively on the economic interest of traders.[87] At the same time, the EU has been trying to gain social legitimacy by introducing various non-economic policies, such as the equal treatment policy, or by adopting harmonising measures aimed at protecting employees. In EU consumer law, consumers are often denied the possibility of expressing their preferences as to the level of protection. This is perhaps justified by the findings of behavioural economics, which show that consumers are not rational decision-makers, that they overestimate certain risks and underestimate others, and that they trade long-term substantial gains for smaller instant benefits. So while the EU consumer should not necessarily be given the power to choose the level of their protection against the price of protection, the EU constitutional framework should be open to arguments of excessive financial burden of regulatory measures for consumers. The possibility to challenge an EU act on the ground that consumers are shown to be bearing its cost would enhance the democratic and justice-promoting credentials of the EU.

[83] Commission, Consumer Policy Strategy 2002–2006 (Communication) COM(2002) 208 final.

[84] H-W Micklitz, 'Social Justice and Access Justice in Private Law' *EUI Working Paper Law* 2011/02.

[85] See Study Group on Social Justice in European Private Law, 'Social Justice in European Contract Law: A Manifesto' (2004) 10 *European Law Journal* 653; U Mattei and FG Nicola, 'A "Social Dimension" in European Private Law? The Call for Setting a Progressive Agenda' (2007) 7 *Global Jurist. Frontiers*; T Wilhelmsson, 'Varieties of Welfarism in European Contract Law' (2004) 10 *European Law Journal* 712.

[86] D Caruso, 'Contract Law and Distribution in the Age of Welfare Reform' (2007) 49 *Arizona Law Review* 665.

[87] S Weatherill, 'The Constitutional Competence of the EU to Deliver Social Justice' (2006) 2 *European Review of Contract Law* 136.

12

Ethical Consumption and the Internal Market

LUCINDA MILLER*

I. Introduction

In our everyday shopping experiences we are constantly reminded that our consumption choices might have 'negative externalities'—that there may be an environmental and social impact associated with our consumption. Whether it is the exhortation to eat locally sourced food, to reuse our plastic shopping carriers (or not to use them at all) or to ensure that the coffee or tea we drink has been 'fairly grown', the terrain we cross as consumers is replete with ethical and moral significance. Surrounded by organic, non-GMO, fair trade, low carbon footprint, dolphin-friendly, energy-efficient product messages, our purchasing choices have become morally and ethically complex.[1]

And yet, although daunting, this market complexity has not deterred consumers from attempting to give meaning to their purchasing activities: ethical consumerism has captured the imagination of consumers across the world.[2] Although not

* Thanks to Marija Bartl, Maria Lee, Dorota Leczykiewicz and Stephen Weatherill for comments on an earlier draft, as well as to participants at the Oxford Conference ('The Image(s) of the "Consumer" in EU Law: Legislation, Free Movement and Competition Law') for helpful feedback on elements of this chapter. All errors remain my responsibility.

[1] The complexity is accentuated by the competing nature of many ethical messages. For example, the ethical promise of 'Fair Trade' goods must be weighed against the carbon footprint of these goods, in comparison to locally grown and locally produced products.

[2] This chapter uses a broad definition of 'ethical consumerism' and the notion is intended to include, but also to go beyond, those aspects of consumption which are commonly defined as 'political' consumption. Instances of 'ethical' consumption, as used in this chapter, do not necessarily have as their objective any political or social transformation (which is often how political consumption is defined) but may simply be important to the individual in allowing them to lead a 'better life'. For an alternative definition which draws a distinction between political consumption and ethical consumption see C Hilson, 'EU Environmental Solidarity and the Ecological Consumer: Towards a Republican Citizenship' in M Ross and Y Borgmann-Prebil (eds), *Promoting Solidarity in the European Union* (Oxford, Oxford University Press, 2010) 144: ethical consumerism is seen to implicate moral or ethical duties, whereas political consumption, it is argued, reflects 'stronger, justice-based duties'.

an entirely recent phenomenon,[3] ethical consumerism is certainly on the rise. This is often explained as the consequence of both a spontaneous maturing of consumer awareness and partly to the growth in both national and transnational pressure groups responding to global concerns. And, naturally, the commercial world is responding to this evolution in purchasing patterns. The exponential increase in the sale and marketing of 'ethical' goods reveals the economic advantages of a business model that pays heed to the ethical consumer's concerns.[4]

However, although clearly of intensifying importance for the individual and their market choices, ethical consumption has played little of a role in the design of the most central area of the EU legal and political order—the internal market.[5] Even though the consumer has been a key component for internal market policy, it is not the ethical consumer that is envisaged. Indeed, the ethical consumer is immediately striking for their incongruence with the image of the consumer that has been constructed in the dominant EU discourse: it is the neoliberal notion of the self-interested individual that has captured the imagination of the EU, undoubtedly because of this individual's purportedly crucial role in the creation of the internal market.

However, the extent to which the EU internal market should be framed and even limited by an ethical consumerist orientation is a matter ripe for investigation. If, as we shall see, the market is to play an increasingly important role in the articulation of ethical (and political) values, then this issue should not be sidestepped. Moreover, although consumers themselves consciously play a role in their own 'making',[6] consumer identity is also fashioned by the cultural, legal, political and economic institutions of a society,[7] which exert 'defining pressures' on them.[8] The role, therefore, of EU law, most notably consumer protection policy and the internal market provision of Article 114, in constituting the consumer and empowering them in their ethical role is crucial and deserves analysis. Such an

[3] The market has long been an important site for the expression of individuals' political and ethical views, even if it is only in more recent times that individuals have developed a sense of themselves as belonging to a constituency of 'consumers', see F Trentmann, 'Knowing Consumers' in F Trentmann (ed), *The Making of the Consumer* (Oxford, Berg Publishers, 2006).

[4] The market for so-called ethical products in the UK, for example, has expanded from £13.5bn (1999) to £47.2bn (2012). Figures from The Co-Operative, *Ethical Consumer Markets Report 2012* <www.co-operative.coop/PageFiles/416561607/Ethical-Consumer-Markets-Report-2012.pdf> accessed 2 March 2015.

[5] Although more recently it has been recognised as an important challenge for the EU and its consumer protection strategy. See, eg, DG SANCO, 'Health and Consumers: Future Challenges Paper 2009–2014' <www.ec.europa.eu/dgs/health_consumer/events/future_challenges_en.htm> accessed 2 March 2015.

[6] See M Hilton and M Daunton, 'Material Politics: An Introduction' in M Daunton and M Hilton (eds), *The Politics of Consumption: Material Culture and Citizenship in Europe and America* (Oxford, Berg Publishers, 2001) 4; Trentmann, 'Knowing Consumers' (n 3) 2–3.

[7] M Everson and C Joerges, 'Consumer Citizenship in Postnational Constellations?' (2006) *EUI Working Paper* 2006/47.

[8] M Dani, 'Assembling the Fractured Consumer' (2011) 36 *European Law Review* 362, 363. See also D Kysar, 'Preferences for Processes: the Process/Product Distinction and the Regulation of Consumer Choice' (2004) 118 *Harvard Law Review* 525, 530 and 579.

examination demonstrates how ethical consumption can test the limits of Article 114 and the consumer protection objectives of the EU. More broadly, it digs deeply into important political and moral questions about the role of government in enabling ethical behaviour in the market place and exposes the societal values that are deemed central to how we live as 'good' Europeans.

Thus, the discussion on ethical consumption is more than simply an interesting, yet peripheral concern about 'alternative' consumer practices. It asks us to think more carefully about the values that should underpin the operation of the internal market, beyond those values typically prized by a capitalist market economy, and which constitute and shape our identities as European consumers and ultimately as European citizens.

The consumer protection provisions of the Treaty are initially instructive as to the place of ethical consumption within EU consumer protection law. Article 169 TFEU sets out the powers for the EU in consumer protection policy. Article 169(1) provides that a high level of consumer protection is to be achieved through protection of the 'health, safety and economic interests of consumers', as well as promotion of 'their right to information, education and to organise themselves in order to safeguard their interests'. Ethical interests, therefore, do not feature explicitly and have not been identified as interests worthy of particular protection within the framework of consumer protection policy. This is perhaps unsurprising, for when we turn to Article 169(2) it is seen that consumer protection is deeply cemented within the internal market objectives of the Union; consumer protection objectives are to be pursued through measures which are adopted under Article 114, the internal market harmonising provision of the TFEU.[9]

Article 114 TFEU is an extraordinarily wide provision that allows measures to be adopted for the approximation of national laws which have as their object the 'establishment and functioning of the internal market'. It has been of crucial importance for achieving the internal market aims of Article 26 TFEU. And it is this internal market corset within which the EU's consumer protection policy has been largely confined. Consumer protection measures emerge not as a result of an independent, and therefore coherent European consumer policy, but instead emerge indirectly as a dimension of internal market policy. It is only those aspects of consumer protection policy which facilitate the functioning of the internal market that are singled out for the Union's attention.

Thus, the *rationality* of the EU's consumer protection policy is that of the single market. So, legislation to protect the health, safety and economic interests of consumers becomes predominantly framed in terms of its ability to establish a genuine internal market across the territory of the EU. Refracting consumer protection policy through the lens of the market might partly explain why the discourse on

[9] The linkage between consumer policy and the internal market is only abandoned where the Union adopts measures that 'support, supplement and monitor' policies pursued by the Member States: Art 169(2)(b). This power has been little used, see S Weatherill, *EU Consumer Law and Policy* 2nd edn (Cheltenham, Edward Elgar, 2013) 18.

ethical consumption has been remarkably muted and it is from this perspective that one might comprehend the absence of any ethical consumer issues from the Treaty. As we shall see, however, one doesn't need to stray far from the logic of the internal market to bring ethical interests within the framework of EU law.

This chapter first addresses the elusive character of the consumer. This is helpful in understanding just how plural and fragmented the consumer identity is and in highlighting how the particular image that is constructed of the consumer dictates a particular regulatory strategy. We further see how reductionist it is for EU law to shoehorn its one-dimensional, ideologically driven version of the consumer into its legal framework. We then turn to explore the character of the ethical consumer, before addressing the extent to which EU law may enable their ethical market practices.

II. Who is the Consumer?

The consumer was once a rather neglected figure in legal, political, and even economic discourse. The analytical and regulatory glare traditionally focussed on the 'supply' side of economic relations rather than on the 'demand' side—in other words, on 'producerist' rather than 'consumerist' considerations.[10] But, with deeper understanding of the transformative implications of consumption on society, as well as increasing concern more generally over protection of the more vulnerable, the tenor shifted during the twentieth century.[11] A consumer-oriented discourse emerged, which was to establish the consumer as a separate social and legal category and distinguish them in their role as consumer from that of worker, tenant, voter or family member. With such a modification in the political and collective register, an ever-deepening and broadening set of regulations materialised, aimed at protecting this category of individuals from the weaknesses in the operation of the market. Initially, such consumer protection measures were a national project that went right to the very heart of the design of the welfare state. More recently, however, and as we will see in more detail below, consumer policy has become an intrinsic part of the EU's regulatory project, most specifically as a key component in the realisation of the single market.

However, despite the way that consumption and the consumer have become central to policy formation and the economy in contemporary national and

[10] See J Whitman, 'Consumerism versus Producerism: A Study in Comparative Law' (2007) 117 *Yale Law Journal* 340. Early economists, such as Adam Smith, lamented the lack of economic interest in consumption: 'the interest of the consumer is almost constantly sacrificed to that of the producer and [the mercantile system] seems to consider production, and not consumption, as the ultimate end and object of all industry and commerce': A Smith, *An Inquiry into the Nature and Causes of the Wealth of Nations* (RH Campbell and AS Skinner eds, Oxford, Clarendon Press, 1976).

[11] Neoliberal political and economic ideology, which normalises individualist self-interest and consumerism, can also explain this shift in status from worker to consumer.

European society, the character of the consumer remains rather elusive.[12] One refers to consumption and the consumer in a 'free and casual manner as if the notions are self-evident'[13] and unproblematic, but this is far from being the case. The consumer image is an intellectually[14] and politically unstable one that is easily manipulated and instrumentalised to reflect the political and economic goals of the polity in which the consumer is located. This is particularly evident in the EU where, as we will see, the confident, active and individualist consumer has been tightly harnessed to the reins of the European market-making programme.

Such a characterisation of the consumer is problematic, however. The EU's approach condenses the richness and variety of consumer identities that prevail within its society into a one-dimensional account of a self-interested individual that seeks personal gain from shopping. This may well serve the political and economic interests of the EU in constructing a post-national polity,[15] but it overly simplifies the consumer character. The consumer has an identity that is fragmented and pluralistic—an identity that reflects the multifaceted nature of the individual and the pluralisation of human identity itself.[16] By suggesting that the range of diverse consumer characters can be reduced to one, EU discourse neglects other facets of the consumer, most notably, for the purposes of this chapter, their ethical concerns and, in turn, has undervalued the potential role that the ethical consumer can play in the EU.

This is not to deny, however, that there are dangers in recognising the plural identities of the consumer. Policy formation and regulatory strategy are predicated on the particular image that is held of the consumer.[17] If the consumer image remains 'fractured'[18] and amorphous, the heterogeneous identities are forced to compete and the potential for regulatory coherence is greatly diminished. Moreover, any number of strategies may count as in the 'consumer interest', thereby increasing the likelihood of its capture by interest groups. In assessing the benefits, therefore, of a more flexible, dynamic understanding of the consumer identity one must be careful to acknowledge its possible downsides.

A related observation when exploring the boundaries of the 'consumer' category concerns its all-encompassing nature: after all, we are *all* consumers[19] and

[12] F Trentmann, 'The Modern Genealogy of the Consumer: Meanings, Identities and Political Synapses' in J Brewer and F Trentmann (eds), *Consuming Cultures, Global Perspectives: Historical Trajectories, Transnational Exchanges* (London: Berg Publishers, 2006) 19.

[13] See Trentmann, 'Knowing Consumers…' (n 3) 2.

[14] Y Gabriel and T Lang, *The Unmanageable Consumer: Contemporary Consumption and its Fragmentation* (London, Sage Publishing, 1995) preface.

[15] M Everson, 'Legal Constructions of the Consumer' in Trentmann, *The Making of the Consumer* (n 3) 116.

[16] A Sen, *Identity and Violence—The Illusion of Destiny* (London, Penguin, 2007).

[17] The various images of the consumer entail 'often radically opposed consumer policy aims and underlying political-philosophical or economic constructions of the consumer' (Everson (n 15) 116).

[18] Dani (n 8).

[19] In JF Kennedy's words, '[c]onsumers, by definition, include us all', quoted from Kennedy's Special Address to the Congress on Protecting the Consumer Interest (15 March 1962).

one might wonder whether addressing the consumer as a 'constituency'[20] does not render the category somewhat abstract and meaningless.[21] At one time or another, we all participate in activities that embody those of a 'consumer', but the label reveals little about the identities of those undertaking the acts, the motivations and objectives underpinning the activity, or the nature of the goods or services that are being 'consumed'.[22] It neither tells us why only some acts of consumption are connected to the sense of 'consumer'—'as an identity, audience or category of analysis'.[23] Within the broad category hides a myriad of identities and characteristics which echo our very distinctiveness as individuals. Reducing this diversity to a 'clearly delimitable and organisable complex of individuals'[24] from which public policy can be formulated may appear as overly simplistic and easily susceptible of manipulation.

Of course, there is an obvious need to rise above the individual and to find a collective consumer interest around which regulatory policies can be constructed.[25] But the diversity of interests contained within the category mean that identifying the appropriate collective interest (as well as deciding that there *is* a mass collective interest) is a potent political exercise. The increasing use of identifiers, such as 'vulnerable', 'average', 'empowered', 'rational', 'active', 'passive' and 'ethical', which have become attached to the consumer label, only emphasises the variety of interests that lie hidden within the broad and vague notion of 'consumer' and 'consumer policy'.

A further observation on the notion of consumer is that the term has tended to signify a neutral individual, stripped of any of their distinctive human characteristics and identifiable solely by their activities in the market place: the consumer simply *consumes*. From this perspective, the consumer is constructed, and then entrenched in the dominant discourse, as an abstract, anonymous, undifferentiated character who operates in an equally abstract mass market.[26] Such a visualisation of the consumer highlights the economic agency of the individual—they are reduced to little more than a *homo economicus*—and reinforces the idea of them as purely self-interested actors whose sole motivational impulse is that of

[20] See R Sassatelli, 'Virtue, Responsibility and Consumer Choice: Framing Critical Consumerism' in J Brewer and F Trentmann (eds), *Consuming Cultures, Global Perspectives: Historical Trajectories, Transnational Exchanges* (London, Berg Publishers, 2006) 219.

[21] As Claus Offe puts it, '[e]veryone and at the same time no one is a "consumer"', C Offe, *Contradictions of the Welfare State* (Cambridge, Cambridge University Press, 1984) cited in Trentmann (n 12) 19.

[22] The act of 'consumption' embraces a range of diverse activities including, for example, the purchase of a luxury item such as a computer, or the 'purchase' of necessities such as health care, education, water, gas and postage services.

[23] Trentmann, 'Knowing Consumers…' (n 3) 2.

[24] Trentmann (n 12) 19 citing Offe (n 21).

[25] Everson (n 15) 105–06.

[26] H Rösler, 'The Transformation of Contractual Justice—A Historical and Comparative Account of the Impact of Consumption' in HW Micklitz (ed), *The Many Concepts of Social Justice in European Private Law* (Cheltenham, Edward Elgar, 2011) 332. This can be neatly contrasted with the notion of 'customer' which has a deeper, relational dimension (ibid 332) suggestive of individualisation and a less impersonal market experience. See also Gabriel and Lang (n 14) 7.

acquisition for personal enrichment. They are simply final purchasers of goods for self-gratification.

This disembodied, individualist image of the consumer sits neatly within the framework of neoliberal economics. Within this narrative, the paradigm consumer is a responsible, rational, utility-maximising individual who, by prioritising self-interest, ensures optimal market outcomes. The interests of such a consumer are best served by ensuring competition and unfettered access to the market with a minimum of government regulation. According to this image, consumer protection becomes justified under the principle of correcting 'market failure' and traditionally addressed in accordance with the objective of informational transparency.[27]

III. The European Consumer

This neoliberal image of the self-interested consumer has had particularly powerful traction in the framework of the EU where the image has been harnessed for instrumentalist goals. Although the consumer is attributed with a highly political role in the life of the Union—they are an influential figure in the creation of the internal market—ironically, the achievement of their political role is dependent on individualist, inward-regarding behaviour. It is through their desire to purchase goods and satisfy their inward-regarding preferences that the self-interested consumer participates in the European market and drives the European economy forwards. The individualist consumer is elevated as the crucial linchpin for internal market success and stimulation of the economy.[28]

In order to fulfil this market-making role, the consumer must have an active, dynamic relationship with the market. She must therefore be encouraged to seek purchasing opportunities beyond national frontiers. The 'entrepreneurial' consumer must be confident to cross the physical and virtual borders of national markets if the vision of a single European market is to be a reality. For this purpose, the consumer could not be a passive individual, sheltering in the comfort of their home market. They needed to be revitalised from their national image as a 'passive recipient of interventionist protection'[29] and fashioned as a 'frontier-busting',[30]

[27] For an overview of the EU consumer *acquis* and its evolution from a philosophy of *market transparency* towards one of greater control over the *substance* of the consumer transaction, see Weatherill (n 9) chs 4 and 5.

[28] It is a point which is demonstrated well by Commission, A European Consumer Agenda—Boosting Confidence and Growth COM(2012) 225 final. Under the title of *Consumer Policy as an Essential Contribution to Europe 2020* it states 'consumer expenditure accounts for 56% of EU GDP and is essential to meeting the Europe 2020 objective of smart, inclusive and sustainable growth'. In addition, the EU Consumer Policy Strategy 2007–2013 COM(2007) 99 final, depicts the consumer as the 'lifeblood of the economy' whose choices 'drive innovation and efficiency'.

[29] Everson (n 15) 102.

[30] M Everson and C Joerges, 'Reconfiguring the Politics-Law Relationship in the Integration Project through Conflicts-Law Constitutionalism' (2012) 18 *European Law Journal* 644, 659.

confident individual, eager to sample the variety of products that foreign markets promised. In consequence, national, culturally embedded consumer protection policies were to give way to the 'European common good'[31] of the internal market project.

This image of the consumer was to be reflected in consumer protection legislation that was to be predominantly founded on empowering the consumer and on inspiring trust in the market to ensure maximum participation. As mentioned in the introduction, the EU's consumer protection policy is tightly woven into its internal market programme through the role of Article 114 TFEU as the legal base for consumer protection measures. All legislative measures must satisfy market-making imperatives if they are to be legitimate. Whilst the court has set a low threshold for this requirement to be satisfied,[32] there is nevertheless a legal threshold and it must be respected by EU lawmakers (see discussion in section V below). This has established a restrictive discourse around which consumer 'protection' policy is framed. 'Protection' is assimilated with the simple, if ideologically tainted, idea that competitive, fully functioning markets optimise consumer welfare. From this perspective, one might be sympathetic to the argument that the 'protective' element of EU consumer 'protection' policy has been neglected[33] and consumer protection policy has been transformed to a 'consumer (*market* protection) law'.[34]

In this vein, the key driver of EU consumer policy has been empowering the consumer through the provision of information that would guide their domestic and cross-border consumption: '[e]mpowered and confident consumers can drive forward the European economy'[35] through their activities as cross-border shoppers, and therefore actively break through the frontiers of national markets. The information model has become entrenched in much of the EU consumer *acquis*, most particularly in legislation for the protection of the economic interests of consumers.[36] Whilst there has been some regulatory evolution towards controlling the content of the bargain (thereby embedding a supplementary and more

31 Everson and Joerges (n 30) 660.

32 The much-discussed *Tobacco Advertising* decision of the CJEU (Case C–376/98 *Federal Republic of Germany v European Parliament and Council of the European Union* [2000] ECR I–08419) seemed to suggest a more exacting judicial review of legislative measures enacted under Art 114 (ex Art 95) than has in fact occurred. Subsequent case law has demonstrated that the European Court's scrutiny of a measure is rather shallow and a measure is likely to pass muster if subjected to the court's review. See, eg, C–58/08 *The Queen, on the application of Vodafone Ltd and Others v Secretary of State for Business, Enterprise and Regulatory Reform* [2010] ECR I–4999.

33 H-W Micklitz, 'Do Consumers and Businesses Need a New Architecture of Consumer Law?' *EUI Working Paper LAW* 2012/23, 6.

34 M Hesselink, 'European Contract Law: A Matter of Consumer Protection, Citizenship or Justice?' (2007) 15 *European Review of Private Law* 323, 329. Note the positive evaluation of consumer protection law's position within the internal market by Unberath and Johnston: 'In a Community which is market-driven and which originates in the creation of a free trade zone, consumer protection is bound to be of merely auxiliary nature and to remain a *corollary* to the internal market. There is nothing wrong with that.' H Unberath and A Johnston, 'The Double Headed Approach of the ECJ Concerning Consumer Protection' (2007) 44 *Common Market Law Review* 1237, 1244 (emphasis in the original).

35 COM(2012) 225 final (n 28).

36 We also find the information disclosure technique being employed in legislation other than that which protects consumers' economic interests. For example, Directive 2001/37/EC of the European

interventionist regulatory technique to the legislative *acquis*),[37] as many of the earlier Directives have been revised the information paradigm can be seen to have deepened its hold even further.[38] Thus, whilst the regulatory philosophy and technique that underpins the body of EU consumer legislation is not limited solely to the information model, the technique is nevertheless widely and consistently employed. As such, it echoes neoliberal tenets of private autonomy and enhanced consumer choice, releasing a confident consumer into the internal market.

If consumer policy is to be largely pursued through an information-driven strategy, then faith must be had in a particular vision of the consumer: the consumer must be rational and discerning enough to process and respond to the informational signals that they receive. This echoes with the CJEU's construction of the consumer identity. As is well known, the Court's view of the 'average consumer' is someone who is 'reasonably well-informed and reasonably observant and circumspect'.[39] This image of the consumer is an instrumental one, intended to assist in the integrationist project that was at the heart of the Court's agenda.[40] In its bid to sweep aside a mass of national consumer protection measures and in order to push ahead with the single market the Court needed a consumer that was perfectly able to look after themself in the market without the over-protective (and therefore potentially protectionist) blanket of national regulation.[41] A rational, circumspect consumer that could be sufficiently protected through the provision of information was to be the Court's weapon in breaking down restrictive national barriers to the European market.[42]

Parliament and of the Council of 5 June 2001 on the approximation of the laws, regulations and administrative provisions of the Member States concerning the manufacture, presentation and sale of tobacco products [2001] OJ L194/26 adopts the information model (detailed labelling requirements under Article 5) to pursue health objectives. The EU's GMO regime has also used the information disclosure technique for health and safety concerns (see discussion below).

[37] See, eg, Council Directive 93/13/EEC of 5 April 1993 on unfair terms in consumer contracts [1993] OJ L95/29; Directive 1999/44/EC of the European Parliament and of the Council of 25 May 1999 on certain aspects of the sale of consumer goods and associated guarantees [1999] OJ L171/12 and Directive 2011/83/EU of the European Parliament and of the Council of 25 October 2011 on consumer rights [2011] OJ L304/64. For broader discussion on this regulatory evolution see Weatherill (n 9) chs 4 and 5.

[38] See Micklitz (n 33) 5.

[39] See, Case C–470/93 *Verein gegen Unwesen in Handel und Gewerbe Köln eV v Mars GmbH* [1995] ECR I–1923; Case C–220/98 *Estée Lauder Cosmetics GmbH & Co OHG v Lancaster Group GmbH* [2000] ECR I–117; Case C–210/96 *Gut Springenheide GmbH and Another v Oberkreisdirektor des Kreises Steinfurt-AMT für Lebensmittelüberwachung* [1998] ECR I–04657.

[40] It should be stressed, however, that when the Court has been required to interpret consumer protection legislation, most notably the Directive on Unfair Terms in Consumer Contracts, it has pursued a more 'consumer-friendly' approach and one that follows a far less instrumental vision of the consumer (eg Case C–473/00 *Cofidis SA v Jean-Louis Fredout* [2002] ECR I–10875; Case C–243/08 *Pannon GSM Zrt v Erzsébet Sustikné Győrfi* [2009] ECR I–4713). This has established a distinction between the Court's free movement case law and its case law which interprets the consumer *acquis*. See Unberath and Johnston (n 34).

[41] See discussion in Everson (n 15) 99.

[42] Case C–362/88 *GB-INNO-BM v Confédération du commerce luxembourgeois* [1991] ECR I–667: 'under Community law ... the provision of information to the consumer is considered one of the principal requirements' (para 18).

The construction of the consumer as a confident, active and self-interested individual is understandable in the context of a legal order that must accommodate a number of different consumer protection traditions amongst the Member States. And, the information-led approach for consumer protection policy obviates the need to choose between opposing national constructions of the consumer and their protective needs. Moreover, the information paradigm is less restrictive of free movement than the enactment of substantive provisions.[43] But, in conceiving of the consumer as having such an instrumentalist role, it could be argued that the consumer is discouraged from building solidaristic bonds with the European community in which they operate. Ultimately, a lack of allegiance to the Union will prove problematic since the implication is that EU citizens will be less willing to be bound by EU law.[44] Similarly, concerns arise about the EU's social, or popular legitimacy if the legal order does not reflect citizens' wider values and ideals.[45]

IV. Ethical Consumption

The narrative of the instrumentalised and self-interested consumer has held considerable sway, chiefly because it coalesces so neatly with the internal market goals of the EU and the dominant narrative of neoliberal economics. And so, the idea that consumers may have *outward* regarding preferences has struggled to find a foothold in the European legal discourse. Ethical consumption feels counterintuitive to the individualist ideology of self-interested consumption. As Jo Shaw observes, 'individual moral virtue in the marketplace is an extremely difficult notion to construct, since the primary moral of the market should be to promote rational, self-interested behaviour'.[46]

However, the consumer's relationship with the market is more complex than this one-dimensional account might suggest and the disjuncture between the individualisation of the internal market consumer and the everyday realities of the shopper needs to be explored. Shopping does not always reflect a process of self-gratification, and the neoliberal account of the consumer depicts only one half of the story. Consumers, rational or otherwise, are not simply utility maximisers whose sole motivation is that of individual self-interest. They are vessels of moral and ethical views too and may make transactional choices that reflect a wider spectrum of concerns, including those rooted in ethical, environmental

[43] See G Howells, 'The Potential and Limits of Consumer Empowerment by Information' (2005) 32 *Journal of Law and Society* 351.

[44] Michelle Everson calls for a departure from 'self-interested constructions' as rapidly as possible if allegiance to the Union is to be fostered. M Everson, 'Legacy of the Market Citizen' in J Shaw and G More (eds), *New Legal Dynamics of European Union* (Oxford, Clarendon Press, 1995).

[45] See G Davies, 'Democracy and Legitimacy in the Shadow of Purposive Competence' (2015) 21 *European Law Journal* 2.

[46] J Shaw, 'Citizenship of the Union: Towards Postnational Membership?' (1997) *Jean Monnet Working Papers* No 6/97.

and political values. Goods are *meaningful* and their significance is deeply embedded in a social and political context.[47] So, for example, the ethical consumer may consciously choose to purchase a product, or brand, in preference to an alternative product because it better aligns with their ethical or political views (the buycott). Or, they may refrain from entering a transaction because of the product's negative associations with a particular political, environmental or ethical stance that they hold (the boycott). As intimated in the introduction, the growth in this more reflective aspect of consumerism has been significant.

Much of the discourse on this aspect of consumption has highlighted the more headline-grabbing concerns that may underpin consumer choices. So, a consumer purchase may be influenced by such things as the labour conditions under which the goods have been produced,[48] the environmental impact associated with getting the product to market,[49] animal welfare concerns,[50] whether the production processes have depleted natural resources,[51] whether modern genetic technology has played a part in its development or whether the company adheres to appropriate tax arrangements.[52] In all these instances, purchasing decisions are not based on the physical attributes and functionality of the product, nor the price, but on the *processes* involved in its production and distribution. Consumers may have a 'preference for processes'[53] that influences their market behaviour. These process preferences offer an 'important vehicle through which individuals influence the world, express their views on public issues and fashion their moral identity in an era of extraordinary interconnectedness, complexity and dynamism in the market'.[54]

In more recent years, there has been a vibrant theoretical scholarship on consumption that has highlighted the linkages between consumption and politics and examined the political potential of this 'private' act, thereby releasing the act of consumption from a purely individualist underpinning. Faced with growing dissatisfaction and alienation from the traditional arena in which political expression can be voiced, the market is seen to offer an alternative forum

[47] As Crocker and Linden put it, 'what is consumed is *meaning*'. D Crocker and T Linden, 'Introduction' in D Crocker and T Linden (eds), *Ethics of Consumption: The Good Life, Justice and Global Stewardship* (Lanham, Rowman & Littlefield, 1998) 7.

[48] For example, whether children were involved in any part of the product's manufacturing process; whether the wages throughout the supply chain were appropriate (or 'fair'); whether the workers' conditions were safe and of a decent standard and whether they suffered any coercion or degrading practices. These illustrations of working conditions can be encapsulated by the term 'sweatshop'. This evocative term depicts the whole range of deplorable working conditions under which goods can be produced before arriving at the European and global markets. Eg LKL Tjon Soei Len, 'The Effects of Contracts Beyond Frontiers: A Capabilities Perspective on Externalities and Contract Law in Europe' (PhD thesis, University of Amsterdam, 2013), on file with the author.

[49] eg the extent to which the products embody carbon emissions.

[50] A long-standing concern for consumers has been over matters of animal cruelty, whether this be related to the living conditions of animals, the manner of their slaughter or capture, or the conditions associated with their use for cosmetics or medicine.

[51] This raises concerns over sustainability.

[52] eg, there has been much public consternation over multi-national companies such as Amazon or Starbucks using tax loopholes to avoid paying corporation tax.

[53] Kysar (n 8).

[54] Kysar (n 8) 624.

for the articulation of political and ethical values,[55] meaning that our consumer purchases can be interpreted as market-embedded 'votes'. This process of 'sub-politicisation'[56]—where politics is played out not in the formal political arena but in the market—is said to open up an increasingly effective avenue through which the private experience of shopping can express public oriented views and even effect social and political transformation.[57]

Recognition of the political dimension of consumption has spawned the notion of the 'citizen-consumer' or 'consumer-citizen', a denomination that has emerged relatively recently in the academic literature.[58] This hybrid character is depicted as combining, even collapsing, the attributes of citizenship with those of consumption: consumers begin to 'assess products through the eyes of citizens'[59] and thereby amalgamate their public role of citizenship with their private role of consumer.[60] Consumer-citizenship can be said to reflect a shift away from the 'politics of the self', where consumption is a communicator about the nature of the individual, towards a 'politics of the collective'. The notion is thus capable of reorienting the perception of the consumer: away from one that is solely aligned to principles, of individualism and welfare maximisation, towards one that is linked to the wider concerns of the citizen.

But, the relationship between consumption and citizenship is both 'complex and tantalising',[61] and the linkages between the two are sometimes rather hastily drawn. The citizen and consumer do not necessarily make such easy bedfellows[62]

[55] Haltern observes that the 'consumption of commodities has supplanted the exercise of the traditional political functions of citizenship as the main mode of the construction—and thus control—of personal identity'. U Haltern, 'The Pathos and Patina: The Failure and Promise of Constitutionalism in the European Imagination' (2003) 9 *European Law Journal* 14, 43.

[56] Sassatelli (n 20) 223.

[57] Even the more 'banal', or everyday, acts of consumption can be deeply imbued with political and ethical significance. And the political and ethical nature of the consumptive act can, itself, be a politicisation of the 'everyday' and ordinary. See M Hilton, 'The Banality of Consumption' in K Soper and F Trentmann (eds), *Citizen and Consumption* (Basingstoke, Palgrave Macmillan, 2008).

[58] eg J Davies, *The European Consumer Citizen in Law and Policy* (Basingstoke, Palgrave Macmillan, 2011); M Micheletti, A Follesdal and D Stolle (eds), *Political Products and Markets: Exploring Political Consumerism Past and Present* (London, Transaction, 2009). But, and as mentioned above, this is not a modern phenomenon for even before this recent interest in 'political consumption' individual acts of purchase have had linkages with civic and collective, political goals.

[59] J Peretti (with M Micheletti), 'The Nike Sweatshop Email: Political Consumerism, Internet and Culture Jamming' in Micheletti, Follesdal and Stolle (n 58) 127.

[60] See M Micheletti, *Political Virtue and Shopping: Individuals, Consumerism and Collective Action* (Basingstoke, Palgrave Macmillan, 2003) 16. Lizabeth Cohen speaks of the 'permeability' between economic and political arenas. L Cohen, 'Citizens and Consumers in the United States in the Century of Mass Consumption' in Daunton and Hilton (n 6).

[61] I Ramsay 'Consumer Law, Regulatory Capitalism & the "New Learning" in Regulation' (2006) 28 *Sydney Law Review* 10, 35.

[62] Mark Sagoff, for example, insists on the distinctive social roles of the consumer and citizen: 'As a citizen I am concerned with the public interest, rather than my own interest: with the good of the community rather than the well-being of my own family … in my role as consumer … I concern myself with personal or self regarding wants and interests; I pursue the goals I have as an individual', *The Economy of the Earth: Philosophy, Law and the Environment* (Cambridge, Cambridge University Press, 1988) 8.

and one might draw a note of caution before making too much of the connections between the two. For one thing, it would often be misleading to talk of the consumer as exercising a political 'vote' when shopping: even if one could objectively ascribe political meaning to their purchasing event, they might not have perceived of their action as a politically eventful one and may have acted without any self-reflexive motivations at all.[63]

This observation reinforces just how difficult it is to unravel the complex amalgamation of stimuli that underpin any one individual's act of consumption, a factor which complicates the issue of whether, and to what extent, regulatory strategy should be aligned with ethical consumer preferences as signalled in the marketplace. For example, a consumer may freely make market choices that do not align with their political or ethical view about the products or services they are purchasing. This might be because they have been overcome by the aggressive pricing strategies of powerful business that force their ethical views into a subordinate position in relation to the price of the product. Similarly, the consumer's faith in individual action to achieve collective goals can be fragile—they may feel that their individual contribution will make little difference to wider objectives. As one author puts it, it is common for there to be a 'discrepancy between consumer and citizen revealed preferences' stemming from the consumer's 'knowledge that one's own contribution will have a minuscule effect on the desired outcome and the fear that not enough others will contribute'.[64] None of this is to deny that the consumer *can* find political meaning in the market place. Nor is it to dismiss the idea that there can be significant implications for policymaking if one takes the role of the responsible citizen-consumer seriously.[65] But it is dangerous to read too much into individual acts of consumption and let them be used too readily as a compass or even as a replacement for regulatory policy. In order to give effect to the real aspirations of the citizenry, government responsibility for its citizenry should not be shirked and public regulation that reflects *citizen* values might be more appropriate, even where it appears to conflict with consumer revealed 'preferences'.[66]

But, despite these difficulties, the notion of the citizen-consumer is helpful to our discussion on ethical consumption. It invites reflection on the more expansive, outward, or public-regarding aspect of consumption and forces consumption out of its individualist straightjacket. This is especially important for the EU consumer who, having been wrenched from their natural habitat in the nation state, has

[63] Sassatelli (n 20) 223. Consumers' interaction with the material world is both an unconscious and conscious one, one of 'habit and routine' just as much as one that attempts to fulfil broader social and political objectives, see Hilton (n 57) 92–93.

[64] D Lewinsohn-Zamir, 'Consumer Preferences, Citizen Preferences and the Provision of Public Goods' (1998) 108 *Yale Law Journal* 377, 379 and 392. The author depicts the consumer as having a sense of 'helplessness'. Also, S Henson and G Harper, 'Consumer Concerns About Animal Welfare and the Impact on Food Choice' ec.europa.eu/food/animals/docs/aw_arch_hist_eu_fair_project_en.pdf.

[65] Ramsay (n 61) 35.

[66] See M Lee, *Regulation of GMOs: Law and Decision-Making for a New Technology* (Cheltenham, Edward Elgar, 2008) 225–28.

been subjected to an economic and scientific reconfiguration through EU law.[67] EU law's construction of the consumer as simply an economically rational and scientifically calculable agent is, in effect, an account of the depoliticisation of consumer law.[68] Bringing the idea of the consumer-citizen within the discourse on EU consumer law forces consideration of the political virtues that the market might be able to offer and of the political role that the consumer can play, beyond that of internal market maker. As such, it might have some potential for 'civilising' or 'humanising' the image of the (internal) market. Additionally, revitalising the consumer as a citizen offers one avenue through which EU law might begin to appeal more widely to its citizenry. At a juncture where the future of the EU is deeply contested, where there is scepticism about EU law's legitimacy and voting apathy among its citizens is high, empowerment of the consumer citizen (and, thus, the ethical consumer) might offer one avenue for meaningful political participation and in turn present a more socially legitimate face of the EU.

V. Ethical Consumption and Article 114 TFEU

We have seen that a consumer's interest in a more ethical relationship with the market has been deemed of little relevance to EU consumer protection law. The central character of the atomistic, individualist consumer, as constructed by European law, left little room for the ethically minded citizen-consumer who attenuated their inwardly regarding market behaviour with concern for the wider impact of their purchasing, or who used the market as a means to pursue political objectives. The self-interested consumer, born to neoliberal economic theory, mapped neatly onto the economic goals of the EU and there found a natural home.

If the EU is to capture some of the political potential of consumerism, the ethical consumer needs to be recognised more explicitly as a subject of EU law and policy. References to a 'responsible consumer practice' and the consumer's role in making socially responsible choices and contributing to a sustainable economy are indeed dotted around policy documents.[69] But there seems little real engagement with the ethical consumer figure as a force for social and ethical change. This might seem surprising since the *empowerment* of the consumer is a much-valued objective of European consumer policy, and seems to fit just as easily with ethical forms of consumption as any other. In this vein, the European consumer may be empowered to make ethical choices that can contribute to a more ethically meaningful market.

Implicit to this understanding of empowerment is the provision of information as a tool for the consumer to make rational, informed and ethical choices about

[67] H Schepel, 'The European Brotherhood of Lawyers: The Reinvention of Legal Science in the Making of European Private Law' (2007) 32 *Law and Social Inquiry* 183; Everson and Joerges (n 30).

[68] Everson and Joerges (n 30).

[69] See Davies (n 58) 56 ff.

the market in which they operate. The information model that, as we have seen, underpins EU consumer protection law, can be placed at the disposal of citizen-consumers. If informed choice is to be the leitmotiv of European consumer policy, then providing information about the ethical credentials of the goods can be cast as a measure enabling ethical consumption. Indeed, there is a strong argument in favour of this proposition—for if consumer policy, or at least one of its aspects, is to 'foster consumer reflection on preference, then greater attention might be given to information policies that address such issues as the sourcing of products'.[70] Still further, if consumers are to play an important citizenship role, then one could argue that they have a *right* to information about the ethical credentials of products on the market.[71]

This fits neatly with the consumer protection objectives of the TFEU. As seen above, Article 169(1) TFEU provides that consumers have a right to information. The *kind* of information to which consumers have a right is not further defined, but one would expect that it was a broad and inclusive notion of information that was intended since this would reflect the neoliberal market vision of the EU. Thus, it would appear counterintuitive to this informational model to exclude from its realm information regarding the process and production methods of goods. Unlike the United States,[72] and the approach adopted under international trade rules,[73] the EU has not developed any analytical distinction between 'process preferences' and 'product preferences'.[74] So, information detailing characteristics of the product need not be treated any differently from information informing the consumer about the *processes* though which the goods are produced, thereby signalling to the consumer the social, environmental and economic impact of production.

We can illustrate these arguments by first turning to the 2011 Food Information Regulation.[75] Although the substance of the Regulation is not directly concerned with *ethical* interests of consumers (we might define these interests as the consumer's process preferences), the Regulation nevertheless supports the contention that the information model can be expanded beyond the European paradigm of the self-interested consumer. Article 3 sets out the general objectives of the legislation:

> The provision of food information shall pursue a high level of protection of consumers' health and interests by providing a basis for final consumers to make informed choices … with particular regard to health, economic, environmental, social and ethical considerations.

[70] Ramsay (n 61) 35. See also Kysar (n 8).

[71] COM(2012) final 225 (n 28), para 3.2: 'Consumers have the right to know the environmental impacts throughout the lifecycle of the products (goods and services) they intend to buy'.

[72] See Kysar (n 8).

[73] See, eg, the 'Shrimp/Turtle' case; WTO Appellate Body Report on US Import Prohibition of Certain Shrimp and Shrimp Products, WT/DS58/AB/R (12 October 1998).

[74] See discussion in G Davies, '"Process and Production Method"-based Trade Restrictions in the EU' (2007) 10 *Cambridge Yearbook of European Legal Studies* 69.

[75] Regulation (EU) 1169/2011 of the European Parliament and of the Council of 25 October 2011 on the provision of food information to consumers [2011] OJ L304/8 (Food Information Regulation).

Thus, it is recognised that consumers' ethical beliefs are relevant to the choices that they make about the food they consume and, in turn, it is acknowledged that choices about food are not simply based on individual health concerns but are also about an 'active contribution to a better society'.[76]

It is also helpful to briefly turn to the EU's GMO regime, most particularly the Food and Feed Regulation[77] in which labelling obligations (see discussion below) are mandatory for all products covered by the legislation.[78] Here, the labelling mechanism highlights how the technique of information disclosure is just as valid when concerned with characteristics of production as when concerned with the characteristics of the product itself.[79] Although the relationship between labelling and ethical concerns might be implicit (on the basis that the authorisation procedure for food products containing GMOs has exhausted the safety and environmental protection issues)[80] it is nevertheless affirmed that ethical consumer preferences can be protected within the current framework of EU law.

These two brief examples illustrate how consumer information about process and production methods can be most easily conveyed: a system of labelling. The consumer's right to information in Article 169 can be (and often is) given concrete application in labelling legislation, transforming the consumer right to information into that of informed choice. Labelling is therefore central to our discussion on ethical consumerism. At the national level, labelling has played an important role in moralising the marketplace and allowing consumers to express political and ethical preferences. It has deep historical roots. In the US, for example, during the late 19th century, the 'White Label Campaign'[81] was an anti-sweatshop labelling scheme that was particularly effective in mobilising consumers (this particular campaign appealed primarily to women) behind an appeal to fair working conditions. But, labelling has become far more prevalent in more times and more global in its character. Contemporary labelling schemes are also more institutionalised than their historical counterparts and are often embedded in the activities of established civil society organisations.[82]

Labelling has a long history in the consumer protection discourse of the EU, reaching back to the early CJEU case law concerned with free movement of goods.

[76] D Chalmers, 'Gauging the Cumbersomeness of EU Law' (2009) *Current Legal Problems* 405, 410.

[77] Regulation (EC) 1829/2003 of the European Parliament and of the Council of 22 September 2003 on genetically modified food and feed [2003] OJ L268/2 (GMO Food and Feed Regulation).

[78] In brief, labelling is required for foods which contain or consist of GMOs or which are produced from or contain ingredients produced from GMOs (Art 12(1)).

[79] See further M Lee, *Regulation of GMOs: Law and Decision-Making for a New Technology* (Cheltenham, Edward Elgar Publishing, 2008) 221.

[80] See Opinion of the Group of Advisers on the Ethical Implications of Biotechnology of the European Commission of 5 May 1995 'Ethical aspects of labelling foods derived from modern biotechnology': 'when [foodstuffs] are authorized to be placed on the market they will have already met the required safety standards both for human health and for the environment' (para 1.5).

[81] K Sklar, 'The Consumer's White Label Campaign of the National Consumers' League, 1898–1918' in S Strasser, C McGovern and M Judt (eds), *Getting and Spending: European and American Consumer Societies in the Twentieth Century* (Cambridge, Cambridge University Press, 1998).

[82] Micheletti (n 60) 108.

In the European Court's drive to reduce national barriers to trade, Member States' claims that national regulation was necessary for consumer protection objectives were often given short shrift via the tool of proportionality. Arguments, for example, that German *bier* drinkers needed protection from those (usually imported) beers that did not comply with the sixteenth-century German beer purity laws were countered with the assertion that compulsory labelling 'giving the nature of the product sold' could meet the state's consumer protection concerns perfectly well.[83] German consumers (constructed as 'average consumers') were deemed sufficiently able to make informed decisions about the content of the beer they drank. The German market was subsequently prised open to beers bearing ingredients other than those required by German law.

The Court's reliance on Member State labelling as a strategy to dismantle restrictive national markets meant that labelling was a regulatory area ripe for positive measures of harmonisation. There are a variety of different forms that labelling can take, each of which can politicise products.[84] Leaving aside industry-led initiatives,[85] EU labelling measures, of which there are many,[86] are framed around two basic techniques: mandatory and voluntary labelling. The aforementioned EU Food Information Regulation and the GMO Food and Feed Regulation are two examples of the mandatory form of labelling. The former sets in place a complex system of mandatory food information disclosure relating to such things as the ingredients, nutrition values and country of origin;[87] and, as we have seen, it is premised on ensuring the consumer's right to information and enabling informed consumer choice, including choice associated with ethical considerations.[88] The latter Regulation provides for a system of mandatory labelling of food products containing GMOs and thereby promises to enable consumers to make informed choices as to purchases involving genetically modified products. Whilst the stated objective of consumer choice might be compromised by exceptions to the labelling requirements found within the Regulation itself,[89] at the very least it signals that the EU is willing to engage with labelling as a mechanism for facilitating ethical engagement with the market.

Both of these Regulations have been enacted under the internal market provision of Article 114 TFEU,[90] which brings us to a central issue concerning

[83] Case 178/84 *Commission v Germany* [1987] ECR 1227 (*German Beer Purity*).

[84] Micheletti (n 60) 89–99.

[85] These may be in the form of self-certification, or self-declaration schemes which are designed to highlight certain (sometimes ethical) values in a company's products or services. An example of this form of disclosure tool is the Marine Stewardship Council which uses fishery certification and the ESC ecolabel to indicate that seafood can be traced to sustainable fishery.

[86] Davies has identified some 79 pieces of EU labelling legislation that cover both food and non-food products. See Davies (n 58) 138.

[87] EU Food Information Regulation, Art 9.

[88] GMO Food and Feed Regulation, Recs 3 and 10.

[89] eg Art 12(2), which provides that the labelling obligation does not apply to foods or individual ingredients containing up to 0.9% GM material, provided that the presence of the GM material is 'adventitious' or 'technically unavoidable'. See further Lee (n 79) ch 9.

[90] Art 114 is just one of several competences under which the GMO Food and Feed Regulation is enacted.

the compatibility of ethical labelling with the internal market objectives of the EU: to what extent can and *should* Article 114 play a role in supporting ethical consumerism? More broadly stated, we are concerned with the extent to which Article 114 and the internal market can constitute the ethical, rather than just the self-interested, consumer.

We have already highlighted how the use of Article 114, the harmonising provision of the TFEU, must meet the market-making threshold as established by the Court. As the Court has reminded us, measures referred to in Article 114 (ex Article 95) of the Treaty 'are intended to improve the conditions for the establishment and the functioning of the internal market' and that measures enacted in accordance with this legislative route must genuinely do just that.[91] There must therefore be a connection between harmonisation under Article 114 and the internal market objectives of Article 26.

Labelling measures enacted under Article 114 have all followed a similar pattern of internal market justification, with a close eye it seems (particularly in more recent legislation) on the requirements established by the Court.[92] The assertion made, in almost syllogistic fashion, is that differences between Member States' rules on labelling may hinder free movement, creating conditions of unequal and unfair competition.[93] This renders necessary harmonised rules on labelling. Where the European Court has specifically examined the legitimacy of Article 114 for labelling legislation[94] it has held that where Member States are contemplating the introduction of labelling regimes for a particular product, the legislative divergence across the EU that this would generate is *likely* to cause obstacles to free movement and, as such, is sufficient to justify the use of Article 114 for an EU labelling regime. Once the labelling measure has complied with this market-making threshold, there is nothing to prevent ethical consumer objectives being decisive in determining the *content* of the measure itself.[95] From this, and with the important

[91] eg *Tobacco Advertising* (n 32) para 83.

[92] S Weatherill, 'The Limits of Legislative Harmonization Ten Years after Tobacco Advertising: How the Court's Case Law has become a "Drafting Guide"' (2011) 12 *German Law Journal* 828, 856.

[93] See, eg, Rec 3 of Regulation (EU) 1007/2011 of the European Parliament and the Council of 27 September 2011 on textile fibre names and related labelling and marking of the fibre composition of textile products [2011] OJ L272/1 and Rec 2 of Directive 2000/13/EC of the European Parliament and of the Council of 20 March 2000 on the approximation of the laws of the Member States relating to the labelling, presentation and advertising of foodstuffs [2000] OJ L109/29 (the precursor to the consolidated Food Information Regulation, discussed above). In relation to GMO Food and Feed Regulation (n 77), the claim is that the free movement of safe and wholesome food and feed is an integral aspect of the internal market (Rec 1). Having established the internal market imperatives, the consumer's 'right to information' as promised in Art 169 TFEU is pursued through a labelling scheme which ensures informed choice for the consumer (Rec 17).

[94] For example, a challenge was made to the legitimacy of Art 114 as a legal base for a Directive on the labelling (health warnings and tar yield) of cigarette packets. See Case C–491/01 *The Queen v Secretary of State for Health, ex parte British American Tobacco (Investments) Ltd and Imperial Tobacco Ltd* [2002] ECR I–11543, relating to the challenge to Directive 2001/37/EC (n 36, recently revised March 2014 and adopted under Art 114).

[95] See, eg, *Tobacco Advertising* (n 32) above, where the court accepted that public health could be a decisive factor in the choices to be made by the legislator, provided that the conditions for Article 114 had been fulfilled (para 88).

proviso that labelling can be convincingly framed as a suitable technique for the protection of the ethical consumer interest (see discussion in the next section), we might begin to view Article 114 in a more ethically favourable fashion.

However, this being said, a number of EU ethical labelling measures have been enacted under alternative (non-internal-market) provisions of the Treaty. So, for example, the EU Ecolabel Regulation[96] was enacted under the environmental provision of the Treaty, Article 192, and the Organic Labelling Regulation[97] was enacted under the agriculture provision of the Treaty, Article 43.[98] The consumer's concern for production processes was nevertheless recognised in both of these pieces of legislation.[99]

These labelling devices can be distinguished from the previous examples by their voluntary, rather than mandatory nature, thereby raising different issues as to the legitimacy of Article 114 as a legal basis; it might be difficult to cast voluntary schemes as internal market measures. But, regardless of this, one might wonder whether the regulatory fragmentation of ethical labelling matters or whether there is something normatively attractive about framing ethical consumerism through the lens of Article 114. Conceptually, it is often difficult to say whether the ethical issue is more about the consumer interest or the underlying agricultural or environmental (etc) concern and the flexibility to pursue ethical interests through a range of Treaty powers might be welcomed. Ultimately, it is a difficult exercise to establish where best to pursue ethical interests and the regulatory fragmentation reflects the diversity and diffuseness in consumers' ethical interests. However, the fragmentation makes it difficult to provide a coherent account of ethical consumption and one sacrifices the opportunity to fashion a more human side to internal market policy, which a more consistent use of Article 114 might have allowed.

That consumers and their ethical interests are implicated in and entangled within a range of policy areas is unsurprising. Consumer law, typically conceptualised as the body of law denominated as 'consumer protection law', sits within the broader framework of a legal order which 'encounters' the consumer in a number of different, and often opposing, ways.[100] Thus, there is a broad range of regulatory measures that are inspired and guided by the distinct categories of law from which they have emerged, but nevertheless directly or indirectly implicate

[96] Regulation (EC) 66/2010 of the European Parliament and of the Council of 25 November 2009 on the EU Ecolabel [2010] OJ L27/1.

[97] Council Regulation (EC) No 834/2007 of 28 June 2007 on organic production and labelling of organic products and repealing Regulation (EEC) No 2092/91 [2007] OJ L189/1.

[98] See also Directive 1999/94/EC of the European Parliament and of the Council of 13 December 1999 relating to the availability of consumer information on fuel economy and CO_2 emissions in respect of the marketing of new passenger cars [1999] OJ L12/16, which was also enacted under Art 192.

[99] In the Organic Labelling Regulation, consumers' preferences for products produced using natural substances and processes was explicitly recognised (Rec 1). In the Ecolabel Regulation environmental impact was recognised as a factor for consumer choice (Rec 6).

[100] Everson and Joerges (n 6).

consumers. In this respect, labour law measures, competition law measures, contract law measures and environmental protection measures (to name just a few) each with their distinctive set of regulatory goals, may interact with and implicate the consumer in a variety of ways. Similarly, tracking the interchangeability of notions such as 'citizen', 'individual' and 'consumer' appearing in a string of EU legislative measures[101] highlights the extent to which consumer protection policy, so defined, is often tightly enmeshed with a wide range of public interest policies, such as health, telecommunications or even animal welfare. In a legal order such as the EU, which is so functionally diverse, a shared conceptual framework under which the distinct functional areas can be understood is lacking[102] and the conflict between the different components of the legal order becomes accentuated. Not only does this render 'consumer law' far more complex and its precise boundaries difficult to pinpoint, but it also makes it challenging for law to construct the consumer and their interests in a coherent way.[103] 'Integrated approaches' may be politically desirable[104] but ultimately the context may be too complex and contested[105] and the identity and interests of the consumer too diverse.

VI. Advantages and Limitations of Labelling

Regardless of the legislative base on which labelling measures are enacted, having established that the disclosure of process information fits reasonably well with both the ethical consumer interest and the EU consumer paradigm, deeper examination is merited on the technique of labelling itself.

There are a number of advantages in labelling as a regulatory tool, which might make it favourable as a mechanism for the protection of consumer's ethical interests. First, its non-interventionist nature obviates the need for the regulator to make substantive decisions on what may be highly sensitive areas of policy where a number of competing interests are in play. So, for example, the recently revived debate concerning halal meat (meat from the 'ritual' slaughter of animals) treads

[101] The string of tobacco advertising legislation is a case in point. Directive 89/622/EEC of 13 November 1989 on the approximation of the laws, regulations and administrative provisions of the Member States concerning the labelling of tobacco products [1989] OJ L359/1 mentioned only the health of 'citizens', whereas Directive 98/43/EC of the European Parliament and of the Council of 6 July 1998 on the approximation of the laws, regulations and administrative provisions of the Member States relating to the advertising and sponsorship of tobacco products [1998] OJ L213/9 mentioned the health of 'individuals'. Finally, Directive 2001/37/EC (n 36) brings the 'consumer' into the protective ambit of the Directive, along with the health of the individual, and the 'citizen' is nowhere present. See Davies, *The European Consumer Citizen in Law and Policy* (n 58) 29.

[102] Dani (n 8) 30–31.

[103] Everson (n 15) 106.

[104] DG SANCO, for example, aspires to have a more integrated, systematic framework for EU policies which affect consumer interests, but the reality may prove rather difficult <www.ec.europa.eu/consumers/strategy/integration_en.htm> accessed 2 March 2015.

[105] Everson (n 15) 115.

a contentious path between the interests of religious groups and the interests of those who are concerned about the cruelty aspects of animals killed in this way. Labelling can act as a mediator between the two explosive issues by giving freedom of choice to the consumer who wishes to consume a product because of its halal credentials and to the consumer who actively prefers *not* to buy products that have been produced following these processes. Labelling dissipates much of the heat that would be present in a regulatory context and respects the private autonomy of market players.[106]

This does not mean that a label serves no 'nudge' value to the regulator, since depending on the form of labelling chosen it is possible for labelling to guide consumer behaviour to a greater or lesser extent.[107] So, in the context once again of halal meat, labels could either simply signal to the consumer that the meat is in accordance with halal processes through a recognisable sign, or it could be more descriptive than that, perhaps indicating through a statement that the animal has not been stunned prior to slaughter. This latter form of labelling is more likely to discourage the purchase of these products by consumers who are concerned about animal welfare issues, thereby subtly guiding consumer behaviour towards a particular regulatory objective.

Additionally, labelling might be viewed as an important conduit for bringing consumers closer to production processes and engaging them with global concerns. There is an assumption that ethical consumer practices are contingent on the individual's knowledge and response to the social, environmental and political embeddedness of the goods they are purchasing. It is argued that the impersonal nature of the global market can insulate the consumer from the deeper meaning of the product and the implications of purchasing behaviour.[108] In addition, it is often a monumental task for the consumer to unpick global supply chains in order to determine the product's 'biography'. The global nature of the marketplace, therefore, facilitates consumer ignorance and indifference about the moral and ethical implications of their activities. According to this line of argumentation, therefore, labelling is one way of bringing home to the consumer, at the point of purchase, the external implications of their purchasing event.

Finally, in some instances, labelling ensures that the market opens up an arena in which political values can be (albeit imperfectly) expressed. As Lee observes

[106] S Grundmann, W Kerber and S Weatherill, 'Party Autonomy and the Role of Information in the Internal Market: An Overview' in S Grundmann, W Kerber and S Weatherill (eds), *Party Autonomy and the Role of Information in the Internal Market* (Berlin, Walter de Gruyter, 2001) 36.

[107] Of course, the very existence of a labelling scheme can have 'nudge' value.

[108] It is common to view spatial and temporal distance as a barrier to responsible action by individuals. Global commodity chains are said to exacerbate the problem of 'caring at a distance' and thus the issue becomes how to reconnect the separated moments of production, distribution and consumption. Informational models such as labelling act as a mechanism for 'reconnection'. This view is prevalent amongst the discipline of human geography (see C Barnett and others, 'Consuming Ethics: Articulating the Subjects and Spaces of Ethical Consumption' (2005) 37 *Antipode* 23) and fits well with neoliberal claims about the value of information as a regulatory tool.

in the particular context of GMOs, the debate on the non-safety-related issues of genetically modified food has been virtually silenced and labelling provides at least one avenue through which the citizen consumer voice can be articulated.[109]

Nevertheless, the limitations of labelling are easily exposed and we can illustrate this through a few key examples. First, labelling has been criticised for its 'extra-territorial' effects and viewed with deep suspicion by less developed nations as a threat to their sovereignty. As a consequence, labelling strategies, from the mandatory to industry-led initiatives, have often been vigorously opposed.[110] Important questions as to the conformity of ethical labelling schemes with international trade obligations have also been raised. Mandatory labelling schemes, for example, have been challenged in front of GATT and WTO panels because of their *de facto* trade-restrictive impact.[111] Voluntary labelling schemes do not seem so vulnerable to challenges for WTO incompatibility since they are less trade-restrictive—products that do not conform to the labelling requirements are still able to access the market. Nevertheless, there is significant debate on this matter, both within academic circles[112] and the WTO Committee on Trade and Environment, and the lack of litigation concerning voluntary labelling may simply attest to states' current unwillingness to litigate.[113]

One might also question whether labelling is an effective instrument for pursuing the ethical objectives that it seeks to promote. Consumers may well feel that the purchase of 'sweatshop-free' labelled goods, for example, is alleviating the working conditions of those manufacturing their goods, but there may be unintended detrimental consequences that exacerbate the conditions of those very workers that the scheme is attempting to assist. For example, consumers may be horrified to learn that their 'ethical' purchasing behaviour has forced factory workers into alternative employment, such as prostitution.[114]

Importantly, any assessment of labelling as a mechanism for enabling ethical consumption must take into account the limitations of informational economics. Although the labelling mechanism takes information asymmetries in the market seriously, it does not take enough account of important factors that might impact

[109] Lee (n 79) 164; see also Kysar (n 8) 534.

[110] V Jha and S Zarrilli, 'Eco-Labelling Initiatives as Potential Barriers to Trade: A Viewpoint from Developing Countries' in S Zarrilli and others, *Eco-Labelling and International Trade* (London, Palgrave Macmillan, 1997).

[111] eg, Shrimp/Turtle case (n 73); Appellate Body Report, *United States-Measures Concerning the Importation, Marketing and Sale of Tuna and Tuna Products* WT/DS381/AB/R (16 May 2012). For more detailed discussion, see J Karbowski, 'Grocery Store Activism: A WTO Compliant Means to Incentivize Social Responsibility' (2008) 49 *Virginia Journal of International Law* 727.

[112] See, eg, US academic arguments that voluntary non-GM labelling could create barriers to trade unless accompanied by a disclaimer informing consumers that 'no significant differences as yet have been shown between foods with and without GMOs'. Kysar (n 8) 550, citing P Bentley, 'A Re-Assessment of Article XX, paras (b) and (g) of GATT 1994 in the Light of Growing Consumer and Environmental Concern about Biotechnology' (2000) 24 *Fordham International Law Journal* 107, 128–29.

[113] See Karbowski (n 111) 743–44.

[114] See discussion in Kysar (n 8) 538 and references within.

consumer behaviour.[115] This informational justification for consumer policy is founded on the assumption that the 'average consumer' is a rational individual who is willing and able to read labels and to understand and respond to their implications. The reality is rather different since consumers are not always capable of making rational, informed choices. Their rationality is 'bounded' and behavioural, or cognitive biases may impact on their ability to process and respond to information provided through labelling mechanisms.[116] This has implications not only for labelling's capacity to provide a 'high level of protection of … consumer interests' as promised in EU legislation[117] but also for its ability to act as an effective enabler of ethical market behaviour.[118]

A further significant issue is that concerning the monitoring of claims made on labels. In order for consumers to put trust in this market tool, they need to feel confident that the label makes accurate claims about the process methods under which the goods have been purportedly manufactured. However, it is often difficult to verify whether the goods in question have indeed been produced in compliance with particular processes, particularly where complex global supply chains are involved, or where production takes place in foreign states. Compliance with labour standards, for example, are difficult 'facts' to verify and it is often problematic to rely on auditors to ensure that advertised process standards are met.[119] This limitation applies to the range of labelling schemes, whether mandatory, voluntary or industry-led, although governmental involvement might provide for more effective institutional monitoring mechanisms. A related matter concerns the use of broader terms, such as 'organic' or 'Fair Trade', and the difficulty in consistent, trustworthy interpretations, particularly when multiple schemes emerge, many of which claim to adhere to standards set by their own private codes of conduct.[120]

115 See generally F Rischkowsky and T Döring, 'Consumer Policy in a Market Economy: Considerations from the Perspective of the Economics of Information, the New Institutional Economics as well as Behavioural Economics' (2008) 31 *Journal of Consumer Policy* 285.

116 See Howells (n 43); O Bar-Gill, 'The Behavioral Economics of Consumer Contracts' (2008) 92 *Minnesota Law Review* 749.

117 eg EU Food and Feed Regulation, Art 1.

118 Critics of GMO labelling, for example, argue that consumers are not able to fully understand the health, safety and environmental benefits of the technology and overplay its risks. See K Goldman, 'Labeling of Genetically Modified Foods: Legal and Scientific Issues' (2000) 12 *Georgetown International Environmental Law Review* 717, 760.

119 See discussion in DJ Doorey, 'Who Made That? Influencing Foreign Labour Practices through Reflexive Domestic Disclosure Regulation' (2005) 43 *Osgoode Hall Law Journal* 382, 383. See also R Locke, *The Promise and Limits of Private Power: Promoting Labor Standards in a Global Economy* (Cambridge, Cambridge University Press, 2013), who gives a detailed account of the limited effectiveness of private compliance programmes in the enforcement of labour conditions (esp ch 2). Note should also be made of the financial cost involved in monitoring compliance.

120 C Macmaoláin, 'Ethical Food Labelling: the Role of European Union Freetrade in Facilitating International Fairtrade' (2002) 39 *Common Market Law Review* 295, 310. Furthermore, one might question the *effectiveness* of these schemes. For example, recent doubts have arisen as to whether so-called Fair Trade products do indeed improve the lives of the poorest workers and thus can be legitimately deemed as 'fair'. See media coverage on the low wages paid to 'Fair Trade' employees working on African farms: J Vidal and C Provost, 'Fairtrade accused of failing to deliver benefits to African farmworkers' *The Guardian* (London, 24 May 2014) <www.theguardian.com/global-development/2014/may/24/fairtrade-accused-of-failing-africas-poor> accessed 2 March 2015.

Perhaps a more profound concern over the use of labelling as an ethically oriented tool is how, in harnessing the notion of choice, it renders the consumer's ethical responsibilities wholly voluntary.[121] Unlike citizen responsibilities that are compulsory, the consumer can choose whether to commit to an ethical purchase or, alternatively, whether to opt out. Of course, this is the whole non-interventionist, neoliberal *point* of a labelling scheme. However, it reinforces the individualist framework in which consumption takes place and gives a self-interested spin on ethical consumerism. On the one hand, this might simply reflect the fact that ethical consumption cannot simply be understood as stemming from altruistic 'other-regarding' motivations, but includes 'self-regarding' and self-interested motivations such as identity formation and the 'emotional expression of individuality'.[122] On the other hand, the voluntary, self-interested nature of labelling might be particularly inappropriate where the problems being addressed by labelling (for example, GMOs) are of concern 'species-wide' and therefore beyond the individual.[123] Moreover, through the reliance on voluntary choice, we are left with a 'starkly limited space to encourage the responsibilities and to develop the knowledge of citizenship'.[124]

Finally, ethical labelling can be criticised for its *responsibilisation*[125] of the consumer and its marketisation of politics. Ethical consumption becomes not just voluntary, but ethical issues become the sole responsibility of the individual rather than being a matter for government. Not only does this paint a rather individualist picture of political responsibility, but it also shifts onto the consumer an overwhelming sense of obligation for political change.[126] Whilst labelling might be *one* way of enabling ethical market behaviour, it should not impede a discourse that explores additional, more interventionist mechanisms for dealing with ethical issues both within[127] and beyond the market.

The deficiencies of labelling clearly stack up and it would be wrong to endorse this market tool as a wholly adequate mechanism for empowering the ethical consumer. Nevertheless, despite all of its limitations, ethical labelling does go at least some way in down-streaming information about *processes* and, in that respect, responds to the increasing ethical consciousness of consumers. If European consumers are to operate in the internal market as European citizens, it is vital that they be armed with the information that might assist them in performing this role.

[121] J Johnston, 'The Citizen-Consumer Hybrid: Ideological Tensions and the Case of Whole Foods Market' (2008) 37 *Journal of Theory and Society* 229, 251.

[122] C Barnett, P Cafaro and T Newholm, 'Philosophy and Ethical Consumption' in R Harrison, T Newholm and D Shaw (eds), *The Ethical Consumer* (London, Sage Publications, 2005) 14.

[123] See Lee (n 79) 454–55.

[124] Johnston (n 121) 251.

[125] The notion of responsibility elides important distinctions and includes the individual's causal responsibility for events and their ability to effect actual change. See Barnett, Cafaro and Newholm (n 122) 14.

[126] ibid.

[127] eg trade bans.

VII. Conclusion

This essay has explored the rather neglected character of the European ethical consumer and the extent to which Article 114 TFEU might play a part in shaping and responding to ethical consumption practices. There is little doubt that ethical consumption is an increasingly prominent issue and that many consumers approach the market with an eye on the social, political and ethical implications of their purchases. Exploring this aspect of consumption expands the dominant, one-dimensional image of the European consumer—the self-interested, market-making figure—and forces us to include the image of the European consumer-citizen within EU legal discourse. If the EU is to respond to the concerns and values of its citizens, important questions need to be addressed about the role that the legal order should play in enabling this ethical market behaviour and whether the internal market driven agenda of EU policy making can be recalibrated to incorporate ethical consumer issues.

As we have seen, process and production method labelling emerges as an obvious, even if flawed, technique for enabling ethical consumption and it is a mechanism that fits rather neatly into the market liberalist rhetoric of consumer choice. Moreover, labelling seems compatible with the logic of the EU internal market and thus legitimate under Article 114 TFEU. The use of Article 114 for the pursuit of ethical objectives has the potential to foster debate on the very *nature* of the internal market and the extent to which moral and ethical values can and should play a defining part. For this reason its use for ethical objectives should be further explored.

However, the notion of ethical consumption encapsulates a diffuse range of direct and indirect consumer interests. Whilst the use of Article 114 TFEU might have valuable expressive potential insofar as it signals a less individualistic, perhaps even a more moral internal market, ethical consumerism spreads beyond the internal market and is entangled within other policy areas such as the environment, agriculture, transport and energy, amongst others. It is to be expected, therefore, that ethical consumer issues will remain fragmented amongst a number of policy areas including, but not limited to, the internal market. The extent to which this impacts on the potential of EU law to empower the ethical consumer remains to be seen.

Finally, we have seen that the use of labelling as a mechanism for empowering the ethical consumer is beset with shortcomings. As such, it should not be viewed as an exhaustive method for enabling ethical consumerism in Europe. Wider debate should be initiated, therefore, not only on the normative question as to the role that the EU should have in this policy area but the available mechanisms through which ethical objectives can best be achieved. This may have broader implications since a commitment to enabling ethical consumerism is one way in which the EU institutions can signal to its citizens that it is concerned with more than market integration at all costs. This might prove especially valuable at a time when the EU must work harder than ever to garner popular appeal.

13

Conformity of Goods, the Network Society, and the Ethical Consumer

HUGH COLLINS*

I. Introduction

In the *Manifesto on Social Justice in European Contract Law*,[1] a central argument was that it would be inappropriate in a post-national multi-level Europe in the twenty-first century simply to repeat the nineteenth-century tradition of codification of civil law. Such an agenda, it was suggested, would fail to accommodate how those civil codes had been revised and even marginalised in respect of most common transactions such as sales to consumers and employment, in order to ensure both procedural and substantive standards of fairness. The strong presumption in favour of freedom of contract with respect to the choice of terms no longer seems appropriate outside transactions between businesses, and even in those commercial contexts where small businesses are involved questions about inequality of bargaining power may sometimes be appropriate. The task for a modern code is not simply to refine and articulate the idea of freedom of contract, but to engage in the analysis of social policy with a view to identifying where regulation is needed to correct market imbalances in favour of the weaker party.

Furthermore, it was pointed out in the *Manifesto* that in an age of respect for human rights, as highlighted by the coming into force of the Charter of the Fundamental Rights of the European Union, one could observe many trends towards the constitutionalisation of private law by means of the insertion of fundamental rights into private law.[2] Although no doubt private law in general

* This chapter was previously published under the same title as an article in (2014) 22 *European Review of Private Law* 619.

[1] Study Group on Social Justice in European Private Law, 'Social Justice in European Contract Law: A Manifesto' (2004) 10 *European Law Journal* 653. Hereafter 'Manifesto'.

[2] D Oliver and J Fedtke (eds), *Human Rights and the Private Sphere: A Comparative Study* (London, Routledge, 2007); C Mak, *Fundamental Rights in European Contract Law: A Comparison of the Impact of Fundamental Rights on Contractual Relationships in Germany, the Netherlands, Italy and England*

upholds many of the values and principles contained in human rights documents,[3] modern interpretations and understandings of some rights such as equal treatment and respect for private life have strengthened and expanded their scope of application. For instance, freedom of contract in the sense of freedom to choose a contractual partner has been radically limited by controls against discrimination on grounds of sex, race, nationality, age, disability and sexuality in many kinds of transaction.[4] The principle of equality or equal opportunity is treated as a fundamental principle of EU law,[5] which is incompatible with the more or less unbridled freedom to choose a partner envisaged in nineteenth-century codes. At the time of their enactment, the embracing of formal equality by the civil codes was a radical measure levelled against prior status-based societies, but in the twentieth century a radical restatement of the law would have to abandon formal equality and replace it with a more substantive notion of equality of opportunity.

Adding to these points regarding protection of weaker parties and the growing impact of human rights on contract law, the *Manifesto* asked further whether broader distributive considerations should be influential in the development of modern European law.[6] Should a modern law of contract be concerned not only with the protection of weaker parties to a contract but also others who might be adversely affected by contracts concluded in Europe? Similarly, given that the protection of human rights is a general moral imperative, should a modern law of contract be concerned not only with the protection and vindication of the human rights of parties to contracts concluded in Europe but also the human rights of others adversely affected by such contracts? Following those lines of thought, the *Manifesto* argued, for instance, that 'the Charter [of the Fundamental Rights of the EU] prohibits child labour, which suggests that products made using child labour should not be placed on the market or at least that consumers should have the right to rescind purchases of such products.'[7]

(Groningen, Wolters Kluwer, 2008); S Grundmann (ed), *Constitutional Values and European Contract Law* (Groningen, Kluwer Law International, 2008); G Bruggermeier, AC Ciacchi and G Comande (eds), *Fundamental Rights and Private Law in the European Union—A Comparative Overview*, vol 1 (Cambridge, Cambridge University Press, 2010); OO Cherednychenko, *Fundamental Rights, Contract Law and the Protection of the Weaker Party* (Munich, Sellier, 2007); D Hoffman (ed), *The Impact of the UK Human Rights Act on Private Law* (Cambridge, Cambridge University Press, 2011); C Busch and H Schulte-Nölke (eds), *Fundamental Rights and Private Law* (Munich, Sellier, 2011).

[3] A Barak, 'Constitutional Human Rights and Private Law' in D Friedmann and D Barak-Erez (eds), *Human Rights in Private Law* (Oxford, Hart Publishing, 2001) 13, 21–22; J Smits, 'Private Law and Fundamental Rights: A Sceptical View' in T Barkhuysen and S Lindenbergh (eds), *Constitutionalisation of Private Law* (Leiden, Martinus Nijhoff, 2006) 9; R Stevens, *Torts and Rights* (Oxford, Oxford University Press, 2007).

[4] H Collins, 'The Vanishing Freedom to Choose a Contractual Partner' (2013) 76 *Law and Contemporary Problems* 101.

[5] Case C–555/07 *Seda Kücükdeveci v Swedex GmbH & Co KG* [2010] ECR I–365.

[6] H Collins, 'The Constitutionalisation of European Private Law as a Path to Social Justice?' in H-W Micklitz (ed), *The Many Concepts of Social Justice in European Private Law* (Cheltenham, Edward Elgar, 2011) 133.

[7] Manifesto (n 1) 668.

This novel suggestion could be generalised. A variety of reasons could be invoked in order to impugn the quality of goods marketed in Europe. As well as production systems that involve the use of child labour, the prohibition could extend to goods produced under conditions of forced labour or in violation of other minimum international labour standards such as maximum hours of work or health and safety conditions. The marketability of the goods might also be challenged on the ground that the production process involved unacceptable degrees of environmental damage by causing heavy pollution that is injurious to human health.

The concern about human rights and the environment in these examples is directed toward third parties who are not directly involved in the contract that is being impugned. The violations of human rights or basic labour standards occur up the supply chain during the manufacturing process or perhaps the distribution process. The consumer contract with a retailer does not involve any rules or practices that interfere with the human rights of the parties. The problem of violation of labour standards and rights is rather with respect to other parties who have helped to produce and distribute the product, and who may be several contractual steps removed from the final purchaser of the product. Under traditional contract law doctrine, usually the interests of such third parties or strangers to the contract are not regarded as relevant to the interpretation and enforcement of a contract. The contract usually only creates rights and obligations between the parties, but does not confer benefits or obligations on others. Economic analysis of contracts labels the interests of third parties as 'externalities', because in making their cost/benefit assessment of the attractions of market opportunities the parties will generally not take them into account. Contract law focusses on considerations relevant to the parties to the contract; the task of protection of third parties is left to public regulation. Under theories of the efficiency of markets, parties to contracts should be entitled to focus on their own interests and preferences, a process which permits the invisible hand of the market to guide economic growth. Where the market produces serious adverse effects, these should be remedied, on the traditional view, by public regulation that sets limits on the scope and content of market activities.

This chapter challenges that traditional division of labour between contract law and public regulation with respect to labour rights. The second section examines the new international division of labour in a network society with a view to suggesting that remote suppliers up the supply chain are in fact semi-integrated into a production system in which the hub business organisation should be (and in fact is) held morally responsible for labour standards among the suppliers. The third section explains the inadequacy of current regulatory tools for addressing the problem of poor labour standards in foreign jurisdictions outside Europe. The next section explores how the remedies available to consumers in sales have been transformed in recent years by a switch from focussing on the content of the seller's promise to the expectation of a consumer. That analysis is then applied in the fifth section to the potential for consumers to use the modern European law of sales with respect to defective products in order to address poor labour conditions in the processes of manufacture of products. The conclusion argues that European contract law is on the verge of empowering consumers to regulate through their rights under sales law the labour conditions under which their goods have been produced.

II. The International Division of Labour in Networks

The mobile phone is surely the most successful new consumer product of the last twenty years. In the USA, the market grew from 5 million subscribers in 1990 to 291 million in 2009, resulting in about 93% of Americans having a cell phone.[8] In the United Kingdom, the regulator OFCOM reported in 2012 that 92% of the adult population use a mobile phone and that there are 81.6 million subscriptions, a number which significantly exceeds the total population.[9] The United Nations reported in October 2012 that worldwide there about 6 billion mobile phone users in a total population of less than 7 billion.[10] The portability and multi-functionality of the mobile phone, especially its access to the Internet, increasingly make it appear an indispensable feature of modern life. Many people love their mobile phones and quite a few would be lost (literally) without one. The mobile phone is also emblematic of two defining features of our contemporary world.

First, the mobile phone is increasingly a vital part of the tools of global instantaneous communications. The phone or 'portable communications device' permits us to discover what is going on in almost any part of the world and to respond to developments, whether they comprise political news stories, market fluctuations, or staying in touch with the needs of friends and family. The 'information society' is better understood as a communications society, where the linkages or networks channel our access to others and society as a whole, whether those groups and associations comprise the workplace, a political association, or friends and family. Texts replace personal meetings, emails diminish the number of committees demanding our presence, podcasts substitute for lectures, and access to the internet and the digital commons removes the need to consult books collected in the public spaces of libraries.

Second, the mobile phone is a characteristic product of the modern international division of labour. Instead of the Fordist mode of production, in which goods are conceived, designed, tested, manufactured and then distributed from a single location owned and managed by a single capital unit or firm, now

8 O Bar-Gill, *Seduction by Contract* (Oxford, Oxford University Press, 2012) 185.

9 Independent Regulator and Competition Authority for the UK Communications Industries, 'Facts and Figures' <http://media.ofcom.org.uk/facts> accessed 19 February 2015.

10 'UN: Six billion mobile phone subscriptions in the world' (BBC News, 12 October 2012) <www.bbc.co.uk/news/technology-19925506> accessed 19 February 2015.

sophisticated products are conceived and developed in technologically advanced countries, then manufactured by different companies in the sweatshops of the developing economies, and are finally marketed and distributed globally under a brand name by other companies. Advanced economies in the West prosper through developing a knowledge economy and providing sophisticated services to others, whilst developing economies such as China and south eastern Asian countries aspire to modern versions of the labour-intensive factory production reminiscent of Victorian England. This productive organisation is aptly described as a network of businesses, bound together by contracts rather than ownership and organisation, united by a common purpose to make profits through a product such as a mobile phone, but simultaneously with each business working in its own interests.[11] It is not simply a supply chain, however, because every detail of the product, its production process, and its marketing is organised and managed by the central hub, as in the case of Apple.

In his analysis of the network society, Manuel Castells observes not only how economic networks diminish the vertical integration of production but also reduce the presence of social hierarchies.[12] Individuals are less likely to identify themselves by reference to the organisations to which they belong, whether these associations are a business, a church, a trade union, or a political party, since their links to those organisations are looser than before. Instead of finding our identity through membership of these hierarchical organisations, we become more autonomous individuals, who have greater freedom to create ourselves rather than finding a niche in an organisation. At the same time as we experience greater autonomy, though, we are not isolated from others owing to the omnipresence of communications technology. Through communications networks we learn about the world and other people, what we want, with whom to associate, and where we want to go. Of course, the dominant feature of the Internet is that it is designed to sell us products, so we are likely to conceive ourselves as needy consumers, anxious to achieve material welfare, and through acquisitions in the online market, we hope to find happiness. But the Internet cannot be confined to marketing of products. It also provides us with knowledge about what is going on in the world; both the organised and the informal media of the blogosphere steer us towards (or market) various political viewpoints.

On our mobile phones, therefore, we can discover (indeed it is hard to avoid) information about the latest features on the new model that are made to appear essential for modern living and personal development, but we can also encounter news stories that reveal that the phone was produced under sweatshop conditions in foreign countries by poorly paid workers who toil for long hours under oppressive working conditions. The iPhones that many of us admire and cherish, though

[11] G Teubner, *Networks as Connected Contracts* (Cambridge, Cambridge University Press, 2010).

[12] 'Our societies are increasingly structured around the bipolar opposition of the Net and the Self' (M Castells, *The Rise of the Network Society, The Information Age: Economy, Society and Culture*, vol 1, 2nd edn (Oxford, Blackwell, 2000) 3).

designed and marketed by Apple Corp, are produced in China in factories not owned or managed by Apple,[13] where the working conditions are clearly harsh.[14] In one factory the workers have been required to sign a new contract under which they promise not to commit suicide, though this does not seem to have been effective.[15] This is an intriguing response (together with higher pay, outsourcing of dormitories, and the termination of compensatory payments to bereaved families) to a spate of suicides that appear to be mostly related to the long working hours at the factory, which far exceed the ILO standard of a maximum 48-hour week. Apple has admitted that at least 55 of the 102 factories that produce its goods were ignoring Apple's rule that staff cannot work more than 60 hours a week.[16] Apple has also admitted that its suppliers and assemblers have used child labour in the factories in the past. Apple has also found 24 of its contractors' factories where workers were not even paid China's minimum wage.

Apple is concerned about the labour conditions in the factories run by its contractual partners because consumers appear to include political concerns when exercising their preferences in making purchasing decisions. Large corporations like Apple manage their network by insisting that their partners conform not only to business efficiency requirements such as Total Quality Management (TQM), but also to a code of conduct that is largely concerned with labour standards, though they may also include environmental standards. Such firms may also create associations for branding mechanisms that consumers value such as Fairtrade coffee or compliance with sectoral codes of conduct. The dominant motivation behind such measures is presumably the concern that, if consumers believe that the processes by which the product was produced violate ethical standards, they may boycott a corporation's products in sufficient numbers to affect sales and profits.

Questions need to be posed, of course, about the wisdom of consumer boycotts and other methods for asserting political and ethical views through purchasing decisions. The well-intentioned consumer who avoids products made using child labour, such as cotton clothing from Asia,[17] may discover that the main group who suffer from a consumer boycott are the children themselves, who may be forced to survive by accepting even worse kinds of jobs such as prostitution.[18] Evidence

[13] The principal factories are owned by Foxconn, a Taiwanese company, which is also a supplier for Microsoft and other major IT companies.

[14] 'Beyond Foxconn: Deplorable Working Conditions Characterize Apple's Entire Supply Chain' (*China Labor Watch*, 2012) <www.chinalaborwatch.org/pro/proshow-176.html> accessed 19 February 2015.

[15] N Arnold, 'More Suicides at Foxconn' (*Wall Street CheatSheet*, 19 May 2013) <www.wallstcheatsheet.com/stocks/more-suicides-at-apple-supplier-foxconn.html> accessed 19 February 2015.

[16] Apple publishers annual reports on the conduct of its suppliers: http://www.apple.com/uk/supplierresponsibility/.

[17] 'White Gold—The True Cost Of Cotton' (*YouTube*, 3 April 2007) <www.youtube.com/watch?v=Hntampr_k7M> accessed 19 February 2015.

[18] J Bhagwati, 'Afterword: The Question of Linkage' (2002) 96 *American Journal of International Law* 126, 132.

suggests that it is not boycotts but willingness to pay a higher price for goods that will diminish child labour and probably other harsh working conditions.[19] Nevertheless, we must remain sceptical about the effectiveness of much-hyped corporate codes of conduct and similar measures in upholding minimum labour standards, for even well-intentioned western corporations cannot properly supervise the daily conduct of management in foreign businesses in the context of the 'organised irresponsibility' of business networks. For instance, Apple must rely on its supplier's records and reports of pay to individual workers to determine whether or not the contractors comply with a maximum of 60 hours' work per week, but those records can evidently be easily falsified. The consumer is probably wise not to trust completely the claims of ethical trading issued by global businesses, but equally needs to be circumspect in participating in product boycotts that may back-fire. Although urgent action may be required for proven violations of human rights, it is always worth questioning whether trade bans and boycotts are the appropriate response. Although these dilemmas are serious concerns, in a network society it is unclear what alternatives are available to individuals to have a political influence other than by using the communications network itself and their purchasing decisions.

III. Regulatory Alternatives

Citizens can hope to influence the political process to do something in response to their concerns about the plight of foreign workers. But in reality a national government cannot exercise much influence over foreign business under a different jurisdiction. The United Nations has never empowered the International Labour Organization (ILO) to go beyond the establishment of optional Conventions of Labour Standards that are unenforceable except through moral persuasion.[20] Other techniques could be developed to try to uphold international labour standards,[21] but in the absence of effective international or regional legal regimes (as in the EU), these regulatory strategies seemed destined for ineffectiveness. International law has also maintained a fairly strict separation between the rules facilitating international trade and concerns about labour standards.[22] As a result,

[19] EV Edmonds and N Pavcnik, 'The Effect of Trade Liberalization on Child Labor' (2005) 65 *Journal of International Economics* 401; EV Edmonds and N Pavcnik, 'International Trade and Child Labor: Cross-Country Evidence' (2006) 68 *Journal of International Economics* 115.

[20] B Creighton, 'The Future of Labour Law: Is there a Role for International Labour Standards?' in C Barnard, S Deakin, GS Morris (eds), *The Future of Labour Law* (Oxford, Hart Publishing, 2004).

[21] K Stone, 'Labour and the Global Economy: Four Approaches to Transnational Labor Regulation' (1995) 16 *Michigan Journal of International Law* 987; B Hepple, 'New Approaches to International Regulation' (1997) 26 *Industrial Law Journal* 353.

[22] B Hepple, *Labour Laws and Global Trade* (Oxford, Hart Publishing, 2005).

national governments or the EU will experience great difficulty in justifying bans on products based on the labour conditions under which they were produced.

The GATT rules governing international trade prohibit product regulations that discriminate between 'like products' of domestic and foreign origin.[23] In the *Tuna/Dolphin* dispute,[24] the WTO panel could not accept that tuna was not a 'like product' whether it was caught by line or by nets which also trapped dolphins, so a ban on imported tuna caught by nets was impermissible. The same reasoning that distinguishes between the product and the process by which it was produced should apply to trainers whether manufactured by children or adults: provided the trainers are a 'like product', a state should not be permitted to discriminate against imported products on the ground that they were manufactured by children. It is true that in the subsequent *Shrimp/Turtle* decisions of the WTO appeal panel,[25] it was accepted that environmental and ecological measures might be saved under the separate provision of Article XX of the GATT agreement on the ground that the policy goal was one that sufficiently concerned the importing nation itself and that the regulation satisfied something equivalent to a test of proportionality. Although the US Government could plausibly claim it was concerned about the fate of turtles in its territorial waters, it would be more difficult to satisfy this exception where the policy addressed poor labour standards of workers in foreign countries. The argument would have to be that the exploitation of workers in south-east Asia was directly causing a loss of jobs and a decline in living standards in Western countries rather than simply causing a new international division of labour to the benefit of all concerned. Assuming the failure of such an argument, in the absence of effective political and legal measures available to governments to use trade regulation to secure better labour standards in foreign countries, all that may remain is consumer purchasing decisions as an expressive and symbolic choice, even if that choice proves ineffective, risky, and sometimes counterproductive.

In a network society, where formal political associations are weak and cannot provide leadership, the citizen's vote becomes partly transformed into purchasing decisions guided to some extent by political, social, and cultural considerations. As the US Supreme Court has recognised, a consumer boycott is an aspect of the right to freedom of speech or expression.[26] It can be used to put pressure on both

[23] Art III, 4: 'The products of the territory of any contracting party imported into the territory of any other contracting party shall be accorded treatment no less favourable than that accorded to like products of national origin in respect of all laws, regulations and requirements affecting their internal sale, offering for sale, purchase, transportation, distribution, or use.'

[24] Panel Report, *United States—Restrictions on Imports of Tuna*, DS21/R (3 September 1991) GATT BISD (39th Supp) 155 (1993).

[25] Appellate Body Report, *United States—Import Prohibition of Certain Shrimp and Shrimp Products*, WT/DS58/AB/R (12 October 1998); Appellate Body Report, *United States—Import Prohibition of Certain Shrimp and Shrimp Products*, recourse to Article 21.5 of the DSU by Malaysia, WT/DS58/AB/RW (22 October 2001).

[26] MC Harper, 'The Consumer's Emerging Right to Boycott: *NAACP v Claiborne Hardware* and its Implications for American Labor Law' (1984) 93 *Yale Law Journal* 409, 415: 'A refusal to buy non-union [products] gains significance as self-definition, as well as expression, when that decision is associated with the decisions of others'.

public and private actors to adopt ethical policies with respect to labour standards, human rights, and environmental concerns. The principal way that consumers can exercise these expressive and symbolic choices is through their purchasing decisions.[27] They can choose a coffee shop that uses 'Fairtrade'[28] coffee and pays a fair amount of taxes in preference to others that do not. As Kyser observes with respect to the Fairtrade label, 'the observed demand for process-labelled goods reflects in part the value that individuals place on the ability to express their moral and political views through the medium of conscientious consumption'.[29] When buying their cappuccinos, consumers are not simply quenching their need for froth and caffeine, but they are also exercising 'voice' in the sense that they may be condemning according to their personal ethical values the conduct of other businesses that do not comply with those standards. 'Consumer behaviour, which appears to be focused and directed at the object and at pleasure, in fact responds to quite different objectives: the metaphoric or displaced expression of desire, and the production of a code of social values through the use of differentiating signs.'[30] Even with the many restrictions on freedom of contract today, unlike governments, the consumer retains the freedom to make such discriminatory purchasing decisions, provided, of course, they are willing and able to pay a bit more in order to align their product preferences with their ethical principles. Despite the fact that most consumers are ignorant about the ethical features of products they purchase, studies have shown that, with some prompting from the media about an identifiable problem such as child labour or animal testing with a particular brand, consumers are likely to rate such issues near the top of the attributes of the product which they select.[31] Many consumers want to affirm a personal moral position through their purchases, even if it may not serve their instrumental goal of the reduction of the violation of labour standards or would not survive rational scrutiny under an objective test of proportionality.

These expressive and ethical dimensions of consumer behaviour clearly inform choices between products and provide the main grounds for boycotts. The law protects consumer sovereignty in these respects, even when similar measures by governments would be prohibited. But what about claims made after a purchase of goods? Suppose the consumer acquires a mobile phone, but discovers shortly afterwards that it had almost certainly been manufactured using child labour, indentured labour, or working conditions that violated international labour standards, human rights, and local labour laws? Is there any remedy for the consumer who now feels that their ethical principles have been compromised?

[27] DA Kysar, 'Preferences for Process: The Process/Product Distinction and the Regulation of Consumer Choice' (2004) 118 *Harvard Law Review* 525, 601 ff.

[28] http://www.fairtrade.net/

[29] Kysar (n 27) 604.

[30] J Baudrillard, 'Consumer Society' in M Poster (ed), *Jean Baudrillard: Selected Writings* 2nd edn (Cambridge, Polity Press, 2001) 49.

[31] P Augur, P Burke, TM Devinney and JJ Louviere, 'What Will Consumers Pay for Social Product Features?' (2003) 42 *Journal of Business Ethics* 281.

One possible avenue of redress may be found in the law of fraud or misrepresentation. If the seller of the goods has represented certain facts about the product, such as that the coffee was produced in accordance with 'Fairtrade' standards or that the trainers were made without the employment of children, and if those representations turn out to be false, a court might rescind the contract under the common law for misrepresentation.[32] Although it will not matter under the common law for the purpose of rescission of the contract whether the misrepresentation was deliberate or the result of a mistake by the seller, it will be necessary for the consumer to establish that the false statement was a material inducement to purchase the product, without which the consumer would probably have purchased a different product. A further obstacle to such a claim for misrepresentation might arise if it is not the retail seller who made the misrepresentation, but the manufacturer further up the supply chain, perhaps in its advertisements for the product. If the retailer has not repeated the representation, the consumer cannot rely on misrepresentation to avoid the contract, but must bring a claim against the manufacturer for pure economic loss caused by a negligent misstatement (or deceit), a claim that would almost certainly fail.

In some European legal systems, it may be possible to invoke a general principle of 'good morals' or public policy for the purpose of invalidating the sale.[33] Given that the purpose of the transaction such as the purchase of a mobile phone is not immoral or contrary to public policy in itself, the legal argument must be that somehow the marketing of this product tends to encourage immorality elsewhere, as in the sweatshops of eastern Asia. That argument might work, for instance, in the case of the sale of child pornography which tends to encourage the production of such images, but in that example, unlike the mobile phone, the product itself is also likely to be regarded by the courts as inherently immoral. English law is, however, reluctant to invoke the nebulous grounds of public policy and immorality in the absence of clear statutory authorisation to invalidate particular kinds of contracts. Just as cotton picked by slaves in the southern United States could be marketed in England without questions being raised about the validity of the domestic sales on moral grounds, despite the widespread and official disapproval of slavery in the nineteenth century, so too the marketing of products manufactured under appalling working conditions in south-east Asia is unlikely to raise the eyebrows of the English judiciary.

This chapter examines instead the possibility of a claim through the law of sales. Here the consumer's claim is that the product failed to comply with the implied obligations of the seller to deliver goods in conformity with the contract. The chapter explores the changing ideas about conformity in the context of a network

[32] False labelling may also be an offence under Directive 2005/29/EC of the European Parliament and of the Council of 11 May 2005 concerning unfair business-to-consumer commercial practices in the internal market (Unfair Commercial Practices Directive) [2005] OJ L149/22.

[33] LKL Tjon Soei Len, 'The Effects of Contracts beyond Frontiers: A Capabilities Perspective on Externalities and Contract Law in Europe' (PhD thesis, University of Amsterdam 2013).

society. The central question is whether the distinction between the product itself and the process by which it was made, or, to express the point in a different way, the distinction between the intrinsic and extrinsic characteristics of the product, still governs the notion of conformity. It is argued that it is possible to discern a transition in the concept of conformity of goods from an analysis of the content of the seller's promise to an assessment of the buyer's expectation. Once the expectation of the buyer becomes the guiding thread for conformity, the distinction between the product itself and the process by which it was made becomes less significant, because the buyer's expectations may be addressed both to the functioning of the product and symbolic and expressive qualities that may include the manufacturing process.

IV. Conformity: From Promise to Expectation

In its primary sense, conformity requires a seller to deliver goods that match the description contained in the contract. The goods must be of the quantity, quality, and description required by the express terms of the contract.[34] This standard mirrors the requirement of the general law of contract with regard to terms expressly agreed between the parties. Sales law in many countries differs from general contract law, however, with respect to the remedy afforded to breach of this primary sense of conformity, with many jurisdictions according the buyer the right to reject the goods for minor deviations from the contractual specifications.[35] But there is an important secondary sense of conformity in European legal systems, which originates from the general requirement of good faith in the Roman law of obligations.

The law of sales in most European countries also makes the seller liable for latent defects in the product that would not have been obvious to the buyer. In France, for instance, Article 1641 of the Civil Code provides:

> A seller is bound by a warranty with respect to the latent defects of the goods sold which render them unfit for the use for which they were intended, or which so impair that use that the buyer would not have acquired them, or would only have given a lesser price for them, had he known of them.

Originally, Roman law only made the seller liable for defects actually known to the seller, but by the time of Justinian's Corpus Iuris, strict liability for latent defects was prescribed for all sales. Interestingly, this strict liability appears to have originated in a special law governing the sale of slaves, where the slave-owner might not

[34] eg United Nations Convention on the International Sale of Goods (CISG), Art 35(1): 'The seller must deliver goods which are of the quantity, quality and description required by the contract and which are contained or packaged in the manner required by the contract'.

[35] Sale of Goods Act 1979, s 13.

be aware of certain 'defects' such as the information that the slave was a vagabond, a runaway, or subject to forfeiture for a tort previously committed by the slave (noxal liability).[36] Liability for latent defects in the product itself could be described as a secondary meaning of conformity, since, for instance, if a mobile phone does not connect to a phone service, the defect could be described as one rendering the goods not in conformity with the contract for the sale of a mobile phone. However one classifies the liability for latent defects, the focus of the seller's obligation with respect to latent defects is clearly on the product itself and how it functions rather than on the process by which it was made.

Although not embracing liability for latent defects as such, English common law achieved a similar result through the implied term in sales of goods of merchantable quality,[37] which was subsequently consolidated in the Sale of Goods Act 1893.[38] The seller had to supply goods that satisfied this term unless the seller alerted the buyer to the defect, excluded the warranty, or the defect would have been discoverable by the buyer when they actually inspected the goods. By characterising the seller's obligation as an implied term, the common law presented the obligation as supplementary to or implicit in the general conformity requirement as specified in the express terms of the contract.

The seller's obligations to supply goods that comply with the terms of the contract, correspond to descriptions of the product, and that are free from latent defects constitute the traditional core of the idea of conformity. These obligations can all be linked to the seller's promise in a sale of goods by describing them as express and implied elaborations of the content of the promise. Assuming the seller to be acting in good faith in the sense of honesty, the promise to sell an item such as a horse, a slave, or a mobile phone implies that the goods are free from defects, will function in the ordinary way, and have the features that the seller has described. The emphasis on the seller's promise tends to restrict the notion of conformity of goods to the qualities of the product itself, because the seller is warranting that the goods are worth buying at the price on offer. The seller is not promising that these are the goods that the purchaser really wants or needs or that the goods will help to establish the purchaser's plans or ethical goals.

The first important shift away from the content of the seller's promise towards the expectations of the buyer occurred with respect to notified special purposes of the buyer. If the buyer told the seller the purpose for which the buyer required the goods and relied upon the seller to select suitable goods, subject to any disclaimers, the seller was held to have impliedly promised that the goods were fit for that particular purpose.[39] This exception for notified purposes could at a pinch be

[36] B Nicholas, *An Introduction to Roman Law* (Oxford, Clarendon, 1962) 181.

[37] *James Drummond and Sons v EH Van Ingen & Co* (1887) 12 App Cas 284.

[38] M Bridge, *The Sale of Goods* 2nd edn (Oxford, Oxford University Press, 2009) 417–23.

[39] eg CISG Article 35(2)(b): 'are fit for any particular purpose expressly or impliedly made known to the seller at the time of the conclusion of the contract, except where the circumstances show that the buyer did not rely, or that it was unreasonable for him to rely, on the seller's skill and judgement'.

included as an elaboration of the seller's promise about the quality of the goods, for, having been told about the particular purpose, a seller acting in good faith could be regarded as having impliedly promised to ensure that the goods could serve that particular function. But in my view it is preferable to recognise the importance of the promisee's expectations in determining the conformity standard in such cases, because the goods supplied may not have any intrinsic defects and be fit for all ordinary purposes for which such goods are supplied. It is the buyer's expectation combined with reasonable reliance on the seller that creates the standard of conformity that governs the contract.[40]

A major shift towards the protection of the buyer's expectation rather than the content of the seller's promise occurred in response to the policy to protect consumers. In UK law, the replacement of the standard of merchantable quality with that of 'satisfactory quality' shifted the focus away from the seller's promise and the inherent qualities of the goods to the expectations of the consumer to acquire a product that satisfied her.[41] To meet the standard of satisfactory quality, new goods have to be not only capable of functioning effectively, safely, and for a reasonable period of time, but also perfect in appearance, free from minor defects, blemishes and scratches. The general question posed to the court is whether a reasonable person would regard the goods as satisfactory in all the circumstances. Though presented as an objective standard, the reasonable person is surely to be understood as a reasonable purchaser, for it is the purchaser who has to find the goods satisfactory. The test of conformity contained in the 'satisfactory quality' standard should therefore be understood as focussed on the buyer's expectations about the product.

This shift towards the consumer's expectation became even more decisive with the European Consumer Sales Directive.[42] Article 2(d) defines the criterion of conformity to include:

> [s]how the quality and performance which are normal in goods of the same type and which the consumer can reasonably expect, given the nature of the goods and taking into account any public statements on the specific characteristics of the goods made about them by the seller, the producer or his representative, particularly in advertising or on labelling.

This formulation speaks explicitly about the reasonable expectations of the consumer. Furthermore, it emphasises that such expectations can be increased and manipulated by advertising and labelling. This standard is repeated, though with a clearer formulation that benefits from the work on the Draft Common Frame of

[40] Not every expectation will be protected, for it must be reasonable for the buyer to rely upon the seller to achieve that particular result, which will not be the case where the buyer must also contribute to its achievement (*Jewson Ltd v Boyhan* [2003] EWCA Civ 1030, [2004] 1 Lloyd's Law Rep 505 (CA)) or the functional failure is attributable to a separate cause (*Slater v Finning Ltd* [1977] AC 473 (HL)).

[41] Sale of Goods Act 1979, s 14(2) (as amended).

[42] Directive 1999/44/EC of the European Parliament and of the Council of 25 May 1999 on certain aspects of the sale of consumer goods and associated guarantees [1999] OJ L171/12.

Reference,[43] in the proposed European Regulation on a Common European Sales Law ('CESL'). Article 100 CESL adopts two broad standards with which goods must comply:

(f) possess the qualities and performance capabilities indicated in any pre-contractual statement which forms part of the contract terms by virtue of Article 69;
(g) possess such qualities and performance capabilities as the buyer may expect.

Again the emphasis of the standard of conformity contained in CESL is the expectation of the consumer rather than the express and implicit dimensions of the seller's promise.

V. Expectations of Process

We can now address the question whether the conformity standard in sales to consumers might include the issue of how the goods were produced as opposed to the intrinsic qualities and functions of the goods themselves. If the goods have been produced down the supply chain under labour conditions that verge on forced labour or breach minimum international standards of safety and fair working conditions, does that mean that the goods disappoint the expectations of a consumer? In other words, does the new emphasis on the expectation of the consumer undermine the traditional distinction drawn between the product itself and the process by which it was produced and open up the possibility of consumers rejecting goods or claiming damages for breach of the implied seller's obligations in a contract of sale?

Such a claim is by no means straightforward, even with the transition to the emphasis upon consumer's expectation. The requirement of conformity in CESL (and the Consumer Sales Directive) is still expressed as a quality that the goods must possess, which suggests some kind of intrinsic quality or function of the goods remains the central focus of the enquiry. Even so, it may be possible to interpret the concept of expectation to influence the scope of the idea of a quality of the goods to encompass at least some aspects of the manufacturing process. If a product is claimed to be ethically sourced, free from genetically modified organisms, or manufactured in a carbon-neutral manner, the reasonable expectation of the consumer is that the product will possess those qualities, even though they relate to the process by which it was produced rather than the performance of the product itself.

[43] C von Bar and E Clive (eds), *Principles, Definitions and Model Rules of the European Private Law: Draft Common Frame of Reference (DCFR)*, vol II (Oxford, Oxford University Press, 2010) 1283, Art IV A-2:302.

Bearing in mind those general remarks about the product/process distinction, it is convenient to consider the two arms of the conformity standard applied to consumer sales in turn.[44]

A. Pre-contractual Statements

Both the Consumer Sales Directive and CESL contain the idea that goods should have the qualities ascribed to them in pre-contractual statements made in the course of advertising and publicity documents. The test under CESL Article 69 is whether the trader, manufacturer, or supplier in earlier links of the business chain or network makes a public statement about the characteristics of what is to be supplied. No doubt some of these statements should be ignored as meaningless or mere puff that cannot be relied upon. But claims about the ethical sourcing of products are surely not in that category of mere puff, even if the consumer is bound to be a little sceptical about their veracity. On the other hand, consumers may reasonably judge that statements about a product and its provenance by its manufacturer or owner of the brand name are more likely to be trustworthy than representations made by a retailer who lacks expertise in the qualities of the product. In particular, the consumer may pay considerable attention to the Codes of Conduct that large corporations that manage extensive production networks claim to impose on their suppliers. Apple Corp is a case in point.

Apple publishes and to some extent enforces its Apple Supplier Code of Conduct, which is available for consumers to inspect on the Internet.[45] There are many statements in this document that might be read by a consumer when considering whether to purchase one of their products. It is worth quoting a few sections from the document that demonstrate how the statements concern the process of production in the network of suppliers.

> The Apple Supplier Code of Conduct requires suppliers to provide safe and healthy working conditions, to use fair hiring practices, to treat their workers with dignity and respect, and to adhere to environmentally responsible practices in manufacturing. To that end, the code includes standards in the areas of Labor and Human Rights, Health and Safety, Environmental Impact, and Ethics and Management Commitment.
>
> Apple's Supplier Code of Conduct is based on the standard established by the Electronics Industry Citizenship Coalition (EICC), an organization established in 2004 to promote common codes of conduct for the electronics and information and communications technology industry. The EICC code was developed using internationally recognized standards from the International Labor Organization and the United Nations, among

[44] According to the *DCFR*, ibid, 1297, in some EU systems the seller's liability for statements made by third persons is not restricted to consumer sales (Austria CC, s 922(2); Finland SGA, s 18; Germany CC, s 434(1); Norway and Sweden SGA, s 18(2)).

[45] Apple, 'Supplier Responsibility' <www.apple.com/supplierresponsibility/pdf/Supplier_Code_of_Conduct_V3_1.pdf> accessed 19 February 2015.

> others. The Apple code includes these standards and goes beyond them in the areas of ending involuntary labor practices, eliminating underage labor, and preventing excessive working hours. Apple is the first technology company accepted by the Fair Labor Association (FLA). As a member, Apple will open its supply chain to the FLA's independent auditing team, measuring our performance against the FLA's own Workplace Code of Conduct. We execute an aggressive compliance-monitoring program that includes Apple-led factory audits, corrective action plans, and confirmation that these plans have been carried out. Our goal is to work with every supplier to meet our expectations. When suppliers don't respect the code or they refuse to take corrective actions based on audits, we terminate our relationship with those suppliers.

Apple does seem to have largely eliminated child labour from its main suppliers and assembly plants, but other labour standards are very poor.[46] For instance, with respect to hours of work, the Code states that:

> Working Hours
>
> Except in emergency or unusual situations, a work week shall be restricted to 60 hours, including overtime, and workers shall take at least one day off every seven days. All overtime shall be voluntary. Under no circumstances shall work weeks exceed the maximum permitted under applicable laws and regulations.

According to Apple's own report, it seems that about 90 per cent of weeks worked in the suppliers' and assembly plants have recorded hours for individual workers of less than 60. That leaves about 10 per cent working more than 60 hours per week. We are not told how reliable the record-keeping is in these factories. Apple does not record how many of their suppliers' employees work over the ILO and EU maximum of 48 hours, though presumably it is a large number. There is no report on the effectiveness and levels of compliance with the requirement for overtime being voluntary. Apple does seem to be trying to respond to consumer concerns about labour standards in its factories and those of its suppliers. This improvement has been achieved simply by adverse publicity in the media.

The question being considered here is whether the threat that, in the EU, every purchase of an Apple product might be terminated on the ground of nonconformity under CESL Article 100(f) (or equivalent national provisions that have implemented the Consumer Sales Directive), because it was produced in breach of Apple's own Code of Conduct and its misleading claim that it conforms to ILO standards, would provide an additional incentive for Apple to revise its Code to comply with international standards and to police the conformity of its suppliers with greater assiduity.

The legal question is, first, whether any of these statements can be described as a public statement about the characteristics of what is to be supplied. The difficulty here is that the statement does not directly claim that Apple products are made in

[46] See the report commissioned by Apple but carried out by the Fair Labor Association into working conditions at the major supplier Foxconn: Fair Labor Association, 'Foxconn Investigation Report' (29 March 2012), <www.fairlabor.org/report/foxconn-investigation-report> accessed 19 February 2015.

compliance with the Code of Conduct. This seems to be the aspiration, but is not a clear promise or statement of fact.

Furthermore, and secondly, Article 69 (and the Consumer Sales Directive Article 2(4)) creates an exception when the consumer is aware when the contract is concluded that the statement was incorrect or could not otherwise be relied on as a term of the contract. Here it might be argued that, given the adverse media coverage of sweatshops in China, many consumers who purchase Apple products are well aware that Apple may have some good aspirations but they have been unable to live up to them.

It is therefore far from clear that CESL Article 101(f) (or the equivalent provisions based upon the Consumer Sales Directive) can assist a claim that the goods are non-conforming on the ground that they are produced in violation of Codes of Conduct that ostensibly uphold human rights and require compliance with international labour standards in the supply chain.

B. The Expectation of Quality

It will be recalled that this definition of conforming goods in Article 100(g) requires the goods to possess such qualities and performance capabilities as the buyer might expect. Under the Consumer Sales Directive the goods must 'show the quality and performance which are normal in goods of the same type and which the consumer can reasonably expect'.[47] The questions to be addressed in this context are whether the compliance with international labour standards or local minimum labour standards or some other criteria is a quality that a good may possess and whether a consumer buyer might (reasonably) expect that the good had a quality of that kind.

In answering those questions, there is a recurrence of a version of the product/process distinction that must be addressed. The ideas of a good 'possessing' or 'showing' a quality are not straightforward. In general, people possess things as an aspect of ownership. The idea of goods possessing something seems to be a kind of metaphor that seeks to express the idea of 'belonging to' or, more loosely, 'associated with'. It seems to me possible to say that goods can possess a reputation; after all, that is what a brand name is all about. The iPhone has a great reputation and brand name, much of it no doubt well deserved. If goods can possess a reputation, that reputation might also include a reference to how it was produced down the supply chain. In other words, if the Apple iPhone name stands for, in part, an ethical and legal production process, in substantial compliance with their Code of Conduct, the products could be said to possess the quality of being produced according to good labour standards.

[47] Art 2(2)(d).

If so, then the second question is whether the ordinary consumer (or average consumer) would expect compliance with good labour standards in the production of iPhones. Apple itself seems to concede that consumers have such an expectation on its website:

> At Apple, we care just as much about how our products are made as we do about how they're designed. We know people have very high expectations of us. We have even higher expectations of ourselves.[48]

Again we encounter the difficulty that adverse media publicity might destroy any such expectation. But I suspect that a court would be unwilling to permit Apple (or its retail outlets) to rely on its well-publicised failings to live up to its Code of Conduct as a defence that no consumer should have that expectation. That would be to permit a company to rely upon its own wrong to escape its legal liability.

In short, once the standard of conformity of goods includes a consumer's expectation, the sharp distinction once drawn between the product itself and the process by which it was produced ceases to be determinative of the scope of liability. A consumer's expectations about a product often include not only the functioning of the product but also the processes by which it was produced. In networks, the hub organisation often goes to great lengths to reassure consumers that their expectation of ethical sourcing is met by their branded products. It is therefore possible to argue that the product itself 'possesses' or 'shows' this quality of ethical manufacturing process. If that quality turns out to be missing in the light of better information regarding the manufacturing process, a consumer may be able to argue that their expectation of conformity in this respect has been dashed. It should follow that the normal remedies for breach of the requirement of conformity should be available, including rejection of the goods or compensation for the reduction in value.

VI. Regulating Production Networks

This chapter has sought to question the traditional regulatory strategy with respect to markets and contracts that limits the law of contract to the justice of the arrangements between the parties and relegates the task of concern about externalities to public regulation. It questions the adequacy of that dominant regulatory strategy in the light of the evolution of aspects of a network society. First, it is evident that the international division of labour found in production networks resists any straightforward regulatory solution. A national government cannot regulate labour standards in another country and nor does it seem likely that it will be permitted under GATT rules to ban imports of products on the ground

[48] http://www.apple.com/uk/supplierreseponsibility/

of violations of human rights or labour rights. The alternative of international legal measures such as compliance with ILO conventions offers a possible avenue for challenging exploitative labour practices in foreign jurisdictions, but the ILO remains fundamentally a voluntary organisation without powers of inspection and enforcement.

Some additional pressure can be applied to the hub of a production network like Apple Corp in the country where it is primarily registered as a legal entity. Although the network consists of formally separate legal entities, without responsibility for the conduct of each other, the hub can certainly use its contractual bargaining power to dictate through measures such as TQM how the spoke businesses should be managed. Political or consumer pressure on the hub business can therefore certainly affect how its suppliers treat their employees. Consumers hold the hub business morally responsible for the activities of its network. The question being considered here is whether the law can and should empower consumers to hold the hub organisation responsible and through the law of sales to enforce minimum international labour standards and related human rights instruments.[49].

A second feature of a network society that has been stressed is the role of consumption as an expression of allegiances and values. If that is correct, it can be argued that the value of the product to a consumer is not simply the intrinsic qualities of the product such as how well it functions or satisfies a need, but also its extrinsic qualities such as its original source, its environmental impact, and the labour standards under which it is produced. The ethical issues are therefore part of the price/quality ratio that the law can assess in an analysis of contracts. This essay has explored the possibility of using the quality standard imposed on consumer sales as a vehicle for consumers to exercise political and moral choice with respect to labour conditions in remote locations up the production chain.

If it is correct that product/process distinction no longer holds the dominant position governing the warranty of quality against latent defects and that it is now qualified by the criterion of the reasonable expectation of a consumer, it becomes possible to link the expectation of the consumer to be able to purchase ethically with the warranty in sales. The standard of conformity of goods in CESL (and the Consumer Sales Directive) certainly tries to move in that direction. Article 100 of CESL comes tantalisingly close to achieving a major breakthrough in aligning consumer protection law with human rights law and minimum international labour standards.

[49] H Collins, 'Ascription of Legal Responsibility to Groups in Complex Patterns of Economic Integration' (1990) 53 *Modern Law Review* 731.

14

The Consumer, the Citizen, and the Human Being

GARETH DAVIES

I. Introduction

The Treaty usually requires national measures to be set aside when they hinder cross-border trade in goods and services.[1] Such a policy is not without its risks. Those measures may well have been adopted or maintained for a sensible reason, and even if not may nevertheless serve some useful and legitimate purpose.[2] Setting them aside because of their effect on trade risks causing harm to other interests, effectively subordinating those interests to free movement. For this reason the Treaty requirement is not absolute. Even where a measure is shown to have an obstructive effect on trade it may nevertheless be maintained if it can be shown that it is necessary to protect some other interest, and that there is no less obstructive way of protecting that interest.[3]

The category of interests that may be pleaded in defence of national measures is open-ended. While a few kinds of interest have been excluded as a matter of principle—purely economic reasons, and protectionist or discriminatory reasons[4]—the Court has repeatedly emphasised that, in general, any legitimate public interest objective may be put forward to prevent disapplication of a national

[1] See Arts 34 and 56 TFEU. See generally C Barnard, *The Substantive Law of the EU*, 4th edn (Oxford, Oxford University Press, 2013).

[2] Many of the ideas in this chapter are developed at greater length in G Davies, 'Internal Market Adjudication and the Quality of Life in Europe' *EUI Working Paper LAW* 2014/07, also forthcoming in (2025) 21 *Columbia Journal of European Law*. The distinction between the original purpose and actual consequences of a law is discussed therein at pp 16–18.

[3] Case 120/78 *Rewe-Zentral AG v Bundesmonopolverwaltung für Branntwein* (*Cassis de Dijon*) [1979] ECR 649; Case C–55/94 *Gebhard v Consiglio dell'Ordine degli Avvocati e Procuratori di Milano* [1995] ECR I–4165; N Nic Shuibhne, *The Coherence of Free Movement Law: Constitutional Responsibility and the Court of Justice* (Oxford, Oxford University Press, 2014) 24.

[4] Case 72/83 *Campus Oil Limited and others v Minister for Industry and Energy and others* [1984] ECR 2727; Case C–452/01 *Margarethe Ospelt and Schlössle Weissenberg Familienstiftung* [2003] ECR I–9743.

measure.[5] If, indeed, the measure is found to be necessary for the achievement of this objective, and generally proportionate, then it will be accepted and the consequences for trade will have to be either accepted too or addressed via positive harmonisation.[6]

One might therefore think that mapping the interests which are pleaded, debated, and accepted or rejected in the numerous judgments on the free movement of goods and services would provide a picture of how European societies relate to their economies: how economic and non-economic concerns interact and perhaps conflict, and how they have been balanced within the Member States. An image would emerge of how trade and economic activity fit within the wider values and concerns of Europeans—or at least how the Court thinks they do.

The thesis of this chapter is that such an image does emerge, but it is an alarming one. While free movement affects many aspects of life, the interests which are put forward to balance it are overwhelmingly those specific to the consumer. The wider social consequences of deregulation are rarely suggested as a reason to limit that deregulation. The position which this implies, it will be argued, is that economic interests and social interests are separable, and the law which regulates the interests of the parties to a transaction is not the same law which regulates matters such as quality of life, social cohesion, and equality. That view is not just factually wrong,[7] it is distinctively un-European, and potentially dangerous for the achievements of European societies, which are notable precisely for their commitment to the integration of the social and the economic.[8] Member State governments need to start pleading their cases more thoroughly, showing more awareness of the character of their own states, and the Court needs to start balancing interests as open-mindedly as it claims that it will.

This book is, however, about the image of the consumer: how is she or he portrayed in the law? The answer which the above argument suggests is that the consumer, in the eyes of the Court, is half a human being. As consumer she buys, and is interested to get the best deal, and to have her expectations protected, and the law recognises this. But the same person who shops is also the citizen who collectively enacts or maintains laws which limit economic freedom in the name of social concerns, and is also the human being whose life is shaped by a certain quality of public economic space. Her relationship to economic activity and economic law is multi-facetted, and many things are at stake for her in a decision to regulate or deregulate. These non-transactional matters, however, are ignored in the case law.

[5] See Case C–123/00 *Christina Bellamy and English Shop Wholesale SA* [2001] ECR I–2795.

[6] G Davies, 'Is Mutual Recognition an Alternative to Harmonisation?' in F Ortino and L Bartels (eds), *Regional Trade Agreements and the WTO Legal System* (Oxford, Oxford University Press, 2006).

[7] See, eg, M Granovetter, 'Economic Action and Social Structure: The Problem of Embeddedness' (1985) 91 *American Journal of Sociology* 481; K Polanyi, *The Great Transformation* (Boston, Beacon Press, 1944); G Becker and K Murphy, *Social Economics: Market Behavior In A Social Environment* (Cambridge, Harvard University Press, 2001).

[8] A Picchieri, 'Social Cohesion and Economic Competitiveness: Tools for Analysing the European Model' (2013) 16 *European Journal of Social Theory* 85; C Offe, 'The European Model of "Social" Capitalism: Can It Survive European Integration?' (2003) 11 *Journal of Political Philosophy* 437.

Apparently, as far as the Court is concerned, only her narrowly material interests in the best and fairest deal are worthy of acknowledgment. When she shops, she ceases to be more than a shopper. There is no space for the citizen or the person in the adjudication of economic law. The Court does not look at Europeans as they are, but as a certain vision of the law would like them to be.

II. Interests within the Transaction: Protecting the Consumer

The range of interests which have been acknowledged as justifying restrictions on movement is quite broad. Where trade in goods and services is concerned, the protection of the consumer has been the most prominent, albeit not necessarily the most successful.[9] However, the creation of a more diverse marketplace, by removing restrictions on the type of goods and services that may be sold, exposes the consumer to the risks that she may be confused, her expectations may not be met, that foreign goods may describe themselves in ways that are deceptive, and that the quality of the goods she buys may be disappointing. All but the last of these have been recognised as legitimate concerns.[10] The latter, the question of quality, has been decided by the Court not to be the proper concern of states.[11] Rather than being guaranteed a certain degree of quality by law, consumers should be reasonably circumspect and aware, and seek it out for themselves.[12]

Where services are concerned the question of access has been particularly important. Many rules limiting the type, location, or behaviour of service providers have been justified on the basis that they guarantee a spread of services, ensuring access to these even for consumers who live in undesirable, remote, or otherwise economically marginal locations.[13] The success of such claims before

[9] See D Chalmers, G Davies and G Monti, *EU Law* 3rd edn (Cambridge, Cambridge University Press, 2014) 781.

[10] In principle, at least: *Cassis de Dijon* (n 3); Case C–470/93 *Verein gegen Unwesen in Handel und Gewerbe Köln eV v Mars GmbH* [1995] ECR I–1923; Case C–315/92 *Verband Sozialer Wettbewerb eV v Clinique Laboratoires SNC and Estée Lauder Cosmetics GmbH* [1994] ECR I–317; Case 178/84 *Commission of the European Communities v Federal Republic of Germany* (*German Beer*) [1987] ECR 1227.

[11] Case C–161/09 *Kakavetsos-Fragkopoulos AE Epexergasias kai Emporias Stafidas v Nomarchiaki Aftodioikisi Korinthias* [2011] ECR I–915; Joined Cases C–158/04 and 159/04 *Alfa Vita Vassilopoulos AE and Carrefour Marinopoulos AE v Elliniko Dimosio and Nomarchiaki Aftodioikisi Ioanninon* [2006] ECR I–8135.

[12] See, eg, S Weatherill, *EU Consumer Law and Policy* (Cheltenham, Edward Elgar, 2005); M Radeideh, *Fair Trading and Consumer Choice in the Internal Market* (Groningen, Europa Law Publishing, 2005); H Unberath and A Johnston, 'The Double-Headed Approach of the ECJ Concerning Consumer Protection' (2007) 44 *Common Market Law Review* 1237.

[13] Case C–570/07 *José Manuel Blanco Pérez and María del Pilar Chao Gómez v Consejería de Salud y Servicios Sanitarios* [2010] ECR I–4629; Case C–169/07 *Hartlauer Handelsgesellschaft mbH v Wiener Landesregierung, Oberösterreichische Landesregierung* [2009] ECR I–1721; Joined Cases C–171/07 and C–172/07 *Apothekerkammer des Saarlandes and Others and Helga Neumann-Seiwert v Saarland and Ministerium für Justiz, Gesundheit und Soziales* [2009] ECR I–4171.

the Court has been mixed, but the issue of access, particularly for health-related services such as pharmacies, has been recognised as important.[14]

The word consumer plays a varying role in judgments, but what links all these matters is that they are consumer protection in the sense that they are about protecting the position of people who do, or would like to, enter into specific kinds of transactions. Their right to engage in cross-border transactions (or internal transactions with cross-border parties) is protected by free movement.[15] The acknowledged restrictions on free movement serve to protect their capacity to competently do this—by ensuring information, access, and so on. There is thus no need to envisage free movement and consumer protection derogations in opposition. If one sees the internal market as a project to maximise the capacities of both businesses and consumers to do business with each other across borders,[16] then the right to movement and the right of states to restrict it for consumer protection reasons are simply two girders in the same construction, and if they lean against each other then this is what gives the whole its strength.

III. Interests Outside of the Transaction: The Quality of Life

However, when two parties transact this can have consequences for others, and the transaction, or even its possibility, can also have consequences for the parties involved that go far beyond the terms and fairness of the sale and purchase. If I buy a car, house, or bottle of whisky, then the impact of these purchases on my life and wellbeing, or indeed of those around me, is very poorly captured by looking just at whether the deal was made on fair and transparent terms.

The Court is not blind to externalities. In its case law there are a wide range of interests recognised as potentially limiting free movement, from the traditional externalities such as the environment, public health, or public order,[17] through to vaguer concerns such as the identity of a nation, or its constitutional values, or its commitment to certain ideals, albeit that these latter have been confined until now to citizenship law and have not yet penetrated the economic.[18] Nevertheless,

[14] ibid; see also R Cisotta, 'Limits to Rights to Health Care and the Extent of Member States, Discretion to Decide on the Parameters of their Public Health Policies' in F Benyon (ed), *Services and the EU Citizen* (Oxford, Hart Publishing, 2013).

[15] G Davies, 'Freedom of Contract and the Horizontal Effect of Free Movement Law' in D Leczykiewicz and S Weatherill (eds), *The Involvement of EU Law in Private Law Relationships* (Oxford, Hart Publishing, 2013).

[16] ibid.

[17] See generally Chalmers, Davies and Monti (n 9) ch 20.

[18] Case C–209/08 *Ilonka Sayn-Wittgenstein v Landeshauptmann von Wien* [2010] ECR I–13693; Case C–148/02 *Carlos Garcia Avello v État Belge* [2003] ECR I–11613; Case C–147/03 *Commission v Austria* [2005] ECR I–5969. See also Case 186/87 *Ian William Cowan v Trésor public* [1989] ECR 195, the case on services which in its discussion of the special relationship between citizen and state

even within the law on goods and services there are a number of cases where the impact of free movement on society and its values is, in some sense, addressed. Examples are the gambling cases, in which the Court is relatively respectful of the different attitudes towards gambling found in different states, or *Las*, where the preservation of the national language was claimed (implausibly) to be at issue, or *Omega*, where a service was banned because it offended public moral sensibilities, or *Familiapress*, where press freedom was put forward to balance trade in goods.[19]

Yet there are profound differences—type differences—between the interests acknowledged in these cases and those which this chapter seeks to address. The cases above concern relatively concrete and discrete concerns by contrast with the somewhat slippery and diffuse idea of the quality of life which this chapter will discuss. More to the point, the cases above contained a relatively clear norm which was offended by a specific act, product, or service either inherently—because the product was offensive—or as a result of a chain of consequences reflecting the imperfectness of law and markets, such as where gambling freedom is claimed to raise the risk of criminal activity. There was a particular type of transaction which the state wanted to stop for reasons linked, more or less directly, to the nature of that transaction.

By contrast, this chapter is not concerned with particular goods or services or activities which are 'dangerous' in some sense. The idea here is not that deregulation allows particular ways of making products or providing services which are inherently problematic or inferior, or inherently likely to lead to some other harm. Rather it is the deregulation as such which is the social risk. The societal value of the alcohol standard in *Cassis de Dijon* was not because of the level at which it was fixed, but because it created a standard. There is no serious argument that French cassis was in any way worse than the German, yet the German rule, this chapter will argue, still had a value simply by ensuring that all cassis in Germany was essentially the same. The claim, in essence, is that restriction of economic activity itself is sometimes a valuable thing, almost independently of what the restriction is. The limiting of choice, the enforcing of shared experiences, and the prevention of market-led change can all contribute to quality of life in a legitimate and even orthodox way. Not only are these restrictions thus arguably socially important in ways that should be considered by the law, but the role of the measures as

come closest to addressing the issue discussed here, and which is generally now regarded to have been superseded by citizenship law. See generally L Azoulai, 'The European Court of Justice and the Duty to Respect Sensitive National Interests' in M Dawson, B de Witte and E Muir (eds), *Judicial Activism at the European Court of Justice* (Cheltenham, Edward Elgar, 2013).

[19] Case C–258/08 *Ladbrokes Betting & Gaming Ltd and Ladbrokes International Ltd v Stichting de Nationale Sporttotalisator* [2010] ECR I–4757; Case C–316/07 *Markus Stoß v Land Baden-Württemberg* [2010] ECR I-8609; Case C–390/12 *Proceedings brought by Robert Pfleger and others*, judgment of 30 April 2014; Case C–201/11 *Anton Las v PSA Antwerp NV*, judgment of 13 April 2013 (*Las* was about free movement of workers, but one may assume that analogous reasoning would have been applied in an analagous establishment or services context); Case C–36/02 *Omega Spielhallen- und Automatenaufstellungs-GmbH v Oberbürgermeisterin der Bundesstadt Bonn* [2004] ECR I–9609; Case C–368/95 *Vereinigte Familiapress Zeitungsverlags- und vertriebs GmbH v Heinrich Bauer Verlag* [1997] ECR I–3689.

restrictions (rather than as guarantees of a particular substantive quality norm) is the primary social importance of the measures in question in the goods and services cases discussed here.

The relevance to this argument of the cases such as *Las* and *Omega* is then limited. What these cases show is that the Court is open to derogations, and clearly not determined to push economic freedom at all costs, and in denial of its consequences. However, the cases do not show the Court engaged with the quality of life interests under discussion here, issues which will be called for convenience social interests, because they are about the subjective experience of living and shopping in a society with a more or less deregulated marketplace, and how that experience affects one's subjective sense of one's relationship with other members of that society.

On one view of private law, the absence of these concerns from the case law is quite sensible. Vulgar material or financial externalities may be the proper concern of the regulator, but other than this, transactions are often seen as essentially private matters. Justice between the parties matters, but what the rest of society may think or feel about the transaction does not. There may then be a fierce, even political, debate about the extent to which the regulator should intervene to protect weaker parties to a transaction, but there is, on this view, a consensus that it is primarily the interests of the parties to the transaction that are at stake. The idea that what I buy might be everyone else's business, even if I do them no concrete harm thereby, would be alien to this view.

That view is, however, normative at least as much as it is empirical. That is to say, it represents a moral or political view of how we ought to regard transactions, and whether the majority ought to have any say in what individuals buy and sell. It does not, however, represent a plausible view of the actual consequences of purchase and sale. Which goods and services are and can be bought and sold, and how, is something which affects us all, whether or not we buy and sell them ourselves. Moreover, even if we do buy and sell, we are also affected in ways that the terms of the deal do not begin to address.

Examples may make this clearer. Two kinds of rules will be considered, both of which have played an important role in free movement law. One of these is the national rule which restricts the kinds of goods, or occasionally services, which may be sold, requiring them to conform to certain quality standards. *Cassis de Dijon* is of course the most well-known example in the case law, but there are many.[20] The other kind of rule is the kind which protects a certain kind of service-market structure, and so restricts market access. Such rules may limit the size, location, or legal form of service providers, with the typical consequence that small, traditional and locally rooted businesses are protected from large-scale

[20] *Cassis de Dijon* (n 3); Case C–14/00 *Commission v Italy* [2003] ECR I–513 (Chocolate); Case 407/85 *Drei Glocken GmbH and Gertraud Kritzinger v USL Centro-Sud and Provincia autonoma di Bolzano* [1988] ECR 4233 (Pasta); *German Beer* (n 10); Case C–442/02 *CaixaBank France v Ministère de l'Économie, des Finances et de l'Industrie* [2004] ECR I–8961.

foreign competition.[21] The rules are usually defended as attempts to guarantee universal access or quality of services. Both types of rules are presented to the Court, and apparently viewed by it, as potentially necessary in order to protect the rights and expectations of the consumer within their transaction: to ensure that they are able to buy, and are not deceived or disappointed.[22] However, a moment's thought shows that the measures are at least as important, probably more so, for wider society.

First, the risks posed to the consumer are relatively limited. Where product standards are concerned they risk, at most, disappointment. Perhaps the product will not be as good as they are used to or had hoped. They may, of course, not notice this, or may consider that the difference was worth the cost saving. However, if they are disappointed then presumably next time they will buy a different product. Since most consumer purchases are relatively small scale, and since serious risks concerning health or safety are addressed entirely differently by the law and not threatened by free movement, the stakes are pretty low.[23] Similarly, the claims that large foreign businesses will concentrate their activities in population centres to the detriment of those in remote areas, or that too much competition will lead to reduced quality or even reduced supply of services, may well be true to some extent, but the risks are largely hypothesised by the pleading states rather than proven, and the fact that such rules have been litigated to the greatest extent in largely protected national markets provides reason for a degree of scepticism as to the extent of the threat.

By contrast, the social consequences of these rules are quite significant. It does not require much experience of different countries to realise that strict regulation of public economic life creates a different quality of society than does a laissez-faire approach.[24] Being in the marketplace in a state where product standards are ubiquitous and economic activity is confined to certain spaces is a different experience from being in the marketplace of a state where the size, location, and character of sellers, and the things that they sell, are largely determined by market forces. But the public economic space of a state is a large part of the life of those who live there: it is the streets, the town centres, the places where people work and travel and meet. How economic activity is regulated is part of the quality of life.[25]

[21] See cases cited at (n 13); Joined Cases C–94/04 and C–202/04 *Federico Cipolla v Rosaria Fazari, née Portolese and Stefano Macrino and Claudia Capoparte v Roberto Meloni* [2006] ECR I–11421; Case C–565/08 *Commission v Italy* [2011] ECR I–2101; Joined Cases C–357/10 and C–359/10 *Duomo Gpa Srl v Comune di Baranzate*, judgment of 10 May 2012; Case C–217/09 *Maurizio Polisseni v Azienda Sanitaria Locale nº 14 VCO and Antonio Giuliano* [2010] ECR I–175; Case C–539/11 *Ottica New Line di Accardi Vincenzo v Commune di Campobello di Mazara*, judgment of 26 September 2013; Case C–140/03 *Commission v Greece* [2005] ECR I–3177; Case C–531/06 *Commission v Italy* [2009] ECR I–4103.

[22] See Davies (n 2) 13–16.

[23] See Chalmers, Davies and Monti (n 9) 781.

[24] Nevertheless, see citations at nn 7 and 8.

[25] JQ Whitman, 'Consumerism versus Producerism: A Study in Comparative Law' (2007) 117 *Yale Law Journal* 340; A Bagchi, 'The Political Economy of Regulating Contract' (2014) 62 *American Journal of Comparative Law* 687.

IV. The Policy of Limiting Market Freedom

More concretely, product standards may reasonably be argued to contribute to social cohesion and equality, and to collective values and identity, and to protect from choice, and to be a rational part of a policy for economic development. Protecting small businesses may reasonably be argued to be part of a policy protecting social interactions and quality of life, and deliberately subordinating consumption to social cohesion.

To expand: product standards reduce the range of goods available, often dramatically, with the consequence that all in the market place, or indeed society, consume the same, or at least more similar, goods. Product standards have traditionally been particularly ubiquitous where foodstuffs are concerned, with the consequence that the degree to which the rich and the poor taste the same food and drink is likely to be increased.[26] It is contestable whether this is a contribution to equality: since standards tend to increase cost, standards may impose the greatest financial burden precisely on the poor who, in a deregulated society, would have access to a wider range of cheap junk and be able to consume more. However, another point of view is that creating shared experiences is a way of linking members of society, and making them less unequal.[27] It is also arguably a way of linking them with their past, and with their nation: foodstuffs are often highly traditional, and part of the way a society describes itself. Protecting them, and their unique place, is protecting that identity. It is not necessarily enough that a certain traditional product be available (if the market so desires). It is the fact that everyone eats and drinks it, just as they have always done, which makes it a contribution to social policy.

Product standards also protect us from choice. Consumer choice is often presented as a good thing, and it is certainly the case that many consumers in many contexts may welcome increased choice, and be frustrated by lack of it. Yet most consumers in some contexts will also welcome its limitation.[28] Particularly where decisions do not matter, because the differences between goods or services are largely trivial, standardisation can be a valuable contribution to quality of life: essentially the state acting as our personal assistant, taking the decisions for us that would be no more than an irritation if we had to take them ourselves.[29] In the

[26] See Case 286/86 *Ministère public v Gérard Deserbais* [1988] ECR 4907; Case 788/79 *Gilli and Andres* [1980] ECR 2071; Case C–12/00 *Commission v Spain (Spanish Chocolate)* [2003] ECR I–459; *Commission v Italy* (n 20); *Drei Glocken* (n 20); Case C–314/89 *Siegfried Rauh v Hauptzollamt Nürnberg-Fürth* [1991] ECR I–1647; Case 178/84 *German Beer* (n 10); Case C–184/96 *Commission v France* [1998] ECR I–6197 (Foie gras); *Cassis de Dijon* (n 3). See also Joined Cases C–158/04 and C–159/04 *Alfa Vita v Elliniko Dimosio and Nomarchiaki Aftodioikisi Ioanninon* [2006] ECR I–8135.

[27] See Davies (n 2) 9.

[28] G Low, 'The Psychology of Choice of Laws' (2013) 24 *European Business Law Review* 363, 367; B Schwartz, *The Paradox of Choice: Why More Is Less* (New York, Harper, 2004).

[29] ibid. See also T Veblen, *A Theory of the Leisure Class* (London, Macmillan, 1899).

purchasing of utilities, insurance, telephony, wine, most consumers will welcome a limitation of choice, a set of guarantees of certain minimum standards rather than an infinite variety, with the associated infinite complexity.

There are certainly reasons to maximise choice, by contrast: it extends the possibilities for competition, and that may lead to increased efficiency and ultimately wealth. Maximising choice is then not about helping the consumer but all about burdening the consumer with a responsibility because the exercise of that responsibility is believed to contribute to the general good. It is decentralisation of economic policy, and brings with it the decentralisation of decision costs too. This is defensible policy. But so is the alternative, limiting choice, even if this has the consequence of reducing total wealth in order to protect the consumer's quality of life.

Finally, while some may believe that all policy should lie in the hands of the market, almost all states continue to try and steer their societies and their populations, and in particular they try to stimulate activities which they think will contribute to general wellbeing: certain kinds of education, innovation, and industry are supported, for example, while others, less immediately valuable, are left alone.[30] So does the EU follow this path, with infrastructure, social and innovation policies which are explicitly aimed at managing social and economic development, rather than just leaving them to market chance?

It may be that the most innovative state is one which innovates everywhere. It may also be that limiting innovation in certain areas pushes creativity into others. Restricting retail may dull the creative sensibilities of the population, or it may push creativity into other activities, from manufacturing to policymaking. The fact that the states most committed to retail freedom are also those least committed to manufacturing suggests that managing retail freedom can be seen as a form of industrial policy.[31]

Turning to services, and rules which protect small businesses, at the price of market access for others, the economic inefficiency of these is obvious. They create the high prices and slow service which one can enjoy on high streets in many Southern European states. Yet not everyone seems to dislike these high streets—many object to their replacement by modern large-scale commerce. Is it perhaps because in those small boutiques people spend time talking, and know each other, and because the shopping street becomes an intimate and friendly place? This is certainly the subjective experience of many, and then it seems hardly strange that at least some communities might collectively decide that such pleasures are worth paying for: that they are willing to pay the price associated with loyalty to their tiny shops, in return for the style of life it allows them to enjoy.

[30] See W Streeck, 'German Capitalism: Does it Exist? Can it Survive?' (1997) 2 *New Political Economy* 237.

[31] ibid. See also W Streeck, 'Beneficial Constraints: On the Economic Limits of Rational Voluntarism' in JR Hollingsworth and R Boyer (eds), *Contemporary Capitalism: The Embeddedness of Institutions* (Cambridge, Cambridge University Press, 1997); J Beckert, *Beyond The Market: The Social Foundations of Economic Efficiency* (Princeton, Princeton University Press, 2002).

Of course, on all these questions one can take many stands. A national choice to deregulate can be as principled and as socially and morally engaged as a choice to restrict.[32] Freedom, opportunity, diversity, and change may also be valued and desired. However, it seems clear that social interests are at stake in regulating the marketplace, so that what is allowed affects the consumer not just as consumer, but also as citizen and human being, and affects also the other consumers, citizens, and human beings who live in the society which her transactions help to shape.[33] Moreover, it seems clear that multiple positions on the regulatory spectrum are defensible, depending on how much particular communities value and feel the need to extend or protect certain things: wealth, profit, freedom, diversity, equality, time, togetherness, and the texture of public life.

V. The Consumer, the Citizen, and the Human Being

When free movement law is used to set aside a national rule of one of these kinds there are therefore (at least) three kinds of interest at stake. First, there are the interests of the parties to the transaction and, in particular, of the more vulnerable party, usually the consumer. Second, there are the interests of those who live in that society, who may enjoy certain styles of life and believe in certain social values, which are protected by the law. Third, there is the democratic interest of citizens of that society, who have made conscious choices or acquiesced in established rules with the consequences that a certain kind of society is created and certain kinds of values are preserved. Their ability to make collective choices expressing their distinctive preferences is also under threat.[34]

Typically, the same person is affected by all these and is concerned by them all. This may lead to behaviour which, while not inconsistent, expresses the tensions between the interests: I may vote for a certain law, or enjoy the quality of life created by a certain kind of regulation, but nevertheless seek to profit from its absence if it is set aside. I would rather not choose, but if I have to then I will behave like the model consumer of old-fashioned economists, seeking my material self-interest ruthlessly, if sadly or perhaps with irritation.

This is not to say that the consumer and society are necessarily at odds. As the literature on *Cassis de Dijon*, and on free movement generally, displays, there is no

[32] See H Dittmar, 'Material and Consumer Identities' in SJ Schwartz, K Luyckx and VL Vignoles (eds), *Handbook of Identity Theory and Research* (Heidelberg, Springer, 2011); S Timmermans and S Epstein, 'A World of Standards But Not a Standard World: Towards a Sociology of Standards and Standardization' (2010) 36 *Annual Review of Sociology* 69.

[33] Whitman (n 25); Bagchi (n 25).

[34] C Sunstein, 'On the Expressive Function of Law' (1995) 144 *University of Pennsylvania Law Review* 2021; W van der Burg, 'The Expressive and Communicative Functions of Law, Especially With Regard to Moral Issues' (2001) 20 *Law and Philosophy* 31.

consensus on what is in the interests of the consumer or of society.[35] These are matters which depend on one's normative vision of the place of the individual in society, of individual responsibility, and collective protection, as well as on more empirical matters such as how we are psychologically affected by choice, loss, and shared experience. They are, in short, political choices, and the allocation of rights and freedoms to citizens, human beings, and consumers, is an essentially political process in which some may see necessary links between certain preferences but others may see them as quite separable. None of the three interests is either a proxy for, nor in necessary opposition to, the others. Precisely for this reason, any Court that claims to take account of all the interests at stake in free movement should consider them all.

VI. The Transactional Fixation of the Case Law

Yet the Court of Justice does not. Its case law is rich in consideration of transactional concerns, while social and democratic ones are absent. The social interests at stake in the free movement of goods and services have never been named or weighed, let alone allowed to prevail.[36]

There is only one possible legal defence of this absence, and while it is tempting, it fails. That is the argument that the Treaty entails that states must pay the price of openness because they have chosen to commit to it. To try and resist movement on the social grounds discussed above is just to try and escape Treaty obligations.

The first problem with this is that it applies equally to consumer protection: it provides no reason why one class of interests should be privileged over others. The second, very similar, problem is that it begs the question of what the Treaty prohibitions mean. How should free movement be understood? The Court has, quite reasonably, found that they should not be understood in the most absolute terms possible, but as prohibiting rules which obstruct movement beyond the extent justified by other legitimate interests.[37] This provides an explicit doctrinal obligation to consider the social interests concerned and makes it all the more mysterious that this does not occur.

[35] See for some small indication of the range of debate concerning free movement and society: H Schepel, 'Constitutionalising the Market, Marketising the Constitution, and to Tell the Difference: On the Horizontal Application of the Free Movement Provisions in EU Law' (2012) 18 *European Law Journal* 177; I Lianos, 'Shifting Narratives in the European Internal Market: Efficient Restrictions of Trade and the Nature of Economic Integration' (2010) 21 *European Business Law Review* 705; A Somek, *Individualism: An Essay on the Authority of the European Union* (New York, Oxford University Press, 2008); Azoulai (n 18); G Majone, *Rethinking the Union of Europe Post-Crisis: Has Integration Gone Too Far?* (Cambridge, Cambridge University Press, 2014); M Dani, 'Rehabilitating Social Conflicts in European Public Law' (2012) 18 *European Law Journal* 621.

[36] See for more discussion, Davies (n 2) 13–16.

[37] Shuibhne (n 3).

The reasons for the absence, which have been discussed elsewhere, are probably several, and the gaps in the judgments are more convincingly understood as the product of a mix of practical, procedural, and doctrinal accidents rather than of any coherent judicial political agenda.[38] Nevertheless, for the purposes of this chapter it is necessary to ask what message is sent by the selective focus on consumer interests at the expense of the social, and what vision of Europe, and of its consumers, the Court invites us to share.

VII. Images of Europe in the Goods and Services Case Law

One way of making sense of the judgment texts is as a statement that social interests simply do not matter. Consumer rights do, but the vague concerns with equality and identity and quality of life which have been discussed above are too trivial, or even immoral, to deserve recognition. That message may certainly be drawn by some, who will then understand the internal market as a project of subordinating the social to the financial, the human to the material, the qualitative to the merely countable, the profoundly important to the tiresomely shallow. Those familiar with the EU may tend to disagree, and to regret such over-simplistic views of what it does, but it cannot be denied that the Court, in its case law on goods and services, is doing its bit to feed these fears.

Another way of reading the judgments is less as a rejection of the social than as a message that the social and the economic are two separate regulatory domains. One can perhaps believe in equality, social cohesion, and the value of traditions and identity, yet also believe that they should be addressed by their own laws and not within the sphere of free movement. Perhaps those in Luxembourg are sympathetic to the view that free movement law should concentrate on keeping trade free and fair, while the relations between those living in society should be addressed elsewhere. The separation of the spheres, as Walzer would have it, may be pursued by judicial decree.[39]

There is something of Chicago economics in this, an echo of the idea that the market should be left free to make the biggest pie possible, and then the state should decide separately how to distribute the pieces.[40] The problem is that, as anyone who has ever made a pie knows, much of the pleasure is in eating it while it is being made. Separating the economic and the social may—or may not—help maximise the total amount of pie in the world but it has nothing to do with making the world a more contented place.

[38] Davies (n 2) 15–22.
[39] M Walzer, *Spheres of Justice* (New York, Basic Books, 1983).
[40] R Bork, *The Antitrust Paradox* (New York, Basic Books, 1978) 82.

The problem with reading the judgments in this way is not, however, that it turns them into bad policy, for policy is always contestable, and it can be a noble exercise for a Court to loyally execute the poor judgment of the legislator. The problem is rather that it is legally inappropriate, both on a narrow view of law and a broad one. Narrowly, the problem is one of doctrinal incoherence: the Court has said it will and must take account of all interests, and so it should do so.[41] If it takes the view that social cohesion should be addressed elsewhere then, on its own doctrine, the proper reasoning is to concede that this may be threatened by regulation, but to express the faith that it can be adequately protected by other means—rather as it does with consumer protection issues in fact.[42] Simple silence makes no sense.

Alternatively, if one sees the Court primarily as a motor of integration, properly more committed to the goals of the Union than to textual niceties, then the problem of silence on the question of social interests is that it is un-European: it is a betrayal of one of the most distinctive hard-earned, and prized achievements of European societies.[43] Like no other countries in the world many European states have struggled to reconcile the social and the economic, and to integrate them rather than push them apart.[44] What makes many European states stand out, from a regulatory point of view, is that economic actors play an important role in social policy, and that social policy is constructed in a way that is integrated with the economy: businesses pay for those who cannot work, but those who cannot work are helped to retrain, for example. The search, in European politics, is always for synergies between the state, society and the economy, not for distance. That the regulation of products, services, and service providers should take account of the broader effects on quality and style of life is precisely what one would expect of a European state and, indeed, for those who value the social market structures of Europe could be seen as an aspect of one of Europe's greatest post-war achievements.

To then deny the need for such integrated policy, in an unspoken parody of old Chicago economics, is to see the Union as a break with the achievements of its states, as a market which should not be social. This would be a very distinctive and controversial understanding of the terms of the contract of the Member States, and not one that would sit very comfortably with the Treaty texts in which that contract is contained. Indeed, while no-one could accuse the Treaties of being determinative of the law, they provide more obvious support for the view that, in EU law, the economic is social and the social economic: integration is the buzzword, not separation.[45]

[41] *Bellamy* (n 5).
[42] See Chalmers, Davies and Monti (n 9) and cases cited at n 10.
[43] See citations at n 8.
[44] ibid.
[45] See Arts 7–13 TFEU.

VIII. Images of the Consumer in the Court's Regulatory Dream

If this is the Union, who then is its consumer? Clearly she is not a European, but more than that, she is, as the Court portrays her, half a person. The Court implies, with its exclusion of the social, that she should seek to separate her consumption from her membership of society and should see herself, when she is in the market, as just a consumer. Her citizenship, indeed her humanity, are matters for the agora or the home, but not for the market. This is a sad and foolish view of the world, but the risk for Europe lies not in the fact that it may persuade, for it will not, but in the chance that it may condition and form: normative assertions lightly disguised as factual ones, such as the Court's claims about when the reasonably circumspect consumer will or will not be confused or deceived, can become self-fulfilling.[46] Consumers are forced to behave as the Court would like them to, in their own interests, and so they gradually do become the consumers that the Court claimed they were. That can be seen as a triumph of law and policy, or simply as a display of brute judicial force. Europeans do not want social interests to be ignored, but if the law does that for long enough they will have to find other ways of creating togetherness, or living without it. In time the Court's implicit claim that social interests do not belong in economic law will become accepted, and even, once Europeans no longer expect or remember or want a European quality of life, perhaps true.

[46] See cases cited at n 10.

15

The Image of the Consumer in EU Trade Mark Law

GRAEME B DINWOODIE AND DEV S GANGJEE*

I. Introduction

Scholars working in the field of consumer law have commented on the 'pluriform' nature of the 'average consumer' in EU law.[1] And that observation rests in part upon analysis of trade mark law, among other areas of law which the 'average consumer' inhabits. In fact, there is a variable concept of the consumer *within* EU trade mark law and this chapter sets itself the task of mapping these variations. We suggest that for structural reasons EU trade mark law may be compelled to work with a differentiated concept of the consumer that varies depending upon whether courts are assessing the validity of rights or their infringement, and by reference to the national or European nature of the marks at issue.

Despite these variations, we argue that most efforts by courts to identify or construct consumers and the marketplace they inhabit are blended exercises that are part-empirical and part-normative. Explicitly recognising this blend and identifying the mechanisms by which a consumer-based assessment is informed by empirical evidence or framed by normative considerations will, we believe, enable a richer debate about the role played by the consumer in EU trade mark law. It also allows us to explore whether EU trade mark law ought—either to achieve its own objectives or to contribute to the broader European project—to adopt an approach to the consumer that is more empirically or normatively grounded.

* We are grateful to Marianne Madden (NYU JD Class of 2016) for excellent research assistance, and to Barton Beebe, Lionel Bently, Colin Birss, Jennifer Davis, Rochelle Dreyfuss, Annette Kur, Vanessa Mak, Ansgar Ohly, Luis Porangaba, Martin Senftleben and Kathy Strandburg, as well as participants in the Engleberg Centre Workshop at New York University School of Law, for comments on prior drafts. Thanks also to Dorota Leczykiewicz and Steve Weatherill for editorial suggestions. The views expressed are, however, attributable only to us (as are any errors that remain).

[1] See V Mak, 'Standards of Protection: In Search of the "Average Consumer" of EU Law in the Proposal for a Consumer Rights Directive' (2011) 19 *European Review of Private Law* 25, 30.

Our analysis also prompts consideration of whether different national courts are (despite different methodological traditions that survive European harmonisation) converging on a common approach to the 'trade mark consumer', and raises for debate the extent to which harmonised EU trade mark law is beginning to (further) subsume aspects of the allied regimes of passing off and unfair competition law supposedly reserved for Member States.

Section II of the chapter sets out the structure of EU trade mark law as established by two pieces of secondary legislation, one Directive and one Regulation, a quarter of a century ago. Section III investigates the principal doctrinal contexts in which the consumer appears. Although the average consumer is often presumed to be a stable constant, the structural bifurcation of EU trade mark law and the different contexts in which this consumer surfaces accounts for the conceptual variation that we describe. Finally, in section IV we step into largely uncharted territory, considering the extent to which these different conceptions of the consumer in EU trade mark law currently do (or ideally should) reflect empirical or normative assessments. Underlying these varied inquiries is a fundamental set of questions, relating to the characterisation of this consumer construct and its functions. For example, in any given legal setting, is the consumer construct normatively 'loaded', perhaps implementing policy preferences by being predisposed to or resistant to being confused through the use of legal presumptions? To what extent can empirical evidence be accommodated—to offset such legal presumptions, or to further flesh out the construct, or to pursue a more real-world assessment? Alternatively, to what extent is this trade mark law consumer an unreflexive, formalistic construct, imported from EU free movement or consumer law but left underdeveloped in significant ways and thus failing to reflect the distinct normative basis of trade mark law? Developing responses to these questions matters, because the consumer construct is at the core of trade mark law both normatively and doctrinally.

Despite the centrality of the consumer to EU trade mark law, there has been little scholarly effort to articulate precisely his or her characteristics, beyond rehashing abstract principles.[2] An emerging judicial consensus (at least in the UK) now suggests that the average consumer is a normative legal fiction whose reactions are not to be determined by mere statistical analysis (that is, the behaviour of a mean, median or mode consumer). But that assertion does not tell us how the content of that fiction is to be determined, nor does it foreclose a role for empirical evidence of marketplace realities. In the concluding part of the chapter, we offer a preliminary sketch of how these questions might be disentangled and usefully approached.

[2] The most notable exception has been Jennifer Davis, who has authored two important assessments. See J Davis, 'Locating the Average Consumer: His Judicial Origins, Intellectual Influences and Current Role in European Trade Mark Law' [2005] *Intellectual Property Quarterly* 183; J Davis, 'Revisiting the Average Consumer: An Uncertain Presence in Trade Mark Law' [2015] *Intellectual Property Quarterly* 15.

II. The Structure of EU Trade Mark Law

The initial treatment of trade mark law by the Court of Justice of the EU ('CJEU') arose in cases adjudicated under primary EU law, mostly involving claims that assertions of national trade mark rights served to impede the free movement of goods within the EU.[3] From the earliest days of the European Communities, however, efforts have been under way to address trade marks in secondary legislation.[4] These efforts came to fruition with the adoption of two instruments: the Trade Mark Directive and the Community Trade Mark Regulation.[5]

The Trade Mark Directive purported to be a limited harmonisation of national registered trade mark laws of the Member States.[6] It expressly did not harmonise protection of unregistered marks under allied regimes such as passing off or unfair competition.[7] However, it is increasingly apparent that the harmonisation

[3] See, eg, Joined cases 56 and 58/64 *Établissements Consten S.à.R.L. and Grundig-Verkaufs-GmbH v Commission* [1966] ECR 299.

[4] See, eg, Commission, Memorandum on the Creation of an EEC Trade Mark SEC(76) 2462 final.

[5] See Directive 2008/95/EC of the European Parliament and of the Council of 22 October 2008 to approximate the laws of the Member States relating to trade marks [2008] OJ L299/25 (Trade Mark Directive), consolidating and replacing Council Directive 89/104/EEC of 21 December 1988 to approximate the laws of the Member States relating to trade marks [1990] OJ L40/1 (original Trade Mark Directive); Council Regulation (EC) 207/2009 of 26 February 2009 on the Community trade mark [2009] OJ L78/1 (Trade Mark Regulation), replacing Council Regulation (EC) 40/94 of 20 December 1993 on the Community trade mark [1994] OJ L11/1. The two instruments were designed in tandem, and their status as an integrated 'package' is evident again from the current legislative revision process. See Max Planck Institute for Intellectual Property and Competition Law, 'Study on the Overall Functioning of the European Trade Mark System' (Munich, 15 February 2011) (Max Planck Study); Commission, Proposal for a Regulation of the European Parliament and of the Council amending Council Regulation (EC) No 207/2009 on the Community trade mark COM(2013) 161 final (Proposed Regulation); Commission, Proposal for a Directive of the European Parliament and of the Council to approximate the laws of the Member States relating to trade marks COM(2013) 162 final (Proposed Directive).

[6] Rec 3 of the original Trade Mark Directive (now Rec 4 of the consolidated Trade Mark Directive) stated that it was not necessary to undertake 'full-scale approximation'. Rather, the Directive claimed to tackle only those national provisions most directly affecting the functioning of the internal market.

[7] See Trade Mark Directive, Recs 5 and 7. Some aspects of national unfair competition laws might, however, be pre-empted by other bodies of EU law that regulate unfair trading such as Directive 2005/29/EC of the European Parliament and of the Council of 11 May 2005 concerning unfair business-to-consumer commercial practices in the internal market (Unfair Commercial Practices Directive) [2005] OJ L149/22. See A Ohly, 'Interfaces Between Trade Mark Protection and Unfair Competition Law: Confusion About Confusion and Misconceptions About Misappropriation?' in N Lee, G Westkamp, A Kur and A Ohly (eds), *Intellectual Property, Unfair Competition and Publicity: Convergences and Development* (Cheltenham, Edward Elgar Publishing, 2014) 58–59 (discussing the possible restriction of Member State autonomy to hold search engines liable for the sale of keyword advertising under unfair competition law, while noting that the CJEU implicitly rejected part of this argument in Joined cases C–236 to 238/08 *Google France SARL v Louis Vuitton Malletier SA* [2010] ECR I–2417). And immunity conferred under Directive 2000/31/EC of the European Parliament and of the Council of 8 June 2000 on certain legal aspects of information society services, in particular electronic commerce, in the Internal Market [2000] OJ L178/1 (E-Commerce Directive) also effects some harmonisation of the scope of possible unfair competition liability. See GB Dinwoodie, 'Secondary Liability for Online Trademark Infringement: The International Landscape' (2014) 37 *Columbia Journal of Law and the Arts* 463, 486.

was in fact close to maximum harmonisation, imposing both floors and ceilings on the extent of protection that Member States could provide under national law. The Court of Justice has given very little scope to those areas where the Directive appeared explicitly to reserve discretion to Member States.[8] And its reading of the Directive has arguably intruded on matters that might have been thought to be questions of unfair competition.[9] As a result, the Directive has begun to mimic a uniform law, and the pending legislative reform of the Directive would take this process even further, making many optional provisions mandatory.[10]

The Directive thus effected substantial convergence in the legal norms applicable throughout the Member States. However, under the Directive, both the rights-conferring and enforcement authorities remained national in nature; the Directive simply harmonised national trade mark laws, but did nothing to disrupt the territorial character of national trade mark rights that had long presented obstacles to the free movement of goods.[11] This explains the necessity for the Community Trade Mark Regulation that created an industrial property title, the Community Trade Mark ('CTM'), which confers EU-wide protection. It is granted by a dedicated EU agency, the Office for Harmonisation in the Internal Market (trade marks and designs) ('OHIM'), based in Alicante.[12] The substantive conditions on which the CTM is granted and the scope of protection it receives parallel (with minor modifications related to geography that will be discussed below) the provisions that the Directive imposes on national offices and national courts with respect to national trade marks.[13]

The principal feature of the CTM was its unitary character. Thus, Article 1(2) of the Trade Mark Regulation provides that:

> A Community trade mark shall have a unitary character. It shall have equal effect throughout the Community: it shall not be registered, transferred or surrendered or be the subject of a decision revoking the rights of the proprietor or declaring it invalid, nor

[8] See GB Dinwoodie, 'The Europeanisation of Trade Mark Law' in A Ohly and J Pila (eds), *The Europeanisation of Intellectual Property Law* (Oxford, Oxford University Press, 2013) 81–83; cf *Oracle America Inc v M-Tech Data Ltd* [2012] UKSC 27, [2012] 4 All ER 338 [12] (Lord Sumption) (suggesting that the 'efficacy [of the Trade Mark Directive] as a harmonising measure uniformly applicable across the whole of the EU depends on treating it as an exhaustive statement of the rights of trade mark proprietors'); see generally S Weatherill, 'Consumer Policy' in P Craig and G de Búrca (eds), *The Evolution of EU Law* 2nd edn (New York, Oxford University Press, 2011) 850–51 (discussing minimum and maximum harmonisation in the context of consumer protection rules).

[9] See GB Dinwoodie, 'Dilution as Unfair Competition: European Echoes' in RC Dreyfuss and JC Ginsburg (eds), *Intellectual Property at the Edge: The Contested Contours of IP* (Cambridge, Cambridge University Press, 2014) 90–92.

[10] See, eg, Proposed Directive, Arts 5(3) and 10(2)(c).

[11] Trade Mark Regulation, Rec 4: '[t]he barrier of territoriality of the rights conferred on proprietors of trade marks by the laws of the Member States cannot be removed by approximation of laws'.

[12] Thankfully, the Proposed Regulation would rename the OHIM. For present purposes, think of it as the EU Trade Mark Office.

[13] The Trade Mark Regulation also had to address procedural matters (which were not tackled in the Trade Mark Directive) and had to make decisions on provisions that were left optional for Member States in the Directive. See Dinwoodie (n 8) 87.

shall its use be prohibited, save in respect of the whole Community. This principle shall apply unless otherwise provided in this Regulation.

That is to say, a CTM is valid for the entire EU, or not at all. So goods bearing a valid CTM can (with few exceptions) freely move throughout the EU without fear of a conflicting national right.[14] Consequently, the 'footprint' of the CTM is impressive: a unitary right to be relied upon by the 500 million residents of the EU, with all the accompanying variations in income, age, education, locations (urban or rural), languages and national cultural contexts that this entails.[15]

If the unitary character of the CTM was *its* defining feature, the intention underlying the package of reforms *as a whole* was to ensure coexistence between the national regimes and the EU-level CTM regime.[16] Thus, the EU legislature recognised that certain businesses of a more local nature would not wish protection for the entire EU and thus should not be compelled to incur the costs of such an application. Moreover, where the business operates in only one or two Member States, protection across the EU via a CTM would clutter trade mark registers throughout Europe.[17] Such 'deadwood' (as US courts call unused marks) would effectively limit the marks that could be used by other producers, even if they were only seeking national protection.[18] The proliferation of 'earlier' marks makes it harder for producers to select and clear marks with certainty that they are not intruding on the rights of others. Finally, given that trade marks are (unlike patents or copyrights) potentially perpetual, a large number of earlier national trade mark rights were in existence in 1996 when the first CTMs were issued. Any of these existing national marks could have priority over applications for CTMs.[19] With so many potential obstacles to CTM registration, national registrations in those Member States where no conflicting mark existed were an important fall-back. Thus, whether for reasons of minimising applicant costs, public interest in an uncluttered register, or practical necessity derived from existing rights, the national systems would have to continue even after the creation of the CTM.

[14] With the expansion of the EU since 1994, first from 15 to 25 and now to 28 Member States, transitional provisions have blurred this principle at the edges. See Trade Mark Regulation, Art 165(5).

[15] European Commission, Eurostat and Directorate-General for Health and Consumers, *Consumers in Europe* (Luxembourg, Office for Official Publications of the European Communities, 2009).

[16] See Max Planck Study (n 5) 45, para 1.1 ('One of the core elements in European trade mark law is the principle of coexistence. Rec 6 in the preamble to the [Regulation] voices this principle by stating that the Community trade mark law does not replace the law of the Member States on trade marks and that national trade marks continue to be necessary for those undertakings which do not want protection of their trade marks at Community level').

[17] See G von Graevenitz and others, *Trade Mark Cluttering: An Exploratory Report* (2012/11, UK Intellectual Property Office, 19 April 2012); G von Graevenitz and others, *Cluttering and Non-Use of Trade marks in Europe* (2015/48, UK Intellectual property office, August 2015).

[18] Prior CTMs are earlier rights for the purpose of determining priority under all national regimes in the EU. See Trade Mark Directive, Art 4(2)(a)(i).

[19] Under the Regulation, prior conflicting rights may consist of a number of different earlier rights: applications or registrations for CTMs, applications or registrations in a Member State of the EU or the Benelux, international registrations having effect in an EU Member State, marks that are well known in an EU Member State, and even unregistered marks or other signs that are of more than mere local significance (provided that the law of the Member State governing such mark or sign grants its proprietor the right to prohibit the use of a subsequent mark). See Trade Mark Regulation, Arts 8 and 42.

After years of debate,[20] the principle of coexistence was understood to require broadly similar substantive provisions in the Directive and Regulation.[21] As the *substantive* provisions in the Directive and Regulation are largely the same, we will address below the role which the consumer plays in trade mark law with respect to both instruments, noting the important points of divergence. However, the overall structure of the system we have described in this section means that EU trade mark law encompasses a consumer concept that operates on two entirely different planes—at the national level and at the unitary or pan-European level. Along with the theoretical complexity we outline below, this difference in market scales helps to explain some of the variations in the concept of the consumer in trade mark law.

III. The Consumer in EU Trade Mark Law

The consumer is ubiquitous in trade mark law. This ubiquity takes two forms. First, the protection of the consumer is a universal justification for trade mark law as a whole.[22] Second, even where trade mark protection is justified on other terms (such as protecting producer goodwill or investments in reputation), consumer interests still play an epistemic role when deciding discrete legal issues. For example, where third parties make unauthorised use of a sign that is the same as or

[20] At different stages in the legislative process, different solutions were contemplated. For example, if the rights secured by the CTM were far easier to acquire and conferred far more extensive protection, applicants would be incentivised to pursue the CTM. See A Sattler, 'Dilution of Well-Known Trademarks—An Analysis of its Foundations in Germany and The European Union' (2011) 3 *Zeitschrift für Geistiges Eigentum / Intellectual Property Journal* 304, 320. A shift to EU-wide marks would enhance the free movement of goods, as well as facilitate the expansion of national businesses to EU-wide enterprises that is one of the other stated objectives of the unitary right. See Trade Mark Regulation, recs 2, 4; but see GG Howells, 'The Rise of European Consumer Law—Whither National Consumer Law?' (2006) 28 *Sydney Law Review* 63, 67: 'in reality consumers' willingness to shop overseas is likely to have less to do with their substantive rights and be more connected to convenience, language and practical questions of complaining about faulty goods and services and access to justice'. Instead novel mechanisms were introduced to encourage applicants with existing national rights to apply for the parallel CTM without imperilling the priority of their national protection, see Trade Mark Regulation, Arts 34–35 (seniority), and to ensure that applicants unsuccessful in securing a CTM because of a prior right (or other problem) in a particular Member State could convert their CTM to a bundle of national applications in the other Member States without loss of priority based on their CTM filing date. See Trade Mark Regulation, Arts 112–14 (conversion).

[21] Nevertheless, there are advantages in applying for the CTM, such as the greater territorial scope of protection, the absence of a requirement to show an intent to use the mark, and the relatively inexpensive application fees.

[22] Max Planck Study (n 5) 55, para 1.40, describing the interests protected by trade mark law as those of applicants in a smoothly functioning registration system; trade mark proprietors in full and efficient protection of their rights; the interests of consumers in protection against confusion that potentially affects their decision-making; and the interest of other market actors in maintaining free competition; United States Senate Report No 79-1333, 3 (1946), offering as one purpose of protection 'to protect the public so that it may be confident that, in purchasing a product bearing a particular trade-mark which it favorably knows, it will get the product which it asks for and wants to get'.

similar to a registered trade mark, confused consumers are unable to claim in their own right. Their actual or presumed reaction to the third party use will, however, determine whether the trade mark owner's action to protect its property interest is successful.[23] Indeed, consumer perceptions and interests function as the litmus test both for the existence and scope of protection; there are few areas of trade mark law where the concept of the consumer is not relevant.[24]

For the purposes of this chapter, we will focus on two crucial doctrinal questions: proof of distinctiveness and determination of confusion. And in so doing we will differentiate between two procedural contexts where these questions arise: assessments of validity (where questions of distinctiveness and confusion can both arise) and analysis of infringement (where confusion is central).[25] In order to frame our analysis in section IV, we will highlight in particular where the approach to the consumer presents (or perhaps conceals) a tension between an empirical and normative conception of the consumer.

An empirical conception of the consumer involves an assessment grounded in actual measured behaviour. In characterising the trade mark law consumer as 'normative', we mean that that consumer is deemed to have certain attributes or default characteristics, such as ascribed levels of attention, care or circumspection, which may be at odds with how some consumers actually behave in the marketplace. Instead, such a consumer is premised on how consumers *should* be assumed to behave in a specific context, in part because by validating those assumptions we ensure an outcome that the law regards as prescriptively desirable (for reasons that may or may not have anything to do with consumer protection). This is a familiar argument for those who have encountered the 'reasonable person' in tort law.[26]

[23] Trade mark is not the only area of law where this approach to standing and enforcement occurs. See, eg, F Henning-Bodewig (ed), *International Handbook on Unfair Competition* (Munich, CH Beck/Hart Publishing, 2012) 256–57, discussing German unfair competition action by trader against competitor for violation of, inter alia, consumer protection provisions. But it is unusual for a trader's property right to turn on consumer reaction.

[24] See J Mellor and others, *Kerly's Law of Trade Mark and Trade Names*, First Supp 15th edn (London, Sweet & Maxwell, 2014) (Kerly 2014 Supplement) 2, para 2-02n-02o: 'The target for all the functions of a trade mark is the notional average consumer. Readers will be aware that the concept of the average consumer arises in many chapters in this work … For this reason, it may be useful to gather some propositions regarding the concept of the "average consumer" in this [chapter of the 2014 supplement], where we discuss some of the fundamentals of EU trade mark law'.

[25] The *extent* of distinctiveness can be relevant to infringement, both as a factor in the confusion inquiry, and in establishing the 'reputation' of a mark (which triggers enhanced protection against dilution). See Case C–39/97 *Canon KK v Metro-Goldwyn-Mayer Inc* [1998] ECR I–5507, para 24; Trade Mark Directive, Art 5(2) (dilution).

[26] M Moran, *Rethinking the Reasonable Person: An Egalitarian Reconstruction of the Objective Standard* (Oxford, Oxford University Press, 2003) 2, referring to 'anxiety about the normative significance of the "default characteristics" of the reasonable person and the difficulty posed when those characteristics do not represent the person actually judged'; cf L Heymann, 'The Reasonable Person in Trade Mark Law' (2008) 52 *St Louis University Law Journal* 781, emphasising that the notional 'reasonable consumer' in trade mark law is an artificial, monolithic construct, representing millions of real people with varying perceptions of the 'sight, sound and meaning' of trade marks, so that judicial abstractions—while necessary—should not stray too far from marketplace realities; V Mak, 'The "Average Consumer" of EU Law in Domestic and European Legislation' in D Leczykiewicz and S Weatherill (eds), *The Involvement of EU Law in Private Law Relationships* (Oxford, Hart Publishing, 2013) 335–37, drawing parallels with other legal fictions such as the reasonable person in tort law.

This normatively infused consumer construct offers (a more objective) vantage point from which to assess certain categories of empirical evidence relating to consumer perception or behaviour.

A. Distinctiveness: When Does a Sign Function as a Trade Mark?

Trade marks are signs that are used by traders to identify their goods or services and distinguish them from the goods or services of others.[27] This origin-indicating function remains the primary basis for trade mark protection around the world. Both the Trade Mark Directive and the Trade Mark Regulation explicitly identify this as the essential function of marks,[28] and the Court of Justice has in fact constructed a substantial body of doctrine around the principle that the rights of the owner are to extend no further than necessary to protect the functions of a mark.[29]

Fortunately, the details of the Court's broader 'functions-based' doctrine, which have been the subject of extensive recent criticism, are not germane to this chapter.[30] However, to serve the foundational origin function and thus to warrant registration—to be 'distinctive' in doctrinal language—trade marks must be understood *by consumers* as pointing to a particular producer as the source of the goods (even if the consumers could not specifically name the producer).[31]

A mark may be inherently distinctive by its very nature—for example, if the sign is a word sufficiently disconnected from the nature of the goods or services on which it is used such that consumers will instantly see it as an indication of origin rather than a description of the characteristics of the goods.[32] APPLE works better as a trade mark for computers than it does for fresh fruit. If registration is sought for a mark prior to its use in the course of trade—as permitted under both the Directive and the Regulation—then this must be the basis on which the applicant establishes distinctiveness. Inherent distinctiveness is in essence a prediction that

[27] See Trade Mark Directive, Art 2.

[28] Trade Mark Regulation, Rec 8: '[t]he protection afforded by a Community trade mark, the function of which is in particular to guarantee the trade mark as an indication of origin'; Trade Mark Directive, Rec 11 (same).

[29] See, eg, Case C–482/09 *Budějovický Budvar, národní podnik v Anheuser-Busch Inc* [2011] ECR I–8701; Case C–235/09 *DHL Express France SAS v Chronopost SA* [2011] ECR I–2801.

[30] The Court has layered advertising and investment functions upon the origin and quality functions of marks. Defining these functions and justifying their protection has proved controversial. See generally DS Gangjee, 'Property in Brands: the Commodification of Conversation' in HR Howe and J Griffiths (eds), *Property Concepts in Intellectual Property Law* (New York, Cambridge University Press, 2013); A Kur, 'Trade Marks Function, Don't They? CJEU Jurisprudence and Unfair Competition Practices' (2014) 45 *International Review of Intellectual Property and Competition Law* 434.

[31] Conversely, if the mark loses its significance to consumers as an indication of source (eg it becomes a generic term, like escalator) it will lose protection as a mark. See Case C–409/12 *Backaldrin Österreich The Kornspitz Co GmbH v Pfahnl Backmittel GmbH* [2014] ETMR 30.

[32] See Trade Mark Directive, Art 3(1)(b); Trade Mark Regulation, Art 7(1)(b); Joined cases C–53 to 55/01 *Linde v DPMA* [2003] ECR I–3161, para 41: '[a] trade mark's distinctiveness must be assessed by reference to, first, the goods or services in respect of which registration is sought and, second, the perception of the relevant persons, namely the consumers of the goods or services'.

consumers will see a proposed mark as a source-identifier by virtue of its (oblique) relationship to the goods in question.[33] At the point of registration, there may be no possibility of the trade mark examiner making a targeted empirical assessment of whether that prediction is correct vis-à-vis the mark in question, although the empirical realities of the broader marketplace and the way that similar marks function might be relevant to any such prediction.[34] We refer to this latter aspect as empirical evidence relating to market conditions; it is essentially evidence that provides background context.[35] But the overall assessment of inherent distinctiveness is notional or predictive in nature, taking into account this market context.[36]

Alternatively, a mark may acquire distinctiveness through use. For example, a term that is descriptive of the characteristics of goods will initially be denied registration. However, if the consistent and extensive use of the mark by a single manufacturer on its products and related advertising causes the consumer to understand the mark as pointing to a single source of the products, the sign will have become a registrable mark.[37] Clearly, here, the actual distinctiveness of the purported mark can be empirically tested; indeed, absent proof of that distinctiveness, the mark will not be admitted to the register. And the Court of Justice has in a series of cases identified the types of evidence that may be relevant to proof of acquired distinctiveness. This evidence includes a range of circumstantial matters: market share/sales, extent of geographical use, length of use, advertising spend, and statements from chambers of commerce and industry or other trade and professional associations.[38]

Of most significance for present purposes, however, the Court has also indicated that public opinion polls or surveys may be relevant to prove acquired

[33] See generally GB Dinwoodie, 'Reconceptualizing the Inherent Distinctiveness of Product Design Trade Dress' (1997) 75 *North Carolina Law Review* 471, 480–81 and 486–87.

[34] ibid, 585–97. See also J Bergquist and D Curley, 'Shape Trade Marks and Fast-moving Consumer Goods' (2008) 30 *European Intellectual Property Review* 17, 20, n 24, noting that under CJEU case law, European consumers are presumed 'not [to be] in the habit of making assumptions about the origin of products, on the basis of either their shape or the shape of the packaging, in the absence of any graphic or word element. [However, when] assessing the habits of relevant consumers, the CFI subsequently held that the normal marketing practices of the product in question should be taken into account', and that for example empirical evidence relating to consumer perception of automobiles' features in general could be permitted.

[35] Overall, distinctiveness is very subjective (see Case C–191/01P *Office for Harmonisation in the Internal Market (Trade Marks and Designs) v Wm Wrigley Jr Company* [2003] ECR I–12447 (Doublemint), Opinion of AG Jacobs) and this factually intensive inquiry generally makes courts and examiners wary of undue reliance on other *registrations*. See Bergquist and Curley (n 34) fn 24 (evidence of other CTMs on motor vehicle grilles). But in a use-based system, such registrations ought to be slightly more persuasive because they are theoretically more reflective of market conditions. See Dinwoodie (n 33) 591–92.

[36] The utility of any survey as regards inherent distinctiveness would depend upon what one thinks surveys are doing. cf *Marks & Spencer plc v Interflora Inc* (*Interflora I*) [2012] EWCA Civ 1501, [2013] 2 All ER 663 [35]: '[t]here is, of course, no doubt that a valid survey can be an accurate diagnostic or *predictive* tool' (emphasis added).

[37] See Trade Mark Directive, Art 3(3); Joined cases C–108 and 109/97 *Windsurfing Chiemsee Produktions v Walter Huber* [1999] ECR I–2779, paras 50–52.

[38] See, eg, ibid, para 51.

distinctiveness, even if they are not mandatory.[39] Such polls are direct evidence of what the Court in its list of factors called 'the proportion of the relevant class of persons who, because of the mark, identify goods as originating from a particular undertaking'.[40] However, they also address with little mediation the ultimate legal question: whether 'the relevant class of persons, or at least a significant proportion thereof, identify goods as originating from a particular undertaking because of the trade mark'.[41] And because that ultimate question is phrased in the past or present (as opposed to future) tense,[42] it has the feel of an empirical inquiry.[43]

Adoption of such evidence should not, however, be taken as a wholesale delegation of decision-making to statistical or empirical proof.[44] The Court has insisted that neither national courts nor the OHIM can require polls to demonstrate a particular percentage of association as a precondition to protection: all circumstances must be considered, suggesting that the empirical data produced by opinion polls remains an input to a broader legal analysis.[45] And in its endorsement of opinion

[39] See ibid, para 53: 'Community law does not preclude the competent authority, where it has particular difficulty in that connection, from having recourse, under the conditions laid down by its own national law, to an opinion poll as guidance for its judgment'; see also L Bently and B Sherman, *Intellectual Property Law*, 3rd edn (Oxford, Oxford University Press, 2008) 845, fn 160: 'One of the factors is stated to be the proportion of the relevant class of persons who, because of the mark, identify goods as originating from a particular undertaking [citing *Windsurfing* (n 37)]. However, in our view this is not really a factor, so much as the essence of the inquiry. Consequently, we think it more helpful to distinguish … between primary and secondary evidence'.

[40] See *Windsurfing* (n 37), para 51.

[41] See ibid, para 52.

[42] See *Enterprise Holdings v Europcar Group UK Ltd* [2014] EWHC 2498 (Ch), [2014] ETMR 50 [33]: '[a] further possible distinction between a confusion survey and a distinctiveness survey is that the former may involve a prediction as to the likelihood of something happening whereas a distinctiveness survey addresses the issue of whether something has happened'.

[43] See Bently and Sherman, *Intellectual Property Law*, 3rd edn (n 39) 841, fn 139: 'acquired distinctiveness is normally a factual inquiry rather than one dependent on a legal construct'. This is not to say that one cannot make an empirically grounded assessment of likely (future) effects; indeed, confusion surveys can be understood as such. But we do not intend to articulate a formal definition of 'empiricism', because confusion surveys are alternatively described in some countries as circumstantial evidence of 'actual confusion' (with a resultant hint of looking backwards).

[44] The test of what must precisely be shown to establish acquired distinctiveness—association by consumers of the sign with a single trade source or consumer reliance on the sign as an indication of origin—was recently considered by the Court on reference from the UK courts. See *Nestle v Cadbury (Four-Finger Kit Kat)* [2014] EWHC 16 (Ch), [2014] ETMR 17. Some scholars had seen in the tentative endorsement by the UK courts of the latter standard a shift towards taking account of 'reality'. See I Fhima, 'Introducing Reality into Trade Mark Law' (2014) 9 *Journal of Intellectual Property Law & Practice* 684. If correct, and the recent opinion of the Court may not settle the question, (see Case C–215/14 *Société des Produits Nestlé SA v Cadbury UK Ltd*, judgment of 16 September 2015), such a conceptual shift might in turn portend a move towards the introduction of different types of evidence. But the adoption of a different legal standard may not of itself necessarily lead down the path of greater empiricism; it might simply re-orient the empirical evidence towards the new legal question. That is, the legal test establishes the normative framework within which empirical assessments occur and provide the standard against which those assessments are measured.

[45] See *Windsurfing* (n 37), paras 51–52. See also Joined cases C–217 and 218/13 *Oberbank AG v Deutscher Sparkassen- und Giroverband* [2014] ETMR 56, paras 43–44, reaffirming that while a sufficiently significant percentage of those surveyed must view the sign as a trade mark, predetermined percentages or cut-offs cannot be used to determine when this sufficiently significant threshold has been met.

poll evidence, the Court (while respecting varied national rules of evidence and procedure) arguably conditions the circumstances where use should be made of such optional evidence, noting that:

> Union law does not preclude the competent authority, where it has particular difficulty in assessing the distinctive character acquired though use of the mark in respect of which registration or a declaration of invalidity is sought, from having recourse, under the conditions laid down by its own national law, to an opinion poll as guidance for its judgment.[46]

This explanation of why courts might have regard to survey evidence—only as part of a broader legal test and where the facts present a particular difficulty for judges—has resonated generally with the judiciary at the national level.[47] The UK courts may be more sceptical about the value of surveys than their continental cousins,[48] and have developed increasingly rigorous gatekeeping devices that may preclude the admission of surveys into evidence.[49] However, it is also clear that even UK courts are more receptive to survey evidence in the distinctiveness context than elsewhere.[50] For example, in *Enterprise Holdings*, Morgan J distinguished between a survey measuring distinctiveness, on the one hand, and a survey of confusion, on the other, on the grounds (inter alia) that:

> In the case of a survey as to confusion, the question whether the survey is likely to be of real value may readily be answered in the negative in a case where the goods or services in question are ordinary consumer goods or services and the judge feels that there will be no real difficulty in the court determining the issue of confusion without a survey. Conversely, in the case of a survey as to acquired distinctiveness, the court may feel that it is not able to determine such a dispute based on its own experience and/or the court may feel the need to guard against an idiosyncratic decision.[51]

That is to say, the reason for using a survey rests in part on the extent to which such evidence usefully fills a gap in judicial knowledge.[52] Surveys do not replace

[46] *Oberbank* (n 45), para 43.

[47] The judicial inability to stand in a consumer's shoes in specialised markets provides some leeway for surveys to be admissible and we explore further reasons why courts could afford to be more open to surveys below (see below section IV.B). In contrast, if costs and unwarranted complexity are the principal concerns with surveys, directly correlated procedural or evidentiary responses may be more appropriate, as opposed to a judicial signal that surveys are generally undesirable. See below section IV.

[48] See Davis, 'Locating the Average Consumer. .' (n 2) 189: 'German courts tended to look favourably on opinion polls or surveys as evidence of consumer perceptions, both in cases of unfair competition and in judging distinctiveness in trade mark cases. By contrast, the UK courts traditionally had a "rather hostile attitude" to opinion poll evidence in trade mark cases'.

[49] See text to nn 177–178 below.

[50] Compare J Mellor and others, *Kerly's Law of Trade Mark and Trade Names*, 15th edn (London, Sweet & Maxwell, 2011), para 8-121: 'The ultimate source of evidence [of acquired distinctiveness] is the body of consumers of the goods or services in question. Well-conducted opinion polls can be persuasive, but require much thought and care and are often very expensive' with ibid, para 21-022: 'Since their introduction in English litigation in the late 1960s and early 1970s surveys have not … achieved great impact, although there have been instances where they have been given great weight'.

[51] *Enterprise Holdings* (n 42) [34].

[52] *Interflora I* (n 36) [54] (Lewison LJ).

judgment; they inform it,[53] especially when the judge is unable with any confidence to stand in the shoes of the consumer.[54] Thus, while the liberal accommodation of surveys within judicial analysis of acquired distinctiveness throughout Europe might be thought to underscore the characterisation of the overarching enquiry as being factually driven, the dispositive nature of the survey can easily be misstated; it is simply one piece of (powerful) evidence. The CJEU's all-circumstances test affirms that proposition.[55]

Surveys have attracted considerable attention in recent months but they form part of a broader taxonomy of empirical evidence, which assists courts when applying the average consumer standard. In general, three categories of empirical evidence inform legal enquiries concerning consumer understanding in trade mark cases (largely, in assessing distinctiveness or confusion). First, parties can introduce circumstantial evidence relating to use of the sign by the particular mark owner or alleged infringer and the effects thereof. For example, when determining whether a mark is highly distinctive or has a reputation (which confers certain advantages during infringement proceedings) or has acquired distinctiveness over time, the OHIM trade mark registry guidelines permit evidence such as certifications or awards for the mark; press cuttings; samples of actual advertising materials; advertising expenditure relating to the mark; market share; and turnover.[56] Such evidence is treated as a circumstantial proxy for consumer perception. If the mark is well advertised and very visible, it is likely that consumers will be familiar with it. Likewise, in assessing confusion, the Court of Justice has articulated a

[53] See T Cohen Jehoram, C van Nispen and T Huydecoper, *European Trademark Law: Community Trademark Law and National Harmonised Trademark Law* (Alphen aan den Rijn, Kluwer Law International, 2010) 291–92, discussing Dutch case law.

[54] UK courts repeatedly distinguish between cases involving ordinary consumer goods and those with which judges will be unfamiliar. See *Interflora I* (n 36) [59], [90] and [137] (in sceptical analysis of the use of survey evidence to assist analysis of likely confusion suggesting, however, that greater latitude might be allowed when the case involves goods with which judges would not be familiar). This seems to be a very small subset of cases, at least as regards confusion (but perhaps less so as regards acquired distinctiveness). Compare *Zee Entertainment Enterprises Ltd v Zeebox Ltd* [2014] EWCA Civ 82, [2014] FSR 26, refusing permission for survey and allowing judge to make assessment in passing off case where claimant broadcast television channels from India, with *Enterprise Holdings* (n 42) [72]: 'I do not consider that a trial judge in this case will be able to determine [the question of acquired distinctiveness of the logo of a car rental company] by using his own knowledge and experience. Even if a trial judge thought that he had relevant knowledge and experience, the trial judge would wish to guard against the possibility that his view might be somewhat idiosyncratic or not fully informed'.

[55] This is consistent with the role that Lewison LJ appeared to contemplate for acquired distinctiveness surveys in *Interflora I*. See *Interflora I* (n 36) [35]: 'a survey may accurately identify that proportion of the relevant public which recognises the mark as a badge of trade origin. It will then be for the fact finding tribunal, *with the aid* of such a survey, to decide whether a significant proportion of the relevant public identify goods as originating from a particular undertaking because of the mark' (emphasis added); *Enterprise Holdings* (n 42) [72]: 'of course, the trial judge will have evidence on the question of distinctiveness over and above the survey evidence'.

[56] Guidelines concerning proceedings before the Office for the Harmonization of the Internal Market (Trade Marks and Designs), Part B: Examination, Section 4: Absolute Grounds for Refusal (2015) 82–86; Guidelines concerning proceedings before the Office for the Harmonization of the Internal Market (Trade Marks and Designs), Part C: Opposition, Section 5: Trade Marks with Reputation, Art 8(5) CTMR (2014), 31–37.

series of factors including real-world evidence of enhanced distinctiveness, which will enable it to determine whether marks are similar and in turn inform a global appreciation of whether confusion is likely.[57]

Second, there can be evidence relating to market conditions—general yet empirically substantiated features of the market, as defined by the goods or services in question, including generalisations about consumer responses for a type of sign (for example, colours) or type of product/service (for example, internet services).[58] This is comprehensively illustrated in the (since over-turned) *Interflora* trial court decision by Mr Justice Arnold, where extensive evidence was submitted regarding internet literacy (where the age of the user was highly relevant) and consumer understanding of keyword advertising in general (in particular, the issue of whether consumers were aware of or could conveniently distinguish between natural and sponsored search results).[59] Recent empirical work in the behavioural sciences has the potential to inform such generalisations about consumer perceptions and marketplace responses.[60] For instance, that scholarship reveals that context matters a great deal during the consumer decision-making process so a legal test which is more open to contextual cues would more accurately map decision making in the marketplace.[61]

Third, there is the potential for direct evidence of consumer perceptions as it relates to the signs in a specific dispute between parties. Frequently, litigants conduct opinion polls or surveys intended to measure whether a mark is distinctive or whether there is likely to be confusion between the proprietor's and a third party's use of similar signs. Alternatively, as to the latter question, parties in the UK have historically conducted so-called 'witness collection exercises', which are a process of identifying witnesses who (although not statistically representative) testify or submit witness statements as to their reactions. We include in this category particular instances demonstrating actual confusion as well as probabilistic assessments of the likelihood of confusion that surveys permit. Of course, surveys ultimately measure consumer responses to a stimulus in an artificial context, and thus might (if one treated this taxonomy as more important than we intend) be strictly classified as circumstantial evidence. In any event, it is often said that proof of actual confusion is the best evidence of likely confusion. And in the wake of the

[57] See *Canon* (n 25), para 22; Case C–251/95 *SABEL BV v Puma AG, Rudolf Dassler Sport* [1997] ECR I–6191; see also *WHG (International) Ltd v 32 Red plc* [2012] EWCA Civ 19, [2012] RPC 19 [79]; *Specsavers International Healthcare Ltd v Asda Stores Ltd (No 2)* [2012] EWCA Civ 24, [2012] ETMR 17 [52]; *Red Bull GmbH v Sun Mark Ltd* [2012] EWHC 1929 (Ch), [2013] ETMR 53 [74].

[58] See *Kraft Foods Group Brands Llc v Cracker Barrel Old Country Store Inc* 735 F.3d 735, 742–43 (7th Cir 2013) (Posner J), discussing alternatives to surveys 'including testimony by experts on retail food products about the buying habits and psychology of consumers of inexpensive food products'.

[59] *Interflora Inc v Marks & Spencer plc* [2013] EWHC 1291, [2013] ETMR 35 [142]–[165].

[60] See TR Lee, ED DeRosia and GL Christensen, 'An Empirical and Consumer Psychology Analysis of Trademark Distinctiveness' (2009) 41 *Arizona State Law Journal* 1033; TR Lee, GL Christensen and ED DeRosia, 'Trademarks, Consumer Psychology, and The Sophisticated Consumer' (2008) 57 *Emory Law Journal* 575; TR Lee, ED DeRosia and GL Christensen, 'Sophistication, Bridging the Gap, and The Likelihood of Confusion: An Empirical and Theoretical Analysis' (2008) 98 *Trademark Reporter* 913.

[61] Davis, 'Revisiting the Average Consumer …' (n 2) 23–26.

Interflora litigation in the UK, where the Court of Appeal provided a clear message that there should be reduced reliance on surveys, courts have tended to highlight particular instances of actual confusion in a number of cases.[62]

However, such empirical evidence (of any type) merely informs the perceptions of the hypothetical or notional average consumer, which remains the legal benchmark. The 'average consumer' was incorporated by the CJEU into EU trade mark law from its jurisprudence on regulation of misleading advertising.[63] In that context, it was clearly understood that the CJEU was articulating a normative conception of the consumer that would instantiate a particular (less paternalistic) European vision of the consumer than might have resulted from national assessment.[64] Trade mark courts appear mostly to have taken over this understanding of the nature of the concept. And even UK courts (which historically might have offered the greatest resistance to the normative label)[65] have, in recent years in particular, made frequent reference to the normative or fictional nature of the 'average consumer'.[66] To be sure, the mathematical connotation of the term 'average' has tempted some British judges to muse about the concept in terms that have appeared to some commentators to contemplate (wrongly) a statistical

[62] See, eg, *British Sky Broadcasting v Microsoft* [2013] EWHC 1826 (Ch) [143] and [155] (confusion shown in 0.000011% of the calls to the customer helpline); *Comic Enterprises v Fox* [2014] EWHC 185 (Ch), [2014] ETMR 46 [120]–[121] (single witness of confusion during 5 years of a hit TV show); *Thomas Pink Ltd v Victoria's Secret UK Ltd* [2014] EWHC 2631 (Ch), [2014] ETMR 57 [160] (evidence of confusion did not support a finding of confusion, but prevented the defendant from arguing that no evidence of confusion). If the effect of *Interflora* is in fact to switch focus on to particular instances of actual confusion, it will be important to inquire as rigorously of that evidence whether (as was asked of surveys and witness collection) it is representative of broader consumer reaction. cf *British Sky Broadcasting* [144]–[145] (concluding that evidence of confused calls to helpline could not be regarded as skewed because of self-selection of callers and spontaneous reaction). Of course, the costs of making these inquiries may be far less than judicial scrutiny of surveys. And courts appear to accept very easily that the weight of such actual confusion evidence has to be considered as input data into a larger legal determination made through the eyes of the average consumer.

[63] See Davis, 'Locating the Average Consumer…' (n 2); *Interflora* (n 59) [194]–[224].

[64] Davis, 'Locating the Average Consumer…' (n 2) 197: 'the ECJ developed the concept of the "average consumer" largely in contrast to the empirical test for customer confusion which had been deployed by the German courts, in particular, and which has been described as "over-regulatory"'; Howells (n 20) 80, noting that the average consumer used by the Unfair Commercial Practices Directive assumes capacities superior to ordinary consumers but allows national courts to take into account social, cultural and linguistic factors.

[65] See text to nn 109–114 below.

[66] See, eg, *Interflora* (n 59) [208]–[211] (Arnold J) (average consumer is a 'legal construct' that provides a 'benchmark'); *Thomas Pink* (n 62) (Birss J) (accepting that the 'average consumer test is normative'); *Jack Wills v House of Fraser* [2014] EWHC 110 (Ch), [2014] ETMR 57 [63–65] (Arnold J): 'the average consumer provides a normative benchmark'); *Comic Enterprises* (n 62) [120] (Wyand QC): '[t]he average consumer is not a real person but is an artificial construct'. These formulations echo the legislative sentiments expressed in the Unfair Commercial Practices Directive, which itself reflected CJEU interpretations of prior consumer legislation. See Unfair Commercial Practices Directive, Rec 18, describing the average consumer as a 'a notional, typical consumer', and a 'benchmark' and emphasising that the 'average consumer test is not a statistical test. National courts and authorities will have to exercise their own faculty of judgement, having regard to the case-law of the CJEU, to determine the typical reaction of the average consumer in a given case'. It should of course be noted that the normative basis of trade mark and consumer protection legislation is not identical. See Ohly (n 7) 46.

exercise.[67] We find criticism of a statistical approach persuasive;[68] the average consumer offers a normatively infused vantage point from which to assess (more objectively) subjective empirical evidence relating to actual consumer perceptions and behaviours.[69]

Potential ambiguities of this sort can also be found in the approach of the CJEU to acquired distinctiveness. Although the CJEU has disavowed a numerical approach, its doctrinal formulations might at first glance suggest a greater attraction to empirical measures. Thus, in *Windsurfing*, the CJEU required that consumer recognition must subsist for 'the relevant class of persons, or least a *significant proportion* thereof'.[70] But the CJEU has also stressed that the question has to be considered through the lens of the 'average consumer', which we have explained as a normative concept.[71] This blending of empirical and normative assessments highlights that the binary choice between an empirical or normative approach to legal tests involving the consumer concept is a false one. In the end, there is a spectrum between empirical and normative assessments, and different issues may lend themselves to being addressed toward one end of that spectrum rather than the other. For instance, it would be uncontroversial to describe acquired distinctiveness as relatively positioned towards the empirical end. But almost all conceptions of the consumer—as circumscribed by the applicable legal tests—reflect a blend.[72]

There is clear evidence of this blended approach within the test for distinctiveness more generally. The fictional character of the average consumer has not stopped the CJEU from trying to put some flesh on its bones, which might be thought of as establishing a general normative framework within which to incorporate and assess empirical measurements. Thus, the CJEU has articulated *the type of consumer* from whose perspective the questions are to be assessed. The Court has offered several forms of guidance.

First, the Court has stressed that distinctiveness has to be assessed based upon 'the presumed expectations of an average consumer of the category of goods or

[67] See *Interflora I* (n 36) [35] (Lewison LJ); Kerly 2014 Supplement (n 24) 8–9, para 2-02n-02o, criticising the language of Lewison LJ in *Interflora I*.

[68] See *Hearst Holding v AVELA Inc* [2014] EWHC 439 (Ch), [2014] ETMR 34 [60] (Birss J): '[t]he word … "average" denotes that the person is typical. The term "average" does not denote some form of numerical mean, mode or median'; *Schutz v Delta* [2011] EWHC 1712 (Ch) [98] (Briggs J): '[t]he search for a statistical average is neither warranted by European jurisprudence, nor sensible in the present context'; *Interflora* (n 59) [211] (Arnold J): 'not a statistical test'.

[69] See nn 26–27 and accompanying text.

[70] *Windsurfing* (n 37), para 52 (emphasis added).

[71] Cf Bently and Sherman, *Intellectual Property Law* 3rd edn (n 39) 841, fn 139: 'In *Philips*, the ECJ stated that the tribunal is to assess acquired distinctiveness in "light of the presumed expectations of the average consumer". This seems strange because acquired distinctiveness is normally a factual inquiry rather than one dependent on a legal construct. Nevertheless, it is a way of screening out the views of real people who are either very attentive or very inattentive'.

[72] See Dinwoodie, 'Dilution as Unfair Competition' (n 9) 93: 'With respect both to absolute grounds for refusal such as distinctiveness and infringement tests such as likely confusion or association, trade mark law remains dominated by a legal fiction (the reasonably well-informed and reasonably observant and circumspect consumer) that is a mix of factual realities and legal policy'.

services in question, who is reasonably well informed and reasonably observant and circumspect'.[73] Second, the Court has detailed how this consumer perceives marks: the average consumer normally perceives a mark as a whole and does not proceed to analyse its various details. Thus, in order to assess whether or not a trade mark has any distinctive character, the overall impression given by it must be considered.[74] Third, the Court has (while nominally applying the same distinctiveness test to all types of marks) developed specific rules of thumb as regards the likelihood that consumers will treat certain categories of signs—often referred to as non-conventional—as marks. Thus, for example, consumers are *deemed in the normal course* not to regard the colour or shape of a product as a source-identifier.[75] Such marks will typically be protected only upon proof of acquired distinctiveness. Although the CJEU has denied this differential treatment,[76] it might be thought that this relatively conservative characterisation of consumer responses to non-conventional marks in the context of inherent distinctiveness—nominally involving judicial assessment of likely 'real world' consumer reaction—is to some extent informed by normative concerns about the greater anti-competitive effects associated with protection for shape or colour marks.[77]

This (not unreasonable) reticence relating to the registration of non-conventional marks such as colours or shapes in practice transfers across to acquired distinctiveness as well. Since the necessary degree of recognition by the relevant public (for example, 60 per cent) is *not* specified by case law, which only refers to a 'significant proportion' of that public, some courts appear to require a relatively higher degree of consumer awareness for such marks, when compared with word marks.[78] As a result, despite CJEU protestations to the contrary in *Windsurfing*, even acquired

[73] Case C–329/02 P *SAT-1 v OHIM*, [2005] 1 CMLR 57 [24].

[74] ibid [28].

[75] See Case C–104/01 *Libertel Group BV v Benelux-Merkenbureau* [2003] ECR I–3793, para 66 ('[i]n the case of a colour per se, distinctiveness without any prior use is inconceivable save in exceptional circumstances, and particularly where the number of goods or services for which the mark is claimed is very restricted and the relevant market very specific'); see also Case C–456/01 *Henkel KGaA v Office for Harmonisation in the Internal Market (Trade Marks and Designs)* [2004] ECR I–5089, para 38: '[a]verage consumers are not in the habit of making assumptions about the origin of products on the basis of their shape or the shape of their packaging'.

[76] See Case C–144/06 P *Henkel KgaA v Office for Harmonisation in the Internal Market (Trade Marks and Designs)* [2007] ECR I–8109, paras 34–39: '[a]ccording to … consistent case-law, the criteria for assessing the distinctive character of three-dimensional trade marks consisting of the appearance of the product itself are no different from those applicable to other categories of trade mark'.

[77] *Société Des Produits Nestlé SA v Cadbury UK Ltd* [2013] EWCA Civ 1174 [13] (Mummery LJ), endorsing the lower court's opinion 'that unconventional or "exotic" marks, such as colours, sounds and smells, give rise to conceptual problems, which are not encountered with more conventional trade names and logos. As the registration of a trade mark creates a form of intellectual property conferring a potentially perpetual monopoly in the mark and excluding everybody else from use in various ways, [the conditions under which they can be registered] has some public importance'.

[78] P Kutschke, 'All Consuming—Consumer Surveys in Germany' [May 2012] *Intellectual Property Magazine* 48, 49. And for word marks where the underlying meaning is generic for the goods or services, courts have been tempted to set a very high recognition threshold, to discourage exclusive rights in such terminology. This is illustrated by the application of the former German state monopoly in postal

distinctiveness should perhaps be seen as only a *predominantly* empirical assessment, with the space for accommodating normative agendas.[79]

B. Infringement by Likelihood of Confusion

The consumer is also central to questions of infringement. Most importantly, the 'consumer' provides the perspective through which a court will view whether a defendant's use is infringement under Article 5(1)(b) of the Directive, which requires proof of a likelihood of confusion.[80] In essence, this test is satisfied when (a) the identity or similarity of the two signs being compared and (b) that of the goods or services on which they are used (c) combines to give rise to a likelihood that the public wrongly believe that the goods or services originate in the same enterprise, or otherwise presume a connection, in the nature of an economic link (such as an authorised licensing arrangement), between the two enterprises. Again, the CJEU has developed a series of guiding principles concerning the nature of the consumer for this analysis, which broadly correspond with those articulated for the purposes of determining distinctiveness.[81] These considerations must be appreciated globally by a court, and this multi-factor, 'global appreciation' approach has become the hallmark of the CJEU's approach to confusion.[82]

services to register the mark POST. Evidence showed that around 85 per cent of the population associated the mark with the former state monopolist. Given its descriptiveness, the Federal Patents Court regarded this as insufficient for acquired distinctiveness and demanded a higher percentage. See BPatG, GRUR 2007, 714—POST. The appeal was successful since the BGH held that in the light of *Windsurfing* (n 37) there could be no fixed percentages, no exceptionally strict requirements for plainly descriptive marks and that the freedom of competitors to use the term descriptively was preserved via limitations. See BGH GRUR 2009, 669—POST II.

[79] See A Kur, 'Strategic Branding: Does Trade Mark Law provide for Sufficient Self-Help and Self-Healing Forces' in I Govaere and H Ullrich (eds), *Intellectual Property, Market Power and the Public Interest* (Brussels, PIE Peter Lang SA, 2008) 213–16 (arguing that room for such an approach exists even after *Windsurfing* (n 37)); see also *Oberbank* (n 45), paras 44–49.

[80] Even where consumer confusion is not a factor, such as in the double identity infringement test in Art 5(1)(a) of the Trade Mark Directive, consumer perception remains relevant (eg when assessing whether marks are identical). See Case C–291/00 *LTJ Diffusion v Sadas Vertbaudet* [2003] ECR I–2799, para 52; cf *Reed Executive Plc v Reed Business Information Ltd* [2004] EWCA Civ 159, [2004] ETMR 56 [25]. To the extent that Art 5(1)(a) is simply the cause of action under Art 5(1)(b) with a different burden of proof, then perhaps the assimilation is less problematic. However, at the time of writing there is an unresolved debate as to whether the 'reverse onus' approach is correct. Contrast *Interflora Inc v Marks and Spencer plc (Interflora III)* [2014] EWCA Civ 1403, [2015] ETMR 5 [71]–[106] and [131]–[151] with *Supreme Pet Foods v Henry Bell & Co* [2015] EWHC 256 (Ch) [84]–[161].

[81] See *SABEL* (n 57), para 23; *Canon* (n 25), para 16; Case C–361/04 P *Claude Ruiz-Picasso v Office for Harmonisation in the Internal Market (Trade Marks and Designs)* [2006] ECR I–643, paras 36; Case C–342/97 *Lloyd Schuhfabrik Meyer v Klijsen Handel BV* [1999] ECR I–3819, para 26.

[82] eg Case T–394/10 *Elena Grebenshikova v Office for Harmonisation in the Internal Market (Trade Marks and* Designs, judgment of 5 December 2013, [2014] ETMR 22, para 16: '[the global appreciation approach] implies some interdependence between the factors taken into account, so that a low degree of similarity between the goods or services covered may be offset by a high degree of similarity between the marks, and vice versa'.

In addition to those characteristics noted above in the context of acquired distinctiveness, the Court has identified other attributes of the consumer relevant to assessment of confusion:[83]

— The average consumer normally only rarely has the chance to make a direct comparison between different trade marks and instead must place their trust in the imperfect picture of them that they have kept in mind.
— Because the average consumer perceives a trade mark as a whole and retains only an imperfect image of it, its predominant and distinctive components are of major importance and will more likely be retained in the mind.
— Consumer sophistication and levels of attention will vary according to the categories of goods and services under consideration. It is presumed to be low for ordinary consumer goods (fast moving consumer goods, or FMCGs) but higher where the products are expensive, durable, relate to health or are intended for use by specialists.

In listing the types of considerations that might be relevant to determining confusion, the Court has again included the option (but not the requirement) of allowing the use of opinion polls. Despite recent judicial scepticism regarding the utility of surveys or polls, discussed below, this is another point at which empirical evidence relating to market conditions or context is potentially admissible, in an otherwise increasingly non-empirical (or, as an OHIM 'insider' has credibly argued, formalistic) test.[84]

This body of CJEU case law has grown up notwithstanding Recital 11 of the Directive. That recital recognises that although an EU-wide interpretation of concepts such as similarity of marks or similarity of goods was essential, 'the ways in which likelihood of confusion may be established, and in particular, the onus of proof, should be a matter for national procedural rules'.[85] Thus, despite articulating these principles, the CJEU will routinely defer to national court application of its global appreciation test in confusion, absent reliance on an incorrect principle of law, and national courts have begun to flesh out the test at a level of detail that is more helpful than the formulaic incantations emanating from the CJEU.[86] And ultimately, of course, to the extent that these determinations *are* empirically

[83] A convenient summary is found in OHIM Guidelines for Examination in the Office, 'Part C: Opposition, Section 2: Double Identity and Likelihood of Confusion, ch 6: Relevant Public and Level of Attention' (2015). The time for assessing likely consumer confusion is at the time of sale, although some recent judgments suggest that the door may be open for liability based on pre-sale and post-sale confusion. See *Och-Ziff Management Europe Ltd v OCH Capital LLP* [2010] EWHC 2599 (Ch), [2011] ETMR 1 [79]–[101]; *British Sky Broadcasting* (n 62) [82]; *DataCard Corp v Eagle Technologies Ltd* [2011] EWHC 244 (Pat), [2011] RPC 17 [276]–[289]; cf *Interflora III* (n 80) [158].

[84] R Morgan, 'Ensuring Greater Legal Certainty in OHIM Decision-Taking by Abandoning Legal Formalism' (2012) 7 *Journal of Intellectual Property Law & Practice* 408. We discuss the relationship between formalistic tests and empirical assessments below in section IV.

[85] But see Max Planck Study (n 5) 107, para 2.194, proposing addition of detail about the confusion test to the preamble of the Directive.

[86] See, eg, *WHG* (n 57) [79] and *Specsavers* (n 57) [52].

grounded, national courts will (as fact-finders) assume greater influence in the outcomes.[87]

C. The Likelihood of Confusion in Registration and Infringement

Unlike determinations of distinctiveness, the question of actionable confusion between competing uses of marks arises in two procedural contexts.[88] A comparison of the claimant's and defendant's use will be made if a registrant alleges infringement of its mark by a competing trader in the marketplace. But the comparison must also be made in the registration context (usually before the relevant trade mark office, but also potentially before a court)[89] when an opponent alleges that the mark for which registration is sought is confusingly similar to its earlier trade mark.[90] Such a ground for opposition to the registration of a mark is known as a 'relative' ground for refusal to register—the applicant encounters someone with prior rights relative to the applicant's filing date.

While the statutory 'likelihood of confusion' language is identical in both situations concerning potentially conflicting signs, the different procedural contexts generate divergences in the approach adopted.[91] In the registration context, the comparison is between the allegedly conflicting earlier *mark* and the *mark* for which registration is sought. The comparisons are 'paper based'—the marks in question are the marks as represented on the register, not as used in reality by traders and perceived in fact by consumers.[92] Again, this method is inevitable in

[87] See Dinwoodie (n 9) 93–95. In fleshing out the legal test, the Court no doubt has reflected and thus embedded some normative concerns as a matter of law. Thus, the Court has held that, consistent with growing international norms, the stronger the claimant's mark the more likely that confusion will occur: *SABEL* (n 57), para 24. This could well be inconsistent with an empirical assessment. Cf *Reed Executive* (n 80) [83]–[86] (Jacob LJ), discussing comments by Pumfrey J [78] who found this 'surprising … but that is the law', and managing to explain the proposition in real world terms; A Griffiths, 'The Impact of the Global Appreciation Approach on the Boundaries of Trade Mark Protection' (2001) 4 *Intellectual Property Quarterly* 326, 336–37.

[88] To be sure, assessments of distinctiveness may occur in a number of settings: upon application, if infringement is asserted, or if revocation of the mark is sought. However, these are largely identical assessments, with small temporal adjustments. cf Trade Marks Act 1994, s 3(1) (proviso) with s 47(1).

[89] The comparison could come before a national court on appeal from a denial of registration, but could also arise if a defendant in an infringement proceeding alleges that the mark of which infringement is alleged was invalid on relative grounds.

[90] See Trade Mark Directive, Art 4(1)(b). The earlier mark upon which an opposition is based can be a registered mark but it can also (in most, but not all, countries of the EU) be an unregistered mark. See Trade Mark Directive, Art 4(4)(b). In the UK, the invocation of an earlier unregistered right effectively initiates a passing off claim against the applicant, the success of which will result in the denial of the registration. See Trade Marks Act 1994, s 5(4). At the CTM level, see Trade Mark Regulation, Art 8(4); C–196/11 P *Formula One Licensing BV v Office for Harmonisation in the Internal Market (Trade Marks and Designs) and Global Sports Media Ltd*, judgment of 24 May 2012.

[91] See *Och-Ziff Management Europe* (n 83) [76]–[78].

[92] See P Maeyaert and J Muyldermans, 'Likelihood of Confusion in Trade Mark Law: A Practical Guide Based on the Case Law in Community Trade Mark Oppositions from 2002 to 2012' (2013) 103 *Trademark Reporter* 1032, 1115: '[o]pposition proceedings … are by their very nature (and in contrast to infringement proceedings) prospective and utterly abstract and are likely to fail to respect

a registration-based system, where registration is not dependent upon prior use. In many instances, the applicant will have not used the mark; indeed, in some instances neither will the opponent, given the five-year grace period in EU law.[93] If this is so, there will be no evidence of actual consumer confusion on which a court could proceed. It must make a prediction, and the comparison thus assumes a notional hue.[94] Moreover, in the registration context it has to be assumed that the trader whose application is being challenged will use the goods across the entire range of the specification of goods in the application, because that is the goods in respect of which (if successful in registration) it will secure exclusive rights, even if it in fact is using the mark on only a subset of those goods.[95]

In contrast, when assessing an infringement claim, the text of the Directive and Regulation calls for a court to compare the claimant's registered *mark* as against the defendant's *sign* (as used). Thus, on the claimant's side, according to the legislation, one must still look at the mark as registered 'on paper', which defines the mark owner's rights. Again, this will often be unavoidable, as the mark may not yet have been used; it can be enforced absent use within the five-year grace period. Here a court:

> [P]resupposes that the plaintiff's mark is in use or will come into use. It requires the court to assume the mark of the plaintiff is used in a normal and fair manner in relation to the goods for which it is registered and then to assess a likelihood of confusion in relation to the way the defendant uses its mark, discounting external added matter or circumstances.[96]

Sometimes, however, the marks in question will have been used. Indeed, the defendant must have been using (or threatening to use) the sign or there would be no infringement claim.[97] Thus, it is clear that, in the infringement context, '*the offending use* [by the defendant] must be seen in context'.[98] As Lord Justice Kitchin explained in *Specsavers*:

> In assessing the likelihood of confusion arising from the use of a sign the court must consider the matter from the perspective of the average consumer of the goods or services in question and must take into account all the circumstances of that use that are likely to operate in that average consumer's mind in considering the sign and the impression it is likely to make on him. The sign is not to be considered stripped of its context.[99]

concrete real-life situations where the transactional decisions for everyday consumer goods are often taken in a manner of seconds'.

[93] See Trade Mark Directive, Art 10 (use requirement).

[94] The full force of this notional approach should be adapted five years after the registration of the earlier mark. At the very least, the earlier right owner should be vulnerable to a claim of partial revocation based on non-use if invoking registered rights with respect to goods beyond those on which the mark has used. See, eg, Trade Marks Act 1994 (UK), s 46(5); Community Trade Mark Regulation, Art 51(2). But in any event the applied-for mark might still not be used, so some degree of notionality might persist.

[95] See Case C–533/06 *O2 Holdings Ltd v Hutchison 3G UK Ltd* [2008] ECR I–4231, para 66.

[96] See *Origins Natural Resources Inc v Origin Clothing Ltd* [1995] FSR 280, 284.

[97] Trade Marks Act 1994, s 10; cf *Google France* (n 7).

[98] *Specsavers (No 2)* (n 57) [67] (citing *O2* (n 95) [64]).

[99] *Specsavers (No 2)* (n 57) [87].

Specsavers usefully illustrates the extent to which an appreciation of context is now permissible under infringement analysis. In that case, the defendant Asda (a supermarket) had alluded to the claimant Specsavers (a retail chain offering optician's services) in promotional material that stated 'be a real spec saver at Asda' and 'spec savings at Asda'. The claimant alleged that this infringed several of its registrations, including the mark SPECSAVERS in both standard and figurative form. The approach adopted by Lord Justice Kitchin took into account that '[t]he average consumer would see the signs "spec saver" and "Spec savings" in the context of the [allegedly infringing] straplines and, indeed, the posters and other materials on which they were used as a whole'.[100] 'Context' meant as seen in the defendant Asda's store and online: as the trial court noted, Asda's own (well-recognised) name was prominently displayed along with the signs and the writing on Asda's sign appeared dark on a light background (the claimant's mark doing the opposite).[101]

However, on the claimant's side (until *Specsavers*) it was only the *registered mark* that was to be considered.[102] To be sure, the British courts had for some time been willing to admit of some concern for reality. So in *Premier Brands*, it was suggested that the way in which the claimant proprietor *actually uses the mark* would be the paradigm case of 'normal and fair use' of the registered mark.[103] In *Specsavers* this concession to reality was taken even further. The claimant's registered mark did not claim colour; it had been registered in black and white. However, Specsavers actually used the logo in a specific shade of green. So which logo should form the basis for the comparison—the monochrome one as registered or the coloured one as used? While referring the matter to the CJEU, Lord Justice Kitchin offered his provisional view that 'a mark registered in black and white is [treated as] registered in respect of all colours'.[104] This conclusion was buttressed by other doctrinal rules on infringement analysis, which consider the distinctiveness and reputation of the earlier mark:

> If, therefore, a logo registered in black and white has acquired, through use, a particular and distinctive character, in, for example, the colour green, that would seem to me to be a matter which ought to be taken into account in the global appreciation analysis.[105]

[100] ibid [88].

[101] See *Specsavers International Healthcare Ltd v Asda Stores Ltd* [2010] EWHC 2035 (Ch), [2011] FSR 1 [137]–[138] (Mann J), explaining basis for denying s 10(2) claim.

[102] See, eg, *L'Oréal SA v Bellure NV* [2007] EWCA Civ 968 [2008] ETMR 1 [109]–[111]: '[t]he test is, and must be, founded on the mark as registered, not material which forms no part of that. There is simply no warrant in the Directive for taking more than the registered mark into account. The global appreciation test does not amount to the proposition that once a registered mark is used in marketing, anything, extraneous to the mark used in marketing, comes in too—as though it formed part of the registered mark. [By contrast, context is permissible when] we are looking at *the defendant's sign*. How *it* would be perceived in practice does form part of a global appreciation on the strict mark for sign test' (emphasis added).

[103] *Premier Brands UK Ltd v Typhoon Europe Ltd* 2000 ETMR 1071, 1083–84 (Neuberger J).

[104] *Specsavers (No 2)* (n 57) [96].

[105] ibid.

The judgment of the CJEU is not as clear as the exposition of the Court of Appeal, but in essence endorsed Lord Justice Kitchin.

> At the very least where there is a trade mark which is registered not in a particular colour or characteristic, but in black and white, the colour or combination of colours in which the trade mark is later used affects how the average consumer of the goods at issue perceives that trade mark, and it is, therefore, liable to increase the likelihood of confusion or association between the earlier trade mark and the sign alleged to infringe it.[106]

D. Converging Approaches in Member States?

These developments, which have allowed courts in the context of infringement to consider the claimant and defendant's marks as actually used, might be seen as more connected to empirical consumer reality than would have been expected in a registration system. Indeed, analysis acknowledging greater contextual marketplace usage may come close to importing into registered trade mark law perspectives more frequently adopted during national passing off or unfair competition proceedings.[107] This would be unremarkable in the use-based regime of the United States, where there has been an effective assimilation of federal unfair competition (essentially, passing off) claims with those of registered trade mark infringement. But in the EU, the Trade Mark Directive quite explicitly did not address unfair competition, for reasons with obvious historical explanations.[108]

The convergence that could not be pursued legislatively may at least partially be occurring via the reconceptualisation of the trade mark consumer, the vehicle for assessing so many core questions. The tentative and fluid nature of the debate in the UK in the last three years may exemplify the potential for movement, and for opening up further discussion of the nature of EU trade mark and unfair competition law through a debate about the nature of the consumer.

Prior to the last three years, once can find little explicit reference in British case law or literature to the 'normative' or 'fictional' nature of the average consumer, although courts have commented on the notional exercise conducted at the stage of registration (which at least suggests some hypothetical or predictive assessment). Before 1994, the absence of such language might not have been a surprise because UK law did not purport expressly to define the scope of rights explicitly by reference to the perceptions of a consumer.[109] But one might perhaps have expected

[106] See Case C–252/12 *Specsavers International Healthcare Ltd v Asda Stores Ltd* [2013] ETMR 46, para 37.

[107] This is not the only doctrinal site at which a convergence of trade mark law and passing off or unfair competition is occurring. See Dinwoodie (n 9), 91; see also Case C–661/11 *Martin y Paz Diffusion SA v Depuydt* [2014] ETMR 6, constructing a reading of trade mark law that might ordinarily have been handled in several member states via principles of unfair competition law and bad faith.

[108] See generally RM Hilty and F Henning-Bodewig, *Law Against Unfair Competition: Towards a New Paradigm in Europe?* (Berlin, Springer, 2007).

[109] See Trade Marks Act 1938, s 4(1).

some development of the nature of the consumer by the UK courts either in 1994 when the UK implemented the consumer confusion-based test of Article 5 of the Directive (or at least in 1997 when the CJEU interposed the 'average consumer' into that test).[110]

Instead, with the notable exception of the work of Jennifer Davis, although references to the 'average consumer' abound, there is little judicial or scholarly development of the concept in these terms until the Court of Appeal began grappling with the admissibility of survey and related evidence in 2012 in *Interflora*.[111] Indeed, those references that did exist (in two opinions by Geoffrey Hobbs QC, sitting as a Deputy Judge) appeared to disavow a normative approach to the consumer. For example, in *Whirlpool v Kenwood* at first instance, the Deputy Judge commented that:

> I am aware that in some Member States the average consumer test is regarded as a means for determining the scope of protection on a 'normative' or 'regulatory' basis. The rationale is that trade mark owners are entitled to the benefit of an exclusive right with appropriate scope of protection, just as patent owners are entitled to the benefit of an exclusive right with appropriate scope of protection. The appropriate scope of protection is a matter of law, not a matter of fact: the notional average consumer in the law of trade marks should, like the notional technician skilled in the relevant art in the law of patents, be viewed as a synthetic person with the 'correct' mindset and behaviour patterns. However, I believe that this approach can be too abstract. In my view, the average consumer is meant to be a person of the type whose mindset and behaviour patterns conform to the norm among reasonably well-informed and reasonably observant and circumspect people in the market for the goods or services in question. That appears to me to bring into consideration the real world thought processes of real people. I therefore think that the appropriate scope of protection should in each case be determined with as great a sense of reality as the circumstances of the case will allow. Empirical evidence should therefore not be ignored. That is the basis on which I am proceeding in this case.[112]

The Directive left open to Member States the ability to choose the ways in which likelihood of confusion may be established, and the reference here to 'empirical' evidence might be thought simply a function of evidentiary rules.[113] By the same, token, however, Hobbs QC appeared to ground this approach in the notion of the 'average consumer', suggesting perhaps that he considered the approach in other Member States to be substantively inconsistent with the conception outlined by

[110] See *SABEL* (n 57), paras 23–24.

[111] See Davis, 'Locating the Average Consumer …' (n 2); cf Griffiths (n 87) 341, noting the 'notional' and 'imaginary' nature of the average consumer.

[112] *Whirlpool Corp v Kenwood Ltd* [2008] EWHC 1930 (Ch), [2009] RPC 2 [70] (Hobbs QC, Deputy Judge). cf *Daimler AG v Sany Group Co Ltd* [2009] EWHC 1003 (Ch), [2009] ETMR 58 [26] (Hobbs QC, Deputy Judge), noting findings in registration proceedings in Germany and France on the confusion question that 'seem to reflect a 'normative' or 'regulatory' approach to protection within the general parameters set by the wording of the opposing specifications of goods, which might not lead to the same outcome as an 'empirical' assessment of the specific circumstances characterising an allegedly infringing instance of use'. However, *Whirlpool* was an infringement proceeding.

[113] See Trade Mark Directive, Rec 11.

the CJEU. He certainly made it clear that he thought a more normative approach may well affect outcomes.[114]

In any event, after the Court of Appeal in *Interflora I and II* sent a strong signal limiting the use of survey evidence (or its witness collection variant), the UK courts have explicitly characterised the average consumer as normative. If this is indeed a shift by the UK courts towards a European approach, it arguably renders *Interflora* a greater watershed than some commentators have suggested; for many, the decision simply tightened up and endorsed existing predispositions in the UK judiciary toward particular types of evidence.[115]

At the very least, more thought needs to be given to the consequences of this fuller and more explicit embrace of the normative approach by the British courts. The leading judgment in *Interflora I* itself reflects what some commentators have seen as ambiguity about what it means to adopt a normative approach, zeroing in as it did on the meaning of the term 'average'.[116] As the editors of the most recent supplement to *Kerly on Trade Marks* usefully suggest, the cause of some of the difficulties in grasping the nature of the 'average consumer' may be linguistic.[117] It might have been better had the term used (in English) been 'ordinary' or 'reasonable' consumer, a usage that can be found in some English decisions.[118]

This 'watershed' reading of *Interflora* has fairly dramatic implications and might liberate a new notion of the consumer, more normative and less empirical, in European (or British) trade mark law. But it is important to note that a normative approach does not preclude empirical evidence, including surveys. Prior to 2012, the most frequent description of the trade mark confusion test as normative would have been found in German literature. Yet German courts had over the last few decades been slightly more receptive to the use of opinion poll evidence, suggesting no necessary tension between empirical evidence and a normative approach.

The *Interflora I* opinion also discussed the relationship between the 'average consumer' concept and parallel concepts in passing off.[119] Passing off requires that a 'substantial number' of members of the relevant public are confused (or likely to be confused in a *quia timet* action).[120] That cause of action (like continental European unfair competition law) was conventionally understood as being more

[114] cf *Daimler AG* (n 112) [26] (Hobbs QC, Deputy Judge).

[115] cf Kerly (n 50), para 21-026, noting pre-*Interflora* that the 'net effect of these rules, necessary as they are, is that it is very difficult to design a survey which will pass muster in court'; *Zee Entertainment* (n 54) [64] (Lewison LJ), noting that the 'general run of cases, both before and after *Interflora*, does tend to show that such surveys have very limited value'.

[116] See above n 68.

[117] Kerly 2014 Supplement (n 24), paras 2-02e-h.

[118] *Reed Executive* (n 80) [82] (Jacob LJ).

[119] *Interflora I* (n 36) [33]–[34] (Lewison LJ).

[120] See C Wadlow, *The Law of Passing Off: Unfair Competition by Misrepresentation*, 4th edn (London, Sweet & Maxwell, 2011).

grounded in market realities than registered trade mark law,[121] and hence more amenable to resolution based upon empirical evidence.[122] Indeed, a passing off claim *requires* more evidence of actual marketplace conditions (such as existence of goodwill through use).

Despite that, and despite language in elements of passing off doctrine that has a quantitative ring, even passing off can be thought to contain a normative dimension.[123] It certainly has been understood as involving more than a statistical exercise.[124] But it *is* more grounded in actual use. Oddly, therefore, although Lord Justice Lewison affirmed that greater latitude for surveys might exist with respect to a passing off claim, evidentiary practice in passing off cases since *Interflora I and II* suggests that the approach to surveys may be converging with those applicable in registered trade mark cases.[125] This may, counter to some of the suggestions above, simply affirm that shifting judicial attitudes towards surveys are influenced by litigation costs and not any conscious reorientation of the nature of the trade mark consumer. But taken with the contextual turn in *Specsavers*, the distinct regimes of trade mark and passing off may be converging via the construction of the consumer and increasingly common ways of measuring his or her perception.

[121] See *Zee Entertainment* (n 54) (Floyd LJ) [44], describing passing off as a 'real world cause of action'; J Griffiths, 'Star Industrial Co Ltd v Yap Kwe Kor: The End of Goodwill in the Tort of Passing Off' in S Douglas, R Hickey and E Waring (eds), *Landmark Cases in Property Law* (Oxford, Hart Publishing 2015) 279: 'the fundamental principles of the law of passing off are generally aligned closely with the reactions of real marketplace consumers'.

[122] See Davis, 'Revisiting the Average Consumer …' (n 2) 26; *Neutrogena Corp v Golden Ltd* [1996] RPC 473, 482 (Jacob J): '[i]t was certainly my experience in practice that my own view as to the likelihood of deception was not always reliable. As I grew more experienced I said more and more "it depends on the evidence."'; see also Ohly (n 7) 45, noting a similar distinction between the 'abstract method of determining confusion in trade mark law and the concrete assessment' of continental unfair competition law.

[123] In some respects, the 'average consumer' is normative in much the same way as the standard of not catering to the 'moron in a hurry' so beloved of passing off cases. See *Morning Star Cooperative Society Ltd v Express Newspapers Ltd* [1979] FSR 113 (Foster J). That standard operated to allocate responsibility ideally as between trader and consumer. So too the average consumer in trade mark law. But of course the consumer conception can be normative along other dimensions. Thus, the scope of trade mark protection also implicates 'deep down ..the philosophy of how competitive the law allows European industry to be'. *O2 Holdings Ltd v Hutchison 3G UK Ltd* [2006] EWCA Civ 1656, [2007] RPC 16 [1] (Jacob LJ). Indeed, it arguably reflects an even broader range of normative commitments sometimes obscured by the beguiling power of the consumer trope. See below section IV.

[124] *Neutrogena* (n 122), 485–86 (Jacob J): '[t]he court in a passing off case is not concerned with statistical precision. What it wants to know is whether or not there is a substantial degree of deception or confusion'.

[125] See Davis, 'Revisiting the Average Consumer …' (n 2) 26–28, discussing *Zee Entertainment* (n 54). In some respects, if courts believe that surveys are truly artificial and fail to replicate real world circumstances, they might (despite the conventional wisdom and the exceptions noted in *Interflora I* (n 36)) find surveys even more unhelpful than in trade mark infringement cases. cf *Zee Entertainment* (n 54) (Floyd LJ) [44]; ibid (Lewison LJ) [62]–[63]. At the very least, the need for context is even more important, although that is of course increasingly true in registered trade mark infringement analysis too. See ibid [62] (Lewison LJ): '[e]ven in the case of … trade mark infringement the acontextual comparison of mark and sign has been abandoned'. See above text to nn 98–104.

IV. Reconstructing the Consumer(s) in EU Trade Mark Law

A. A Normative Conception of the Consumer in EU Trade Mark Law

As discussed above, the possibility for registration prior to use in EU trade mark law clearly requires that analysis of consumer perception *has* on some occasions to be based on something more than current empirically testable marketplace perceptions because it will often need to be anticipatory and therefore hypothetical or notional. The *likelihood* of confusion test is also designed with its anticipatory deployment in mind.

However, the assessments of consumer perceptions that are required by such a system might not necessarily be normative. A notional or hypothetical analysis, because it inevitably predicts consumer perceptions with lesser regard for current real-world conditions, might appear less empirically grounded. But, as discussed above, that analysis can still proceed in light of some empirical measures. Moreover, a non-empirical consumer may simply be a formal construct—for instance, on the basis of a small universe of facts, if certain conditions of the doctrinal test are satisfied, confusion is inevitable as a logical (and legal) consequence.[126] The double-identity rule in trade mark infringement operates somewhat on this basis.[127] We do not mean to suggest that formalistic concepts do not sometimes conceal normative preferences; very often, they do.[128] Formalism can mask or translate (sometimes, but not always, for good reason) those normative choices. But there may be something else at play.

As we noted above, the roots of the average consumer concept in trade mark law, which most national courts have recognised to require more than an empirical or statistical exercise,[129] lie in the jurisprudence of the CJEU on misleading advertising, which became easy to transfer to the context of trade mark law when the CJEU first tackled case law under the Trade Mark Directive.[130] But this apparently

[126] See Morgan (n 84).

[127] Trade Mark Directive, Art 5(1)(a) (use of identical marks on identical goods amounts to infringement); cf Agreement on Trade-Related Aspects of Intellectual Property Rights (adopted 15 April 1994, entered into force 1 January 1995) 1869 UNTS 299 (TRIPS Agreement), Art 16(1) (confusion should be presumed where identical mark used on identical goods).

[128] See FS Cohen, 'Transcendental Nonsense and the Functional Approach' (1935) 35 *Columbia Law Review* 809. Jennifer Davis persuasively traces the historical antecedents of the apparently hollow 'average consumer' in both the British and European contexts, exploring their normative underpinnings in the process. See Davis, 'Locating the Average Consumer …' (n 2) (British aspects); Davis, 'Revisiting the Average Consumer …' (n 2) (European context).

[129] Kerly 2014 Supplement (n 24) 8–9, paras 2-02n–02o.

[130] See Davis, 'Locating the Average Consumer …' (n 2) 198. Davis notes several ways in which the social and economic climate in the UK was favourable for such a transposition, and how developments in non-legal research enable us to contemplate the move. See ibid. But of course the implementation of the Trade Mark Directive and the growing centrality of the CJEU were also hugely significant.

reflexive adoption of the 'average consumer' from EU advertising law occurred without much (if any) consideration of whether EU trade mark law possessed a different normative basis than consumer protection or advertising law.[131] Perhaps adoption of the formalism embedded in the consumer law concept reflected mere (administrative) convenience rather than an overt prescriptive agenda to limit judicial paternalism?[132]

Alternatively, in some instances what appears to be a non-empirical consumer construct might simply be one that operates as a rough and ready approximation of empirical reality, enforcement costs suggesting that it is not worth more finely-grained assessments.[133] That is, consumer reaction might be deduced using heuristic devices designed to short-circuit the factually intensive and messy enquiry into how real world consumers actually perceive signs.[134] Multi-factor legal tests for assessments of consumer reactions (both as regards acquired distinctiveness and likely confusion) might be seen as falling into this category, though evidence about the actual nature of the market is often led to help courts apply the formal tests. Such devices lead to faster decision-making, and are as a result especially attractive to trade mark registries with large caseloads and indeed potentially to courts concerned with the use of judicial resources or keeping a lid on the costs of litigants (although the balance between speed and granular assessments of reality might differ in infringement proceedings). However, where such heuristic techniques have limited predictive value in the real world, such a 'quick-and-dirty' approach could undermine the normative foundations of trade mark law, which claims to meaningfully engage with and protect consumer interests.

[131] See Ohly (n 7) 46–50 (discussing normative bases of similar laws). Some scholars (more so in the US) see trade mark law as a subset of advertising law. See, eg, R Tushnet, 'Running The Gamut From A To B: Federal Trademark and False Advertising Law' (2011) 159 *University of Pennsylvania Law Review* 1305, arguing that 'false advertising law, though vastly undertheorized compared to trademark law, has several important lessons for trademark' and that '[t]rying to understand the Lanham Act solely through the lens of trademark law [without taking account of the role of false advertising law] is like trying to write a story with only half the alphabet'. But what does this suggest about the nature of EU trade mark law, because trade mark law could be viewed as more multifaceted than a mere part of advertising law. To be sure, it shares consumer protection goals. But is it a more affirmative and empowering force for consumer (or other, trader) interests than a prohibition against misleading information?

[132] See above text to n 65 (purpose behind adoption of concept in consumer law). Indeed, the Court of Justice continues to expand the assessments into which it injects the average consumer. See Case C–26/13 *Árpád Kásler and Hajnalka Káslerné Rábai v OTP Jelzálogbank Zrt*, judgment of 30 April 2014, para 74, interpreting the Directive on Unfair Terms in Consumer Contracts (Council Directive 93/13/EEC of 5 April 1993 on unfair terms in consumer contracts [1993] OJ L95/29) by considering the average consumer. One could argue that a preference for administrative or judicial convenience within an EU institution itself reflects some degree of prior political commitments. But we are not trying to push the 'empirical', 'normative' and 'formalistic' labels here to sustain a fundamental philosophical truth. Rather, we suggest only that the choice between an empirical and normative consumer is not a binary one; there is a spectrum and the consumer may be a different blend of the two in different contexts for a variety of reasons.

[133] See GB Dinwoodie, 'What Linguistics Can Do For Trademark Law' in L Bently, J Davis and JC Ginsburg (eds), *Trade Marks and Brands: An Interdisciplinary Critique* (Cambridge, Cambridge University Press, 2008).

[134] A Carter-Silk and J Leighton, *Confusion, Heuristics and the Consumer* (Speechly Bircham, Report for the British Brands Group, 2012).

As opposed to a hollow 'formal' consumer or consumer-as-heuristic, the specifics of the consumer construct *could*, however, be based on an overtly normative commitment. In the broader EU regulatory context of consumer protection, free movement cases led the CJEU to describe the average consumer as one who is 'reasonably well-informed and reasonably observant and circumspect'.[135] The relatively high level of attention attributed to this consumer was designed to counteract paternalistic consumer protection rules adopted by national Member States, which acted as an obstacle to the free movement of goods and inhibited consumer choice. The consumer was 'presumed to be capable to work out for him- or herself whether products or services live up to their description or quality requirements'.[136] As Stephen Weatherill observes in his contribution to this volume, these shifts were about consumer empowerment.[137] In a similar vein, in *Interflora III* Lord Justice Kitchin characterised the average consumer in trade mark law as 'a person who has been created to strike the right balance between various competing interests including, on the one hand, the need to protect consumers, and, on the other hand, the promotion of free trade in an openly competitive market'.[138]

Since the transposition of the 'average consumer' from advertising law, the CJEU has fleshed out the concept of the consumer in trade mark cases by implicit reference to the goals of trade mark law, such that the nominally identical concepts may have diverged to reflect different normative groundings.[139] And in a similarly prescriptive vein, the CJEU has recently re-envisioned consumer responses when applying the standard of trade mark infringement in the context of internet advertising.[140] In *Google France*,[141] the CJEU was clearly influenced by the policy of transparency embodied in the E-Commerce Directive.[142] It concluded that the purchase of keyword advertisements would infringe trade mark rights by threatening their origin-indicating function:

> [W]here [such an] ad does not enable an average internet user, or enables that user only with difficulty, to ascertain whether the goods or services referred to therein originate

[135] Case C–210/96 *Gut Springenheide GmbH v Oberkreisdirektor des Kreises Steinfurt* [1998] ECR I–4657, para 37.

[136] Mak (n 1) 30.

[137] Stephen Weatherill in this volume.

[138] *Interflora III* (n 80) [113].

[139] See n 87, discussing stronger protection for stronger marks via the consumer confusion rubric.

[140] In these cases, the CJEU has characterised the average consumer as the 'average internet user'. Some scholars have seen this as an attempt to construct a different test in the internet context, see Davis, 'Revisiting the Average Consumer …' (n 2), whether because of a different normative framework or because the internet is in fact a different consumer environment. It is too soon to know whether the elements of the consumer that the CJEU has devised in crafting the 'average internet user' will give rise to more generally applicable evolutions in the construct of the consumer. cf *DataCard* (n 83), applying internet-based changes in doctrine in the offline environment. This may to some extent depend upon whether the CJEU discerns that the internet offers a unique normative or empirical context, because the normative or empirical assimilation of offline and online may occur at a different pace.

[141] *Google France* (n 7), para 84 and 99.

[142] ibid, para 86.

from the proprietor of the trade mark or an undertaking economically connected to it or, on the contrary, originate from a third party.[143]

The CJEU also suggested that where an ad was vague about the origin of goods or services, this would constitute infringement.[144] This is a far more paternalistic standard than the CJEU routinely applies outside the internet context: mere uncertainty or difficulty in ascertaining the origin of the product appears far short of the likely confusion that would normally threaten a mark's source-indicating function.[145] By the same token, the CJEU's decision to situate the *sale* of such advertisements outside the scope of trade mark law, and hence immunise search engines from liability for trade mark infringement, might likewise have reflected a judgment about the social and commercial value contributed by the search engines. Although that motivation is not apparent from the CJEU's judgment, the opinion of Advocate General Maduro (although not faithfully followed by the Court in terms of the *basis* for its decision) is much more explicit.[146]

Likewise, in *Interflora*, the CJEU readjusted the level of paternalism that it had imposed in *Google France* in its articulation of when a consumer would be confused such that the origin function of the mark would be affected.[147] The CJEU's judgment in that case was clearly influenced by recognition that trade mark law has long been an important part of the EU's goal of facilitating undistorted competition and that third party use of marks might be consistent with that objective (along with the promotion of consumer choice).[148] And free movement of goods clearly informs both trade mark law and EU law generally.[149] The rising prominence of fundamental rights in EU intellectual property law further enriches the normative palette into which the CJEU can dip, as it has already shown.[150] Indeed, at the very least, the CJEU might even more explicitly take into account the different normative grounding of trade mark law and unfair competition or consumer protection law from which the average consumer was transplanted.[151]

[143] ibid, para 99.

[144] ibid, para 90.

[145] See, eg, Case C–48/05 *Adam Opel AG v Autec AG* [2007] ECR I–1017, para 24.

[146] *Google France* (n 7), Opinion of AG Maduro, paras 70–73 and 101–113.

[147] Case C–323/09 *Interflora Inc v Marks & Spencer plc* [2011] ECR I–8625, para 50.

[148] ibid, paras 57–59, discussing effect on advertising function.

[149] See Case C–63/97 *Bayerische Motorenwerke AG v Deenik* [1999] ECR I–905, para 62, noting that 'Article 6 seeks to reconcile the fundamental interests of trade-mark protection with those of free movement of goods … in such a way that trade mark rights are able to fulfil their essential role in the system of undistorted competition which the Treaty seeks to establish and maintain'.

[150] See Case C–314/12 *UPC Telekabel Wien GmbH v Constantin Film Verleih GmbH and Wega Filmproduktionsgesellschaft mbH*, judgment of 27 March 2014, [2014] ECDR 12; *Cartier v British Sky Broadcasting Ltd* [2014] EWHC 3354 (Ch), [2015] ETMR 1 [86] and [133]; see generally C Geiger (ed), *Research Handbook on Human Rights and Intellectual Property* (Cheltenham, Edward Elgar, 2015).

[151] See Ohly (n 7) 46, supporting the abstract method of determining confusion in trade mark law rather than the concrete method found in unfair trading law in the policy that 'trade mark gives its owner the possibility to develop a business strategy under the protected mark, [and so other] traders must respect the defensive perimeter which is drawn around the mark, even if actual confusion can be avoided under the concrete circumstances'. In the context of the CTM, this might involve a set of normative commitments beyond those found in national law. See Trade Mark Regulation, Recs 2–4, 16.

Thus, we do not believe it is beyond the CJEU to approach EU trade mark law from a more explicitly normative direction. An indirect and perhaps more palatable approach to pursuing normative objectives may well be achieved through painting a picture of the consumer.[152] But it is, and always will be, to some extent a normative picture.[153]

In its voyage of prescriptive reengineering, the Court is of course influenced by the arguments made to it by litigants. And litigants likewise frequently argue for a scope of permissible competition that best advances their interests by refracting it through the consumer construct. That is, they tailor the relevant consumer to fit their interests; consumer interests have a public-regarding feel that is rhetorically useful. Indeed, these actors may argue for a consumer that is constructed differently for the purposes of distinctiveness (for example, a claimant mark owner will suggest an astute consumer capable of reading origin indicating significance into signs relatively easily) and infringement (for example by the same party, a relatively inattentive consumer who may be easily confused).

Barton Beebe has noted perceptively that in the United States litigants selectively advance a consumer construct that alternates between Sovereign and Fool in such situations.[154] Evidence for this same phenomenon in the European context can be found in the numerous 'stripes' disputes. When producers seek to register design marks consisting of a particular number—whether two, three or four—of parallel stripes on sports shoes, they argue that consumers of this class of products possess sufficient nous, attention or sophistication to identify the source of the shoes on this basis, as opposed to seeing the stripes as mere embellishments or decoration.[155] Subsequently, as trade mark proprietors asserting infringement by competitors selling shoes bearing a slightly different number of stripes, they argue that the same class of consumers will be easily confused between three and four (or two) stripes and lack the capacity to differentiate between them.[156]

[152] A normatively 'pre-loaded' consumer construct is not the only option for having prescriptive debates within trade mark law, but is clearly one important option for courts and policy makers. See Ohly (n 7) 48–49, noting that trade mark policies could be incorporated into the interpretation of the Unfair Commercial Practices Directive, thus reconciling potential conflicts between those regimes, either by altering the presumptive knowledge of the reasonably well-informed consumer or by a balancing of competing interests.

[153] Of course, there may not always be consensus as to how broadly trade mark should reach out in search of relevant norms. See Kerly (n 50), para 9-100, discussing whether confusion is to be assessed differently in cases of pharmaceutical products because of nature of the harm flowing from confusion; Max Planck Study (n 5) 106, para 2.193.

[154] B Beebe, 'Search and Persuasion in Trademark Law' (2005) 103 *Michigan Law Review* 2020. Trade mark litigants are of course not unique in this respect. See Howells (n 20) 71, noting inconsistencies in the vision of consumers and traders used by the Commission to sustain its jurisdiction over consumer matters and that embodied in the resultant legislation.

[155] The potential distinctiveness of stripes was considered twice by the CJEU in Case C–408/01 *Adidas-Salomon v Fitnessworld* [2003] ECR I–12537; Case C–102/07 *Adidas AG v Marca Mode CV* [2008] ECR I–2439. Whether the class of sports shoes consumers was attentive enough to view five stripes as a trade mark was recently considered in Case T–85/13 *K-Swiss Inc v OHIM* [2014] OJ C245/13.

[156] *Adidas-Salomon AG v ALYSIDA AEBE* [2010] ETMR 23 (Athens Court of Appeal, Greece) (Adidas successful against retailer selling shoes with two and four stripes); *Adidas AG v Almacenes*

This opportunistic behaviour is not unique in trade mark law; there are parallels, for example in European design law, where it might be advantageous for one party to argue that the 'informed user' (the equivalent design fiction) is more or less informed at the infringement stage than in assessing validity. Doctrinally, this strategic revision of the consumer could be checked by devices that insist on a constant perspective at the stage of both validity and infringement.[157] However, this is hard to achieve in trade mark law because the range of actions subsumed under the heading of infringement is so varied that the consumer relevant for distinctiveness analysis may not be the same as the relevant consumer for infringement.[158] Moreover, there is a sense among courts that assessment of acquired distinctiveness may involve a more empirical inquiry than the relatively normative exercise of assessing likely confusion.[159]

Finally, any normative vision of the consumer in EU trade mark law would, by reason of the Europeanisation of trade mark law, tend towards a single, autonomous conception. To the extent that normative preferences are best effectuated by rules of law, the CJEU would be well placed to enforce that vision. The more that the reasonably well-informed and reasonably observant and circumspect consumer is a normative fiction, the greater the scope for the CJEU to create *legal* rules that establish EU-wide standards. The more empirical that question becomes, the greater the role of national courts and the more likely that divergent market realities in Europe will result in different outcomes with adverse effects on the creation of an integrated market.[160]

Kaymo SA, 31 July 2009 (Zaragoza Commercial Court, Spain) (successful on similar facts); *Adidas v Patrick Portugal-Artigos de Desporto Ltda*, 21 June 2012 (Valencia Court of Appeal, Spain) (successful on similar facts).

[157] Cf D Stone, *European Union Design Law: A Practitioner's Guide* (Oxford, Oxford University Press, 2012) 11.09 (noting this full parallel in design law); FK Beier, 'Basic Features of Anglo-American, French and German Trademark Law' (1975) 6 *International Review of Industrial Property and Copyright Law* 285, 303 (discussing German theory of *Abstandslehre*).

[158] See L Bently and B Sherman, *Intellectual Property Law* 4th edn (Oxford, Oxford University Press, 2014) 991–92, noting confusion variants. In determining distinctiveness the relevant consumer is determined by reference to the goods in respect of which the applicant seeks to register its mark. See Kerly (n 50) para 8-016. At the infringement stage, however, the goods on which the defendant is using its sign may be different, causing courts to adapt the relevant consumer. See Bently and Sherman, above, 989, noting General Court case law suggesting that the relevant public is composed of users likely to use both the claimant's and defendant's goods; cf *Jack Wills* (n 66) [59]–[68] (Arnold J), discussing average consumer when parties targeting different markets, as opposed to selling different goods. The role of the average consumer in the dilution cause of action may diverge even further because that action extends to uses on dissimilar goods and one variant focuses on defendant's benefit. cf ibid [81]–[83] (Arnold J), considering effects of unauthorised uses on defendant's consumers.

[159] See *Enterprise Holdings* (n 42).

[160] See Dinwoodie (n 8) 94–95, comparing *Adam Opel* (n 145) and Case C–206/01 *Arsenal Football Club plc v Matthew Reed* [2002] ECR I-10273. See also n 38, discussing stronger protection for stronger marks via definition of confusion factors.

B. An Empirical Assessment of Consumer Perception in EU Trade Mark Law

It is also clear, however, that trade mark law *is* at least to some extent concerned with market realities. The protection of actual consumers is in fact a prime concern of trade mark law. To be sure, consumer protection is not the only objective of trade mark law, but the consumer is not simply a fiction through which to determine appropriate forms and levels of competition.[161] And while normative goals may structure the formulation of legal tests of distinctiveness and confusion and generate applicable presumptions, the application of those tests to the facts of a specific dispute creates meaningful opportunities for empirical assessment. Courts (not just in Europe) are inevitably attracted to the notion that they are legitimately making factual assessments rather than formulating normative policies about the appropriate nature of competition or consumer choice.

However, judges may also be persuaded that it is their responsibility to make decisions that determine the outcome of legal tests rather than sign off on conclusions mechanically flowing from supposedly neutral measures of empirical reality, such as a responsibly designed consumer confusion survey. Certainly, UK decisions (on passing off and trade mark infringement) are replete with statements that the likely confusion of customers is a matter for judges to decide,[162] even if the judgment called for is more instinctive than scientific.[163] Although courts have little compunction in concluding that the reactions of particular members of the public who testify before them are quite different from the average consumer,[164] the purportedly scientific character of a survey may be instinctively harder for some judges to dismiss and thus reconcile with the exercise of judgment.[165]

161 Cf MP McKenna, 'The Normative Foundations of Trade Mark Law' (2007) 82 *Notre Dame Law Review* 1839, challenging the conventional wisdom that trademark law traditionally sought to protect consumers and arguing that consumer deception was historically relevant only to the extent it was the means by which a competitor diverted a producer's trade).

162 See, eg, *Neutrogena* (n 122) 482 (Jacob J), noting in assessing passing off that '[t]he judge must consider the evidence adduced and use his own common sense and his own opinion as to the likelihood of deception. It is an overall "jury" assessment involving a combination of all these factors. Ultimately the question is one for the court, not for the witnesses'. See also *General Electric Co v The General Electric Co Ltd* [1973] RPC 297, 321–22; *Spalding AG v AW Gamage Ltd* (1915) 32 RPC 273, 286 (Parker LJ).

163 See *Wagamama Ltd v City Centre Restaurants Plc* [1995] FSR 713, 732 (Laddie J) (the question is more a matter of 'feel than science').

164 See, eg, *Specsavers* (n 101) [149] (Mann J).

165 See G Vos and T Iserief, 'The Rise of Market Surveys in Trade Mark Cases' in *BMM Magazine* 2012/3, 2–3, translated from Dutch <http://www.klosmorelvosenschaap.nl/_images/uploads/Vos%20&%20Iserief%20-%20The%20rise%20of%20market%20surveys%20in%20trade%20mark%20cases.pdf> accessed 27 April 2015: '[a] greater role for the market survey automatically implies a smaller role for the discretionary authority of the court. The court would hand, as it were, part of its judgment over to empiricism, and experience has shown that, in general, they are not keen to do so. They are the ones appointed to give their own judgment in, in this case, trade mark law disputes. If the role of market surveys were to increase, the feeling might arise that part of the court's characteristic legal authority was being handed over to (market) researchers, which some people would find inappropriate'.

But once it is accepted that no single item of empirical evidence is dispositive, as opposed to merely potentially helpful and considered within a broader (normatively structured) framework, the use of empirical evidence will be less threatening to the judicial role. And that is how empirical evidence should be conceived: factual evidence (whether direct or circumstantial) that assists a court in making a legal determination of validity or infringement.

In this regard, the use of empirical evidence in trade mark cases is not unlike that adduced in patent cases. Judges called upon to assess the validity of a patentable invention may be asked to consider whether it satisfies the 'inventive step' or non-obviousness threshold. In this situation, judges must adopt the perspective of the notional person of ordinary skill in the art, who is familiar with the state of the art in the relevant technological sector. Here, empirical evidence is submitted regarding the state of the art, which would allow the judge to determine whether the invention is non-obviousness to the notional skilled person. In such situations there would be no question that the ultimate legal question remains one for the judge. Recognising this purely intermediate role for empirical evidence is important; courts appear more sceptical of evidence that appears to opine on the ultimate legal question than on matters that provide background context. And this is an understandable fear in trade mark law where the legal fiction is very close to one of the primary objects of legal protection, namely, the consumer. Patent protection does not so obviously exist to protect the interests of the person of ordinary skill in the art. This misapprehension could be alleviated by courts stressing what is apparent in CJEU jurisprudence, namely, that opinion polls on distinctiveness or confusion (which come closest to the ultimate legal question) are simply one factor to be considered among many.[166]

Attitudes towards surveys have historically varied quite widely among Member States.[167] The admissibility of survey evidence (whether a full-blown survey or via a witness collection exercise) has been extensively reviewed by the UK Court of Appeal in recent years and it is fair to say that such evidence has not been welcomed with open arms (at least as regards the question of confusion).[168]

There are two principal reasons why such evidence is treated with caution. First, UK courts have been sceptical about whether surveys are reliable in their methodological rigour, impartial implementation, and accuracy of the conclusions drawn.[169] In short, surveys might be thought of as second-best 'constructed'

[166] See n 53 and accompanying text.

[167] See n 48.

[168] *Interflora I* (n 36); *Interflora Inc & Anor v Marks & Spencer plc (Interflora II)* [2013] EWCA Civ 319. Similar sentiments have been expressed by courts in other countries. See, eg, *Masterpiece Inc v Alavida Lifestyles Inc* 2011 SCC 27 (Supreme Court of Canada); *Australian Postal Corporation v Digital Post Australia* [2013] FCAFC 153 (Federal Court of Australia); see also *Kraft Foods* (n 58) 735 F.3d, 741 (Posner J), listing numerous problems that academic literature has identified about surveys, but acknowledging that '[o]f course, judges and jurors have their own biases and blind spots'.

[169] For an elaboration of these methodology and implementation concerns and ways in which sufficient objectivity might be established, see A Niedermann, 'Surveys as evidence in proceedings before OHIM' (2006) 37 *International Review of Intellectual Property and Competition Law* 260; K Swaine and

evidence, both because the artificial environment in which they are asked differs from actual purchasing experience and because of the 'hired gun' dimension to duelling party-adduced surveys. Thus, surveys in the UK had for 30 years prior to *Interflora* to comply with the arduous requirements of the so-called 'Whitford Guidelines' if they were to be admitted as evidence.[170] These included selecting a relevant cross-section of the public to be surveyed; the scale of the survey being sufficient to produce statistically significant results; full disclosure of the number of surveys and the manner in which they were conducted; avoiding leading questions or ones inviting speculative responses; and faithfully recording and disclosing all responses.

Second, surveys can be expensive to design, conduct and critique, so courts or registries tightly regulate the admissibility of such evidence in order to keep costs down. Concern about costs of litigation generally has become more prominent in recent years, and this was referenced by the Court of Appeal in *Interflora*. It clearly is driving a lot of this debate. Courts have performed a 'gatekeeping' function not just by tightening formal rules on admissibility, but also through case management techniques that require court supervision to conduct potentially admissible surveys.[171]

On its own terms, each of these concerns could be addressed. If unsatisfied with the artificiality of surveys, courts could contemplate alternative forms of expert study that do speak to the actual particularities of the market (if there has been sufficient use of the mark by the defendant).[172] The fear of bias in using hired guns could be ameliorated by the use of a court-ordered survey.[173] Alternatively, if the principal concern behind a reluctance to admit survey evidence is the costs of such evidence, then reform would focus on other techniques that could be imposed through case management or perhaps (in the UK) with some reform of the 'Whitford Guidelines'. Ironically, tackling the costs objection is hampered by the concern of reliability. Guidelines (such as the 'Whitford Guidelines') that seek to establish the reliability and representativeness of surveys by imposing rigorous standards paradoxically increase the costs of surveys. Less rigorous surveys *might* be cheaper.[174] Indeed, witness collection pilots (though savaged by the Court of

others, 'The Value and Treatment of Survey Evidence in Different Jurisdictions' (2010) 100 *Trade Mark Reporter* 1373; S Diamond and D Franklyn, 'Trade Mark Surveys: An Undulating Path' (2014) 92 *Texas Law Review* 2029.

[170] See *Imperial Group plc v Philip Morris Ltd* [1984] RPC 293 (Whitford J).

[171] See *Enterprise Holdings* (n 42) [21]–[34], describing practice adopted in the UK of requiring litigants to seek the advance permission of the court to conduct potentially permissible surveys.

[172] See, eg, *Kraft Foods* (n 58) 735 F.3d, 742 (Posner J), musing about the possibility of a statistical study analysing sales in areas where defendant was—and was not—using and comparing results, but suggesting that would not have confidence in the reliability of such a study either.

[173] See Vos and Iserief (n 165) 5, discussing Dutch practice.

[174] cf *Enterprise Holdings* (n 42) [35], noting that interlocutory 'gatekeeping' proceedings on the admissibility of surveys may in certain circumstances increase costs over what would have been incurred by dealing with survey evidence at trial.

Appeal in recent opinions to the extent that they are surely beyond rehabilitation) might have been seen as driven in part by such concerns.[175]

Given the scepticism shown by UK courts towards full-blown surveys, this of course seems wholly counterintuitive. But it would also address what we earlier ventured as a possible reason for judicial discomfort, namely, the abdication of judgment and usurpation of the judicial role. Surveys of the cheaper, less rigorous variety would very clearly be admitted on the assumption that they be afforded lesser weight and were simply to assist the exercise of judgment. The reaction of UK judges to the admissibility of surveys in recent years suggests that they, at least, would be comfortable dismissing the dispositive weight of such surveys and exercising independent judgment. Paradoxically, it is that scepticism that should allow courts to reconcile this form of evidence with their judicial role.[176]

But the appetite and room for these types of reform is surely limited after *Interflora*. As Lord Justice Lewison summarised the state of affairs in *Interflora II*:

> [T]he general message [is] that evidence from consumers in this kind of case (i.e. trade mark infringement involving ordinary consumer goods or services) should only be admitted if it is of *real* value; and even then only if the value justifies the cost; and that judges should be robust gatekeepers in that respect.[177]

Although the Court of Appeal has not completely foreclosed the admissibility of surveys,[178] especially as regards unusual goods and to test distinctiveness,[179] no

[175] Cf *Neutrogena* (n 122), 485–86 (Jacob J), expressing a preference for live witnesses over market surveys in assessing passing off.

[176] On gaps between input and judgment, litigants may be on the horns of a dilemma: are surveys too dispositive or insufficiently helpful? See *Zee Entertainment Enterprises* (n 54) [65] (Lewison LJ), noting in a passing off case that 'Mr Malynicz does not submit that the answers go to the question of deception. The survey goes to the question of whether the public or the relevant public has a propensity to make a connection between the mark and the sign. But, as Floyd LJ has said, that is not the real issue in cases of passing off, where the real issue is deception, so the fact that the survey only goes to a peripheral or subsidiary issue is itself a reason for degrading its value and not allowing it into evidence'; cf *Neutrogena* (n 122) 482 (Jacob J): 'It was certainly my experience in practice that my own view as to the likelihood of deception was not always reliable. As I grew more experienced I said more and more "it depends on the evidence"' (although expressing a preference for live witnesses over market surveys).

[177] *Interflora II* (n 168) [5].

[178] See *Interflora I* (n 36) [138]: '[I] would not accept the proposition that evidence from respondents to a questionnaire can never be called in the absence of a statistically valid and reliable survey. But (apart from those I have mentioned) the cases in which that kind of evidence might be of real use are difficult to imagine. I would not therefore hold that such evidence is inadmissible as a matter of law'; ibid [150]: '[i]n a case of trade mark infringement in which the issue is one of deception in relation to the provision of ordinary consumer goods or services, these criteria are likely to be satisfied only in a special or unusual case'.

[179] See ibid [137]: '[t]hat is not to say that there can never be evidence called in a case of trade mark infringement. The court may need to be informed of shopping habits; of the market in which certain goods or services are supplied; the means by which goods or services are marketed and so on. In addition I must make it clear, however, that different considerations may come into play where: (i) Evidence is called consisting of the spontaneous reactions of members of the relevant public to the allegedly infringing sign or advertisement; (ii) Evidence from consumers is called in order to amplify the results of a reliable survey; (iii) The goods or services in question are not goods or services supplied to ordinary consumers and are unlikely to be within the judge's experience; (iv) The issue is whether

surveys have been successfully admitted in the UK courts to date on the question of consumer confusion since the *Interflora II* court emphasised its '*real* value' test.

As Lord Justice Lewison noted, and several courts have since emphasised, this test is really a cost–benefit calculation: is the game worth the candle?[180] Is the expense of conducting a survey, having it analysed by experts to draw conclusions and having these challenged in the course of litigation worth the additional insight that it provides, especially in a likelihood of confusion context? And the value side of the ledger is affected not only by the ruling on admissibility of surveys and the use of witness collection exercises, but also by the fuller embrace of the normative consumer by the UK courts.[181] If the consumer is a fictional subject of the law which may be inhabited by the judge in the given dispute, and where the judge can be assisted by other categories of evidence, and must consider policy values of trade mark law that might discount precise consumer understanding, in reaching a conclusion, how much do surveys add?[182] Here other values, such as the cost and efficacy of the legal process, offset the relatively modest advantages of survey evidence, which once again raises the prospect of normative choices to be made in designing the consumer construct under EU trade mark law.

In sum, the normative (at the level of the test and its encoded presumptions) can and does coexist with empirical evidence relating to consumer perceptions as well as with behaviour in real world contexts. But that mix may vary across legal contexts. Acquired distinctiveness is seen as implicating a far more empirical inquiry, resulting in a more liberal attitude to surveys than in the confusion context. Moreover, empirical evidence can be used to rebut presumptions. For example, one could imagine that empirical evidence could support the argument that a European consumer would react differently than a British consumer in determining the appropriate scope of an injunction in a case involving a CTM.[183] Or empirical evidence can add detail to attenuated aspects of the test. As an illustration, courts assume that *generally* goods are not presented side by side; but in fact, some categories of goods might be, thus altering the confusion inquiry. Finally, there can also be variations as to when and where such evidence is considered relevant, the calculus potentially being different at the trade mark office or in courts adjudicating cases of infringement.

a registered mark has acquired distinctiveness; or (v) where the cause of action is in passing off, which requires a different legal question to be answered'. Despite exception (v) in *Interflora I*, the message from that judgment appears to have informed attitudes to surveys in passing off cases too. See, eg, *Zee Entertainment Enterprises* (n 54).

[180] See *Interflora I* (n 36) [150]; see, eg, *Zee Entertainment Enterprises* (n 54) [28]–[30].

[181] However, reliability of surveys might also matter less if the assessment is more avowedly normative.

[182] Therefore the relevant consumer perspective is adopted by the trial judge as a 'notional juror', using their own common sense and experience of the world. See *Cosmetic Warriors Ltd v Amazon.co.uk Ltd* [2013] EWHC 2470 (Ch), [2014] FSR 15 [26]–[31].

[183] *DHL Express* (n 29); *Interflora Inc v Marks & Spencer plc* [2013] EWHC 1484 (Ch), [2014] FSR 2 [31]–[38].

C. Institutional and Structural European Questions

As noted above, the consumer is a fictional figure through whose eyes doctrinal questions are answered in both the registration and infringement contexts. The CJEU hears appeals from registration determinations at OHIM as well as preliminary references from national courts (and so-called CTM courts) on issues of both registration and infringement.[184] The Court readily adopts doctrinal and methodological statements about consumer reaction from one context and applies them in the other, though it has been careful to note the different (more limited) supply of information given to a notional consumer in the registration context.

In section III above, we noted that where there *had* been use of the marks in question, the Court appears to be growing more comfortable with the notion that actual context should be allowed to inform how the notional consumer views both the claimant and defendant's marks. But because of the continued importance of enforcing registration in unused marks, the default rule will often be for courts to proceed without evidence of current empirical realities. Since neither the Directive nor the Regulation addresses the characteristics of the consumer directly, the image has been painted by the CJEU. However, pursuing the EU goal of a unitary market, the Regulation contributes uniquely to the construction of the average European consumer in at least one way. A trade mark registration will only be granted if the purported trade mark avoids being descriptive. But the 'consumer' through whose eyes questions of trade mark law are assessed differs in cases involving national marks (litigated under the Directive) and CTMs (litigated under the Regulation). In the latter case, the Regulation is concerned with the average European consumer. Reflecting that fact, if the term for which a CTM is sought is descriptive or generic in any part of the Community, Article 7(2) requires that registration be denied.

The practical upshot of this rule is that one of the characteristics of the consumer through whose eyes distinctiveness determinations are made is that he or she speaks every language of the Community. An application to register the Portuguese term for biscuits as a mark for biscuits would be denied registration notwithstanding that consumers throughout the rest of the (non-Portuguese speaking) Community would not regard the term as descriptive and likely see it as distinctive. Such a consumer is clearly not empirically grounded; certainly the 'average consumer' does not speak all 24 official languages of the EU. There is a normative construction of the consumer, reflecting the core goals of the European project.[185]

[184] To administer the CTM, the Regulation had to establish EU institutions, leading to the creation not only of the OHIM to administer the system of registration, but also of CTM courts to enforce the rights conferred. The CJEU is not the only court to hear cases under both the Directive and the Regulation. CTM courts are national courts designated by the Member States to hear CTM infringement actions. See Trade Mark Regulation, Art 95.

[185] In this regard, trade mark law is to some extent adopting a proactive approach to the consumer, seeking to construct a legal fiction and shape markets in Europe, rather than reactively mirror reality.

Some countries make similar (but not identical) assumptions in assessing their national marks either because they recognise (empirically) that some of their citizens might speak the foreign language and thus view the mark differently, or because (normatively) free trade concerns counsel in favour of not protecting marks that would be generic in other countries and thus likely on the packaging of any goods imported from that country. But Member States of the EU are not required to follow this rule (sometimes called the doctrine of foreign equivalents). For example, in *Matratzen Concord AG v Hukla Germany*, an applicant sought to register the mark MATRATZEN for mattresses with the Spanish Trademark Office.[186] This term would have been regarded as generic for mattresses and unprotectable in Germany. But the Spanish office reasoned that Spanish consumers would not appreciate this, and would regard the word as the mark for a single brand of mattresses. The CJEU was not willing to overrule this approach, notwithstanding the barriers that the ownership of the Spanish mark by a single producer might have had on the import of mattresses from Germany to Spain. The empirical reality was not trumped by normative commitments. Empirically, the Spanish consumer is not the European consumer. But should this reality prevail normatively? Recent Commission proposals for reform of the Trade Mark Directive and Regulation would have required Member States to adopt as national law the rule found in Article 7(2) of the Regulation, namely that a lack of distinctiveness in any country of the EU will doom a national mark as well as a CTM.[187] But national offices, lacking the linguistic infrastructure that exists in Alicante, objected and the proposal is lacking from the most recent text of the proposed directive.[188]

A similar dilemma arises in the context of infringement. The same average European consumer determines whether two marks are confusingly similar for purposes of infringement of a CTM. But such judicial assessments are made by CTM courts.[189] These are *national* courts (and national judges) masquerading as federal courts.[190] Indeed, typically these are simply the same courts that hear cases under national trade mark law.[191] Does this institutional structure affect the construction of the consumer? When an application is made before the OHIM, there

See GB Dinwoodie, 'Trademarks and Territory: Detaching Trademark Law From the Nation-State' (2004) 41 *Houston Law Review* 885.

186 Case C–421/04 *Matratzen Concord AG v Hukla Germany* [2006] ECR I–2303.

187 See Proposed Directive (n 5), Art 4(2).

188 See Council, Proposal for a Directive of the European Parliament and of the Council to Approximate the Laws of the Member States relating to Trade Marks—Presidency Compromise Proposal (2013/0089 (COD), 19 November 2013) 16 (deleting Art 4(2)). For the latest text, see Council, Proposal for a Directive of the European Parliament and of the Council to Approximate the Laws of the Member States relating to Trade Marks—Presidency Compromise Proposal (2013/0089 (COD), 18 July 2014) 25 (deleting Art 4(2)).

189 A CTM court with international jurisdiction can hear an invalidity counterclaim. See Trade Mark Regulation, Arts 96(d), 98(1).

190 See Trade Mark Regulation, Art 95.

191 See, eg, The Community Trade Mark Regulations 2006, SI 2006/1027, reg 12.

will likely be consideration of the mark in all languages of the EU.[192] As a result of the institutional framework chosen for the creation of CTM courts, however, (national) judges pragmatically tend to decide cases involving the CTM through the eyes of a local consumer (or judge, notionally being a consumer).[193]

If infringement of a CTM is found, and the CTM court has what is called 'international jurisdiction', the CTM court should ordinarily grant an injunction that is EU-wide in scope.[194] That is the normative basis of the unitary right system. However, in *DHL Express France SAS v Chronopost SA*, the CJEU recognised an exception to this rule where infringement has occurred in only a particular group of Member States because the existence of confusion is dependent on a specific linguistic usage in those territories.[195] To be sure, the burden to show variation among other consumers of the EU is imposed on the party seeking to deny the national–Community level assimilation.[196] However, here the Court has allowed empirical reality potentially to modify the normative vision of a single European consumer that underlies the unitary right.

In both these cases—languages relevant to the distinctiveness of a CTM and scope of relief for infringement of a CTM—the EU has elevated a normative conception of the European consumer reflecting the ideals of the European project, although the latter doctrine leaves open the possibility of empirical modification. The approach that has been adopted in the infringement context seems to us to be a pragmatic reconciliation of normative market integration goals and other objectives of trade mark law that are more tied to the realities of how real consumers react to marks.

But could other approaches be envisaged, and how would they affect the image of the consumer in EU trade mark law? Clearly, the most single-minded pursuit of market integration (from which the Commission has pulled back in its current reform of the Directive) would construct at the national and CTM level a fictional European consumer who would speak all 24 official languages and react uniformly to marks throughout Europe (both when we assess distinctiveness and determine confusion). Despite decades of European integration, there would with respect to many goods and services be a large gap between this vision and marketplace realities.[197] And, because of the consumer's schizophrenic existence as both the legal fiction driving the system and the actual real world object of trade mark protection, the gap between reality and normative ideal cannot become too wide lest the policy goal of market integration undermine the consumer protection objectives of trade mark law.

[192] See OHIM Guidelines, Part B, Examination, Section 4, Absolute Grounds for Refusal (n 56) 37.

[193] As a contrast, consider the design of the unitary patent court system, and the composition of panels. See Council Agreement on a Unified Patent Court [2013] OJ C175/01.

[194] *DHL Express* (n 29), para 44.

[195] ibid, para 48.

[196] *Interflora* (n 183) [31]–[38].

[197] See Howells (n 20) 72–73, noting that 'signs of a homogenous European consumer protection culture are still fledgling' in terms of what different consumers rely on.

Of course, to some extent we already tolerate such gaps at the national level; this is implicit in recognition that the average consumer is not a policy-blind reflection of reality. But the average national consumer channelled by national judges is (at least with respect to goods with which a judge is familiar) not too far removed from reality. Could mechanisms be developed to help national judges sitting as CTM judges more closely approximate a European consumer? Indeed, paradoxically, could empirical evidence assist in the construction of this notional character (in ways that increasingly we deem unnecessary in the national context)? If the relevant assessment has (for normative reasons) to be of the European consumer, could not a court require opinion polls to be constructed that test the reactions of consumers throughout the entire EU?

Such an approach is unlikely to occur without aggressive legislative prompting. As noted above, there has historically been a divergence of opinion about the use of such evidence among different national courts. And in a CTM court, procedural matters are left to the national law of the country in which the CTM courts sits. More fundamentally, of course, the costs of imposing such a requirement may outweigh the gains (as the default assimilation of national and European consumers, subject to proof otherwise, adopted by UK courts might suggest).

V. Conclusion

Trade mark law recognises and protects proprietary interests in signs. However, both formal recognition (when does a sign qualify as a trade mark?) and protection via the infringement provisions (has a mark's signalling ability been harmed?) turn on consumer perception. Provoked by the other contributions in this volume, this chapter seeks to make two contributions to EU trade mark law scholarship. First, it has identified a variable consumer construct. Structural features stemming from the coexistence of national and unitary trade mark rights, as well as different doctrinal reasons for turning to the consumer (assessing distinctiveness or the likelihood of confusion; during registration or when applying infringement tests) ensure that such variations are hard-wired into the trade mark regime. Second, this variation is often expressed in the divergent degrees to which empirical evidence is incorporated within a notional average consumer test. Inherent distinctiveness analysis is a light touch best-guess or prediction as to whether an average consumer will perceive a sign as a trade mark qualifying for protection. Yet, despite viewing the matter from the same vantage point, analysis of acquired distinctiveness typically accommodates far more empirical evidence relating to how the mark has been used and its visibility in the marketplace. Empirical heft is also required to support claims that a mark should no longer be protected because it is generic in the eyes of relevant consumers, or where a mark is alleged to possess such reputation that it deserves a greater scope of protection. For likelihood of confusion, recent debates over the admissibility and utility of survey evidence have foregrounded the extent to which the average consumer is a fictional construct. If we are ultimately asking whether a normatively infused 'reasonable' consumer would be confused, survey evidence can only provide a partial answer. Is it worth the time and expense?

At the same time, in drifting too far from empirically grounded consumer responses, trade mark registries and courts could stray into contested territory. Will the average consumer vantage point become a set of heuristic techniques used to process large volumes of opposition decisions or distinctiveness claims? Can it collapse into an abstract, formalistic infringement test which relies on a visual comparison of the signs and their goods and services, as applied for on paper? Would it be deployed such that assumptions about consumer behaviour further trade mark proprietors' agendas in pursuit of bright line property rules? At present, each of these characterisations is recognisably familiar at different doctrinal sites within EU trade mark law. Unreflexive assumptions that we are working with the same 'one size' notional consumer construct could lead to dangerous cross-fertilisation (or cross-contamination) across EU trade mark law. Expanding our horizons further, what are the sources of normativity—both within EU trade mark law and across EU law more generally—which inform this objective construct? To the extent that consumer interests may conflict with other normative agendas, how should such normative dissonance be managed? To take one illustration, what if consumers are becoming habituated to seeing pure or single colours as trade marks, regardless of the anti-competitive effects and colour depletion this could generate? Thus the two contributions we seek to make in this chapter lead to a third embryonic contribution—setting out a research agenda for developing a more nuanced, diagnostically accurate, normatively robust and reflexive approach to understanding the average consumer in EU trade mark law.

16

The Consumer in European Regulatory Private Law

VANESSA MAK

I. Introduction

The 'image' of the consumer in law is a fictional image. In seeking to balance the rights of consumers against those of businesses the law makes a choice that applies to all consumers, regardless of their actual characteristics, their ability to express or enforce their preferences or their need for guidance or protection. For the law, Homer's self-reliant Ulysses is treated the same as the less sophisticated Homer Simpson.[1] The choices that have been made in relation to consumer images in law, in other words, are simplifications of reality, which have been modelled to fit with certain rationales or policy goals. And different choices fit different markets.

The question that I will seek to answer in this chapter is what normative choices have been made with regard to the image(s) of the consumer in European regulatory private law ('ERPL'), and whether these choices may (or may not) need revision as insights on consumers' needs for protection evolve. European regulatory private law can be defined as the rules laid down by the EU legislator that seek to facilitate private law relationships whilst also pursuing specific policy goals, such as consumer protection or the integration of the EU internal market. They can be rules of private law—for example, introducing mandatory contractual terms in consumer contracts—but often take the form of administrative law or even, in a broader definition of ERPL, competition law.[2] In the definition used by Hans Micklitz, ERPL is regarded as (the emergence of) a self-sufficient European private

[1] The example is taken from RH Thaler and CR Sunstein, *Nudge* (New Haven, Yale University Press, 2008). For an insightful discussion see S Frerichs, 'False Promises? A Sociological Critique of the Behavioural Turn in Law and Economics' (2011) 34 *Journal of Consumer Policy* 289, 294–95.

[2] cf H-W Micklitz, 'The Visible Hand of European Regulatory Private Law—The Transformation of European Private Law from Autonomy to Functionalism in Competition and Regulation' (2009) 28 *Yearbook of European Law* 3.

law, which exists alongside national private laws.[3] My focus will be on a relatively small part of this field, relating to EU legislative intervention in consumer contract law.

In this chapter, consequently, I will focus on the 'active' side of ERPL. By that I mean the rules of EU law that have sought to enhance consumer protection through positive measures of harmonisation, such as EU directives in contract law. They can be contrasted with measures of negative harmonisation, which also pursue harmonisation but instead of through the introduction of legislation do this by taking away barriers posed by national laws to the integration of the internal market.[4] It has been noted that this active branch of harmonisation takes a markedly more pro-consumer stance than rules of negative harmonisation do.[5] Fitting with this approach, the image of the consumer for whom these rules are written—although it is not spelled out in any of the legislation—seems to lean towards a weak(er) party who is in need of protection to make up, for example, for a lack of bargaining power or for cognitive limitations to rational choice.[6] Consumers can be regarded as weak vis-à-vis businesses, for example, because they do not have access to the same product information that businesses have, but also because of more personal attributes such as age, mental or physical infirmity, or perhaps even poverty.[7]

The image of the weak consumer, however, does not sit well with the general framework for economic regulation of private law relationships in the EU as laid down for instance in competition law; nor does it fit with the general principle of party autonomy that underlies most national private laws.[8] In either of these systems, the consumer is regarded as a rational actor who—like other private actors—makes autonomous decisions and for whom the law normally only offers a facilitative back-up, rather than protection. The choice of ERPL to focus on weaker consumers, therefore, seems to diverge from the norm. That divergence, as we will see in the discussion of, for example, the protection against unfair contract terms, is increasing as a result of the Court of Justice ('CJEU') case law in which consumer protection is steadily drawn out further both in the context of procedural law and more recently even in the substantive test for unfairness.[9]

[3] See the description of the ERPL project at: H-W Micklitz, 'Project Description—The Visible Hand of European Regulatory Private Law (ERPL)—The Transformation from Autonomy to Functionalism in Competition and Regulation' <http://blogs.eui.eu/erc-erpl/project-description> accessed 12 April 2015. Also H-W Micklitz, Y Svetiev and G Comparato (eds), 'European Regulatory Private Law—The Paradigms Tested' *EUI Working Paper LAW* 2014/04.

[4] Such as the rules on the free movement of goods; Art 34 TFEU.

[5] H Unberath and A Johnston, 'The Double-Headed Approach of the ECJ Concerning Consumer Protection' (2007) 44 *Common Market Law Review* 1237.

[6] The latter as a response to insights from behavioural sciences with regard to 'bounded rationality'; see A Tversky and D Kahneman, 'Judgment Under Uncertainty: Heuristics and Biases' (1974) 185 *Science* 1124.

[7] See section II of this chapter on unfair commercial practices.

[8] cf S Grundmann, 'Information, Party Autonomy and Economic Agents in European Contract Law' (2002) 39 *Common Market Law Review* 269, 270 ff.

[9] See section III of this chapter.

The question whether these inroads into party autonomy in private law can be explained, or even justified, in the light of the EU's internal market policy become newly relevant as the Court discovers the 'sleeping beauty' of consumer protection rules laid down in EU directives.[10] To assess whether they can be, it is submitted that a functional approach may provide some guidance. With this I mean that a focus on the function that consumer protection standards have in the broader framework of regulation in which they operate can explain why certain policy choices have been made and why they make sense in that context. An example is the 'average consumer' of EU law as a benchmark but also as a means by which to mediate between EU law and national laws.[11] The notion of the average consumer, and the level of protection attached to it, is in that case chosen with particular policy goals in mind. As will be seen, the goals are different in other areas, such as ERPL and national private laws, and as a result the consumer protection standards adopted there also come out differently.

The structure of the chapter is as follows. I will first describe the 'standard' consumer image that has emerged in EU law in a broader sense, that is, encompassing not just consumer (contract) law but also competition and intellectual property law (section II). I will then elaborate the image of the consumer as it has developed in European regulatory consumer contract law, that is ERPL in the narrow definition (section III), and compare this with the consumer notion in national private laws (section IV). National regulatory laws relating to private law—contractual—transactions are not discussed in this chapter. They form an interesting field of investigation, for example, because they often also introduce stricter protection for consumers, like ERPL. The type and level of regulatory consumer protection, however, differs greatly between the Member States' laws, not to mention that sometimes enforcement of consumer protection laws is also pursued through criminal laws.[12] An investigation of the overlaps and differences between ERPL and national regulatory laws therefore goes beyond the scope of this chapter. I will focus on EU law to provide a bird's-eye view of ERPL's position in the broader framework of the EU internal market, and national private laws as a way to compare it to images of the consumer in general private law relationships.

In each section, I will seek to describe not only which images of the consumer exist, but also what the ratio behind them is and their function in a particular area of law. To illustrate these approaches, I discuss selected examples from the CJEU's case law. In section V, I connect the various consumer images. It will emerge that function is a determinative factor in defining consumer images in ERPL and beyond. A functional perspective can explain the balance that has been struck

[10] H-W Micklitz and N Reich, 'The Court and Sleeping Beauty: The Revival of the Unfair Contract Terms Directive (UCTD)' (2014) 51 *Common Market Law Review* 771.

[11] See below, section II.B.

[12] That is, eg, the case for remedies relating to the infringement of unfair commercial practices law in France; see G Howells, H-W Micklitz and T Wilhelmsson, *European Fair Trading Law. The Unfair Commercial Practices Directive* (Ashgate, Aldershot, 2006) 7.

between responsibility, protection and empowerment of consumers, and why in this context a more lenient consumer image has been adopted in ERPL. Whether this is also a justification, however, is doubtful.

II. Image I: The 'Rational' Consumer in EU Law

The prevailing image in EU law appears to be that of the consumer as a 'rational actor'. This image implies that:

> [e]ach individual in the market is assumed to be the best judge of his own interests and to act rationally, maximising his utility (or personal satisfaction) within the constraints of his economic resources.[13]

This notion of the consumer, as can be seen, emphasises a number of economic rationales. The consumer is defined purely in economic terms and the focus lies on their role as a market participant, not on other roles that individuals may have in society (for example, citizen, subject of fundamental rights). Further, a specific goal is defined which the consumer is assumed to pursue, namely the maximisation of utility or personal satisfaction.[14] In this context, the consumer is assumed to be the best judge of their own interest, to take rational decisions, and to do so within the constraints of their economic resources.

The rational consumer in EU law appears in a number of instances in unfair commercial practices regulation, competition law, and in intellectual property law—albeit that some discussion is possible with regard to the degree of 'rationality' that is required of a consumer. I will explore these areas with reference to the case law (section II.A) and will then elaborate on the rationales for these consumer images in the context of EU market regulation (section II.B).

A. Image

One of the core images of the consumer in EU law is the 'average consumer'. This consumer type is encountered in unfair commercial practices regulation,[15] but has its origins in the regulation of the free movement of goods.[16] In a number of cases, the CJEU was asked to rule on the compatibility of national rules with EU free movement law where national measures to protect consumers against misleading marketing or advertising could constitute barriers to intra-Community trade.

[13] I Ramsay, *Consumer Law and Policy* 3rd edn (Oxford, Hart Publishing, 2012) 47.

[14] On this, see further below, section II.B.

[15] Directive 2005/29/EC of the European Parliament and of the Council of 11 May 2005 concerning unfair business-to-consumer commercial practices in the internal market ('Unfair Commercial Practices Directive') [2005] OJ L149/22, Art 5.

[16] Art 34 TFEU, formerly Art 28 EC.

In *Mars* it was noted that 'reasonably circumspect' consumers should be able to understand that a marking on product packaging indicating a quantity increase is not necessarily linked to the size of that increase.[17] National law should therefore be set aside if it sought to impose stronger protection for consumers. In a further set of cases,[18] culminating in *Gut Springenheide*, the Court developed this benchmark to that of the 'presumed expectations' of a consumer who is 'reasonably well-informed and reasonably observant and circumspect'.[19] Again, this notion sets a high bar for consumer protection measures.

It is worthwhile noting that parallel to the development of this 'average consumer' notion sometimes similar cases used the criterion whether 'a significant number of consumers' would be misled as their benchmark.[20] The CJEU has more recently indicated that it regards this quantitative assessment as a measure that may be interchangeable with the average consumer test. In assessing whether advertising with regard to parallel imports should be considered misleading, the national court should determine whether a 'significant number of consumers' would have been deterred from a purchase had they known the true state of affairs.[21] That finding appears to fit with some approaches seen in national systems, such as in German law, where the assessment of whether consumers will be misled is often tested through empirical studies.[22] It should be noted, however, that the 'average consumer' in EU law is foremost a normative concept. As the CJEU indicates in *Gut Springenheide*, national courts may determine the presumed expectations of an average—reasonably well-informed and reasonably observant and circumspect—consumer 'without ordering an expert's report or commissioning a consumer research poll'.[23] The CJEU's reference to a 'significant' number

[17] Case C–470/93 *Verein gegen Unwesen in Handel and Gewerbe Köln eV v Mars GmbH* [1995] ECR I–1923, para 24.

[18] The CJEU refers to Case C–362/88 *GB-INNO-BM v Confédération du commerce luxembourgeois* [1990] ECR I–667; Case C–238/89 *Pall Corp v PJ Dahlhausen & Co* [1990] ECR I–4827; Case C–126/91 *Schutzverband gegen Unwesen in der Wirtschaft eV v Yves Rocher GmbH* [1993] ECR I–2361; Case C–315/92 *Verband Sozialer Wettbewerb eV v Clinique Laboratoires SNC and Estée Lauder Cosmetics GmbH* [1994] ECR I–317; Case C–456/93 *Zentrale zur Bekämpfung unlauteren Wettbewerbs eV v Privatkellerei Franz Wilhelm Langguth Erben GmbH & Co KG* [1995] ECR I–1737; and Case C–470/93 *Verein gegen Unwesen in Handel und Gewerbe Köln eV v Mars GmbH* [1995] ECR I–1923. Van Dam notes correctly that the earlier cases, unlike the Court seems to suggest by its reference to them, do not explicitly engage with the 'average consumer' benchmark; see Cees van Dam, 'De gemiddelde Euroconsument—een pluriform fenomeen' (2009) *Sociaal-economische wetgeving SEW* 3, 6.

[19] Case C–210/96 *Gut Springenheide and Rudolf Tusky v Oberkreisdirektor des Kreises Steinfurt* [1998] ECR I–4657, paras 30–31. This definition was followed in Case C–220/98 *Estée Lauder Cosmetics GmbH & Co OHG v Lancaster Group GmbH* [2000] ECR I–117, paras 27 and 30; Case C–44/01 *Pippig Augenoptik GmbH & Co GK v Hartlauer Handelsgesellschaft mbH* [2003] ECR I–3095, para 55; Case C–99/02 *Criminal proceedings against Linhart and Biffl* [2002] ECR I–9375, para 32.

[20] See Case C–373/90 *Criminal proceedings against X (Nissan)* [1992] ECR I–131, para 15.

[21] Compare Case C–356/04 *Lidl Belgium GmbH & Co KG v Etablissementen Franz Colruyt NV* [2006] ECR I–8501, paras 78 and 82; and see *Nissan* (n 20), paras 15–16, as well as the Opinion of AG Tesauro, para 9.

[22] See *Gut Springenheide* (n 19), para 36.

[23] ibid, para 31.

of consumers therefore should probably be interpreted in a normative manner, without the need for empirical evidence.[24]

The standard by which conduct is assessed is adopted in other areas too. The 'average consumer' has since been included in Directive 2005/29 concerning unfair commercial practices as a benchmark by which to measure whether consumers should be protected against specific practices.[25] The standard is used to assess whether a practice is unfair, in the sense that it has misled the consumer and causes or is likely to cause them to take a transactional decision that they would not have taken otherwise.[26] In this context it copies the consumer image used in the free movement case law of the CJEU. It includes further definitions of the image of the consumer in two respects. First, besides the 'average consumer' another 'targeted average consumer' is defined. In cases where practices are directed at a specific group of consumers (for example, children) it is deemed desirable that practices are assessed from the perspective of an average member of that group.[27] Second, the Directive protects 'vulnerable consumers'. It specifies that the protection of consumers who, because of their 'age, mental or physical infirmity or credulity', are more susceptible to being misled by commercial practices should be assessed from the perspective of an average member of that group.[28] These further definitions are, however, not easy to apply in practice and the categories mentioned may be under-inclusive; they do not, for example, reckon specifically with poverty.[29]

In the regulation of intellectual property rights, another area of internal market regulation, the image adopted is also that of the consumer as a rational actor. It is given a more specific definition there. In the regulation of models, reference is made to the 'informed consumer', whereas in patent law the standard is that of the 'man skilled in the art'. Both reflect a standard of informed reasonable behaviour from the consumer that is higher than that of the 'average consumer', albeit to different degrees. For patent law, the standard is really that of an expert in the field.[30]

B. Function

The function of the consumer image(s) in EU law that emerges from this overview is two-pronged. First, the consumer image provides a normative benchmark for

[24] Support for this conclusion can also be gleaned from the Opinion of AG Tesauro in *Nissan* (n 20), which seems to conflate the two concepts: 'that the average consumer, who I am convinced is not wholly undiscerning, is inclined, not least in view of the considerable expense he is contemplating, to make a careful comparison of the prices on offer' (para 9).

[25] For a comprehensive analysis, referring also to national case law in Germany, England and Italy, see B Duivenvoorde, *The Consumer Benchmarks in the Unfair Commercial Practices Directive* (doctoral thesis, University of Amsterdam 2014).

[26] Unfair Commercial Practices Directive, Art 5.

[27] See Unfair Commercial Practices Directive, Rec 18.

[28] Unfair Commercial Practices Directive, Rec 19.

[29] P Cartwright, 'The Image of the Consumer in EU Law' in C Twigg-Flesner (ed), *Research Handbook on EU Consumer and Contract Law* (Edward Elgar, 2015, forthcoming).

[30] cf Joined cases C–101/11 P and 102/11 P *Herbert Neuman v José Manuel Baena Grupo SA*, judgment of 18 October 2012.

the substantive rules that should be adopted in a business–consumer relationship. Further, this benchmark has a broader function in EU internal market law as an instrument for mediating the competences of the EU and the Member States.

Looking at the normative content first, the consumer image gives guidance to the type of intervention in consumer markets (in the form of regulation) that is introduced through EU law. The image of the 'average consumer' as a reasonably well-informed and circumspect actor fits with the neo-classical economic school. The neo-classical view starts from the premise that intervention in consumer markets can be justified if it addresses market failures, that is to say, factors that hinder the optimal operation of a competitive market, in particular factors hindering efficiency.[31] The key example is that of information asymmetries between businesses and consumers, for example in relation to the characteristics or the quality of goods.[32] The model assumes that such failures can be addressed by, for example, providing relevant information. That should enable the consumer to make a decision that maximises their utility (or personal satisfaction). Of course, for that model to work, the assumption is that the consumer is a 'rational' actor who only needs this additional information to be in an equal position vis-à-vis the business to make a sound—or in economic terms, optimal—decision.

It should be noted that this perspective underlies many consumer laws in the world—for example in the US but also in most European private laws—and explains why these laws seek to increase the bargaining power of consumers by focussing on information requirements. Their aim is to create equality between consumer and business by taking away the asymmetry that exists between on the one hand the consumer (who has limited information about the product) and on the other hand the business (who is in possession of, presumably, full information about the product). As a basis for intervention in consumer markets this view is likely to encounter the least resistance because its intervention will be of the minimum degree deemed necessary to correct market failures. Regulation will be introduced sparingly, taking account also of the costs that regulation is likely to have, such as compliance and enforcement costs.[33]

Regulatory intervention, when it occurs, will often take the form of information requirements but can also appear as a delimitation of options. A common case is where regulation is used to steer consumers towards a default option, such as for a specific pension scheme which will give them adequate pension payments upon retirement.[34] The creation of options may be regarded as a form of (soft) paternalism but it is not entirely excluded from the neo-classical school of thought. In the neo-classical perspective, one could also say that by more clearly defining

[31] cf Ramsay (n 13) 42–43.

[32] R Epstein, 'The Neoclassical Economics of Consumer Contracts' (2008) 92 *Minnesota Law Review* 803.

[33] cf O Bar-Gill, 'The Behavioral Economics of Consumer Contracts' (2008) 92 *Minnesota Law Review* 749.

[34] Thaler and Sunstein (n 1).

options consumers have better information and are therefore better able to make (rational) choices. Soft paternalism is then turned into empowerment.[35]

The consumer image in EU law, based on neo-classical economic thought, has a second function. That function is to mediate between the EU and the Member States levels of regulation. Choosing a restrictive notion of the 'average consumer' and (by corollary) a lower level of consumer protection makes it harder for Member States to maintain or introduce stricter rules of consumer protection. The 'rational' consumer image chosen by EU law therefore has the effect that it supports EU internal market law. The threshold for unjustified barriers to trade in the internal market is set higher.[36] From the perspective of market regulation in the EU, therefore, the benchmark of a rational, well-informed consumer not only fits normatively with the neo-classical economic view, and the neo-liberal politics of the EU. That normative image is also given support by its central function as a mediating instrument in the EU's internal market or free movement regulation.

The notion that the consumer in EU law is only seen as a 'rational' actor in the utility maximising sense, however, can be downplayed.[37] Weatherill has pointed out that much of the case law concerns situations in which—rather than taking issue with the content of the consumer notion in national laws—the CJEU had difficulty with particular measures of national law because they were hard to justify, and that the Court has accepted restrictive measures where compelling justifications were given.[38] In other words, the case law itself has made it hard to engage the Court in a constructive dialogue with the Member States as to what degree of protection a consumer requires in the European internal market. Some support may even be found in the cases for the notion that the consumer is not regarded as a rational consumer in the strictly economic sense, but that instead a less demanding average consumer test is used.[39] Whichever way this should be understood, it is clear that some degree of rationality or competence must be assumed on the part of the consumer in order to maintain a workable regulatory framework.[40] The purpose of the framework, after all, is not to give unqualified protection to consumers, but rather to strike a fair balance between the interests of consumers, businesses and—on a more abstract level—the conditions for trade and competition in the EU internal market. Consumers therefore also have a responsibility to look out for their own interests and to prevent themselves from entering into

[35] Y-H Alex Lee and K Jeremy Ko, 'To Empower, Prohibit or Delegate? Regulatory Strategies for Modernizing the Consumer Credit Market' *University of Pennsylvania Business Law Journal* (forthcoming) <http://ssrn.com/abstract=1903595> accessed 12 April 2015.

[36] cf Unberath and Johnston (n 5); see also V Mak, 'The "Average Consumer" of EU Law in Domestic and European Litigation' in D Leczykiewicz and S Weatherill (eds), *The Involvement of EU Law in Private Law Relationships* (Oxford, Hart Publishing, 2013) 333.

[37] See also Cartwright (n 29).

[38] S Weatherill, 'Who is the "Average Consumer"?' in S Weatherill and U Bernitz (eds), *The Regulation of Unfair Commercial Practices under EC Directive 2005/29* (Oxford, Hart Publishing, 2007) 115.

[39] cf Weatherill (n 38), and see Cartwright (n 29).

[40] ibid.

economically detrimental transactions if they could have avoided doing so by, for example, reading the product information more carefully.

That the internal market function can also be supported in other ways, with use of a different consumer image, becomes clear when we consider ERPL. It is to this area of EU law that I now turn.

III. Image II: The 'Calimero Consumer' in European Regulatory Private Law

The image of the consumer in ERPL has taken various forms. I will, in this section, elaborate a number of these. One connecting factor is that all of these images appear to take a very protective stance towards consumers, viewing them generally as a weak party in need of protection. An image that fits well with this notion is the cartoon character Calimero—created in Italy and famous in some other European countries too—who is a small, black chicken that gets into trouble often and does not quite understand why grown-ups around him are angry at him for his clumsiness. The phrase that he utters invariably at the end of each episode is: 'They are big and I is [sic] small and it's not fair, oh no!'

The consumer as a weaker party, or the 'Calimero consumer', is prevalent throughout ERPL. I will first describe the instances in which this consumer appears in ERPL and will then elaborate on the function of this consumer image.

A. Image

ERPL, in the form of EU secondary law relating to consumer contracts, is based on the idea that consumers are weaker parties who need to be protected. The image of the consumer, therefore, although it may start from the presumption of consumers as 'rational' actors, tends to pay greater heed to the weaknesses and biases that prevent consumers from making rational choices. As a result, the rules laid down in these instruments not only seek to empower consumers—for example by imposing information duties on traders—but often also to lay down substantive rights aimed at consumer protection. The notion of the consumer's right to protection by law has also given rise to far-reaching measures to achieve effective protection of these rights through national remedies. Remedies, in this sense, include secondary rights laid down in legislation such as the right to repair non-conforming goods, but also the enabling of remedial actions through procedural law, with a prime example in unfair terms regulation.[41]

[41] The right to repair non-conforming goods follows from Art 3 of Directive 1999/44/EC of the European Parliament and of the Council of 25 May 1999 on certain aspects of the sale of consumer goods and associated guarantees [1999] OJ L171/12. On unfair terms, see section III.A.i.

The scope of this chapter does not allow for a full discussion of all the case law. I will therefore only discuss a few selected highlights to illustrate the position of the consumer in ERPL. The selection below focuses on two types of case that have been particularly influential in the case law of the Court since, roughly, 2000.

It should be noted that, unlike in the examples from EU law that I discussed in section II, ERPL does not normally refer to specific notions or images of the consumer. In other words, a benchmark such as the 'average consumer' or the 'man skilled in the art' is not identified in the legislation or in the case law. Nevertheless, it is possible to distil from the cases what kind of attitude is taken towards consumer protection in ERPL. Comparing it to the 'average consumer' case law—and similar EU regulation—it can be surmised that the image of the consumer to which ERPL is attuned must be more protective towards consumers.[42]

i. *Unfair Terms and Other ex Officio Protection*

The first, and perhaps most extreme, example of consumer protection through ERPL is the policing of unfair terms in consumer contracts. Directive 93/13 on unfair terms stipulates that terms which have not been individually negotiated should be regarded as unfair and should not bind the consumer if, contrary to the requirement of good faith, they 'cause a significant imbalance in the parties' rights and obligations arising under the contract'.[43] Content-wise, the goal of the Directive is already more focussed towards protection than the examples seen in EU internal market law. The rule that unfair terms will be regarded as non-binding has very little to do with the expectations of the EU 'average consumer', or of an otherwise informed consumer. The test is more objective: it looks at the effect that a term has on the balance of the parties' interests under the contract. Recent case law moreover reflects that the CJEU is gradually filling in more of the substance of the test,[44] whereas it had in the early years of the Directive not interfered much with the substance and left it to national courts to make the assessment of unfairness within the context of national law and the circumstances of the case.[45]

Although one could in theory expect a reasonably well-informed, observant and circumspect consumer—such as the 'average consumer' in EU internal market law—to consider the rights and obligations which they enter into more carefully, that is not what the Directive requires. Of course some of this protective attitude can be explained by the fact that most consumers are unable to properly assess the effects of general terms and conditions before signing a contract.[46] That, however,

[42] See also Unberath and Johnston (n 5).

[43] Council Directive 93/13/EEC of 5 April 1993 on unfair terms in consumer contracts [1993] OJ L95/29, Arts 3(1) and 6(1).

[44] eg Case C–415/11 *Mohamed Aziz v Caixa d'Estalvis de Catalunya, Tarragona i Manresa (Catalunyacaixa)*, judgment of 14 March 2013; Case C–226/12 *Constructora Principado SA v José Ignacio Menéndez Álvarez*, judgment of 16 January 2014.

[45] See also Micklitz and Reich (n 10).

[46] For a critical perspective, see eg O Ben-Shahar and CE Schneider, 'The Failure of Mandated Disclosure' *University of Chicago Law & Economics Olin Working Paper* No 516 <http://ssrn.com/abstract=1567284> accessed 12 April 2015.

does not explain why a consumer is not protected against equal nonchalance in reading the information on products in the supermarket or adverts in the newspaper, as is the case for the 'average consumer' in unfair practices regulation.[47]

Apart from the substantive component of the test laid down by the Directive, unfair terms protection has also received a significant boost from the CJEU's case law concerning the ex officio assessment of unfairness by national courts. In a line of cases, starting with the judgment in *Océano*,[48] the CJEU has established that an effective protection of consumers against unfair terms in certain circumstances requires active involvement of the judge. Article 3(1) in combination with Article 6(1) of Directive 93/13 requires that unfair terms should be 'non-binding' on the consumer. In order for this protection to be effective, the Court reasoned, a national court should be able to determine of its own motion (or: ex officio) whether a contract term is unfair. If consumers were obliged to raise the unfair nature of such terms themselves, the Court states, there is a 'real risk' that they will not do so either because of ignorance of their rights or because the fees for obtaining expert assistance, for example, by a lawyer, are too high in comparison to the amount at stake in the litigation.[49] This protection was taken further in subsequent judgments, where the CJEU ruled that this ex officio protection of consumers is not just possible, but mandatory for national courts. Accordingly, a national court must examine, of its own motion, whether a contract term is unfair,[50] where it has available to it the legal and factual elements necessary for that task.[51]

The ex officio protection of consumers on the basis that their weaker procedural position may make it harder, if not impossible, for them to give effect to substantive consumer rights arising from EU law extends into other areas than unfair terms too. Examples to which this applies are off-premises contracts (*Martín Martín*),[52] consumer credit (*Rampion*)[53] and consumer sales (*Duarte Hueros*).[54] It is noteworthy that protection in these cases seems to be more restricted than

[47] See above, section II.A.

[48] Joined cases C–240/98 to 244/98 *Océano Grupo Editorial SA v Roció Murciano Quintero* [2000] ECR I–4941.

[49] See *Océano* (n 48), para 26. Also Case C–473/00 *Cofidis SA v Jean-Louis Fredout* [2002] ECR I–10875.

[50] Case C–168/05 *Elisa María Mostaza Claro v Centro Móvil Milenium SL* [2006] ECR I–10421, paras 27 ff; Case C–40/08 *Asturcom Telecomunicaciones SL v Cristina Rodríguez Nogueira* [2009] ECR I–9579, with an important addition, namely the ruling that 'Article 6 of the directive must be regarded as a provision of equal standing to national rules which rank, within the domestic legal system, as rules of public policy', para 52.

[51] Case C–243/08 *Pannon GSM Zrt v Erzsébet Sustikné Győrfi* [2009] ECR I–4713, para 32. Note also that the court is obliged, if it finds that a term is unfair, not to apply it, unless the consumer opposes that non-application; *ibid*, para 33. See also Case C–137/08 *VB Pénzügyi Lízing Zrt v Ferenc Schneider* [2010] ECR I–10847.

[52] Case C–227/08 *Eva Martín Martín v EDP Editores SL* [2009] ECR I–11939.

[53] Case C–429/05 *Max Rampion and Marie-Jeanne Godard, née Rampion v Franfinance SA and K par K SAS* [2007] ECR I–8017.

[54] Case C–32/12 *Soledad Duarte Hueros v Autoriba SA, Automóviles Citroën España SA*, judgment of 3 October 2013. Note also that the CJEU has recently adopted far-reaching consumer protection in relation to the notification duty in consumer sales law; Case C–497/13 *Froukje Faber* (nyr).

in the unfair terms cases. Whereas protection under Directive 93/13 requires a court to test the unfairness of a term, in the case of the other Directives the Court is not obliged but has the *possibility* to, of its own motion, assess whether rules of national law hinder the effectiveness of substantive rights arising out of EU law.[55] Still, the Court's overall attitude seems to be that national procedural restrictions should not create barriers to substantive consumer protection. In order to enable consumers actually to make use of their rights, the Court is willing to make significant inroads into national procedural autonomy where it finds that national procedural law imposes restrictions on consumers' possibilities to exercise these rights.

Across a wide area of ERPL, therefore, the CJEU has backed up substantive rights with procedural mechanisms to give effect to those rights. The consumer image that is central to these cases is that of the consumer who is in 'a weak position vis-à-vis the seller or supplier, as regards both his bargaining power and his level of knowledge'.[56] This consumer is given protection through the ex officio involvement of the court, to counter 'the real risk that he is unaware of his rights or encounters difficulty in enforcing them'.[57]

ii. The Right of Withdrawal, Extended Version

Another set of cases that offers a good example of the pro-consumer approach taken in ERPL are cases in which the trader or supplier had omitted to inform the consumer about their right to withdraw from the contract. The right to withdraw, which in essence gives consumers some time to consider their purchase and/or to inspect or test the goods or services, has become a common feature of European regulatory contract law. It is included in the Consumer Rights Directive, which of course replaces two earlier Directives in which a right of withdrawal was already included (Directive 85/577 on doorstep selling and Directive 97/7 on distance contracts).[58]

The case law of the CJEU makes clear how important the right to withdraw can be in terms of consumer protection, and in particular how its reach can be extended in cases where the seller has failed to inform the consumer that they have the right to withdraw. In *Pia Messner*,[59] a distance contracting case, the consumer of that name had bought a laptop from an online seller. When the laptop's screen

[55] In Dutch: JHM Spanjaard, 'Pénzügyi/Lízing: HvJ EU verzet de bakens inzake ambtshalve toetsing van algemene voorwaarden' [2011] *Maandblad voor Vermogensrecht* 75, with reference to Van der Beek. Also A Ancery [2014] *Tijdschrift voor Consumentenrecht* 153, 154, with a different reading of *Rampíon*.

[56] *Océano* (n 48), para 25.

[57] *Mostaza Claro* (n 50), para 28, with reference to *Océano* (n 48), para 26 and *Cofidis* (n 49), para 33.

[58] Directive 2011/83/EU of the European Parliament and of the Council of 25 October 2011 on consumer rights [2011] OJ L304/64 (Consumer Rights Directive), Art 9; Council Directive 85/577/EEC of 20 December 1985 to protect the consumer in respect of contracts negotiated away from business premises [1985] OJ L372/33 (Doorstep Selling Directive), Art 5; Directive 97/7/EC of the European Parliament and of the Council of 20 May 1997 concerning the protection of consumer in respect of distance contracts [1997] OJ L144/19, Art 6.

[59] Case C–489/07 *Pia Messner v Firma Stefan Krüger* [2009] ECR I–7315.

started to malfunction, some eight months after the purchase was concluded, the seller refused to repair it free of charge. Ms Messner then sought to undo the contract by invoking the right to withdraw.[60] Although this right would normally have expired for distance contracts after seven days, in this case the seller had failed to inform Ms Messner about her right to withdraw. Under German law, which applied to the contract, no prescription period applied and the consumer would therefore be able to invoke the right to withdraw indefinitely.[61] Moreover, as the right of withdrawal prescribes, she would be able to do so without paying compensation to the seller apart from the direct cost of returning the goods.[62]

The CJEU confirmed that consumers are in principle able to withdraw from distance contracts without paying compensation for use to the seller. To hold otherwise could impair the effectiveness and efficiency of the right to withdraw by imposing a financial burden on consumers—which could deter them from making use of the right to withdraw—and by curtailing their possibility to test (as opposed to use) the goods free of charge.[63] The consumer therefore could, even after almost a year, invoke the right to withdraw and, in principle, incur no expenses. This conclusion was somewhat attenuated by the Court's ruling that the consumer could be required 'to pay fair compensation in the case where he has made use of the goods acquired under a distance contract in a manner incompatible with the principles of civil law, such as those of good faith or unjust enrichment'.[64] Also, the Consumer Rights Directive now contains not only a codification of this case law but also a specification of the requirements regarding compensation for use.[65]

Another instance in which the right of withdrawal gave rise to an extensive interpretation by the Court was in the *Schulte* and *Heininger* cases.[66] These cases concerned investments in immovable property which for many consumers turned out to be unprofitable. In an attempt to escape such contracts, consumers invoked the Doorstep Selling Directive. The CJEU applied the Directive with great emphasis on consumer protection. First, it held that the contracts at issue fell within the scope of the Directive and that the fact that consumers had not been informed of their right of cancellation meant that the right was valid indefinitely.[67] That did not solve the problem, however, as it allowed consumers to get out of the credit agreement but not automatically also to cancel the underlying contract for the

[60] Which, although it may not be the most obvious action in these circumstances, has the advantage that the consumer does not have to supply evidence to support her claim that the non-conformity was present from the time of delivery. Messner's choice to invoke the right of withdrawal was in this respect a clever alternative.

[61] See *Messner* (n 59), para 6.

[62] Directive 97/7 (n 58), Art 6(1).

[63] *Messner* (n 59), paras 17–29.

[64] ibid, para 26.

[65] Consumer Rights Directive, Art 14.

[66] Case 481/99 *Georg Heininger and Helga Heininger v Bayerische Hypo- und Vereinsbank AG* [2001] ECR I–9945; Case C–350/03 *Elisabeth Schulte and Wolfgang Schulte v Deutsche Bausparkasse Badenia AG* [2005] ECR I–9215.

[67] *Heininger* (n 66), para 40 and 48.

purchase of immovable property. The Court, in a very consumer-friendly judgment, gave an opening for doing that by holding that 'if the bank failed to comply with the obligation to inform the consumer of his right of cancellation, then the bank should bear the consequence that the risks "associated" with the failure to comply actually materialize'.[68] Essentially, the CJEU therefore extended the right of withdrawal to enable consumers not only to get out of contractual obligations years after the conclusion of the contract, but also to get out of linked contracts. It should be noted that this protection proved of only limited use in the ensuing litigation in Germany. By ending the credit agreement, consumers would be liable for immediate repayment and would therefore on balance be worse off. The CJEU's decision in *Schulte* opened the door to alternative solutions but in their search for these national courts get very little help from the rather vague pronouncements of the Court of Justice.[69]

What emerges from the case law, nonetheless, is an image of a consumer who is in need of protection. The CJEU is willing to extend protection very widely on the basis that consumers in comparison to businesses have a weaker bargaining position and less access to relevant information.[70] This type of protection goes much further than in the 'average consumer' cases discussed above, where vulnerability is defined in relation to specific concepts such as age, mental or physical infirmity or credulity.

B. Function

Observing the function of the consumer image in this field, it is noteworthy that ERPL, although it is referred to as 'private law', has a distinct policy influence that is absent in particular in (national) contract laws. Contract law—stereotypically—is based on the autonomy of parties and has a facilitative character. This means that parties are free to decide with whom to contract and on what terms. Contract law does not interfere with the content but provides the legal backup to enforce the rights that are created in this way.[71] Although inroads on this ideal type are present also in national systems, not least because those systems have also developed consumer protection law through mandatory contract rules, ERPL is by its

[68] Unberath and Johnston (n 5) 1260; *Schulte* (n 66), paras 94–103.

[69] cf N Reich, 'The Social, Political and Cultural Dimension of EU Private Law' in R Schulze and H Schulte-Nölke (eds), *European Private Law—Current Status and Perspectives* (München, Sellier, 2011) 70–73.

[70] See above, n 57.

[71] See further section IV of this chapter. See also, inter alia, Grundmann (n 8), PS Atiyah, *The Rise and Fall of Freedom of Contract* (Oxford, Oxford University Press, 1979), G Gilmore, *The Death of Contract* (Columbus OH, Ohio State University Press, 1974), SA Smith, *Contract Theory* (Oxford, Oxford University Press, 2004) and F Bydlinski, *Privatautonomie und objektive Grundlagen des verpflichtenden Rechtsgeschäftes* (Wien, Springer, 1967).

nature based on and influenced by such policy goals. In other words, ERPL is instrumentalist in nature.[72]

The function of *European* regulatory private law, therefore, is fundamentally different from regulatory contract law at the national level. In national private law, regulatory elements have been introduced, for example, to strengthen the position of weaker parties in contract (consumers, or employees), or to redistribute losses in cases where liability can be established in tort law. In these instances regulation intervenes to achieve a re-balancing of responsibility between private parties.[73] The law shifts from responsibility to protection. Where in contract law parties would otherwise be regarded as autonomous actors, instead consumers are given protection because they are considered to be 'weaker' parties. In tort the starting point is that 'losses lie where they fall, but this perspective changes if damage can reasonably be attributed to another party' (the tortfeasor).

ERPL, although it pursues similar regulatory goals *in* private law, also seeks to achieve policy goals *through* private law. The goals that it seeks to achieve through private law are related to the role of law in the EU in a more general sense: namely, to install measures that support the integration of the internal market.[74] It has been noted that ERPL through positive harmonisation seeks to achieve what free movement regulation seeks to achieve through negative harmonisation: namely to support the integration of the internal market.[75] That can explain, and perhaps justify, why a 'weak' consumer image seems to underlie this field. It requires that regulation is put in place to protect the consumer.

IV. Image III: The 'Autonomous' Consumer in National Private Laws

In national private laws, a third image of the consumer can be found. Contract laws are based on the principle of party autonomy,[76] which entails that private parties are free to decide whether and with whom to contract, but also that they are responsible for the choices that they make. In tort law, similarly, responsibility lies first with the party who suffers a loss and can only be reverted to another party

[72] R Michaels, 'Of Islands and the Ocean: The Two Rationalities of European Private Law' in R Brownsword and others (eds), *The Foundations of European Private Law* (Oxford, Hart Publishing, 2011).

[73] On responsibility in (Dutch) private law, see eg KJO Jansen, *Informatieplichten. Over kennis en verantwoordelijkheid in contractenrecht en buitencontractueel aansprakelijkheidsrecht* (Kluwer, Deventer 2012).

[74] The competence of the EU in private law, therefore, is normally found in the internal market provision, Art 114 TFEU.

[75] Unberath and Johnston (n 5).

[76] See citations at n 71.

if certain conditions (such as a duty of care, causation) can be established. The image of private parties, therefore, is foremost one of autonomous actors.

For consumers, the same applies as a default. General doctrines in private law, for example, relating to mistake or misrepresentation at the stage of pre-contractual negotiation but also at a later stage the interpretation of contracts, will not normally be applied in a more protective or consumer-friendly way than they would for other parties. Consumers, like other parties, have their own responsibility to take reasonable care in private law relationships. In some instances, however, exceptions may be introduced, for example, through a particular application of private law doctrine to take account of an ad hoc or a generally weaker position of consumers, or of course through the introduction of specific consumer protection laws. I will describe a few examples from national systems and will then elaborate on the function of the consumer image.

A. Image

An apt illustration of the way that private laws take account of consumers is given by doctrines relating to non-disclosure or misinformation of the consumer. In English law, one would think of mistake or misrepresentation; in civil law systems of doctrines like *dwaling* (Dutch law) or *Irrtum* (German law), or fraud. In many consumer cases problems will arise because consumers are under a false impression with regard to the characteristics of goods or services. In some cases that impression has even, wilfully or not, been induced by the trader. The doctrines of misrepresentation or mistake—or equivalents in other systems—establish under what circumstances a party may be protected against such false impressions.

English law takes the most restrictive approach to protection. Non-disclosure is in principle not an actionable omission. As the case of *Smith v Hughes* established, a seller is not obliged to disclose information about the goods, even if they are aware that the buyer is operating under a mistaken presumption.[77] That becomes different only if the mistaken term becomes part of the contract. In that case, the buyer can bring an action for misrepresentation—also referred to as 'induced mistake'—on the basis that the seller has provided them with false information. An action for misrepresentation exists for fraudulent or negligent statements, but also for false statements that were innocently made.[78] The ratio of the rules is that buyers have a responsibility to acquire the necessary information before entering into a contract. Where they fail to enquire, they will have to bear the consequences of their own mistake. Only where the seller has actively done something to mislead the buyer does the law give an action.

[77] In this case, the buyer mistakenly believed that he was buying old oats instead of new oats. The latter were not suitable as horse feed. See *Smith v Hughes* (1871) LR 6 QB 597.

[78] Misrepresentation Act 1967.

Dutch and German laws are more protective. Rescission is possible in both systems if a party is mistaken about the 'essential characteristics' of the subject-matter of the contract, that is to say, if they would not have entered into the contract if they had been aware of the actual characteristics.[79] One can think of cases where a consumer believes a DVD to be playable in their home country, only to find out later that they are unable to do so because of a different region code. If the seller had failed to inform the consumer about the existence of different region codes, an action may lie for mistake. Further, if the seller had provided the wrong information about the envisaged use of the DVD, an action may exist for misrepresentation. In both cases, the consumer may rescind the contract.

Even though Dutch and German laws give wider scope to actions for, in particular, mistake that does not mean that they require a generally lower level of responsibility from the consumer. For an action in *dwaling* in Dutch law to succeed, for example, a balance has to be struck between the trader's duty to inform and the consumer's duty to enquire.[80] Where information is ambiguous, or where the consumer has their mind set on specific characteristics of the goods which are not common, they have a specific duty to enquire with the trader whether the goods do indeed have the characteristics that they require.

The image of the consumer as an 'autonomous' actor is continued in related areas of private law. Even in cases where more protection is given by law, the starting point of the enquiry is that consumers have their own responsibility to take reasonable care. Duties of care, for example, are recognised in Dutch or German law for specific cases in which consumers are deemed to be dealing with situations of a complexity that they are unable to navigate, like the purchase of complex financial products.[81] In the Netherlands, the provider, as the expert party, is obliged to take account of the interests of the consumer and to protect them against the risks associated with their lack of insight or their own rash decision-making. More specifically, this means that banks and investment firms are obliged to warn consumers about the specific risks of a product, to investigate the financial position of the client, and if the circumstances demand it even advise the client against purchase of the product.[82] It may seem that such a duty of care goes further in protecting consumers than duties arising under the doctrine of *dwaling*. However, that is not the case per se. It has been suggested that the Supreme Court chose the route of recognising a special duty of care because that would make it possible

[79] cf Art 6:228 Dutch Civil Code; s 119 German Civil Code.

[80] Dutch Supreme Court (Hoge Raad) 17 November 1957, *Nederlandse Jurisprudentie* 1958, 67 (*Baris/Riezenkamp*). In Dutch, see AS Hartkamp and C Sieburgh, *Asser/Hartkamp & Sieburgh 6 III. Algemeen overeenkomstenrecht* (Deventer, Kluwer, 2013), no 218 ff. For a comparative overview, see R Sefton-Green (ed), *Mistake, Fraud and Duties to Inform in European Contract Law* (Cambridge, Cambridge University Press, 2005).

[81] See on this Mak (n 36).

[82] Dutch Supreme Court (Hoge Raad) 5 June 2009, *Nederlandse Jurisprudentie* 2012, 182, ECLI:NL:HR:2009:BH2815 (*De Treek/Dexia*), para 4.8.1. cf Dutch Supreme Court (Hoge Raad) 5 June 2009, *Nederlandse Jurisprudentie* 2012, 183, ECLI:NL:HR:2009:BH2811 (*Levob*), paras 4.5.4, 4.5.6 and 4.5.10.

to divide responsibility between the bank and the consumer: unlike with *dwaling*, where the remedy would be rescission plus full compensation, the court was now in a position to divide the loss between both parties. In many cases, consumers had to bear up to 40 per cent of the loss themselves.[83]

B. Function

The picture that emerges from national private laws, therefore, is that consumers are regarded as autonomous, responsible actors. The general doctrines of private law may be adjusted to give some protection—as in the financial services cases—but will not take all responsibility away from the consumer.

Naturally, these rules may be complemented with mandatory rules of consumer protection in areas where the legislator deems such protection necessary. The choice for the introduction of such rules is a policy decision and, like in ERPL, is motivated by the desire to protect consumers as 'weaker' parties in comparison to businesses. However, it may be that the assessment of protection is by comparison more restrained. Autonomy, as a starting point, can imply that parties (consumers) who are not on equal bargaining terms with their counterparties (businesses), for example, because they lack relevant information, are assisted by law to achieve a more equal bargaining position. On that ground, the law may for example introduce information duties or other measures of consumer 'empowerment'.[84] Such measures, however, should go no further than necessary to support autonomy. They would not, one may assume, go quite as far as some of the developments that can be seen in ERPL with regard to, for example, the ex officio assessment of unfair terms.

Functionally, the consumer image in national private laws therefore can be explained mostly from a perspective of party autonomy. Protection of the weaker consumer in that light is an ancillary goal.

V. A Functional Approach Towards Consumer Images

Based on the foregoing, an overview of consumer images in EU law, ERPL and national private laws reveals a spectrum ranging from a reasonably well-informed and circumspect, 'rational' average consumer to—on the other end—a weak 'Calimero' consumer who is protected strongly through measures of ERPL. In the middle, we find the 'autonomous' consumer of national private laws who gets protection but only to the extent that it is necessary to ensure autonomy.

[83] See case note J Vranken, *Nederlandse Jurisprudentie* 2012, 184.

[84] G Howells, 'The Potential and Limits of Consumer Empowerment by Information' (2005) 32 *Journal of Law and Society* 34.

From a functional perspective, the choice for these images can be explained by the context in which they operate. These functions have been elaborated in the previous parts of this chapter. It is noticeable that the various images are nevertheless not easy to match. In this section, I will bring together some of the lines set out above in order to determine whether a functional perspective can clarify the relationship between the consumer images in the various fields.

First, it is clear that the starting point for regulation in each of these areas is the same. The legislature only intervenes if market failures exist.[85] Consumer law, from that perspective, only seeks to address such failures in order to create a new equilibrium in the market.

Second, intervention may nevertheless take different forms. Two degrees of intervention can be discerned. On the one hand, the images of the EU 'rational' consumer and the 'autonomous' consumer in national private laws—although they differ—appear to reflect a similar caution to intervene too soon or too strongly. Protection of these types of consumers is justified when it puts them back 'on par' with the businesses that are their counterparties. That can be because even a reasonably well-informed consumer would be misled by a particular practice and therefore deserves protection. It can also be because the consumer does not have equal bargaining power in comparison to the business and therefore does not have the same degree of autonomy. In either case, the legislature will exercise restraint before it intervenes with new regulation. Responsibility and empowerment are promoted, but strong protection not per se.

For ERPL, on the other hand, it appears that different policy choices have been made. In this field, protection is taken very far. Case law on unfair terms protection and the extensive application of withdrawal rights reveals that the CJEU is willing to take protection as far as can reasonably be justified within the scope of European Directives. In terms of protection, the outcomes go beyond what could be expected for the 'average' or 'autonomous' consumer. Even passive consumers are sometimes granted protection, as seen in the unfair terms cases.[86]

As a third point, the different degrees of intervention may be explained by the function that the consumer image has in ERPL, as opposed to its function in the other areas. All fields use the consumer image as a benchmark for assessing the appropriate level of consumer protection. However, that function is the most clear-cut in national laws, where it is the only consideration. Both EU law and ERPL bring in—different—considerations relating to market integration. In EU law market integration is helped by a consumer image that enables the Court to set aside measures of national law that, by adopting a higher level of protection, create barriers to trade in the internal market. ERPL approaches integration from an opposing perspective: the use of a 'weak' consumer image justifies intervention through EU regulation and thereby promotes the use of ERPL to contribute to the integration of the internal market.

[85] Ramsay (n 13).
[86] cf *Asturcom* (n 50).

Finally, can a justification for the different consumer images be found in their functions? That is a difficult point. Explanations may be given, but a normative framework that can justify the coexisting choices—for example, for a well-informed consumer or a weak consumer image—is hard to devise. In all likelihood, such a framework would combine justifications from various perspectives: neo-classical economics, market integration, behavioural studies, perhaps ideas of (social) justice or fairness. These are hard to combine into one theoretical framework; many of these perspectives conflict even.

It should be noted, however, that the contrast between the various choices may be less great than it is perceived. In order to have a workable regulatory framework, it is recognised at all levels that some responsibility must be assumed on the part of the consumer, but that this does not per se require fully rational behaviour in the economic, welfare-maximising sense.[87] A realistic approach, focussing on what can reasonably be expected from consumers, fits with the consumer images discussed here. It would seem for ERPL that the balance is sometimes struck very far towards protection. There may, however, be reasons to justify such a choice,[88] and it is also possible to correct certain choices through regulation at a later point in time.[89]

Perhaps the only realistic conclusion, then, is that consumer law in the EU functions with different consumer images and different degrees of protection. Is that problematic? Perhaps not if we consider that the problem of different degrees of protection is not unique to EU regulation. Also within national systems, differences may exist between areas of consumer law. Still, these systems are able to develop and to adopt new solutions when they are needed. An example can be seen in the cases concerning complex financial products, where new solutions—a duty of care—could be developed within the broader framework provided by public regulation and private law.[90]

That different images of the consumer exist does not mean, however, that no effort should be made to keep reassessing regulation in these areas. Businesses and consumers benefit from transparency and predictability of outcomes—that is, legal certainty—and it would help if regulation pursued these goals. Perhaps by looking at the images of the consumer, we can determine with greate precision which balance should be struck at different levels of regulation between responsibility, empowerment and protection.

[87] Above, section II.B.

[88] eg grounds of public policy; cf *Mostaza Claro* (n 50) and *Asturcom* (n 50).

[89] eg the rules on withdrawal in the Consumer Rights Directive, discussed above, section III.A.ii.

[90] cf *Dexia* (n 82).

17

The Court of Justice's 'Paradigm Consumer' in EU Free Movement Law

SYBE A DE VRIES*

I. Introduction

Excavations in the Italian town of Modena have made clear that oil lamps were one of the first mass-produced goods in Roman times, each bearing the stamp of a producer. The most well-known brands were *Stroboli*, *Communis*, *Fortis*, *Eucarpi* and *Phoetaspi*.[1] Fortis was the trendiest of all pottery brands, the *Artemide Tizio* under the lamps. They were distributed across the Roman Empire until the trade routes broke down and Germanic tribes took over the production centres. A functioning retail trade was vital to the survival of Rome considering the dense concentration of consumers. Ancient Rome could be regarded as a consumerist society, at least where people purchased goods and services in excess of their basic needs.

Similarly, the success of the EU Single Market depends on consumers and their willingness to purchase goods and services across borders. In a Europe with different regulatory traditions and solutions, protecting different groups of consumers coming from different cultural backgrounds, there is no real Euro-consumer. But as we will see, the Court of Justice of the EU (CJEU) has in its search for a 'paradigm consumer' found one: a consumer who plays a crucial role in building Europe's Single Market. But is this concept of a paradigm consumer sufficiently robust to make consumers not wholly dependent on the market for their survival, like in ancient Rome? And if the paradigmatic consumer is dependent on the market, does the paradigm meet the current requirements of the Treaty of Lisbon?

* This chapter is partly based on a previously published article: S de Vries, 'Consumer Protection and the EU Single Market Rules—The Search for the Paradigm Consumer' (2012) 4 *The Journal of European Consumer and Market Law* 228.

[1] http://www.archeobologna.beniculturali.it/modena/viale_reister_fornace/factory_08_en.htm

II. The Relationship Between the EU Single Market and the Consumer

A. The Consumer as a Beneficiary of the Internal Market Process

If we assume that market integration serves the consumer interest and optimises consumer welfare, then the EU rules on free movement and competition could, according to Weatherill, be seen as a form of consumer policy.[2] This can be well illustrated by the Premier League case on the compatibility of territorial restrictions on broadcasting rights for the English Premier League matches.[3] The European Court of Justice decided that a consumer was able to rely on EU law to challenge a criminal conviction for the use of a relatively cheap Greek satellite decoder card in contravention of UK law, allowing her to watch football matches in the United Kingdom which would otherwise have required the payment of a much higher fee. Hence, '[t]he internal market is at the service of the consumer who wants to shop around'.[4]

It will be shown that *consumer choice* plays a pivotal role in the case law of the CJEU, breaking down national market regulation.[5] The Court has particularly condemned national rules which crystallise given consumer habits that offered national industries concerned to comply with these, a competitive advantage. Instead, the Court relies on the capacity of the consumer to process information and to make informed choices about available products and services.[6]

B. Balancing Consumer Interests with Economic Freedoms According to the CJEU

In the following it will be shown how the European Court of Justice has developed and consolidated a system of trade liberalisation based on prohibitions imposed on the Member States and has thereby enhanced consumer choice. Yet at the same time the CJEU has acknowledged that certain national consumer measures, even though restricting free movement, may under conditions be upheld.

[2] S Weatherill, 'Consumer Policy' in P Craig and G De Búrca (eds), *The Evolution of EU Law*, 2nd edn (Oxford, Oxford University Press, 2011) 838.

[3] Joined cases C–403/08 and C–429/08 *FA Premier League Ltd et al v QC Leisure et al and Karen Murphy v Media Protection Services Ltd* [2011] ECR I–9083. See also S de Vries, 'Sport, TV and IP Rights: *Premier League* and *Karen Murphy*' (2013) 50 *Common Market Law Review* 591.

[4] See also S Weatherill, *EU Consumer Law and Policy* 2nd edn (Cheltenham, Edward Elgar Publishers, 2013) 34.

[5] ibid 840.

[6] S Weatherill, *EC Consumer Law and Policy* (London, Longman, 1997) 48.

i. *Prohibitive Treaty Rules on Free Movement*

Trade liberalisation and market integration are first boosted through the broad applicability of the Treaty provisions on free movement requiring Member States to set aside national laws and measures that restrict trade and free movement for non-justifiable reasons. In the following three ways, which will be elaborated hereafter, the Court has developed and consolidated the EU system of trade liberalisation: first, through a wide interpretation of the terms 'goods', 'services' and 'persons', the Court has applied a functional test and has thereby couched non-market values 'in the language of economics'.[7] Second, by distinguishing the actual origin of the restriction and what it consists of from who causes the restriction, all kinds of acts or measures can be brought within the scope of 'measures having equivalent effect' or restrictions within the meaning of the EU rules on free movement. Whether the restriction consists of legislation, binding decisions, contractual provisions or actual practice then becomes irrelevant.[8] And, lastly, the Court has determined that all kinds of obstacles to trade and free movement are in principle prohibited unless justified on public interest grounds.

a. The Concept of Economic Activity

Activities generally fall within the scope of the provisions on free movement insofar as they can be considered to be economic activities. Where there is no gainful activity involved, or where certain goods are not subject to commercial transactions, the Treaty rules on free movement will not be applicable.[9] Where certain activities in particularly sensitive areas are involved, Member States may want to retain the right to protect consumers in full by prohibiting these activities or imposing stringent conditions upon the exercise of these activities, irrespective of the impact of such legislation on trade between Member States. However, the CJEU generally does not exclude the applicability of EU law merely on the basis of the specific nature of the activity. In the *Schindler* case, for example, concerning national legislation prohibiting certain lotteries the question was raised whether lotteries form an economic activity within the meaning of Article 56 TFEU. The Court held that 'it is also the case that like amateur sport, a lottery may provide entertainment for the players who participate. However, that recreational aspect of the lottery does not take it out of the realm of the provision of services. Not only does it give the players, if not always a win, at least the hope of a win, it also yields a gain for the operator'.[10]

[7] SA de Vries, *Tensions within the Internal Market: The Functioning of the Internal Market and the Development of Horizontal and Flanking Policies* (Groningen, Europa Law Publishing, 2006) 28; D Chalmers, 'The Single Market: From Prima Donna to Journeyman' in J Shaw and G More (eds), *New Legal Dynamics of European Union* (Oxford, Clarendon Press 1995) 63.

[8] S Prechal and S de Vries, 'Seamless Web of Judicial Protection in the Internal Market?' (2009) 34 *European Law Review* 5, 7; De Vries (n 3) 606–07.

[9] Case C–2/90 *Commission v Belgium (Walloon Waste)* [1992] ECR I–4431; Case 263/86 *Belgian State v René Humbel and Marie-Thérèse Edel* [1988] ECR I–5356.

[10] Case C–275/92 *Her Majesty's Customs and Excise v Gerhart Schindler and Jörg Schindler* [1994] ECR I–1039, para 34.

The most peculiar *Josemans* case is also illustrative in this respect. According to Advocate General Bot in this case, the Treaty rules on the free movement of services did not apply to activities of 'coffee shops' in the Netherlands, which sell soft drugs as well as fizzy drinks and sandwiches. According to the Advocate General the activities related to the sale of soft drugs operate outside the legal economic sphere of the internal market. The case concerned a Dutch measure preventing non-Dutch nationals from having access to Dutch 'coffee shops' (selling soft drugs).[11] Although the CJEU ruled that the sale of soft drugs did not fall within the scope of application of the Treaty provision on services, since trade in soft drugs is prohibited in all Member States, it did rule that the sale of other products in coffee shops was covered by the Treaty rules on services. As a consequence the Dutch government needed to invoke a justification ground to keep non-Dutch consumers of soft drugs outside the border towns. In other words, the measures restricting the sale of these products needed to be justified on grounds of public order.[12]

b. Broad Scope of the Concept of 'Measure' or 'Restriction'

A broad scope of the notion of 'measures' or 'restrictions' entails that a considerable number of rules, irrespective of their origin, may fall within the prohibitions of the Treaty. Regarding the concept of 'measures having equivalent effect' within the meaning of Article 34 TFEU, the Court has provided for a wide interpretation of this term in a series of cases starting with *Dassonville*. Many arrangements, such as licences, inspection and monitoring, safety requirements, advertising and labelling requirements and price measures can be covered by the term 'measure'.[13] With respect to Article 56 TFEU on the free movement of services, where market access has become the main criterion for adjudicating national measures under the prohibitive rules on free movement,[14] the test employed by the CJEU appears to include various types of measures, such as certain licence requirements, authorisation requirements for medical treatment abroad or other mandatory provisions, but also the selection rules determining that Christine Deliège was not allowed to compete in the Paris International Judo Tournament in the under-52 kg category—even though these rules were in the end not considered to be in breach of Article 56 TFEU.[15]

[11] See Case C–137/09 *Marc Michel Josemans v Burgemeenster van Maastricht* [2010] ECR I–13019.

[12] See HJ van Harten and H van Eijken, '"Lookin" for a little green bag…' en de werkingssfeer van het Unierecht' (2011) 4 *Nederlands tijdschrift voor Europees recht* 105.

[13] Case 8/74 *Procureur du roi v Benoit and Gustave Dassonville* [1974] ECR 837.

[14] Case C–384/93 *Alpine Investments BV v Minister van Financiën* [1995] ECR I–1141.

[15] Joined cases C–51/96 and C–191/96 *Deliège v Ligue francophone de judo et disciplines associées ASBL* [2000] ECR I–2549. In the *Grogan* case a prohibition issued by an Irish court to provide information on the availability of legal abortions in the United Kingdom was, however, not considered a restriction within the meaning of Art 56 TFEU, since, according to the Court, the link between the activity of the students' associations of which Mr Grogan and the other defendants are officers and medical

In the above-mentioned *Premier League* case the disputes in the main proceedings essentially concerned horizontal disputes between private parties, including Football Association Premier League Ltd ('FAPL') and Karen Murphy (a pub owner). The Court also declared that the

> actual origin of the obstacle to the reception of such services is to be found in the contracts concluded between the broadcasters and their customers, which in turn reflect the territorial restriction clauses included in contracts concluded between those broadcasters and the holders of intellectual property rights.[16]

But this did apparently not constitute an obstacle to assess the case under EU free movement law,[17] an approach that fits in emerging case law, where the actual origin of the restriction and what it consists of are distinguished from who causes the restriction and to whom the restriction can be attributed. A *self-standing test* is used in which it is first of all determined what exactly the restriction comprises—does it consist of legislation, binding decisions or also of actual practice—and related to this, who causes the restriction. This may be the legislature, the central or local government, a civil servant, a public organisation, a sporting federation or a trade union, or even individuals holding demonstrations.[18] If the question of whether a restriction exists is separated from the addressee issue, it would also imply that contractual provisions could in principle qualify as a restriction on the free movement of goods or services within the meaning of Articles 34 or 56 TFEU and only on a second analysis could they be removed from the scope of free movement, namely if the obstacle can in no way be attributed to an authority which is bound by the free movement provisions.

c. The Market Access or Restriction Test

Lastly, through the use of the market access criterion,[19] or 'restrictions approach',[20] the Court has managed to bring most national consumer protection rules within

terminations of pregnancies carried out in clinics in another Member State is too tenuous for the prohibition on the distribution of information to be capable of being regarded as a restriction within the meaning of Art 56 TFEU: Case C–159/90 *The Society for the Protection of Unborn Children Ireland Ltd v Grogan* [1991] ECR I–04685.

[16] *Premier League* (n 3), para 88.

[17] A reason for the Court to feel inclined to adopt a 'total approach' on both the aspects of free movement and competition in *Premier League* (n 3) was possibly the interplay between the contractual provisions of the FAPL licences and the national law offering FAPL certain rights and remedies against a person who imports, distributes, and installs for commercial purposes 'any apparatus designed or adapted to enable or assist persons to access programs or other transmissions or to circumvent conditional access technology related to the programs or other transmissions when they are not entitled to do so'. And the national court had emphasised the role of the national law in conferring legal protection on the restrictions, which may suffice to trigger the application of EU free movement law and in particular Art 56 TFEU (De Vries (n 3) 606).

[18] See Prechal and de Vries (n 8).

[19] See also J Snell, 'The Notion of Market Access: A Concept or a Slogan?' (2010) 47 *Common Market Law Review* 437.

[20] See with respect to the Treaty provisions on persons and services: C Barnard, *The Substantive Law of the EU—The Four Freedoms* (Oxford, Oxford University Press, 2010) 253.

the scope of the prohibitive rules on free movement. This obviously leads to more competition between domestic and foreign, unfamiliar goods and services. Regarding the type of obstacle under the free movement regime, the *Dassonville* case[21] and subsequent cases, in particular *Cassis de Dijon*,[22] make clear that not only discriminatory measures, but also indistinctly applicable product requirements are caught by the prohibition on restricting trade in goods as contained in Article 34 TFEU.[23] In fact, it appears that *how* a restriction should be classified has become increasingly irrelevant.[24] The legal commitment to free trade and free movement entails a regime which is directed at prohibiting any unjustified obstacle to trade rather than at merely eliminating discrimination and protectionism.[25]

In the context of the provisions on services and persons, the Court made clear that these provisions also apply to indistinctly applicable measures. In the *Säger* case the Court held that

> article 49 (now Article 56 TFEU) requires not only the elimination of all discrimination against a person providing services on the grounds of his nationality, but also the abolition of any restriction, even if it applies without distinction to national providers of services and to those of other Member States.[26]

In the *Gebhard*[27] and *Bosman*[28] cases, the Court provided for a similarly broad interpretation of the freedom of establishment and the free movement of workers respectively.

And now also in the context of *exportation* of goods, the Court has been willing to modify its approach to Article 35 TFEU, which had always been more narrowly interpreted than Article 34 TFEU. In the *Gysbrechts* judgment the Court reinterpreted the *Groenveld* test, which implied that Article 35 TFEU only covered discriminatory export measures, by applying Article 35 TFEU also to an indistinctly applicable national consumer measure (see section II.B.ii.c below).[29]

[21] *Dassonville* (n 13).

[22] Case 120/78 *Rewe-Zentral AG v Bundesmonopolverwaltung für Branntwein* (*Cassis de Dijon*) [1979] ECR 649.

[23] Barnard (n 20) 80; P Oliver (assisted by M Jarvis), *Free Movement of Goods* (London, Sweet & Maxwell, 2003) 115–18.

[24] De Vries (n 3) 609.

[25] See for the dispute which cut to the heart of the international trade regime: JHH Weiler, 'The Constitution of the Common Market Place' in Craig and de Búrca (n 2) 352.

[26] Case C–76/90 *Manfred Säger v Dennemeyer & Co Ltd* [1991] ECR I–4221.

[27] Case C–55/94 *Reinhard Gebhard v Consiglio dell'Ordine degli Avvocati e Procuratori di Milan* [1995] ECR I–4165, para 37; See also Case C–19/92 *Dieter Kraus v Land Baden-Württemberg* [1993] ECR I–1663, where the Court considered a mere obstacle to the right of establishment as incompatible with Art 49 TFEU.

[28] Case C–415/93 *Union royale belge des sociétés de football association ASBL v Jean-Marc Bosman, Royal club liégeois SA v Jean-Marc Bosman* [1995] ECR I–4921, para 96.

[29] Case C–205/07 *Lodewijk Gysbrechts v Santurel Inter BVBA* [2008] ECR I–9947; Case 15/79, *Groenveld BV v Produktschap voor Vee en Vlees* [1979] ECR 3409. See also the annotation by WH Roth, 'Case Law' (2010) 47 *Common Market Law Review* 509; SA de Vries, '"Goods Revisited": Nieuwe inzichten in de rechtspraak over het vrij verkeer van goederen' (2009) 4 *Nederlands Tijdschrift voor Europees Recht* 121.

As is well known, the Court provided for a more restrictive interpretation of the free movement of goods provision in *Keck*. In this case the Court placed national rules on selling arrangements outside the scope of Article 34 TFEU, provided that these rules apply to all affected traders operating within the national territory and provided that they affect in the same manner, in law and in fact, the marketing of domestic products and those from other Member States. Here the legal commitment to free trade appeared to entail the abolition of discrimination, or protectionism, but no more.[30] Where national rules address particularly local interests, such as the opening hours for shops or the prohibition of resale at a loss, the impact on trade must be assumed negligible. But also *Keck* appears to be limited in scope as the Court decided in *Mickelsson and Roos* and *Commission v Italy* that rules restricting or prohibiting the *use* of certain goods—like personal watercraft on waters other than general navigable waterways in Sweden[31] and trailers for motorcycles or mopeds in Italy—did impede market access. According to the Court, such a prohibition has a considerable influence on the behaviour of consumers which in turn affects the access of that product to the market.[32]

ii. Exceptions for the Protection of Specific Consumer Interests

The foregoing makes clear that, if the State wishes to uphold consumer protection rules, this can only be done within the context of the exceptions. The important consequence of this approach is a shift in the burden of proof. The consumer rights proponents will have to justify their actions. As so often, the sting is in the 'tail': the proportionality principle will be extremely relevant here, determining the borderline between justifiable and non-justifiable restrictions.

Consumer protection as such is not mentioned in the Treaty as a justification ground for trade restrictions. But since consumer protection is concerned with the exposure of individuals, as consumers, to risks which face any of us in everyday life, it is also concerned with health and safety risks. Health and safety are grounds of justification for restrictions to free movement as recognised in the Treaty in Articles 36 and 51 TFEU. The case law shows that where a national measure is designed to protect (sensitive) consumers from a health risk, Article 36 TFEU may be invoked.[33]

[30] At dawn, just before the Court gave its judgment in *Keck*, AG Tesauro, in his search for the rationale behind the Court's case law, asked himself the following question: 'Is Article 30 (now Art 34 TFEU) a provision which seeks to liberalise trade between Member States, or quite simply does it seek to liberalise the pursuit of economic activities within a Member State as well?' AG Tesauro in Case C–292/92 *Ruth Hünermund et al v Landesapothekerkammer Baden-Württemberg* [1993] ECR I–6787. See G Tesauro, 'The Community's Internal Market in the Light of the Recent Case-law of the Court of Justice' [1996] *Yearbook of European Law* 5.

[31] Case C–142/05 *Åklagaren v Percy Mickelsson and Joakim Roos* [2009] ECR I–04273; Case C–110/05 *Commission v Italy* [2009] ECR I–519.

[32] *Commission v Italy* (n 31), para 56.

[33] Case 97/83 *CMC Melkunie BV* [1984] ECR 2367; Case 53/80 *Officier van Iustitie v Koninklijke Kaasfrabriek Eyssen BV* [1981] ECR 409.

More general consumer protection measures, originating from mandatory civil rules in favour of consumers, should be justified on the basis of the Court's case law and the protection of the economic interests of consumers has now a prominent place in the list of mandatory requirements developed by the CJEU in its case law under the rule of reason.[34] In *Cassis de Dijon* the Court held that national laws which give rise to obstacles to the free movement of goods must be accepted in so far as these provisions may be recognised as being necessary to satisfy mandatory requirements relating inter alia to the *defence of the consumer* and the fairness of commercial transactions.[35] This recognition of the protection of the consumer as mandatory requirement has had the result that Member States are allowed to uphold their national protective measures, as long as the national legislation applies to domestic products and imported products alike.

a. The Notion of Consumer in EU Law

Although the Court has accepted that consumer protection constitutes a mandatory or overriding requirement in the general interest, it depends on the context of each case which particular consumer has to be protected. Since national consumer protection law may impede free movement, which in itself is designed to advance the consumer interest, the Court, as stated above, has developed its own notion of consumer interest.[36] The basic notion of consumer in EU law is that the consumer is considered an individual who can, if provided with the necessary information, make their own choices and defend their own interests. In *GB-INNO-BM* the Court held that 'Article 28 (now Article 34 TFEU) cannot be interpreted as meaning that national legislation which denies the consumer access to certain kinds of information may be justified by mandatory requirements concerning consumer protection'.[37] This is also referred to as the notion of 'reasonably circumspect consumer' considering the Court's perception 'that most consumers are sufficiently robust and well informed to take care of themselves in the market place'.[38] The question is whether the Court's approach meets the current challenges that European consumer policy faces, where consumer behaviour and its impact on the market has changed considerably. Due to economic, environmental and technological

[34] Even though the notion of consumers as a separate group that needs particular attention has only recently developed: J Stuyck, 'European Consumer Law After the Treaty of Amsterdam: Consumer Policy in or Beyond the Internal Market?' (2000) 37 *Common Market Law Review* 367, 368–69.

[35] *Cassis de Dijon* (n 22).

[36] Weatherill (n 6) 41. For the notion of the consumer in Community law, see K Mortelmans and S Watson, 'The Notion of the Consumer in Community Law: A Lottery?' (1995) *Tijdschrift voor Consumentenrecht* 229; S Weatherill, 'Recent Case Law Concerning the Free Movement of Goods: Mapping the Frontiers of Market Deregulation' (1999) 36 *Common Market Law Review* 51.

[37] Case C–362/88 *GB-INNO-BM v Confédération du commerce luxembourgeois* [1990] ECR I–667, para 18. In his opinion AG Lenz emphasised the importance of information—in the form of advertisements—for consumers: 'Information should only be withheld from the consumer for his own protection for *convincing* reasons. After all, it must be assumed that any accurate information can only be useful to the consumer' (para 34).

[38] S Weatherill and P Beaumont, *EU Law* (London, Longman, 1999) 699–702.

developments and due to developments in, for instance, behaviour economics, the informed and rational consumer hypothesis has been challenged: consumers are in their opinion all vulnerable as they struggle to make rational decisions; they are irrational and sometimes uneducated (see section IV.A below).[39]

In several cases relating to misleading advertising, the Court refused to accept measures aimed at protecting the consumer whose intelligence and attention is less than average.[40] In *Mars*, for example, the question arose as to whether a German prohibition of the marketing of Mars ice-cream bars presented in wrappers marked '+10%' constituted a measure having equivalent effect and could be justified by reasons related to the protection of consumers against misleading information. According to the German government the '+10%' marking could lead the consumer to think that the new product was being offered at a price identical to that at which the old product had been sold. Furthermore the '+10%' marking induced the consumers to believe that they in fact gained more product because the band bearing the '+10%' marking occupied more than 10% of the total surface area of the wrapping. The Court, however, held that this justification could not be accepted: '[r]easonably circumspect consumers may be deemed to know that there is not necessarily a link between the size of publicity marking relating to an increase in a product's quantity and the size of that product'.[41]

The strong belief in the consumer as an active and critical information-seeker at the cost of some consumers being possibly misled as to the characteristics of certain products is also reflected by the *Clinique* ruling.[42] Here, a German law prohibiting the use of the name *Clinique* for the marketing of a cosmetic product could not be justified on grounds of consumer protection. The products were ordinarily marketed in other Member States under the name *Clinique*. Besides, the clinical or medical connotations of the word *Clinique* were not sufficient to make the word so misleading as to justify the prohibition of its use. The prohibition therefore did not appear to be necessary to satisfy the requirements of consumer protection and the health of humans. The Court thus rejected the notion that confusion suffered by German consumers could be sufficient to justify a prohibition to use the name *Clinique*.

Where national rules require the use of certain ingredients or additives in the manufacture of certain products the Court will regard these rules often as disproportionate or unnecessary restrictions to free movement. Instead, appropriate labelling could sufficiently inform consumers about differences between various products. In *Drei Glocken*, Italian rules required the use of durum wheat only for

[39] I Benöhr, *EU Consumer Law and Human Rights* (Oxford, Oxford University Press, 2013) 84.

[40] Stuyck (n 34) 392.

[41] Case C–470/93 *Verein v Unwesen in Handel und Gewerbe Köln eV v Mars GmbH* [1995] ECR I–1923, para 24.

[42] Case C–315/92 *Verband Sozialer Wettbewerb eV v Clinique Laboratoires SNC and Estée Lauder Cosmetics GmbH* [1994] ECR 317. See also G Howells and S Weatherill, *Consumer Protection Law* (Aldershot, Ashgate Publishing, 2005) 116.

the manufacture of pasta products.[43] The Court found these rules disproportionate since it remained possible for the Italian authorities to restrict the description 'pasta made from durum wheat' to 'pasta made exclusively from durum wheat', and adequately inform the consumer.[44]

Where the approach of the Court in cases on the free movement of foodstuffs could be criticised for its finding that labelling is more proportionate to the aim of consumer protection and the free movement of goods, where doubt has been cast on the fact that consumers actually read or even comprehend labelling disclosures,[45] it also stimulates cross-border trade in products that consumers are not familiar with. According to Weatherill, this case law shows 'the strength of the Court's impetus against "crystallization" of consumer habits caused by national choices about market regulation'.[46]

Although the notion of consumer has been given an autonomous meaning by the CJEU, this does not mean that the Court does not take into account certain 'national' requirements or particularities, that is to say, the fact that consumers of a Member State must be able to seek information in a language that is understandable for them. Or, in other words, the notion of consumer in EU law does not necessarily entail that European consumers become Euro-consumers. In the *Juvelta* case, for instance, the CJEU specifically referred to the *Lithuanian* reasonably circumspect consumer, who should be able to understand the information in an intelligible fashion. This case concerned Juvelta, an undertaking that engages in retail trade in articles of jewellery made of gold (amongst other things), which is required to have its articles stamped at an independent State assay office in accordance with Lithuanian legislation. But the articles had already been stamped by an independent office in Poland. According to the mutual recognition principle, articles which are lawfully traded and hallmarked in accordance with the legislation of the country of origin should be able to be sold in the country of importation. But the question was whether the Polish stamp provides information intelligible to an average *Lithuanian* consumer who is reasonably well informed and reasonably observant and circumspect. The CJEU stated that

> it must be held that it is probable that that mark is not intelligible to such a consumer, since such a person is not, in principle, deemed to know the Polish system of indicating standards of fineness for articles of precious metal. However, although the restrictive effects of the legislation at issue can thus be justified by the objective of ensuring effective protection for Lithuanian consumers, and providing them with information relating to

[43] Case 407/85 *Drei Glocken GmbH and Gertraud Kritzinger v USL Centro-Sud and Provincia autonoma di Bolzano* [1988] ECR 4233.

[44] AG Mancini's argument of Italian consumers not being adequately informed by labels about production of differently constituted pasta in other states, given the depth of cultural expectation in Italy about pasta, was not followed by the Court. See also Case C–448/98 *Criminal proceedings against Jean-Pierre Guimont* [2000] ECR I–10663.

[45] eg C MacMaolain, 'Free Movement of Foodstuffs, Quality Requirements and Consumer Protection: Have the Court and the Commission Both Got it Wrong?' (2001) 26 *European Law Review* 422.

[46] Weatherill (n 2) 842.

> standards of fineness for articles of precious metal imported into Lithuania which are intelligible to them, such justification can be accepted only if that legislation is proportionate to the objective pursued, that is to say if, while appropriate in order to fulfil that objective, it does not go beyond what is necessary to attain it.[47]

b. (More) Protection for Certain Groups of Consumers

In some cases the Court is willing to accept that certain groups of consumers need enhanced protection. The first category of measures concerns the measures that protect the economic interests of (particularly vulnerable) consumers. The *Buet* case, for example, involved a French measure prohibiting canvassing in connection with the sale of educational material.[48] According to the Court

> it is common ground that the French legislature adopted the prohibition of canvassing in question out of concern to protect consumers against the risk of ill-considered purchasers. [...] In that respect canvassing at private dwellings exposes the potential customer to the risk of making an ill-considered purchase. To guard against that risk it is *normally* sufficient to ensure that purchasers have the right to cancel a contract concluded in their home.[49]

Apparently, in normal situations a right of cancellation is sufficient for the protection of consumers. This case did, according to the Court, not reflect a normal situation, as there was a greater risk of an ill-considered purchase when the canvassing is for enrolment for a course of instruction or the sale of educational material. The potential purchasers are persons who are behind with their education and are seeking to catch up. That makes them *particularly vulnerable*.[50] The Court concluded that the ban on canvassing was necessary at private dwellings in particular to protect vulnerable consumers. As a result less restrictive means were unavailable.

A second category consists of measures that restrict certain activities, particularly sensitive areas, like gambling or insurance. The Court allows Member States a considerable margin of discretion where the specific nature of the activity requires so. In *Schindler* the Court held that 'given the peculiar nature of lotteries, which has been stressed by many Member States, those considerations are such as to justify restrictions, as regards Article 49 of the Treaty (now Article 56 TFEU), which may go so far as to prohibit lotteries in a Member State'.[51] In this case the Court was not prepared to test the necessity of the measure, if the matter was sufficiently sensitive.[52] Member States have an adequate degree of latitude to determine what measures are required, and the Court leaves it to the Member States whether less restrictive means are available.

[47] Case C–481/12 *UAB "Juvelta" v VĮ "Lietuvos prabavimo rūmai"*, judgment of 16 January 2014, paras 28–29.

[48] Case 382/87 *R Buet and Educational Business Services (EBS) v Ministère public* [1989] ECR 1235.

[49] ibid, paras 11 and 12.

[50] *Buet* (n 48), paras 13 and 14.

[51] *Schindler* (n 10), para 59.

[52] JH Jans, 'Proportionality Revisited' (2000) 27 *Legal Issues of Economic Integration* 245.

Ever since, the Court, although having refined its *Schindler* judgment, has been considerably receptive to Member States' arguments relating to the prohibition or restriction of the organisation of lotteries and the provision of gambling services,[53] including the offering of games of chance via the Internet.[54] Member States have wide discretion in determining what system of protection works best in their country, as long as the gambling policy is not inconsistent with its policy aims—the so-called 'hypocrisy test'—and restricts free movement.[55]

The *German Insurance* case also illustrates how the Court took into account the sensitive nature of the regulated area. The Court accepted that the insurance sector is a very sensitive area particularly because of the *specific nature of the service* provided by the insurer, which is linked to future events, the occurrence of which, or at least the timing of which, is uncertain at the time when the contract is concluded.[56] The German *Sicherungsaufsichtsgesetz* provided that insurance companies which wished to provide services in Germany in relation to direct insurance business must be established and authorised in Germany. The authorisation procedure could, according to the CJEU, 'provide an effective means of ensuring the supervision which, having regard to the foregoing considerations, is justified on grounds relating to the protection of the consumer both as a policy holder and as an insured person'.[57] The requirement of establishment, however, was not considered indispensable, unless it concerned compulsory insurance or insurance for which the insurer either maintains a permanent presence equivalent to an agency or branch, or directs his business entirely or principally towards the territory of the Federal Republic of Germany.

The self-restraint in the application of the proportionality test, also compared to the proportionality test employed in other consumer cases, can be explained by the particularly sensitive nature of the area concerned where Member States are primarily competent to take action.[58] However, these cases may be limited, as is shown, for example, by the *Caixa-Bank France* case, where the notion of consumer

[53] Case C–124/97 *Markku Juhani Lääräet et al v Kihlakunnansyyttäjä (Jyväskylä) and Suomen valtio (Finnish State)* [1999] ECR I–6067; Case C–67/98 *Questore di Verona v Diego Zenatti* [1999] ECR I–7289; Case C–243/01 *Piergiorgio Gambelli* [2003] ECR I–3031; Case C–203/08 *Sporting Exchange Ltd (Betfair) v Minister van Justitie* [2010] ECR I–4695.

[54] Case C–42/07 *Liga Portuguesa de Futebol Profissional and Bwin International Ltd v Departamento de Jogos da Santa Casa da Misericórdia de Lisboa* [2009] ECR I–7633; Case C–258/08 *Ladbrokes Betting and Gaming Ltd and Ladbrokes International Ltd v Stichting de Nationale Sporttotalisator* [2010] ECR I–4757.

[55] J Mulder, 'A New Chapter in the European Court of Justice Gambling Saga: A Stacked Deck?' (2011) 38 *Legal Issues of Economic Integration* 243.

[56] Case 205/84 *Commission v Germany* (*German Insurance*) [1986] ECR 3755.

[57] ibid, para 46.

[58] Jans (n 52) 250. According to Barnard there may be two explanations for the Court's approach: 'The judicial deference towards the Member States may partly be explained by the fact that, in these cases involving an activity which is legal in one State but illegal in another, the Court is wary of imposing the values of the majority of the States (where lotteries are lawful, albeit highly regulated) on the minority (where lotteries are unlawful). Another explanation is that these cases concern the situation of a service which moves but the provider and the recipient do not', Barnard (n 20) 383–84.

as reasonably circumspect European citizen has been emphasised also in relation to banking activities.[59] Consumers were prevented from choosing between an unremunerated sight account with certain basic banking services remaining free of charge and a remunerated sight account with banking services being charged for. The measure was considered suitable for the encouragement of long-term saving, but was nevertheless disproportionate without further explanation by the Court.

A third and last category constitutes measures that protect certain fundamental rights, which are particularly relevant for consumers. Consumer protection is even explicitly mentioned by the EU Charter of Fundamental Rights under the Solidarity Title in Article 38, which calls upon the EU to ensure a high level of consumer protection (see below).

c. Extraterritorial Protection of Consumers

The analysis has so far been confined to the protection by the national State of *domestic* consumer interests. As some cases reveal, the State may also be induced to protect consumers outside its own boundaries. This is generally referred to as extraterritorial protection, which has become pertinent now consumers themselves are increasingly aware about the environmental or social conditions under which consumer goods are produced. But extraterritorial protection is controversial as it is regarded as an unwarranted burden for international business. The Court is reluctant to accept such 'altruistic policies', as they seem to be incompatible with the idea of an EU Single Market prohibiting export restrictions and restrictions on the movement of services. In the following two cases the CJEU has had the chance to pronounce itself on this issue in respect of national consumer protection measures. The *Alpine Investments* judgment concerned a Dutch law prohibiting financial institutions from contacting individuals by telephone without their prior written consent in order to offer them various financial services.[60] This prohibition of 'cold calling' applied to consumers located inside and outside the Netherlands. Alpine Investments, a Dutch financial institution with clients in the Netherlands and Belgium, contested the validity of this prohibition. The case was brought before the Court, which found that the Dutch rules restricted the free movement of services (Article 56 TFEU).

The Netherlands had argued that the purpose of the prohibition on cold calling was to protect consumers and to preserve the reputation of the Dutch financial sector. The Court held that '[a]lthough the protection of consumers in the other Member States is not, as such, a matter for the Netherlands authorities, the nature and extent of that protection does none the less have a direct effect on the good reputation of Netherlands financial services'.[61]

[59] Case C–442/02 *CaixaBank France v Ministère de l'Économie, des Finances et de l'Industrie* [2004] ECR I–8961.

[60] *Alpine Investments* (n 14).

[61] ibid, para 43.

Without explicitly rejecting the possibility of extraterritorial protection of consumers as a legitimate objective which can be relied upon to justify a trade restriction, the interest of consumer protection is being rephrased into a domestic interest, or 'recycled in order to recognize a new imperative reason relating to the public interest'.[62] Hence, behind the interest of consumer protection (here the protection of investors as consumers) other interests are hiding (for example, the good reputation of the financial services).

The more recent *Gysbrechts* case does not explicitly address the issue of the extraterritorial protection of consumers.[63] A Belgian law prohibited a supplier in a distance selling transaction from requiring an advance or any payment before expiry of the period of withdrawal of seven working days after receipt of the goods. According to the Belgian authorities, this prohibition also implied that suppliers may not require consumers not residing in Belgium to provide the number of their payment card during that period. Gysbrechts argued that these prohibitions were contrary to the EU rules on free movement of goods. As stated above, the law was considered to contravene Article 35 TFEU and needed to be justified. As a consequence, the CJEU accepted consumer protection as an overriding legitimate objective in the public interest within the framework of Article 35 TFEU for the first time.[64]

This ruling indirectly acknowledges that the protection of consumers in other Member States may justify trade restrictions. Although the Belgian rules apply to both local and cross-border transactions, the Court focussed on the latter aspect:

> As is clear from the order for reference, the consequences of such a prohibition are generally more significant in cross-border sales made directly to consumers, in particular, in sales made by means of the internet, by reason, inter alia, of the obstacles to bringing any legal proceedings in another Member State against consumers who default, especially when the sales involve relatively small sums.[65]

The Court could have referred to its previous ruling in the *Alpine Investments* case and stated that Belgium cannot rely on the objective of consumer protection alone in respect of cross-border transactions. However, neither the Court nor Advocate General Trstenjak in her lengthy opinion addressed this issue; neither did the Court look for another objective public interest ground 'hidden' behind the protection of consumers, as Advocate General Jacobs had done in his opinion in *Alpine Investments*.

In the absence of an explicit allusion to the issue of extraterritorial protection of consumers in the *Gysbrechts* ruling, the divergent approach compared with *Alpine Investments* leaves one with speculations. One possible explanation lies in the development of distance selling contracts most notably in the online market

[62] V Hatzopoulos, 'Case-Note on *Alpine Investments*' (1995) 32 *Common Market Law Review* 1443.
[63] *Gysbrechts* (n 29).
[64] See also Roth (n 29) and de Vries (n 29).
[65] *Gysbrechts* (n 29), para 47.

for trading goods and services. This growing market raises new questions in terms of consumer protection such as the choice of law applicable to a consumer contract and the enforcement by Member States of their national rules on consumer protection. Consumers are not necessarily protected by the laws of their State of residence. Under Article 5(1) of the Rome I Regulation,[66] consumer contracts shall be governed by the law of the country where the consumer has their habitual residence.[67] However, the Rome I Regulation also provides for a number of exceptions to that rule. First, the law of the country of the consumer applies only insofar as the supplier '(a) pursues his commercial or professional activities in the country where the consumer has his habitual residence, or (b) by any means, directs such activities to that country or to several countries including that country'. It is at this stage unclear whether this provision covers all online trading and in particular all situations where the supplier and the consumer are located in different States. In any case, Article 5(2) of the Rome I Regulation provides for the possibility for the parties to a consumer contract to choose another law than the law of the country of residence of the consumer subject to certain conditions. Besides, the fact that we are dealing with distance selling via the Internet, there is a good case for Belgium to treat distance selling in a more uniform fashion.[68] Furthermore, Belgium may have been induced 'to assist another Member State in the enforcement of its policy justified by a mandatory requirement'.[69]

Hence the statement of the Court in *Alpine Investments* according to which 'the protection of consumers in the other Member States is not, as such, a matter for the Netherlands authorities' may partly lose its significance in relation to distance contracts and online trading.

III. Interlude: The Lisbon Treaty and Consumer Protection

The choice of the Court of the paradigm consumer as a sufficiently robust and well-informed consumer has never been explicitly recognised by the Treaty.[70] It is clear that the Lisbon Treaty infuses the EU with deeper commitments to, inter alia, fundamental rights and social protection, but the exact consequences for, inter alia, EU consumer policy remain vague. The following important features

[66] Regulation (EC) 593/2008 of 17 June 2008 on the law applicable to contractual obligations [2008] OJ L177/8. Note that the Regulation, which replaces the Rome I Convention, was adopted prior to the Court's judgment in *Gysbrechts* (n 29) but had not entered into force at the time of the dispute between Santurel and Mr Delahaye.

[67] See also Roth (n 29) 518.

[68] ibid, 519.

[69] ibid.

[70] Weatherill (n 2) 839.

of the Lisbon Treaty may nevertheless have reinforced the consumer dimension of EU Single Market law, which should also be to the benefit of more vulnerable consumers.

A. Concept of Social Market Economy

Whereas the internal market originally seemed to be mainly concerned with the abolition of trade barriers, later a broader conception of the internal market can be found, conceptualised in more holistic terms, including consumer safety and environmental protection.[71] The realisation of an internal market and the liberalisation of trade are not ends in themselves, but important tools to increase welfare and promote sustainable development. This is confirmed by the inclusion of the concept of 'social market economy' in Article 2 TEU, which emphasises that market integration is not pursued in isolation but must be counterbalanced by social considerations and public interests.[72]

B. Integration Clause

In addition the integration clause contained in Article 12 TFEU states that 'consumer protection requirements shall be taken into account in defining and implementing other Union policies and activities'. Now that the consumer integration clause has been incorporated in Article 12 TFEU, it has been placed on an equal footing with the environmental integration clause, making it stronger and more fundamental than before.[73] But the exact legal consequences of this provision—also referred to as the 'horizontal clause', as there are so many linkages between horizontal and flanking policies such as environmental, health and consumer policies as well as between these policies and the internal market—are rather unclear, mainly owing to the still-developing case law.[74] The legal value of the principle of integration is generally presumed to be limited, but its legal status can certainly not be disregarded.[75] The integration principle delimits the Union's discretionary powers in the sense that the full effect of the internal market must be mitigated where horizontal and flanking policy interests, such as consumer

[71] This developed over time, see P Craig, 'The Evolution of the Single Market' in C Barnard and J Scott (eds), *The Law of the Single European Market—Unpacking the Premises* (Oxford, Hart Publishing, 2002).

[72] See with respect to the economic constitution of Europe: C Joerges, 'The European Economic Constitution and its Transformation through the Financial Crisis' in D Patterson and A Söderstn (eds), *A Companion to European Union Law and International Law* (Oxford, Wiley-Blackwell, 2013).

[73] Stuyck Law (n 34) 386.

[74] cf de Vries (n 7) 18.

[75] See with respect to the environmental integration clause: N Dhondt, *Integration of Environmental Protection into other EC Policies—Legal Theory and Practice* (Groningen, Europa Law Publishing, 2003) 183.

interests, are at stake.[76] The integration principle thus reaffirms the view that consumer interests must be promoted within the context of the internal market. Consumer protection requirements probably concern the health, safety and economic interests of consumers, as well as their right of information, education and to organise themselves, as mentioned in Article 169 TFEU.

C. EU Charter of Fundamental Rights

A third important feature of the Lisbon Treaty is the EU Charter of Fundamental Rights, which got binding force through Article 6(1) TEU, and its possible impact and significance for consumer rights. Article 38 of the Charter of Fundamental Rights (see also above) states that 'Union policies shall ensure a high level of consumer protection'. This provision is not couched in terms of individual enforceable rights,[77] but as it is placed under the title 'Solidarity', it emphasises a dimension of the EU that transcends the originally economic one. The inclusion of consumer protection in the Charter shows the EU's commitment to a more 'human' dimension of consumer policy, possibly leading to an improvement of consumers' rights of access to justice. The Charter shows that the EU is committed to a high level of consumer protection and that consumer law 'has received recognition as a fundamental social value'.[78]

In addition fundamental rights may enhance consumer protection in a number of ways.[79] In the field of consumer health, the recognition of human dignity and the right to integrity of the person as fundamental rights, now enshrined in Article 3 of the Charter, are relevant. Furthermore, the consumers' use of the Internet may call for a strong protection of personal data and a right to privacy as contained in Articles 7 and 8 of the EU Charter. The importance of EU citizens' rights to privacy and protection of personal data has been underlined by the CJEU in recent judgments, like *Digital Rights Ireland* on the validity of the Data Retention Directive in the light of the Charter, and *Google Spain* on, inter alia, the so-called 'right to be forgotten' on the Internet (see section IV.C).[80] Other fundamental rights that enhance consumer protection are the freedom of expression and information (now Article 12 of the Charter), access to services of general economic interest (now Article 36 of the Charter), the protection of the rights

[76] B De Witte, 'The Cultural Dimension of Community Law' in Academy of European Law (eds), *Collected Courses of the Academy of European Law (Yearbook)—European Community Law* vol 4 (Dordrecht, Martinus Nijhoff Publishers, 1993) 295.

[77] Probably it is framed as a principle that needs to be further elaborated and not as a right within the meaning of Art 52(5) of the Charter: Benöhr (n 39) 64.

[78] ibid 61.

[79] See, in particular, Benöhr (n 39).

[80] Joined cases C–293/12 and C–594/12 *Digital Rights Ireland Ltd v Minister for Communications, Marine and Natural Resources and Others and Kärntner Landesregierung and Others*, judgment of 4 April 2014; Case C–131/12 *Google Spain SL and Google Inc v Agencia Española de Protección de Datos (AEPD) and Mario Costeja González*, judgment of 13 May 2013.

of children, the elderly and persons with a disability (now Articles 24, 25 and 26 of the Charter), access to preventive healthcare (now Article 35 of the Charter) and effective judicial protection (now Article 47 of the Charter). The fact that the Charter, since the Lisbon Treaty entered into force, is now legally recognised and binding is significant 'as it can now more easily and more vigorously be deployed as a standard for judicial review of Union measures and national measures implementing Union law and as an aid to interpreting national and Union measures'.[81]

The CJEU has confirmed that the scope of application of the EU Charter of Fundamental Rights is similar to that of the general principles of EU law, which had already, long before the proclamation of the Charter in Nice (2000) and before the Charter was given binding force by the Lisbon Treaty (2009), been discovered and recognised by the CJEU in its case law.[82] The Charter thus also applies within the context of EU free movement law.[83] In several cases the Court made clear that the economic freedoms could be seen as a specific amplification of the EU Charter.[84] In that sense a number of Charter provisions, namely Article 15(2) on the freedom of every EU citizen to exercise the right of establishment and to provide services in any Member State, Article 16 on the freedom to conduct a business, and Article 17 on the right to property, enhance the market integration process and may thus, as stated previously, serve consumer interests and optimise consumer welfare. At the same time the Court held that the EU Charter applies whenever a Member State restricts one of the four freedoms and relies on a justification ground.[85] Normally, where the EU Charter provisions can be applied alongside the free movement rules, the Court will focus on the latter.[86] Interestingly, in the *Pfleger* case, which concerned an Austrian law prohibiting the provision of gaming machines, the Court went along with the Opinion of Advocate General Sharpston, who held that 'Articles 15 to 17 of the Charter impose no greater obligations to be satisfied for a restriction on the freedom to provide services to be permitted than is already established by the case law of the Court in relation to Article 56 TFEU'.[87]

According to Benoehr, the Charter could have three major effects in the field of consumer protection.[88] First, the Charter could give a new direction to legislative action at EU and national level. That the EU institutions' obligations under the Charter must be taken seriously appears most notably from the *Digital Rights*

[81] D Chalmers and G Monti, *European Union Law—Updating Supplement* (Cambridge, Cambridge University Press, 2008) 69.

[82] Case C–617/10 *Åklagaren v Hans Åkerberg Fransson*, judgment of 7 May 2013.

[83] Case C–390/12 *Proceedings brought by Robert Pfleger*, judgment of 30 April 2014.

[84] Case C–233/12 *Simone Gardella v Istituto nazionale della previdenza sociale (INPS)*, judgment of 4 July 2013, para 39: 'Article 12(2) of the Charter reiterates inter alia the free movement of workers guaranteed by Article 45 TFEU'; Case C–367/12 *Proceedings brought by Susanne Sokoll-Seebacher*, judgment of 13 February 2013, para 22: 'Article 16 of the Charter refers, inter alia, to Article 49 TFEU, which guarantees the fundamental freedom of establishment'.

[85] *Pfleger* (n 83).

[86] ibid.

[87] ibid, Opinion of AG Sharpston, para 70.

[88] Benöhr (n 39) 66.

Ireland case, in which the CJEU declared the Data Retention Directive invalid as it constituted a disproportionate interference with the right to data protection contained in the EU Charter (see section IV.C below). Second, contractual provisions between consumers and companies may be affected by the Charter, when EU legislation and national implementing measures are assessed in light of the Charter.

It is so far not clear to what extent certain Charter rights may be invoked directly in a purely horizontal dispute between two private parties, or in other words have horizontal direct effect. The Court in its recent judgment in the *Association de Médiation Sociale* case seems to accept that certain provisions in the Charter may have horizontal direct effect.[89] *Google Spain* concerned a 'horizontal dispute' between, inter alia, Google Spain and Mr Consteja Gonzalez before the Spanish court, which raised questions on the interpretation of Spanish legislation implementing Directive 95/46/EC on data protection (see section IV.C).[90] In *Google Spain* the Court held that Google as a search engine operator falls within the scope of the current Data Protection Directive and that it may fall under an obligation to remove links to web pages which are returned when a person is searched for by name.[91] The Spanish national Mr Gonzalez requested that Google remove website results that referred to his social security debts and resulting real estate auction in Spain back in 1998. By first establishing that the Data Protection Directive seeks to ensure a high level of fundamental rights of persons, in particular the right to privacy in the context of processing of data, and that the Directive should be interpreted in the light of Articles 7 and 8 of the Charter, the Court did not hide its enthusiasm for the rights to privacy and data protection. And the Court held in paragraph 97 that

> [a]s the data subject may, in the light of his fundamental rights under Articles 7 and 8 of the Charter, request that the information in question no longer be made available to the general public by its inclusion in such a list of results, it should be held … that those rights override, as a rule, not only the economic interest of the operator of the search engine but also the interest of the general public in finding that information upon a search relating to the data subject's name

Third, the Charter may help to justify an exception to the free movement rules, such as consumer health, human dignity[92] or the protection of the child. The Charter may in this respect have an important, additional value in consumer-type cases where particularly vulnerable consumers are concerned, which can be illustrated by the Court's judgment in *Dynamic Medien*. Here the Court expressly referred

[89] Case C–176/12 *Association de médiation sociale v Union locale des syndicats CGT (ASM)*, judgment of 15 January 2014. See also S Peers, J Kenner, T Hervey and A Ward (eds), *The EU Charter of Fundamental Rights: A Commentary* (Oxford, Hart Publishing, 2014) 1413.

[90] *Google Spain* (n 80); Directive 95/46/EC of the European Parliament and of the Council of 24 October 1995 on the protection of individuals with regard to the processing of personal data and on the free movement of such data [1995] OJ L281/31 (Data Protection Directive).

[91] *Google Spain* (n 80).

[92] See Case C–36/02 *Omega Spielhallen- und Automatenaufstellungs-GmbH v Oberbürgermeisterin der Bundesstadt Bonn* [2004] ECR I–9609.

to the Charter, in particular Article 24, to justify a new 'mandatory requirement', namely the protection of the child. This judgment is thus particularly interesting for the possibilities Member States have in protecting a vulnerable, if not the most vulnerable, group of consumers, that is, children.[93] In this case the dispute concerned the importation of Japanese cartoons called 'anime' in DVD or video cassette format into Germany from the United Kingdom. The cartoons were examined before shipment by the British Board of Film Classification ('BBFC'). The image storage media bore a BBFC label stating that they may be viewed only by adolescents aged 15 years or older. German law on the protection of young persons, however, prohibits the sale by mail order of image storage media which have not been examined in accordance with that law, and which do not bear an age-limit label corresponding to a classification decision from a higher regional authority or a national self-regulation body (competent authority). Dynamic Medien, a competitor of the company importing the Japanese cartoons, started a procedure before the German court, which submits preliminary questions to the CJEU. The questions were whether such a prohibition is contrary to the free movement of goods and, if so, whether this could be justified.

In examining the justification of the German law the CJEU held that the protection of the rights of the child is recognised by various international instruments and that those international instruments are among those concerning the protection of human rights of which it takes account in applying the general principles of Community law. Furthermore, the Court, inter alia, refers to the Charter of Fundamental Rights, which provides in Article 24(1) that children have the right to such protection and care as is necessary for their well-being. Regarding the proportionality of the German law and the examination procedure established by the national legislature in order to protect children against information and materials injurious to their well-being, the Court reiterated that

> the mere fact that a Member State has opted for a system of protection which differs from that adopted by another Member State cannot affect the assessment of the proportionality of the national provisions enacted to that end. Those provisions must be assessed solely by reference to the objective pursued and the level of protection which the Member State in question intends to provide.[94]

D. Constitutional Diversity: *Sayn-Wittgenstein* and *Omega*

A fourth and last interesting feature of the Lisbon Treaty is signified by Article 4(2) TEU, which states that '[t]he Union shall respect the equality of Member States before the Treaties as well as their national identities, inherent in their fundamental structures, political and constitutional, inclusive of regional and local self-government'. This provision may support regulatory diversity and

[93] Case C–244/06 *Dynamic Medien Vertriebs GmbH v Avides Media AG* [2008] ECR I–505.
[94] ibid, para 49.

enhance the national identity of Member States. It will, however, not detract from the principles of primacy, unity and effectiveness of EU law.[95]

The following two cases illustrate the (potential) scope of Article 4(2) TEU. In the fairly unique *Sayn-Wittgenstein* case the Court referred to this provision for the first time. The case involved a refusal by the Austrian authorities to register the name Fürstin von Sayn-Wittgenstein, which was a title acquired in Germany. Under the Austrian law on the abolition of the nobility, which has a constitutional status in accordance with the Federal Constitutional law, it is prohibited to use titles like 'Fürst' or 'Fürstin'. According to the CJEU a refusal to recognise all the elements of the surname of a national as determined in another Member State constitutes a restriction on the freedoms conferred by Article 21 TFEU on every citizen of the Union.[96] For the justification of this restriction the Austrian authorities refer to the objective of public policy. The Austrian government had stated that the law on the abolition of the nobility constitutes implementation of the more general principle of equality before the law of all Austrian citizens and, considering this argument, the Court referred to the Charter of Fundamental Rights, which includes the principle of equality as a general principle of Union law. Interestingly, it also, within the context of the proportionality test, referred to Article 4(2) TEU. The EU thus recognises and respects the national identity of her Member States, which also encompasses the republican state form. By its explicit reference to Article 4(2) TEU the Court appears to be very sensitive to the argument based on the constitutional identity of Austria.[97] The question is: to what extent may an argument based on Article 4(2) TEU be relevant for the protection of consumers under EU free movement law?

A case that was comparable to *Sayn-Wittgenstein* was the *Omega* case, which was decided six years earlier. This case involved a prohibition ordered by the police of the German state Nordrhein-Westfalen of laser games as they constituted a danger to public order. Acts of simulated homicide and the trivialisation of violence were contrary to fundamental values prevailing in public opinion. After the CJEU concluded that the free movement of services was affected, it held that it was clear that the commercial exploitation of games involving the simulated killing of human beings infringed a fundamental value enshrined in the national constitution, namely human dignity. The Court then held that 'the Community legal order undeniably strives to ensure respect for human dignity as a general principle of law'. And '[t]here can therefore be no doubt that the objective of protecting human dignity is compatible with Community law, it being immaterial in that respect

[95] Case C–399/11 *Stefano Melloni v Ministerio Fiscal*, judgment of 26 February 2013. See also N de Boer, 'Addressing Rights Divergences Under the Charter: *Melloni*' (2013) 50 *Common Market Law Review* 1083, 1092.

[96] Case C–209/09 *Ilonka Sayn-Wittgenstein v Landeshauptmann von Wien* [2010] ECR I–13693, para 71.

[97] Regarding this, see in particular: L Besselink, 'National and Constitutional Identity Before and After Lisbon' (2010) 6 *Utrecht Law Review* 36. See also L Besselink, 'Case Law' (2012) 49 *Common Market Law Review* 671.

that, in Germany, the principle of respect for human dignity has a particular status as an independent fundamental right'.[98]

After having defined human dignity as a general principle of EU law, it went on to assess the proportionality of the German order in light of the protection of human dignity. According to the Court, the need for and adoption of provisions such as the German prohibition on laser games are not excluded merely because one Member State has chosen a different system of protection than another. In other words, there is no need for one conception which is shared by all Member States as to the way in which the fundamental rights are to be protected. And it came—rather quickly—to the conclusion that the German measure corresponded to protecting human dignity, which the national constitution seeks to guarantee in the territory of the Federal Republic of Germany.

The particularity of this case is that the Court first defines a typically *German* concept of human dignity as a general principle of *EU* law, and then, while applying the proportionality test, it shows a predominantly Member State-friendly approach.[99] Both cases emphasise that the Court takes nationally sensitive matters seriously, which may also be relevant for national consumer policies. And Article 4(2) TEU 'is a route to soften free movement law yet further'.[100] In the *Ladbrokes Betting & Gaming* case the Court had already held that[101]

> moral, religious or cultural factors, as well as the morally and financially harmful consequences for the individual and for society associated with betting and gaming, may serve to justify a margin of discretion for the national authorities, sufficient to enable them to determine what is required in order to ensure *consumer protection* and the preservation of public order

and that the Member States 'are free to set the objectives of their policy on betting and gambling according to their own scale of values and, where appropriate, to define in detail the level of protection sought'.[102] Article 4(2) TEU may further enhance the discretionary power of the Member State in these areas of national competence, where consumer interests also play an important role.

IV. Some Current Challenges for EU Consumer Policy

The continuous interplay between legal developments, societal changes and technological developments, for instance in the field of the Internet, dynamically

[98] *Omega* (n 92), para 34.

[99] N Nic Shuibhne, 'Margins of Appreciation: National Values, Fundamental Rights and EC Free Movement Law' (2009) 34 *European Law Review* 230, 254.

[100] S Weatherill, 'From Economic Rights to Fundamental Rights' in S de Vries, U Bernitz and S Weatherill (eds), *The Protection of Fundamental Rights in the EU After Lisbon* (Oxford, Hart Publishing, 2013) 32.

[101] Emphasis added.

[102] Case C–258/08 *Ladbrokes Betting & Gaming* [2010] ECR I–4757, paras 19–20.

inform the relationship between the EU Single Market rules and consumer policy. These developments offer challenges but also possibilities for the paradigm consumer.

A. Informing the Consumer and Protecting the Weaker Party

Although the Court's perception of consumers as being reasonably circumspect has been a powerful tool for market integration, it has also been criticised.[103] The Court's case law, which is still heavily influenced by the market consumer approach and puts emphasis on the average consumer, should not undermine the protection of the weaker party, which is at odds with the changed Treaty framework after Lisbon, embracing a model based on justice and social values (see section III above). Besides, differences in linguistic, social and cultural conditions could have the result that something which does not mislead consumers in one country might do so in another according to AG Gulmann in the *Clinique* case.[104] One State may regard something as unsafe or unintelligible, whereas another may not, confirming that EU law does not force regulatory protection down to the lowest common denominator among the Member States. Furthermore, the lack of homogeneity among the traditions of the Member States may cause something seen as harmless in one State to have a different impact in another.[105] The Opinion of AG Gulmann in *Clinique* reveals the remarkable difference between the activist approach of the Court in considerably restricting Member States' discretion in determining the level of protection they deem necessary, and the more reluctant attitude of the Advocate General in favour of the vulnerable consumer. The Court places a focus on the more 'ordinary confident consumers', ie the informed or reasonably circumspect consumer, for whom the virtues of information provision may be questioned.[106] The implication is that the Court finally establishes the level of consumer protection,[107] which may not always allow for the highest level of protection.[108] As will be seen hereafter, the current economic and societal challenges also reveal that the Court's approach to consumer protection, insofar as it is still influenced by market-building and market integration, may have to be revised.[109]

[103] The 'information paradigm' according to G Howells and T Wilhelmsson, 'EC Consumer Law: Has It Come of Age?' (2003) 28 *European Law Review* 370, 380–82.

[104] *Clinique* (n 42), Opinion of AG Gulmann, para 25. See also with regard to different consumer cultures: T Wilhelmsson, 'The Abuse of the "Confident Consumer" as a Justification for EC Consumer Law' (2004) *Journal of Consumer Policy* 328.

[105] Weatherill, 'Recent Case Law…' (n 36).

[106] Howells and Wilhelmsson (n 103) 381.

[107] Jans (n 52) 252.

[108] Weatherill (n 6) 58.

[109] Benöhr (n 39) 107–08.

B. The Economic, Food and Climate Change Crises

The economic crisis, the persistent food crisis and climate change have challenged the EU Single Market and the role of the paradigm consumer therein.[110] The European Commission's cry for more action back in 2011, when it stated in its Single Market Act that 'the crisis could have a lasting effect on potential growth and on employment, affecting both the standard of living of Europeans and their future',[111] is still applicable. In its Europe 2020 report, in which goals for, inter alia, sustainable and inclusive growth are formulated, the Commission urges prioritisation of measures that are likely to foster growth and employment and to put an end to market fragmentation.

Looking at their role in the internal market, consumers are a little like Janus, the Roman god represented with a double-faced head, each looking in opposite directions.[112] On the one hand, consumers as active market participants and cross-border purchasers of goods and services are an important 'instrument' for increased movement of goods and services, but on the other hand, the increased Europeanisation and globalisation of national and world markets seem to make consumers more concerned than ever with their own culture and identity.[113] Hence, whereas on the one hand consumers may be more receptive to imported products, ethnic sentiments may enhance market fragmentation and protectionism on the other. But ethnocentric campaigns supported by a national government have been considered to be contrary to the free movement of goods in the *Buy Irish* case. In this case the compatibility of an advertising campaign supported by the Irish government to encourage the sale and purchase of Irish products with Article 34 TFEU was at issue. According to the CJEU, although the advertising campaign was carried out by a private organisation, it could not be seen as separate from a government programme. And as the potential effect of the campaign was comparable to that resulting from government measures of a binding nature, the practice could not escape the prohibition of Article 34 TFEU simply because it was not based on binding measures.[114] The Court held that 'even measures adopted by the government of a Member State which do not have binding effect

[110] J Kojnik, 'Free Movement of Goods in a Labyrinth: Can Buy Irish Survive the Crises' (2012) 49 *Common Market Law Review* 293.

[111] Commission, Single Market Act: Twelve Levers to Boost Growth and Strengthen Confidence 'Working Together to Create New Growth' (Communication) COM(2011) 206 final, 3.

[112] Janus was the Roman god of gates and doors (*ianua*), beginnings and endings, and hence he was represented with a double-faced head. 'He was worshipped at the beginning of the harvest time, planting, marriage, birth, and other types of beginnings, especially the beginnings of important events in a person's life. Janus also represents the transition between primitive life and civilization, between the countryside and the city, peace and war, and the growing-up of young people', MF Lindemans, 'Janus', *Encyclopedia Mythica* (3 March 1997) <http://www.pantheon.org/articles/j/janus.html> accessed 14 April 2015.

[113] Kojnik (n 110) 291.

[114] Case 249/81 *Commission v Ireland* [1982] ECR 4005, paras 26–29.

may be capable of influencing the conduct of traders and consumers in that state and thus of frustrating the aims of the Community'.[115]

The question is whether ethnocentric campaigns, considering environmental, food security and other concerns, could ever be justifiable in the light of the EU single market rules. Invoking consumer protection (including preserving national and local traditions) as a justification might, as the case law discussed above shows, be difficult. Nonetheless, the changed Treaty framework allows for more regulatory diversity and more room for national traditions. If Member States can convincingly show that their policy's aim is the protection of national tradition and not economic, the CJEU might be willing to uphold such a measure. It has been rightly observed, though, that more general, protectionist 'buy local' campaigns would not fall under this category.[116] In addition developments in the case law in the field of the environment show that the CJEU is increasingly willing to uphold national discriminatory measures.[117] But whether this entails that ethnocentric campaigns with an environmental dimension, for instance to reduce the amount of 'food miles' and stimulate the consumption of locally produced food, are more readily justifiable, is the question. In any event, *Buy Irish* makes clear that protectionism and extreme xenophobia should be prevented.[118]

Suppose that the promotional campaigns are carried out *without* governmental support or state intervention. Could such private action be caught by the free movement rules? This question touches upon the scope of prohibitive rules on free movement, in particular Article 34 TFEU, and the (potential) horizontal direct effect of the EU free-movement rules. Regarding the Treaty provisions on persons and services, it can be deduced from the Court's case law that these rules constitute horizontal direct effect. But to what extent these provisions apply to private persons acting individually is not (yet) clear. Several arguments have been raised in the legal literature to give these provisions under certain conditions limited or even full horizontal direct effect.[119] The situation with regard to Article 34 TFEU seems to be more complicated and horizontal direct effect of the free movement of goods provisions is less self-evident. But there are voices calling upon the Court to recognise at least a limited form of horizontal direct effect, which may cover cases where 'buy national' campaigns are involved, but where a link to the State is missing.[120]

[115] ibid, para 28.

[116] Kojnik (n 110) 312.

[117] De Vries (n 7) 59–62.

[118] Kojnik (n 110).

[119] Prechal and de Vries (n 8) 15–18. See also *Premier League* (n 3); De Vries (n 3) 610–13.

[120] C Krenn, 'A Missing Piece in the Horizontal Direct Effect "Jigsaw": Horizontal Direct Effect and the Free Movement of Goods' (2012) 49 *Common Market Law Review* 177–216. The Opinion of AG Trstenjak in Case C–171/11 *Fra.bo SpA v Deutsche Vereinigung des Gas- und Wasserfaches eV (DVGW)—Technisch-Wissenschaftlicher Verein* [2012] ECR I–453, where AG Trstenjak proposes, interestingly, to grant Art 34 TFEU a limited horizontal effect. But it must be noted that this case concerned a private law association drawing up technical standards, a task which in other Member States may well

Interestingly, parallel to the ethnocentric consumer approach a more polycentric attitude of consumers can be discerned, inducing the state to adopt extraterritorial measures protecting 'out-of-state' interests of consumers (see section II.B.ii.c above). Next to these ethnic sentiments, there is an increasing number of groups of consumers who simply have difficulties in adjusting 'to fast-changing complex markets and technological developments'.[121] As stated above, the CJEU in its case law has recognised that certain vulnerable consumers may need extra protection, which justifies restrictions imposed by the national legislator on EU free movement. But the Court's case law is still rather limited and centres on the concept of 'reasonably circumspect consumer'. Within the context of the Lisbon Treaty and the EU Charter of Fundamental Rights with more emphasis on sustainable development, environmental protection and social justice and social protection, the case law in this respect could be developed further, whereby a better compromise must be found between consumer autonomy and the protection of social and ethical concerns.[122] In this respect it should be noted that the Court, in respect of the environment, gives Member States considerable discretion to implement environmental objectives, even by means of discriminatory measures, allowing the Member States to support schemes that stimulate national consumption of green electricity and thus sustainable consumption.[123]

C. The Digital Age and the Internet

The digital age and the Internet offer challenges for consumers as well as possibilities for the EU Single Market by promoting cross-border sales and use of services. According to the Commission in its Single Market Act, 'the development of the digital single market is hindered by lack of consumer confidence, the prime causes of which are payment security and enforcement of consumer rights in cross-border transactions, particularly with regard to product safety and counterfeiting'.[124] But apart from the benefits of a well-functioning digital internal market for consumers, there are obvious dangers relating to the use of the Internet. Personal data of consumers are transferred and exchanged, not only across Europe but around the

be performed by public authorities. See also: R van Mastrigt and S de Vries, 'The Horizontal Direct Effect of the Four Freedoms: From a Hodgepodge of Cases to a Seamless Web of Judicial Protection in the EU Single Market?' in U Bernitz, X Groussot and F Schulyok (eds), *General Principles of EU Law and European Private Law* (Deventer, Kluwer Law International, 2013) 262.

[121] Benöhr (n 39) 81–85.

[122] ibid 93.

[123] Case C–204/12 *Essent Belgium NV v Vlaamse Reguleringsinstantie voor de Elektriciteits- en Gasmarkt*, judgment of 11 September 2014; Case C–573/12 *Ålands vindkraft AB v Energimyndigheten*, judgment of 1 July 2014.

[124] COM(2011) 206 (n 111) 12. This part does not explicitly return in the Single Market Act II. See Communication from the Commission, 'Single Market Act II: Together For New Growth' COM(2012) 573 final.

whole world. The European Court of Justice has been confronted with cases like *Promusicae*, in which it has had to balance consumers' rights to data protection with the copyrights of Promusicae. In this case the Spanish right holder group Promusicae wanted to oblige the Internet Service Provider Telefonica to disclose the identity data of peer-to-peer users of Kazaa, a file-sharing application allowing consumers to illegally upload copyrighted musical works, in a civil dispute. In its judgment the Court does not force the Member State to allow the disclosure of personal data to private entities; instead it offers a balancing approach that is mostly in favour of consumer fundamental rights.[125]

Similarly in *Scarlet Extended SA* the CJEU in referring to *Promusicae* held that 'national authorities and courts must strike a fair balance between the protection of copyright and the protection of other fundamental rights', which in this case included the freedom to conduct a business enjoyed by operators such as Internet Service Providers pursuant to Article 16 of the Charter.[126]

That the privacy of European consumers is a 'top priority' for the European Court of Justice appears in particular from the judgments of the Court in *Digital Rights Ireland* and *Google Spain*. In *Digital Rights Ireland* the entire Data Retention Directive was held incompatible with the Charter, in particular Articles 7 (respect for private life) and 8 (protection of personal data).[127] According to the CJEU the Directive 'affects in a comprehensive manner, all persons using electronic communications services, but without the persons whose data are retained being, even indirectly, in a situation which is liable to give rise to criminal prosecutions',[128] and comes to the conclusion that

> Directive 2006/24 does not lay down clear and precise rules governing the extent of the interference with the fundamental rights enshrined in Articles 7 and 8 of the Charter. It must therefore be held that Directive 2006/24 entails a wide-ranging and particularly serious interference with those fundamental rights in the legal order of the EU, without such an interference being precisely circumscribed by provisions to ensure that it is actually limited to what is strictly necessary.[129]

The Court held that in cases where fundamental rights like the right to protection of personal data and privacy are seriously impaired, the EU legislature's discretion is reduced and the review of that discretion should be strict.[130] In the end the Directive did not meet the requirements of proportionality as laid down in Article 52 of the Charter.

[125] X Groussot, 'Case C–275/06, *Productores de Música de España (Promusicae) v Telefónica de España SAU*, Judgment of the Court (Grand Chamber) of 28 January 2008, not yet reported—Rock the KaZaA: Another Clash of Fundamental Rights' (2008) 45 *Common Market Law Review* 1745; F Coudert and E Werkers, 'In The Aftermath of the Promusicae Case: How to Strike the Balance?' (2008) *International Journal of Law and Information Technology* 1.

[126] Case C–70/10 *Scarlet Extended SA v Société belge des auteurs, compositeurs et éditeurs SCRL (SABAM)* [2011] ECR I–11959, paras 44–46.

[127] *Digital Rights Ireland* (n 80).

[128] ibid, para 58.

[129] ibid, para 65.

[130] ibid, para 48.

Also, the abovementioned *Google Spain* judgment is exemplary for the way in which these rights may easily take precedence over the economic rights of the operator of the search engine and the interest of the general public in having access to information. The freedom of expression implications of such extensive protection of privacy and data are, in fact, largely ignored in the judgment of the Court.[131] Meanwhile the European Commission adopted a proposal for a General Data Protection Regulation reforming the data protection rules and more explicitly incorporating citizens' rights to be forgotten.[132] The European Parliament voted in favour of a compromise text in March 2014. We will have to wait and see whether and when this far-reaching legal act will be adopted and whether it will help to reinforce consumer confidence in online services, as the Commission suggests.[133]

V. Conclusion: An On-Going Endeavour for Closer Harmony

Looking at the case law of the Court, we see that in the construction of the EU Single Market the Court resolves the tension between the EU single market and consumer protection by opposing national policies which underestimate the ability of consumers to make informed choices. At the same time, national rules protecting specific groups of consumers are upheld, even though they restrict free movement and even though they have an extraterritorial effect.

More particularly, the Court, in accepting the limits of consumer choice, takes account of a number of factors: different standards of protection in the Member States, the sensitive nature of the regulated sector, the fact that certain consumers need extra protection because they are vulnerable, which may be reinforced by the EU Charter, and linguistic, social and cultural considerations as consumers should be able to process information in an intelligible way.

Hence, although the Court of Justice, by establishing the concept of a reasonably circumspect consumer, enhances a notion of a paradigm consumer that reflects the 'rational homo economicus', EU free movement law contains a number of safeguards for consumers who are not in a position to make these informed choices.

[131] *Google Spain* (n 80), para 99. See also O Lynskey, 'Rising like a Phoenix: The "Right to be Forgotten" Before the CJEU' *European Law Blog* (13 May 2014) <http://europeanlawblog.eu/?p=2351> accessed 14 April 2015.

[132] Commission, Proposal for a Regulation of the European Parliament and of the Council on the protection of individuals with regard to the processing of personal data and on the free movement of such data (General Data Protection Regulation) COM(2012) 11 final.

[133] Commission, 'Commission proposes a comprehensive reform of data protection rules to increase users' control of their data and to cut costs for businesses', Press Release IP/12/46 (25 January 2012) <http://europa.eu/rapid/press-release_IP-12-46_en.htm> accessed 14 April 2015.

The consumer is not (always) a rational person who wants or is able to choose; the dichotomy between the vulnerable consumer and the circumspect consumer is not always clear-cut.

The recognition of these limits should be developed further in the still rather limited and market-led case law of the Court. It fits in a more holistic conception of the EU Single Market with a more inclusive consumer concept. Furthermore, various legal developments, most notably the entry into force of the Lisbon Treaty, and societal changes and technological developments, call for continued critical reflection on the notion of consumer as rational homo economicus. The aim is to guarantee an adequate level of consumer protection in the face of market integration and also to take account of an increasing number of different groups of consumers. Here there is also a clear role for the EU legislature, which has not been addressed in this chapter, in providing for a more coherent, uniform and harmonious approach to the development and future shaping of the EU Single Market, which includes a (reasonably) high level of consumer protection.[134]

And, although the notion of a paradigm consumer should perhaps not be too conflated with human rights thinking, thereby putting citizenship and 'consumerism' on an equal footing, the social and human rights dimension of the EU Single Market reinforced by the EU Charter of Fundamental Rights could prevent an outcome in which consumers become wholly reliant on the market for their survival.

[134] See also S de Vries, 'Consumer Protection and the EU Single Market rules—The Search for the Paradigm Consumer' (2012) 4 *The Journal of European Consumer and Market Law* 228, 241–42.

18

Europe's (Lack of) Vision on Consumer Protection: A Case of Rhetoric Hiding Substance?

GERAINT HOWELLS

I. Introduction

There is a sense that times are changing in Brussels as regards consumer protection and some are uneasy about the extent of the EU's commitment to consumer protection. No one can doubt that the EU has engaged heavily in consumer protection. It has implemented a raft of substantive provisions[1] and in recent times has started to address enforcement and access to justice.[2] There is now a specific

[1] eg Council Directive 90/314/EEC of 13 June 1990 on package travel, package holidays and package tours [1990] OJ L158/59; Council Directive 93/13/EEC of 5 April 1993 on unfair terms in consumer contracts [1993] OJ L95/29; Directive 1999/44/EC of the European Parliament and of the Council of 25 May 1999 on certain aspects of the sale of consumer goods and associated guarantees [1999] OJ L171/12; Directive 2002/65/EC of the European Parliament and of the Council of 23 September 2002 concerning the distance marketing of consumer financial services [2002] OJ L271/16; Directive 2005/29/EC of the European Parliament and of the Council of 11 May 2005 concerning unfair business-to-consumer commercial practices in the internal market (Unfair Commercial Practices Directive) [2005] OJ L149/22; Directive 2008/48/EC of the European Parliament and of the Council of 23 April 2008 on credit agreements for consumers [2008] OJ L133/66; Directive 2008/122/EC of the European Parliament and of the Council of 14 January 2009 on the protection of consumers in respect of certain aspects of timeshare, long-term holiday product, resale and exchange contracts [2009] OJ L33/10; Directive 2011/83/EU of the European Parliament and of the Council of 25 October 2011 on consumer rights [2011] OJ L304/64 (Consumer Rights Directive).

[2] On enforcement in general see Directive 2009/22/EC of the European Parliament and of the Council of 23 April 2009 on injunctions for the protection of consumers' interests (Codified version) [2009] OJ L110/30 and Regulation (EC) No 2006/2004 of the European Parliament and of the Council of 27 October 2004 on cooperation between national authorities responsible for the enforcement of consumer protection laws [2004] OJ L364/1. For example, on redress, see Regulation (EC) No 805/2004 of the European Parliament and of the Council of 21 April 2004 creating a European Enforcement Order for uncontested claims [2004] OJ L143/15, Regulation (EU) No 524/2013 of the European Parliament and of the Council of 21 May 2013 on online dispute resolution for consumer disputes [2013] OJ L165/1, Directive 2013/11/EU of the European Parliament and of the Council of 21 May 2013 on alternative dispute resolution for consumer disputes [2013] OJ L165/63 and

consumer protection provision in the Treaty,[3] internal market provisions should take as their base a high level of protection[4] and indeed consumer protection is one aspect of competition policy.[5] Why then do some commentators criticise the EU's commitment to consumer protection?

There are two main strands running through such criticisms. First, the move to maximal harmonisation. The arguments about this have been well rehearsed elsewhere by myself[6] and others[7] and so will not be dwelt upon. In particular I will not rehearse the argument as to why this approach is unlikely to achieve by itself the objective of increased cross-border trade.[8] However, in essence there has been a move away from seeing the goal of Europe as being to create a platform of harmonised rights that gives consumers the confidence to shop anywhere in the Union towards a policy of uniformity so that businesses become willing to trade across borders as they have no surprising national provisions to contend with. Some argue that consumers will also be more confident as they will be less confused about their rights,[9] but that argument sounds rather specious as consumers could only benefit from more protective national laws. At the heart of this debate is an argument as to whether consumers are better off by having some more protective national rules or a more competitive environment. One suspects the empirical answer to that will depend upon just how competitive local markets already were before attempts are made to open them up.

This chapter will not dwell upon the harmonisation topic more than necessary, but rather seeks to focus on the second criticism that there is an empty soul

Commission Recommendation of 11 June 2013 on common principles for injunctive and compensatory collective redress mechanisms in the Member States concerning violations of rights granted under Union Law [2013] OJ L201/60.

[3] Art 169 TFEU. With regard to the development see N Reich and others, *European Consumer Law* 2nd edn (Cambridge, Intersentia, 2014) 8–21; see also with regard to its infrequent use as a legislative basis M Loos, 'Full Harmonization as a Regulatory Concept and its Consequences for National Legal Orders' in M Stürner (ed), *Vollharmonisierung im europäischen Verbraucherrecht* (München, Sellier, 2010) 51.

[4] Art 114(3) TFEU.

[5] Arts 101(3) and 102(b) TFEU.

[6] G Howells, 'European Contract Law Reform and European Consumer Law—Two Related But Distinct Regimes' (2011) *European Review of Contract Law* 173, 184–86; G Howells and N Reich, 'The Current Limits of European Harmonisation in Consumer Contract Law' (2011) 12 *ERA Forum* 39; G Howells and R Schulze, 'Overview of the Proposed Consumer Rights Directive' in G Howells and R Schulze (eds), *Modernising and Harmonising Consumer Contract Law* (Munich, Sellier, 2009) 6–8.

[7] For comments related to specific aspects see the contributions in Howells and Schulze (n 6); more generally see Loos (n 3) 47–98; V Mak, 'Review of the Consumer *Acquis*: Towards Maximum Harmonization?' (2009) *European Review of Private Law* 55; H-W Micklitz and N Reich, 'Crónica de una muerte anunciada: The Commission Proposal for a "Directive on Consumer Rights"' (2009) 46 *Common Market Law Review* 471; P Rott and E Terryn, 'The Proposal for a Directive on Consumer Rights' (2009) *Zeitschrift für europäisches Privatrecht* 456, 458–65.

[8] See Howells (n 7) 184–86; see also Loos (n 3) 61–65 for an overview of the various arguments. See also A De Vries, 'The Aim for Complete Uniformity in EU Private Law: An Obstacle to Further Harmonization' [2012] *European Review of Private Law* 913; Rott and Terryn (n 7) 460.

[9] For a summary of this argument and criticism see H-W Micklitz, 'Targeted Full Harmonisation' in Howells and Schulze (n 6) 71–73.

to EU consumer protection policy. This substantive critique is linked to the first question because the substantive content becomes more crucial under maximal harmonisation regimes where the European rules are the only source of protection. Also, as the main motive becomes more transparently increased cross-border sales there is a danger that despite the constitutional requirement to take a high level of consumer protection, there may be incentives to adopt lower standards to encourage trade. As part of the context, it should also be noted that responsibility at the Commission for the bulk of the consumer *acquis* has been moved from DG SANCO to DG JUSTICE. This in fact mirrors academic trends as there has been a shift in scholarship from a focus on studying consumer protection to European private law as a field of study.[10] There is a danger that even enlightened officials or academics looking through the prism of traditional legal science may not be sensitive to all the concerns of consumers. Consumer activists tend to have learned the need for particular forms of protection as a result of many battle scars.

What aspects of consumer policy seem to be at risk from the developing *acquis*? Two touchstones are often cited: an overemphasis on information and empowerment at the expense of substantive regulation and a reduced concern for vulnerable consumers by applying the average consumer benchmark. These arguments have been well rehearsed in Stephen Weatherill's chapter in this collection and so this will allow me to be briefer on the background materials.[11]

Weatherill is concerned that the Commission is over-emphasising empowerment at the expense of traditional consumer values. This chimes with my own view that information is a necessary but not sufficient form of protection.[12] This EU approach is reflected in a preference for information over substantive protection and less focus on protecting the vulnerable. The EU seems to have a lot of faith in the ability of consumers to take advantage of information rules, often in the face of its own discussion of the need to be aware of the lessons of behavioural economics.[13] In fact the legal rules themselves are, to be fair to the Commission,

[10] eg C Twigg-Flesner (ed), *The Cambridge Companion to European Private Law* (New York, Cambridge University Press, 2010), R Brownsword and others (eds), *The Foundations of European Private Law* (Oxford, Hart Publishing, 2011), and J Basedow, K Hopt and R Zimmermann (eds), *The Max Planck Encyclopedia of European Private Law* (New York, Oxford University Press, 2012).

[11] Stephen Weatherill in this volume.

[12] See G Howells, 'The Potential and Limits of Consumer Empowerment by Information' (2005) 32 *Journal of Law and Society* 349.

[13] See Commission, A European Consumer Agenda—Boosting Confidence and Growth (Communication) COM(2012) 225 final, para 3.3, and Commission Staff Working Document: On Knowledge-Enhancing Aspects of Consumer Enforcement 2012–2014 SWD(2012) 235 final, where it cites at 2.2 BEUC's view that '[t]his increase in disempowerment, the reverse of what official strategies aim for, is compounded by the fact that current policy initiatives do not necessarily take into account the different information needs of people according to their particular conditions or vulnerabilities. Ultimately, this "confuseopoly" makes choices difficult, as there are so many dimensions to consider for each product and service. The "right" choice is not an easy one. Searching for the necessary information—if it's available—is not only complicated, but demands a great deal of time, which most consumers in their hectic daily lives cannot and do not want to spend'. See also 2.73, 'Behavioural studies warn that policy efforts in information/education do not always have the desired effect in terms of applied consumer skill' and also 3.1, 'Looking at The Consumer Challenge: Information Overload vs Knowledge Deficit' and s 5, 'Vulnerability and Vulnerable Consumers'.

only part of its understanding of empowerment. This empowerment framework also involves consumers knowing their rights and how to enforce them as well as being educated to understand the options available in the market place.[14] All these aspects of empowerment have of course their own debating points.

My thesis is that there are many instances when the Commission and the Court of Justice (CJEU) have in fact shown themselves sensitive to consumer concerns. The *acquis* contains many substantive rights and when faced with concrete cases the CJEU has shown itself willing to protect consumers. Why then do some people criticise the EU so much for not being sufficiently consumer protective? The bad press the EU gets might be due to its rhetoric and dogmatism on issues such as maximal harmonisation. But it also needs to learn the lessons it preaches about the value of behavioural economic insights and refocus its policy so that a high level of consumer protection is demonstrated to be a central concern and not merely a subsidiary consideration. In other words I do not think the EU lacks a soul to its consumer policy, but its emphasis on the internal market and maximum harmonisation has risked making people forget the core values and rights it has guaranteed EU citizens. There is a danger that over time the EU listens to its own rhetoric too much and can forget the importance of the core values it has established. Thus my message to the Commission is that it needs to build bridges with consumer stakeholders by restating its commitment to a high level of consumer protection. Explaining the philosophy that underpins its belief in substantive consumer rights (of which EU law offers many examples) will both reassure the consumer community and ensure that policies are guided by those protective principles which should be at the core of any law reform agenda.

II. Free Movement Cases

The free movement cases are often seen as prime examples of the EU being anti-consumer protection. The CJEU rejected national images of the consumer as a vulnerable person unable to make sensible judgments on marketing practices and replaced this with the model of the 'average consumer who is reasonably well-informed and reasonably observant and circumspect'.[15] The obvious criticism is that this standard sacrificed the vulnerable consumer, who by definition is less capable than the average, on the altar of integration. However, the motivation for this is important to recognise as these cases sought to challenge national practices which had more to do with protectionism than real consumer protection. I have previously argued that this case law was in fact willing to take on board genuine

[14] See Commission documents cited at n 13.

[15] Case C–210/96 *Gut Springenheide GmbH and Rudolf Tusky v Oberkreisdirekyto des Kreises Steinfurt—Amt für Lebensmittelüberwachung* [1998] ECR I–4657; Case C–220/98 *Estée Lauder Cosmetics GmbH v Lancaster Group GmbH* [2000] ECR I–117. Cf New Zealand case *Godfrey Hirst v Cavalier* [2014] NZCA 418 that used the standard of 'all consumers in class except outliers', but assumed they 'will not be lacking in perception and can be expected to bring to bear a reasonable degree of common sense.'

consumer protection arguments to justify the maintenance of national protective rules.[16] Stephen Weatherill makes a similar point in his chapter and so I will not repeat the details. Moreover, the assessment of the national law has been said to be capable of being applied sensitively taking account of 'social, cultural or linguistic factors'.[17]

How many of these protected national laws relating to marketing would now be struck down because of the maximal harmonisation approach of the Unfair Commercial Practices Directive is another matter. Indeed this might be seen as an almost unwitting side effect of the Commission's determination to impose maximal harmonisation. Consumer protection is overridden as a side issue. National marketing measures would have to be challenged as unfair practices and this would be hard to do if accepted in most states. The reference to 'social, cultural or linguistic factors'[18] in Recital 18 of the Directive might allow some scope for national diversity of protective approaches, but as Bram Duivenvoorde notes, the scope for this to be a source of diversity might be limited by the tendency of the CJEU to interpret it restrictively and in particular to emphasise the more limited linguistic justification rather than the social and cultural.[19]

Even accepting that an average consumer test is appropriate, two problems seem to exist with the EU's adoption of the average consumer test. First, it has been expanded from the realm of negative harmonisation to the field of positive harmonisation through the Unfair Commercial Practices Directive and probably indirectly also the Unfair Terms in Consumer Contracts Directive.[20] A tool used to challenge national restrictive practices should not necessarily become the general standard for consumer protection. It was useful in the negative harmonisation context as a counter to arguments that consumers could not be trusted to make any evaluation of marketing practices and so should be judged by the standards of the least capable. However, that should not apply to positive law where there may indeed be reasons why protection should be fixed at a level below that suitable for the most aware. This connects to the second criticism, which is that the average consumer standards as defined in fact relate to an image of the consumer very different from any average consumer who might be empirically discovered. Ignoring the finding of behavioural economics[21] it assumes the average consumer

[16] G Howells, H-W Micklitz and T Wilhelmsson, *European Fair Trading Law* (Farnham, Ashgate, 2006) 17–18.

[17] *Estée Lauder* (n 15).

[18] See also ibid.

[19] B Duivenvoorde, *The Consumer Benchmarks in the Unfair Commercial Practices Directive* (PhD thesis, University of Amsterdam 2014) 71–73.

[20] See below at text around n 55.

[21] See generally R Ellickson, 'Bringing Culture and Human Frailty to Rational Actors: A Critique of Classical Law and Economics' (1989) 65 *Chicago-Kent Law Review* 23; C Jolls, C Sunstein and R Thaler, 'A Behavioural Approach to Law and Economics' (1998) 50 *Stanford Law Review* 1470; R Korbkin and T Ulen, 'Law and Behavioural Science: Removing the Rationality Assumption from Law and Economics' (2000) 88 *California Law Review* 1951; C Sunstein (ed), *Behavioral Law and Economics* (New York, Cambridge University Press, 2008); A Tversky and D Kahneman, 'Rational Choice and the Framing of Decisions' [1986] *The Journal of Business* 251.

is 'reasonably well-informed and reasonably observant and circumspect'. In reality we know consumers are not like that, if such a standard assumes they read terms and conditions carefully and ponder the meaning of advertisements. Possibly there is scope for a more relaxed interpretation by reliance on the use of 'reasonably' but there is no tendency in that direction.

Information of course plays an important role in the freedom of movement cases. The free flow of information across borders is promoted.[22] In many cases information is seen as a substitute for substantive regulation, but when you look at the facts of these cases one again sees the national laws are often disguised protectionism.[23] Little consumer protection is lost by opening up the markets to new products, subject to labelling provisions if desired.

The free movement rules might well be judged to evince a desire to continue to protect real consumer protection ideals, whilst eschewing the use of consumer protection as an excuse for protectionism. It is the use that has been made of the concept of the average consumer in other substantive regulation contexts that has become problematic. There is also a risk that many of the national measures left in place are threatened by the Unfair Commercial Practices Directive.

III. Unfair Commercial Practices

The Unfair Commercial Practices Directive perhaps typifies the reasons why the EU is viewed with scepticism by consumers, despite its efforts to put in place a comprehensive regime against unfair practices. A lot of wrath has been spent criticising the maximum harmonisation character of the Directive. The CJEU case law has underlined the firm principle of making the Directive the sole source of EU law. Indeed the proposal for a Sales Promotion Regulation[24] that proved too controversial hardly seems needed as the Directive has been interpreted so as to pre-empt automatic bans unless provided for in the Directive. Combined with the challenge to measures left in place by free movement provisions, the Directive has done a pretty good job of clearing out national laws.

The Directive does, however, offer a fairly strong protective regime, with an annex setting out 31 practices which are considered unfair in all the circumstances,

[22] See Case C–362/88 *GB-INNO-BM gegen Confédération du commerce Luxembourgeois* [1990] ECR I–667.

[23] See, eg, Case C–788/79 *Criminal proceedings against Herbert Gilli and Paul Andres* [1980] ECR 2071 (vinegar); Case C–130/80 *Criminal proceedings against Fabriek voor Hoogwaardige Voedingsprodukten Kelderman BV* [1981] ECR 527 (bread); Case C–178/84 *Commission v Germany* [1987] ECR 1227 (beer); Case C–90/86 *Criminal proceedings against Zoni* [1988] ECR 4285 (pasta).

[24] Proposal for a European Parliament and Council Regulation concerning sales promotions in the Internal Market COM(2001) 546 final.

three small general clauses (on misleading action, misleading omissions and aggressive practices) and a general duty to trade fairly.[25]

As noted, concern has focussed on the uncritical acceptance of the (in reality not so) average consumer standard. Weatherill notes, however, that the standard is adapted to take into account the vulnerable, albeit that there is a limited list of vulnerabilities listed.[26] However, a close reading of the provision amending the average consumer standard to take account of vulnerabilities illustrates how hard it will be potentially to apply it to protect vulnerable groups.

Article 5(3) provides:

> Commercial practices which are likely to materially distort the economic behaviour only of a clearly identifiable group of consumers who are particularly vulnerable to the practice or the underlying product because of their mental or physical infirmity, age or credulity in a way which the trader could reasonably be expected to foresee, shall be assessed from the perspective of the average member of that group. This is without prejudice to the common and legitimate advertising practice of making exaggerated statements or statements which are not meant to be taken literally.

There must be a clearly identifiable group of vulnerable consumers. They must be vulnerable because of the specific characteristics listed—mental or physical infirmity, age or credulity. These may seem sensible caveats, but the phrasing states that the variable standard only applies when only this group would be likely to have their behaviour materially distorted. So if members of this group and some others would be misled, but not the hypothetical average consumer, there would be no protection. Also the trader should reasonably be expected to have foreseen they would be misled. One can appreciate how a trader could see that a mentally ill person might make decisions differently from the average consumer, but can this be expected just because someone is elderly or physically infirm? Do these groups necessarily have lower cognitive abilities? Moreover, how are traders expected to determine whether individuals are particularly credulous? This provision was inserted in response to concerns that the provision was not sufficiently protective. It demonstrates that the Commission was keen to address these concerns, but it did so as a secondary consideration. This shows that the special measure on vulnerability fits uneasily into a framework whose primary objective is market liberalisation. It looks overlaid on top of the basic principles in a rather slapdash manner. Its practical application may or may not be reasonably protective. It may be that the court will not dissect its wording as set out above. But, there are enough questions raised to at least make one concerned that the actual protection of the vulnerable may be difficult to deliver.

[25] It was confirmed in Case C–435/11 *CHS TOURS v Team4 Travel*, judgment of 19 September 2013, that the court should start from the specific practices in the annex, then move on to the small general clauses and only finally sue the general unfairness text.

[26] Weatherill (n 11), citing J Stuyck, E Terryn and T Van Dyck, 'Confidence through Fairness? The New Directive on Unfair Business-to-Consumer Commercial Practices in the Internal Market' (2006) 43 *Common Market Law Review* 107.

Most of the Directive's provisions are aimed at improving market practices including making sure information that is provided is accurate. Moreover, its rules on omissions have won many plaudits. It seems to strike a sensible balance by only requiring necessary or material information to be provided and so should not unduly add to any information overload problems.

Most of the CJEU case law has confirmed the market liberalisation thrust by striking down national rules which prohibited practices not on the Directive's black list. The practices have to be assessed under the Directive's general criteria.[27] The Court did, however, accept that different rules applied in the financial services context.[28] Consumer protection seemed to be to the fore in some Court decisions on substantive matters. The Court held that transactional decisions included the decision to enter a shop.[29] It applied the rules to public bodies providing health insurance[30] and gave consumer friendly interpretations of the rules on pyramid selling schemes[31] and prize lotteries.[32] On the other hand, consumers might be more concerned by the Court allowing entry-level pricing advertisements,[33] although this may be understandable given the nature of the travel services involved.

The Unfair Commercial Practices Directive is perhaps indicative of the general perception of the Commission and consumer protection. There are many good features and certainly examples in particular cases (in the annex or litigation) of a desire to protect the consumer. Useful features include incentives to provide material information and a general obligation not to behave unfairly. However, the main driver was internal market concerns with consumer protection being secondary. In particular the maximal harmonisation approach of the Commission (resoundingly endorsed by the Court) has meant that the principles of the abandoned Sales Promotion Regulation have been reintroduced by the back door, and national measures protected under free movement rules fall for renewed scrutiny. This does little to inspire confidence in the Commission's concern for consumer protection as a goal in itself. The amendment to take into account vulnerable consumers is factually and symbolically evidence that consumer protection is an add-on to the basic policy. In summary this Directive is a good example of a measure, which should have underpinned the EU's commitment to consumer

[27] Case C–540/08 *Mediaprint Zeitungs- und Zeitschriftenverlag GmbH & Co KG v 'Österreich'-Zeitungsverlag GmbH* [2010] ECR I–10909; Joined Cases C–261/07 *VTB-VAB NV v Total Belgium NV* and C–299/07 *Galatea BVBA v Sanoma Magazines Belgium NV* [2009] ECR I–2949.

[28] Case C–265/12 *Citroën Belux NV v Federatie voor Verzekerings- en Financiële Tussenpersonen (FvF)*, judgment of 18 July 2013.

[29] Case C–281/12 *Trento Sviluppo srl and Centrale Adriatica Soc. coop. arl v Autorità Garante della Concorrenza e del Mercato*, judgment of 19 December 2013.

[30] Case C–59/12 *BKK Mobil Oil Körperschaft des öffentlichen Rechts v Zentrale zur Bekämpfung unlauteren Wettbewerbs eV*, judgment of 3 October 2013.

[31] Case C–515/12 *'4finance' UAB v Valstybinė vartotojų teisių apsaugos tarnyba and Valstybinė mokesčių inspekcija prie Lietuvos Respublikos finansų ministerijos*, judgment of 3 April 2014.

[32] Case C–428/11 *Purely Creative and Others v Office of Fair Trading*, judgment of 18 October 2012.

[33] Case C–122/10 *Konsumentombudsmannen v Ving Sverige AB* [2011] ECR I–3903.

protection, being undermined by rhetoric and dogma around the need for maximum harmonisation to promote the internal market.

IV. Unfair Terms

Although adopting minimum controls on unfair terms throughout the Community is a significant achievement in terms of harmonisation, when judged against the highest standards in Europe, the Unfair Terms in Consumer Contracts Directive is modest in ambition. It only applies to non-negotiated terms,[34] excludes review of core terms and the adequacy of price and remuneration[35] and has no black list of terms always unfair, merely a grey list of indicatively unfair terms.[36] Even the much heralded adoption of good faith is not as progressive as might be thought as it is not an independent test of unfairness, but rather an additional condition that has to be met beyond the finding of a significant imbalance to the detriment of the consumer.[37] However, as it is a minimum harmonisation measure, the latitude given to Member States to increase protection meant that its consumer protection standards were not subject to intense scrutiny. This changed when the proposal for a Consumer Rights Directive[38] sought to convert this to a maximum harmonisation directive. In particular Nordic states were concerned that they would lose the ability to control core terms and price.

The proposals on unfair terms were dropped from the final Consumer Rights Directive[39] and indeed several commentators have noted that in practice the CJEU has used the Directive in a manner that is protective of consumers.[40] This was seen in one of the first judgments where an unfair jurisdiction clause was struck down by the Court.[41] The Court pulled back from being as definitive in the assessment of terms in *Freiburger Kommunalbauten*,[42] but has been very alert in ensuring the

[34] Council Directive 93/13/EEC of 5 April 1993 on unfair terms in consumer contracts [1993] OJ L95/29, Art 3.

[35] ibid, Art 4(2).

[36] ibid, Art 3(3) and Annex.

[37] See discussion in R Brownsword, G Howells and T Wilhelmsson, 'Between Market and Welfare: Some Reflections on Article 3 of the EC Directive on Unfair Terms in Consumer Contracts' in C Willet (ed), *Aspects of Fairness in Contract* (Oxford, Blackstone Press, 1996) albeit that some terms may be so shocking that their use would always be against good faith and so not involve good faith in necessarily imposing a requirement for procedural unfairness.

[38] Proposal for a Directive of the European Parliament and of the Council on consumer rights COM(2008) 614 final.

[39] Consumer Rights Directive (n 1).

[40] V Trstenjak and E Beyson, 'European Consumer Protection Law: Curia Semper Dabit Remedium?' (2011) 48 *Common Market Law Review* 95; H-W Micklitz and N Reich, 'The Court and Sleeping Beauty: the Revival of the Unfair Contract Terms Directive' (2014) 51 *Common Market Law Review* 771.

[41] Case C–240/98 *Océano Grupo Editorial SA v Roció Murciano Quintero* [2000] ECR I–4941.

[42] Case C–237/02 *Freiburger Kommunalbauten GmbH Baugesellschaft & Co KG v Ludger Hofstetter and Ulrike Hofstetter* [2004] ECR I–3403.

Directive is available to consumers. It has required that national procedural law ensures that the issue of unfairness can be assessed;[43] that the Court is under an obligation to review unfairness *ex officio* without a consumer raising the issue;[44] that the remedies regime allows meaningful redress;[45] and that collective decisions are given effect to in other cases involving use of the same terms with other consumers (indeed this would seem in any event to flow from the *ex officio* obligation of the court to assess redress).[46] However, all these issues relate to the effectiveness of European law rather than directly affecting the interpretation of the substantive rules.

There have, however, also been some CJEU decisions on the meaning of the substantive provisions. One important dimension is the CJEU's discussion of transparency. This is evident in the *Invitel*[47] and *RWE*[48] cases concerning a price variation clause[49] and in *Kásler*[50] where the issue was the transparency of the difference between currency rates in buy and sell transactions in foreign currency loans. Many commentators applaud and are excited by this transparency principle as they see it as giving an edge to the information obligations.[51] These are viewed as not merely formal obligations, but rather real obligations with bite, which not only require the terms to be formally clear but also comprehensible to consumers. However, these same commentators often also point to the limits of information policy due to the lessons of behavioural economics. Does anyone really believe the average consumer would have read these contract terms carefully? Even assuming they did, would they therefore not have entered into the contract because of them? There is plenty of evidence that consumers rarely read contracts and if they are not put off by disclosures of exorbitant interest rates it is unlikely that the litigated clauses, even if clearly spelt out, would affect many consumer decisions. Indeed the consumers may have had few practical alternatives. These cases instead seem to be a way to find a consumer-friendly solution despite the limitation on substantive review possible under the Directive. The transparency principle provides a positive outcome

[43] Case C–168/05 *Claro v Centro Móvil Milenium SL* [2006] ECRI–10421; Case C–40/08 *Telecomunicaciones SL v Cristina Rodríguez Nogueira* [2009] ECR I–9579.

[44] Case C–243/08 *Pannon GSM Zrt v Erzsébet Sustikné Győrfi* [2009] ECR I–4713; Case C–472/11 *Banif Plus Bank Zrt v Csaba Csipai und Viktória Csipai*, judgment of 21 February 2013.

[45] Case C–415/11 *Mohamed Aziz v Caixa d'Estalvis de Catalunya, Tarragona i Manresa (Catalunyacaixa)*, judgment of 14 March 2013.

[46] Case C–472/10 *Nemzeti Fogyasztóvédelmi Hatóság v Invitel Távközlési Zrt*, judgment of 26 April 2012.

[47] ibid.

[48] Case C–92/11 *RWE Vertrieb AG v Verbraucherzentrale Nordrhein-Westfalen eV*, judgment of 21 March 2013.

[49] As an aside it might be questioned how the Court's requirement that the consumer be informed of 'clear, intelligible criteria' (para 49) sits alongside the English consumer credit cases that have allowed interest rates to be varied without needing to specify the rationale behind any increases: *Lombard Tricity Finance v Paton* [1989] 1 All ER 918 (CA) and *SBC Bank Plc v Brophy* [2011] EWCA Civ 67, [2011] ECC 14.

[50] Case C–26/13 *Árpád Kásler and Hajnalka Káslerné Rábai v OTP Jelzálogbank Zrt*, judgment of 30 April 2014.

[51] Weatherill (n 11); Micklitz and Reich (n 40).

for consumer redress in the instant cases, but is not necessarily going to improve the overall lot of consumers. It can be viewed as an example of over-reliance on information, even in transparent form as a means of protection. Traders can make contracts clearer and continue to act just as they were with legal impunity under the Directive. That may, however, be a rather harsh assessment, for it does signify the CJEU's desire to be proactive in using the tools available to protect consumers.

In *Aziz*,[52] there was a very positive statement about the content of the unfairness test and in particular what is meant by 'substantial imbalance' and 'good faith'. Substantial imbalance could be found by comparison with what the normal rule would be under national law absent the term in question. Agreeing with Advocate General Kokott, the CJEU went on to state:

> the national court must assess for those purposes whether the seller or supplier, dealing fairly and equitably with the consumer, could reasonably assume that the consumer would have agreed to such a term in individual contract negotiations.[53]

Recital 16 had hinted at a strong version of good faith by requiring that the other party's interest should be taken into account.[54] The judgment seems to have taken a similarly strong interpretation by not only mandating disclosure, but also an obligation not to supply on terms consumers would not have reasonably agreed to.

When judging the fairness of terms an important question to ask is: by whose standards are the terms to be judged? The answer from *Kásler* seems to be that they should be judged by the standard of the average consumer, for the Court stated:

> As regards the particularities of the mechanism for conversion of the foreign currency such as those set out in Clause III/2, it is for the referring court to determine whether, having regard to all the relevant information, including the promotional material and information provided by the lender in the negotiation of the loan agreement, *the average consumer*, who is reasonably well informed and reasonably observant and circumspect, would not only be aware of the existence of the difference, generally observed on the securities market, between the selling rate of exchange and the buying rate of exchange of a foreign currency, but also be able to assess the potentially significant economic consequences for him resulting from the application of the selling rate of exchange for the calculation of the repayments for which he would ultimately be liable and, therefore, the total cost of the sum borrowed.[55]

This seems to apply not only to injunctive procedures, but also to individual assessments, as was the case in *Kásler*. Is that appropriate? Although one is dealing with standardised contracts the individual sales may vary from highly depersonalised sales, such as on the internet, to very personalised sales, such as mortgage products where the seller knows the individual well. The average standard may be

[52] *Aziz* (n 45).

[53] ibid, para 67.

[54] For discussion of versions of good faith see R Brownsword, '"Good Faith in Contract" Revisited' (1996) 49 *Current Legal Problems* 111.

[55] *Kásler* (n 50), para 74 (emphasis added).

appropriate for the assessment of terms used in standard form contracts for mass sales of goods and services. However, especially in the context of good faith assessments one would have thought it relevant that in some contexts the trader would be expected to be aware of the limitations or personality of the consumer he was dealing with and to take these factors into account. It may be against good faith to use a term where its use may be unfair if a trader knows the particular consumer is unable to comprehend it at least without the trader taking additional steps to explain the term and its consequences.

Equally there is an irony in relation to the use of the average consumer standard in the context of regulating standard form contracts. A major motivation for the regulation of standard form contracts is precisely that consumers are not reasonably circumspect and so need substantive regulation, but here it is assumed that consumers will read contracts or at least that the protection of the law only extends to protecting them by transparency on the assumption they have read the contract.

V. Conclusions

There is much to commend the EU for in the field of consumer protection. Yet, whilst some suggest it is too protective of consumers,[56] others criticise it for sacrificing consumer protection on the altar of internal market integration. We have focussed on a few key points that give the EU a bad press. The over-reliance on information strategies to protect consumers is viewed as using the cloak of empowerment language to implement a deregulatory approach. The use of an unrealistic conception of the average consumer benchmark has been simply imported into the positive consumer *acquis* from the free movement context without appreciating the different purposes it serves in each context. It has been further cross-fertilised from unfair competition law to unfair terms without the full ramifications being thought through. Underpinning these substantive law policies is the philosophical starting point of the Commission that maximum harmonisation is the optimum solution. Therefore EU laws, unless pitched at the highest standard throughout the Community, threaten national traditions of consumer protection. This is done without convincing empirical evidence on the extent to which such uniformity will increase cross-border trade.

In assessing EU law one might want to distinguish between the Commission-driven legislation and the CJEU. The legislation sets the standards and it is for the CJEU to interpret them. The legislation has provided a slate of consumer rights, which whilst promoting a consumer information strategy also respects the need for firm underpinning rules. If they were minimum rights few commentators

[56] H Unberath and A Johnston, 'The Double-Headed Approach of the ECJ Concerning Consumer Protection' (2007) 44 *Common Market Law Review* 1237.

would be critical. It is the attempt to place a ceiling on consumer rights by the use of maximal harmonisation which has brought the Commission into conflict with consumer advocates. The CJEU has been enthusiastic in robustly upholding the maximum harmonisation philosophy of recent legislation,[57] but it has also shown itself to be sensitive to consumer protection. We have seen that the CJEU was sympathetic to real evidence of the need for protective rules in the free movement cases and has been keen to ensure that the unfair terms legislation protection is available to consumer litigants as well as providing some consumer-friendly interpretations of both it and the substantive provisions on unfair commercial practices. In other contexts it has provided pro-consumer interpretations on matters such as extending withdrawal periods where information was not supplied[58] and ensuring that remedies are not diluted by the consumer's obligation to compensate for the use of goods when exercising remedies such as the right of withdrawal[59] or termination.[60]

My view is that the EU is supportive of strong consumer protection, although it has not always articulated what that basis is. Whilst the value of information allowing consumers greater freedom to make choices is stressed, there are many other examples of the EU setting strong minimum consumer protection rights. The maximum harmonisation debate has opened up a chasm between the Commission and the consumer movement. Its attempts to extend this principle more broadly in the proposal for a Consumer Rights Directive provoked much opposition.[61] It deflected the opposition of national lawyers by dropping the provisions from the proposal for a Consumer Rights Directive and inserting them into its now-withdrawn proposal for a Common European Sales Regulation.[62] There was therefore no longer a threat to national sales law, as it would only have applied to cross-border consumer sales. But the proposal still inflamed those concerned with protecting national levels of consumer protection for, as regards consumer sales across borders, there would have been the same result of a *de facto* European sales regime that was less protective than some national laws. This lower level of

[57] In addition to unfair commercial practices cases, see product liability cases such as Case C–52/00 *Commission v France* [2002] ECR I–3827; C–154/00 *Commission v Greece* [2002] ECR I–3879; Case 183/00 *González Sanchez v Medicina Asturiana SA* [2002] ECR I–3901; Case C–402/03 *Skov Æg v Bilka Lavprisvarehus A/S* [2006] ECR I–199; Case C–127/04 *Declan O'Byrne v Sanofi Pasteur MSD Ltd and Sanofi Pasteur SA* [2006] ECR I–1313.

[58] Case C–481/99 *Georg Heininger and Helga Heininger v Bayerische Hypo- und Vereinsbank AG* [2001] ECR I–9945.

[59] Case C–489/07 *Pia Messner v Firma Stefan Krüger* [2009] ECR I–7315.

[60] Case C–404/06 *Quelle AG v Bundesverband der Verbraucherzentralen und Verbraucherverbände* [2008] ECR I–2685.

[61] See, eg, Howells and Schulze (n 6); Micklitz and Reich (n 7); Rott and Terryn (n 7); C Twigg-Flesner and D Metcalfe, 'The Proposed Consumer Rights Directive—Less Haste, More Thought?' 3 (2009) *European Review of Contract Law* 368. With respect to the final version of the Consumer Rights Directive see E Hall, G Howells and J Watson, 'The Consumer Rights Directive—An Assessment of its Contribution to the Development of European Consumer Contract Law' (2012) *European Review of Contract Law* 139–66.

[62] Proposal for a Regulation of the European Parliament and of the Council on a Common European Sales Law COM(2011) 635 final.

protection would have been imported into national law through the creation of a parallel regime for cross-border trade. The regime would have side-stepped choice of law rules safeguarding traditional mandatory national consumer protection rules. This would have been achieved by the making the rules in the Regulation the relevant applicable national rules for cross-border contracts. The Commission portrayed the rules in the Regulation as an optional regime. This characterisation seemed to ignore or be uncaring as to the reality. In practice the regime would have been optional only for traders. Traders would decide whether or not to operate under the new regime, but once that decision was taken consumers would have been left with a 'take it or leave it' offer.[63] The proposal has now been withdrawn and we are promised a more focussed measure, perhaps restricted to online or digital services.

Several involved in developing the Common European Sales Regulation were frustrated with the consumer movement for failing to welcome a measure which they point out offers a high level of protection.[64] It is true that the background history may have set the consumer movement against this measure.[65] There was also a fear, not without some support from past experiences,[66] that the final product might not have been as protective as the original proposal. For instance, one could imagine lobbying on the issues of remedies with a desire by traders to be allowed to cure defects before the right of rejection arises. If that one seemingly small amendment had been adopted the assessment as to the protective level offered by the Regulation would have altered significantly. Once the measure was in the legislative process it would have a momentum that might make it difficult to stop it being enacted with the lowering of protection being characterised as marginal.

The EU might reflect on its philosophy and rhetoric. There may be only a few differences between Member States' consumer laws. That is to the credit of the EU as it is a consequence of its policy of developing the consumer *acquis* that familiar means of protecting consumers are firmly established in all Member States' legal systems. But those remaining differences are often important ones, reflecting

[63] J Cartwright, '"Choice is Good." Really?' (2011) *European Review of Contract Law* 335; G Howells, 'European Contract Law Reform and European Consumer Law—Two Related But Distinct Regimes' (2011) *European Review of Contract Law* 173.

[64] H Beale, 'The CESL Proposal: An Overview' (2013) 1 *Juridica International* 21; M Hesselink, 'How to Opt into the Common European Sales Law? Brief Comments on the Commission's Proposal for a Regulation' (2012) *European Review of Private Law* 20. See also the 2012 report drafted by H Schulte-Nölke for the European Parliament: 'Consumer Protection under the Proposal for a Common European Sales Law' (PE 462.507) 14–16.

[65] U Pachl, 'The Common European Sales Law—Have the Right Choices Been Made?' (2012) 19 *Maastricht Journal of European and Comparative Law* 180.

[66] cf the use of the good faith standard in the Unfair Contract Terms Directive and in its original proposal (Proposal For a Council Directive on Unfair Terms in Consumer Contracts COM(90) 322 final)—the latter included good faith as an independent means of determining fairness. cf also the remedies in the Consumer Sales Directive and in its original proposal (Proposal for a European Parliament and Council Directive on the sale of consumer goods and associated guarantees COM(95) 520 final)—the latter did not contain the two-tier system of remedies therefore allowing the consumer to choose between all four remedies.

national values that support providing substantive controls and recognising that consumer law has a protective element to support not only the particularly vulnerable, but also all consumers who are structurally vulnerable in most consumer contracting situations. The EU needs to show that it is concerned with its citizens and is not merely a free trade zone for the benefit of business interests. It should leave the last remaining space for national diversity. It should follow through on its policy as regards behavioural economics to reflect on (i) its concept of the average consumer and (ii) the balance between empowerment and regulation in consumer policy. It is already refocussing its efforts away from substantive law reform towards improving regulatory enforcement and access to justice.[67] This arena of activity gives it a chance to reconnect with the consumer movement by promoting their role as active enforcers.[68] Unfortunately the CJEU seemed to have too much confidence in the resources of the consumer movement when it failed to extend its protective approach to consumers to encompass consumer organisations in a case assessing the fairness of jurisdiction clauses.[69]

Europe has done a lot of good work in the consumer field. It risks undermining this by pushing for more uniformity. It is not insensitive to consumer needs when they are pointed out, such as the amendment to take account of vulnerable consumers in the average consumer standard in the Unfair Commercial Practices Directive. They should, however, have been at the centre of Commission thinking when developing a fairness regime. Equally, empowerment has a role and in practice EU law does strike a fairly good balance with a lot of substantive protection. Something has, however, gone wrong with the mood music, for consumer initiatives have recently very often in the private law field come to be viewed sceptically by the consumer movement. As regards private law the stakeholders seem to be in entrenched positions.

The Commission needs to break this deadlock. I am willing to believe that the Commission does want a high level of protection; the problem has been that it has preferred to emphasise the internal market function of consumer protection. It would be helpful if it reflected on whether it had overstated the benefits of maximum harmonisation. At times it has expressed a desire to step back and refocus on targeted harmonisation, but it still seems wedded to the idea that private law distortions are impeding the internal market. It is unlikely to retreat from its position favouring maximum harmonisation, but it can change the tone of the debate by reiterating that it wants to emphasise the need to offer a high level of protection and explaining that at the heart of its consumer policy are strong minimum consumer rights. What has perhaps been lacking is a clear statement

[67] See legislation cited in n 2.

[68] eg the Consumer Law Enforcement Forum (CLEF) <http://www.clef-project.eu> accessed 14 May 2015, and the Consumer Justice Enforcement Forum (CoJEF) <http://www.cojef-project.eu> accessed 14 May 2015.

[69] Case C–413/12 *Asociacion de Consumidores Independientes de Castilla y Leon v Anuntis Segundamano Espana*, judgment of 5 December 2013.

of the rationale underpinning consumer protection, but in this respect the EU is no worse or better than most national governments. It might be too much to hope for a thorough restatement of all consumer policy, but the EU-led discussion on behavioural economics might be the occasion to open a discussion about its implications for consumer information and the notion of the average consumer. A willingness to engage with these issues in a mature way should enhance communications between the Commission and the consumer stakeholders. The internal market rhetoric has dominated discussions so that the EU is subject to criticism, whereas it should have a good measure of praise for the rights it has established. The valuable rights the EU has granted risk being forgotten in the internal market rhetoric.

Fortunately the next phase of EU consumer policy is likely to have a fresh policy focus where it will be easier for the Commission and the consumer movement to find common ground. The shift of emphasis to enforcement and access to justice agendas affords the Commission an opportunity to build bridges and rekindle a positive desire to promote positive consumer protection objectives. The EU is moving into a new era, when its challenge will be to make the rules it has established work for the benefit of consumers and fair competition in the internal market. This should be more about practical delivery of results than the rather technical debates about harmonising substantive rules. Legislators and consumers will have much common ground, but areas such as class actions will again provide a litmus test of the nature of the EU's commitment to consumer protection.

19

A Short History of Consumer Policy in the EU

SIDNEY FREEDMAN*

The Treaty of Rome of 1957 brought into existence the European Economic Community, at its heart a 'common market', a market without barriers to trade. It barely mentions consumers. Only with the adoption of a Resolution of the Council of Ministers in 1975 did a consumer policy first come into existence in the EU.[1] The Resolution is no more than a statement of political will. It did not establish a legal basis for the new policy. That lacuna has since been remedied by Article 169 TFEU, which now enshrines consumer policy in law. However, what the Resolution did do, and did rather well, was to set out a reasoned justification for introducing consumer policy into the EU and to identify the policy's objectives. It proclaimed that the improvement of the quality of life is one of the tasks of the Community and that, while consumer protection has long been an established fact in the Member States of the Community, the concept of a consumer policy is relatively recent. It has developed in response to the abuses and frustrations of consumers in an ever-widening market, in which the balance has become weighted in favour of suppliers.

The discovery of new materials, the introduction of new methods of manufacture, the development of means of communication, the expansion of markets, and new methods of retailing have had the effect of increasing the production, supply and demand of an immense variety of goods and services. The consumer has become merely a unit in a mass market. Trade practices, contractual terms, consumer credit and the very concept of competition itself have all evolved to meet market conditions. A new perspective has emerged. Thus practices once regarded as unfair solely in terms of competition between producers (misleading advertising, for example) are now also considered from the point of view of relations between producers and consumers.

* Head of Division (1978–1990) in the Consumer Service of the European Commission. The views expressed are personal and not to be attributed to the Commission. No distinction is drawn between the European Union and the European Economic Community, one being a continuation of the other.

[1] Council Resolution of 14 April 1975 on a preliminary programme of the European Economic Community for a consumer protection and information policy [1975] OJ C92/1.

Significantly, the Resolution draws a distinction between consumer protection and consumer policy. Whereas consumer protection has negative, defensive overtones, consumer policy foresees the empowerment of consumers as a balancing force in the economy. Mapping out a comprehensive programme of action, the Council Resolution identified five consumer rights: health and safety, economic interests, redress, information and education, and representation. It also laid down a number of priorities for action. The European Commission duly responded with proposals for directives on product liability, sales made away from business premises, misleading and unfair advertising, consumer credit, package travel, and unfair contract terms.[2] It was an ambitious programme. The proposed directives were diverse and potentially wide ranging. Respectively they covered:

— manufacturing industry;
— marketing: advertisers, the media, advertising agencies;
— credit: banks and finance houses;
— contracts: including standard forms of contract and warranty;
— travel: packaged air/road/rail transport, hotels, tour organisers; and
— distance selling: mail order sales (e-commerce had not yet been invented).

While at first sight it might appear a random selection, it met the major concerns expressed by consumers at the time, concerns which some Member States met better than others. The level of consumer protection across the EU was uneven. In the case of product liability, a gap in the law of some Member States left the victims of defective products without a remedy. The injustice of their situation was thrown into stark relief by the case of babies born crippled because their mothers had taken thalidomide, a pharmaceutical product prescribed during pregnancy to calm morning sickness. The case became a *cause célèbre* and caused a public outcry.

Consumers wanted truth in advertising, but the reality was often that advertisements left them none the wiser and no better informed. They complained that publicity added to the cost of goods and services merely to establish brands and trademarks in the mind of the public without serving any useful purpose. They also disliked the way psychologically astute advertising undermined the ability of consumers to make rational purchasing decisions. Advertising to children was a source of complaint because it tended to lead children to nag their parents to buy

[2] Proposal for a Council Directive to protect the consumer in respect of contracts which have been negotiated away from business premises [1977] OJ C22/6; Proposal for a Council Directive relating to the approximation of the laws, regulations and administrative provisions of the Member States concerning liability for defective products [1976] OJ C 241/9; Proposal for a Council Directive relating to the approximation of the laws, regulations and administrative provisions of the Member States concerning misleading and unfair advertising [1978] OJ C70/4; Proposal for a Council Directive relating to the approximation of the laws, regulations and administrative provisions of the Member States concerning consumer credit [1979] OJ C80/4; Proposal for a Council Directive on package travel, including package holidays and package tours [1988] OJ C96/5; Proposal for a Council Directive on unfair terms in consumer contracts [1990] OJ C243/2.

what was on offer, toys, cereals or whatever. The topic of comparisons in advertising was also an issue. All advertising is implicitly comparative wherever there are competing products or services. However, explicitly comparative advertising, while potentially informative and approved of by consumers, was lawful in some Member States but not in others.

The ready availability of credit often led to over-indebtedness on the part of consumers, who were sometimes badly informed of the true rate of interest payable and had no easy means of comparison between competing offers of credit. Most Member States had laws governing hire purchase contracts, but not more recent forms of credit such as credit cards or running accounts. Some suppliers of credit were regulated and others were not, which created unfair competition; some consumers were protected and others were not, which was unfair. The UK Consumer Credit Act 1974 provided a model for modern legislation because it covered all forms of credit, but not all of its concepts exist in continental legal systems, such as that of a holder in due course of a negotiable instrument. It is not readily understood on the continent that negotiable instruments should not be used as security for a debt, because they can be transferred to a holder in due course free from the equities and leave the debtor defenceless in cases where he might otherwise have had a defence.[3]

As to unfair contract terms, the weasel wording of standard form contracts and warranties often deprived consumers of their rights in law. Generally in minuscule print, their terms were incapable of being read by anyone with sufficient maturity to understand their meaning or significance. To a consumer buying goods or services across a frontier in a foreign language they posed even more of a problem. In the 1980s quite a few British consumers found that they could buy the identical model of car in the Netherlands cheaper than at home, but most were unable to understand a contract of sale in Dutch.

According to one of the leading consumer associations the only certainty about package holidays was that they had to be paid for in advance and having paid before departure, consumers who bought a travel package were especially vulnerable. Many found their travel plans changed, often without notice. Charter flights might be consolidated or cancelled, causing disruption and delays, and there were scandals over fuel surcharges. They were liable to find the hotel of their choice was overbooked, in some cases unbuilt or unfinished, and, having paid in advance, were tied to alternative choices proposed by the tour operator. Across the EU there were literally millions of complaints about package holidays, many of them fully justified. Tour organisers frequently rejected claims for compensation, blaming hotels and airlines for the disappointments suffered by consumers, while refusing responsibility for performance of the contracts to which they—and not the hotels and airlines—were party.

[3] Consumer Credit Act 1974, s 123(3). The Geneva Convention on Bills of Exchange 1930 makes no mention of negotiable instruments.

The EU's consumer policy not only addressed these complaints and concerns, it also had the aim of improving the position of consumers in every production, distribution and service sector.[4] Thus it was forward looking and intended to create confidence in the common market among consumers, so that in time they would take full advantage of the benefits it had to offer. Already the market was beginning to open up. Many consumers live in border areas. A glance at a map shows it to be true. Cities such as Nice, Strasbourg, Lille, Antwerp and Rotterdam are less than an hour's drive from a neighbouring state. Studies showed that consumers living in such places frequently crossed national boundaries to make purchases whenever and wherever the prices and the range of goods on offer were more attractive than in their home country. It was foreseeable that consumers would increasingly take advantage of their freedom to make purchases across national boundaries as the common market developed. Over the years cross-frontier purchases have become commonplace with the advance of technology.

However, consumers can only take full advantage of the benefits the common market has to offer if allowed to do so. Protectionist forces were still active in the Member States as the consumer policy programme unrolled. In Germany a marketing regulation prohibited the sale of the French liqueur Cassis. The German government argued that the regulation was justified on the grounds of consumer protection, being intended to avoid the proliferation of drinks with a low level of alcohol in case they induced a tolerance or liking for stronger drinks. The government also claimed that consumers would be deceived by the marketing of a liqueur with a lower alcohol level than liqueurs normally sold in Germany, because to a large extent the level of alcohol determined price.

The European Court of Justice ('ECJ') dismissed the German government's case.[5] A wide range of alcoholic drinks were already available on the German market. Moreover, strong drinks may be diluted before drinking. As to the second line of argument, the ECJ pointed out that the level of alcohol could be printed on labels. It ruled that, in the absence of EU measures, Member States were entitled to regulate the marketing of products in order to protect consumers but, subject to a number of conditions, if such regulation hindered the free circulation of goods between Member States it infringed Article 30 of the Treaty of Rome and was consequently illegal.[6] The ECJ extended the principle in a judgment on a case brought by the Commission against France, where regulations permitting wine-based products to be advertised discriminated against foreign products such as whisky or gin.[7] France argued that the regulations were justified for reasons of consumer protection, claiming that whisky and gin are a danger to health. They

[4] Council Resolution of 14 April 1975 on a preliminary programme of the European Economic Community for a consumer protection and information policy [1975] OJ C92/4, para 14.

[5] Case 120/78 *Rewe-Zentral AG v Bundesmonopolverwaltung für Branntwein* (*Cassis de Dijon*) [1979] ECR 649.

[6] Art 30 TEC has been replaced by Art 34 TFEU.

[7] Case 152/78 *Commission v France* [1980] ECR 2299.

are drunk as aperitifs before meals and enter the bloodstream rapidly. Alcoholism was a problem in France. The ECJ recognised the seriousness of the French government's contentions with regard to alcoholism. It acknowledged consumer protection may justify national measures, even if they create an obstacle to the free circulation of goods, and also that advertising of alcoholic drinks encourages their consumption. Nevertheless, the ECJ condemned the regulations for not meeting their intended aim. Aperitifs are generally followed by a meal. A good malt whisky is frequently drunk as a digestif after a meal. The regulations handicapped the marketing of alcoholic beverages from other Member States, thereby restricting the volume of imports.

The *Cassis de Dijon* case established a principle of equivalence and mutual recognition. Simply stated, any product lawfully produced in a Member State must be admitted to the market of any other Member State. The Commission saw the principle as the basis for narrowing down the harmonisation of laws to cases where national provisions admissible under the criteria set by the Court created barriers to trade in the common market.[8] There were even some who advocated leaving the development of the common market entirely to the ECJ, letting it decide on problems as they arose, rather than try to foresee and eliminate problems by legislation. However, there is a limit in the extent to which general provisions of the Treaty can be made to prevail over the laws of Member States, even when such laws create obstacles to the free movement of goods and services. In the absence of Community law, national rules may have to be respected. Consequently, when five years later a British Commissioner, Lord Cockfield, launched the Commission's programme to complete the internal market (as the common market was renamed), by 1992 he listed some 300 legislative proposals necessary to that end.[9]

In most cases the procedure for drafting and negotiating directives to their final adoption by the Council of Ministers is lengthy and arduous. A great deal of preparatory work has to be done. The aforementioned consumer directives were preceded by studies of the law of the Member States and of the markets in question, as well as by consultation in working groups with government and private experts. The Commission also had the advantage of work done by other bodies. For example, the Council of Europe had already undertaken work on product liability; an OECD report on consumer credit had shown that the law of some countries was not up to date with recent developments. Another input came from within the Commission, as its internal working procedures enabled all departments with an interest in the directives to comment on them, the aim being to maintain an even balance between consumers and commerce and industry.

The Commission does not live and work in an ivory tower. It set up a Consumer Consultative Committee to tap consumer opinion. It also created the European

[8] Commission, Communication from the Commission concerning the consequences of the judgment given by the Court of Justice on 20 February 1979 in Case 120/78 (*Cassis de Dijon*) [1980] OJ C256/2.

[9] Commission, Completing the Internal Market—White Paper from the Commission to the European Council COM(85) 310 final.

Consumer Law Group,[10] both to have an input on the consumer law of the Member States and to comment on the Commission's own proposals. The fact that the Commission's proposals were all published in the Official Journal, and in the public realm at a very early stage, meant that a very wide range of comments were received from associations representing commerce and industry. Of an estimated 2,000 lobbying organisations in Brussels in the 1980s only one, Bureau Européen des Unions de Consommateurs (BEUC—the European Consumer Organisation), represented consumers.

Commission officials were frequently invited to address conferences to explain their thinking in public and never hesitated to do so, but despite every effort to draft balanced proposals and to explain them widely, the new European consumer policy was greeted with considerable hostility. Commerce and industry opposed it strenuously. They were represented by strong and well-financed lobbies, which exercised considerable influence in the European Parliament as well as in national parliaments. Their voice was to be heard at every stage of committee procedures and in plenary sessions. They also had the ear of government ministers and senior civil servants. Opposed to consumer protection root and branch, they contended that consumer protection had nothing to do with the common market. There is a simple answer to that contention. Every market has two sides—supply and demand—and consumers are the demand side of the market. As a concept it is simple and true, and so wide it could potentially cover a huge range of business and private activities.

The Council Resolution of 1975 gave it focus and narrowed it down to private consumers only.[11] However, as is so often true of simple answers, the devil is in the detail; in this case, the absence of any article of the Treaty of Rome expressly relating to consumer policy. In the event, the Commission adopted as the legal basis of the consumer directives Article 100 of the Treaty, which related to the establishment and functioning of the common market. Even before 1975, Article 100 had been the legal basis of directives to protect the health and safety of consumers, notably harmonising national rules on food additives (colouring agents, emulsifiers, anti-oxidants etc), which previously created barriers to trade. The directives opened up the common market, allowing products to cross national borders unhindered by differing national regulations. Although not part of a consumer protection programme as such, the standards set by these directives also protect

[10] The Group was set up and chaired by a very gifted German lawyer in the service of the Commission, Ludwig Kraemer, and included some of the best academic minds in the field, including Professors Norbert Reich and Hans Micklitz (both contributors to the present volume), Thierry Bourgoignie, Jean Calais-Auloy, Erwin Hondius, and two lawyers who worked for consumer associations: Benedicte Federspiel and David Tench.

[11] 'The consumer is no longer seen merely as a purchaser and user of goods and services for personal, family or group purposes but also as a person concerned with the various facets of society which may affect him either directly or indirectly as a consumer' (Preliminary programme of the European Economic Community for a consumer protection and information policy [1975] OJ C92/2, para 3).

consumers.[12] It is a good example of the law meeting the interests of both business and consumers. They do not necessarily conflict.

However, some of the Commission's proposals relating to the economic interests of consumers did not at first sight have a similar cross-border character. For example, during a debate in the House of Commons one MP queried the need for a doorstep sales directive. Was it the case, he wondered, that British housewives were being harassed by French onion-sellers mounted on bicycles peddling their wares from house to house? To be sure, the French onion-seller was not the Commission's major concern, which was much more the mail order trade, very substantial in the clothing sector at that time. For their part the mail order traders claimed that they did not sell clothes across national frontiers because consumers were so different physically from one Member State to another that it was difficult to produce catalogues indicating accurate sizes. The success of catalogue sales at present enjoyed by mail order traders would seem to contradict that statement. It is part of an irreversible trend of sales made away from business premises, currently including telephone sales and sales via the internet, which increasingly makes national borders in the common market irrelevant.

Eventually, the doubts about the legal basis of the consumer directives were resolved and the directives progressed through the lengthy procedure necessary to their adoption. It involved discussions in the European Parliament and in the Economic and Social Committee, both adopting reports on the proposals. Simultaneously, working groups of officials from the national administrations, meeting in the Council of Ministers, examined and debated the Commission's proposals in minute detail. The UK Parliament was also very active and Commission officials were sometimes invited to answer the questions of the House of Lords Scrutiny Committee on European Affairs, which also produced reports in depth after hearing witnesses.

The EU is often accused of having a democratic deficit. It all depends on one's definition of democracy, but a good definition is government by discussion. By that standard the EU ranks very high among the world's democracies! The dialogue seemed never-ending and even extended beyond the borders of the EU. Interest groups in Spain, Portugal and other candidates for membership increasingly sought information about the EU's work in the field of consumer policy. From much further abroad, the Australians—in addition to a general interest in the EU's consumer programme—had a special interest in product liability, because their Law Reform Commission was preparing a report to inform the debate on whether to introduce product liability into the law of Australia.[13] The meetings of the OECD consumer committee in Paris were a profitable forum for the exchange

[12] ibid, para 16.

[13] As the result of a talk on product liability at a meeting of the International Bar Association, I was invited to address the Bicentenary Australian Legal Convention in 1988 in Canberra on the directive. The organisers timed it to take place on the day the Law Reform Commission published its report, which I had previously discussed with them.

of views, particularly with the non-member Scandinavian countries, Norway and Sweden, whose social democrat governments had created consumer-orientated societies. Together with Denmark, already a Member State, they were world leaders in consumer affairs with their system of consumer ombudsmen and market courts. Those more to the right of the political spectrum than the Scandinavians tend to be less comfortable with consumer policy. They oppose the 'nanny state', which, as they see it, mollycoddles consumers from the cradle to the grave. They oppose big government and complain about excessive regulation. They tend to see the public good in the prosperity of commerce and industry, and consumer protection as a costly burden. They disapprove of 'consumerism', a notion with ugly connotations of a society which is shallow, materialistic, ruled by greed and, perhaps, a touch of envy too. Consumer policy is highly charged politically. Not surprising, therefore, that much of the comment on the proposed directives was extremely hostile.

The Commission had given the task of implementing the consumer programme to a small directorate. Progress was slow, in part for lack of human resources,[14] but also because consumer policy did not have a great deal going for it politically. The portfolio was generally given to a Commissioner from one of the small Member States, Ireland or Greece. Even in the hands of a Commissioner from a large Member State, the UK or Germany, the consumer portfolio tended to be overshadowed by environment or the internal market, the other EU policies for which Commissioners Stanley Clinton Davis and Karl-Heinz Narjes respectively were also responsible at various times. Progress was also slow because in the early days there was no Consumer Council. During the Greek Presidency of the Council in 1983 a short but decisive meeting took place between the Commission and the Greek minister of commerce, Dr Pangalos, who found a date and fixed the very first meeting for a Consumer Council. When in the following year France took over the Presidency, the ministers for consumer affairs of the 10 Member States adopted the directive on misleading advertising at a meeting of the Consumer Council.

It was a very significant step in the implementation of the consumer programme, particularly as the directive's adoption at one time seemed doubtful because of fierce opposition on the part of the advertising lobby. They raised a variety of objections. The UK Advertising Association contended that there was no misleading advertising. The Commission countered with several examples. One was an advertisement for a medium priced car, a standard production model, claiming that it accelerated faster in top gear than a Ferrari or a Porsche. And so it did! But the gear ratios were entirely different. It had four gears whereas the Ferrari and Porsche had six gears. Another advertisement for a well-known brand of paraffin (kerosene for domestic heaters) claimed it did not rust the can in which it was sold, which implied that other inferior brands did rust metal, contained an impurity, and perhaps leaked away. In fact, paraffin does not rust metal. Water

[14] Fortunately, a colleague in another Commission department, Hans Taschner, undertook the heavy burden of the negotiations on product liability and did so in a masterly fashion.

rusts metal. Another case of *suppressio veri*. The lobby also argued that advertisements do not cross frontiers for language reasons, if for none other. Even at that time the argument was false and, given the technical advances which would make possible television advertising via satellite, untenable. In 1971 a World Administrative Radio Conference had already set the direction for the orderly development of satellite broadcasting. Subsequent conferences allocated high frequency bands and geostationary satellite orbit locations 30,000 kilometres above the equator.[15] In Europe the satellite footprints would spill over national frontiers to such an extent that broadcasts from the French and German satellites would potentially be received in 11 or 12 countries, with multiple language versions possible.

In the light of these developments the directive took on special importance, because there was virtually no international law governing the transmission of misleading advertising across frontiers. The Paris Convention 1883, Article 10*bis* requires Convention countries to assure effective protection to their citizens against unfair competition; defined as any act of competition contrary to honest practices in industrial or commercial matters, including indications or allegations the use of which in the course of trade is liable to mislead the public as to the nature, the manufacturing process, the characteristics, the suitability for their purpose, or the quantity of the goods. The Convention clearly covers misleading advertising.

However, the law has developed differently from country to country. If the words 'unfair competition' can be translated exactly from one language to another, in French *concurrence déloyale*, in German *unlauterer Wettbewerb*, the concept of unfair competition does not translate so readily. In Germany for many years businessmen have brought legal proceedings to take misleading advertising out of circulation. They sue to protect their own commercial interests, but in doing so they also protect the consumers who would be deceived. Whereas in the United Kingdom no comparable cause of action existed; the concept of unfair competition, at least until the recent unfair commercial practices directive,[16] being more or less limited to trademark infringements and passing off. On the other hand, comparative advertising, permitted in the UK, would in the past have swiftly led to an action for unfair competition on the continent.

The UK has not enacted the Paris Convention's articles specifically and is almost alone among EU Member States in that it does not have any distinct law of unfair competition or of unfair practices that private rights holders can enforce.[17]

[15] The negotiations were protracted, but by the early 1980s the deal had been done, despite the claim of six equatorial nations that the allocation of satellite positions infringed their sovereignty, the so-called Bogotá Declaration. See DD Duverney, 'Implications of the 1983 Regional Administrative Radio Conference on Direct Broadcast Satellite Services: a Building Block for WARC-85' (1985) 9 *Maryland Journal of International Law* 117.

[16] Directive 2005/29/EC of the European Parliament and of the Council of 11 May 2005 concerning unfair business-to-consumer commercial practices in the internal market (Unfair Commercial Practices Directive) [2005] OJ L149/22.

[17] Law Commission, *Patents, Trade Marks and Design Rights: Groundless Threats* (Law Com No 346, 2014).

There was also a distinct preference in the UK for self-regulation of advertising as against public law supervision. The International Chamber of Commerce ('ICC') explains it well:[18]

> Advertising and marketing self-regulation is a system by which the advertising, marketing, agency and media industry set voluntary rules and standards of practice that go beyond their legal obligations. Self-regulatory organisations are responsible for enforcing industry's commitment to these rules. They offer consumers increased protection and a cost-effective, accessible and responsive alternative to legal avenues.

In the UK the self-regulatory organisation responsible for advertising, set up and financed by the advertising industry, is the Advertising Standards Authority ('ASA'), a private body. It publishes a code of practice and seems to work well as a supervisory body. However, at the time when the directive on misleading advertising was being negotiated, it was an open question whether there was any recourse to the courts of justice from a decision of the ASA, as provided by the proposed directive.[19] Eventually it was agreed to amend the proposal by introducing recourse to an administrative authority as well as to the courts of law. This brought the Danish consumer ombudsman and the British Office of Fair Trading within the ambit of the directive. In some quarters the amendment was seen as a surrender to the advertising industry. In fact, the Commission was taking a long view. The English courts were beginning to create a body of law on the judicial review of administrative decisions. After its adoption the directive was transposed into UK law as the Misleading Advertising Regulations. Effectively it was administered by the ASA. Subsequent decisions of the Court of Appeal, upheld in the Lords, decided that the ASA, private body though it is, was exercising a public law function. In the words of Lord Hoffmann, the ASA had been integrated into a system of statutory regulation. 'What one has here is a privatisation of the business of government itself.'[20]

There was a price to pay for the adoption of the directive on misleading advertising. As originally drafted the directive also covered unfair advertising and comparative advertising.[21] They were dropped in the face of opposition from two of

[18] http://www.iccwbo.org/advocacy-codes-and-rules/areas-of-work/marketing-and-advertising/self-regulation/.

[19] Proposal for a Council Directive relating to the approximation of the laws, regulations and administrative provisions of the Member States concerning misleading and unfair advertising [1978] OJ C70/4, Art 7.

[20] *R v The Disciplinary Committee of the Jockey Club ex parte the Aga Khan* [1992] EWCA Civ 7, [1993] 1 WLR 909; see also *R v Advertising Standards Authority Ltd., ex parte the Insurance Service plc* (1990) 2 Admin LR 77, 81–82 and 86.

[21] 'Unfair advertising' was defined in Art 2 of the Proposal (above n 19) as any advertising which:

'(a) casts discredit on another person by improper reference to his nationality, origin, private life or good name, or

(b) injures or is likely to injure the commercial reputation of another person by false statements or defamatory comments concerning his firm, goods or services, or

(c) appeals to sentiments of fear, or promotes social or religious discrimination, or

the Member States. Unanimity was the rule in the days before qualified majority voting was introduced in the Council of Ministers. A single Member State could block the adoption of a directive. One of the frustrations of negotiating with governments is that from time to time there is a general election and a new government takes power. In the case of unfair advertising an agreement reached with one of the Member States proved worthless after a change of government. Concessions also had to be made to enable some of the other directives to be adopted.

As originally proposed by the Commission, the product liability directive imposed strict liability for damage, loss or injury on the producer of a defective product whether or not the producer knew the product was defective. No defence was allowed for development risks, that is, the risk of defects unforeseen and unforeseeable at the date of production. The point proved highly contentious. The Commission argued that the loss should fall on the producer who put the offending goods into the stream of commerce. By the act of placing goods on the market the producer represents by implication that they are safe and suitable for use and should be held liable if this proves false. Moreover, it is unacceptable that consumers should be treated as guinea pigs and bear the risk, without remedy, of defects being discovered during use. It was also argued that to exclude development risks from strict liability would leave a gap in the compensation cover through which the victims of another thalidomide disaster might slip. It is not a case of blaming producers for putting defective products into circulation. The issue is purely one of compensation. These cases ought to be covered by insurance, if the risk is too great for the producer to bear.

What sort of burden would this rule have placed on industry? It is clear that certain industries would hardly be affected at all. Manufacturers of writing paper, clothing or furniture, for example, would barely feel the impact. Others would be affected. Pharmaceuticals and aviation are prime examples. Nevertheless, even in these cases, one must keep a sense of proportion. The characteristics of products which have been in existence for years are well known. Problems get ironed out. New products are often based on existing products and do not constitute a step into the unknown. The real risk would arise from totally new developments. But is it not right that the producer who puts a totally new product on the market should take special care in the development and quality control of that product?

These arguments did not win the day. Product liability was cloaked in a mantle of fear emanating from the USA, where juries in class actions award huge damages—sometimes including punitive damages—for death or personal injury caused by defective products. The fear that huge awards of damages might be made in Europe (despite the differences between American and European legal

(d) clearly infringes the principle of the social, economic and cultural equality of the sexes, or
(e) exploits the trust, credulity or lack of experience of a consumer, or influences or is likely to influence a consumer or the public in general in any other improper manner'.

systems) influenced the debate on the scope of the directive. In the end the product liability directive as adopted allows producers a defence for development risks, while permitting Member States an option to create or maintain liability for such cases.[22] France, Belgium and Luxembourg already had strict liability for defective products for many years before the adoption of the directive. These countries assimilated the legal position of the producer to that of the seller of goods under the Code Civil. It was considered bad faith for a seller to deny that he knew the existence of a defect. He was deemed to know the quality of the goods. The rule was strict liability in all circumstances, even for latent defects. France and Belgium have not exercised the option to maintain strict liability for development risks. Consequently, the directive reduced their standard of consumer protection.

As proposed by the Commission the package travel directive would have imposed strict liability for performance of a contract solely on the tour organiser. It provided that the services to be provided for the consumer under the contract should be rendered punctually and efficiently. The travel industry asserted that to do so would substantially increase their costs. It was a most extraordinary claim. It would reflect very badly on the travel industry if there were a substantial cost involved in guaranteeing that consumers get what they have contracted and paid for because it would suggest that there was a high degree of risk in package travel. Of all the EU Member States France had the strictest law, obliging the travel industry to insure against failure to supply the agreed services. Taking the figures for 1985, on a turnover of 16 billion French francs the insurance cover was 12.6 million francs. As there were 5 million package travellers, premiums therefore represented a cost of 2.32 French francs per traveller, a very modest sum to compensate consumers for the disappointment and frustration when their travel arrangements went wrong. Nevertheless, a major concession had to be made at the insistence of one Member State. The directive as adopted required the tour operator to do no more than use due diligence or best endeavours to provide the consumer with the services contracted and paid in advance of departure.

The early directives were measures of minimal harmonisation. Member States were free to maintain or introduce higher standards if they wished. On one view it is politically undesirable to require Member States to reduce their standards of consumer protection for the sake of harmonisation. According to another point of view harmonisation should be strict and not allow for national variations. There are strong arguments on both sides. In some cases it is possible to lay down a rule to produce an identical result in all of the Member States. For example, compensation for passengers whose flights have been delayed can be calculated precisely by taking account of how long the flight was delayed and the length of the journey being undertaken. Again, whether a food additive is safe for use may be a matter of scientific opinion, but the opinion will generally be clear and can be tested.

[22] Council Directive 85/374/EEC of 25 July 1985 on the approximation of the laws, regulations and administrative provisions of the Member States concerning liability for defective products [1985] OJ L210/29.

Strict harmonisation is appropriate in such cases. On the other hand, an award of damages in an action for personal injuries is subject to many variables and there are wide differences from one Member State to another in the quantum of damages awarded. In the case of product liability, therefore, the unifying effect of harmonisation is limited. That is probably also true of the directive on misleading advertising. The market for consumer goods and services is robust. Advertising claims are not made on affidavit. Truth in advertising is a broad enough concept to allow for a modicum of humour and exaggeration, but given the cultural differences between the Member States judgments may vary. The same applies to the legitimate expectations of holidaymakers who buy package travel deals.

The early directives relating to the economic interests of consumers were far from ideal. Too many concessions had to be made to secure their adoption. Nevertheless, in part they laid the foundations of consumer law in the EU, foundations upon which the Commission has subsequently built by introducing directives to make good the concessions. Thus the Unfair Commercial Practices Directive allows comparative advertising and introduces a rule against unfair advertising, albeit subject to many qualifications.[23] The economic interests of consumers must also be viewed in the wider context of the EU's other activities. For instance, the EU's open skies transport policy has enabled low-cost airlines to operate out of regional airports at prices extremely advantageous to consumers. It has democratised air travel. To take another example, the private international law of the EU makes special provision for consumers. Subject to certain conditions they are entitled to sue and be sued in their country of domicile.[24] It is bad enough for any consumer to be involved in litigation, but the prospect becomes very daunting if the litigation is in a foreign country.

Even in their country of domicile there is little point in giving consumers rights under EU law unless they are able to exercise or defend those rights. Their value depends very largely on the availability of redress or access to justice. Litigation is rarely the answer. It is generally formal, slow and expensive. It has been said that the doors of the Royal Courts of Justice, like the doors of the Ritz Hotel, are open to all.[25] In many consumer cases the amount of money in issue does not justify the cost of conventional litigation and would not qualify for legal aid, even were it available. Considerations such as these led the Commission to consider simplified small claims procedures and alternative dispute resolution. Ideally, legal procedures should be simple, rapid, cheap, effective and fair to all parties. In the Commission's view a directive stating those principles at that time would not have

[23] Directive 2005/29/EC (n 16).

[24] Regulation (EU) No 1215/2012 of the European Parliament and of the Council of 12 December 2012 on jurisdiction and the recognition and enforcement of judgments in civil and commercial matters [2012] OJ L351/1, s 4. For a full discussion of the issues see ZS Tang, 'Consumer Contracts and the Internet in EU Private International Law' in A Savin and J Trzaskowski (eds), *Research Handbook of EU Internet Law* (Cheltenham, Edward Elgar, 2014) 259.

[25] Perhaps quoting a nineteenth-century Irish judge, Sir James Mathew, to whom this *bon mot* is sometimes attributed.

advanced the state of the art very far. Instead, the Commission funded a series of pilot projects on access to justice in some of the Member States, namely the UK (Scotland), Belgium, France, Greece, Italy and Portugal. They were genuinely collaborative ventures, which created a lot of interest and were very well received.

The first of the pilot projects, in Scotland, was particularly encouraging. It began with a meeting chaired by the Solicitor-General for Scotland, subsequent meetings were chaired by a future Law Lord and the legal profession was also well represented. Based in the Sheriff's Court of Dundee, the project relied on a preliminary hearing of an informal nature, with the Sheriff intervening to discuss and identify the issues so as to take a view of the likely outcome of further proceedings. Often, that was enough to settle the matter. This is not the place to describe in any detail the procedures adopted. They have already been more fully described in documents published by the Commission.[26] However, the French project, based in the courts of the *juge d'instance* at Dijon and Le Creusot, perhaps deserves a special mention. It introduced a conciliation procedure in the presence of the judge, designed to lead to an agreement having the same binding force as a judgment. The procedure appears to have been particularly effective.[27] In a recent conversation with a *juge conciliateur* in the Alpes Maritimes he confessed that he had a failure rate of 25 per cent in the cases in which he officiated, that is a 75 per cent success rate. However, he refused to accept that a 75 per cent success rate was acceptable, which is perhaps overly self-critical. The pilot project in Portugal, based in Lisbon, relied on compulsory mediation, but it was not centred in a court of law. It proved very successful, to some extent thanks to the personal intervention of the mayor of Lisbon.

The interest shown in these pilot projects at a high level was a good omen for what followed, when the procedures were adopted countrywide for Scotland,[28] France and Portugal respectively. The projects also had a wider significance, because they incorporated new ideas emerging in the early 1980s. Beginning with interest in alternative dispute resolution in American academic circles, notably at Harvard, the approach rapidly caught on nationwide in the United States. Of especial interest was the notion of a 'two-door court', channelling claims into initial stages of neutral evaluation and mediation at which disputes could be resolved before the due process of a formal hearing at law was reached. In the EU these were still early days for consumer dispute resolution, but the projects represented the first steps in an approach now widely accepted.[29]

[26] Supplementary Communication from the Commission on Consumer Redress COM(87) 210 final, Commission Green Paper on Access of consumers to justice and the settlement of consumer disputes in the single market COM(93) 576.

[27] Decree No 88-209 of 4 March 1988, Code of Civil Procedure, Art 829.

[28] Law Reform (Miscellaneous Provisions) (Scotland) Act 1985.

[29] eg Directive 2008/52/EC of the European Parliament and of the Council of 21 May 2008 on certain aspects of mediation in civil and commercial matters [2008] OJ L136/3; Directive 2013/11/EU of the European Parliament and of the Council of 21 May 2013 on alternative dispute resolution for consumer disputes [2013] OJ L165/63. See also Lord Woolf, *Final Report to the Lord Chancellor on the Civil Justice System in England and Wales* (HMSO, 1996).

One of the images of the consumer in the law of the EU is that of the humble seeker after justice, always the weaker party, with neither the time, nor the inclination, nor the funds to enter into an unequal contest with the big battalions of commerce and industry; be it the purchaser who did not read or understand the small print in the terms and conditions of contract, one-sided and very much to his disadvantage; the holidaymaker whose hotel bore no resemblance to the photographs in the tour operator's glossy brochure; the naïve person who took advantage of easy credit, up to the ears in debt and worried stiff about repaying the money owed; the sorrowing mother who took pills to relieve morning sickness during her pregnancy and her crippled children born without limbs. For them and others like them the EU first undertook its work in the field of consumer policy. The work continues to this day.

INDEX

www.ingramcontent.com/pod-product-compliance
Ingram Content Group UK Ltd.
Pitfield, Milton Keynes, MK11 3LW, UK
UKHW020130290926
15471UKWH00003B/398

9 781509 921171